Civil Litigation Handbook

CIVIL LITIGATION HANDBOOK

General Editor: **John Peysner**
Consultant Editor: **Suzanne Burn**

The Law Society

© The Law Society 2001

ISBN 1–85328–592–7

Published in 2001 by the Law Society
113 Chancery Lane, London WC2A 1PL

Typeset by J&L Composition Ltd, Filey, North Yorkshire
Printed and bound by TJ International Ltd, Padstow, Cornwall

Contents

PART III: NEW PROCEDURES

APPENDICES

Notes on contributors

General editors

John Peysner, MA(Cantab), has worked as a solicitor for Tottenham and North Kensington Law Centres and for Oxley and Coward (now Beachcroft Stanley) and was a Partner at Peysner and Foley. He was a Senior Lecturer at Leeds Metropolitan University and is currently Professor of Civil Justice at the Centre for Legal Research at Nottingham Law School. He has written extensively on a number of aspects of litigation for a wide variety of journals and publications and was Editor of *The Litigator*. He is on the editorial board of *Nottingham Law Journal*. He is a Fellow of SALS and was a member of the Lord Chancellor's Committee on Non-Qualified Claims Assessors and co-author of the report. He was also on the Nottingham Law School team that advised the General Council of the Bar on the ethical impact of conditional fee arrangements and the Leader of the Consultation Exercise for the LCD on recoverability rules under the Access to Justice Act. He is currently undertaking research for the LCD evaluating case management.

Suzanne Burn was the solicitors' profession main voice on Woolf and the CPR from 1994–9, serving on many LCD working groups. She was the main author of the personal injury and clinical negligence pre-action protocols. Since 1999 she has been implementing the CPR as a Deputy District Judge and continuing to train and guide the profession as a Senior Consultant to the College of Law, a trainer for CLT, APIL, Hawksmere, LAG and Bond Solon and a contributor to many publications on the CPR including the *White Book* & Sweet & Maxwell's *Litigation Practice*. Suzanne is also a member of two of the Civil Justice Council Sub Committees – Litigant Information and Court Fees.

Contributors

Sarah Ahmed has worked as a commercial litigation solicitor at Clifford Chance and then at Anthony Gold where she was a Partner heading up the Commercial Department. She obtained an LLM in Advanced Litigation from Nottingham Law School. Having mastered legal practice, she decided to pursue her interest in wine full-time and is currently enjoying a career in the wine trade.

Tim Aspinall is Managing Partner and Head of Litigation at DMH. Tim's practice focuses on commercial litigation including intellectual property and computer-related litigation. He has particular experience in the high technology sector, but deals with the full range of commercial disputes on behalf of national and international clients. Skilled at managing complex and difficult cases to a successful conclusion he has been involved in numerous major disputes of this kind over the years. He regularly speaks at conferences and lectures to other lawyers throughout the country on litigation topics including the strategy and tactics of winning cases, project management of cases and managing risk.

Susan Barty obtained an LLB at Bristol University and an LLM in Advanced Litigation at Nottingham Law School. She is a Partner at CMS Cameron McKenna, London. She specialises in commercial litigation and advises on effective dispute avoidance and resolution. She is an accredited CEDR mediator, has considerable experience in mediation and has lectured extensively on alternative dispute resolution.

Julian Boardman-Weston, after reading law at Cambridge, practised at the specialist bar and then as a Partner in a firm of solicitors in the East Midlands. In 1994 he set up Computer Counsel, an IT consultancy working exclusively with lawyers and law firms. He is one of the directors of Sherwood, a management consultancy specialising in work with professional service firms, and a principal tutor at the Centre for Lay Firm Management at Nottingham Law School. He has an MSc in management and is a Sloan Fellow of London Business School. Julian has worked with law firms of most sizes, and writes and speaks widely on law firm IT and related issues.

James Burnett-Hitchcock, BA(Hons) Oxon, was admitted as a solicitor in 1971 and has practised in the areas of banking, insolvency and commercial litigation, defamation and media law. He is a CEDR and ADR Group accredited mediator and is currently a consultant to CMS Cameron McKenna and a Visiting Professor at the College of Law specialising in Civil Procedure and Litigation/ADR skills. He is past President of the London Solicitors Litigation Association, a former member of the Law Society's Civil Litigation Committee and a current member of their ADR Group.

Anthony Cherry is an insurance Partner, based at the London office of the commercial law firm Beachcroft Wansboroughs, and a member of the Law Society's Civil Litigation Committee.

Jane Ching, MA(Cantab), is a solicitor who has worked for Nottingham Law School since 1993 and is currently Principal Lecturer in Course Design and Curriculum Development in civil litigation. She was a contributor to

Blackstones' *Guide to the Civil Procedure Rules* and a member of the Law Society's Working Party on incorporation of CPR into the Legal Practice Course. She has recently become Assistant Editor of the Nottingham Law Journal.

Roger Clements was a Consultant Gynaecologist and Obstetrician at North Middlesex Hospital from 1973 to 1994 and is currently a Consultant Gynaecologist practising from 111 Harley Street W1G 6AW. He is also the Editor of *Clinical Risk* and a Founding Governor of the Expert Witness Institute.

David Greene is Head of Litigation at Edwin Coe Solicitors. He qualified in 1980 and since then has practised in the areas of insolvency and commercial litigation/arbitration. He is an accredited CEDR mediator and a Fellow of the Chartered Institute of Arbitrators. He is a member of the Civil Procedures Rules Committee, having been appointed by the Lord Chancellor in 1997, and has thus overseen the inception of the new CPR. He was a member of the Working Party on Practice Directions and is on the Executive Committee of the London Solicitors Litigation Association. He has written and lectured extensively on civil litigation and CPR.

Caroline Harmer, FRSA, is a barrister. She has been President of APIL, Editor of the *Journal of Personal Injury Litigation* and member of the Law Society's Civil Litigation Committee, and has been involved in many working parties, drafting guidance on early rehabilitation in personal injury cases. She is a member of the Council of the University of Reading and of the working party preparing a Code of Guidance for the use of experts. She currently writes and lectures on civil litigation, and has contributed to several titles published by Butterworths.

Neil Hext is a barrister at 2 Temple Gardens, London. He practises in commercial law, professional negligence, insurance and construction.

Vicky Ling was one of the first staff recruited by the then Legal Aid Board to implement its quality assurance standard in the early 1990s and is now an independent consultant specialising in legal practice. She has an MPhil in an education topic and is a Member of the Institute of Quality Assurance.

David Marshall is Managing Partner of London solicitors, Anthony Gold. He specialises in personal injury work, but also undertakes employment and commercial work. He is Treasurer of APIL. He has written and lectured extensively on the subject of CFAs and is a member of the Law Society's CFA Task Force.

Simon McCall is a founder member of Sherwood PSF Consulting Limited. He undertakes management consultancy, facilitation and training work with law firms, particularly in the areas of strategy, marketing and organisation design. Simon is also a principal tutor on the MBA in Legal Practice at Nottingham Law School. He had a first career as a solicitor in private practice and then in industry and has an MBA from the Cranfield School of Management.

Geraldine McCool is a Partner at Leigh Day & Co., Manchester, specialising in personal injury and fatal claims arising out of commercial and military air crashes, and personal injury claims against the Ministry of Defence in general. Geraldine is Chairman of the Manchester Law School Civil Litigation Committee and a past National Chairman of the Young Solicitors Group. She is a mediator in the Court of Appeal for personal injury cases and an American Express/Cosmopolitan Career Award winner.

Penny Owston is a solicitor and Senior Partner in franchised, IIP and Lexcel accredited provincial firm Martin and Haigh. She is a graduate of the Nottingham Law School MBA in Practice Management and visiting tutor and trainer for Business Legal Support (BLS). Penny is also a Member of the Law Society's Children and Family Law Panels as well as a Law Society Council member.

Simon Parrington was admitted as a solicitor in 1975. As a Partner with Hill Dickinson he has a wide and varied practice as a civil litigator with a special interest in health and safety law. He is a member of the Law Society's Civil Litigation Committee and a Deputy District Judge. In 1995 he sat on Lord Woolf's Working group on the Fast Track and thereafter lectured extensively on the CPR.

Nigel Tomkins is a training and legal consultant and Associate Professor of Civil Litigation with the College of Law. He is a consultant with solicitors Freethcartwright, of Nottingham, Derby and Leicester and Consultant Director to and a Fellow of the College of Personal Injury Law, the training arm of APIL, the Association of Personal Injury lawyers. He was a working party member on Lord Woolf's Civil Justice Review and was a major contributor to the pre action protocol for personal injury claims. He lectures and trains widely on a variety of subjects including civil litigation, personal injury matters, and health and safety law. He has recently completed a book on repetitive strain injuries for the TUC and is digest editor of JPIL, the *Journal of Personal Injury Law*.

Foreword

The Right Honourable Lord Woolf, Lord Chief Justice

I very much welcome the publication of this *Handbook*. Solicitors will do so as well. The implementation of the Civil Procedure Rules marked a new era in civil litigation. In particular, the transfer of responsibility for the progress of cases from practitioners to the judiciary is a fundamental change to the way in which the civil justice system traditionally worked. Users of the civil justice system, and practitioners in particular, have therefore not only had to cope with a completely new, unified set of Rules. In addition, they have had to embrace a change of culture and restructure the way in which they manage and organise their practices.

This *Handbook* will, I am sure, assist greatly in that process. Old habits have a tendency to die hard. The *Handbook* gives solicitors in particular the pragmatic guidance they need to organise their methods of working so as to conduct successfully their litigation in the new landscape. The Civil Procedure Rules cannot themselves bring about the systemic changes which are so badly needed. It is the effective operation of the Rules, together with the adoption of their spirit, by practitioners and judges that will produce the scale of change required. The *Handbook* sets out in authoritative but clear and well-balanced terms how to manage civil disputes in the new world. It will be a valuable resource for every firm involved in litigation. I congratulate the Editor and his distinguished team of authors on what is an excellent achievement. Their experience means that this *Handbook* provides practitioners with what they need to know to tame the 'Woolf' reforms.

Preface

Preparing the Law Society's *Civil Litigation Handbook* has been an enormous challenge for myself and for all of the contributors. Not only have they had to deal with my demands but also the working out in practice of the greatest revolution in civil procedure this century: the Woolf reforms. Lord Woolf's name is not attached to the recent changes just as a convenient tag, but because his commitment and drive have been fundamental to reforming a civil procedural system beset by problems. Lord Woolf's reports identified a system that did not come close to providing access to justice to its users and he provided both a comprehensive critique of its failings and a far-reaching response that effectively represents the creation of a new system. For these reasons I am delighted that Lord Woolf has contributed the Foreword to this book.

Two factors have been vital in the rapid implementation of the civil procedural changes. The first is a happy conjunction of reforming elements, or to put it another way, luck. Lord Woolf's inquiry spanned the period in office of one reforming Lord Chancellor, Lord McKay and then another, Lord Irvine. The previous and present governments' modernising objectives in this area are virtually identical. The judiciary, under the driving influence of Lord Woolf and Sir Richard Scott, Lord Phillips and Lord Justice May, together with the co-ordinating role of the Judicial Studies Board, have been comprehensively committed to the reform effort. The legal professions, with some exceptions, have accepted the need for restructuring and have exhibited an unexpected degree of enthusiasm for its implementation. The second factor was both the instigating cause of the reform effort but also its constant background: the deluge of changes in the environment within which solicitors work. A huge cultural change is taking place: from financing, to clients' needs, to legal training, to organisational arrangements, nothing has remained static; it has been a period of unprecedented sustained change. In many respects, the legal profession has simply caught up with business in general; the processes of modernisation and globalisation rule everywhere.

I would proffer a small but pointed example of change, one close to my heart. When I started as a solicitor, civil litigation was one of a series of activities in the office. Solicitors, legal executives and articled clerks (remember them?) carried out litigation work. Nobody was called a 'litigator', a term commonly used in the USA. Even now, an irritating aspect of working in this area is that the word 'litigator' is unknown to most computer spellcheckers and to many dictionaries. I have contemplated for some time a campaign to win wider acceptance of the term. However, I now wonder if I should miss a step and try to popularise the term 'dispute resolver', as litigation is now only part of the work of solicitors involved in resolving civil disputes. This is yet another idiom unknown to the spellchecker and as it has a rather ugly sound, I propose to stick to litigator for the foreseeable future. It does appear, however, that change in legal practice and organisation is now proceeding at a pace faster than conventional responses and structures can cope with and that change will now be a permanent feature of this area. The message seems to be 'hang on, we're in for a bumpy but exciting ride'.

The *Civil Litigation Handbook* provides a comprehensive guide to one of the most challenging and rapidly changing areas of practice; Part I addresses the running of a litigation practice in the post-Woolf era; Part II covers litigation as project management, and Part III deals in detail with the new procedures. The book offers a strategic overview, together with practical day-to-day advice on the dispute process and the way in which litigators can face the challenges of the litigation revolution; it should be on the litigator's bookshelf alongside the Civil Procedure Rules. The future will still be an exciting ride, but, hopefully, the *Handbook* will help make it less bumpy!

JOHN PEYSNER
April 2001

Table of cases

xv

Table of statutes

Table of secondary legislation

STATUTORY INSTRUMENTS

PRE-ACTION PROTOCOLS

EUROPEAN LEGISLATION

Abbreviations

ADR	alternative dispute resolution
AEI	after the event (legal expenses) insurance
APIL	Association of Personal Injury Lawyers
AVMA	Action for the Victims of Medical Accidents
CAB	Citizens Advice Bureau
CBI	Confederation of British Industry
CCR	County Court Rules 1981, SI 1981/1687
CEDR	Centre for Dispute Resolution
CFA	conditional fee agreement
CLSQM	Community Legal Service Quality Mark
CMC	case management conference
CMP	case management plan
CPD	continuing professional development
CPR	Civil Procedure Rules
ECHR	European Convention on Human Rights 1950
FOIL	Forum of Insurance Lawyers
IIP	Investors in People
IP	intellectual property
ISP	Internet service provider
IT	information technology
LAB	Legal Aid Board
LAFQAS	Legal Aid Franchise Quality Assurance Standard
LAN	local area network
LCD	Lord Chancellor's Department
LSC	Legal Services Commission
lEI	legal expenses insurance
LIP	litigant in person
LSC	Legal Services Commission
NAO	National Audit Office
OSS	Office for the Supervision of Solicitors
PTR	pre-trial review
RAID	redundant array of inexpensive disks
SFLA	Solicitors Family Law Association
SJE	single joint expert
SMART	specific, measurable, attainable, realistic target
TEC	Training and Enterprise Council
TQM	total quality management

Mapping the new litigation landscape

John Peysner

Change and growth

How will growth be managed?

Influences on thinking about litigation

Response to the challenge of change

What are the factors moving litigators from the old to the new model?

Inter-connecting factors influencing the modern litigator

Publication of the *Civil Litigation Handbook* comes at a time when the work of the litigator and the organisation of firms dealing with litigation have been subject to a greater period of sustained change than at any time since the period when the solicitors' profession emerged from that of attorney. This Introduction will examine these changes and attempt to predict the direction we are moving in. While the *Handbook* as a whole offers a practical approach to solving litigation problems in the new environment, I am going to take the liberty of speculating a little.

CHANGE AND GROWTH

Before looking forward let us look back. I started to practice in 1973 in a medium-sized long established provincial firm. Litigation was an important element in the practice but it still took second place to non-contentious commercial work and domestic conveyancing was a vital element. How things have changed. What has caused the change? The reason is growth; growth in litigation which started in the 1960s and has developed at a pace. In a recent publication by Frank Furedi, *Courting Mistrust: the Hidden Growth of Litigation in Britain* (Centre for Policy Studies, 1999) it was reported that the sum of up to £6.8 billion was currently spent on an annual basis in compensation and fees to lawyers. Whilst this figure is a 'guestimate' and the pamphlet approaches the topic of the growth of litigation from a critical perspective, it is clear that litigation has increased and the role of the litigators has moved from the periphery of practice to the centre.

What drove this change? There were two main reasons. First, Britain has been unique in developed nations in offering a comprehensive legal aid system. The availability of legal aid has meant that a substantial part of litigation practice – both claimant and defendant – has ultimately depended on state support. Whilst the growth in this area has come to a halt (in common with the experience of more limited legal aid schemes for civil work in the rest of the world) the burden has been taken up by litigation insurance. It seems likely that this method of funding will be the engine behind continuing, and perhaps escalating, growth in demand for dispute resolution services by individuals and some parts of the public and corporate sector. The world is getting increasingly complicated and citizens are becoming increasingly assertive and aware of their rights. At the same time individual rights – not to be discriminated against, to be paid equally, to have a safe environment, not to be mis-sold pensions – have increased. Hazel Genn in *Paths to Justice: What People Do and Think about Going to Law* (Hart, Oxford, 1999) reports on a mass survey of people's attitudes to non-trivial problems and their approaches to resolving them. It demonstrates that in a five-year period, 40 per cent of people interviewed had at least one problem for which a legal remedy is available. Whilst a number of these problems are in areas which have not attracted much interest from private practice, e.g. faulty goods or landlord disputes, this may be changing. Of the total number interviewed, 3 per cent had lost a job in disputed circumstances in the period and 7 per cent had suffered an injury or health problem, potentially caused by a third party, serious enough to warrant medical intervention. Whilst the research demonstrates that an enormous number of people 'lump it' and don't take action, the potential market for advice and assistance is huge. Increasingly litigators will seek to share the risks and benefits of this increased activity.

The second river behind litigation is the growth in the economy that has been matched by an increasing sophistication of the legal environment faced by businesses: a substantive law explosion. It goes without saying that our lives are becoming more and more complicated in this modern age. I always made the assumption that the USA – the land of the brave and the free – would be a place where the law exercised a light touch. In fact, in areas such as antitrust or immigration, this paradigm of an advanced capitalist state has the most mind-numbing and complex legal system in the world. It seems impossible in the modern world to escape from the complexities of law and the continuous generation of new laws and regulations. As technology develops into new areas, such as the Internet, telecommunications, e-commerce or genetic modification of food, then regulations and law follow. When there is more 'law' bearing down on businesses and organisations there are, inevitably, more disputes. The effect of this is that throughout the developed world the need for lawyers has outpaced the growth in economies.

Change has been continuous, from every side, and constant. The response to growth has not been met by a simple increase in the activity of solicitors operating in traditional ways. Growth has been a complex matrix of legal aid changes, more assertive clients, more complex legal systems; all happening at the same time. The traditional ways of operating have been subject to attack. It is not surprising that litigators feel they are constantly under pressure from the process of change.

HOW WILL GROWTH BE MANAGED?

In talking about growth and its impact on litigation, I would choose to use the phrase 'dispute resolution services'. There is absolutely no inevitability that a rise in demand for dispute resolution services equates with an equal rise in demand for traditional lawyer-led, court-based litigation. The introduction of the Woolf reforms, in particular Pre-action Protocols, has created a dip in the number of issued cases, which is continuing. However, this tells us very little about the volume of dispute resolution activity. There is now an increasing challenge to any idea that solicitors practising litigation have a monopoly in this area and this goes far beyond the somewhat sterile debate as to how far alternative dispute resolution will replace court-based adjudication. I see that argument as about the *tools* that litigators adopt on behalf of their clients. It is only part of wider and more fundamental questions that ask what is the purpose of civil justice, what is the role of the litigator and what method or methods of resolving disputes will arise in the coming period.

INFLUENCES ON MY THINKING ABOUT LITIGATION

Although I have been an academic since 1991, I spent some 17 years working as a litigation lawyer practising for both claimants and defendants. Since leaving practice my work has involved thinking about litigation, writing about litigation, teaching litigation skills and talking to litigators. For the first time in my life I have had a little time to think about what practice means, rather than concentrate on the daily struggle to meet deadlines, make money, please clients and satisfy staff while, of course, never forgetting that time is measured not in decades or days but in six minute units. What has helped to develop my thinking? Two books have been most useful. Neither are substantive law books: I rarely read a black letter law book. My interest is not in the material that the lawyer sculpts – the substantive law clay – but the way in which the sculpture is built and paid for.

My concern is how litigators fit into modern business practice and the skills they will need to be effective and successful. The books that had the most influence on my thinking are *The Age of Unreason* (Harvard Business School,

3

1991) (and many others) by Charles Handy and *Against the Gods* (John Wiley, New York, 1996) by Peter Bernstein. What are they about? They both offer fascinating and readable glimpses into the two major challenges for modern businesses and organisations: the management of change and the management of risk.

Charles Handy deals with pressures on organisations from cultural change; in other words when old ways of doing things are replaced by new methods and new challenges. He demonstrates how this works out on the global stage under the influence of technological change. These changes have crept up so insidiously that it is hard to imagine what the world was like before computers were ubiquitous and e-mail the communication system of choice. I remember that in the firm where I did articles the high chairs and desks for conveyancing clerks to prepare documents by hand were still present and some of the staff recalled their use.

Peter Bernstein demonstrates that successful business depends on the manipulation of risk and that risk is ubiquitous. Until recently many practitioners felt that they were immune from such pressures and that as professional service providers with a high social standing, society and the economy needed them and would pay for their services in any event. One shock after another – the collapse of domestic conveyancing, legal aid franchising, legal aid withdrawals, the reduction of client panels, the introduction of conditional fees, the driving down of hourly rates and the arrival of American firms and claims management companies – has convinced all but the most conservative solicitors that massive change is inevitable. No business is immune from the pressures of modernisation and globalisation, and risk is the new agenda for the litigator: risk to the firm and risk to the client.

RESPONSE TO THE CHALLENGE OF CHANGE

Commentators describe a fundamental change in approach as a 'paradigm shift'. This is an overused term, but looking back at the last 10 years it is hard not to recognise that the average litigator in the twenty-first century is going to be a very different beast from one practising at the end of the twentieth century. This litigator can be characterised as changing from the *'uninvolved proceduralist'* to the *'partner-problem solver'*.

In litigation it has not been uncommon to come across litigators who churn and grind files, appear to have no clear idea where a case is going and whose bill for taxation discloses frequent pauses for reflection, or for want of anything better to do. The bill may also disclose diversions into areas of fact investigation or seeking counsel's opinion on matters that should have been within the litigator's competence or do not seem vital. The litigator does not appear to have a grip on the case. Whilst we all have had such files, it is surprising how many litigators, or firms, seem to have adopted this as a work style. At worst the uninvolved proceduralist becomes the '*taxi driver*'. This litigator picks up the client, sets the taxi meter running and heads off in the general direction of trial but explores every cul de sac, takes every diversion and appears to be more interested in the journey than the destination. He or she may be 'part-time', not specialising but running a caseload alongside a range of other types of practice.

Of course, most litigators are committed to their clients' hopes and dreams and fully engaged on their behalf. However, a large swathe of the profession turned to litigation in the heady days of the 1970s, when legal aid was readily available and institutional and commercial clients were less cost conscious than they are today. While hourly rates for legal aid work were hardly generous and at times cash flow problems could be widespread, the business environment was not too hostile. Hourly rates offered relatively sanguine terms of trade and not much incentive to be efficient. Across the country small firms and sole practitioners set up and flourished alongside traditional commercial litigation departments of larger firms.

That relatively comfortable position has been rapidly eroded and the prospects are for a further heightening of the pressures on litigators, litigation departments and firms. Whilst City litigation departments grew from strength to strength, they are not immune from competitive pressures, not least from the American giants. A great swathe of the profession may appear to be relatively unaffected but the ground is moving under their feet and one key feature is the increasing influence of risk management.

To illustrate the point, some of the broad features of the two species outlined above are suggested below in stark fashion. Most litigators will have characteristics of both 'animals' but in common with the nature of paradigm shifts, the key issue is about the turning of the tide and the change in overall direction.

The old model: the uninvolved proceduralist

Characteristics include the following:

(a) rather dispassionate and detached from the client: whilst described as a 'family' or 'firm' solicitor and, possibly, involved in the managerial or organisational side of businesses, for example, as a director, this may be incidental to the separate legal role required, from time to time, in resolving disputes;

(b) paid on an hourly rate with mark up (the 'taxi driver's meter'). Billing tends to be an arcane and opaque discipline; clients may be unclear about their financial commitment to the case – clarity arrives with

5

the delivery of the bill, alongside other emotions such as anger and despair;

(c) no direct financial interest in the outcome of the claim;

(d) re-active: not instructed until the dispute fructifies;

(e) concentrating on fact-gathering (the 'taxi driver's route') and whilst competent on the basic legal approach, leaving the ultimate legal theory to counsel;

(f) concentration on the mechanics, the nuts and bolts, of rules and procedures;

(g) no sharing of real time information with the client;

(h) may be located in a generalist firm and may conduct litigation alongside other activities such as conveyancing.

The new model: the partner-problem solver

Characteristics include the following:

(a) closer to the client; in an ongoing 'partnership' relationship on the particular problem, or series of projects, or permanently knitted into the client's structure;

(b) often paid on a fixed fee, by the piece, following tendering for a contract, or within a procedure allowing for fixed party and party costs; billing is predictable and transparent, clients are aware of the costs position at any time;

(c) increasing direct financial interest in the outcome having been engaged under conditional fee arrangements under the Access to Justice Act 1999 or on fixed fees;

(d) pro-active; often involved in planning and advising on disputes *before* they happen. Of course, solicitors have always been instructed to assist in advance of and in expectation of disputes, e.g., in the drafting of standard form contracts intended to limit or remove liability for future default, however, the pro-active solicitor will hold a much wider brief considering not only legal text but all the surrounding organisational matrix;

(e) operating a project management, case theory approach to dispute resolution with a firm view of the legal theory in a matter;

(f) approaching civil procedure and court-based methods as only one way of resolving disputes and solving problems; a keen interest in problem solving techniques (characterised as ADR), use of alternative pressure points (e.g. the media);

(g) may interface IT with the client, i.e. allow the client to see the state of progress on a matter in real time;

(h) likely to be a specialist litigator, or even a specialist in a discrete field of litigation; may be located in a large commercial firm, i.e. any firm operating for commercial or institutional clients, including the highly formalised and structured contractual arrangements which will increasingly represent the 'terms of trade' available from the Legal Services Commission, or as a specialist in a boutique or studio set-up.

WHAT ARE THE FACTORS MOVING LITIGATORS FROM THE OLD TO THE NEW MODEL?

In my view a litigator operating *all* or *most* of the elements of the new model will be the *only* viable way of running a successful dispute resolution business in the future. This is because a whole series of factors are pressing litigators to become closer to the client, to take more risks and to be more business-minded.

Globalisation and modernisation

The difficulty in attempting an analysis of the continuing change from the old model of litigator to the new is that the description is complicated by the fact that everything is changing at once. This is not a chronological movement but a chaotic development. The saving grace of this is that solicitors have demonstrated over the years that despite their conservative reputation they are extremely flexible in responding to market pressures. The engine behind the changes can be found in the process of globalisation and modernisation. You may be tempted to ask why would globalisation matter to a high street solicitor struggling with the implications of legal aid contracts, litigation insurance and competition from banks and estate agents? However, even if you practise in a small country town, you may well work alongside estate agents owned by multi-national companies, do your banking over the Internet and enter into the new arrangements with others looking for professional indemnity cover on the European insurance market. The most humble 'slip and trip case' may be covered by after the event insurance provided by a subsidiary of an American insurance company. The reason is that globalisation is not only, or not mainly, about an increase in world trade. At one level it is correct to say that the market for legal services at an international level is intense and growing. There are multitudes of examples of this which are evident from any reading of the professional press. The Da Heng Law Office in Beijing has now opened a law office in Amsterdam. Many European and American firms are opening offices in the Far East in response to pressure from clients whose base is now moving from a national to an international, or even virtual platform. World trade is massively increasing and the demand for service industries, whether they be IT, accountancy or legal services, follows behind.

A key driver is telecommunications. The creation of real time systems for communication across the globe allows multi-national companies to exist. Whilst in the nineteenth century such companies did exist, they were limited by the delays in the flow of information consequent upon a system dependent on the telegraph and the steamship. Now, there is no technological reason why a company's communication cannot be as simply operated across continents as within one state. The implications of this have spread inexorably into the domestic sector. We have seen the rise of call centres that have revolutionised the domestic insurance industry. We can also see that this technology is increasingly applying to the provision of legal services. The first group to become active in this field were the domestic insurers who have bolted legal advice onto their services. Now, the claims management companies are operating national campaigns to attract new work (personal injury and employment cases) that are initially serviced by a network of call centres. That work is first of all directed to franchised claims managers and then ultimately ends up in the hands of panel solicitors. Many of those panel solicitors are the high street firms that I mentioned, but the generation of this work (which is mostly new work) is entirely due to a technique – the remote call centre and communication network – that underpins the globalised economy. In this way, techniques which might immediately seem only of interest to companies like Ford and McDonald's have become highly relevant to small and medium-sized enterprises.

Globalisation proceeds hand-in-hand with modernisation, which is generally expressed to be the creation of a political and economic system based on complex commodity-based industrial systems. Again at first sight that might seem irrelevant to the interests of ordinary solicitors in the UK and of more interest to third world countries struggling with the cost of development. In fact, the process has an immediate bearing. One example is the worldwide reduction in public expenditure in the developed world in favour of the market. This has many aspects, including a reduction in welfare benefits, but also it has changed the way in which states, across the developed world, have financed those areas that they wish to continue to fund. An attempt is being made to introduce the invisible hand of the market into the provision of state support. Thus, our rail companies now compete for a subsidy from the state on which baseline they then operate a limited market pricing system. Legal aid in England and Wales has proceeded on the same basis. Instead of providing a case by case funding system, all legal aid will ultimately be provided by way of contracts whereby the decisions and risks of work are transferred to the contractee with what is intended to be a light management touch from the contractor. This 'contract culture' represents the process of modernisation.

Alongside these developments is a growth in assertiveness by clients who, faced with the creation of a market approach in all aspects of modern life, including education and health, are increasingly looking for value for money.

Service changes

These pressures lie behind the process of changing litigation to dispute resolution. Dispute resolution indicates a range of services provided by the litigator including pre-issue activity, arbitration and alternative dispute resolution. Whilst the 1970s and 1980s saw a slow growth in alternative dispute resolution – predominantly mediation in England and Wales – there is no doubt that the pressures of the market and new procedures are increasing the pace of this type of dispute resolution system. The pattern in the USA has been that mediation has taken off when it has been promoted by the court (sometimes called court annexed mediation). The incentive here was for the court to find a method to resolve the pressures of criminal litigation on the system where judges had both criminal and civil lists. Pressures on the criminal calendar meant that judges were increasingly unable to cope with civil work and looked for new methods of resolving such issues. A requirement that cases should be mediated, together with a not uncommon requirement in American law that parties negotiate 'in good faith', meant that a substantial amount of cases could be successfully mediated. (In fact, it may well be that mediation would have been even more successful in the USA if it had not been for the omnipresence of the jury. As such, claimants might be more prepared to mediate their cases except that they wish to enjoy the advantages of having juries set the damages.) Although cases issued in the courts of England and Wales are down at present and may remain suppressed because of the influence of the Pre-action Protocols, the courts anticipate being under future pressure because of increasing numbers of criminal trials and human rights litigation. It may well be that pressure from the courts to divert cases away from trial, particularly in the multi-track, and pressure from clients, may result, as is demonstrated in Chapter 14 below, in increasing interest in alternative dispute resolution.

These service changes, as will be demonstrated throughout this book and particularly in Chapter 3 below, impact on the human resources of solicitors' firms. Instead of the uninvolved proceduralist, described above, what the modern firm requires are individuals with the ability to apply risk management and effective entrepreneurial values to legal work, rather than simply the ability to manage large caseloads. That species of management is a very particular one – juggling. A litigator carrying a caseload of 200 or 300 cases acts like a Chinese juggler attempting to keep a series of plates spinning – a little touch here, a little touch there, keeps the plates going round. Failure to pay attention to all the plates means that some will come crashing to the ground. An attempt to devote equal attention to all the plates is impossible. An attempt to pay proper, appropriate and deep attention to a single plate is also impossible. Under the old procedures, such plate-spinning was possible and might be regarded as very profitable. However, new procedures mean that it will no longer be sustainable.

INTER-CONNECTING FACTORS INFLUENCING THE MODERN LITIGATOR

The factors outlined below represent a network of interrelating and sometimes opposing influences on the modern litigator. However, there is no doubt in my mind that the survivors of this great shake out will generally join the new model army of partner-problem solvers.

The rise of management

It is implicit in the change from the old to the new model that management becomes more and more vital to the success of litigators and firms. In the past, solicitors' firms operated in an environment where competition, and rewards, were less intense, the need to organise teams of personnel was less evident, capital investment was lower and the pace of work was slower. Everything has changed. On the one hand, the sole practitioner personal injury lawyer in Nottingham scours the market for new insurance products to back litigation whilst in Tokyo the branch of a globalised solicitors' firm starts the day by spewing out reams of current client information to track down potential conflicts of interest. Both examples illustrate a move away from the central idea of a litigator as a proceduralist getting the *rules* right, to litigators as managers making sure the *process* is right. This *Handbook* is essentially about the necessary skills and knowledge to manage the process of dispute resolution in all its phases: from getting the work in the first place to being paid for it at the end. In short hand terms we can see a change from a service profession to a modern business. One cause was the lifting of the limit on the number of partners allowed under the Partnership Acts which have facilitated the mega-partnerships which stride across the national and international stage. Multi-disciplinary partnerships (MDPs) and cross-jurisdictional practices will further enhance this process. It goes without saying that the task of managing such huge businesses is very different from the double figure partnership firms of the past, which were often little more than groups of individual practices in a more or less collegiate setting. It has now become impossible to practise without devoting more and more time to entrepreneurship, and financial and human resources management.

New methods

In 1993 I joined Nottingham Law School. Why? The reason was very simple. I had been involved in training solicitors by fairly traditional chalk and talk methods but I was dissatisfied with this approach, which concentrated on the knowledge that solicitors needed rather than the method and work-style that would make them more efficient and effective.

One day I wandered into a litigation summer school run by Professor Peter Jones. There I saw the astonishing sight of a High Court judge (Otton J as he then was) moderating a hypothetical case dealing with an environmental problem. He created a tale of intrigue and excitement and followed a tangled web of tactics and strategy which allowed the panel of litigation experts to bring the problem to life. This was the way to teach litigation. The approach of the Law School was to treat litigation as a goal-orientated activity; identifying the clients' interests and objectives and pursuing them in a single-minded way. At its simplest this establishes that in litigation, as in most practical legal subjects, black letter law must be partner to a thorough understanding of ends and means; after all, with very few (and often painful) exceptions, clients are not interested in the minutia of the law that applies and the potential of exciting points to be taken on appeal, but rather mundane but important questions such as: will I win and how much will it cost? The approach developed by the Law School with collaborators in practice and academic life in the UK and USA, was to view litigation as a multi-faceted discipline, as shown below.

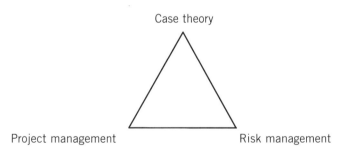

Case theory

Project management

Risk management

Figure 0.1

In the lead has been and will always be case theory. In the past I would listen to litigators, often highly successful lawyers, say that their job was simply to be 'commercial', to do the deal and issues of law and procedure were secondary to tactics. In fact, a deeper analysis of their approach indicated that they adopted and used case theory – they simply didn't articulate it and this approach marked them off from less successful litigators.

What is case theory and what does it mean in practice? An analogy can be drawn with painting. The simplest approach to painting is to do it by numbers; slowly but inexorably the picture emerges but it is far from clear how the picture will end up. (Unless, of course, you sneak a look at the finished product on the outside of the box, not an approach available in litigation.) The skilled painter has a mental idea *from the start* about the end result and strives to reproduce it, shifting and changing the picture as it develops. The skilled litigator approaches a problem by gathering the basic facts – the initial interview, the first documents – and constructs from them the initial case theory. By using techniques that can be learnt and which are not wholly dependent on experience the litigator develops an analysis of the case.

Case theory

A theory of the case that draws on initial fact investigation, and knowledge of the substantive law applying that demonstrates how and why the client, claimant or defendant, should win.

It hardly needs saying that in the era of conditional fee agreements and after the event insurance, often signed up at first instructions, an initial theory of the case is vital. The theory will alter as new facts, new legal interpretations or more rarely new law, intervene but the course is always laid towards the final clash of the client's case against an opponent in trial or across the negotiating table. What should never happen is an aimless approach, collecting facts to which the litigator's mind is applied at a later stage or, even worse, in which counsel is belatedly asked to advise. Even though every solicitor will have an idea about the nature of the problem (tort, contract, regulatory or a mixture) and a feeling about the odds ('looks like a good case'), case theory offers a much more rigorous approach. At this point many litigators new to the game may say: 'so what?' This approach has now become almost universal in the training of young solicitors, in continuing education and in the daily working of many firms. However, it must not be forgotten that less than 10 years ago the theory of the case was not the normal way of conducting litigation in this country and, indeed, was often regarded as yet another unnecessary import from across the pond, such as confessional TV. Times have changed.

Case theory wills the ends but it does not will the means. For this further work is required to translate the theory into a viable plan.

Case planning

Planning what are the resources necessary to win the case and in what order they should be deployed.

Case planning uses the theories and experience of project management: the powerful technique that has transformed the world, organised the construction of the bridges, the software, the company structures and the public services that control our lives. In legal work project management has always been part of organising merger and acquisition transactions where large teams have to be deployed across firms and clients to move towards a final pre-planned denouement: the transfer of ownership. Litigators have tended to say that litigation is more like war – litigators need to be flexible and quick on their feet to meet the unexpected challenge from their opponent. If this was ever true – in litigation or in war where generals know that an army marches on its stomach and resources planning is key – it has been replaced by the post-Woolf 'cards on the table' approach. Ambush has been replaced by case management. As explained in Chapter 6 below, the techniques of project management are not 'mumbo jumbo' but are an easily accessible, comprehensible and essential element of modern litigation practice.

The final element in this triangle is risk management.

Risk management

The identification, elimination, transfer and management of risk: risk to the client, the case and the firm.

Risk management has little or no role for the 'uninvolved proceduralist' who is, essentially, a free standing service professional, task-orientated, not paid by results and, often, not in the bigger picture. Conversely, the 'partner-problem solver' is much more likely to be in an ongoing relationship with the client where the identification, elimination and management of risk is central to the task; whether those risks are legal, financial or organisational and whether centred on the business of the client or the solicitors' firm; in other words, a genuine partnership.

Risk management is the 'new kid on the block'; the latest element in the dispute resolution equation. My own view on this subject has rapidly developed over the last four years. At that time, I led a seminar in the Law School on what I saw, in the context of conditional fees, was likely to be of fundamental importance to the organisation of litigation: the management of the risk of individual cases. It seemed clear to me that the concept of a success fee meant that the calculation of risk in a particular case must inevitably involve views as to the profile that the firm took to risk across its present and prospective cases. A firm that was risk averse might lose fewer cases but was unlikely to build new work and attract the volume that seemed to me to be the key to success in this new, highly competitive, environment.

13

Nothing that has happened in the intervening period has changed my mind about the basic requirement to risk manage individual cases. In the funding environment which has now unfolded after the Access to Justice Act 1999 the decision made by the fee earner when taking instructions will increasingly become a complex matrix involving: the view taken of the client (can the instructions be believed, should the instructions of the finance director be double checked with the managing director?); the type of funding arrangement (hourly paid, some type of individual fee) and whether, and to what extent, insurance should be involved in identifying and managing risk. However, it is now becoming increasingly clear that risk management cannot be restricted to the individual fee earner and individual interest. Firms need to be re- engineered so that *all* of their activities are constructed on a risk management model. The process is well developed in the commercial area with litigators being called in to advise on the drafting of contracts to make them less likely to generate claims or to channel claims in more user friendly directions. One example of the latter approach is to ensure that commercial contracts incorporate time-limited mediation processes before the parties embark on litigation or arbitration (which is becoming as arcane, expensive and long-winded as the court process). Some clients may well resist this pro-active approach as they may prefer only to pay lawyers to resolve issues using court-based techniques, and feel they can otherwise resolve problems under their own steam and avoid using lawyers. They need to be persuaded that the pro-active approach is likely to be more effective and will reduce legal bills. Does this not involve litigators cutting their own throats? I believe not. If, as I discuss below, litigation work is splitting into 'commodity litigation' and 'added value litigation' then the choice seems to me to be increasingly between joining the race to the bottom – low fees and less control – or 'adding value' to the process by keeping the value and cost of the work high and being effective in what, with globalisation and increasing economic progress, is a competitive but growing market.

My work on risk management for litigators is just beginning but I suspect that if case theory and project management have been the theme of the 1990s, risk management will be the theme for the twenty-first century.

New workstyles in the new procedural regime: the bombshell of the overriding objective

This *Handbook* is different from most works on litigation because it considers managing the process of dispute resolution as being central to the work of the litigator. Knowledge of technical procedural rules forms only part, although a vital part, of that process and these are dealt with in Chapters 9 to 15 below. However, there is one aspect of the new CPR that must take centre stage: Part 1, the overriding objective. The overriding objective Rule sets the stage for a revolutionary change in procedural approach: from a 'hands off' to a 'hands on' approach which influences all stages of litigation activity.

The overriding objective is centrally important for three reasons. First, dispute resolution in all its many forms is played out against actual or potential litigation with state-imposed sanctions – damages or injunctive remedies – in the background. The CPR and its overriding objective hang like a shadow over all negotiations or discussions between parties even before a claim is issued *or where it is unlikely that a claim will be issued*. Parties in the UK do not agree to settle their quarrel because they prefer consensus to argument. One party feels injured and wants recompense. The *form* of dispute resolution may alter according to circumstances, where the parties have a need to preserve a continuing relationship or whatever, but there is always the prospect that if discussions break down there is the possibility of involving the state court system. Secondly, the overriding objective permeates the whole of the CPR, filling in any gaps and helping with interpretation. Thirdly, as is explained below, the overriding objective, together with the CPR as a whole, have a substantial influence over pre-litigation behaviour. The new costs rules and case management powers dictate that early issue is not viable: 'jaw, jaw' must precede war. Fourthly, the overriding objective impacts on the role of the trial. In practical terms the trial was theoretically unimportant to litigation because so few cases came to trial (less than 2 per cent). However, the influence of the trial was extreme, the whole of the process of litigation being adapted to produce before the judge pleadings and evidence generally in the form generated by the parties' lawyers along the lines of which they wished to advocate their case. This can be compared with the procedure in civil law countries where the trial is downgraded and many decisions are made in the pre-trial period. Woolf procedure moves towards a similar process of limitation of trial effort, by decision-making on key issues before the trial. This was already hinted at by automatic directions but now is fully in force, in parti-cular, in the fast track and in the prescriptive approach adopted by many case managers in the multi-track.

Analysing the overriding objective

The overriding objective has a central objective of dealing with cases justly. In fact justice is not tempered with mercy but with expediency. In common with procedural rules in every jurisdiction, the CPR represent a compromise between allowing parties to litigate according to their own wishes and establishing fairness between the parties and being fair to the taxpayer by rationing the amount spent on the court system, buildings, staff and judges. How does this inevitable compromise work out in practice and how will this affect litigators and clients?

The concept of procedural justice is broken down into four areas:

(a) establishing equality between the parties: the court cannot make parties equal but they can equalise *litigation effort;*

(b) saving expense: parties should be economical with their litigation activity; to do otherwise is to put an unfair burden on the loser (who should only pay reasonable costs), on the client (who picks up the balance) or the court (which prefers to provide a stage for short, snappy and well focused performances);

(c) encouraging proportionality: while expense as a whole should be reduced, parties should gear their litigation effort to the task in hand (let us take scalpels rather than hammers to the task of cracking nuts);

(d) issues should be dealt with expeditiously and fairly: litigation is not to be a game for the amusement of solicitors or clients wishing to exhaust their opponent. If litigation is launched then it is to be concluded with an amount of effort that is consistent with justice. If not, then the court can impose penalties or withdraw its services and throw the case out.

These objectives are specifically promoted in two ways:

(1) Protocols approved by the Head of Civil Justice lay down arrangements for the exchange of information prior to the start of proceedings. If no protocol is applicable for the type of case, by Practice Direction parties should 'act reasonably in exchanging information and documents relative to the claim and generally avoid the necessity for the start of proceedings', in penalty of costs.

(2) Active case management gives the court all the necessary powers to take steps to direct litigants and lawyers to direct their effort to areas of fact investigation or legal argument that the *case manager*, rather than the parties, think is important to the trial judge's decision in the case. This should be based on two objectives: first, to 'allot to [the case] an appropriate share of the Court's resources whilst taking into account the need to allot resources to other cases', in other words, a rationing system; secondly, as the means whereby all the objectives and, in particular, the issue of proportionality are given life.

The implications of the overriding objective in practice

It is still too early to attempt a definitive analysis of the impact of the Civil Procedural Rules. Together with Professor Mary Seneviratne I have embarked on research for the Lord Chancellor's Department to see what effects can be measured in the use of case management by track or within a track. There may well remain areas of practice, or areas of the country, where the aim of active case management is honoured in the breach. The tradition of a neutral umpire runs very deep in the common law world. However, in a sense, the activities of individual case managers are fundamentally irrelevant to the change in culture worked by the totality of these new rules. The argument is a simple one. The CPR creates a fundamental shift in the cost benefit analysis for parties in determining whether their disputes should be resolved by litigation or ADR or by negotiation. First, litigation now offers a risk that the case manager will remove freedom of action from the solicitors and retain it in the court (the fast track institutionalises this risk). This makes the outcome and the ultimate distribution of costs much more unpredictable for a litigator and it is hardly surprising that the volume of commercial litigation declined after the introduction of the CPR and remains flat. ADR and, in particular, arbitration offers a more attractive alternative to litigants who do not require state power to back them. Secondly, as is discussed throughout this book, the process of pre-issue exchange of information, allied to the new cost regime, increases the advantage of early settlement and will also divert cases from the courts. The effect of these structural pressures will be to limit litigation activity in favour of other methods of resolving disputes. The courts will remain busy because new areas of jurisdiction, such as human rights, are emerging and also because the total numbers of disputes are rising for the reasons explained at the beginning of this Introduction and, inevitably, a proportion will not be resolved pre-issue or diverted away.

Examples of the new rules in practice

What follows is an incomplete and entirely arbitrary snapshot of elements of decisions in a few cases to demonstrate how some of the concepts in the overriding objective and the rest of the CPR are being interpreted.

Biguzzi v. Rank Leisure Plc ([1999] 1 WLR 1926, CA) was an application to strike out. Following an injury in 1993, proceedings were begun in 1995, and automatic directions applied from December 1995. There was incomplete compliance by both parties with directions. The claimant applied to set down then had it vacated on a condition that was not complied with. In 1997, the defendant successfully applied to strike out. On appeal to the judge in 1999, the case was reinstated. The Court of Appeal held that it was essential that parties did not ignore timetables. If they did the court must show by its conduct that it would not tolerate failure. When deciding whether to strike out the court should also consider the administration of justice generally: the effect on the court's ability to hear other cases if default was allowed to occur in this case. Judges had to be trusted to exercise their wide discretion fairly whilst recognising the responsibility to litigants in general not to allow the same defaults to occur in the future as in the past. The whole purpose of making the CPR was that they should be a self-contained code and the earlier authorities were no longer relevant now that the CPR were applicable.

Charlesworth v. *Relay Roads Ltd (No 2)*, (*The Times*, 31 August 1999, Patents Court) was an application to amend a statement of case and to call further evidence after hearing and judgment but before the order was drawn up. It was held that there was jurisdiction to apply CPR, Part 1 to balance the desire of parties to put forward every point they wanted against the strain of litigation, legitimate expectation, efficient conduct of the case and the interests of other litigants; that discretion must be exercised in a way best designed to do justice. So, the order would not be granted just because the other side could be compensated in costs.

BCCI v. *Ali and others* (BCCI Employees (No 4) (1999) 149 NLJ 1734, Ch D) was a breach of contract claim in which breach was established but none of the claimants could establish any loss. The costs of each side exceeded £1m. It was held that the pre-CPR approach to costs was inappropriate, there were no constraints beyond those in the CPR. 'Success' was not a technical term but a result in real life and the question as to who succeeded was a matter for common sense, taking a realistic view of the outcome in the context of the case, including conduct at trial. On an overview, 'honours were even' and the proper course was no order as to costs.

In *Townshend* v. *Superdrive Motoring Services Limited* (unreported, 4 February 1999, CA), the claimant in a county court case wanted orthopaedic, psychologist, maxillo-facial, care/rehabilitation and employment experts. The Court of Appeal held that the orthopaedic surgeon could deal with the maxillo-facial issues, the court did not need an employment expert and the care consultant could deal with employment issues as well. 'In the present climate of change, and noting the content of Parts 32 and 35 of the new rules, the order of the judge was not wrong.'

In *Daniels* v. *Walker* ([2000] 1 WLR 1382, CA), a joint expert was appointed by consent. After the report had been provided, the defendant objected to its conclusions and sought permission to have the claimant examined by his own doctor. A further report was refused but further written questions to the joint expert were allowed. The defendant appealed on the basis of CPR Part 1 and Article 6, of the ECHR. The Court of Appeal held that judges should be robust in resisting human rights arguments. However, if it would be unjust under CPR Part 1 not to allow the subsequent evidence, it should be allowed. If, for reasons that were not fanciful, the defendant was not satisfied with the joint report then he should be allowed to seek further information and where large sums are involved it might be reasonable for the defendant to have his own expert. Oral evidence should only be given as a matter of last resort.

In *Securum Finance Ltd* v. *Ashton* (*The Times*, 5 July 2000, CA), the Court of Appeal held that it was no longer open to someone who had had proceedings struck out for inordinate delay to rely on the principle that a second action within the limitation period would only be struck out in exceptional circumstances. The court had to consider CPR Part 1 and to consider whether the claimant's desire to have a second go outweighed the need to allot resources to other cases. Some claims made in the second action but not in the first could not be struck out for abuse of process and those issues would have to be resolved whether or not the claims that had been brought twice were struck out or not.

In *Carr* v. *Bemrose* ([2001] EWCA Civ 194, CA), negotiations began between the parties before the issue of proceedings on 26 October 1998 and continued throughout. On the issue of costs the district judge directed herself to the provisions of CPR Rule 44.3(2)(a) that, as a general rule, the successful party should recover its costs. The judge held that the conduct of the parties had been 'too close to call' before 13 January 1999 but that the defendants should have their costs thereafter. The Court of Appeal held that the judge had not erred in principle and had not failed to consider everything relevant to the exercise of her discretion. In so doing she had looked at whether to depart from the general rule and, in exercising her discretion under CPR Rule 44.4, had looked at the conduct of the parties both before and after the issue of proceedings. There was nothing that flawed the exercise of her discretion.

Stocznia Gdanska SA v. *Latvian Shipping Co.* (*The Times*, 15 March 2000) was an application by the claimants to adduce further documentary evidence. The application was made after the close of the trial but before judgment was handed down. It was held that the document was relevant to the case between the parties and had become available before judgment. It would not be just to ignore it in accordance with the overriding objective.

Other chapters in this book deal with the interpretation of the CPR in detail but I would suggest that some themes are beginning to emerge in the cases:

(1) The overriding objective is taken seriously in reported cases. However, the objective has different elements, stressing both the rights of the parties and of the wider community, in particular those waiting in the queue for the judge's time.

(2) Not all problems can be resolved by awarding costs. There may be occasions where this simply rewards a party who uses unfair tactics and has a deep pocket to support them.

(c) While excessive appeals to the Human Rights Act 1998 may be unwelcome, concepts of a fair trial in the overriding objective have great influence.

(d) The runaway expert industry is beginning to have its wings clipped.

In any system involving thousands of hearings with a myriad of different facts it is impossible to be sure that the views of the appellate courts are reflected in the day to day work of district judges and masters. However, appeal cases do set the tone. Does this mean the end of the 'Rottweiller' litigator? In so far as this beast tended to be more active in the heavy end of commercial litigation it may be that even taking proportionality into account, there will be more room to take interlocutory points. However, costs related to conduct may well act as a increasing brake on this activity.

One issue lurking in the shadows is the question of the long term impact of pre-issue activity as, increasingly, litigation can only be mounted after going through a protocol. Will failure to act reasonably during the protocol stage influence the distribution of resources and costs by the case managing judge?

Added value or commodification?

Not so very long ago on a Sunday the roads around my house in Sheffield would be filled with bored children mooching around, while, in the distance, a Salvation Army band could be heard patrolling the streets. Now those same streets reverberate to the sound of lorries delivering guavas from Madagascar to the local supermarkets where workers on flexible (i.e. zero hours contract) jobs stack the shelves according to plans laid out by the store's IT system calculated overnight in a back office in Bangalore. That same office calculates the spending patterns of royalty cardholders and ensures that they receive information about goods that they 'want' from the supermarket and a host of other companies. (Meanwhile in another part of Sheffield sandwiches are being made and flown out on a daily basis to Saudi Arabia!) The process of shopping has been transformed from an experience involving an intimate relationship with a shopkeeper and the sale of items linked to service elements into a process known as commodification: the action of turning something into a commodity; an article to be bought and sold as opposed to a service. Whilst supermarkets are keen to promote their service elements (if you ask where something can be found the shelf-stackers will now insist on going with you to the right aisle rather than simply pointing at it), in reality supermarkets are not about service but about selling.

What has this got to do with solicitors? I suggest quite a lot. The Great British public likes this anonymous approach and seems to want to receive some legal services in a rather similar way. How is this developing? Whilst the debt collecting end of commercial litigation has always been subject to the commodification process, with clients provided a mass of anonymous raw material (the claims) to be processed; the personal injury market has begun to exhibit the same characteristics. In particular, the relatively recent emergence of claims management companies and credit hire companies has given impetus to this change. Whilst working under legal aid or for trade unions has increasingly mandated a 'no frills' approach, the emphasis has remained on making and keeping a relationship, albeit, sometimes rather limited, between solicitor and client, with a continuing stress on service delivery. It looks as though times are changing.

Claims management companies have a long history in the USA where they are known as 'claims farms': companies who solicit for claims and then farm them out to attorneys. They have made limited impact in the personal injury market because in the USA, with contingency fees, it is always possible to find a lawyer to take a case, even if he turns out to be 'my cousin Vinny'. However, these methods are now being imported into the UK with some significant additions and improvements. Claims management companies operate in various ways but the system generally has three elements. First, a franchisee who is not normally legally qualified visits clients in their homes who have seen the advertisements and have telephoned asking for help. The franchisee/claims investigator passes on the details to a central body who carries out a preliminary sift. The cases that get over this first hurdle are sent to one of the panel solicitors, who then progresses the claim if he/she thinks that it is likely to be successful. While different companies operate in different ways, one scheme often sends claims to solicitors who are not in the area of the client. This 'doling out' approach – perhaps, to make sure everyone on the panel gets a fair crack of the whip – appears to reduce the time that the solicitor will spend on client contact and may make the system more efficient. However, it begs the question for whom is the solicitor working: client or claims management company? In any event, it does seem that a solicitor in this type of case is involved in the processing of a commodity, a fungible or traded commodity, rather than a personal service.

Credit hire companies seem to me to present an even more extreme example of commodification. These companies farm out work to solicitors on referrals they have obtained through advertisements or repair garages. They advance hire vehicles, or repair a client's own vehicle, following an accident and then claim their charges through the client. Often, the client has a personal injury claim in addition. Again, the question must be asked, who is the client in this situation, the injured party or the credit hire provider?

One effect of the process of commodification, linked to powerful IT systems, can be found in the emergence of the free Internet service provider. The ISP offers the basic commodity, Internet access and now the cost of the telephone call, for free or relatively cheaply. Money is earned by advertising, e-commerce and the gathering and distribution of information about customers to third parties. There is no reason to assume that solicitors' firms will be immune from this type of development. Already, we have seen a solicitors' firm offering a free will writing service to the clients of a company that purchases endowments. The key is the use of IT, allied to volume. This allows the firm to produce the legal commodity, in this case the will, very cheaply and sell the product to the company who will cover the solicitor's cost within the marketing budget. If such an approach might work with will writing could it not spread to other legal services, such as debt collecting? Of course it will, because it already has: firms who 'eat what they kill' and rely on 'both sides costs' do not look to clients to pay them for debt collection work.

As I discuss below, one aspect of these emerging arrangements will be the depressing effect on the real level of fees but this is already common in such areas as defendant insurance. It is hardly surprising, then, that many firms are looking to break out of the cycle of low fees, centralisation and commodification to an approach that stresses the 'added value' of the service they provide. In my view this is a very healthy development because it concentrates on the core values of litigators: risk management, negotiation skills, written and oral advocacy and, above all, sound judgement rather than the mere processing of claims. Any approach that concentrates on the process without considering the strategy and tactics of dispute resolution is bound to de-skill and undervalue legal work. While this process-based approach is viable for some firms and some practices it begs the question: what does the client need a solicitor for? It is clear that some areas of solicitors' work are vulnerable to emerging IT-based expert systems organised and run by individuals who may not need any deep legal knowledge. The modern litigator needs increasingly to 'work smart not hard'; in other words to move away from a concentration on viewing litigation as a task with a start (instructions), a middle (exchange of information between client, experts, counsel, opponent and solicitor) and a conclusion (taking a view and settling), towards a more global view that the dispute is a problem which needs a solution. That solution should be creative; it may involve negotiation; it may encompass ADR; it will not involve issuing a claim and spending months on cases before taking a view. Increasingly, litigators will want to be involved pro-actively at the start of problems or in advance of problems emerging as claims. I accept that claimant personal injury work is unlikely to come into this category but what about the defendant side? Claims arising out of the activities of large organisations such as the NHS or manufacturing industry need solicitors to intervene at the earliest possible stage to identify problems that are waiting to happen and then advise on speedy resolution.

Partnering or centralised control?

In some areas of practice the future has already arrived. At its height, the partnering idea is represented by the Du Pont chemical company 'wheel'. This involves the client in a close and long term relationship with a group of solicitors' firms closely integrated into the client's business and IT systems (this can extend to requiring the firms to recruit new staff using the client's own agency and to standards agreed with the client). In return for long term security the firms share information, for example about potential litigation threats, both with the client and each other. To this extent competition between firms is replaced by cooperation. It might be said that this is an unusual example in a very high powered area of litigation, quite untypical of normal practice. However, the logic of partnering is increasingly present in many more instances. For example, the franchising model adopted by the Legal Aid Board forces firms into a form of partnership with the Board: there is no other choice. Failure to obtain a franchise eliminates a firm from the relationship. One criticism of this analysis is that the idea of being close to the client suggests that a partner-problem solvers is involved in a relationship between equals. In some cases this will be true. Certainly, the increase in in-house lawyers in many companies and the corresponding growth in secondments of solicitors from firms into those companies suggests a 'team' model. Many beauty parades will include not only proposals on charging but also the ability of a firm to interface electronically with the client and, crucially, the ability of the in-house lawyer to 'see' progress on cases by electronically dipping in and out of the firm's files.

In some areas of practice, central control seems more in the ascendant than partnering. It seems inevitable that solicitors acting in the 'claims farming' area will be increasingly caught between two interrelated pressures: the demands of the 'real' clients and pressure on fees. One of the claims management companies has introduced a scheme that involves its panel solicitors being required to attend and pay for training courses it has brokered. At one level this is sensible risk management but it smacks more of control than partnering and, of course, it represents a discount against the fees that the solicitor can obtain.

However, the logic of modern litigation practice suggests that partnering will be imposed on *both* parties in almost every case. Let us look again at the example of the Legal Aid Board. It might be thought that the arrangements between the Board and firms is very one-sided, with the Board dictating the terms. However, when the current arrangements shake out, the Board will increasingly rely on a reducing number of well-organised firms to deliver on contracts in accordance with government targets of which cost will be only one factor. Running huge legal aid contracts dictates that only firms with advanced and expensive IT will be able to service the Board. To some extent the Board and its providers are handcuffed together and have to cooperate. Further down the line, only firms tied in to the Board's system will be candidates for a franchise: a shot-gun marriage may well lead to true love.

The idea that the logic of the marketplace and the demands of IT dictate partnering is not limited to heavy commercial litigation or the public sector. The defendant insurance market exhibits very similar features. Most public liability insurers have culled their panels and reduced their numbers from hundreds of firms to dozens or fewer. Whilst, this type of work, as I discuss below, is highly cost sensitive, the information required to run such panels effectively, to organise consistent reserving policies and to create common reporting systems will involve close working relationships between firms and their insurance client. As time passes it will be inevitable that insurers will see that locked into the files of their panel firms is information that would be of interest to the insurer both directly and also, by exchange with other firms, in creating a levering of the effort of the panel as a whole. Firms themselves have not settled back and been picked off one by one, many have reacted defensively in mergers which tend to equalise the power relations between big clients and their solicitors. If the number of firms is reduced and those remaining firms can offer a full service profile, then the freedom of movement of the client is reduced: the number of candidates in the beauty competition is limited to a few equally gorgeous candidates and the odds of winning the prize are increased.

Changes in funding arrangements

When I talk to non-legal aid firms at the moment, the message I am often given is that things haven't changed as much as I believe: the old ways of billing and charging continue and there is still plenty of work about. I am not so sure. As is set out so cogently in Chapter 7 below, the new cost rules, allied to the changes under the Access to Justice Act 1999, constitute a fundamental shift in the system of litigation costs with more to follow.

From a strategic point of view the changes can be divided into three areas:

Does time equal value?

It might seem that our current system of billing clients per six minute unit has been around forever: in fact it is only a couple of decades old. In the early 1970s, files were normally charged on a value billing basis (sometimes technically described as 'weighing' the file!). In other words the client was charged what the case was worth – an equation that included, but was not exclusively tied to, time. Two factors changed this arrangement. First, the growth of solicitors' firms and the need to increase efficiency meant that management felt they needed more information about what employees did and they also wanted to incentivise and control them, hence targets and time recording. Secondly, time recording developed because of that old but sound reason: it could happen. The growth of IT offered the possibility of capturing information cheaply and efficiently.

No doubt, time recording will remain central to the cost bargain between solicitor and client and between parties in litigation, but the picture is rapidly becoming more complicated. Larger commercial clients are increasingly looking for systems that offer payment for results. In other words a bargain is struck that sets out a regime for service delivery – who does the work, what is the timescale, what results are predicted, what is the reporting regime and so on – and this matrix, rather than a crude equation of time equals money, will be audited and the bill paid. At the commodity end there are already signs that clients who pay bills are increasingly attracted to fixed costs and certainty.

There will always be clients who will pay for the best and solicitors' firms who provide the best at a price. After all, to quote the old adage 'no purchase manager ever got sacked for buying IBM' (an adage that went out of fashion when 'Big Blue' had its problems, but now seems fashionable again). If you are an in-house lawyer of a large PLC with a serious piece of litigation then instructing a top solicitors' firm has a number of advantages: it is a safe decision and it convinces your opponent that you mean business. While the solicitors' firm's part of the bargain offers top class service it will come at a high price (too high according to the OFT). That is the way of the world but it is not the only way.

Let us consider the profit pyramid, as shown in Figure 0.2.

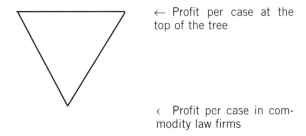

← Profit per case at the top of the tree

‹ Profit per case in commodity law firms

Figure 0.2

Whilst far from completely reversed the caseload model will look different, as shown in Figure 0.3.

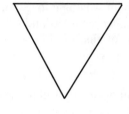

← Profit per caseload in commodities if firm case loads are large enough

← Profit per caseload at the top of the tree if firm caseloads are too low

Figure 0.3

Of course, the big city firms have, in general, solved the dilemma by marrying high fees per case with substantial and growing activity in the world market: they are highly profitable businesses. However, efficient solicitors' firms operating in the commodity market using IT, economies of scale and high turnover are, and will remain, highly profitable: trading volume against value per case.

The challenge lies for the firms in the middle: niche firms and small partnerships who do not offer 'must buy' services but are not big enough to dip into the mass market. There seems little option here but to offer 'added value' and to join in the new and exciting game: the 'risk business'.

Risk money, funding and 'eating what you kill'

The launch of conditional fees caused a very small splash in the pool of legally aided work. Whilst some practitioners have exploited them profitably they continued to have a limited impact. After all, why take a risk when relatively risk free work was available on legal aid. No longer. The withdrawal of legal aid and the arrangements to allow recovery of the success fee and premium will mean that conditional fees will colonise the whole of litigation except for the 'must buy' firms whose unique selling qualities will enable them to insist on being paid the high and certain hourly rate. (Even in this stratospheric area, clients will be putting pressure on to try to persuade solicitors to take risk.)

Risk taking is then the wave of the future but it will take a number of different forms, closely related to the added value/commodity split.

Added value cases, as explained above, where solicitors have special skills, knowledge or access to information, will continue to allow them to charge premium rates for their work. Will it or should it free them from taking risks? There will be pressure from clients who want to be able to limit and control costs and to get a good price on the insurance premium. After all, if the solicitor takes part of the downside risk then this should be reflected in the price of AEI insurance. If the work is done on a conditional fee with a success fee, with no charge to the client if the case is lost, then the premium should be cheaper. Even if no success fee is charged the downside can be limited by offering discounted hourly rates. It all comes back to a calculation of where the risk is and who should bear it. Let me suggest possible alternatives for the financing of a case, as shown in Figure 0.4.

Example A	Conditional fee with success fee	Lower AEI premium	Higher risk to lawyer than client	High reward
Example B	Ordinary litigation – lawyer paid full fee if case is lost	Higher AEI premium	No risk to lawyer, all the risk to client	No reward
Example C	Conditional fee without success fee, e.g. 'normal' rates if case won, discounted rates if case lost	AEI premium negotiated	Risk is part of the bargain	Reward?

Figure 0.4

Many litigators would prefer to remain in 'B', leaving the risk to the client and the insurer and accepting that they get no reward because, of course, they earn their profit within the fee. However, in a case with a good chance of success, 'A' might be more attractive as the risk appears to be high, and so might be the reward. Why would this be of interest to the client? Possibly, because the client cannot fund a higher premium and, of course, if the case is won under the recoverability regime the cost of the premium and the level of the success fee is irrelevant to the client. It might be said that this argument is flawed because there is no such animal as a good case with a high success fee: if the case is good then the risk is low and the success fee should be restricted. I am not so sure that, in practice, things will work out in such a neat mathematical way. I suspect that assessing judges will find relatively high success fees difficult to challenge *ex post facto* particularly if the calculation of the fee is well reasoned and documented. Again, time will tell.

Example 'C' offers a more potent brew for the negotiating commercial client and will represent a key element in the work of the future litigator. The process of assessing case theory and projecting the resources necessary to complete the task (project management) will form part of the partnership with the client: what is this case worth; how much will it cost to mount; what is the downside and the reward structure, including calculation of what 'normal' actually means in practice – do risky cases have higher 'normal' costs? The argument about risk seamlessly knits with the argument about the merits.

27

In *Commodity litigation*, 'You eat what you kill'. Commodity litigation simply does not suit the complex calculation of risk and reward suggested above. What will happen in the future, outside the now limited world of legal aid, is what happens now: no win, no fee, classic 'speccing'. It is clear that many debt collecting, legal expenses, claims management or credit hire operations do not involve the client paying if the case is lost. Overall, the calculation is made that the *caseload* will be profitable, at the expense of some individual lost cases. This arrangement now proceeds into a brave new world where the risk is muddied by the adoption of success fees and insurance. Only time will tell whether the insurance premiums in this area truly reflect risk (or are, perhaps, paying for the administration and profits of a claims management company or intermediary) and whether high success fees are sustainable.

In reality, insurance may increasingly look like a funding arrangement; simply providing the collateral to a bank that allows the litigator to draw down payments on account to fund cash flow where the work is carried out on an ordinary litigation basis. The bank can even advance the premium so that, if it is set at a recoverable level, it never needs to be paid by the client. It is hard to see conditional fees being attractive to the high volume practice in this situation; they may well accept limited reward in return for limited risk (that is ordinary litigation rather than success fees) trusting that their skill in getting the caseload mix right, allied to driving down costs and volume, will produce higher profits overall.

The future of both sides costs

The new conditional fee arrangements will in due course signal the end of the indemnity principle. What else will change? Britain is unique in having a system of cost recovery where winners get a substantial amount of their lawyers' fees plus outpayments and expenses. Additionally, it is unusual for recoverable lawyers' fees to be a moveable feast calculated only after a trial or acceptance of a court-based offer. These arrangements, allied to the new costs rules, introduce an element of uncertainty that does not fit well with an insurance supported litigation market. If a litigation insurer does not know the level of the client's lawyers' fees or the opponent's lawyers' fees or whether winning the case may still leave the insurer picking up 'own side' costs (for example, the judge decides that costs follow the event only on some issues) then premiums are bound to be higher than they need be to give a cushion. The German model offering a band of fixed fees looks very attractive and simple. Equally, the American system of pure contingency fees, with no transfer costs, has substantial advantages. The debate over this area has a considerable way to go but I suspect that in the fast track, costs will be inexorably transformed into fixed costs, not just for the trial.

In any event, the question of litigation costs may well become less important as dispute resolution becomes increasingly forward loaded and concentrated on the protocol stage. Fixed costs work in Germany partly because the court carries out a great deal of work rather than the parties. There is much more court-based activity but this does not necessarily lead to higher legal fees. In England and Wales we may be involved in a permanent move away from the courts with litigation as a last resort. If more cases are resolved pre-issue to what extent will the courts want to intervene on pre-issue costs? While this issue has been raised first in relation to pre-issue AEI, it also raises broader issues that may take some time to work through. Broadly, parties are either negotiating or exchanging before going to court, or litigating. Can the same cost rules apply to both or will it simply be a matter of traditional long term deals between parties?

This is far from an academic discussion. If, in the fast track, litigators are funding more and more work in progress through conditional fees, turnover becomes crucial to avoid over-trading. It may well be that a case on which the work is forward-loaded is most profitable at an earlier stage than under the old rules when costs (and potential profit) peaked just before trial. If this analysis is right, and it may vary from firm to firm, the question of the costs of the litigation process from the filing of the defence may be less important than the quantum of costs prior to this stage and who pays them.

New relationships

With the Bar

The speech by the President of the Law Society at the 1999 Law Festival was distinguished in one respect by a call for a single legal profession:

> One unified legal profession. No more solicitors or barristers – just lawyers. With one code of conduct, one set of rules, one regulator. One legal profession offering the public whatever legal help they need. Advocacy at every level, mediation, financial services, business consultancy, investment advice. From Legal Aid to corporate takeovers. Every legal service. All provided by one unified profession regulated and represented by the Law Society

It isn't necessary to accept this argument to understand that the relationship between solicitors and barristers in the post-Woolf environment is undergoing a sea-change. The position of the barrister has been, historically, that he/she were paid in any event. Indeed, it was a matter of professional requirement for a solicitor to ensure that a barrister's work was paid for when he or she had been instructed on a case, *even* if the solicitor was not paid by the client for the work. As such the Bar exhibited both the qualities of the independent 'gentleman' and the building sub-contractor, without a 'you won't get paid until the main contractor pays me' clause in the contract. Whatever the advantages of such a system it seems singularly old-fashioned for a system where the solicitor increasingly shares risk with the client, or in many cases takes all the risk of the case. There is some argument that some elements of the system may retain the ability to be paid in any event, such as experts (although I think that this is not an absolute requirement, e.g., experts routinely operate on a 'no win, no fee basis' in Eire). In a solicitors' firm there will always be some out-payments, such as secretaries, the electricity bill, etc., which will have to be met irrespective of the success or failure of an individual case or caseload. However, it seems contrary for that arrangement to apply to a fellow professional, capable of making similar risk assessments to the solicitor. Whilst that fellow professional expects to be paid, and well paid at that, then their position remains vulnerable. I certainly consider that the Bar has a healthy future but only as a profession of highly specialised and sort after 'stars' or as the specialised advocacy or advising element of a broader profession which is predominantly made up of solicitors. Certainly, from the point of view of the public the idea that one consults a 'lawyer' would be much clearer and would save a tremendous amount of explanation as to the difference between solicitor and barrister.

IT

IT with all its limitations is one of the prime examples of globalisation – 'nowhere will be there any more, it will all be here'. The space between clients and firms and between firms and the court will be compressed.

As well as the advice contained in Chapter 2 below we are fortunate to have two other incisive thinkers in this area: Professor Richard Susskind (see *The Future of Law* (OUP, 1998)) and Charles Christian *Legal Practice in the Digital Age* (Bowerdean Publishing Company Ltd London, 1998). I characterise Susskind as writing about 'what might and should be' and Christian as writing about 'what is and could be'. It is vital to have an overview of this rapidly changing area because opting out of IT is no longer an option for litigators. While Susskind introduces ideas of legal information engineering and expert systems, Christian concentrates on the client–firm interface.

Whilst both contemplate an eventual outcome where it will be routine for the client to see the firm's file (no more excuse that the papers are with counsel!), and for the procedural judge to communicate directly with the lawyers, we are some way off this. There is an inherent difficulty in the nature of litigation. In transactional work, it is possible for all parties and their solicitors to agree on a common protocol for communication and to use new web-based technology such as 'deal rooms'. In litigation, the parties' solicitors might agree but is the

30

court in the loop? Although some facilities can deal with bulk issue, it is likely to be many years before the courts as a whole introduce a system of electronic filing and issue which would also allow case managers to track cases and conduct audits of cases which have fallen behind the timetable, calling in the parties for explanation. However, the future is with us. Have a look at the webpage for the United States Bankruptcy Court for the District of Minnesota (http://www.mnb.uscourts.gov). If a lawyer wishes to initiate proceedings then all that is required is a simple click on the case-filing box. If the lawyer wishes to track the progress of the case, then there is another box that allows access to the electronic records. According to their latest announcement, over 2,000 cases have been issued electronically and after February 2001 all motions for relief *must* be filed electronically.

Just as the courts had to accept the use of faxes, so they will be unable to resist the onslaught of e-mail. The comparison is a useful one. If the litigant has the right to issue a writ within the limitation period and that right might be lost because of the administrative limitations of the court, then there may be a challenge under the Human Rights Act 1998. The court has had to allow for faxes to be recognised in the same way as a formal writ although, in reality, the paper fax is what it says it is, merely an electronically created facsimile of the original document.

If court IT will increase productivity and create a seamless web between clients, firms and the court, can solicitors afford to leave the pace of development of IT to the courts? Perhaps, like the road hauliers demanding better roads, it's time for the legal professions to lobby for increased investment in the courts to allow litigators to continue to compete successfully in the global legal market.

PART I

Running a Litigation Practice in the Post-Woolf Era

CHAPTER 1

Quality and standards

David Greene and Vicky Ling

INTRODUCTION

This chapter argues that changes engendered by the Woolf reforms are part of a general development in the environment of all businesses. Lawyers will find that the need to improve the quality of practice to meet the challenges posed by the Civil Procedure Rules will help them to gain and retain clients.

The whole litigation process has undergone a radical change. The Civil Procedure Rules (CPR) introduced as part of the Woolf reforms have an impact on every stage, from the moment that a client enters a solicitor's office for the first time to the date when the matter concludes. Practitioners have had to adapt to the more rigorous litigation climate and many are beginning to feel that the major challenge has been faced successfully. However, an examination of the wider environment suggests skills in managing change will continue to be essential to legal practice for the foreseeable future.

De-mystification and the information age

Changes in litigation practice are not just the result of administrative or legislative developments. Legal practice is undergoing a fundamental transformation. In the same way as hand loom weavers were rendered niche players by powered looms, the craft of law is being exposed to the scrutiny of the information age. Light has been let in on the mystery. Clients' knowledge and their reverence towards the law and lawyers has changed. Information about the law and legal process is more widely available, for example through the Internet. If clients are going to be prepared to pay for services, then lawyers will have to demonstrate that they add value. Meeting client need is a crucial element in any quality system, so lawyers will have to address quality seriously in order to attract and retain clients.

The quality of service provided by litigators is a mixture of subjective and objective standards. Clients are rarely in a position to determine whether their lawyers are technically competent. Surveys conducted for the Law Society indicate that they are usually content with their solicitors' knowledge of law, although it may be argued that clients' views are likely to be heavily influenced by the perception of whether they succeeded or failed in relation to a particular dispute. As clients' perceptions may well be conditional on the result, winning cases will remain vital.

Clients do not need any legal knowledge to compare the quality of legal service delivery with other services. In her 1998/9 Annual Report, *Modernising Justice . . . Modernising Regulation?* the Legal Service Ombudsman identified that 35 per cent of complaints against solicitors were about service provided. Of these 13 per cent were due to delay or inaction; 11 per cent, disregarding instructions; 7 per cent, failing to keep the client informed, and 4 per cent, lack of reply to letters or phone calls. In a world where the defining characteristic of successful organisations is quality of service, solicitors need to ensure that clients' experiences match or exceed their expectations.

COMPETITION AND THE LEGAL MARKET

In 1989 the Government issued a Green Paper *The Work and Organisation of the Legal Profession*. It examined the manner in which legal services were delivered to the public and identified that most services described as 'legal' were in fact administrative services which happened to be performed by lawyers and which could just as easily be provided by non-lawyers. The logic is reversible and lawyers may be uniquely positioned to provide new services as they can offer professionalism and regulation in the uncertain world of the Internet.

Competition in the litigation market comes from three major areas:

- within the profession;
- outside the profession;
- litigants acting for themselves.

Within the profession

There has been a substantial growth in law firms, both in overall numbers and the size of firms. Initially, this was restricted to London and particularly the City of London; but recent years have seen the balance shift towards growth in the provinces and the birth of large provincial firms. Larger practices based in other parts of the English speaking world, such as the USA, are increasingly opening offices in the UK. However, size is not necessarily a defining characteristic of success. As the market is growing and becoming more segmented, there is also room for a growing number of lawyers offering niche services – the number of sole principals has increased every year for the last ten years.

Competition between solicitors and between solicitors and barristers has never been fiercer. Under the Access to Justice Act 1999, solicitors can compete openly with barristers in the provision of advocacy services. Conversely, the pressure is on to allow clients direct access to the Bar.

A buoyant, competitive market is forcing practices to invest in staff, premises and information technology. Lawyers are beginning to concentrate on the costs of providing services including the output and profitability of fee earners. It is increasingly clear that business skills are required to prosper when a client is no longer yours for life.

Outside the profession

Accountants have been setting up separate associated legal practices for some years. In due course these may merge to become multi-disciplinary practices offering a full range of services, including litigation, to financial and corporate clients.

At the other end of the litigation spectrum, independent advice centres and Citizens Advice Bureaux, which meet the appropriate quality standard, are being given contracts by the Legal Services Commission to provide advice and assistance in 'social welfare' areas of law, including debt, welfare benefits, housing, and employment.

Currently, solicitors are the advisers of first choice in relation to litigation. Professor Hazel Genn (in *Paths to Justice* (Hart Publishing, Oxford, 1999)) found that 24 per cent of people whose problem was capable of resolution through the court system, approached a solicitor first, and 49 per cent of all those seeking help stayed with their initial adviser. These figures are encouraging; but could be improved if more people went to solicitors initially and stayed with them after the first contact.

All those offering legal services will find that their costs and quality of client service are being compared. Purchasers are looking for the right combination of quality and price.

Litigants acting for themselves

One of the policy developments furthered by the Woolf reforms is to simplify legal process to allow people to represent themselves. For example, a company can act in person in both the High Court and the County Court. Anyone acting in person may want to 'unbundle' the services offered by solicitors. Litigants may dip into solicitors' services from time to time when it comes to dealing with the more complex aspects of a piece of litigation, for example the preparation of witness statements or disclosure of documents, whilst conducting the matter themselves. The CPR allow the litigant in person to recover the cost of professional services used in this way even when the solicitor is not on the court record. There is a growing number of solicitors able to provide 'unbundled' services to meet clients' needs.

It seems inevitable that in smaller claims where no costs are recoverable or there is a fixed limit on recovery, there will be a growth in litigants representing themselves. If solicitors are to be instructed to represent parties in such claims, services will have to be offered on a cost-effective basis to provide a commercial proposition.

Quality: essential for success

At the heart of the quality revolution are three things:

- the power of client choice;
- the need to be able to respond to client choice effectively;
- the drive towards continuous improvement.

From a consumer's point of view, quality is based on the following guiding precepts:

- value for money;
- fitness for purpose;
- meeting agreed and implied specifications;
- delivery on time;
- right first time;
- reliability;
- satisfaction.

38

A joint DTI/CBI report, *Competitiveness: How the Best UK Companies are Winning*, identified key characteristics for successful companies. These include:

(a) management and leadership style: recognising the need for change and providing the drive to carry it through over an extended period;

(b) using the full potential of people already working in the business;

(c) meeting the needs of customers, identifying their needs and securing their comments;

(d) developing new and differentiated services or products;

(e) providing services that meet or exceed client expectations.

THE SOLICITORS' PROFESSION: A QUALITY ASSURANCE STANDARD IN ITSELF?

What is quality?

A common misunderstanding is to confuse quality with excellence. Sometimes we need 'the best'; but most of the time 'good enough' will be perfectly acceptable, especially when you consider the costs implications. International standard ISO 8402 defines quality as: 'The totality of features and characteristics of a product or service that bear on its ability to satisfy stated or implied needs'.

What do quality assurance schemes do?

All quality assurance systems set out an agreed standard and ensure that the standard will be planned and implemented in the provision of goods or services. All solicitors are subject to the general law, the Solicitors' Practice Rules, the Solicitors' Accounts Rules, and other requirements set out in *The Guide to the Professional Conduct of Solicitors 1999*, published by the Law Society. Some solicitors think they are subject to sufficient standards without seeking any outside those imposed by their own professional body.

A quality assurance system should meet the needs of the organisation's customer or client and be implemented consistently throughout the organisation. Until recently, solicitors would act in their clients' best interest without necessarily involving them overly in the decision-making processes concerning their cases. This approach is fast becoming outdated as solicitors find themselves part of the wider service sector of the business community which has a strong customer focus. The CPR is reinforcing this change by emphasising the involvement of the client in litigation.

39

It has been argued that the existence of the *Guide* and the Solicitors' Practice Rules act as a quality assurance measure for clients in themselves. Although in reality few clients are aware of the detailed requirements of the self-regulated profession, they do operate to ensure a professional standard of service to the benefit of the client.

Unlike self-imposed professional standards, many externally defined systems require quality audits to provide an independent assessment of the way systems are working. Identifying areas where systems are not working well enables the organisation to improve. Historically, solicitors have operated a system of mutual respect for each other's professionalism which has precluded reviewing each other's work. This has meant that solicitors' firms could not provide assurance about consistent standards of technical expertise or standards of service.

There are significant differences between the kind of quality assurance offered by professionalism and that provided by similar standards which are not self defined. Perhaps the most significant of these differences are:

- increased emphasis on what the client wants;
- independent validation.

What the client wants

Any standard which is developed with an outward focus, sets its sights firmly on the customer: 'the customer is always right'; whereas a self-regulating profession is likely also to consider issues relating to its membership – 'what sort of people do we want in our club?' – as well as its customers.

Independent validation

Solicitors are disciplined by their professional body if their standards are shown to fall significantly short of those required; but that does not provide as high a standard of quality assurance as being able to demonstrate that all requirements are actively being implemented.

Standards which are independently, externally validated, provide a higher degree of quality assurance.

More and more firms of solicitors are adopting standards, which incorporate an emphasis on meeting client needs and are externally validated. The Law Society itself has adapted the Practice Management Standards and created a system by which these can be assessed, 'Lexcel'. This and the other most significant quality standards for solicitors are discussed below.

Solicitors' Practice Rules 1990

The Law Society has done much over the years to assist the development of quality assurance standards. This development has taken place both within its regulatory regime and its advisory role.

Practice Rule 15

Within the framework of quality of service provided, the exertion of the regulatory hand of the Law Society has historically been light. This changed in May 1991 with the introduction of Practice Rule 15. This, the first compulsory practice rule, made a determined attempt at regulatory control of the quality of the relationship between the client and solicitor. As client care is a key component of quality, this was a significant development.

Practice Rule 15 addressed the issue of good communication between solicitor and client, which plays a crucial part in the client's perception of the quality of service. If the client is unaware of what the solicitor is doing and how much it is costing, he or she is unlikely to feel that a good service is being provided, regardless of the technical quality of legal service.

The Law Society (in *Client Care: Guide for Solicitors*) has acknowledged that 'Failure to give adequate information on costs frequently gives rise to complaints about solicitors'.

The requirements of Practice Rule 15, were that solicitors should:

- tell the client who was dealing with their matter, and his/her status;
- provide information about costs;
- have an internal complaints procedure and tell the client about it.

Solicitors were generally slow to comply with Practice Rule 15 and many litigators were reluctant to provide estimates of costs. They believed that it was too difficult to predict the course of a piece of litigation, and it is a truism to state that the cost of litigation may not depend on the amount in dispute. However, part of the professional's service is to advise the client of the cost/benefit of starting or continuing to litigate and in reality experienced practitioners do have benchmark figures for different types of case.

It is difficult to think of many examples where consumers make a free choice to use services without finding out what the cost might be at the end of the day. Estimates of costs are particularly important in relation to private client litigation, where the client is likely to be a first (and only) timer. Most members of the public have no idea at all of the costs of litigation, apart from the telephone

41

number fees quoted in articles about 'fat cat lawyers' in the press, which are hardly representative of fees in general.

One may have sympathy for the litigators who said that precise costs were difficult to predict, and who, as lawyers, were aware of the potential consequences of providing figures which proved, through no fault of theirs, to be inaccurate. Partly as a result of the open market in conveyancing, where private clients started to telephone for quotes, and partly due to the Legal Aid Board's requirements to carry out a basic cost benefit analysis when applying for public funding, the climate affecting advising clients on costs began to change.

By 1999, the requirements of Practice Rule 15 were strengthened and the definition of 'best possible information about costs' made more explicit in the Solicitors' Costs Information and Client Care Code. Failure to send a 'client care letter' with an estimate of likely cost may amount to a disciplinary offence of inadequate professional services under the Solicitors Act 1974 s.37A.

Information about costs

Information about costs must:

(a) be transparent: references to costs must include fees, VAT and disbursements, and a warning given to the client if charging rates may be increased;

(b) give the best information possible: including agreeing a fixed fee; giving a realistic estimate; or a forecast within a range; explaining the likely time to be taken, if relevant to the fee structure;

(c) cover the next stage in the matter: if it is not possible to give a realistic estimate of overall costs, the reasons why not;

(d) explain that the client can agree a ceiling on costs, not to be exceeded without authority;

(e) explain when payments to third parties may be needed;

(f) be updated as the matter progresses.

The Code provides that information given to the client must be given 'clearly, in a way which is appropriate to the client. Any terms with which the client may be unfamiliar, for example "disbursement" should be explained'. In addition, information given to the client orally has to be confirmed in writing as soon as possible, which gives the client something for reference and makes it easier to establish from the solicitor's file that the information has actually been provided.

The Code was framed to take the introduction of the CPR into account. Solicitors are now required to discuss the cost/benefit with the client at the outset and to keep the client informed of any changes during the lifetime of the case.

Estimate or quotation?

The CPR and Practice Directions provide for the provision of estimates of costs at certain stages of the proceedings. A solicitor may be bound by such an estimate given in a fast track case at the listing questionnaire stage. This accords with Lord Woolf's desire to provide predictability about litigation and particularly the amount of recoverable costs.

The Solicitors Act 1974 s.74(3), provides that, where a solicitor and client bill is subject to detailed assessment in the county court, the solicitor may not recover costs from the client unless there is a written agreement between them to that effect. This has not been used much in the past; but may be used more frequently if, as predicted, costs fall. This would mean that more solicitor and own client bills under £5,000 could be subject to detailed assessment in the county court. In addition, CPR Rule 48.8(1A) was introduced at the Law Society's behest, simply drawing attention to Section s.74(3) by repeating that the section applies unless written agreement has been reached to the contrary. As the agreement has to be in writing, it should be signed by the client for the solicitor to be able to rely upon it.

Practice Rule 13

This Rule has also been subject to clarification and development since its inception. The Rule provides that a solicitor's office must be supervised by a solicitor holding a practising certificate for at least 36 months in the previous 10 years and who has completed training specified by the Law Society.

It provides a key element of quality assurance for clients, as effective overall supervision should ensure that people within the practice (admitted and un-admitted) work within their own levels of competence and that they have opportunities for development. There will also be systems in place to ensure that individual matters are being progressed and 'sleeping files', the old enemies of client, solicitor and court alike, are avoided. Practice Rule 13 covers the following key quality issues:

- competence;
- supervision;
- process;
- legal requirements.

Specialist panels

The Law Society operates a number of specialist panels. In order to be accredited, solicitors must demonstrate a depth and breadth of experience in a particular area of law, for example; family, children work, personal injury, clinical negligence, mental health, immigration. Accreditation lasts for three years after which it must be renewed.

This scheme allows clients to see that their solicitors have substantial experience in the relevant area and that this level of competence has been independently assessed.

Professional standards or pious hopes?

In the areas of quality and standards of service provided by solicitors, the Law Society has increasingly moved from guidance to regulation. The Solicitors' Practice Rules set some minimum standards; but too often even these modest targets are not met, as statistics from the Office for the Supervision of Solicitors (OSS) suggest. There is a strong argument that clients are only provided with real quality assurance when standards are externally validated. This demonstrates that standards are honoured by observance rather than enforced by Law Society penalties when breached.

REVIEW OF QUALITY STANDARDS

Development of quality assurance

An understanding of the development of quality assurance standards can provide an insight into their structure and assist solicitors' firms in deciding which standard is appropriate for their needs and the needs of their clients.

It can be argued that the first quality standard was the Egyptian 'Book of the Dead' which set out in detail all the steps required in the process from death to entombment. At the end of the process, the work was checked by the Superintendent of the Necropolis before the tomb was sealed, which signified among other things that the procedures had been correctly followed.

The type of standard we are familiar with today first emerged in the defence industry in the Second World War, and many of those in current use are direct descendants of the NATO procurement policies of the 1950s and 1960s. NATO members wanted some form of assurance that producers of armaments would be able to provide the desired level of quality, so that regardless of the country of production materiel supplied would be suitable for purpose and with the objective that it could be used by any NATO country.

Quality assurance can be applied at any or all of the stages involved in producing products or services:

(a) *inputs*: resources or raw materials: in a solicitor's practice this would mean complying with Practice Rule 13, employing fee earners with the right skills and experience to work on matters, making sure that reference materials were available, and that continuing professional development takes place;

(b) *process*: ensuring that the right procedures are applied, for example in complying with the CPR;

(c) *outputs*: products or services produced, for example correct legal advice, being available at times and in locations as specified to meet clients' needs;

(d) *outcomes*: results or effects of outputs, successful results obtained for clients, client satisfaction with services.

In time, major customers were able to define the sorts of systems which they knew produced the products they needed. These were codified and published so that organisations wishing to tender for contracts would know what was required and it would be easier to compare bids. The Japanese motor manufacturer, Toyota, refined this approach and adopted the concept of 'Total Quality Management' or TQM. Total quality management goes beyond simply codifying processes and attempts to generate a culture aimed at ensuring that everyone gets everything right first time, every time. It stresses the complex interdependence of organisations and encourages cooperation between departments. It is based on three components:

- client-focused improvements (both internal and external);
- a documented quality system;
- management and staff commitment and involvement in achieving continuous improvement.

TQM means different things to different people; but Toyota understood that it had to have cohesive and continually improving internal systems. It also realised that in order to develop its products it had to work closely with the organisations which supplied it with components and raw materials. Toyota found that the best results were gained from long-term relationships between the supplier and the customer so that they could work together to improve cost effectiveness and performance. In turn, Toyota's approach influenced the Legal Aid Board as it conceived its Franchise Quality Assurance Standard in the early 1990s.

Initially, the development of agreed standards concentrated on manufacturing industries and their products. As service industries became more significant, it was necessary to develop a standard which related to them. The most widely recognised of these is the ISO 9000 series (previously known as BS5750). A key feature of ISO 9000 is that it can be applied to any type of product or service, since it concentrates on the management systems required rather than the detailed features of the production or service delivery process. However, some commentators (see e.g. John Seddon, *The Case Against ISO 9000* (Oak Tree Press, 2000)) find that ISO 9000 may stifle creative activity and this may explain why it can be difficult to apply in legal practice.

Organisational systems

Since quality systems are designed to ensure that defined objectives are met, it is usually easier to evaluate whether or not internal systems will be effective if they are documented. Some quality standards specify that some or all systems must be documented. As everyone working within the organisation has to be involved and follow the defined systems, documented procedures are useful because they are explicit and accessible. It is also much easier for an external auditor to validate the system, because it is easier to establish what people should be doing.

In order to be effective, the detailed requirements of a quality assurance system should be 'tailor-made' to fit the organisation and the successful systems it already has. This is why quality standards set out requirements, but tend not to specify the precise ways in which they can be met.

A system which is appropriate for a large organisation may be unwieldy and cumbersome in a small one. The best procedures are those which meet customers' needs, the standard required and the needs of those within the business. There must be sufficient flexibility to enable practices to be changed to suit new requirements or to be improved.

Benefits of quality systems

Solicitors' firms benefit from quality assurance systems in the following ways:

- promotion of good practice throughout the firm;
- objective evidence that the firm is meeting standards;
- problems are identified at an early stage;
- reduction in the amount of time taken to correct mistakes in individual cases;
- improved efficiency.

All the standards reviewed below provide practical management tools which will benefit solicitors and their clients. They provide benchmarks against which practices, whatever their size or type of work, both private and in-house, can measure the way they currently manage themselves. Once the benchmark has been established, the practice can use a checklist approach to planning improvement and development.

Improving office and case management through adhering to standards should lead to profitability and success. First, the organised and professional approach to management and administration advocated by the standards will reduce the risk of mistakes and wasted expense. It will ensure that the practice's resources (and fees paid by the client) are used most effectively. Secondly, in an increasingly competitive climate, standards help practices to provide services that meet clients' requirements and expectations, encouraging repeat business.

Types of quality assurance system

There are three types of quality assurance system: internal systems defined by the practice itself and monitored internally; supplier/customer schemes such as Legal Aid Franchising (to become Community Legal Service Quality Mark at Specialist Help Level); independent systems such as the ISO 9000 series.

Internal standards

Practices frequently define their own standards, for example time taken to reply to letters or the way in which the telephone should be answered. These are monitored internally, for example through supervision and file review (first party audits).

Supplier/customer standards

The Legal Services' Commission Scheme is a supplier/customer scheme. Increasingly, it is becoming mandatory for a practice to meet the quality assurance standard before it is permitted to supply services to clients who are eligible for public funding. Audits are conducted by the Legal Services Commission (second party audits).

Independent standards

Some practices want to be able to demonstrate that they meet standards which are set independently and are not determined internally or by a particular customer. The advantage is that many of these standards are recognised by clients, suppliers and competitors alike. More practices are becoming accredited to ISO 9000, Investors in People and Lexcel.

The assessors who carry out the assessment must themselves conform to a set of requirements and must be totally independent of the organisation which they are auditing (third party audits).

STANDARDS DESIGNED FOR SOLICITORS' PRACTICE

There are two standards which are specifically designed for solicitors' practice:

(a) Lexcel, the certification to the Practice Management Standards, accredited by the Law Society;

(b) the Legal Aid Franchise Quality Assurance Standard (shortly to be re-launched as the Community Legal Service Quality Mark – Special Help Level), which is accredited by the Legal Service Commission.

However, there are other standards which may assist practices to develop particular areas or may appeal to particular client groups. This section sets out the main quality assurance standards which are relevant to solicitors' practices, giving a summary of their requirements so that practices can make an initial appraisal and identify which may be particularly appropriate for them. It will be noted that some of the standards overlap or share common features.

Lexcel

In parallel with quality developments generally, the Law Society took steps to assist solicitors to interpret those standards for the purposes of providing legal services. As discussed above, Practice Rule 15 was introduced and the Law Society also provided briefings on how to interpret standards (see *Quality, A Briefing for Solicitors* and *BS 5750 Code of Quality Management for Solicitors* (1991)).

The market was moving towards establishing practice management standards and the Law Society rose to meet the challenge. The profession was also having to deal with continued and growing criticism of its record in negligence, which came to a head in 1993, when the Solicitors' Indemnity Fund announced a record number of claims against solicitors. In its review of the year, the Law Society identified that technical knowledge of law was but a small part of the problem. The major causes were delays and obvious errors, which might have come to light before reaching the point of negligence had there been better quality standards.

Following consultation within and outside the profession, the first Practice Management Standards were published in June 1993. At first these were a voluntary set of standards, recommended to solicitors; but there was no accreditation process to enable solicitors to demonstrate that they met their requirements.

This changed in 1998, when the Law Society authorised independent assessment organisations to carry out assessments against the Practice Management Standards. All the authorised assessment organisations have established track records in quality assurance assessment, either in relation to Investors in People or ISO 9000. All assessors undergo an approved training course before carrying out Lexcel assessments. They also operate established internal quality verification processes so that any practice can be confident that assessments are carried out competently and fairly. The assessor makes a recommendation and the certificate is awarded by the Law Society. The certificate is valid for three years, subject to annual maintenance visits.

The Lexcel standard has recently been revised to emphasise client care and risk management procedures. This has ensured that the standard is in line with the Law Society's strategic priorities and remains a credible scheme, which is 'substantial but not onerous' (see *Lexcel Practice Management Standard* (August 2000)).

What do you need to meet Lexcel?

This section summarises the main features of Lexcel to enable a practice to see what areas are covered. As Lexcel is arguably the most comprehensive standard tailor-made for all types of legal practice, it is worth providing some detail in the summary. Before considering any serious preparation, a copy of the current standard must be obtained. (For contact details see Appendix 6.)

MANAGEMENT STRUCTURE

- A written management structure with a named supervisor for each area of work.

SERVICES AND FORWARD PLANNING

- A three year business plan, reviewed every six months;
- a policy on equal opportunities.

FINANCIAL MANAGEMENT

- Documented responsibility for financial affairs;
- annual budget, variance analysis, profit and loss account, balance sheet, cash flow forecast;
- time recording system.

MANAGING PEOPLE

- Job descriptions;
- recruitment;
- appraisal;
- training;
- communication;
- supervision;
- equal opportunity policy.

OFFICE ADMINISTRATION

- Maintenance and support services, reviewed annually;
- health and safety, reviewed annually;
- office manual;
- legal reference material.

CASE MANAGEMENT SYSTEMS

- Index of matters;
- conflict checks;
- key dates back-up;
- authorisation and monitoring of undertakings;
- risk assessment of the types of work carried out;
- risk manager for the practice;
- procedures for managing problem cases with contingency plans;
- annual review of risk assessment data.

CLIENT CARE

- Compliance with Practice Rule 15;
- best possible costs information;
- consideration of funding sources.

OUTSET OF THE CASE

- Agree and record instruction, action and advice;
- advise name and status of person with conduct and supervision;
- provide information about complaints procedures;
- advise client on cost/benefit of matter;
- consider risk to practice of matter type.

PROGRESS OF MATTER

- Information to the client at appropriate intervals;
- monitoring cost/benefit to client;
- updates on costs;
- identification of all documents relating to a matter.

END OF CASE

- Report outcome to client;
- account for money;
- return original documentation;
- advise on storage;
- concluding risk assessment.

SERVICES FROM OTHERS

- Procedure for using barristers, experts etc.;
- consultation with the client where appropriate;
- maintenance of lists of 'others' used;
- clear instructions;
- checking material supplied;
- procedures for payment of fees.

FILE MANAGEMENT

- Status of file easily checked;
- orderly files;
- key information shown clearly.

FILE REVIEW

- Supervision of casework;
- procedures for allocation of casework;
- independent file review procedure;
- corrective action carried out promptly.

COMPLAINTS

- Definition of complaint;
- procedure accessible to clients;
- central reporting;
- appropriate response;
- corrective action.

Choosing a standard: Lexcel's features

All quality standards will provide a positive contribution to any practice. It can be difficult to decide which to adopt. The following are some of the features which solicitors have identified as particularly helpful in Lexcel:

- written in familiar language;
- suitable for any kind of solicitors' practice;
- joint assessment with Investors in People and ISO 9000 is available.

Legal Aid Franchise Quality Assurance Standard (LAFQAS)/Community Legal Service Quality Mark at Specialist Help Level

The Legal Aid Board (LAB) started to consider supplier quality assurance in the early 1990s. The work produced by the various solicitors' firms offering legal aid was not of consistent quality, nor comparable in price. At the same time, expenditure rose inexorably. The LAB realised that the technique of working with suppliers through a quality assurance system, similar to that used by the automotive industry, could be applied to publicly funded legal services.

Initially, the LAB set up a pilot scheme with six firms of solicitors in the Birmingham area. The firms implemented the LAB's quality system and in return were franchised and allowed to use devolved powers to grant certain kinds of legal aid. The LAB's quality assurance standard was based on the Practice Management Standards; but included some additional very detailed requirements in relation to the legal aid scheme.

In 1994, the franchise scheme became available nationally, with improved payment rates for franchised firms. Increasingly, the scheme has become a prerequisite for any firm wanting to do publicly funded legal work. In order to have a contract to provide legal services it will soon be essential to meet the quality standard. The Legal Services Commission (LSC) (which replaced the LAB in April 2000) is continuing to develop the scheme to assist it in meeting its new broad remit of promoting access to justice.

LAFQAS will become the Specialist Help Level of the Community Legal Service Quality Mark, the other levels being 'General Help' (broadly equating to advice and assistance) and 'Information' (Sign-posting and leaflets).

What do you need to meet LAFQAS/Specialist Help Quality Mark?

The original specification was based on the Practice Management Standards, so there is a great deal of overlap. However, there are no specific risk management requirements, which are increasingly being stipulated by insurance companies.

There are a number of additional contract compliance requirements. There are also requirements which emphasise the network aspects of Community Legal Service providers. These are designed to improve cross-referral, gather information on need for advice and ensure that services meets clients' needs, for example referral and client satisfaction.

ACTIVE SIGN-POSTING AND REFERRAL

- Operating a referral policy and procedures;
- recording feedback from clients about the receiving agency;
- recording instances where no suitable provider can be found;
- providing information to the Community Legal Service Partnership.

CLIENT SATISFACTION

- Providing opportunity for client satisfaction feedback;
- analysis of feedback to improve the organisation's performance.

TRANSACTION CRITERIA

- Analyse the procedures applied throughout a case.

These are audit checklists applied by LSC trained quality auditors to closed files. Transaction Criteria are regarded as a proxy measure to provide a degree of quality assurance about the technical competence of the lawyer, although they cannot assess whether or not the legal advice was correct. The scores must reach pre-set levels and a firm must pass the Transaction Criteria audit as well as the Management Standards in order to be accredited.

Choosing a standard: LAFQAS/Quality Mark's features

The following are some of LAFQAS/Quality Mark's features:

- essential for practices operating public funding schemes;
- assessment is currently free (but the Access to Justice Act 1999 has given the LSC the power to charge).

GENERAL QUALITY STANDARDS

As pre-action protocols have been developed by various specialist practitioners, so the number of quality assurance standards grows as different business sectors develop appropriate standards. A recent publication (Rowan Astbury and Heather Mayall, *A Map of Quality Standards* (NVCO, November 1998)) listed 10 different approaches to quality assurance, most of which would be of interest to lawyers in some respect. A thorough review of the quality environment is beyond the scope of this chapter; but it is appropriate to examine the leading general standards as they may provide a useful complement to those designed for solicitors.

Investors in People

The Investors in People (IIP) Standard was developed in 1990. It provides a framework for improving business performance and competitiveness, through good practice in human resources development. The standard was created by Investors in People UK, a public body whose main stakeholder is the Department for Education and Employment. A revised standard was released in 2000.

Local delivery is through the Training and Enterprise Councils (TECs). These will become part of the Learning and Skills Council network (to be known as LSC, confusingly enough to those in the legal sector!) in 2001.

There are four principles which underpin IIP:

(a) *Commitment*: an Investor in People is fully committed to developing its people in order to achieve its aims and objectives;

(b) *Planning*: an Investor in People is clear about its aims and its objectives and what it needs its people to do to achieve them;

(c) *Action*: an Investor in People develops its people effectively in order to improve its performance;

(d) *Evaluation*: an Investor in People understands the impact of its investment in people on its performance.

There are 12 indicators which show that the organisation is meeting the standard, and 33 evidence requirements specify the evidence an organisation needs to demonstrate. The revised version of IIP concentrates on outcomes, so the organisation needs to monitor the impact of training and development activities and the way that these enable organisational objectives to be achieved. A cycle of commitment, planning, action and evaluation can be applied to both individual and team performance so that high level plans are translated into successful day-to-day reality.

IIP can complement other quality standards as the management and staff of the business are the ones who achieve its goals. Investors in People UK believes that IIP acts as a framework which brings together other standards.

Choosing a standard: IIP's features

The following are some of IIP's features:

- emphasis on training and development;
- wide recognition in the business community and general public.

ISO 9000 Series (9001 and 9002)

Designed by the International Organization for Standardization as a standard which can be applied in any situation, equally applicable to manufacturing as to the service sector. The current standard was first released in 1994, and work on finalising a revised standard to be known as ISO 9000:2000 is nearing completion. In summary, it is likely to cover the following key requirements:

MANAGEMENT RESPONSIBILITY

- Customer and legal requirements;
- policy and planning;
- quality policy;
- internal communication;
- quality manual and control of documents.

RESOURCE MANAGEMENT

- Human resources;
- assignment of personnel;
- competence and training;
- infrastructure and work environment.

PRODUCT OR SERVICE REALISATION

- Identification of customer requirements;
- communication with customers;
- design and development;
- purchasing;
- process control;
- control of nonconformity.

MEASUREMENT, ANALYSIS AND IMPROVEMENT

- Measurement of system performance;
- measurement of customer satisfaction;
- internal audit;
- analysis of data;
- corrective and preventative action;
- improvement processes.

The main differences between ISO 9000:2000 and ISO 9000:1994 are: an increased emphasis on customer satisfaction; assessing availability of resources, measurement generally; and analysis of data on the performance of the quality management system to produce continuous improvement.

Choosing a standard: ISO's features

The following are some of ISO's features:

- internationally recognised by the business community;
- strong on process control.

Which standard for our legal practice?

As shown above, many features of the different quality standards overlap, and all of them produce beneficial results. Every practice needs to consider what it does and who its clients are before making a final decision.

The business reality is that clients in growing numbers are looking for accreditation to a quality standard and litigation requires reliable, consistent systems.

QUALITY WITHIN THE CIVIL PROCEDURE RULES

The overriding objective of the CPR (see Rule 1.1(1)) 'enabling the court to deal with cases justly' provides a deceptively simple and demanding quality standard against which the conduct of all litigation is now tested.

The key elements relating to quality assurance are:

- proportionality: parties must be placed on an equal footing and cases conducted appropriately to their value and complexity;
- economy: expense must be saved where possible;
- expedition: lawyers must comply with judicial management of cases;
- involving the client.

Proportionality

An impetus to improve quality in terms of value for money can be seen at the heart of Lord Woolf's inquiry. In the Final Report (*Access to Justice* (HMSO, London, July 1996)) he identified the problem as follows:

> The . . . present system . . . (is) . . . too expensive in that the costs often exceed the value of the claim; . . . too uncertain: the difficulty of forecasting what litigation will cost and how long it will last induces the fear of the unknown.

The CPR solution was to ensure that the costs regime encourages litigants to comply with case management procedures. More stringent costs penalties have been introduced, particularly where litigation is conducted in an oppressive or unreasonable manner. The quality challenge for solicitors is to ensure that cases are carefully planned from the outset and that each stage is given a budget which is then approved by the court before costs are incurred. Case management must now track case costs effectively to ensure that budget limits are not exceeded and that estimates provided to the court are accurate.

One illustration of proportionality catches the imagination: if the client is driving a Mini, they should receive the service appropriate for a Mini rather than a Rolls-Royce (see *Access to Justice*). An implication is often drawn that the consumer must pay substantially more for a 'better' product and that cheaper is necessarily inferior. However, to do so neglects the question of fitness for purpose, for example, if parking space is a problem, the Mini may be a 'better' product than the Rolls-Royce.

Claims in the fast track are subject to a regime of fixed costs, so solicitors must find ways to offer the best possible service within budget constraints. This has led many firms to implement computerised document production and case management systems, which allow them to provide a good service at competitive cost.

Economy

It had been recognised that prior to the reforms, preparation of expert reports resulted in huge costs and that these had become in effect a second tier of written advocacy (see Freshfields, *The Woolf Reforms in Practice: Freshfields Assess the Changing Landscape* (Butterworths, London, 1998)). A significant step in reducing the cost of cases was a new approach to the use of experts.

Lord Woolf believed that the use of single experts would be more likely to save time, money and increase the prospects of settlement. Although the CPR do not go as far as proposed in the Final Report, the emphasis is on the expert's duty to the court and the parties are required to cooperate wherever possible. The court also has powers to appoint a single joint expert and to determine remuneration.

Further, the court can require disclosure of instructions, so inevitably the degree of control exercised by an instructing party has been reduced. It may be that the reduction of experts' costs will take longer than envisaged; but practitioners are already responding to the clear indications that the pressure on legal costs and disbursements is heading in a downward direction.

One of the aims of Lord Woolf's reforms was to make justice more affordable for those on middle incomes. The rich had been able to afford to pay and the poor had been supported through legal aid; but many others with good cases were deterred from litigation by the fear of costs, both their own and their opponents.

Sir Peter Middleton's review of the civil justice system (*Review of Civil Justice and Legal Aid* (LCD, July 1997)) suggested that clients and their lawyers should 'share the risks' of litigation through conditional fee agreements (CFAs).

The combined pressures of fixed and conditional fees are likely to have an impact on the propensity to settle. It could be argued that more predictable costs and 'no win no fee agreements' would tend to encourage litigants to pursue litigation rather than to settle at an early stage. On the other hand, the introduction of other parties with financial interests in a case, notably legal expenses insurers and conducting lawyers, seem likely to exert a restraining influence.

Government policy has identified CFAs as an alternative to public funding for the majority of claims where damages are sought. This has engendered a fierce debate on the impact of CFAs on access to justice. Opponents of government policy argue that decisions about funding cases for impecunious litigants should be taken by decision-makers in a system which is open to challenge. Replacing public funding with CFAs effectively privatises the process. Unless a case has a very good chance of success it may be difficult to find solicitors to take a case at all; but such a decision has ceased to be an issue of public policy and is redefined as a matter of individual commercial judgement.

Solicitors are having to develop a more sophisticated approach to litigation funding, adopting a 'mix and match' approach where different sources of funding may be available at different stages of the case. They also need to develop data to assess and manage risk as the firm increasingly shares the risk with the client.

Expedition

Speed and cost are inextricably linked, so Lord Woolf took the radical step of removing the control of the litigation process from the parties and put the judge firmly in charge. The courts have become responsible for effective case management, including the regular scrutiny of costs, to ensure that the case justifies the costs incurred.

Rigorous pre-action protocols and strict timetables must be observed, from giving directions, with limited discovery, to trial. This creates a much more demanding quality standard for solicitors to meet in terms of case manage ment. Their internal systems must comply with the court's, and the penalty for failure is costs awarded against the solicitor rather than the client.

Successful post-Woolf litigators will have the ability to case plan, identifying key milestones at an early stage and anticipating the various critical paths that a case may take. Stages, which might have been taken at a leisurely pace over months or years, are now telescoped so that the solicitor needs excellent project management skills to ensure that witnesses, experts and counsel will be available at the right time. Systems to get case management right will increasingly be IT-based, and freed from some of the more pedestrian aspects of case management, lawyers will have more time to concentrate on the law and client care.

Involving the client

Lord Woolf's Final Report made significant proposals to increase client involvement, which have been adopted in the CPR, for example:

(a) *Statements of truth*: these declare the belief of the party that the contents are true and accurate; even where these are made by the representative on the client's behalf, the form of the statement makes it clear that it belongs to the party, not the representative;

(b) *Disclosure*: the person giving disclosure is required to make a statement setting out the extent of the search which has been made to locate the documents which are being disclosed; further, the person must certify that the duty to disclose has been understood and complied with, to the best of the party's knowledge;

(c) *Notification of costs*: if the client is not present when a costs order is made, the solicitor is under a duty to notify the client;

(d) *Costs and conduct*: the court should have regard to the parties' conduct (including conduct before the proceedings), for example, the manner in which the claim was pursued or defended and whether a claim was exaggerated.

A QUALITY SYSTEM IN PRACTICE

There are three elements involved in creating and maintaining an effective quality system:

(a) *a commitment to quality* made by the senior management and implemented through the line management structure; documentation demonstrating the commitment is not likely to change very often;

(b) *quality procedures*, which explain why each is necessary, what each covers and who is responsible for what; documentation detailing the procedures is like the skeleton holding the system together, it is not likely to need changing unless the practice makes major changes in its working methods;

(c) *work instructions*, which explain in detail how the quality policy is translated into day-to-day objectives; these are like the muscles on the skeleton, which respond quickly to frequent activity and atrophy quickly if not exercised! These are likely to change most frequently.

It is easier to follow a quality system which is documented (and many standards require documented systems). Legal practices often document all three elements within one Office Manual, which has the advantage of simplicity. However, it is important to remember that different layers within the overall system are likely to need changing at different intervals, which has implications for the way the documented system is put together. It must be clear how a procedure is put into practice through work instructions and as easy as possible to change them to ensure that they reflect current good practice.

The process for creating a quality system can be summarised as:

- say what you do;
- document it;
- do what you say;
- prove it;
- review and improve.

Starting from scratch?

The principal or partners need to make a commitment to achieving consistent quality throughout the practice, and identify the standard or standards which would be appropriate. The Management Charter Initiative (MCI) is an independent body set up by employers and backed by the Department for Education and Employment. Its aim is to promote competence-based management development. Individuals can demonstrate competence through National Vocational Qualifications. MCI has identified the knowledge and understanding required to establish quality assurance standards within an organisation. Their Management Standard 'Quality Management' (Level 4) may assist principals and partners to identify the managerial contribution to implementing a quality system.

Everyone within the practice needs to be involved because in one way or another everyone is affected, so communication is essential. Staff will quickly be able to tell whether or not senior management is committed to achieving a standard, and unless they can see that it is considered to be a priority at the highest level, they are unlikely to make it a priority on a day-to-day level. This can perhaps cause most difficulty when the reason for achieving a standard is because it is imposed from outside, such as Legal Aid Franchising, rather than arising internally. Even in these circumstances, the only way to achieve the standard will be to identify within it those aspects which are compatible with the practice's own culture and values.

The people involved need to be able to contribute to the development of the quality system, they are the ones with the practical experience of what works and what does not on a practical basis. Everyone who has contact with clients will also be in a position to provide information on what clients want.

Investors in People UK has identified a phenomenon where an early flush of enthusiasm fades away because the practice has underestimated the amount of detailed work which is needed to implement the standard. How can this be avoided?

Benchmarking

The practice needs to carry out a review of current practice against the standard and produce a realistic action plan. An appropriate consultant can provide a useful contribution as he or she will be familiar with the interpretation of the standard's requirements and will be able to make an objective assessment. The Law Society has lists of approved consultants who are familiar with the legal sector and the Lexcel, IIP and ISO standards. Depending on current government policy, grants are sometimes available to subsidise consultants' fees through the local Business Links organisation. For other useful contacts see Appendix 6.

Timetabling: how long is a piece of string?

There are many factors which affect the amount of time needed to implement a quality system. Some are external, for example deadlines set by the Legal Services Commission or Best Value programmes for solicitors working in local authorities. Some are internal, such as the size and location of departments and the degree of shared commitment to achieving the standard.

If the commitment is strong and external factors are compelling, it may be possible to achieve full implementation and compliance quickly. If other circumstances permit, a more leisurely pace can help standards to become firmly embedded. Investors In People UK suggests a time period of between six to 18 months. It is important to make sure that everyone can see the progress which is being made.

The implementation process: positive in itself

Whilst it is important to focus on achieving accreditation, the benefits of implementation should not be underestimated. This is an opportunity for practices to examine why they do what they do and whether their systems are the best way of achieving objectives. Very often systems build up gradually, layer on layer as they are adapted incrementally. The result of an incremental approach can be a system which is cumbersome and was not actually designed for the purpose it is trying to achieve.

One pitfall for the unwary is to create over-elaborate systems which go way beyond the actual requirements of the standard and do not contribute positively to running the practice effectively. It may be useful to take advice from a consultant who is familiar with legal practice and is familiar with the relevant standard, so that the review and implementation phase results in simple and effective systems.

Creating a quality system has the same benefits for administration and operational activity as introducing an appraisal system has for staff. It provides an opportunity to set time aside and focus on business needs and identify potential development to produce improvements.

Assessment

Again, it is important that everyone knows what will happen during the assessment process itself and what their roles will be. Examination of any kind creates anxiety and people may fear that one error or omission by them as individuals may prevent the practice from being successful. Everyone needs to understand that achieving a standard is a team effort with everyone doing his or her best.

Quality is for life, not just for assessment

Having achieved accreditation to the desired standard, it is all too easy to rest on one's laurels. Celebrating successful achievement is important and helps to motivate people; but maintaining a quality standard is an integral part of everyone's daily work.

It is important not to break the cycle of planning, implementation, evaluation and improvement. People within the practice must be given the opportunity to suggest improvements to the quality system. Any changes or developments in working practices need to be introduced over a realistic timescale.

Responsibility for quality is both individual and collective. It requires synergy of effort, but does not subsume individual creativity. It contributes to effectiveness by providing efficient support and an effective organisational framework within which to operate.

SUMMARY

It is likely that practices which understand what their businesses do and where they are going in the way needed to achieve any quality standard have had less difficulty in adapting to the CPR than others.

Adapting to change is the key measure of business success. For lawyers in particular, the business environment is changing rapidly. The combination of developments in law and practice, clients demanding better quality of service, pressures on price, and increased competition, create a climate which will have as fundamental an impact on legal practice as the industrial revolution had on the production of raw materials and commodities.

Quality is about fitness for purpose, and fitness is essential to survival. A practice which fails to address the issue of quality risks finding itself struck out of the market place.

CHAPTER 2

The litigator's guide to IT

Julian Boardman-Weston

Introduction

Understanding IT

IT: a big subject

Just choose what everyone else has?

What is on the litigator's IT menu?

Finally

INTRODUCTION

This chapter aims to cover, among other things, the following topics: networks; word processing; spreadsheet software; forms software; diary; e-mail; accounts and time recording; case management software; project management software; know-how and knowledge management; legal research and sources; the electronic court room and IT skills.

Before getting into the detail let us walk round the subject and weigh up how to approach it.

UNDERSTANDING IT

> I never understood much about computers and at 55 years of age I think it is too late for me to learn. Anyway I've got enough to do as partner in charge of litigation.

> I installed an Ultra-SCSI interface in our fileserver so that we can increase the data transfer rate from our DAT drive and I'm a whiz with C | | since I got the new Pentium III. I'm the one to explain the technology to those litigation partners.

Solicitors have many different attitudes to technology but the two above are not uncommon. This chapter is built on a simple premise: if you are in litigation you *must* understand enough about IT to be able to do your job properly; and you *can*.

65

Nowadays most people who work in litigation have a PC on their desks and have the skill to use it. This hands-on, 'getting things done' sort of skill is important, even vital for those who are doing the work of litigation day by day.

This chapter is about a different sort of skill, one based on what you need to understand if you are in a position of responsibility in a litigation department or for the department's IT. A litigation partner, practice manager or managing partner needs to know things such as:

- What sorts of IT are used in litigation?
- What are they good for?
- What might they cost?
- What issues will you face as you choose them and put them in?
- How will they affect the work you and your colleagues do?

IT: A BIG SUBJECT

It is indeed a big subject. Rather than jump into detailed descriptions of different types of IT, it is best to start with the big picture.

Very often when solicitors' firms think about IT, particularly as they go through the process of buying it, they begin with the technology, the hardware and software. In fact it is a big mistake to see the *paraphernalia* as the most important element in a firm's IT systems. Let me add in two more Ps to go with paraphernalia: *people* and *processes*.

Most of our best and worst moments in life are to do with *people*. It is people who bring successes and problems into legal practice. It is the people in a department who do the work which brings in fees and gains clients. It should come as no surprise that the most important component of a firm's IT system is the people.

IT does affect people enormously. Sometimes they have fears which are unfounded or expectations which will be disappointed. Some people equate IT with loss of work and others with a bright new future. The point is to treat seriously the people dimension within a firm. People can make or break IT systems.

Then there are *processes*. This is an interesting area and a controversial one. It is tempting to fit the computers to the people – to get computers to work just the way that the people did before the computers came on the scene. In some ways this is attractive. It reduces the change and lessens resistance to the new IT. It treats people with respect, by showing them that they are more important than technology. Unfortunately it does not allow much scope for saving money

66

or increasing the quality of service or the amount of work which goes through the department.

There is a widespread view that computers should save money or earn you more. This is encouraged by the computer suppliers who want users to see the cost of IT as a prudent investment. In fact most of the available statistics show the massive investment in computers throughout the developed world has brought no discernible improvement in productivity. Why is this? Diana Coyle (in *The Weightless World* (Capstone, 1997) p. 6) says that one of the explanations for this 'productivity puzzle' is that it takes a long time for new technologies to be diffused. Computer technology is like earlier innovations such as steam power and will take many years before it brings its full benefits. This is due in part to the enormous task of learning how to use any new technology effectively. Whole industries may have to be reorganised, numerous processes redesigned and vast numbers of workers retrained.

In a solicitors' firm, to overlay the old way of doing things with expensive new technology might lead to little more output in return for the extra expense, and you may be not be any further forward. The real benefits are for those firms who can do things in a new way. Perhaps they can cut the cost of doing the job (that is the cost to the firm, not the fee charged to the client). Perhaps they can reduce mistakes or the need to 'reinvent the wheel'. Perhaps they can increase the amount of work which flows through a department without making people work harder. All these will require changes to their processes.

An example of a changed process in litigation was the introduction of computerised debt collection systems. This automation led to reduced manual working. This allowed people with fewer legal skills to progress a standard debt matter. Also case management systems in defendant personal injury work have often gone hand-in-hand with the introduction of team working, which allows better spreading of expensive partner time across large numbers of cases. Even humble word processing encourages firms to change from drafting each document afresh when it is needed towards advance preparation of precedents and their repeated re-use.

We need to be willing to redesign the way we do things. This will take time – time to work out what to do, time to persuade ourselves that it is really necessary to do things differently and time to train ourselves how to do it. In thinking this through for a firm, it may help to talk to other people who have been through it before, perhaps a friend in another firm, an employee who recently joined from elsewhere or a consultant who specialises in this sort of work.

It is an individual decision whether any processes need to be altered to make the best use of computers. But if major benefits are desired from computers in terms of productivity, cost reduction or improved service then, unless processes are streamlined, you are likely to be disappointed.

JUST CHOOSE WHAT EVERYONE ELSE HAS?

I have been in many solicitors' firms and have never found two the same. The same ingredients do crop up time and time again, it is just that they are mixed in different proportions. It is unlikely that there is another firm so like yours that it is possible simply to copy everything they have done in IT. Even in a firm fairly similar to your own, very often the people there will state that they would not do things exactly the same if they were starting over again.

The bottom line is that, to really get the best out of IT in litigation, there is no simple shopping list of hardware and software which will solve all problems.

So does this mean that we have to treat every firm as a unique case as regards IT, starting 'ground up'? Far from it. Consider the Chinese restaurant set meal. If the Chinese restaurants in the UK had not invented the set meal, the novice customer might still be faced with a choice of 200 items written in Chinese with an English description as unfamiliar as it is literally accurate. What does it all mean? Where do you start? What will combine well with what else? The solicitors' firm might well ask the same questions about the variety of technology – hardware, software, suppliers – on offer today. So why not start with the set meal and see if it will suit us? If not we can always plunge into the full menu.

Below there are some suggested set meals for IT in different types of firm. Perhaps none will suit exactly but they may provide a starting point.

Set meal A: for a general litigation department with only one fee earner and secretary:

- one modern PC for each person;
- local area network connection between the two and with the rest of the firm;
- modem and connection to the Internet;
- CD-Rom reader on at least one PC;
- one shared laser printer with dual bins;
- word-processing software;
- spreadsheet software;
- fax software;
- e-mail software with encryption software;
- web browser software for Internet access;
- legal forms software;
- virus checking software;

- on-screen time recording and account enquires from firm's accounts software.

Set meal B: for a general litigation department with 10 fee earners:

As for set meal A plus:

- five heavy duty multi-bin laser printers;
- network fileserver computer;
- CD multi-player on network;
- e-mail gateway software providing desk-to-desk e-mail facility within the department and with the outside world;
- proxy server and firewall software to allow controlled access to the Internet and to prevent unauthorised access in from the outside world.

Set meal C: specialist personal injury litigation department with 10 fee earners:

As for set meal B plus:

- departmental case management system.

Set meal D: for a specialist building litigation department with 10 fee earners:

As for set meal B plus:

- litigation support/imaging software;
- a heavy duty document scanner;
- project management software for team leaders to help them plan and coordinate large cases.

The full litigation IT menu contains a number of types of technology from which you can choose. What are they and when might they be wanted?

WHAT IS ON THE LITIGATOR'S IT MENU?

A reliable network

The basic foundation for any software anywhere in a solicitors' firm is a reliable local area network (or LAN). A network has a number of parts. A typical network includes:

hardware:

- computers (sometimes called workstations or PCs), one for each person;
- printers, one or more;
- on most networks an additional computer called a fileserver which is there to store information;
- network wiring to connect everything together;
- on a simple network, a hub – where all the wiring meets – and, on a more complex network, there may be several hubs and more devices such as switches and routers which control communication on the network and with other networks.

software:

- the network operating system, to allow the computers to communicate with the fileserver, the printers and with each other;
- the operating system on the individual PCs;
- application software, the software which actually does something useful such as word processing, e-mail or case management, to which we will return in more detail below.

Networks come in a bewildering array of shapes and sizes. There is no single design which suits all. In general the larger the firm and the network the more complicated it will be. For example, take the fileserver. On a small network this may be a single computer with a single hard disk and network port. On a larger network the single fileserver may have duplicated components for increased reliability – perhaps two power supplies, a number of hard disks arranged so as to minimise the effects of breakdown of any one of them (a redundant array of inexpensive disks or RAID) and so on.

Let us imagine a hypothetical litigation department of six people in a firm totalling 20 people. A typical network in such a firm will comprise around 20 PCs, a single fileserver with some built-in reliability features and a number of laser printers, perhaps one for each two users. There will be a modem to allow users to send and receive faxes and e-mails and a tape back-up device for data security.

Operating system software on this hypothetical network includes Microsoft 'Windows 98' on individual PCs. The overall network operating system will be Microsoft 'Windows NT' or 'Novell Intranetware'.

If all this means little to you, then the details can be left to whoever in the firm deals with the network. In a small firm this may be one of the partners and in a larger firm it will be the systems administrator or IT manager. Essential points to remember are:

(a) if there is more than one computer, the firm should have a network; it is essential to allow the sharing of data, whether this data is basic word-processing files or the information stored by a complex case management system;

(b) reliability should be high up any list of priorities; an unreliable network will cause litigators needless and costly delays and aggravation;

(c) to network a small number of computers within the same building costs almost nothing per computer; the additional cost above that of stand-alone PCs may be literally zero as it may be possible to pay for the network costs by having fewer printers;

(d) on anything other than a very small network, it is essential that a member of staff is properly trained in systems administration such as file back-ups, cleaning up the file system and administering passwords.

In most cases, there is no need for a separate network dedicated to the litigation department. It is best for the firm to run the minimum number of networks, which in the case of most single-site small and medium sized firms will be just the one. If the firm is big enough to require several networks then it will – or should – have an IT manager who will advise.

Assuming we have a reliable network, what are we going to do with it?

Word processing

Word processing is to solicitors what tractors are to farmers. Word processing is the single most important computer technology in litigation practice.

So much of the solicitor's productive effort ends up in the form of documents. It is pretty obvious that anything which can improve the accuracy, speed of production and attractiveness of these documents is useful – and word processing does all three.

Everyone knows that we can create and store precedent documents to take the donkey-work out of drafting when we come back to a similar situation in the future. However the true benefits of creating precedents are often underestimated. Part of the value of creating precedents is that it makes us take a step back and consider what needs to go into a particular document and the relationship of that document with others which will be produced on the same matter. As we begin to think like this we are taking the first significant step along the road of re-designing our processes and ways of working. We are starting to get to grips with the productivity puzzle.

There was a time a few years ago when 'Wordperfect' software (particularly 'Wordperfect 5.1') was almost universal in solicitors' firms. Nowadays most UK offices use Microsoft 'Word' in one version or another. Modern 'Word-perfect' software designed to run under Microsoft 'Windows' is good but is not widely used. Because 'Word' is more popular there are a number of benefits for the firm which uses it:

- it is easier to recruit secretarial staff who have existing skills in 'Word';
- training in 'Word' is widely available;
- it is easier to exchange documents in electronic form with clients and other firms if these are in 'Word' format.

Standardisation is the name of the game. Even if 'Wordperfect' is a better product (as some say it is) 'Word' is the de facto standard.

Spreadsheet software

If you use a spreadsheet program already, you will know that it is one of the twentieth century's greatest inventions. If you do not and are a litigator, then I recommend looking into it without delay.

What does it do? It allows us to make, save and re-use calculations; it formats the output so that it is ready to print without the need for any layout typing; it will perform date arithmetic, so that it can tell you instantly how many days (even how many weekdays) there were between any two dates in history.

For example, if a calculation of wage loss is made including pre-accident average earnings, very often the client will remember that he had longer off work than he mentioned at first, perhaps because he needed to take time off for an operation; also, he might, e.g., have received a 3.7 per cent pay rise half-way through his absence. If the first calculation was made using pencil and paper, a recalculation could take some time – with a spreadsheet it might take seconds.

The industry standard is Microsoft 'Excel'. At the time of writing it costs around £250 plus VAT. A good idea is to ask someone who uses it to show it to you and let you try it on their computer, as there is no substitute for trying it out for yourself. It is hard to describe but pretty easy to use.

Forms software

Anyone can be excused for finding forms software pretty unexciting but it is another bread-and-butter area of computerisation. While the courts and the

Legal Services Commission continue to require firms to use their forms – and they are unlikely to drop this requirement for as long as they require paper at all – litigators will have to produce forms.

There are a number of ways of producing forms using computer technology. The first is for the firm to create its own versions of the forms using word processing. While it is cheapest in cash spent, the problem is the amount of work involved and the fact that unless the form is exactly right, in the sense of complying with the recipient's specification for boxes in the right place and so on, it runs the risk of rejection.

The most popular high-tech replacement for the old cabinet of printed paper forms is forms software such as that produced by Laserforms and Capsoft UK. These and other suppliers have long lists of available forms and, of course, bear the work of keeping the forms up to date and making sure that they will be acceptable to officialdom. A selected number of forms are now available for free. At the time of writing the Courts Service website (www.courtservice. gov.uk) has a large number of court forms available for free download. Also you can get many Legal Services Commission forms published by Hotdocs free from the Law Society (lawsociety.hotdocs.co.uk). The World Wide Web changes fast and very likely what is available will change frequently.

Diary

In the days before computerisation the paper diary was one of the litigator's most important tools. There is nothing to prevent continued use of a paper diary in the time-hallowed way, and if you have any doubts at all about the reliability of a computerised diary system, continue with the tried and tested method. However a good computerised diary is one of the best things that IT can bring the litigator.

Broadly speaking there are two types of computer diary. They are:

(a) a diary facility which is part of legal software such as a case management or practice management system;

(b) a diary which is a piece of general office software running on a PC or palmtop computer.

General office software diaries are usually cheap and easy to use. Examples are Microsoft 'Outlook' (not 'Outlook Express' which is an e-mail program only), Lotus 'Organiser' and many others. Outlook has appointment, reminder and address book features and can be used to send and receive e-mail (if the computer is set up for e-mail, that is). Information can be carried across to 'merge' with a Microsoft 'Word' document template so as to insert name and address information into a letter, for example.

The limitation of this first type of diary is that, with rare exceptions, the information in it is quite separate from the firm's main store of information in its practice management database and accounting system. This means that every time a new matter arrives, the information has to be entered up twice, once onto the accounts and practice management system and once into the diary software. This is extra work. Worse, as anyone who has operated computer systems like this knows, the two lots of information never quite match – there are clerical errors and changes which never quite made it to the second system. Unreliable data is a hassle at best and at worst – where you are relying on it for reminder information – a potential source of mistakes and negligence claims.

The second type of diary is that which forms a part of legal software such as a case management or practice management system. The advantage of this type of diary is that it works on data which is held in common by the diary, the practice database and the accounts. So, if a client phones the cashiers to say that she has got married and changed her name, the cashiers can change the name just once. The same new information is made available instantly to the fee earner without any separate entry into the diary system. Similarly the data integration works in the other direction; for example, if the fee earner makes a time entry from the diary it works its way through the system into the accounts. At least, this is how it works if the diary is part of one of the better modern systems which provides this level of integration. There are still some older systems around where the level of integration is not as good as it should be.

Electronic mail

E-mail is simple, cheap and invaluable to all lawyers including litigators. A text message is created at the computer, put into the e-mail system and, provided it is correctly addressed, it will pop up at the recipient's computer. Just as a letter can have an enclosure attached by a paperclip, an e-mail can have an 'attachment' in the form of a draft document, a picture or most other types of computer file.

So why is e-mail becoming so popular when solicitors' firms already have telephones, faxes, post and DX? E-mail has a number of advantages over each of these other means of communication.

E-mail is cheaper to use than fax or phone, usually by a large margin. Nearly all e-mail services allow an e-mail to be sent with a single call at local rate even if the recipient is at the other side of the world. The sender only pays for the call to place the e-mail with the sender's Internet service provider (ISP). Nor does the recipient face a large charge, as he picks up the e-mail from his own ISP at a local call rate.

Unlike letters and normal faxes a document sent as a routine attachment via e-mail is received in word processable form. So for example you can receive a draft from counsel in the form of a word processing file which needs no retyping in the office.

What do you need?

(a) a subscription to an ISP; some ISPs like Freeserve and Tesco.net are free to use, although for many firms the extra features of a paid-for service will be worth the extra cost;

(b) a modem and phone line;

(c) e-mail software on the PC; the best known e-mail software is Microsoft's 'Outlook Express' which comes free with most new PCs.

For a simple e-mail installation, that is all there is. The limitation of this simple system is that all e-mails are sent from and arrive at one PC in the firm's offices, the one which has the modem. This is adequate for a small firm which does not expect to have much e-mail traffic. After all, the same firm probably manages with a single central fax machine.

The sophisticated installation adds another bit of software, called the e-mail gateway. This acts like an electronic post clerk. At regular intervals, it dials up and drops off the outgoing e-mail. At the same time it collects all the e-mail incoming for everyone in the firm. It then sorts the incoming e-mail by addressee into electronic pigeon holes where it waits for collection. Each PC on the network checks at regular intervals for any messages addressed to the user of that PC and, if there is one, it picks it up and puts it into the individual PC. The whole process is automatic and users do not have to leave their desks. Often this is called desk-to-desk e-mail.

It should be possible, even with only basic computer skills, to set up the simple installation. Desk-to-desk e-mail is not difficult to set up but you do need to install the additional gateway software and make sure that each PC 'speaks' to the gateway. It may be necessary to ask the network supplier to do this if there is no-one in the firm who can do it.

E-mail pitfalls

E-mail is a powerful technology and there are a number of possible problems. These include:

(1) E-mail attachments can be used to transmit computer viruses and some of these are very nasty, particularly those that are able to pretend to be messages from trusted sources: a recent one was designed to

destroy all word processing documents and spreadsheets on the computer. Virus checking software should be installed on the network and users trained in which types of attachment show danger signs. Unfortunately virus hoaxes are common. I have a policy of never passing on a virus warning without checking that the information is genuine, as nearly all of the 'Watch out for this dangerous virus' e-mail messages are hoaxes, the electronic version of the chain letter. The systems administrator should be able to advise about and deal with viruses and hoaxes. An authoritative source of information about viruses is Symantec's Anti-Virus Research Centre website (www. symantec.com/avcenter/).

(2) The content of e-mails can be a problem. People sometimes send unwise or illegal e-mail messages. Like any other form of communication sent out from the office, policies are needed about what is and is not permissible content and use. Who may give the firm's undertaking by e-mail and what record will be kept? What rules will you have about not sending harassing, threatening or simply embarrassing messages to others inside or outside the firm? E-mail can tempt people to the ill-considered and hasty response. Also, it can seem to be an ideal medium for lovers' small talk – until the wrong person gets the message, that is.

(3) As regards identification and confidentiality, it is wise to require the same type of standard wording on office e-mails as are included on faxes, identifying them as coming from the firm, giving phone and address details and requiring confidentiality if they go astray. There is more advice and some sample wording in the Law Society's e-mail guidelines, which can be found at [2000] *Gazette*, 31 May or obtained from virginie.claeys@lawsociety.org.uk or by logging on to the Law Society website.

(4) E-mails might be intercepted and read as they pass through the Internet. This is technically possible but the chances of any particular e-mail's being intercepted depend on its passing through the hands of someone who wishes to intercept it. Many governments have the ability and inclination to intercept e-mail. Employees of ISPs may have the opportunity to read commercially sensitive e-mail. Probably an e-mail is about as secure as a letter entrusted to the international post or to a motorcycle messenger. If your e-mail is confidential and sensitive then you should use encryption. The Law Society e-mail guidelines (as above) point out the danger of interception and go on to say 'Firms should not include confidential information in non-encrypted e-mail without the informed consent of the clients, whether corporate or individual. In the case of individual clients, solicitors are advised to ensure that their clients fully appreciate the

risks'. Encryption is technically easy to perform with special encryption software. Most of the difficulties are practical ones relating to administering passwords and keys. If there is a network administrator, he or she should be asked to advise about a suitable encryption system or help should be sought from suitable outside experts. Remember, the guidelines do not require you to encrypt in every case, just not to use non-encrypted e-mails with clients without the informed consent of the client. It is wise to be able to encrypt for those cases where the client requires use of e-mail but will not consent to non-encryption, or where in the exercise of your professional judgement you feel that encryption is preferable.

Accounts and time recording

Regardless of the requirements of the new Woolf arrangements, any modern law firm should have computerised accounts and time recording. Since 1 August 2000 it is a requirement of the Legal Aid Franchise Quality Assurance Standards that a firm should have computerised accounts and time recording and, even where a firm holds no franchise, there is every reason why the firm should choose to install and use this software. The main purpose is to assist management and financial control of the firm. A further reason is to assist specifically with litigation. It is much easier to estimate costs incurred to date and to produce evidence justifying costs claims and bills where up-to-date time records are kept on computer.

In most firms, time recording software is provided as part of or linked to the accounts software and this is as it should be. The software varies in its features and quality, and it is important to assess whether any particular software is suitable for the firm's purposes before buying it. See below on case management software for tips on choosing a supplier.

Case management software

The first thing to know about case management software is that often cases can be managed perfectly well without it. Long before 'case management' acquired its present technical meaning to the litigator-in-the-street, legal software suppliers coined the expression to describe software for tracking and progressing matters, both contentious and non-contentious.

What is case management software? It has four components:

(a) an 'engine' which drives the various processes; in modern case management systems from any one supplier this engine is identical, whether the software is used for personal injury litigation, domestic conveyancing or industrial tribunal work – it is not different for different matter types;

(b) skeleton documents; these are matter specific and very often will be written specially for or by the firm;

(c) data – details of clients and their matters, other parties, the courts, experts and so on;

(d) one or more 'workflows' or 'agenda'. These describe the steps to take, which data is to be combined with which skeleton documents and how the records are to be updated and so on.

The whole process is rather like cookery. The workflow is a recipe. The documents and the data are ingredients. The engine is a robot chef which reads and follows the recipe before combining the ingredients to produce a finished dish – that is, all the actions taken by the system over the life of the matter. In practice the case management software cannot do everything. In simple work types such as uninsured loss recovery and debt collection it can do most of it. In more complex litigation the system does some of the work in cooperation with people who do the rest.

A typical case management system is set up to:

(a) produce documents (any standard and semi-standard documents) at the push of a button; it can produce 'top-and-tail' letters including references and matter specific information, leaving the main text to be inserted by the fee earner direct or by a typist from dictation;

(b) keep up to date matter information;

(c) give reminders either in the form of notification to the user or chasing letters or e-mails;

(d) provide reports: unlike word processing systems, case management software is aware of the status of the matter and can provide reports, for example for a trade union client listing all current matters broken down by type of accident and showing current situation and damages estimate.

Case management systems are expensive but can be well worthwhile in some circumstances. The hard part is deciding which. The two key factors to take into account are as follows.

How standardised is the work?

It is a mistake to think that work is either standardised or it is not. There is a continuous spectrum from completely identical matters to those which are completely one-off with no common features. Standardised work is much easier for case management systems to handle. But even work which overall is not very standardised can have some highly standardised elements, such as file review procedures, checks and reminders for limitation purposes and reporting.

The work of creating skeleton documents and workflows is less the greater the degree of standardisation in the work.

Is it worth the cost and effort?

The more people there are doing work of the same type, the easier it is to justify the cost of buying and implementing case management software.

(1) First, consider the money cost. These systems are typically more expensive per user for the first few users than for additional ones because some of the costs, such as installation, administrator training and so on, are incurred however few users are being put onto the system.

(2) Secondly, consider the firm's internal cost of implementation, most of which is proportional to the number of work types which are going onto the system. Usually it makes little difference to the cost of setting up the documents and workflows whether one or 20 users are involved, provided that they are doing work of the same type.

If these two factors point in the same direction, the decision is simple. If they point in different ones then you will need to think through whether case management software would be beneficial.

how standardised is the work?	very much	perhaps – think carefully – per-user cost of system likely to be high	yes – suitable for case management systems
	not much	no – unsuitable	perhaps – think carefully – work of implementation may be excessive or too difficult
		small	large

number of fee-earners doing work of the relevant type

Figure 2.1 Factors in deciding on case management software

It has to be said that some of the computer sales people either do not understand this, or if they do then they see that it is not good for business if they explain it to prospective customers. One supplier has run an advertising campaign which stresses the supposed advantage of being able to reduce the ratio of secretaries to fee earners with case management software. But of course this presupposes that the work is of a type where reduction in the number of secretaries is both possible and desirable. In many firms, it is fee earners who are the expensive ones and it would be far better for cost reduction to decrease the number of fee earners rather than that of the less expensive secretaries – provided of course output and the ability to charge are not adversely affected. The point is that any ratio of this sort is a blunt instrument and suppliers are not always ready or able to see the implications of the options which you face.

Post-Woolf litigation and case management software

Case management software has been around since long before the civil justice reforms but in some ways the two were made for each other. Case management software works best where the steps in the case can be planned and where it will follow a timetable, however flexible this might need to be. Cases where 'anything might happen at any time and anyone might do it' do not lend themselves to case management software. But as we know, modern litigation is not like this. Solicitors are required to be on top of what is happening and the courts monitor the steps in the case and the timetable. Courts have begun to think like the case management systems. What will happen next and when will it happen? What series of steps will be taken and what total time needs to be allowed for all of them? If we have to answer these questions for the court, why not set them up in case management software? And what better way of providing the information for the court than to computerise the monitoring of the case within the office. Then the same information and monitoring satisfies the court, makes life easier and helps to keep the client informed.

I am still not convinced that all litigation should be run on case management software but the Woolf reforms do urge us further in that direction.

Some other factors: supervision and client requirements

There is no doubt that a well implemented case management system can be a useful aid to supervision. The software enables a team leader or head of department to view progress and any outstanding tasks on files being handled by those whom they are supervising. Of course the Legal Aid Quality Assurance Standards impose detailed supervision requirements on firms doing publicly funded work. Case management software is not required by LAFQAS but might form a useful part of the firm's plan for compliance. Even where work is privately funded, supervision is an increasingly important activity. It ensures that work is carried out to a high, consistent standard. It is even more vital under conditional fee agreements where the financial consequences of error may be more than a lost case and an irate client – even one lost case may wipe out the profit from many successful ones. A comprehensive and properly executed computerised case management system can help to a significant extent, but it is important to buy the right software and take the time to set it up to suit you. Simply buying case management software is not the answer to file and staff supervision.

Increasingly, clients feel free to request or even dictate the way in which the firm will do the work, and requiring the use of computerised case management systems may become increasingly common. In one sense it does not matter whether the clients are right in making the connection between computerisation and higher standards of work. They are the clients and if they are important enough there may be little alternative to meeting their demands. Perhaps the clients are right to use a firm's willingness to invest in computerisation and skill to get it working well as indicators of commitment and professionalism: 'If they will do this for us then they are serious about our business'.

One very practical benefit of case management software is that a firm can supply reports and matter status information in electronic form. This can be on disk, by e-mail or increasingly over the Web. If you are going to provide links into your system at all, the Web is a very good way to do it. The client or referrer of business needs no special software, hardware or communication links. Normal web browser software, an Internet connection – and of course the necessary passwords and authentication – are all that is required at the client's end. It is usually more complicated at the solicitor's end as the information must be organised into a form and a place where it is accessible from the Web.

At the time of writing, the most advanced software is capable of providing live links across the Web from the firm's case management system to clients and referees of business. This enables them to issue instructions and check progress without any manual intervention by the firm. It is pretty clear that this is the way of the future, with quite a few firms now promoting heavily their legal e-commerce capability. Things happen quickly on the Web and it is possible that e-commerce links into case management software will become the norm quite quickly.

What do these systems cost?

A significant part of the cost of the total system is incurred for the first user, so each subsequent user is much cheaper to put on the system. This means that there is no simple '£X per user' rule. For a heavy duty case management system suitable for a department the minimum cost including software, set up, training and some basic workflows and documents is probably about £15,000, which does not include any hardware. This might put say the first two users on the system. But a 15-user system might cost less than twice as much.

There are cut down systems available for less. Typically these miss out some of the heavier-duty features which are good for a departmental system, such as:

(a) integration with the accounting and time recording system;

(b) ability to send reminders to a different person – for example a supervisor – rather than the person who has failed to act on the first reminder;

(c) sophisticated reporting facilities.

Also the cheaper systems may be dedicated to one type of work rather than be general purpose.

What are the shortcomings with case management software?

(1) The main problem is the temptation to use case management software where it is not suitable – see above.

(2) Work of implementation: typically firms who implement case management systems find that there is more work involved than they expected. This means that often it takes some time to get a system running well – 12 months is probably a reasonable estimate. The job can be done quicker but not unless suitable people – which often includes a partner – are deployed onto the implementation as a top priority. If the work-flows and documents have to be created in evenings and at weekends then the implementation will be long drawn out.

(3) Cost savings may not be possible: if you are looking for productivity gains or cost savings then case management systems have a good deal in common with low calorie foods – they will help only as part of a controlled diet. If you have expensive methods of working and these are overlaid with expensive case management systems, this will increase not reduce expense – it is essential to alter your way of working in order to obtain these gains. All the case management system can do is to help a firm to work in a new way, if it wants to.

(4) Need for adequate skills and support staff: once you have a case management system, this brings computers into a critical activity. It might be possible to manage for a day or two without time recording or electronic fund transfers, but the firm will not be able to tolerate any protracted breakdown of the case management system. The inability for a whole team to produce any work will be a serious problem. So if a firm has case management, it must also have reliable hardware and networks, and also the right combination of qualified computer

people in-house and external support and maintenance. To get by on a shoestring is not an option. If cost is an objection then the firm should think seriously about not having case management.

Choice of product and supplier can be a challenge. If there is one key thing to do to ensure success it is *choose a good supplier*.

Customers for case management systems are highly dependent on the supplier for support and upgrades. Users whose experience is of packaged general office software such as word processors do not always understand this. With a case management system the supplier is the only source of support, training and technical documentation. Remember that you are going to be in a long term relationship with the supplier lasting for as long as the firm continues to use the software. It is essential to have suppliers who are competent, helpful and going to stay in business.

With all kinds of legal software, case management included, getting the right supplier is usually even more important than getting the right software. The things to look for in a supplier are:

- a helpful attitude;
- a good track record of service to similar firms;
- adequate skills and number of people;
- the financial health to stay in business.

Project management software

Project management software is a general purpose tool used in many industries and professions for planning and coordinating complex projects. Engineers, architects and software project managers have been using project management techniques for years. Many litigators have come across project management techniques used by their own clients in building and civil engineering litigation and will recognise the bar-charts and critical path analysis. These techniques predate the use of software but as in many areas of life computers have arrived to make the donkey-work easier.

Outside the law, project management is about juggling time, quality and budget to come up with a successful outcome. Unpredictable events such as weather and labour disputes have to be accommodated and complex interrelations of cooperating and competing parties have to be managed. Sounds a bit like running a complicated piece of litigation, does it not?

Always litigation has been subject to unpredictable events and has involved coordinating the actions of others such as witnesses, experts and other parties.

Nowadays the solicitor is expected to be able to set a timetable and keep to it, to budget fees and to stick to that budget. This means that litigation, particularly complex, multi-party litigation, has much in common with complex projects in other fields. Litigators can consider the use of the same techniques of project management.

There is not space in this chapter to go into detail about how to do project management, which is a professional discipline in its own right. A good introduction to the subject is Field and Keller, *Project Management* (Open University, 1998). This is not about litigation specifically but is an excellent introduction and explanation of the general concepts and techniques of project management.

Project management software is readily available from many suppliers. It prepares charts and schedules automatically from dates and information which you enter. It re-calculates them if you change something. To that extent it is a bit like spreadsheet software but with output in a number of specialised charts and diagrams.

One of the common software packages is Microsoft 'Project'. This has the familiar 'Windows' interface. It is easy to install but probably a little harder for the litigator to learn to use than is word processing or spreadsheet software. This is because it assists in preparing the standard project management charts and schedules, which assumes that the user knows more or less what these are for and why they are being used. Having said this, it can be a good way into learning more about project management in general – but it cannot be bought on a Monday with the hope of learning from scratch how to plan complex litigation on it by Tuesday morning.

At the time of writing Microsoft 'Project' costs about £320 plus VAT. This makes it much cheaper than case management software but it has to be emphasised that it is not a substitute as it does a different job.

Large and complex cases are the obvious ones where project management techniques are likely to be worthwhile and to pay off. There is no reason in theory why they cannot be used in small cases – the objection is normally that the fees to be earned do not encourage the same detailed case planning. Nevertheless *appropriate* case planning is necessary in every case and simple project management techniques are useful in smaller cases. An interesting hybrid situation is where a firm has a high volume of smaller cases. In some ways planning how to do the work can be treated as a single large project: acquiring the office space, setting up systems of work, putting in the computers and so on make a classic project which needs to be properly planned. Actually doing the individual cases may be more of a job for case management software which can help with the repetitive tasks of document production, reporting and case supervision.

It is fair to say that project management software appears not yet to be widely used by litigators. This is not because of any problem with the software but simply because formal project management is not yet the norm. Personally I think its use will grow as litigators reach out to use the same tools and techniques as do their counterparts in other professions.

Know-how and knowledge management

This is another big subject. Knowledge of the law, procedure and how to conduct litigation is any litigation department's biggest asset. The words 'knowledge' and 'know-how' are sometimes used interchangeably although perhaps the latter includes an element of practical skill – 'knowing how' to do something.

There is a knowledge management bandwagon rolling and many firms will be faced with IT suppliers urging them to embark on a knowledge management project. Other firms will have a feeling of unease about whether this might be nothing more than today's fashion, to be followed or ignored depending on how much the firm is willing to stand out from the crowd. So what is it all about?

Probably for years if not centuries, individual solicitors have kept paper collections of useful bits and pieces from books and files. Probably they wanted to save the wasted expense of doing the same research twice. Some years ago a few solicitors' firms began systematically to develop know-how systems to collect, structure and disseminate their collective knowledge and experience.

A common mistake is to think of knowledge as a sort of data. Computers handle data extremely well, much better than do humans. But knowledge is hard for computers to handle while humans are in their element with it. This is the nub of the problem when it comes to trying to use computers to manage knowledge. It is also why some of the IT-based knowledge management projects are fundamentally misconceived – those undertaking them believe 'computers will have this knowledge stuff sorted out in no time' which is a fallacy.

IT is only one aspect of knowledge management and you should not believe anyone who tells you that there is a mainly computer-based answer to knowledge management needs.

Having said all this, IT can help as part of a knowledge management task. What types of technology are being used? In ascending order of cost and sophistication they include:

(1) Paper: it is quite feasible to manage knowledge without computers and for small firms this may be quite an effective method. A paper system is better than nothing, and certainly a great deal better than an inadequate computerised system.

85

(2) A well organised word processing system: again this seems mundane but in many solicitors' firms a good deal of knowledge is in – or can be put into – word processable form. This starts with precedents but can include practice notes, in-house commentaries, lists of experts and counsel with comments on their abilities and so on. What 'well organised' means depends on the size and type of practice. In small and medium sized firms it may be sufficient to have a good directory structure and adequate document naming conventions. Modern word processing software and operating systems allow increasingly sophisticated text and key-word searching and subject classification. In larger firms document management software allows tracking of larger collections of documents, for example across multiple servers.

(3) Databases: these are in their element with structured information and are not ideal for messy, unstructured information. Trying to force some sorts of know-how into strict categories is likely to deprive it of much of its meaning. However some firms, particularly large ones, use databases to provide indexes and directories to tell people where to go to find the knowledge rather than to hold the knowledge itself.

(4) Intranets: these are simply private versions of the World Wide Web – firm wide webs. Several pieces of software go to make up the typical intranet. The basic two are: a web server which provides documents in standard form on request; and a browser which makes the requests and displays the documents. In addition an intranet will involve the use of other software: a method of turning documents into the appropriate format (an HTML editor and possibly a bulk document translator); and most larger intranets will have some sort of text search facility which typically is a separate piece of software running on the web server at the request of the browser; some intranets will have a connection to a relational database which stores structured information and responds to requests coming from users via the intranet – this is a 'database-backed' intranet.

Knowledge or know-how management is a specialist subject and before getting involved in a major IT project it is vital to talk to someone with experience – and not just experience of IT.

Legal research and sources

As time goes by, more and more legal information is available in electronic form. There are three main types of information service and provider.

(1) The CD versions of traditional legal books and journals: these are available from the well-known publishers. These CD-Roms are the

familiar shiny plastic disk and can be inserted into a computer CD player in the office or at home. A typical CD contains the same as several volumes of paper books and costs about the same as the paper version.

(2) On-line legal books, journals and updating services: typically these are available by subscription and are accessed by web browser over the World Wide Web;

(3) Free information available over the Web: this may be produced as a public service or by those who are using a free service as 'a taster' or an advertisement for a subscription-based service.

What is available is changing all the while. Rather than try to advise which products and services you should have – which of course will depend on the firm's specialisation and the type and size of the practice – let us look at the technology which is needed to get started and then give some guidelines about how to choose what you want.

For access to CD-Roms, the minimum requirement is a PC with a CD-Rom player. Most new PCs come with these, so probably the firm has one already. Any special software will come from the publisher as part of the purchase of the CD 'book' or subscription to the service.

The drawback with a single PC method of access is that each user will need to walk to the PC and insert the disk in order to use it. This is not usually a problem in small firms, although even there the CDs have a habit of disappearing. No sane person will take home 12 volumes of law reports but it is all too easy to slip the equivalent CD into a file and forget to bring it back. One answer is to put the PC in a library and to have strict rules about not taking the CDs away.

In order to make these CDs available across a larger firm or department it is usual to put a CD multi-player on a central machine attached to the local area network. This may have slots for all the CDs at once and will allow selection remotely from the PC on the user's desk. This arrangement is more expensive but worthwhile if a number of people will want access to a number of different CDs.

Web access is now easy to arrange provided that the firm has a local area network. The systems management or network suppliers can provide the means to connect the network to the Internet. In most solicitors' firms this will be by means of a dial-up connection to an ISP from a single point on the network which then allows any authorised users anywhere else in the office to route their Internet access through the single point. In computer-speak the single point is a 'gateway' or a 'proxy server'. Strictly speaking these are different things. A proxy server stores copies of web pages as they pass through to the user's PC so that they do not have to be downloaded a second time when someone else requests them. Again the systems manager or network supplier should be able to advise on the best set-up for the firm.

What factors are relevant in choosing the services and publications to take?

(1) It is a good idea to look at what is available for free as some of it is excellent. For example the Lord Chancellor's website has all the Civil Procedure Rules, protocols and Practice Directions. The Courts Service website has many forms available for download.

(2) It should be borne in mind that CD-based publications are not going to be much cheaper than books. The cost is in producing and updating the content.

(3) It is best to use the same sort of selection criteria as for the traditional law library. Is this publication good value? How high is it up your list of priorities?

(4) Be wary about taking CD versions without having the traditional book as well. What will happen if the computer crashes when you need to look something up? And how will you take a CD to read in bed?

Online pay-per-go services may be a good choice if occasional access is needed to a large number of sources rather than frequent access to a small number.

Another attraction of online information, both free and paid for, is that it is not necessary to be on the office network to do research. Access can be gained from home, a hotel or client premises.

The best source of information of what is on the Web is the Web itself. A good collection of links to all sorts of information for UK lawyers is Delia Venables' website at www.venables.co.uk. Also the usual search engines and index sites such as Hotbot, Yahoo and Alta Vista can help to find what you are seeking.

Electronic court room

It is still early days for IT in the UK court room. At the moment there is no standard country-wide IT. There are a number of different technologies in use.

Electronic transcripts

The shorthand writer creates the transcript straight into a computer rather than taking notes to transcribe at the end of the court day. As the note goes into the computer it becomes available for others to read. This technology allows the judge and counsel – and anyone who is equipped – to receive a transcript as the shorthand writer produces it. The special software allows the users to watch the transcript as it appears or to scroll back through earlier evidence. The result is that the parties have an electronic note which can be searched, marked up on screen, taken away during adjournments and so on.

The best-known product and service is Smith Bernal's 'LiveNote' which is used extensively in the UK.

Litigation support software

This description covers a number of technologies which are designed to organise large collections of documentary evidence.

Some litigation support software contains images – electronic pictures of individual documents – and some only list and index paper documents. Even the latter may be very helpful from the point of view of producing lists of documents and keeping track of who holds which originals, where they are stored and so on. But the addition of imaging brings some valuable benefits:

(a) once a document is scanned into the system it can be printed off any number of times without the need to take a copy from a paper original or master copy;

(b) documents can be inspected on screen lessening the need to produce multiple copies of the same bundles of paper for all and sundry;

(c) it becomes easy to produce bundles which can be printed off, collated and page-numbered by the software;

(d) different versions of the bundles can be produced to include or exclude privileged documents, to cover just particular issues such as quantum or to instruct expert witnesses on single issues;

(e) the electronic documents can be 'packed up' onto CD to allow someone such as counsel to take them home on the train rather than needing a small van for the purpose.

In practice imaging is not going to replace paper but it can reduce the requirement for so many different copies to be produced, and computers arc good at mechanical tasks like page numbering and ensuring that two bundles really are the same.

There are a number of products in use. These include the quaintly named 'R/KYV' (pronounced 'archive') from Valid Information Systems and 'Egami-Legal' from DPA-Egami. Often firms use specialist contractors to scan the documents and they will have their recommendations about software.

Using litigation support software does tend to incur costs earlier in a case than traditional methods of inspecting, collating and copying documents. This is because every document needs to be inspected and classified (for a database) or imaged (for an image-based system), otherwise it will not be in the computer system. The pay-off is that once in there the costs of locating, reading and producing copies of any particular document are very much less than for a paper-based system.

Electronic interface with court offices

As we all become used to online shopping and banking there will be increasing pressure to bring these technologies into other fields. There is no technical reason why all filing of courts documents could not be handled electronically but this will require standardisation and changes in the way that the courts and lawyers work.

Perhaps we should look for steady improvements rather than a sudden revolution. Various court lists now appear on the World Wide Web at www. courtservice.gov.uk and no doubt other innovations will come along.

IT skills

Firms need IT skills at a number of different levels. Most of us now readily accept the need for training the firm's computer users how to use any new software. In many ways this is easy to arrange. Many suppliers welcome the opportunity to sell training services as part of a new IT package. Most of us are familiar with the now legendary British dislike of spending money on training and we do what we can to overcome it.

Firms do not always see the need for some other IT skills such as those in systems administration, support and IT management.

The more IT you have and the more you depend on it, the more need there is of the right level of skill and experience available at a moment's notice. In practice this means that every firm needs at least one person who can sort out routine network problems, see that back-ups are being taken and can give informal advice and training when someone runs into problems. The important thing is that this help must be on hand: often quick application of a sticking plaster is more useful than being able to call in a brain surgeon sometime next week.

There is no rule of thumb for how many and what kind of IT staff are needed. Probably you will know without any prompting when you see that things are not getting done, or being done by expensive fee earners in odd moments rather than by efficient professionals as part of their routine duties. Of course IT staff are expensive and are not fee-earning – they are overheads. But then again many of the most valuable things in a solicitors' firm are overheads and there is no point in economising on essential services.

The need for IT people can come as a shock to anyone who has bought the promise that IT will reduce staff. That promise is often false. There may be some skill-shifting: the firm can manage with fewer or less highly qualified fee earners but at the same time more help is needed with IT. It is rather like smoothing wrinkles out of a carpet – as you reduce the need for expensive skills in one place the need pops up in another.

At the start of the chapter we mentioned that very important skill – that of being able to understand IT at the level necessary to be able to manage the firm and the department. This requires an ability to buy wisely, understand the implications of IT for people and finance and to keep an eye on developments which may be relevant to the firm. Some of this is what is expected from any litigation partner in a modern practice. Some of it falls to an IT partner in a smaller firm. In a larger firm it may be the job of a head of department or managing partner, probably assisted by a systems manager or IT director.

FINALLY

One of the problems with technology – or perhaps it is a problem with you and me – is that we look for a simple IT answer to what is often quite a complex problem. In litigation the clients are more demanding, the Legal Services Commission wants to limit expenditure, the courts are trying to reduce delays and costs while at the same time improving access to justice. Often the litigator has to do more, know more and work down to a price. It is all too easy to see IT as the easy answer. Old hands know that IT is never an easy answer to anything.

In truth there is a complex interrelation between the parts of a firm's litigation IT 'system'. We started this chapter by looking at the three components of a firm's IT system:

- people;
- processes;
- paraphernalia.

It is when these three components are working well together that the whole system runs smoothly and successfully. The trouble with many IT innovations in firms is that they concentrate mainly on the paraphernalia. Avoid this trap! People and processes are important too.

IT in litigation, and in solicitors' firms generally, need not be a bizarre and complex technical subject, understood only by IT experts who speak an unintelligible language of their own. In the modern litigation practice IT costs enough and plays a big enough part to make it hard to ignore. We owe it to ourselves to get on top of it. All my experience suggests that, if we really want to, we can.

CHAPTER 3

Human resources and team management

Geraldine McCool

Introduction

Supervision

Caseloads, workloads

Teamwork on large cases

Unbundling: sharing of work with the client

Use of counsel

Recruiting and keeping of quality staff

Need for staff at the right level

Use and training of paralegals and unqualified staff

Conclusion

INTRODUCTION

Managing litigation fee earners and support staff in the post-CPR landscape requires clear leadership, strategic thinking and a constant and structured exchange of information. It is not possible to predict the medium to long term effect of CPR on the basis of its short term features so flexibility is essential; there is no room for dogmatic assertions against a backdrop of prohibition of reference to past cases, regular amendment of present rules and cases on interpretation that give limited guidance because of the diverse nature of the overriding objective. Training gives familiarity, knowledge of CPR builds confidence. However at the end of the day litigators are going to stumble now and then when getting to grips with all the implications of CPR. Managers too are going to make mistakes which is why constant reappraisal and teamwork are vital. It is easy for managers to lack confidence. There is now a focus on risk at every stage and payment by results but there always has been risk and a good litigator will survive. If the firm is to survive, good litigators have to be created, nurtured and retained.

SUPERVISION

Supervision of all staff is a well established feature of solicitors' offices. It goes on in fee earner teams, between fee earners and support staff and in support staff groups. It is required by outside bodies such as the Law Society, the Legal Services Commission, insurers, unions and commercial clients. It ensures quality, efficiency and that the client's needs are being met. It is important to maintain supervision when dealing with CPR because there is less room for mistakes, less time to rectify mistakes and immediate costs penalties attached to rectification. This section will concentrate on fee earner supervision of litigation fee earners. This is important as an exercise in teamwork to ensure a good outcome for the client, to give those managing the firm knowledge of the team and to increase the likelihood of obtaining further work from clients. Those managing the firm will also want to assess the effect of CPR on billing across different litigation work-types.

One to one

Fee earners run cases for clients and the largest element in supervision is the conduct of the case. However, anyone familiar with practice management standards will know that supervision is about more than file reviews. It includes supervision of the following aspects:

- caseloads and workloads;
- monthly billing against monthly target;
- monthly time recording;
- 'lapsed' cases with no recent time recording;
- relationships with secretaries and support staff;
- relationships with external team members such as barristers and experts;
- the transfer of files to other firms of solicitors;
- risk assessment for conditional fee work;
- client complaints;
- incoming and outgoing post and e-mails;
- office balances;
- trials;
- undertakings (those on a fee earner's file must be given by partner);
- claims and wasted costs orders against the firm;
- problem cases;
- unpaid bills;

- archiving;
- training needs and professional development;
- working environment;
- IT skills.

This type of supervision involves a supervisor at an appropriate level who will also conduct the annual appraisal and regular review meetings probably every month where notes are kept. It involves setting criteria for the work which the supervised fee earner understands. Much of the supervision will be linked to a concentration across the litigation team on one aspect at a particular time such as a blitz on unpaid bills or office balances. This type of supervision has been little affected by CPR.

Teamwork

Supervision also takes place through team meetings. These provide a mechanism for communicating management guidelines and receiving feedback plus an opportunity to observe individual fee earners participation. The agenda will regularly include:

- new client inquiries;
- risk assessments on conditional fee work;
- breakdown of caseloads;
- changes to legal expenses and after-the-event legal expense insurance policies;
- training courses;
- computerised forms;
- hourly rates;
- problems on ongoing cases;
- matters of interest arising from counsel's opinions/notes;
- matters of interest arising from cases generally;
- latest experiences at court;
- membership of organisations;
- annual analysis of cases that are lost or discontinued after service;
- consultation documents such as Law Commission consultation papers;
- marketing.

These team meetings are also the venue for discussion of the impact of CPR. Because the changes are new to fee earners at every level each team member has the opportunity to share experiences which are equally valid and valuable. The team should discuss these and any appropriate changes to working practices. Aspects of CPR covered at these meetings are:

- the latest cases on interpretation of CPR;
- the latest amendments to CPR;
- arguments raised by both sides under the overriding objective and the court's interpretation of the overriding objective;
- operation of pre-action protocols particularly where a lot of work in the team is against a particular opponent;
- operation of case management conferences and preparation time;
- orders made by the court upon reading allocation and listing questionnaires;
- the extent of intervention by the court;
- the effectiveness of CPR Part 36 offers/payments before and after issue;
- venue provisions and transfer of cases;
- the court's attitude towards experts under CPR Part 35;
- striking out statement of case under CPR Rule 3.4;
- the amount of time taken up in compiling the costs information required at various stages of the case and for summary assessment;
- interim payments and whether there is a need for them;
- exaggeration of claims under CPR Rule 44.3(5)(d);
- split issues and orders;
- listing and trial windows;
- detailed assessment: waiting time and interim payments of costs;
- use of counsel.

Support staff

It must not be forgotten that the culture shock of CPR is felt by all members of the litigation team. That includes support staff. In-house or external training is essential as is monitoring their views on differences under CPR. Many commercial providers and local law societies have identified the training need and provide training at reasonable prices. Support staff also have vital contact with the courts and benefit from attendance at the open evenings that most courts now hold. Training can usefully include:

- the overriding objective;
- court forms;

- CPR additions to legal aid forms;
- feedback to the local law society and courts;
- telephone court hearings;
- file organisation including identification of work that has been included in summary assessments;
- deadlines (including particular problems at Christmas and New Year);
- relationship with counsel;
- trial bundles;
- format of witness statements;
- the CPR Part 36 procedure;
- cover for holiday periods.

Case supervision

Case supervision includes choosing broad parameters across cases and reviewing the cases highlighted. Many of the parameters will remain the same as in the post-CPR landscape: files opened more than five years ago and cases issued more than three years ago which are unresolved. New parameters can be worked in, in keeping with CPR: cases opened when no letter of claim has been sent within six months, cases not issued six months after the expiry of the protocol period. This supervision is more effective if cases can be identified through the database rather than relying on feedback from fee earners. However, it is unlikely that many firms will have case management systems in place containing details of all cases in the first period of the CPR.

This type of supervision is important to bring out trends across individual fee earner caseloads and across the firm but it is no substitution for file review. This is because under the old rules if a fee earner faced difficulties on the case it would often 'go to sleep'. There would be delay and the defendant would have no interest in awakening the case before making an application to show that the case has been automatically struck out under the County Court Rules (CCR) Order 17 or an application for dismissal for want of prosecution. Under CPR there is less advantage to defendants in condoning delay and they can keep the pressure on a fee earner who is struggling with a particular case by a series of applications to split and resolve issues. Case management by the court is likely to lead to tight deadlines imposed at the hearing of these applications leaving the fee earner requiring support as well as supervision. Computerised case management is ideal for keeping track of cases and it is important that any program has adequate provision for 'escalating' problems in set circumstances to the supervisor. Any computerised or manual case management system should have built in stages at which the fee earner requires supervisor approval such as issuing.

File reviews

File reviews conducted by the supervisor should take place about once a quarter involving an in-depth analysis of a small number of cases. There should be a balance between those chosen by the supervisor at random, those chosen because the supervisor has seen something that has happened on the case and those where the fee earner has identified the need for advice and guidance. This is a two-way process. The starting document on each file should be a case analysis. This is to assist not just the supervisor conducting the file reviews but any member of the team including support staff who have to refer to that file when the fee earner is out of the office, on holiday or ill. It also helps the fee earner handling the case to refresh the memory about the details. The case analysis should include the following information:

- reasons to believe the client will win;
- chance (per cent) of succeeding on liability/causation/quantum;
- three most important issues in the case;
- client's objectives;
- parties;
- existence of duty of care/statutory duty/contract;
- extent of duty;
- breach of duty;
- causation;
- heads of damage and valuation;
- costs, financing, proportionality;
- good facts, bad facts;
- evidence;
- insurance;
- limitation;
- timescale.

Beyond the case analysis there may well be checklists on the file at key stages such as after the protocol period, before issue, before a CPR Part 36 Offer is made, after a CPR Part 36 payment is made or before trial. Checklist compilation can seem mechanical and tedious but it addresses the mind to agenda. Omission errors can occur through the arrogance of familiarity, repetition and speed of work. Checklists help. They are also useful for supervisors to see whether minimum standards are being met. A mixture of tick box items and items requiring narrative is often used.

After the case analysis and checklists, it is useful to examine the legal file for the procedural status if the case is issued, to look at party and party correspondence, and see when and how counsel has been used as part of the team. Witness evidence, expert evidence and quantum documentation can then be read together with the portion of the file that relates to funding. However the general correspondence file should also be read if only on a cursory basis because this sort of supervision can be used to ascertain the regularity at which the case has been worked on, the relationship between the fee earner and the client and style and tone of letters as well as the substantive nature of the advice that has been given to clients. Provided that the preparation is done by the supervisor in advance, feedback to the supervised fee earner may in fact be brief. A note of the file review should be kept on the file and by the supervisor in a file relating to that fee earner's supervision and any corrective action that is needed should be highlighted on the file review note and entered into the diary of both the supervisor and supervised fee earner so that it is picked up and checked without the necessity of a further file review. Standardisation of the file review form is useful.

One of the criticisms that is often voiced about practice management standards is that the substantive nature of the legal advice given is not assessed. This is certainly not the case under the Legal Service Commission's transaction criteria which look at all the necessary steps that need to be taken in a particular type of case and the matters to be reviewed and advice to be given to the client at those stages. Checklists which include these criteria are easy to draw up, useful for the fee earner and ideal for the firm to demonstrate compliance to any independent auditors. These can be on paper or held on IT. If the latter it must be clear on the file that further information is stored electronically.

File reviews look at the substantive nature of the legal advice given and that is one of the reasons why the case analysis is such an important document. The fee earner should be thinking about the trial from day one and updating the case analysis as further evidence becomes available. It is always important for the supervisor to check that the supervised fee earner has an understanding of what the client is trying to achieve but at the same time is not being inappropriately influenced by the client's wishes if these hamper progress of the claim. The case analysis identifying the important issues also identifies those issues which are less important and may be a distraction upon time resources.

It may be that these 'distractions' are important to the client and advice on costs and proportionality, often through a standard CPR briefing, given at an early stage is essential. If the client understands that they are paying for a particular aspect whatever the outcome of the case they may well reconsider. If they understand that under proportionality they may in addition be paying for something that cannot be used in any event they are likely to reconsider. This advice also needs to be given to work providers who are indemnifying individual cases.

Another important document in the file review is the case plan. Planning, time management and prioritisation are essential skills for today's litigator. A supervisor can deduce personal strategic planning and budgeting characteristics of individual fee earners from these. All files should have one; less complex cases require shorter case plans. A copy of the case plan should be sent to the client and it should be updated at a minimum of six-monthly intervals. It should be kept in a prominent place on the file. In addition to recording the steps that are to be taken, together with an associated time deadline, it can be used as an aide memoire for features of the case such as a reminder to return certain documentation to clients at the conclusion of the case.

The stages through which the case progresses can be clearly seen from CPR but the time associated with those stages is not so clear. The protocols have clear time limits but it may take some time for a consistent pattern to emerge on orders given on consideration of allocation questionnaires and at case management conferences. Yet planning is more important under CPR to comply with the court's case management. Setting out the timescale of the stages of the case helps to manage client's expectations. As the time goalposts will inevitably move, review of the plan with the client is necessary. It is also common for aspiring partners to have a selection of cases reviewed by a partner outside their department, and of course partners' files must not escape the file review system. On these occasions problems can, however, arise if different litigation departments have different systems, as the aspiring partner needs to be judged for compliance within their home environment. The supervisor for this is almost inevitably another partner. It is becoming increasingly common for bulk work providers to review files at their leisure and a costs judge will dip in and out of files at a detailed assessment.

This supervision is designed for fee earners who are running their own cases under supervision. If a fee earner is assisting another fee earner, supervision will consist of review of the work product rather than the full file and monitoring the ability to keep to timescales. This is particularly important where the fee earner is assisting more than one member of staff with the associated competing demands on time requiring prioritisation.

Membership of the appropriate specialist panel by the supervisor is useful but not essential. The supervisor will routinely be a partner and some aspects, such as supervision of incoming post, require partner input. However, experience and ability is not the exclusive domain of partners, and experienced legal executives, associates and assistant solicitors should not be precluded if the make-up of the team warrants it.

It is difficult for a busy supervisor to maintain the required regularity and depth of supervision for more than three fee earners. Problems can arise when a partner has a larger number of fee earners working on a particular work provider's cases, but it is better to have proper supervision than to insist on control. If a whole team of fee earners are working on low volume, standardised litigation which is IT intensive, then a large number can be supervised by one supervisor.

CASELOADS, WORKLOADS

Controlling the size of caseloads of fee earners in the firm is an essential function involving dialogue and review; it is not a paper exercise. The print-out of fee earners' cases is only the starting point. It is, however, a management function that managers will be familiar with and under the CPR the question is whether there is any need, in broad terms, for caseloads to increase or decrease.

Ascertaining caseloads

Management information in the form of generation of lists of cases by fee earner is a basic tool. They may contain basic information about work type by code. Archiving must be kept up to date and archived cases taken off the print-out at the earliest opportunity. Fee earners can then provide further information, including a breakdown of fast track/multi-track, issued, non-issued, concluded but costing. Most firms will have assessed the overall number of fast track cases prior to the start of the CPR when looking at the impact of the reforms on their practice, but the breakdown of these by fee earner is also important.

Information beyond this level includes the stage which the case has reached, likely quantum range and complexity of liability. Firms carrying out any volume of conditional fee work will have produced this type of information when assessing the spread of risk taken on, as opposed to risk assessment in individual cases, and fee earners should be used to cooperating in the provision of information. Instructions and categorisation must always be clear and when asking fee earners to participate in time-consuming exercises the firm's objective must be clear so the fee earner knows the importance of cooperation and the need for accuracy. Accuracy is more likely to result from consultation on an individual basis rather than a team discussion. Feedback to fee earners is essential even if it cannot be immediate.

Information about what is known about the case is fairly easy to provide. The more difficult assessment is information about likely outcomes both in terms of time and result. Views are influenced by experience. Assessing risk and then managing risk within the case is a skill fee earners will be focusing on in conditional fee cases. The Woolf Reforms were designed to get fee earners to budget for time and costs associated with the case. The link between time and money was clearly spelt out and the overriding objective requires cases to be conducted expeditiously (CPR Rule 1.1(2)(d)). The timing of fast track trials should be easier to assess than multi-track where listing practices vary widely, but the pace of procedural steps prior to trial is often similar as multi-track cases in many courts are proceeding with great speed. Too great an emphasis on track is often not warranted. Early experience of CPR Part 36 offers and CPR Part 36 payments is that they are concluding a significant number of cases including pre-issue, but that disputes over costs are in danger of becoming disproportionate in time. However, assessment of outcome is difficult for junior fee earners with little experience of the end product under the old rules to use as a starting point for the new rules.

Ascertaining work loads

Getting from the basic information on the number of cases per fee earner to ascertaining workloads is not easy and involves subjective assessments. Fee earners will be subjective about the level of pressure they are working under and will be influenced by the demands of the present. They may feel very differently about the workload even within the space of a few weeks. Those managing caseloads may herald from an era when work done on each case was not so intensive and caseloads were traditionally higher. It is also difficult for managers with acquired status and experience to remember the challenges of inexperience; it is easy for them to underestimate the complexity of a junior fee earner's caseload. Any combination of running individual cases and individual multi-party casework is notoriously difficult to assess as the peaks and troughs in terms of the demand of a latter are often difficult to predict. Generic multi-party work is unlikely to be combined with individual cases within a caseload. Broad indicators of workload include the record of chargeable hours and volume of typing produced, and supervision and file reviews should give managers a feel for the combination of competing pressures arising out of a caseload.

Maintaining a database of outcomes

An important management tool which produces objective information is formed from recorded details of concluded cases. File closing information should include the following details:

- identification of file and fee earner;
- multi-party action (yes/no);
- type of funding;
- outcome:

1 ongoing;

2 finished: abandoned after investigation either before issue or before service of a protective writ;

3 finished: abandoned after service but before trial;

4 finished: settled before issue of proceedings;

5 finished: issued. served and settled or won at trial;

6 finished: lost at trial;

7 finished: obtained a non-financial win;

8 finished: non-financial loss;

9 damages: actual if won/settled; estimate if not;

- total profit costs, disbursements, experts' fees, counsel's fees and VAT;
- costs attached to stages of the case: investigative, protocols, pre-issue, pre-case management, to trial/settlement and recovery of costs;
- success fee and counsel's success fee and VAT if case run on a conditional fee;
- date to destroy.

If the information is combined with destruction dates, then provision of the information can be made a compulsory step in the archiving process. Completion of the form as each case concludes and inputting into a database is not onerous but it will take some years for meaningful data to be produced. Retrospective completion over archived cases is extremely onerous. Such a database also raises the question as to how far the past can be used as a guide to the future, but the past under 'the old rules' is still a very useful starting position upon which to view the changes brought about by CPR.

There is no point in gathering this information unless it is analysed in detail at least annually and assessed by managers to ascertain specific information. As soon as meaningful numbers of cases are included, the information will show the actual as opposed to the anecdotal. The following matters can be ascertained:

- length of time to conclude cases settled at fast track and multi-track levels;
- percentage of cases abandoned after investigation;
- percentage of cases lost or discontinued after issue;
- average costs on cases which would be fast track under CPR;
- percentage of cases where costs exceed damages recovered;
- success rate of multi-party actions;
- fighting fund of success fees, made up of winners and losers;

- cases that are costly in terms of experts' fees;
- cases that are costly in terms of counsels' fees.

The information can be accessed as required – by department, fee earner, year. Individual cases can also be identified and then analysed further. Such a management tool will be essential to arguments at detailed assessment over recovering the risk element of success fees as the winners subsidise the losers so the firm's statistics on the fighting fund will have to become public knowledge.

Number of cases

Most firms will start with the pre-CPR position. It is impractical to start with a clean sheet of paper because cases are ongoing and the impact of the new rules is uncertain. However, trends can be seen. There has been front-loading of cases. The CPR Part 36 procedure appears to be working to conclude cases early and often pre-issue. There is a different view as to what work a claimant can do under any pre-action protocol without a costs risk and because the courts can only start case management once the case has been issued there is likely to be tension created between issued and unissued cases. The temptation is to concentrate on the former, and this was a necessity in the early days of CPR due to the pace of the court case management and work generated by it. Cases allocated to the fast track are on exactly that and all old cases that come before the court are quickly being case managed even if they are not being allocated to a track. Even issued cases without applications pending are coming under scrutiny, with many district judges making directions orders from the files and even communicating these by e-mail. In reality there has been little by way of 'transitional' breathing space. Managers have therefore been keen to ascertain numbers of unissued and issued cases and to track this breakdown over time over individual caseloads.

Early indications show that more detailed information has to be provided to the court, and there is a need to deal with all issues when looking at one on the case so that the file stays in front of the fee earner for longer. Preparation for case management conferences includes case synopsis, draft directions and costing a file for summary assessment, and compiling the costs information at allocation and listing can take a considerable time. However, there is also the opportunity to settle in a shorter amount of time. Whether there will be a significant reduction in the time worked on the file as opposed to the period of weeks over which the case is concluded remains to be seen but this is likely, particularly if benchmark costs for certain interlocutory applications are introduced. However, in an increasingly competitive market, litigators will also worry about the new cases coming in to replenish those they have concluded. In that sense, whilst working for institutional work providers brings with it the difficulty of having to cater for the whole package it also brings with it a guaranteed flow of new cases which can be spread out among a number of fee earners. Defendant firms are likely to see a decrease in issued cases and will be seeking to be involved pre-issue, traditionally the domain of insurers. Managers may find fee earners looking at the work coming into the firm with a keen interest.

Firms have taken a markedly different approach to the number of cases. Some have reduced the number of cases operated by the fee earners at managerial level so that they can spend more time in a supervisory capacity. This is particularly so where the number supervised is high or the supervisor is operating over different locations. Some have reduced the top layer of fee earners and concentrated on the middle rank of skilled fee earners who require less supervision than junior fee earners. There appears to be an increase in senior fee earners recruiting paralegal support to facilitate strategic decisions by delegating the more mundane tasks. Indeed, there has been renewed emphasis on support and research staff. Defendant insurance solicitors have made efforts to reduce caseloads but their views are likely to be influenced by the agreement they reach with insurers as to the level of their involvement on unissued work. This was formally the province of insurers but given the need to take an early view on liability and instruct joint experts, insurers may wish to use solicitors firms as a pre-issue resource.

Many firms have agreed the need to staff up and provided the work is coming in are likely to have made some expansion. There are many indicators of reduced profitability per case, including lower hourly rates assigned to grades of fee earners by the courts, stagnant public funding, fixed trial costs and the spectre of benchmark costs. Firms are therefore cautious about expanding salary costs and overheads associated with administrative support for new fee earners. This is particularly so if they have needed to invest in training and IT to meet the needs of CPR. However major change, and CPR is certainly that, is often a catalyst for more regular appraisal of workloads and early identification of recruitment needs.

Fee earners who carry out multi-track work are unlikely to feel any need radically to alter their caseload numbers but some adjustment is likely. The numbers will depend upon the value of the case and work types. For those handling fast track cases another significant factor will be the proportion of issued cases. Delays will not be tolerated on issued cases and will be penalised in costs. In both tracks, fee earners have got to feel comfortable with the case in terms of recalling and understanding the issues, monitoring risk and being able to persuade the court about the directions that are appropriate to the case. The increased need for a dialogue with opponents in an effort to agree issues will itself increase the time spent on a file.

Some examples of caseloads scrutinised in a personal injury practice are as follows.

Case study

Experienced partner: 30 unissued, 19 issued (16 multi-track), 8 negotiating costs.

No acute problems after CPR but five issued cases where liability complex (as opposed to issued catastrophic injury cases where liability not complex) taking a lot of time in case management conferences and applications. Wants to maintain these numbers. Able to meet court deadlines but a constant battle and difficult if several deadlines coincide. Slight increase in billing.

New partner of five years' call: 76 unissued, 23 issued (8 multi-track), 48 negotiating costs.

Under some added pressure since CPR casework done at expense of costing. Should settle at least 60 per cent of unissued cases in CPR Part 36 offers. Issued cases where liability/causation complex taking time. Wants to reduce unissued to 60 and no more than 30 issued. Slight decrease in billing.

Assistant solicitor of three years' call: 117 unissued, 48 issued (5 multi-track), 33 negotiating costs.

Intense pressure since CPR on all issued cases due to pace of fast track. Small number of multi-track cases but take time. Should settle at least 65 per cent of unissued cases in CPR Part 36 offers. Need to reduce caseload of which vast majority fast track to 90 unissued and 40 issued maximum. Significant increase in billing but workload unsustainable.

Assistant solicitor of one years' call: 85 unissued, 15 issued (all fast track), 18 negotiating costs.

Should settle 80 per cent of unissued cases in CPR Part 36 offers. Building up caseload before CPR as had only just qualified. Capacity to take more as unissued cases settling at good pace. Below anticipated billing. Wants to get to 100 unissued bearing in mind number need to issue on will rise to around 35 level.

The rules have coincided with a number of initiatives which are also time-consuming. A lot of firms carrying out legal aid work were applying for a franchise and undergoing preliminary or pre-contract audits. Those carrying out conditional fee work were in the process of assessing the overall risk taken, risk portfolio, viewing the conditional fee insurance policies available and assessing the impact of funding disbursements and premiums on the firm's overdraft. Many firms also saw CPR as an opportunity to review their investment in IT and case management, which is time-consuming in terms of assessing the precise requirement, analysing the choices available and training. There has been little respite. The many amendments to CPR and the new regime of conditional fee regulations has meant that the heat has remained on.

TEAMWORK ON LARGE CASES

Large cases are not confined to large firms. Niche practices and individual fee earners with complex caseloads abound. The Multi-Party Action (MPA) Solicitors' Panel announced by the Legal Action Board on 1 February 1999 contained 18 firms of differing sizes. Involvement could arise due to geographical links or links with client groups. These are resource implications. When a large case comes to the firm or a contract is awarded, the firm has to examine how far it can use existing people or how far it has to buy in new people (see below 'Recruiting and keeping of quality staff'). The timescale of recruiting could be a factor. There may well be use of short term contracts, even where these are contrary to the general employment ethos of the firm. The skills bought in may be fairly unusual for the profile of the firm such as a skill in a discovery package/document management system or scientific link to a liability/causation issue.

If existing members of staff have been recruited into the team, there is always an issue as to how far junior fee earners risk specialisation at too early a stage of their career. This is keenly felt in small/medium sized firms, or if the fee earner is off-site, perhaps at the client's office or at an Inquiry. The junior fee earners may feel that they are being taken out of the mainstream experience and will miss out on progression of their careers if they become too specialised in one case. Indeed, they may feel that job security is being undermined if their future is linked with one case. Even though they may welcome the teamwork approach they might be apprehensive about the fact that their work is likely to come under increased scrutiny. The same consideration is also relevant in respect of support staff, who may also be taken out of the mainstream of the firm.

Personal relationships within the team are more important than when fee earners progress cases themselves under supervision. The team will work closely together and is likely to be under stress at the same time. There must always be clear lines of responsibility in terms of instructions down and feedback up. Support staff will also come under stress at the same time and may be required to work outside routine office hours, which can cause difficulty as it is less typically their working day.

The case is likely to be operating to a budget. This will have been put to the funder of the case, whether this be the client, public funding or Insurer and will be determinative of the size and level of the team. The budget will also be influenced by the need to buy in resources that cannot be provided in-house, such as counsel and experts. If the case is large enough there are going to be a number of counsel involved and there will be a closer cooperation between counsel and solicitors than is usual. Difficult strategic issues benefit from team opinions and any negligence risk is spread across several indemnity policies.

Clear lines of responsibility have to be drawn up for who is to deal with:

- the client(s);
- the funder;
- other solicitors with linked cases;
- opponents' solicitors;
- the media;
- counsel;
- experts.

These roles are visible but in addition there will be a raft of support staff without whom the case will halt. Client-handling skills are not part of their routine tasks, although they will be providing a service to fee earners in the firm.

It is likely that the team will be operating at different geographical locations. This will certainly be the case in the sense that the team includes outside counsel and experts, and communication by e-mail is preferable but needs to be secure. There may also be a need for video conferencing, particularly if any of the experts are overseas.

UNBUNDLING: SHARING OF WORK WITH THE CLIENT

Teamwork between solicitor and client is required whether it is a client with no previous experience of litigation or a client used to the requirements that litigation imposes. The nature of the information sought will differ but the type of information and the date of the request are broadly similar. It is likely that firms will have briefed work-providing client such as companies, insurers or trade unions about the Woolf Reforms before they took place and have information such as booklets to provide to new clients. This is advantageous because those with past experience of litigation need to understand the far-reaching reforms and the new litigation landscape, including topics such as ADR with which they may not be familiar. Whilst the client is an important part of the management of the case the opportunities for the sharing of work may be limited. It is perhaps more a question of the Reforms tending to involve the client in what the lawyer is trying to achieve on their behalf. There is a greater concentration on timescales both before and after issue and the prospect of split issues and split orders and penalties for overexaggerating a claim mean that the client will need to understand how they will suffer in costs if they take a course of action that is against the solicitor's advice. It is also important that all clients understand the overriding objective and their solicitor's obligation to the court.

The first interview

The fact that the firm will be making important judgements on costs-benefit analysis for the client and the firm after the evidence-gathering first interview requires liability, quantum and funding options to be dealt with in detail. Protocols require letters of claim to detail quantum but it is also vital for the client to have an early preliminary range. It is unrealistic to have a short initial interview followed by a longer one unless the overall quantum is very high, so it is likely that some filtering of the claims will be operated usually by telephone contact. Whilst it is important to discuss the CPR and protocol at the meeting, it is also vital to supplement this with written briefings that the client can take away and refer to at the various stages of the case. These briefing tools can be highly specialised if the work justifies it. The complexity of conditional fee agreements has expanded into video explanations viewed at the solicitors' office prior to the appointment with the fee earner, but the CPR is not a one-off occurrence and is difficult to approach in this format.

Written briefings to the client should include:

- the firm's funding protocol and how it relates specifically to the client's case;
- case plan with dates and costs estimates for each stage;
- client care regime and complaints procedure (see Chapter 5 below);
- aims of the Woolf Reforms and overriding objective;
- explanation of any protocol: obligation on both sides, aims and timescale, disclosure before issue;
- opportunities to settle before issue;
- CPR Part 36 payments and CPR Part 36 offers;
- case management by the court after issue;
- experts: CPR Part 35;
- timescale, once issued to trial;
- statements of truth;
- disclosure;
- proportionality;
- split issues, split orders, split costs;
- summary assessment and what it means to the client;
- ADR;
- recovery of costs during and after case concluded.

As time goes on it will be possible to tell the client your knowledge of how the courts and regular opponents are operating CPR.

It is important to consider not only what the client can tell you about the evidence that they can produce on liability and quantum but also the evidence that the client expects the other side to have. This will be important if acting for a claimant and having to 'go first' by sending a letter of claim under a protocol.

The claimant should go away with a clear idea of the case plan, timescale and a broad idea of quantum. It can be useful to do broad case analyses by simply picking out for the client factors in the case which will help with the judge, and those which will not. It is easier to get involved in this if the firm is bound to take on the case than if the case has to be risk-assessed and approved.

The client also needs a clear understanding of what is required of him in the future in terms of keeping ongoing records and the requirement to give instructions at key stages. The setting of a timetable raises a client's expectations and fulfilment of these expectations relies not only on the performance of the solicitor but also on external factors such as court listing and responses of experts, and it is useful to draw a distinction between matters that are within the solicitors' control, and those out of the solicitors' control which have to be chased.

The client is an important human resource. Changes to the timescale need to be promptly communicated. Regular communication is vital but must be planned. It is useful to mark on the case plan the stages at which you need detailed consultation. Do not over burden. Part of the client-handling skills is to assess the level and means of communication the client will require.

Consultation and certificates of truth

The majority of fee earners have always obtained the client's approval to documents, such as an expert's report, regardless of how far the client's views can actually be taken into account in terms of revision. The expertise of clients should not be underestimated. Corporate clients are termed 'sophisticated' clients who have an understanding of the business they run and individuals within the business may be lawyers or know a lot of law. However, lay clients may carry out research into their case and opportunities for client research have certainly been enhanced by the Internet. They may also have been given access to documentation by contacts. The introduction of joint experts' reports needs to be broached and that means that the client will have less opportunity to choose the evidence which ultimately comes before the court. It is a concept which clients and lawyers feel makes sense, avoids duplication of costs, and is one they approve of until they see a report that they do not like.

Because of the court rules it is important to consider when to get clients to sign certificates of truth. This will routinely apply to statements of case and disclosure but signature on interlocutory applications and written evidence in support is likely to be by the solicitor as under the old rules. The person who has to sign these may be very senior in the client organisation so difficult to contact but it is difficult to provide these in batches given timing requirements under CPR.

IT

Proportionality and fixed costs have raised issues as to whether clients' access to solicitors conducting cases needs to be reviewed. The debate is partly influenced by the traditional lack of solicitor and own client bills in areas of work such as personal injury law. Such bills are particularly discouraged by institutional work-providers who provide and indemnify a package of work which will often have the majority of cases in the fast track. Firms will already have management systems in place which ensure that work is delegated to the right level and it is vital that clients are informed about the status of the people dealing with their case, as failure to broach this could lead to negation of the bill (Practice Rule 15.7(a)(ii)(b)(1)). Under the client care regime which commenced in Autumn 1999, detailed client care letters and regular information about costs will be the norm. Most firms have a process whereby some screening of client's calls is carried out by fee earners' secretaries. Many fee earners seem permanently 'on divert'. This is appropriate as long as the secretary is familiar with the case, which means that it is not appropriate for a pool-type system. IT is available whereby clients can check on the progress of their case by accessing the timetable through their PC. This accords with the Lord Chancellor's Department strategy for IT and set out in the strategy paper *civil.justice.2000* (June 2000). However, if part of the strategy behind this development is designed to reduce the telephone contact, then before investing in such a system it is important to speak to those who have tried it out to make sure that it does not in fact increase the number of enquiries due to desire for clarification of the information accessed.

IT has generally increased the ease of contact between clients and solicitors. It has for years been part of communication between corporate clients and their solicitors but many individual clients now have access to the Internet and e-mail. It is also a good way of capturing data on potential claims through the firm's website. Firms need to be confident about the e-mail system before completing that particular box on the application notice and will need to have policies as to whether contact by e-mail from the client is encouraged or discouraged. It is important to have a system whereby fee earners' e-mail is checked so that if they are absent for any number of days it is dealt with and the sender of the e-mail appreciates the reason for lack of response. Standard replies to senders can be programmed during holiday periods. It is important for hard copies of the e-mail to get on to the file as a record of dealings and for costing the case. Widespread use of the PC means that many clients and witnesses are able to put their statements onto disk which can easily be downloaded at the solicitors' offices and edited to deal with the new procedural technicalities with regard to the format of statements.

It is important that clients understand the strengths and weaknesses of the case by early case analysis and the areas upon which they need to concentrate. It is also important that less experienced fee earners are not influenced by the client's agenda when analysing these issues. A mechanism whereby a fee earner has to seek approval before taking on a one-off client also shields junior fee earners from client pressures.

Disclosure

You would expect to send the following documents to the client for comment:

- documents obtained through the protocol;
- statements of case;
- documentation produced on disclosure;
- opponent's witness statements;
- quantum details;
- experts' reports: liability and quantum;
- written evidence in support of applications and draft orders sought;
- orders which contain directions timetables;
- schedule of loss and damage and counter schedule;
- case summaries, statements of outstanding issues and observations on experts required for case management conferences;
- skeleton arguments;
- counsel's opinions;
- past and future estimates of costs, VAT and disbursements provided at allocation, for case management and on listing;
- the same information provided by the opponent's solicitors;
- both parties' Form 1 on any summary assessment of costs application.

It can be seen that the client is involved at many stages, sees a lot of original documentation and work products, and has an opportunity to work on the case.

USE OF COUNSEL

More or less?

Rumours of the demise of the barrister's profession following the CPR are exaggerated but it is certainly the case that there are pressures on individual barristers and chambers from a number of sources. It may be that firms of significant size will look at the new culture as an opportunity to alter radically the use of counsel but this will be by substitution of services in-house and not by way of deletion. Many litigation firms will not have the confidence or the inclination to commit resources to this in-house in the earliest years of CPR and there is a continuing role for an independent second opinion, often in a quasi-supervisory role. Practitioners who operate across different areas of litigation will still value specialist counsel chosen for a particular case and specialist practitioners still need an overview. Counsel can also 'think trial' because they see more trials, and can think like a judge because they are still more likely to become a judge. The Bar should be keen to offer the continuing service at a competitive price. Of course the cost of the service is an issue but one that is often seen in the context of highly paid QCs (a title in itself unpopular in some quarters) and the number of young juniors starting off in the profession will mean continued scope for spotting and nurturing talent at a reasonable cost.

In publicly funded work, old certificates still refer to the need for counsel's opinion in the limitation section and work is generated under the terms of the conditional fee agreements with counsel, which include keeping counsel informed of the progress of the case through consultation, on the need for advice on evidence, merits and quantum, and through bringing evidence to the attention of all counsel if it may have a material effect on the prospects of success on liability. In addition, some of the work previously done by counsel on a standard basis (particularly drafting pleadings) will be done by solicitors in most claims. However there may be use of counsel at an earlier stage in multi-track cases in a conference (which is also an ideal opportunity to discuss taking the case on on a conditional fee basis) or in a conference timed just before a case management conference.

Choice of counsel: who to use?

This is an important decision that demands an organised approach. Many firms operate practice management standards which include a register of experts and counsel, being services provided by others to the client, and it needs to be up to date to be meaningful.

Useful reference points for choosing counsel are:

- colleagues;
- counsel register in-house;
- *Chambers Directory* and *Legal 500*;
- Specialist directories, e.g. *Chancery Bar List*;
- polls and tables in legal magazines;
- brochures from Chambers (also needed to cross-reference year of call for statement of costs for summary assessment);
- advice from clerks
- reference to who is writing articles, appearing in case reports.

You should bear in mind also the following:

- if new counsel are used, feedback should always be given;
- operate an equal opportunities policy;
- partners should not dictate; they might be out of touch with newcomers;
- keep the register up to date;
- record the reason that counsel was chosen on the file.

After counsel has been chosen, set and monitor performance criteria to include:

- cost: are they recording preparation hours and conference time on fee-notes?
- availability, including on telephone;
- speed of return of paperwork: discuss with clerk and put a deadline in covering letter;
- familiarity with CPR;
- returned briefs: is there depth in chambers?
- CFA work: is counsel receptive? Is the agreement fair ? What risk assessment do they carry out? Will they charge for this if they turn the case down? Will the success fee be different from the solicitor's?
- client-handling skills;
- advocacy skills;
- use of IT in keeping up to date and communicating documents to instructing solicitors;

- understanding of practical case management issues for CPR and of costs;
- views on experts.

The relationship between solicitor and counsel is essentially a personal one and personal preferences should be accommodated as long as it does not compromise the service. It is usual and sensible to choose counsel close to your offices but if the case is proceeding to trial in a different centre then counsel local to the trial court, particularly in London, should be considered. In an increasingly corporate marketplace, many Chambers are seeking and listening to the views of existing and potential customers. The Bar Council has emphasised client care skills for a number of years so solicitors' views will be welcome.

When and how to use

Unless the case is so large that the client/solicitor/counsel team has to be established on day one it is unlikely that counsel will be seeing papers at an early stage or before the protocol period has expired. It is unlikely also that counsel will be spending significant amounts of time in pleadings, affidavits or witness statements. The practice of counsel drafting witness statements has always been a hostage to fortune and the rules of CPR make it clear that the statements should be in the witnesses own words. In his Final Report, *Access to Justice*, at paragraph 54, Lord Woolf deplored the development of lawyer participation turning this into 'an elaborate, costly branch of legal drafting'.

Using counsel to settle pleadings is a well-established, often cost-effective practice and is still relevant in post-CPR days. Counsel will still be used in contesting interlocutory applications when the stakes are high such as summary judgment applications under CPR Part 24 and striking out a case under CPR Rule 3.4. Many firms located away from the court appear to be instructing barristers to appear alone at case management conferences and in larger cases. Many provincial courts do not operate an issuing system which accommodates counsel's availability, as dates are assigned after the application has been handled or of the court's own motion on the allocation questionnaire. However, a list of available dates accompanying an application notice and request for liaison is very likely to be accommodated.

The role of independent second opinion will continue, not least because the client respects this, a fact which can be harnessed by solicitors facing difficult issues, and because fee earners are sometimes so busy and it is a way of ensuring the case gets consideration. Counsel is likely to be involved in a similar proportion of cases as under the previous rules in terms of reacting to a CPR Part 36 offer or payment, but as the frequency of these has increased and as the stakes are higher on the defendant's side, this is likely to be a fruitful source of work. In addition, counsel will be involved in the proactive practice of making CPR Part 36 payments or offers and these are often an issue on the agenda for the conference. Instructions which conclude with an agenda assist all parties.

The early conference and identifying the issues

After the pre-action protocol period, where one applies, or the investigative period where it does not, an early conference with counsel fits in with the CPR landscape in multi-track cases. The purpose is to identify the issues and identify the evidence obtained and that needed to win at trial. Identifying issues and facts to prove them is a skill practitioners require more than ever given the importance of risk assessments and the prospect of split costs orders. It is also an area where they need help, if only by way of reassurance. In spite of increased emphasis on the teaching of evidence in the Legal Practice Course the narrower focus of the training of a barrister is more litigation and evidence intensive.

Evidence includes:

- witness statements (CPR Part 32);
- disclosure (CPR Part 31) including pre-action and protocol disclosure;
- notices to admit facts (CPR Rule 32.18);
- notices to admit or produce documents (CPR Rule 32.19);
- Notice of intention to rely on hearsay evidence (CPR Rule 33.2).

The stages at which to consider Counsel are:

- conference after protocol period: liability, if still in issue, quantum and CPR Part 36 offer, funding;
- prior to case management conference in multi-track cases;
- large interlocutory hearings on both tracks;
- conference on evidence in multi-track cases after disclosure, exchange of reports and of witness statements: prepare for trial; agreed issues and those in dispute;
- fast track and multi-track trials.

The early conference is also an opportunity to review whether or not the barrister is prepared to work on a conditional fee basis and to agree on the future involvement of counsel. It may be an opportunity for CPR Part 36 offers to be dealt with. The new rules are likely to mean that quantum issues and special damages in particular are raised with the client from the first meeting and so will be available at the conference, but it is unlikely in multi-track cases that a final decision can be made at the early conference.

A conference at any stage involves preparation to be of maximum benefit in the client. The preparation of instructions to counsel in a systemised manner involves a review of the issues (in the instructions) and in the evidence (enclosures) and a conference note afterwards, whether or not signed by counsel, sets the agenda for future work and can be sent to the client as part of the case plan. The new way of working under CPR is likely to involve use of time-set deadlines associated with the work and steps on the agenda. Timing is a factor as conferences need to be listed many weeks in advance for the popular counsel.

However a practical difficulty has recently arisen in conditional fee cases backed by Accident Line Protect. The conditional fee agreement and insurance needs to be in place before the letter of claim is sent. Conferences need to await the expiry of any pre-action protocol period otherwise there is the risk that the defendants will admit liability and costs will be incurred unnecessarily. If the defendant denies liability, then counsel will need to consider the document accompanying that denial obtained through the protocol. Conferences will therefore by definition take place after a conditional fee agreement has been entered in to by the solicitor, and this presentation of *fait accompli* for counsel is difficult for both counsel and solicitor. Counsel need to understand the difficulties that solicitor's face. Like most of the problems in connection with conditional fees and CPR this benefits from dialogue at personal level in addition to that at Law Society and Bar Council level.

Advocacy

Under the old rules, counsel appeared at trials with great frequency, although solicitors did not necessarily see them in action as solicitors' attendance at trials of their own cases was infrequent and they would be more used to seeing counsel in conference. By attending at trial, counsel's skill in advocacy can be observed. The skill is not likely to have been observed in a formal sense amongst colleagues in small and medium sized practices, let alone formally assessed. It is also a skill that fee earners may be reluctant to exercise.

Much advocacy in Chambers is dealt with by solicitors. This trend is marked outside London. A factor under CPR is that issues are unlikely to be dealt with in isolation. A summary judgment or strikeout application is likely to be combined in the alternative by case management directions (a real difficulty for benchmark costing). Well researched legal argument therefore has to be combined with a practical and in depth understanding of the file (issues, experts, timing). Sometimes it is simply easier for the fee earner involved to do the hearing rather than to instruct counsel. Case management conferences in clinical negligence and industrial disease work may involve counsel, and the district judge/Master is not likely to object to certificates for counsel (still considered by some district judges as necessary under CPR) but may take a different view if both counsel and instructing solicitor are present.

The early signs in connection with fast track trials is that the attendance of both solicitor and barrister will have to be sacrificed due to the fixed costs matrix and solicitors are reluctant to extend their advocacy skills into this new area. The problem is that, as with much of CPR, it gives rise to fear of the unknown. This will be lessened through observing fast track trials and recently qualified solicitors will have been assessed for this skill in the Legal Practice Course. However, if a barrister is instructed on these trials it is unlikely in the long run that the solicitor will be there to observe. The fee earner may well want to be present for the summary assessment of costs and to conduct this advocacy. Barristers will continue to be involved in multi-track trials as these are unlikely to be carried out by solicitors unless they are solicitor advocates.

It is possible to increase confidence by setting up rôle playing, which is most pertinent if it is rehearsal for actual negotiation or court hearing. Advocacy in the wider sense as influencing can include negotiations or persuading the decision-making panel of the firm to fund a case on a conditional fee basis.

Advocacy at trial will be influenced by court listing. Court listing has implications for the choice of advocate. Short trial windows, when starting on a particular day cannot be guaranteed, may be difficult for barristers to accommodate and may lead to changes of barrister late in the day, which under the present law is not routinely going to lead to a judge granting an adjournment of the action. The prospect of these returning briefs will also cause problems for teamwork on conditional fee cases due not least to the self-employed status of the barrister.

Higher Court solicitor advocacy is an important development in political terms and is important to some individuals and firms, but it has not revolutionised the majority of small and medium sized litigation practices and can be a controversial area. Some solicitor advocates complain that the judiciary is not as well-disposed to them as counsel which will mean solicitors with no such resource in-house will be cautious about employing solicitor advocates on behalf of their client.

Costing structure

The charging structure may alter after the CPR as barristers understand the need to justify non-trial work on an hourly rate. However, brief fees on trials which settle still remain the cream for them, which has resulted in increased pressure from clerks for solicitors to send in the brief. If this lessens because of less involvement in fast track trials or a reduction in the number of cases issuing and going to trial, then barristers will have to look at increased hourly rates on non-trial work to make up the difference. It is unlikely that the difference could be made up by success fees on conditional fee cases as experience shows that it only takes one loss to write off wins on a significant number of cases. It is envisaged that hourly rates of counsel in demand will increase and this in turn is going to influence the choice of counsel.

RECRUITING AND KEEPING OF QUALITY STAFF

CPR has been accompanied by an increased emphasis on risk. One of the biggest risk factors in a case is the fee earner. It is important to recruit, motivate, reward and retain quality staff. Staff mobility is high. Salaries are currently running at high levels. Investment in the right litigation fee earners is as important as ever.

Once the need for a litigation fee earner has been established, a short job specification can be drawn up looking at whether the vacancy is for a qualified or unqualified fee earner; if the former what qualification level is required; whether the fee earner will have their own caseload or assist another fee earner, the caseload numbers and work types; billing targets and the extent to which the fee earner will require secretarial support. There will still be occasions on which a candidate who is not ideal for the job specification impresses to such an extent that the job specification is effectively changed to recruit them. Flexibility is not a bad thing.

The decision is then taken as to who will do the recruiting and whether recruitment agencies need to be involved. The job description can form the basis of an advert, in the legal press if agencies are not being used and otherwise for agencies. It is preferable for CVs provided through recruitment agencies or from individual candidates to be targeted at the job specification, but candidates do not always take the time to do this as they are pursuing a significant number of varied options and recruitment agencies may want to send a selection of candidates on their books. CVs can be vetted by a fee earner or a member of any human resources department and should be vetted with the job description and the firm's equal opportunities policy in mind, and appropriate records kept. Many practice management standards require recruitment papers to be retained for a year.

Most firms still operate a system of first and second interviews. Use of psychometric testing is not widespread outside large firms but it is always useful to test out legal knowledge by setting one question requiring preparation in advance and asking a series of shorter questions at interview. This provides a useful matrix when interviewing a number of people over a short period of time, particularly if some candidates are known to you. Always provide the answers if the candidate cannot, rather than simply moving on. Any litigation fee earner should be questioned about CPR in terms of understanding its requirements such as the overriding objective and to see how the fee earner assesses that CPR is operating in practice across e.g. a controversial area such as CPR Part 35 on experts. It is always useful to hear another perspective or learn of another firm's choice of counsel and experts. It is common for candidates to be well informed about the firm as websites give more information than Directories.

Keeping

Fee earners should know the job they are required to do by reference to the job description and by being provided at an early stage with an Office Manual to read. The induction process is important and most effective if carried out by a number of different individuals, which also gives variety; it will rarely be appropriate for the same person who is talking about the files to talk about the time recording system or building security. The fee earner needs to understand what is required in terms of case numbers and billing by set targets and the supervisory process. The fee earner needs to understand the ethos of the firm and how far they are expected to follow that, and how far there will be flexibility for individual preferences (such as on choice of counsel). Consistent fair boundaries are required for new staff to settle in. Many firms are adopting dignity at work policies, seeing the need from surveys and anecdotal evidence of harassment and bullying. Mistakes occur in litigation. Fee earners do not want to be part of a firm which sues its employees for uninsured losses, a practice that has gone on for years and will become the subject of a Practice Rule.

Litigation fee earners under CPR need to feel comfortable with the quantity and level of work that they have and the work products and outcomes they are producing for the client. Under CPR they need to have a sense of control over their caseload, given the time limits that are put upon them particularly by the court; they will not want to incur the wrath of the local judiciary. The fee earner will need to be reassured that the firm has a strategy for keeping up to date with cases decided under CPR and monitoring CPR generally, and has committed resources to a library and IT. IT is of particular interest to junior fee earners, who will have been familiar with it as a tool from an early age. CPR itself is commonly accessed on CD Rom. The fee earner will also need the reassurance that the firm has a mechanism in place to share experience of CPR to which all fee earners can contribute and that the firm is participating in and shaping the debate about forthcoming developments such as benchmark costs. It is important that the fee earner feels part of the team, no matter how small the team is, and that there are other people in the team that fee earners can learn from, however senior that fee earner might be.

Administrative back-up, such as the services of a legal secretary if required and the services of office junior and court clerk, is important and should not be underestimated. There is nothing more demoralising for a junior fee earner than to have tapes constantly at the back of the typing queue. Feedback to general progress, file reviews and supervision generally and team meetings are also important, as is a review after any probationary period. Risk assessment meetings for claimants will give fee earners an opportunity to team and to contribute. If mistakes are picked up this can be some comfort to fee earners in terms of knowing the mechanisms that assist within the firm to highlight these and thereafter support them. Salary and perks need to be competitive and reviewed annually or on an ad hoc basis when the need arises. It is not difficult to obtain details of the appropriate level through job adverts and published surveys and fee earners can do their own research. For many qualified fee earners, progression through the partnership is still the goal even though many firms do not have any written criteria for this elevation. There therefore needs to be a mechanism whereby fee earners' aspirations can be discussed at regular stages and there is a set time of year and mechanism whereby other partners can put forward potential candidates for promotion. The debate may well bring out tensions between departments and teams in large firms.

Training

All solicitors now need to fulfil the Continuing Professional Development requirements of the Law Society and may in addition be required to secure membership to specialist panels or higher rights of advocacy. Training should be seen as an opportunity not a burden. In most firms, it is fulfilled by a combination of ad hoc and final in-house training and external training. Litigation training is well catered for in the external market through commercial providers and specialist networks and CPR has been the subject of many courses. There will be little reduction in the quantity of these during its early years as decided cases and trends in case management need to be analysed and solicitors reach the end of their three-year period for points gathering. In addition, some insurers require panel members to attend courses on risk management.

Training to be a specialist in a particular area of litigation requires a commitment to spend time on that area, which requires sacrificing other aspects. It requires embracing work practices of others working in that field (these can only safely be adapted after experience is gained) and going on external training courses and wide reading. Training in skills is now embraced in the Legal Practice Course but it remains more difficult to persuade firms to pay for this than for litigation courses. Training for partnership and management roles is now more commonplace, with certain providers enjoying a good reputation in the field.

NEED FOR STAFF AT THE RIGHT LEVEL

There has always been a need for work to be done at the level of fee earner having the appropriate experience for the case, but whose level of expertise the case will stand so that the client can get a good financial result and the firm can earn a profit. There is a distinction between civil litigation that routinely produces solicitor and own client bills and that which does not, such as personal injury. In the first category, inter partes costs at the rates set by the court (standard practice outside London since the late 1980s) can be supplemented and to some extent the clients can be given more choice as to the level of fee earner they wish to pay for as opposed to require. In the latter, there has to be a closer relationship between the level of fee earner and the rate that the level of work will stand on an inter partes basis.

The Practice Direction first issued on summary assessment of costs on 1 February 1999 (see [1999] *Gazette*, 10 February) produced a matrix of the hourly rates across four categories of fee earner, with a composite rate. The basis for the figures was never clear and the figures were always default figures leading to dialogue at local level. The matrix quickly changed to three levels and following the pilot scheme in the Manchester County Court will revert to four from June 2001. However, the principle of composite rates appears to have been established. Across the various categories there are bound to be winners and losers when compared to the old rates. The discretion to uplift the guideline rates and banding across grades will alleviate the problems on some cases but only when the complexity of the case itself demands it. Firms which have contracts with institutional work-providers based on the old rates may be tied in for several years to rates that have now been radically revised. Hourly rates at reduced levels may have influenced recruitment of new team members as efforts are made to adjust the existing team to what the work will now stand. The paying party is bound to take points about work which could have been delegated and the level of appropriate delegation and the grade of fee earner who was able to handle the case.

Recruitment of fee earners will be influenced not only by the job specification but also by the hourly rate that that fee earner would command across the majority of the cases. The need for any assistance will in itself be influenced by the effect of the different hourly rates on the existing litigation fee earner team. The explicit desire in the three grade matrix to avoid a partner rate by putting in place a rate which combines partners and assistant solicitors of more than four years post-qualification experience appears to be borne of a concern that firms will be encouraged to admit fee earners to partnership so as to enable them to take advantage of an enhanced rate.

Although the expansion of a fixed cost matrix to fast track cases seems some way off (well surpassed by the arrival of benchmark costs) it is still important to look at the level of the fee earner doing those cases. The work will have to be supervised but it is not cost-effective for the supervision to be intense and the case must be pushed on by the fee earner involved who is able to analyse the case, know when to bring in third parties including experts and barristers, has an understanding of the CPR and its application and is able to deal effectively with the client and deal appropriately with the other side. It is possible to underestimate the pressures associated with a significant amount of fast track work (any combination of issued and unissued in excess of 130) and the work cannot be distilled. Exceptions may be routine road traffic cases with modest value injuries, and debt actions.

There has been consultation by the Supreme Court Costs Office on benchmark costs for certain interlocutory applications, and prices on 20 have been put forward for consultation. If the benchmark figure is the same whatever the grade of fee earner who prepares and attends, the court can expect delegation downwards which may well be inappropriate.

Specialisation

It is easier to skill up fee earners at any level if there is specialisation of work type. This brings familiarisation with issues, learning from past experience and confidence in repetition. Specialisation is even easier if a lot of work is carried out against the same opponent. That opponent's attitude to CPR will be particularly interesting. Knowledge of the opponent was important under the old rules and the opponent's reaction to any protocols, ADR, agreed experts and breach of case management directions will be important. There is also a requirement under CPR to work more closely with your opponents in terms of assisting the court. Specialisation also includes belonging to networks and gaining experience from outside the firm.

Delegation and supervision

Delegation of work includes both delegating individual cases and delegation in the case. Large work-providers provide many cases and need to have files delegated according to the complexity of issues and quantum, but the client's partner will often retain a hands-on role in addition to supervision as a poor outcome on any case can lead to repercussions. Supervision also needs to be at the right level, but firms' approaches under CPR have differed markedly. Some have reduced the number of equity partners, whilst some have reduced the billing targets of partners who supervise, particularly across different offices. Some have increased the middle layer of experienced assistant solicitors who require less supervision, but in the early days of CPR every fee earner will need help and to participate in the team meetings.

USE AND TRAINING OF PARALEGALS AND UNQUALIFIED STAFF

Firms which employ significant numbers of paralegals and unqualified staff either have bulk work-providers where the level of work can be done by these members of staff with significant assistance from IT systems, or have team and supervisory arrangements whereby these staff play an assisting function without handling cases of their own. These staff will be in the lowest grade of fee earner for summary and other costs guidelines and are likely to suffer the largest reduction from the pre-CPR arrangements. Firms employing significant numbers of paralegals and unqualified staff will have taken a big hit in the reduction of hourly rates. To some extent these staff may well have been targeted by those responsible for setting the rates on the basis that previously they have been entitled to the same rate as assistant solicitors, whereas their remuneration packages were considerably less, particularly as they are unlikely to require secretarial support. This in turn will have caused problems for firms signed up to contracts for bulk work-providers where the bulk of the work is carried out by this type of staff. This will necessitate either an attempt to renegotiate the contract terms or a gradual replacement of paralegals and unqualified staff by those in the middle layers of categories of fee earner on the costs guidelines. However, the job specification may not fit easily with the new categories of fee earners who are unlikely to be able to produce their own typing at the same speed and who are also less likely to be satisfied by that quality of work as their career progresses.

The clients, including bulk work-providers, will also want to be clear about the level of the person doing the work. The firm will need to be clear about this to ensure that they get paid at the conclusion of the case. Client care requirements and information on costs does include provision for identification of fee earner and level and accompanying hourly rates at the present time, and the client care regime which commenced in Autumn 1999 was higher in this regard.

Where there are significant numbers, training can be carried out in-house which being tailor-made is ideal. Where the numbers do not merit it there are external organisations geared to this type of training.

If paralegals and unqualified staff are working in a large pool of similar staff carrying out their own caseloads, the named supervisor will have to be someone who is familiar with the IT systems and who is available to answer regular queries. It is more effective if the numbers of fee earners being supervised merit a supervisory post which is not combined with other work demands. The named supervisor can also be involved in the training of the fee earners, particularly as the larger the team the higher will be the staff turnover.

Paralegals and unqualified staff carrying out assistant roles are likely to be assisting named fee earners on cases and carrying out research. They may also be responsible for keeping and maintaining computerised or manual records across the team, such as level of general damages for pain, suffering and loss of amenity on settlement and at trial in personal injury forms, and the experts register. These documents are unlikely to be maintained by the firm's librarian.

Paralegals are often delegated the following tasks:

- obtaining police reports or other documents in the public domain;
- speaking to witnesses in investigative stages of cases;
- drafting protocol letter of claim;
- drafting claim forms;
- obtaining and keeping track of medical records;
- perusing medical records, perusing personnel files;
- instructing medical experts;
- sending out witness questionnaires;
- valuing general damages for pain, suffering and loss of amenity in personal injury cases;
- analysing disclosure documents;
- researching similar cases on databases;
- analysing judgments;
- preparing documents for detailed assessment.

When work is delegated to the right level within a case there is going to be some duplication, not all of which can be put to the opponent. Indeed, in so far as it comprises training it also cannot be put to the client. There is likely to be duplication of attendances at conferences, but it is far more effective for the paralegal to be present if they are going to be taking action steps afterwards. There is also likely to be duplication at client interview, but rarely duplication when meeting opponents or attendance at court.

When delegating work on a case to paralegals the deadline for the work should always be clearly stated and reviewed if necessary. Instructions should be full and clear and sometimes an oral briefing will be necessary. Paralegals who work for more than one person are a useful resource in the sense that they will know a particular area has been covered by another fee earner previously. Assistance on casework is more effective if the fee earner who remains in conduct of the case is sufficiently high in status to merit assistance at various stages, thereby ensuring that the paralegal is familiar with the case and the case plan and case analysis in particular.

CONCLUSION

Litigation in the CPR landscape is about risk. It is about risk assessment, risk monitoring and risk management. One of the biggest factors in risk management is the litigation fee earner. Firms need to support and supervise those fee earners they have chosen to be in their team and to provide easy feedback mechanisms so that fee earners can contribute to the debate about how CPR has and will change litigation working practices.

CHAPTER 4

Marketing litigation and ADR

*Penny Owston, Simon McCall and
Geraldine McCool*

A. MARKETING LITIGATION AND ADR

INTRODUCTION

The main purpose of this chapter is to help solicitors ask the right questions about how to market the litigation services the firm offers. We appreciate that every firm is different in terms of specific services and types of client. Each will have a different approach and style. Accordingly, it would not be appropriate to give specific and prescriptive advice: there is no 'right' way to draft a brochure or design an advertisement. Indeed, some solicitors may well already be thinking: 'What use would a brochure or advertising be to us?'. We can, however, prompt you to examine all the options and provide some guidance. Additionally, each solicitor will have their own views, based on their own experience, as to how different the marketing of litigation is (or should be) to the marketing of other legal services. We feel that to a large extent the same principles apply.

We would encourage solicitors to extend their understanding and source of ideas by looking at the expanding range of articles and books on solicitors' firm marketing. Also, it can be very useful to examine and learn from the way other businesses go about winning and keeping clients and customers. For some this will involve abandoning certain instincts (or are they prejudices?) about how different a solicitors' firm is to any other type of business.

A health warning

There is no marketing fairy-dust that can be sprinkled over litigation services in order to create a long queue of new clients. We have to accept that marketing litigation services has always been difficult. This is because for clients it is a distress purchase (whether suing or being sued) that people try to avoid. It is impossible to make this seem an attractive prospect.

So marketing is going to be a combination of:

- profile raising (so people know about the firm);
- providing a reason why people should take legal advice, and
- providing a reason why they should take it from you.

Above all, the fundamental marketing activity of doing a good job for clients so that they return or recommend others will be paramount.

The Woolf changes are designed to make litigation more 'customer friendly' which in itself is an obvious advantage for solicitors. That fact, however, and any explanation of it, are not likely to overcome easily hundreds of years of ingrained prejudice that litigation is slow, complicated, uncertain and that the only people apparently guaranteed to benefit are the lawyers.

Marketing is more risky than law – even litigation! The solicitor's instinct is, quite properly, to get everything absolutely right, first time, every time. Anything less is regarded as failure. This attitude is, undoubtedly, healthy when giving legal advice, but it is likely to be fatal when dealing with marketing, or for that matter other aspects of managing the firm. Marketing is a mix of art and science. You can greatly increase the chances of success through a structured and imaginative approach but you cannot guarantee success. This has to be recognised and accepted, otherwise individuals will, at best, be depressed if marketing initiatives 'fail' and, at worst, will be paralysed into inactivity by the fear that they may fail. The fact of uncertainty and risk is the very reason why careful planning of marketing is necessary. It should not be an excuse for a haphazard approach of one-off initiatives.

If that all sounds very gloomy it should not do. For those solicitors who have addressed the issue of marketing, whether in respect of litigation or other aspects of their practice over recent years, it should only reflect reality. Effective marketing (combined with effective client service) can help the practice gain and keep satisfied clients.

AIMS OF MARKETING

Definitions of marketing that we may come across will probably range from the succinct, 'meeting client needs' to the more formal, 'the management process of understanding, meeting and anticipating client needs in a way that meets the economic and other requirements of the firm'. The important element is 'client needs'. This should distinguish legal marketing from what many of us would regard as some of the excesses of consumer advertising, where the intention may seem to be to persuade people to buy something they do not need. As we will see, persuading clients through promotional activities (such as advertising and brochures), is only one among the marketing tools available to us and not necessarily the most important.

Accordingly, the fundamental marketing questions that we will need to ask ourselves are: How do we:

(a) *get and keep the type of clients (and referral sources) that we want?* i.e. there needs to be some initial focus and purpose to marketing rather than a willy-nilly grabbing of any new client;

(b) *meet their needs?* and their needs are going to be a combination of a good legal result *plus* good service when dealing with the firm (particularly through a lack of uncertainty, surprises and misunderstandings);

(c) *meet the firm's needs?* and these are likely to be a combination of profit *plus* job satisfaction *plus* longer term development of the firm and its capabilities;

(d) *effectively handle the whole business of marketing?* and this is going to be a combination of the attitude of mind of everyone in the firm towards marketing *plus* the quality of specific marketing activities *plus* the management of the process.

If you want to review past marketing experience or set about planning future marketing then these questions can form a simple checklist.

LINKING MARKETING TO THE FIRM'S OVERALL STRATEGY

It (almost) goes without saying that a firm's marketing should be consistent with and support the firm's overall business strategy. Most firms now readily understand the necessity for an explicit strategy, however formally or informally this may be expressed. Written business plans for the firm are, of course, a requirement under the legal aid franchise requirements and Lexcel.

Increasing competition (and a consequent need to stand out of the crowd) and a requirement to specialise (in order to avoid claims and increase profitability) are compelling reasons why firms are now clarifying what their long term objectives are and how they expect to achieve them. What range of work the firm wants to do (and for whom) will be at the heart of the strategy. There are a number of ways to address this question. At some stage, and perhaps fairly regularly, we should ask ourselves questions such as:

- what work do we enjoy doing?
- what are we good at?
- what services do people locally need?
- what types of work actually make us a profit at the moment? (This may be an uncomfortable question but it has to be answered.)
- what can we make a reasonable profit doing in the future?
- how does all this fit with the type of firm we want to be?

Each firm needs to decide which are the most important criteria on which to base its own strategic decisions.

Another good reason for being clear about the overall direction is that it can help attract and retain good staff (both fee earners and support staff). They are more likely to join, stay with and be committed to a firm which has communicated to them its aims for the future. More pragmatically, a bank manager who is being asked to lend money to a firm will, quite properly, need to be persuaded that the firm has planned ahead, which will mean more than a one year financial forecast.

When it comes to the marketing side of the firm's strategy the important questions are going to be:

- who do we want as clients?
- what services do they require?
- how can we be different to and better than the competition, and how can we communicate this?

The last question and its implications are particularly important. The thought that goes into answering it can bring a purpose and vitality to marketing that will be key to its success. Solicitors do frequently say: 'Well, my firm is really very similar to many others'. While this may be true on the surface in terms of size or spread of work, if one then says to a specific solicitor: 'So you would be quite happy then to go and work for X & Co., who are like your firm, would you?', very often the reaction (quite rightly) would be: 'Good heavens – I couldn't possibly work for them!'. So there is going to be something distinctive about any firm that clients too can recognise and value.

It is not necessary to start thinking about marketing by reassessing the whole firm strategy although that might seem logical. The best advice is very pragmatic: just start thinking about and start planning marketing somewhere. But do start. This may well mean assessing specific promotional activities. (See below for the difference between marketing and promotion.) This may not be the textbook place to start but realistically it is what is likely to happen. It will, however, be important that at some stage you step back and think about the desired client base and range of services, if only to confirm that the current strategy does make sense. For example, many firms are reconsidering, in the light of the legal aid franchise (and particularly the supervision) requirements, what work they should do and what they should refer elsewhere.

Advocate

∧

Client

∧

Customer

∧

Prospect

Figure 4.1 The client relationship ladder

THE CLIENT RELATIONSHIP LADDER

It is helpful to think through the way in which a client relationship starts and develops (or should develop) in order to pitch marketing at the right level (see Figure 4.1). So starting at the bottom of the ladder:

'Prospect': this is a person (or business) of the type that you would like to be a client of the firm, but to date has never used the firm and may not even know of the firm's existence. The marketing task here is to ensure that the person knows about the firm and hears about it in a positive light so that they can become a . . .

'Customer': this is when the prospect uses the firm for the first time. The use of the term 'customer', rather than client, here is very deliberate and important. It is meant to look at the relationship from the viewpoint of the person using the firm. It is not meant to dilute the way in which the firm regards and should deal with the first time client, in fact the opposite. If asked about his or her relationship with the firm this person would probably say: 'I used Smith & Co. when I had that problem with my builders'. Now the job of marketing (and especially client service) is to turn this passive 'customer' into an active . . .

'Client': this is the person who, in contrast to the 'customer' of a firm, would say: 'Smith & Co. are my solicitors'. They see an enduring relationship and would use (or may have already used) other services of the firm and dealt with a number of people in the firm. Because of their satisfaction with the firm they will say good things about it to relatives, friends and business contacts and formally recommend the firm. Here the marketing task is to develop the client relationship and, if possible, turn this person into an . . .

'Advocate': this is the person who feels so strongly about the firm that they go out of their way to assist it and help develop it. This person would for example be delighted to provide a reference for a prospective client, or contribute a named testimonial (or case study type feature) in a brochure or newsletter, or

attend a seminar as a speaker or guest. We probably all know people among our clients (and also, importantly, referral sources) who are in this category. In addition, it is quite possible that we fulfil this role for another professional or business that we deal with and so can ask ourselves: 'What have they done for me that makes me so enthusiastic about them?'

In short the job of marketing can be seen to be to move people up the ladder. And it will be readily apparent that the promotional side of marketing plays a lesser role as we address the development of the client relationship further up the ladder.

THE 'SEVEN Ps' OF MARKETING: HOW MARKETING IS PUT INTO ACTION

It can be helpful to take an overall view of the marketing tools that are available. We can use this partly as a checklist to ensure that all aspects of marketing have been considered. We can also use it to track down why our marketing activities have or have not produced the results we hoped.

1 Product (what litigation services to offer)

This is a fundamental decision that is now more important than ever. For many reasons (e.g. economic and competitive) it does not make sense to stray into areas of work where we cannot be confident of doing a good job for the client. The Woolf regime simply is not designed to tolerate the firm or practitioner 'making it up, or looking it up, as they go along' or using delay as a tactic to take the pressure off in a difficult case. So, unpalatable as it may seem in terms of the potential loss of clients and work, most firms should (as noted above in the case of legal aid) be seriously asking: 'do we need to narrow our range of services?' Or more positively, they can ask: 'what investment in terms of recruitment, training and development of existing staff and new facilities/support (e.g. information technology) do we require to reach the necessary standard to maintain our existing range of services effectively?'. And, of course, 'effectively' here means both from the viewpoint of the client in getting a good service and also the firm in making a sensible profit.

Beyond the traditional litigation service there are now products that solicitors can offer that facilitate the process of resolving a dispute. After-the-event insurance is an obvious example that can help make fast track litigation, in particular, more attractive. There is also the possibility with cases in the small claims track of 'unbundling' services to clients, i.e. providing assistance to clients so that they can help themselves rather than actually representing them. This is considered further in Chapter 3 'Human Resources and Team Management'.

'Litigation' is now an inadequate description for the different ways we can help clients resolve disputes. The alternatives under the ADR umbrella, such as arbitration and mediation, offer opportunities that may be attractive to prospective clients who would shun the traditional 'court battle'. Of course, the new legal labels will mean nothing to most clients: you need to explain the practical benefits to them of these alternative approaches.

It cannot be stressed too highly, as other parts of this book will reflect, that a thorough understanding of the thinking behind and the procedures supporting the Woolf regime is fundamental to successful litigation practice. So the first stage of marketing is to get the 'product' right.

2   Price (what and how to charge for services)

Where you can choose the price charged for litigation services (which will be the case unless fixed fees are introduced) then this requires careful consideration. There are 'how much' issues, for example, the rates for different levels of fee earner and the uplift in conditional fee agreements. There are also 'how' issues, for example, interim billing and the acceptance of credit cards for the payment of fees. The latter option, which is used by some firms, but not widely, has the advantage of making buying legal services more like paying for other significant goods or services. This is consistent with the 'demystification' of law that is part of the aim of the Woolf reforms.

3   Place (where to offer the service and the image projected)

For most firms where their offices are situated is not something that can be easily changed. However, this question should be kept under review and, of course, there will be times, such as at the end of a lease or when establishing a new office, when the matter has to be considered. The relative merits of cheaper upstairs premises have to be weighed against the advantages of more accessible and attractive groundfloor offices that can literally be the firm's shopfront to the world. Also there are questions of accessibility for different types of transport that clients may use. For example, is it more convenient to have a town centre/high street location or be closer to where people live or shop or work which may increasingly be out of town, in housing estates and retail or business parks?

As to how the office looks, that comes down to what image the firm wants to project. There is no right or wrong between 'traditional wood-panelled' and 'modern steel and glass', but it is as well to be aware that the way the offices look will send a message about the firm, whether you want it to or not. Think about the other environments where clients will go for services (such as banks, building societies, doctors and dentists surgeries) and consider how the firm compares.

Thinking more imaginatively, there are different ways that solicitors can take their services to clients rather than waiting for them to walk through the office door. Ideas such as, the mobile legal surgery and electronic kiosks, may seem extraordinary but in fact they are already happening. Some of these ideas work on the basis that increasingly the role of the solicitor will be to provide legal information to let clients help themselves. On the other hand, as Hazel Genn memorably put it in her research (see further below) '[some clients] did not want to be *empowered*, they wanted to be saved'.

4   People (who delivers the service: their approach, style and development)

Even more than the firm's offices, the people and the way they behave will send out a strong marketing message to clients. This is obviously different to and goes beyond the technical legal skills the staff may possess. Just about every firm in existence claims, in its advertisements or brochures, to have a 'friendly yet professional approach' (or some close variation). But what does that really mean? More importantly, what actual behaviour does everyone in the firm have to demonstrate to live up to that sort of promise? Small (and not so small) examples will be: the way the phone is answered and calls put through, the use of plain English in letters to clients, not keeping clients waiting for appointments, and returning calls promptly. The simple test is how do we like to be treated when we visit or telephone our bank, doctor, garage or supermarket. And for those who think that, because of their professional status, firms of solicitors should obviously aim to exceed the standards set in the 'commercial' sector, then that is a challenge that should be taken up wholeheartedly!

5   Process (what systems/procedures to use for delivering the service, including the use of IT)

If we take an example from the world of banks the relevance of the (admittedly ugly) word 'process' will quickly become apparent. It has always been one of the services (or to use the terminology in this section, products) of banks to give customers cash. For many years it was simply a case of queuing in the bank, writing out a cheque and being handed cash by a bank employee. Then came the ATMs, the 'hole in the wall' machines, outside banks. Now many of us will obtain our cash via a bank debit card at the checkout in a supermarket at the same time as paying for goods. So we have the same service but delivered in fundamentally different ways to reflect both customer convenience and the desire of banks to control their costs – and all made possible by information technology. The analogy with legal services, for example conveyancing, to take an example outside litigation, is striking. There are very different ways in which solicitors (not to mention non-solicitors) can deliver that service.

Looking ahead, another possibility might be to use Internet and e-mail technology to allow clients to update themselves on progress on their case by giving them access to their electronic file in the office.

This is not to say that all firms must go down the 'hi-tech' route in delivering their services. Some will chose to, using the Internet to make themselves known and available to potential clients and then expert systems to assist with tasks such as client interviewing and fact gathering. What is significant here is that IT is given a front-office role assisting the solicitor rather than a back-office role helping support staff with tasks such as word processing, time recording and accounting. Other firms will want to stress the traditional, personal nature of their services and that is fine too if it is done actively and thoughtfully. In either case, to repeat a point made above, the firm can be different to and better than another (type of) firm.

This consideration of how services are delivered brings us back to a fundamental element of marketing strategy; who does the firm want to have as clients and, in turn, how can the firm market to different types of clients. Over recent years an increasing number of firms (and not just the large ones) have been taking an innovative approach to this question and certainly going beyond simply thinking of very broad categories of client such as legally aided, private client and business. An example is services for, and marketing suited to, the elderly. Equally some firms may think that the hi-tech route is a good way to appeal to a younger generation of clients. (But beware of over-simplistic generalisations!)

6 Promotion (how to make people aware of services and persuade them to use/keep using them)

Many will regard promotion as what marketing is all about. The message we are advocating here is that promotional activities are important, but not, by themselves, sufficient for successful marketing. A separate section on promotion appears below.

As noted above, promotion is going to be most important at the early stages of the client relationship ladder when the goal is to achieve awareness of the firm and its particular advantages. However, its relevance to existing clients should not be ignored. For example, it may be surprising but research has shown that among the most avid readers of consumer advertisements are people who have already purchased the product or service being advertised. They are looking for confirmation about the choice they have made. Equally, you can imagine that existing clients will be impressed and reassured if they see good promotional material from their own solicitors. It can help to remind them about the firm when they may have no reason to use it and make them feel confident about recommending the firm.

7   Providing client service (the overall experience of the client)

'Providing client service' is the coming together of all the marketing elements mentioned above. The moral here is to emphasise the point just made, that promotion (advertising, brochures etc.) on its own, or inconsistent with the rest of the marketing initiatives, will not succeed. The best and simplest way to know if you are succeeding here is to talk to and listen to clients. This can be done informally on a continuous basis and from time to time formally through client surveys. A key point is that marketing in the sense of client service is not a one-off but a continuous activity that needs to be emphasised and monitored throughout the conduct of a matter whether on the fast or multi-track.

Keeping the client informed has always been a fundamental aspect of good client service

PROMOTIONAL ACTIVITIES

It will be useful to start by categorising the different types of activities that we can consider:

- personal (face to face with the (potential) client), this includes:
  - informal meeting;
  - giving a talk;
  - in-house seminar;
  - 'beauty parade'/client presentation;
  - client entertainment;
  - attending social/business functions;
  - joint training;
- impersonal (no contact with (potential) client), this includes:
  - brochure;
  - newsletter;
  - mailshot;
  - articles;
  - media/PR (local, trade, legal press; radio; TV);

- advertising (press, directories, poster, radio);
- sponsorship;
- website;
- 'give-aways' (e.g. pens, mousemats);
- client survey questionnaires.

This list is a long one, and probably not complete. It would be very surprising if any firm was using all or even most of these activities, particularly all at the same time! As to the '$64,000 question': 'Well, which should we use?', the answer must, of course, be 'it depends'. It will depend on what type of client you are targeting for what sort of litigation. What will be appropriate and effective for complex commercial litigation for a multi-national will be very different to trying to attract plaintiff personal injury litigation. Even then, for the same type of client, different activities may or may not suit the style (or budget) of a particular firm. Indeed, at a general level, it is probably good advice that if, when thinking about any particular way of promoting the firm, you find yourself thinking (for example, in the case of radio advertising), 'that is just not our style', then avoid it altogether. The firm that goes into a promotional activity enthusiastically has a much greater likelihood of success.

This leads onto another general point: the need to try to avoid what can be described as 'lowest common denominator marketing'. There is often in firms an approach by which an idea for a marketing activity is put forward (or, by way of a more specific example, an advertisement is drafted) and then other individuals contribute their input, often by finding fault. Gradually the proposal gets watered down so that nobody in the firm objects, but the result is fairly anaemic in terms of creating an impact with clients. Our suggestion, which does involve dropping some of the natural instincts of a lawyer, is not to try and market so that 10 out of 10 people would find the brochure, article, presentation etc., acceptable. Instead, aim to have seven out of 10 potential and existing clients finding what you have done *really* interesting and memorable. Just accept that three out of ten may find the message or style not to their taste (e.g. too commercial or too light-hearted or whatever). This, more bold, approach will be easier if there has been thought applied to which types of client you are aiming for and which you are not.

Always aim to run promotional campaigns rather than one-off activities so that for example a series of advertisements, PR initiatives and a circular to clients are coordinated.

Specific promotional activities: some guidelines

Brochures

Why you need one and how to use it: start by thinking about what role a brochure should play in the particular circumstances of your firm's approach to marketing. Most likely it will be seen by existing clients – otherwise how will they come to have it? Brochures can be expensive so do not produce one just because other firms do.

Think from the perspective of the client: for very good internal reasons the firm may have been organised into departments or at least specialist individuals covering litigation (and, quite likely, different types of litigation) and other types of legal work. This does not mean you have to market the firm in this way. Clients, particularly private and small business clients, who may not be frequent users of legal services, will almost certainly not see the world as divided into legal specialities or understand the distinctions. These types of client are more likely to see themselves as a home-owner or young entrepreneur or retired couple etc., who will have legal needs that potentially span a range of litigation (and other) services. Recognising them and their circumstances and then introducing the firm's services in a way that is relevant to them is genuinely client friendly.

What is really important and interesting about the firm: it is probably not that it was founded in 1848 or 1953 or whenever, so do not necessarily start with that information.

How much information should be permanent and how much should be flexible and easily changed: think about the use of home-produced inserts that can be updated quickly and cheaply.

What clients say about a firm is more persuasive than what the firm says about itself: think about using mini-case studies and client quotes to bring the brochure to life.

Press advertising

Can be a way of reaching 'prospects' and letting them know that the firm exists: think about alternatives (or additions) to the simple box advertisement giving details of the firm and a list of services in the local paper. If you want to reach a particular type of client what do they read or look at? It can be very instructive to look at a press directory (available in the local library) and see the extraordinary variety of specialist publications that exist and through which you can target a particular group of people. We know of one firm that advertises exclusively in motorbike publications and another in hairdressing magazines. Also, if using the general local press think about promoting very specific litigation services (e.g. disputes with builders or business suppliers). If a series of advertisements is booked, they can be used on a rotating basis. Of course not everyone will find every advertisement relevant to them, but for some it will be very relevant.

Visuals can add impact: solicitors are used to dealing in words, but we do live in a very visual age, so if you do want to stand out think about the power of pictures.

Humour can be appealing: if, and only if, the use of humour does naturally suit the style of the firm, it can be a refreshing change. It is true that the law, and particularly litigation, is a serious matter but so are banking, mortgages and insurance and think about how the public are used to having those services promoted to them. Humour can, for example, be a way of punching holes in the stereotype that some potential clients may have about solicitors and the experience of using them.

Getting value for money: always negotiate the price of advertising space or ask about special deals (e.g. accepting last minute spaces on an irregular basis at a large discount).

Radio and TV advertising

Reach and cost: solicitors have generally shied away from this form of advertising on grounds of appropriateness and/or cost. It may be time to look again. Claims Direct, the Law Society sponsored Accident Line and similar organisations work on the basis that most people are not aware that they may have a valid claim and if they are, assume it will be complicated and costly to pursue it. Radio and TV advertising are ways of raising that awareness and giving confidence about the process of making a claim. Those factors, of course, apply equally to solicitors. The advantage of radio and TV advertising is the number of people who can be reached and the geographical and socio-economic targeting that is possible. TV advertising, particularly, is expensive when compared to conventional promotion by solicitors, but there is evidence of results. The Hertfordshire firm Underwoods are renowned for having spent £350,000 on a TV ad campaign on Anglia Television that produced 100 new cases in the first two weeks at an estimated cost of £100 per case. With the growing number of radio and TV stations the cost of advertising is likely to go down rather than up. As to horror stories of 'tacky' American-style advertising, the style and content of radio or TV advertising is up to the firm concerned. But remember that any advertisement is not (or should not be) designed to appeal to the solicitors and 'tacky' may just be a pejorative way of describing something that creates an impact and prompts a response, which is the whole idea.

Public relations and media

Be aware of the possibilities: this will include obtaining editorial (i.e. not paid for) coverage in the press or on radio and TV. Also, if you are thinking of making radio or TV appearances a regular part of marketing, it is essential to invest in some appropriate training.

Create possibilities: editors are always looking for ways to fill their publication and so will be interested in newsworthy stories. Remember, however, that it is 'stories' that they will be interested in, not just information (however interesting that information may be from the viewpoint of the firm) and certainly not just marketing puff (that is why they have an advertising section!). One feature that a number of publications run is a legal/consumer questions and answers section.

Building relationships: we sometimes find that in the local press or specialist trade press relevant to an area of our work, someone from another firm is regularly quoted as an authority on a particular subject. The likelihood is that they have taken the trouble to build up a relationship with an editor or specific journalist over a period of time. This does require effort in terms of returning calls promptly, meeting their deadlines and being prepared to have 'quotable' opinions. There is also the inevitable frustration of the legal story getting 'bumped' at the last minute for something (apparently) more important. So this is not something to be taken on lightly, but it can be valuable if a solicitor does want to be known as one of the experts in a particular field.

MARKETING MESSAGES

As we said at the start of this chapter, the intention behind the Woolf reforms, to make the resolution of disputes faster, cheaper and more certain, should appeal to the public, whether individuals or business people. These advantages should form the basis of the messages we want to get across in our promotional activities. It is not realistic to expect potential or existing clients to have much understanding of, or interest in, the mechanics of litigation. Accordingly, detailed technical comparisons of the old and new procedures are not likely to be persuasive. On the other hand, comparisons of real life cases that illustrate, in concrete terms, that litigation is genuinely faster, cheaper or more certain, while obtaining a similar or better result for the client, may impress people. It is accepted that it may take some time for a firm or the Law Society or some other body to compile these statistics.

Another message that will probably be attractive to clients and is consistent with the purpose of the Woolf reforms is that the solicitor can act as a 'one-stop-shop'. The solicitor can assist without the need to bring in outsiders such as counsel and experts who (as the client is likely to see it) may add to the complication and cost. Many clients may come to a solicitor assuming that he or she has the capability and capacity to fulfil that role in any event.

The matter of litigation being 'more certain' referred to above is important. Of course, only time will tell how the reforms work out in practice, but this issue of greater predictability could well be of advantage to firms in their marketing. Here we are talking about predictability, not in the sense of necessarily being able to forecast the result of a piece of litigation. Rather it is about being able to give reasonably reliable indications of the steps that need to be taken and the time involved. It must be the case that at the moment many potential clients avoid litigation because it is just too much trouble. We can all imagine, or perhaps have heard, words such as 'minefield', 'maze' and 'wild goose chase' being used. It is (or should be) the case that someone who claims expertise and experience in a particular field can make reasonably reliable indications of how a matter will progress. We all know how frustrating it is to be told by a garage or builder: 'Well, how long is a piece of string . . . We shall just have to wait and see how things turn out'.

One of the messages we should be considering is that people should come to a solicitor, rather than another organisation such as a claims assessor or accountant to resolve their problem. The reasons why they should need to be spelt out in practical terms and will probably include issues such as wide-ranging experience and understanding the different possible routes to resolving a dispute.

One guiding rule of marketing that is applicable here is to talk to prospective clients about benefits not features. Features of a firm might be that it has three local offices, four partners and six other specialist staff and up-to-date technology. Think about a client turning round and responding: 'So what? What does that mean for me?'. The reply could be: 'Well, no one in Anytown is more than 15 minutes from one of our offices and we can see you in whichever is most convenient; the lawyer you deal with will have relevant experience and back-up, and we can get fast access to your file via our computer system even if the lawyer handling your case is out of the office'. These are the benefits that are of practical value to the client and which should be stressed in promotional literature. Try using the 'so what?' test on any marketing materials.

THE 'USER-FRIENDLY' SOLICITOR

Recent research by Professor Hazel Genn (*Paths to Justice: What People Do and Think About Going to Law* (Hart Publishing Ltd)) and Hilary Sommerlad (*Legally Aided Clients and their Solicitors* (Law Society Research Study No. 34)) has focused on what clients are looking for from a solicitor. For those who want a wider, or perhaps more objective, understanding of this issue beyond personal experience, these publications are worth studying. They are useful in helping understand why people do not go to lawyers, or even try to resolve disputes formally at all; what type of advice they are looking for, and what they expect when going to a solicitor. As is to be expected there is a lot of common sense here but sometimes the reminder is worthwhile. 'Clients wanted efficiency, consisting of prompt, regular and clear communication; they also wanted full information – honesty as to their chances; speedy action. They wanted solicitors to do what they said they would do' (Research Study No. 34).

REFERRAL SOURCES: DEVELOPING RELATIONSHIPS

Establishing and developing referral sources – people and organisations who recommend clients to go to a particular firm – has always been an important element of solicitors' firm marketing. Often, it will (quite rightly) be more important than the use of promotional materials, PR or advertising.

Every firm should think about its most likely sources of recommendations and have a plan to extend the range of referral sources and to make sure that the relationships are nurtured. For example, if the relationship is with just one person in an organisation, what will happen when they retire or if they leave? How many people in the firm know the relevant contact? It can be a problem if people 'hoard' good contacts for their own, rather than the firm's, benefit. Perhaps the simplest piece of advice in relation to referral sources is the most important – remember to say 'thank you'.

Below is a checklist that may be helpful to see if the firm is exploring all the relevant referral options, some less obvious than others.

- other firms of solicitors: if, as we suggested earlier, firms are thinking about narrowing down the range of services they offer, there are likely to be increasing opportunities to obtain referrals from other firms. This could be done on a reciprocal basis. For referrals between firms to work effectively, for the benefit of both themselves and the clients, it will require firms to be more open and prepared to share information than, in many cases, they have in the past. And, of course, another effect of firms restricting their range of services is that there will be more cases of conflict of interest requiring clients to be directed to another firm;
- Citizens Advice Bureaux and other voluntary agencies: particularly in the case of legal aid work, the not-for-profit sector may be seen as a serious competitor rather than potential supplier of work. However, these relationships are going to remain important and valuable;
- other professional firms and businesses (such as accountants, surveyors, banks, estate agents, doctors' surgeries);

143

- specialist panels (such as for family and personal injury work);
- specialist associations (such as SFLA and APIL);
- regional Legal Services Committee: this is the body that will have drawn up the regional strategy for legal aid provision in the local area;
- local courts.

SUMMARY

Think about the firm's overall strategy so that there is a firm foundation for marketing activities. The key questions will be: who do we want to act for, what services should we offer and how, how can we be different? Use the seven Ps (see above) as a marketing checklist – it is not all about promotion. Above all be imaginative – and persistent.

B. SHARING INFORMATION THROUGH NETWORKS

Networking opportunities exist within firms, amongst friends, at court and through specialist networks. In spite of uncertainty as to its effect upon sitting in a judicial capacity, membership of specialist networks remains popular. Large generic networks with active participation in the Law Society have been around for years but smaller networks linked to specialist areas of practice are a fairly recent phenomenon. The Association of Personal Injury Lawyers has reached its 5,000th member and has an administrative staff of nearly 20 having grown from modest beginnings in 1990. The sharing of information with competitors has always been a difficult issue and whilst individuals and individual firms will give and take at different rates the fact that these networks are successful is a testament to the overall balance.

WHY JOIN?

Membership of specialist networks gives access to:

- newsletters, including updates and articles;
- bulletins, shorter than newsletters communicating urgent news;
- database of experts;
- training courses: CPD points, subsidised prices;
- Annual Conference: lots of CPD points;

- joint seminar with Bar, opposing networks, lawyers in other jurisdictions;
- opportunity to respond to consultation papers;
- special interest groups: sub-divisions within the organisation by speciality;
- other members;
- ideas on cases, litigation but also management techniques and IT;
- discounts on legal products: outside training courses and journals;
- discounts on non-legal products and services: hotels, car hire.

The majority of practitioners join with the broad aim of sharing and this means active participation and collaboration. Few networks operate like the Richard Grand Society where membership is by invitation only and is limited, thereby presenting a marketing opportunity for the individual members. Most specialist networks will not offer work-getting opportunities for the majority of its members, but information gleaned through the network can be put to good use in briefing potential and actual work-providers. Individual profiles are undoubtedly assisted by becoming a spokesperson for the network on a particular issue even if this is a handy by-product rather than a central motivating factor. The dynamic tension on these occasions is always to represent the network rather than an individual's or individual firm's views.

Whilst most networks are accessible through payment of a membership fee and satisfaction of eligibility criteria, the work type carried out by the prospective member means that the appropriate network can be easily identified. Payment by the firm is then not always routine (see below 'Value for money'). Specialist networks are particularly important for sole practitioners or firms with a small number of practitioners operating under CPR, and are also useful for practitioners who regularly have to operate outside their home court. These networks are not confined to solicitors and this is a strength. Solicitors within the networks who sit as deputy district judges and barristers bring an important dimension which focuses on the teamwork approach and trial experience.

SHARE INFORMATION ON CPR IN PRACTICE

There has never been a more important time to share information, as it is essential for practitioners to see how CPR is being operated in practice. There are certain key issues such as to what extent cases under the old rules are being applied to the merits of a particular argument and how the new concepts of the overriding objective and proportionality are being applied. There will be a bedding down period before the Court of Appeal decides issues through satellite litigation and most practitioners realised in advance of 26 April 1999 that there was considerable scope for interpretation of the Rules. Whilst local

145

discretion and local practice directions may be frowned upon, it is unrealistic to expect total uniformity when a host of varied human beings are dispensing judgment in so many cases every day at interlocutory level. This was seen in meetings which took place between practitioners and district judges, Masters and designated civil judges prior to 26 April 1999, when it became clear that the scope for individual interpretation is wide even on issues where Lord Woolf's own views were well known.

TRAINING COURSES

The overwhelming selection of training courses leading up to implementation of CPR sometime led to rejection of the training courses offered by specialist networks, but now that the Rules are being interpreted networks are coming into their own. Sporadic but targeted attendance on other commercial training courses to gain an overview is still very useful. In addition to capturing CPD points, which all practitioners now need, speakers are usually drawn from specialist networks in any event. However, for sharing the latest information on particular work types, networks are essential. This is particularly so because several networks were involved in pilot studies on the operation of protocols and the CPR (fast track cases in particular), so they already have an agenda of advantages and pitfalls which they would like to see worked through in practice.

IT

Information sharing relies on communication. It now helps networks through websites, e-mails, and intranets. There is a particular role for networks in connection with IT associated with CPR. In spite of the fast track framework, in many ways the running of the case is less standard under CPR and case management systems are difficult to design until the application of CPR in practice has been seen. The commercial opportunities mean that there is already a significant range of choice, including the opportunity for some elements to be tailor-made to individual practices. There are key issues as to the timing of any investment, and the size of investment in IT means it is a crucial decision for the future operation of firms (see further Chapter 2 'The Litigator's Guide to IT'). Specialist networks and local law societies often have IT committees which can express views based on practitioners who have operated systems, and are likely to pass on the things they would have really liked to have known before making the investment. These committees have often been difficult to keep going in the past but are now enjoying a new lease of life.

146

VALUE FOR MONEY

There are many networks with no associated membership fee. These comprise loose associations of practitioners or firms operating in the same area of work, networks amongst different offices of the same firm, or consortia of firms who are brought together by the fact that they are on the same panel carrying out work for institutional work-providers. Where membership fees exist they are usually small but become significant when multiplied across the number of eligible members within medium and large firms.

It is essential to adopt an organised approach to membership:

- decide a notional budget based on balancing the benefit to the firm and individuals who wish to join;
- ascertain membership fees: student discounts, group discounts?
- nominate someone to be in charge of the budget (there will not be much work on finances as fees are coordinated once a year);
- ascertain existing and prospective members;
- if the budget exceeds the account, either save money or nominate if the firm needs the coverage of that network;
- if a demand exceeds the budget, decide criteria but try to ensure opportunities for non-partners;
- publish the membership criteria;
- ensure members cover different special interest groups;
- monitor attendance and include a level of attendance in membership criteria;
- share newsletters, bulletins and minutes of special interest groups centrally;
- share training course material centrally and ask fee earners who go on courses to brief team on it, preferably orally;
- review benefit to the firm and individuals, and budget annually.

The benefit in terms of information received can be taken to a different level by increased individual participation in the network, such as going on to the executive, organising regional groups or performing secretarial functions to special interest groups. These positions are often the subject of elections. The increased benefit is accompanied by a significant time commitment, so again the firm will need to look to see that the overall burden is not too great. Monitoring of the membership is recorded centrally in the firm to ensure that those who are paid up members are attending and sharing. It is important to ensure that membership is not limited to the senior practitioners.

147

THE FIRM AS A NETWORK

Specialist networks include the following (see Appendix 6 for contact details):

- Association of Personal Injury Lawyers;
- Forum of Insurance Lawyers;
- Association of Victims of Medical Accidents;
- Legal Aid Practitioners Group;
- Commerce and Industry Group;
- LSLA;
- Young Solicitors Group;
- Trainee Solicitors Group;
- Local Government Group;
- Child Poverty Action Group;
- Freelance Solicitors Group;
- Pan-European Organisation of Personal Injury Lawyers.

Whilst networks are useful, if more than one practitioner within the same firm is affected by CPR, then it is equally important to look at the firm as a network. The fact that CPR changes are such a talking point sets the scene. Prior to the introduction of the reforms many firms will have asked fee earners to analyse files for allocation to tracks, sent fee earners on training courses and set up channels through which fee earners can spread and share their knowledge of the new system. Standard documentation will also have been produced. Feedback on this and the operation of the court administrative staff as well as judicial decisions should continue to be spread, with monitoring of how individual fee earners are coping.

THE COURT CORRIDOR

The fact that the person having conduct of the file needs to attend on inter-locutory applications under CPR before the Master or district judge could result in attendance by senior practitioners who have to be reminded of the location. This should be viewed as a benefit not a burden. The court waiting room is an important source of information sharing as to the different approaches being taken by different district judges/Masters. First hand experience will have more impact than a report from someone delegated to attend on your behalf and so it is worth giving thought in advance to some areas to chat about to your opponent, and make maximum use of waiting time. This prin-

148

ciple is now being formalised as several designated civil judges, often at the instigation of local law societies, are introducing CPR surgeries where practitioners can ask general questions after giving advance notice. These are mostly held once a month for an hour and provide a useful insight into interpretation of the CPR.

THE LAW SOCIETY AND LOCAL LAW SOCIETY

Practitioners involved in the Law Society at national level were involved in the various committees that assisted Lord Woolf and some are now involved in the Civil Justice Council. However, this participation is open to a relatively small number of senior practitioners. The dissemination of information from the Law Society through the *Civil Litigation Newsletter* is universally viewed as a good development and practitioners involved at this level often participate in training courses. The development of the specialist network rather detracted from the role of the local law society, as specialist practitioners came to the view that they had more in common with practitioners specialising in their area of work at the other end of the country than practitioners specialising in other areas of work on their doorstep. CPR may cause those who hold that view to revise it.

The new rules have encouraged practitioners to think widely about the different types of civil disputes and the importance of the operation in the local county court/district registry has given renewed emphasis to the local law society. This occurred when in [1999] *Gazette,* 10 February, was published the Practice Direction of 1 February 1999 entitled 'Summary Assessment of Costs'. The rates contained in it for the provinces at least were largely acclaimed to be low and a reduction of previous rates, in spite of the words of CPR Practice Direction at Part 44 para 3.2 indicating that 'solicitors are not required to conduct litigation at rates which are uneconomic'. Whilst the rates announced for London do not appear to have led to many raised eyebrows, provincial practitioners were blinking in disbelief. The effect on the firm as a business in a competitive marketplace tied in to contracts with work-providers geared to particular rates was acutely felt, as was the effect in areas such as personal injury where solicitor and own client bills are rarely rendered to make up any shortfall. The attention became quickly focused on the phrase 'local arrangements' and the consultation process local law societies have with district judges on an annual basis in setting the guideline hourly rates. The emphasis has continued as the network set up on summary assessment (see [1999] *Gazette*, 12 May, for helpful table) has expanded into coordination of information on CPR generally. Most local law societies are currently continuing to operate civil litigation committees with the designated civil judges and district judges and should be seen as a specialist network.

INTERNATIONAL NETWORKS

Although these are not directly relevant to CPR, there is a place for inter-national networks even if the number of people participating is small. They are important if practitioners have cases with jurisdictional choices and want to locate agents, if they carry out multi-party work where litigation is being conducted in other countries and if they are practising in areas of law in which decisions in other countries have a direct relevance. This applies to interpreta-tion of international conventions such as the Warsaw Convention 1929 in aviation law. The Human Rights Act 1998 may require solicitors to contact other jurisdictions for interpretation.

DIALOGUE BETWEEN NETWORKS

One of the fundamental touchstones of CPR is the scope for agreement between the parties. Whilst these agreements will be scrutinised by the court, if they are sensible they will probably be approved without the need for court attendance. There is a particular role for specialist networks in this area in setting the parameters. The Association of Personal Injury Lawyers (APIL) and the Forum of Insurance Lawyers (FOIL) singularly failed to agree a list of experts at national and local level but the debate gave both sides a better under-standing of their opponent's problems. It remains to be seen whether dialogue can set parameters for reasonableness in the recoverability of the risk element of success fees and insurance premiums.

The debate has at least led to a significant expansion to the APIL database as experts needed to be on the database before they get on to any agreed list. There remains interesting scope for giving real bite to the specialist networks in terms of monitoring not just the performance of joint experts but also fee levels and contractual conditions such as cancellation charges. APIL may also wish to consider its own CFA insurance product. All practice management standards appreciate the importance of having procedures to monitor services from others, including selection criteria, performance criteria and payment of fees, and networks are more able to influence terms than individual firms.

CHAPTER 5

Ethics, conduct and client care

Suzanne Burn

Introduction

The implications of the 'change of culture'

A renewed interest in ethics, conduct and client care in the profession

Client care and funding

Other client care issues

Duties to other parties

Advocacy and conduct

The Civil Procedure Rules, ethics and client care

Conclusions: what the civil justice reforms might mean for solicitors

---

INTRODUCTION

This chapter inevitably covers much territory. It attempts to pick out the key threads of ethics, conduct and client care for litigators in the post-Civil Procedure Rules era, especially in relation to Lord Woolf's change of culture. Inevitably there are overlaps with a number of other chapters, especially Chapter 1 'Quality and standards', Chapter 7 'Costs and financing', Chapter 9 'Early settlement and the protocols', Chapter 14 'Alternative dispute resolution'.

This chapter covers the following: the general implications of Lord Woolf's culture change for ethical conduct; a survey in outline of the current themes in ethics and client care of particular relevance to litigation; client care and ethics in decisions on funding and costs; other client care issues including conflicts of interest and Chinese Walls, inexperienced and difficult clients, client confidentiality and privilege; duties to other parties in litigation; conduct issues in relation to advocacy, and the CPR: conduct and client care issues.

THE IMPLICATIONS OF THE 'CHANGE OF CULTURE'

The conduct and culture of litigation is changing rapidly, partly as a result of Lord Woolf's civil justice reforms. These seek to alter not just the procedures but also the approaches to civil disputes and litigation and what clients and solicitors see as appropriate outcomes. But Lord Woolf's inquiry acted as a catalyst to concerns about the ways in which traditional litigation techniques have served litigants.

The limitations of the old system

The limitations of the old system can be summarised as:

(a) *accessibility*: the severe problems of access for those individuals too well resourced to qualify for legal aid (almost everyone with a job), but with insufficient resources to fund even relatively modest claims;

(b) *formality*: the over-formality and complexity of the procedures, which tend to keep the litigants at arm's length, encourage an adversarial approach and deter many individuals and even some businesses from using the courts;

(c) *delay*: it took a considerable time for many cases to reach trial; the average interval between issue of proceedings and trial in 1998 was 85 weeks in the county court and over three years in the High Court;

(d) *costs*: litigants often have a very real and understandable fear of the costs; costs are difficult to estimate at the beginning and the loser pays rule meant litigation too often became a dangerous game of 'double or quits'.

Demands for Change

Not surprisingly, some of the demand for change came from litigants. Many began to choose other agencies than lawyers, such as debt collectors and claims assessors or turned to less adversarial methods of dispute resolution than litigation, such as complaints systems, ombudsmen and mediation. Business clients increasingly require lawyers to tender for litigation services, and to work for fixed or discounted fees for repeat business, rather than be rewarded on an hourly basis. The early experience of conditional fee arrangements in personal injury cases, which transfer the risk from litigant to solicitor, suggests they are popular with clients..

Finally, an increasing number of litigants are pursuing their own cases in court without legal advice or representation, even as far as the Court of Appeal: a trend likely to grow with a better educated public, and easier access to legal information, especially through the Internet.

Developments in other jurisdictions

Another force for change has been developments in other jurisdictions. England and Wales, for longer than most other common law countries, have retained the tradition of strongly adversarial litigation with oral evidence being presented at length before a judge with no prior knowledge of the case. In other jurisdictions such as the USA, Canada, Australia, New Zealand, Hong Kong and Singapore, control of judicial dockets, case management by judges, time-controlled trials, multi-door court houses which siphon off litigants to other services, especially arbitration and mediation, have become commonplace. In civil law countries the courts have inquisitorial powers.

Lord Woolf's culture change

Underpinning Lord Woolf's main proposals was his belief that there needed to be a major culture change in the way civil litigation was conducted. There are three main strands to this new approach:

(a) litigation should be viewed as a last resort, with other ways of resolving disputes being tried first;

(b) proceedings should be less adversarial, and conduct during litigation should be more cooperative;

(c) there should be a transfer of power in the control of litigation from lawyers to the courts.

This culture change affects all those involved in the litigation process:

(1) *Judges* have a new hands-on interventionist role in encouraging the parties towards earlier settlement or to a shorter more effective trial of the key issues.

(2) *Lawyers* are expected to be more open with clients, the other parties and the court, particularly over costs, and to make less use of procedural tactics which can delay resolution.

(3) *Litigants* should expect to find more user-friendly courts, facilities which enable them to conduct all or parts of their cases themselves, and above all, greater certainty that their disputes might be settled in a reasonable time for a reasonable cost.

In conjunction with the specific procedural reforms these culture changes are intended to make litigation less complex, quicker and more certain and make the costs of litigation more affordable, predictable and proportionate to what is at issue between the parties.

153

In his Final Report *Access to Justice*, in describing his 'new litigation landscape', Lord Woolf said that eight key principles should govern the new system. These are that it:

- is *just* in the results it delivers;
- is *fair* in the way it treats litigants;
- is able to offer appropriate procedures at *reasonable cost*;
- can deal with cases with *reasonable speed*;
- is *understandable* to those that use it;
- is *responsive* to the needs of those who use it;
- provides as much *certainty* as the case allows;
- is *effective*, adequately resourced and organised.

The Civil Procedure Rules enshrine those principles in an 'overriding objective' on the very first page as Rule 1.1. The Rules also emphasise that the court must look to this overriding objective when it exercises any discretion and that the parties are expected to help the court in promoting these goals. This has important consequences for conduct issues, as will be discussed below.

Litigation as a last resort

A new *settlement culture* prevails. Parties are expected to try to settle their dispute before issuing proceedings and to explore alternatives to litigation. Protocols or codes of best practice for pre-action steps have been developed for some areas of litigation, partly to facilitate early settlement. The courts expect compliance with the protocols, and that detailed letters of claim are sent by prospective claimants a reasonable time in advance of issuing proceedings.

The courts have an express power to stay proceedings for one month while the parties try to settle, and may even direct that they use alternative dispute resolution to do so. This remains a controversial reform when mediation and other forms of ADR are still in their relative infancy in England and Wales, when mediators are largely unregulated and in the light of Article 6 of the ECHR (the right to access to the courts and a fair trial).

A claimant's offer to settle has been introduced to counter-balance the defendant's weapon of a payment into court. In fact, both parties are able to make offers to settle 'with teeth', even pre-action. The penalties on the defendant if the claimant's offer is not accepted and is equalled or beaten at court are additional interest on the damages and/or indemnity costs: although some argue that this is not a sufficient incentive.

Judicial Statistics 1999 (Stationery Office, 2000) confirm that there has been a 25 to 30 per cent fall in new proceedings since April in most courts. This *could* be the 'litigation as a last resort' message getting through very quickly.

Alternatives to litigation

In recent years there has been growing interest in less formal and more conciliatory approaches to resolving disputes. The ADR supporters claim that ADR saves cost and time, and offers substantive and procedural benefits for the participants, particularly 'catharsis', increased empowerment and control, and more creative extra-legal settlement terms.

The increasing interest in ADR amongst policy-makers, practitioners and litigants has manifested itself in several ways. In addition to the Practice Directions issued during the late 1990s which encouraged litigants to consider the use of ADR in the course of proceedings, and the express powers given to the courts in the CPR to encourage settlements, several pilot schemes were set up by government departments in order to test the case for mediation of claims. Pilot civil schemes were established in the Central London County Court, the Commercial Court, Bristol County Court and the Court of Appeal. These have now been made permanent and the Government is considering introducing schemes in more courts.

At the same time as Lord Woolf's reforms were being formulated and considered, the Department of Health decided to test whether mediation would resolve cases in a more satisfactory way than the courts were able to. A major concern amongst patients has been that the litigation system is unable to provide the range of remedies which they desire. A survey of litigants' needs commissioned by the Department of Health as part of their mediation initiative supported Lord Woolf's assertion that in addition to compensation, claimants wanted apologies, explanations, investigations, to feel that the other side cared, to improve quality for the future and prevent recurrence, to meet with the other side and put their case, and be listened to. When asked to prioritise these needs the majority of plaintiffs listed compensation as their most important goal but most sought a package of remedies, the majority of which were not achievable through the courts.

The development of ADR as a new technique, and the emergence of a new body of ADR professionals, introduces new ethical and conduct issues outside the scope of this chapter. Some of these are touched on in Chapter 14 below.

But for litigation solicitors the main ethical/conduct issue now is whether, when, and how to recommend ADR to a client, particularly when the client's wish for an early settlement, possibly at a discount on damages, conflicts with the possibility of achieving a 'better' result, or the solicitor's interest in making new law, by litigating to trial. Almost certainly it is negligent not to consider ADR.

But it could be unethical to try to use ADR cynically for a fishing expedition, and, in future, the court may have specific powers to inquire into conduct in relation to ADR processes and take this into account in costs orders. The court already has the power to take conduct generally into account when assessing costs.

More cooperation, less adversarialism

Adversarial systems give control to the party and their lawyer, particularly in investigating and presenting evidence. They also create 'winners and losers', although frequently the 'winners' do not leave trial feeling at all satisfied with either the process or the result.

The adversarial process can tempt lawyers to do things for clients about which the lawyers have 'moral' qualms, including manipulating the evidence; misleading the other parties, witnesses, experts or even the court; or adopting 'bullying' tactics, especially where there is an imbalance of power.

The development of litigation as a separate, and profitable, discipline in solicitors' firms, from about the 1950s, seemed to spawn a particular 'macho', 'hardball' approach to handling disputes typified by:

(a) a two-line letter before action followed by the writ the next day;

(b) sending a 10-page unnecessary fax at 9 p.m. followed by another at 7 a.m. the following day demanding a reply;

(c) holding back information to the very last minute, especially expert reports or 'surprise' video evidence;

(d) brinkmanship on settlements: making a payment into court a few days before trial and caving in at the court door or during the trial.

Ironically, the development of specialised firms, who worked only for plaintiffs or defendants, particularly in areas such as personal injury and medical negligence, encouraged this approach, although in most other respects specialisation has led to a more rational approach to dealing with cases.

For some years the courts had been giving out the message that a more cooperative approach to dispute resolution should be the norm. The reforms implemented after the Civil Justice Review of the 1980s specifically encouraged a more 'cards on the table' approach, through the introduction of the exchange of witness statements and expert reports as a routine step.

In the 1990s there was a trickle of decided cases penalising parties for:

- refusing to negotiate pre-issue;
- refusing to disclose medical evidence pre-issue;
- serving late evidence;
- running up unnecessary costs – the wasted costs jurisdiction.

On occasions, games playing tactics were punished by striking out or costs sanctions. But in the main the court rules did not encourage the judges to be tough, and few of them were.

Lord Woolf's inquiry was partly prompted by the need to do something about this. During the inquiry he and his team worked hard at trying to develop a consensus and at prodding the partisan camps to work together e.g. on the pre-action protocols.

Strong themes which run through his report and the CPR include:

- cards on the table from first contact;
- earlier service of evidence;
- sanctions for non-compliance with rules and orders and for 'conduct' including pre-action;
- transferring much of the control of the timetable and management from the parties and their solicitors to the judges;
- settling early.

Perhaps surprisingly this particular change in culture seems to have been accepted quite readily by many solicitors, at least for the time being. Within a few months of April 1999 there was anecdotal or actual evidence of:

- fewer exchanges of hostile correspondence;
- extensive use of offers to settle;
- the protocols working;
- cooperation on selection of single joint experts;
- meetings and conferences between 'opposing camps', e.g. APIL and FOIL's cooperation on rehabilitation initiatives in serious personal injury claims.

In 1999, the Lord Chancellor's Department began to say there were 'cautiously euphoric' about how the changes were working. The adversarial system is at least for now in decline (or under wraps). This provides an opportunity for solicitors to review their ethical commitments.

A RENEWED INTEREST IN ETHICS, CONDUCT AND CLIENT CARE IN THE PROFESSION

Reasons for the new interest

For other reasons than the civil justice reforms, the last few years has seen a renewed interest in ethics and conduct in debates about the future of the solicitors' profession. This has been prompted by a number of factors:

(a) the increasing volume of complaints against solicitors, which predominantly relate to quality of service rather than legal skills (poor communication, management of client expectations, not involving the client in decision-making, an intimidating or patronising manner and lack of information about charging);

(b) the requirements of funders and clients for the adoption of quality standards;

(c) competition from the Bar and from other professions, especially accountants and from debt collectors, claims assessors and ADR professionals;

(d) the demand for 'pro bono' services and the emergence of a pro bono movement;

(e) the reaction of many young solicitors to the long hours culture in the commercial part of the profession.

Evidence of this renewed interest comes from:

- a spate of new 'think books' on ethics;
- the College of Law appointing a Professor of Ethics;
- commercial training providers offering courses in ethics;
- the new Solicitors' Practice Rule 15 and related Code which requires all firms to operate a complaints handling procedure (which must be in writing, copies to be given to clients on request and the client must know who to contact in the firm if they have a complaint).

Core values for solicitors

Solicitors Practice Rule 1 requires solicitors to act in the best interests of their clients. Research in the USA has suggested that lawyers are generally more conscientious when acting for repeat player clients on whose work the success of the firm might depend. By contrast, some lawyers adopted a patronising, limited consultation attitude, when acting for one-off clients. There has been very limited work in this area in the UK.

Are there core values and duties which solicitors should adopt? This question was posed by a Law Society consultation paper in late 1999 in preparation for drafting a shorter, more user-friendly (including client-friendly) up-to-date Code of Conduct to replace the 900-plus page seventh edition, published in August 1999. The core duties suggested in the paper were:

(a) *integrity* towards clients, courts and lawyers, to include never knowingly giving false or misleading information;

(b) *independence*: not allowing independence to be compromised in the face of pressure from clients, courts or others;

(c) *acting in the clients' best interest*: this is paramount provided there is no conflict with the solicitor's obligations in professional conduct or the public interest in the administration of justice;

(d) *confidentiality*: keeping all information with regard to a client confidential, subject to any overriding legal obligation;

(e) *conflicts of interest*: not acting when there is a conflict between the interests of two or more clients, or between the solicitor's own interest and that of the client;

(f) *competence*: acting only when the solicitor can provide a competent service;

(g) *fairness*: treating clients fairly;

(h) *client care*: maintaining appropriate client care procedures including information on costs to clients;

(i) *management*: operating appropriate business systems;

(j) *professionalism*: not behaving in a way which damages the reputation and integrity of the profession.

Although this is a general bible for all solicitors, the principles are applicable to litigators and will be discussed in this chapter. Also particularly relevant to litigators are conduct in relation to other parties than the client (namely witnesses, experts, advocates, other parties' lawyers and the court) and 'acting in the public interest'.

Client care and codes of conduct

A culture of client care needs to be at the heart of all firms – bolting it on as an extra to comply with Law Society rules is no longer enough. The client's perception of the way they and their case is handled is often as important as the work which is actually undertaken.

Firms might consider adopting their own 'code of conduct' tailor-made to the work and style of the practice, which covers:

- policies on telephone calls and letters: who takes the calls, when calls and letters should be replied to, use of plain English and giving clear explanations;
- meetings with clients: the importance of first interviews and the need for face to face discussions to deal with difficult issues: funding and costs, decisions on whether to issue/defend proceedings, settlements etc. and to deal with client complaints;
- a complaints procedure (see above).

The case belongs to the client: a client, not a solicitor centred approach

The old-fashioned approach to litigation, only slightly caricatured, assumed:

- it was all too technical for the lay client to understand;
- the client should simply 'retain' the solicitor and leave him to get on with the task of winning;
- the solicitor could charge the client pretty much what he liked and 'after the event' regardless of the result;
- at best the client would be consulted about a proposed settlement and/or told the date of the trial.

More demanding clients, especially business clients, have been working on changing this for years and so, latterly, have the professional organisations, as complaints and claims against solicitors have grown, and as increasing numbers of potential litigants have voted with their feet, either not pursuing cases at all because of the costs, stress and sense of alienation, or increasingly acting as litigants in person.

Lord Woolf reached the view during his inquiry that a shift in the balance of power between solicitor and client, and between solicitors and the courts, would bring greater 'reality' back into the litigation process. In particular he wanted clients to have greater control over the costs and to play a more active part in the key steps hitherto seen as 'procedural' and hence solicitors' territory .

Client involvement: unbundling

Most solicitors' firms offer, and clients expect, a traditional 'full service' package, especially in litigation, which is usually regarded by solicitors as too technical and complex for clients to understand. Typically the client 'retains' the solicitor, who, often unilaterally, decides the scope of the service, runs the case, does all the work, and bills the client, usually on an open-ended hourly basis.

But there are other approaches. In the USA a limited service approach, known as 'unbundling' is rapidly gaining popularity. The term was coined by Forrest 'Woody' Mosten, who has been running a successful family law practice in Los Angeles in this way for some years (see F. Mosten, 'Unbundling of legal services' in R. Smith, *Shaping the Future* (Legal Action Group, 1995)). A possible definition of unbundling is: 'providing legal help to those of moderate means by sharing the work between the lawyer and the client, i.e. by dividing up the tasks in the legal bundle'.

Unbundling can take a number of different forms:

(a) providing advice to a client willing and able to conduct their own case: through an initial consultation for a flat fee, or from time to time during the case as determined by the client and his/her needs and means;

(b) agreeing to share the specific tasks required in a case between the lawyer and the client, with the lawyer usually remaining 'in charge' and conducting any litigation. Typical tasks for the lawyer in this scenario will be providing advice on the merits and tactics, research, drafting formal documents, 'coaching' the client for negotiation, mediation or court appearances or for undertaking advocacy. Typical tasks for the client might include assembling information and documents, organising the witnesses, in some cases, drafting letters and court documents, and conducting negotiations or undertaking advocacy;

(c) in the USA, lawyers who practise this approach may also offer one-off representation at mediations and 'legal wellness' preventative check-ups.

The reaction of lawyers, clients, and even judges in the USA to unbundling is very positive because of the potential for increasing access to justice. The benefits for the clients are obvious: they pay only for what they need, they retain ownership of their problem and its resolution, and may develop a better understanding of the legal system. But there are potentially equal benefits to the lawyers in gaining new clients or new areas of work (or at least not losing work especially with the small claims limit in the UK now at £5,000), and in acquiring new skills. Also if lawyers become less paternalistic and remote, respect for the profession might even improve!

Why do we need to re-evaluate our approach to litigation services at a time when the civil justice reforms have simplified the system and there are increasing options for funding the full service package? I would suggest the reasons are as follows:

(1) Surveys show that many citizens are very mistrustful of solicitors, and identify going to court with 'being in trouble', yet there is a large, latent legal market, particularly for claims and disputes (see Professor Hazel Genn, *Paths to Justice* (Hart, Oxford, 1999)).

(2) Very few individual citizens can afford to pay for the full service package, many do not even approach solicitors for fear of the costs.

(3) Legal aid is being withdrawn or is harder to obtain for many types of civil case, particularly personal injury, yet it may be some time before conditional fees backed by affordable insurance can fill the gap.

(4) The public are much more aware of their rights and can access legal information through advice agencies and advice lines, and especially through the Internet. Increasing numbers are choosing to act 'in person' but would use and pay for *some* legal help if the right service was on offer.

It would be wrong to pretend that there are no problems with the unbundled approach, particularly in the post-Woolf world of fast track and tightly timetabled litigation:

(a) skilful screening is required as only some clients will be able to work in partnership in this way;

(b) the division of tasks needs careful planning and recording in writing: important work must not slip down the middle or be expensively duplicated;

(c) financial arrangements must be crystal clear;

(d) either the solicitor or the client must be and stay on the court record to avoid muddle for the other party and the court.

But so far clients appear to be happier, pay their bills, complain and sue less often, and the professional indemnity insurers are being supportive.

There are enthusiasts in the UK. Peter Browne has been running private practice law shops in Bristol for many years; his current one has a front of house manager, provides information packs, court forms and DIY legal books, and access to Peter's back office legal service incurs modest charges for 10 minute units of his time.

The next stage might be combined law and coffee shops as exist in some parts of the USA.

Many other solicitors probably adopt the unbundled approach without attaching the label. The advice sector and solicitors' firms who specialise in welfare law frequently offer no or low cost surgeries and help with small claims or tribunal hearings. At the other end of the spectrum, many businesses and insurers conduct the pre-action stages of claims themselves, only bringing in solicitors for specific tasks until proceedings are issued and many firms now offer extensive services by e-commerce initiatives and on the Internet. The Government's Community Legal Service is adopting the same approach.

Client involvement: key stages

Post-Woolf, clients need to be involved at many more stages of the case than in old style litigation. In particular:

(a) in deciding if and how to proceed at all – approving a case plan and strategy;

(b) agreeing the funding: method, charging and budgets/estimates;

(c) approving letters of claim and response, statements of case and all key litigation documents;

(d) organising the search for disclosure documents and completing the disclosure statement;

(e) attending key interim hearings and some case management conferences;

(f) preparing and signing witness statements;

(g) being advised of adverse costs orders and kept informed of costs generally;

(h) approving any offers to settle before they are made and before acceptance/settlement.

CLIENT CARE AND FUNDING

Selecting the best option for the client and explaining funding and charging

A vital aspect of client care in the current climate is deciding how to fund the case in the best interests of the client. The details, and pros and cons of the choices, are set out in Chapter 7.

The important issues to highlight are:

(a) solicitors need to know what the options are – this is not easy with so many choices which change so quickly;

(b) they need to be able to advise the individual client in a particular case on the best option (or options) for them, taking into account the risks and possible changes during the life of that case. Failure to do this can be a breach of the Client Care Code and Practice Rule 15, and can amount to negligence;

(c) however, firms must continue to have regard to running their business and making at least most of their litigation work profitable.

This has a number of implications for the way firms run their practices and poses a number of dilemmas:

(1) It is vital someone in the firm spends time keeping up with funding and costs issues and disseminates the information to all litigation fee earners.

(2) At least basic information on the current range of 'after the event' insurance products needs to be available if conditional fee work is to be undertaken, although this could be achieved by working with a broker. The Law Society has taken the view that it should not be negligent not to know about every single product on the market, provided the firm makes it clear to a client they need to take responsibility themselves for checking this out. But is this really practical? How many clients are that sophisticated? Paying parties are already challenging the 'reasonableness' of insurance premiums.

(3) Both strategic decisions on which methods of funding the firm is going to offer, and decisions in many individual cases, especially conditional fee cases, must be centralised to ensure objectivity from both client and firm perspectives: this could be one partner or a small committee;

(4) Clients need to be given information on the choices in as digestible form as possible – this is extremely difficult to achieve and keep up to date. A combination of oral and written material is ideal, but the latter is very problematic as it is not easy to produce summary simple letters or leaflets which are sufficiently detailed or accurate. The Policy Studies Institute's research on conditional fees has shown that few clients understood the material and agreement sent to them by their solicitors. The Law Society Client Care Code letters are a good start; these need to be supplemented by information on the choice of funding methods.

(5) A checklist or questionnaire is useful for the initial meeting with a client, to ensure no viable option for that client is overlooked (e.g. trade union membership, or add-on LEI cover in other insurance.

(6) If the right option for the client is one that the firm does not offer, the client must be told and if necessary advised to go to another firm.

(7) How specific is it necessary to be about the success fee in a conditional fee agreement (CFA) case? If the firm does not calculate an individual fee for each client for each case but has a standard mark-up for types or values of claims is this unethical? Is it lawful when the indemnity principle still exists? Each success fee has to be justified to the client, the court and the other party, including if necessary, on assessment. In the past some firms have 'specced' in low risk winnable cases: should the client be told if the firm is likely to make a profit from the case without a success fee? Does the introduction of recoverability make any difference to the ethics when the other side, rather than the client, is paying? It is not possible to give definitive answers to these questions because so much will depend on a firm's charging structure and profits from different types of case. Many firms do not yet know the real profitability of cases in their workloads, but increasingly they need to do so.

(8) Should the Law Society recommended voluntary cap on the success fee of 25 per cent of the damages always be applied? Ethically, does it make a difference if the client has a serious 'need' for the money, particularly if their loss is ongoing?

(9) Is it unethical to take on a large complex case on a CFA basis if it is very difficult to estimate the likely overall costs and to take a clear view of whether the firm will be able to cope financially and see the case through? This may be feasible for a large firm with good risk assessment in place and a reasonable cashflow, but possibly not for anyone else.

(10) Is it wrong for a firm to check their own client's creditworthiness? The way round this is to always work from money on account but some clients are less willing to provide this in a 'no win no fee' environment. The answer, otherwise, is almost certainly to tell the client that a check is being run, and why, and to advise them of the outcome.

(11) Similarly, in a CFA case, checking the client's version of events before taking the risk can only be common sense. Also, building into the agreement clear client responsibilities, and escape clauses for the firm, surely cannot be unethical. The client also needs to be told clearly of their potential liability for the other side's costs, and after the event insurance sought if necessary.

(12) How far is it necessary to investigate the other parties' financial positions before advising the client to sue and to keep checking during the litigation? Most firms do this for high risk, high value cases and take steps to protect the client's position, e.g. by applying for security for costs, but it is arguably as important in smaller cases for individual clients, especially if they are paying privately.

Funding: ethical issues later in the case

Chapter 7 covers Practice Rule 15, and the Solicitors' Costs Information and Client Care 1999 in some detail. Rule 15 was introduced in September 1999, and the Code has replaced the Written Professional Standards. The Law Society has produced draft specimen client care letters.

The Code (and the CPR) both, in effect, require clients in litigation matters to be given at the outset:

(a) a cost benefit assessment of the case;

(b) details of the firm's charges: how these are calculated and whether they may be subject to change during the life of the case;

(c) advance costs information (which is not inaccurate or misleading) including the best information possible about the likely overall costs, which may include realistic estimates for the whole case, or forecasts within a range;

(d) information on the position and likely liability for the other party's costs (which is much harder to predict than before since the CPR gives judges a very wide discretion and costs no longer automatically 'follow the event;

(e) information on when payments will be needed to the solicitor and/or a third party.

Solicitors must also keep this information up-dated during the life of the case.

CPR Rule 48.8 provides that if the client has not signed terms of agreement which allow costs to be recovered from the client to be greater than the costs which may be recovered from the other side, the solicitor can only charge what is recovered from the other party.

It is also necessary to advise a client if a non-solicitor will have conduct of the action. The penalty may be not to recover any fees at all.

Failure to observe any of the above can amount to a breach of the Rule/Code and lead to a finding of inadequate professional services (and disallowing of all or part of the costs and an order to pay compensation) or found a claim in negligence.

Some of the main ethical/conduct questions issues arising from this are as follows:

(1) Only sending information and advice at the beginning may no longer be sufficient, as a client's circumstances and the right choice for them may change. However, some options do not allow for this, e.g.

Accident Line Protect will not allow cases to opt in at a later stage when it appears the risk has increased.

(2) What are the ethical implications of taking on a case for a budget and/or giving estimates which turn out to be much too low? I suggest it depends on the knowledge of the firm when the budget/estimates were given, the degree of sophistication of the client, and the reasons the figures proved to be inaccurate. Recklessly 'pitching low' to get the work could well be negligent, but the situation could be less clear when the firm simply made an innocent miscalculation.

(3) When a third party is funding the case (e.g. trade union, insurer, LSC) the client is still the lay person/business and it is their interest which comes first. This can be very difficult to achieve if the funder takes tough decisions on budget, disbursements etc., or tries to control the entire running of the case, especially to take decisions which should be the client's. The bottom line is whether the funder will withdraw, leaving the client with no way of pursuing the case. Also the principle of client confidentiality remains: the funder is not entitled to see the client's papers without their consent. On the other hand, if the solicitor becomes aware of fraud by the client which affects the funder's interest, the solicitor should tell the funder and inform the client of what has been done and why, and probably advise the client to seek independent advice or terminate the agreement.

(4) Another issue is how 'transparent' to be with the other party and the court about charging. The CPR require parties to provide information to the court/other party on costs to date and future estimates to trial on the allocation and listing questionnaires, on demand, at case management conferences and when presenting bills for assessment. This may need to include the client care letter (see *Bailey* v. *IBC Vehicles* [1998] 3 All ER 570). The Rules also require early disclosure of the existence of a conditional fee agreement, but not the success fee or the amount of the insurance premium. But in practice the basis of charging will often need to be disclosed much earlier, particularly when trying to settle the case pre-issue.

(5) When to settle, for how much, and whether the costs need to be agreed at the same time, is an ethical issue, in sharper focus with the introduction of CFAs, especially when the success fee element is not related to a clearly measurable 'degree of success' or to a settlement date. Solicitors must resist any temptation to settle early for a lower figure to maximise their own fee from the case without telling the client. Some clients are quite happy to compromise to end the dispute, and agree an early deal to mutual benefit, but the lines can be very fine to draw. A peer review system within the firm is one option, involving counsel or the insurer is another.

(6)   Finally, there is the very difficult issue of relating the amount of work to the agreed costs and to the client's expectations, particularly if a case is taken on for a fixed fee or on a budget, especially if this is imposed by a third party, or when CPR 'proportionality' dictates that costs need to be carefully controlled. Does the client need to be advised that this may affect the level of service or even the approach to the work? Managing client expectations is increasingly difficult but has to be faced especially if the particular client is an inexperienced litigant who wants 'no stone to be left unturned'. This will become even tougher if and when there are fixed recoverable costs for litigation under the CPR. Many firms have coped with this in the past by delegating less profitable work to more junior fee earners, but in this era of the more sophisticated client, it is likely to be much more difficult not to be explicit about this. Managing expectations well in a cost-cutting environment will increasingly be a very serious dilemma for many firms.

OTHER CLIENT CARE ISSUES

When to say 'no' to a client

Principle 12.01 of *The Guide to the Professional Conduct of Solicitors 1999* makes it clear that solicitors are generally free to decide whether or not to accept instructions, provided they are not discriminating unfairly.

Taking on all or even most of the cases offered is not good for the clients or the firm. Firms need carefully thought out, usually centralised and monitored, systems in place for deciding which cases to take on.

Having the basic expertise and general capacity are obvious prerequisites but other factors to consider are:

(a)   whether a client is transferring from another firm and why, especially if they have moved more than once; they may have been poorly served by firms who were not specialists or were badly organised, but they could also be very demanding clients with a less than strong case;

(b)   whether the firm can provide a good service in all the circumstances: the factors to consider include:

   – type of case;

   – prospects of success;

   – available funding options;

   – client agenda and expectations;

168

- expertise;
- available staff and other resources;
- timetable;
- anticipated profitability.

It is also much better to take an early decision to say 'no' if the firm cannot provide the service rather than take on a case on and 'hope for the best'. Most clients are reluctant to change firms and it is very dissatisfying for all concerned if a solicitor pulls out of the case after some investment in the relationship has been made by solicitor and client.

Conflicts of interest and Chinese walls

Until recently, conflict of interest problems have not generated much interest in England and Wales. Prior to 1999, the case law relied upon dated back to 1912. The traditional view has been that to work out what a conflict is a solicitor should put him/herself in the client's shoes and ask 'would the client like you doing what the other client has asked you to do'.

Two important cases in 1999 suggest solicitors need to develop a more sophisticated approach to conflicts in the future. The House of Lords in *Bolkiah* v. *KPMG* ([1999] 1 All ER 517) decided that the courts should intervene when there was a real risk that confidential information obtained in litigation for a former client might become available to the team in a firm acting for a different client in separate proceedings. Lord Millett said that no solicitor should, without the consent of his former client, accept instructions unless, viewed objectively, his doing so would not increase the risk that information which is confidential to the former client might come into the possession of a party with an adverse interest.

In *R* v. *Bow Street Magistrates, ex parte Pinochet Ugarte* (No. 2) ([1999] 1 All ER 577) the House of Lords set aside its own previous decision because of the failure of Lord Hoffmann to disclose his involvement in the charity wing of Amnesty International. This case, and the impending implementation of the Human Rights Act in 1998, triggered, during 1999, a spate of decisions concerning judicial conflicts of interest. In November 1999 a special Court of Appeal consisting of the Lord Chief Justice, the Master of the Rolls and the Vice-Chancellor determined five related cases of alleged judicial conflicts and laid down general principles (*Locabail UK Ltd* v. *Bayfield* [2000] QB 451). The perception of a conflict or bias was held to be as important as an actual conflict – a point of equal relevance to solicitors as to judges.

Some of the other important recent decisions involving solicitors include *Re a firm of Solicitors* (LTL 7 September 1999 TCC), where a solicitor was in possession of confidential information in relation to a client who was a party to ongoing litigation. He joined a firm which was acting for the opponent in the litigation. The court held that the new firm would be restrained from continuing to act for the opponent because there was a real risk that the confidential information would not remain secret. In *Morgans* v. *Needham* (The Times, 5 November 1999), a firm of solicitors were involved in a professional negligence claim in which they were counterclaiming against the former client for unpaid fees. The court held that it was undesirable that the person against whom the allegation of negligence had been made should have the day-to-day conduct of the action because he lacked objectivity.

There has not, as yet, been any significant reported cases involving alleged conflicts of interest where barristers acting for opposing parties in litigation are in the same chambers, but in *Laker Airways Inc.* v. *FLS Aerospace Ltd* ([1999] 2 Lloyd's Rep. 45) a challenge to an arbitrator on the ground that counsel instructed was in the same chambers failed.

Are there any general principles to be followed in a litigation context?

(1) Where the issue is an actual or potential conflict between two existing clients the problem for the solicitor is the difficulty of operating with two competing sets of fiduciary obligations of loyalty; in any event, the solicitor can only do so with the truly informed consent of both clients.

(2) Where the issue is an actual or potential conflict between an existing and a former client, any obligation of loyalty ceases at the end of the retainer with the former client, and the only obligation thereafter is one of confidentiality. The options are to terminate the old retainer, or to obtain the consent of the former client. If the solicitor does neither he is still under an obligation to protect the confidentiality of the former client, and taking reasonable steps to do so may not be enough.

While small to medium-sized law firms should not experience great difficulties in following these principles, large multinational firms, especially multi-disciplinary ones, will have much greater problems: indeed it is no coincidence that many of the recent cases concerning conflicts of interest have involved international firms of accountants. It can be extremely difficult for large firms to know, when taking on a litigation portfolio for a business, whether among opponents in any particular action there may turn out to be an existing or former client of the firm. One city firm has set up a specific unit to screen not just new cases, but new clients for potential conflicts, including into the future.

The so-called Chinese wall, or information barrier within a firm, is not necessarily a solution, and has little or no place in existing client conflicts. As Lord Millett said in the *Bolkiah* case, there is a real difference between ad hoc walls, temporarily 'erected' for the life of a particular case, and walls that are an established part of the structure of a firm, such as the physical barrier between two offices some distance apart. The latter might, on occasions, be sufficient to protect the firm.

In terms of practical considerations and remedies there are generally two types of cases:

(a) where the issue arises at the beginning of litigation, as soon as one party realises that the other is represented by the allegedly conflicted solicitor: here the obvious remedy is an injunction to restrain the solicitor from acting, and might relatively easily be obtained, given the heavy burden placed on advisers by the *Bolkiah* case;

(b) when the issue arises after the litigation has concluded and one party claims that the professional who represented them was negligent or in breach of fiduciary duty because he continued to act despite a conflict: here the remedy would lie in damages but these types of claims are not easy to substantiate.

The subject of conflicts of interest and Chinese walls is explored in detail by Charles Hollander QC in *Conflicts of Interest and Chinese Walls* (Sweet and Maxwell, 2000).

Conflicts of interest between individual clients in a group or multi-party action can easily arise especially if and when the other part make a global offer to settle the entire case. The court's new powers in CPR Part 19 assist to a degree but do not specifically provide for the court to hold a settlement or disposal hearing. Involving Counsel or another firm of solicitors may sometimes be the only answer.

Conflicts of interest – a checklist

- Identify who is the client from when first approached.
- Check for conflicts with existing clients from firm's database.
- Consider running company searches against new corporate clients and checking solvency of others.
- Check again at first meeting with the client and before accepting instructions.
- If there is a third-party funder carefully separate instructions and loyalties and put lay clients first.
- In long-running litigation review all the above positions from time to time.

Inexperienced clients

The particular ethical and client care risks in acting for inexperienced clients include:

(a) failing to take adequate instructions at the outset, particularly from a client with poor communication skills, limited literacy, and/or very limited experience of keeping and organising documents and records;

(b) failing similarly to establish clearly what the client wants, i.e. assuming the client and solicitor agendas are the same. The client may want the following as much as or more than a hard fight to maximise compensation:

- an explanation;
- an apology;
- assurances that the same will not happen to others;
- help to get over the problem/damage;
- an early settlement;

(c) some clients can be very naïve about how thorough an investigation their solicitor, the other side and the court might carry out, and may be tempted to hold back 'unhelpful information' in the belief that it can stay hidden;

(d) other clients will do themselves grave disfavours by failing to reveal vital facts without considerable prompting, e.g. with regard to heads of loss in a personal injury claim through embarrassment;

(e) assuming too readily that clients understand and remember oral discussions or read and understand very complex paperwork, especially about such difficult issues as funding options or settlement proposals. This is particularly so in relation to conversations which take place at an especially stressful time, such as in the court corridor before the hearing or trial.

Establishing a good understanding and working relationship at the outset may take a significant investment of time, potentially very difficult in low value 'routine' fast track type cases. This means having a streamlined but client friendly initial screening and interviewing process.

Inexperienced clients need to be kept informed in the same way as repeat player litigants (and arguably more so). Cutting corners on:

- progress letters;
- updating information on charges, costs and future estimates;
- checking on the client's needs and current agenda can be a recipe for disaster.

Settlements are a particularly difficult area with a less experienced client who will usually have very limited knowledge of what can be achieved. There are particular dangers for the solicitor in:

(a) not checking the client's agenda and needs carefully at the outset, especially close to trial, and when a payment into court or updated offer to settlement has been received or is to be made;

(b) not explaining all the implications fully to the client and allowing enough time for him/her to consider/take family advice/ask questions;

(c) putting the solicitor's/the firm's own interests ahead of the client's, even subconsciously, especially when:

 – the case is an 'exciting' one which might make new law or be reported if it goes to trial;

 – the firm is acting on a CFA and the case is risky, particularly where an offer to settle is within the 'reasonable' bracket;

 – there have already been problems in running the case, including adverse costs orders, or unexpected problems or work, which cause the estimate or budget to be exceeded, possibly irrecoverably from either client, funder or the other side.

All of these are situations where obtaining a more objective opinion from the intended advocate/counsel, another solicitor in the firm, or a claims manager at the funding organisation, can be very worthwhile.

Dealing with difficult clients

The skills which solicitors conventionally require are not necessarily those which are needed most when coping with demanding or difficult clients. Putting yourself in the client's position can be effective, especially if the client's problem/case is inherently stressful and/or there is a considerable amount riding on the outcome.

For those practising for some time it can also be difficult to come to terms with the fact that increasingly clients do not accept legal advice at face value. Many will do some homework themselves especially through the Internet, e.g. on medical issues; some will seek second opinions, and the majority will expect high standards of customer care, especially as regards responding to telephone calls, answering letters and transparency on costs. Client care policies are no longer 'the icing on the cake': they are essential.

Good office and administrative systems will prevent some problems occurring including:

(a) prompt, helpful and friendly receptionists/call takers are vital;

(b) consider whether calls might go straight to the fee earner, or their voicemail: levels of filtering can be very frustrating;

(c) consider a pairing scheme: if one fee earner is out for a day or longer another takes their calls and at least finds out whether the request can await their return;

(d) consider an office protocol that requires letters to be answered within a set time: one firm pays compensation to clients if their telephone or letter reply protocol is breached;

(e) ensure fee earners have good easily accessible client information systems, so they can quickly 'recall' sufficient details to take a call effectively; case plans and case management systems online can be very beneficial, especially for solicitors with large case loads;

(f) set up regular bring-forward and reporting systems; clients prefer to have a letter that says not much has happened, than no letter at all;

(g) 'attendance notes' might have old fashioned connotations but are vital for telephone work and are easier to prepare when all fee earners have and use a computer;

(h) consider file 'swap' systems for the unpopular cases/clients – to be used very selectively, and handled carefully, of course;

(i) have excellent incident reporting and complaint handling systems in place (the latter is now required under the Law Society Costs and Client Care Code). Encourage fee earners to share a problem rather than try to bury it, and have a firm protocol for dealing with complaint letters, i.e. referral to a partner etc. Dealing with complaints can seem tiresome, is time-consuming and sometimes dispiriting, but there is no substitute for trying to resolve them quickly. Handling a complaint badly only adds insult to injury, and unhappy clients damage a firm's reputation.

Managing client expectations

A few pointers:

(a) be honest and specific about difficult issues such as limited prospects of success, disproportionate or fast track fixed costs, difficult opponents;

(b) a combination of oral and written advice, especially about bad news, is usually the best strategy, but always be sure to confirm key advice or client instructions in writing, if only to protect the firm's own position;

(c) ensure clients know who in the firm is conducting their case and the fee-earner's status. A firm inadvertently held out a legal executive as a solicitor and was unable to recover their costs from the client on a solicitor/client taxation.

Client confidentiality and privilege

The basic law and professional responsibility remains unchanged:

- communications between solicitors and clients are privileged;
- communications in contemplation of, or during litigation are also privileged;
- solicitors are under a professional duty to maintain client confidentiality.

The Guide to the Professional Conduct of Solicitors 1999 includes useful advice, of which the following is particularly pertinent in a litigation context:

(1) Solicitors should not encourage clients to obtain access to confidential material belonging to or intended for the other side and even very old client papers should be shredded, not left in dustbins outside the office.

(2) When documents come into a solicitor's possession where it is not obvious they have been mistakenly disclosed the party who has inspected them may only use them with the court's permission (CPR Rule 31.3).

(3) However, when documents are obviously mistakenly disclosed the solicitor should immediately cease to read the documents, tell the other side and return them (but the solicitor may tell the client what happened, see *English & American Insurance Co Ltd* v. *Herbert Smith & Co.* [1988] FSR 232 and *Ablitt* v. *Mills & Reeve, The Times*, 25 October 1995).

If the solicitor mistakenly discloses privileged documents, the opponent should still hand them back, as under the pre-CPR law (see *Breeze* v. *John Stacey & Sons Ltd, The Times*, 8 July 1999).

The CPR attempted to make significant inroads into the law of privilege in two instances:

(a) Rule 48.7(3) re wasted costs, which purported to give the court the power to order disclosure of solicitor–client correspondence to the court and the other party on a wasted costs application;

(b) Rule 35.10(4) re instructions to experts, which gives the court the power to order disclosure of the actual instructions to experts when there are

reasonable grounds for believing the summary in the expert's report is
inaccurate or misleading.

However, in one of the most important case law developments since April 1999,
Toulson J attacked the 'vires' of the Rules on legal professional privilege in the
wasted costs jurisdiction (*General Mediterranean Holdings SA* v. *Patel* [1999]
3 All ER 673). This was not a surprise to the author, as the Law Society had
tried hard to persuade the Rule Committee (during the final stages of the rule
drafting) that secondary legislation (such as Rules of court) cannot change
fundamental principles of the common law. Sensibly the Rule Committee has
since decided to omit Rule 48.7(3).

However, Rule 35.10(4) has not been changed: the court still has the power to
require disclosure of the 'actual instructions' to experts if there is a reasonable
suspicion that the expert's summary in the report is inaccurate or misleading.
A circuit judge did decide that this Rule too was ultra vires (in *Burt* v. *Greer*,
New Law Journal, 10 December 1999). This decision was not appealed, but
neither has the Rule Committee changed the Rule!

But when a client sues their former solicitor the position changes – the solicitor
can use confidential information to prepare a defence, including a complaint
(but this does not apply when a solicitor is suing a client for unpaid fees unless
the client counterclaims in negligence).

When and how to cease to act for a client

Ceasing to act for a client is not a decision to be taken lightly, especially if the
case has progressed a long way. Abandoning a client close to trial should be a
very rare occurrence. Important points are:

(a) if a client is paying privately and the solicitor wants money on account
or to interim bill, he/she must set up a clear regime from the beginning
and keep to it. It is the solicitor's fault, and not the client's, if he/she
suddenly wakes up to how much unbilled time there is on the case, and
finds that the client cannot or will not pay;

(b) always seek and confirm instructions on key issues/decisions;

(c) if a client is clearly not cooperating (or even not telling the truth),
warn them politely and firmly and if necessary confront them;

(d) if it is decided to 'terminate the retainer' pre-warn the client; consider
whether help might be given for them to transfer elsewhere; do not be
over-difficult about releasing files unless there are substantial amounts
of fees outstanding, and if proceedings have been started follow the
court procedures for coming off the record promptly and carefully (see
CPR Part 42).

Handling a dispute with a client

Resolving a dispute with a client speedily is in everyone's interest, especially in a litigation matter when the client is likely either to:

- transfer the case to another firm;
- consider a negligence action against the firm

and in either case he or she will very likely give the firm a bad press with friends and colleagues.

Firms are now obliged to have complaints procedures under Practice Rule 15, but the following are also worth bearing in mind:

(a) relationships with professional advisers which have broken down are often good candidates for ADR, especially mediation (see Chapter 14 below);

(b) suing a client for relatively small amounts of unpaid fees can be a hostage to fortune as they may well counterclaim in negligence and handle the matter themselves if the sum is less than £5,000. This can be a painful, time-consuming and ultimately unrewarding process. It is better to transfer the file to a different fee earner for the debt collecting, to ensure greater objectivity, particularly if the ex-client raises negligence in defence, or consider offering mediation.

Stress on solicitors

Most litigation is hard work and very demanding: heavy caseloads, emotional clients (e.g clinical and professional negligence, traumatic personal injury, employment work for employees and defamation), trials, too much responsibility too soon and the long hours culture can be demoralising and damaging. Stories of firms routinely exploiting junior staff are now legion and alcoholism is rife in the profession.

How the firm copes with this very much depends on the type of work but a few suggestions are:

- instituting teamwork and mentoring schemes, even if fee earners work on their own;
- monitoring timesheets: excessive hours are not necessarily to be praised (although sickness records can also be revealing);
- flexibility about working arrangements: taking time out after a heavy trial may be good sense;
- knowing how to access help when it is needed, e.g. counselling.

DUTIES TO OTHER PARTIES

Witnesses

The issues regarding witnesses of fact and payment to witnesses are covered below.

Other parties

The Guide to the Professional Conduct of Solicitors 1999 states that a solicitor should not interview or contact a party directly when he/she is legally represented, without the other solicitor's consent. This generally poses few problems except where the party's solicitor has a limited retainer and, in effect, the party is acting in person at least some of the time.

There has been a significant increase in litigants in person (LIPs) in the last few years, as a consequence of tighter controls over legal aid and increasing education, especially through the Internet. The CPR effectively encourages this trend: the small claims limit is now £5,000, the rules, at least in theory, are simpler and there are more generous provisions for LIPs to recover costs.

Lawyers should not take advantage of opponents acting in person; in fact there is a positive duty to assist them on the law and procedure and not to 'score points' based on their lack of knowledge and experience, e.g., entering judgment in default knowing full well that the LIP has a very arguable defence, or negotiating a glaringly 'unfair' settlement Also CPR Part 52 invites a represented party to provide a LIP with their notes of the judgment to assist in an appeal where no transcript is readily available (Practice Direction to CPR Part 52, para. 5.12(3)).

Other lawyers

The Code of Conduct requires solicitors to treat other lawyers with professional courtesy (para. 19.01). Again this is reinforced by the CPR, which emphasise a non-adversarial approach to litigation, and by the powers of the court under the costs rules to take 'conduct' into account and to make wasted costs orders. Games playing in litigation will incur costs penalties at best and may lead to a strike out at worst.

The CPR makes dealing with difficult opponents (see also Chapter 15) easier because the court has case management powers to level the playing field and to impose sanctions, including costs penalties for unreasonable conduct such as:

- failing to comply with court directions and timetables especially after 'unless orders' or repeatedly;
- refusing to negotiate or put cards on the table pre-action;
- exaggerating the claim or introducing new heads of claim, or defence, or evidence, late in the day;
- using greater resources to make pursuit of the case difficult for the other party – excessive disclosure, repeated unnecessary applications, seeking permission for too many or expensive experts;
- over adversarial correspondence or conduct – bullying tactics.

It is also important to avoid the opposite problem of developing too cosy a relationship with a regular opponent – easy to slip into if two solicitors share a workload, when professional camaraderie can get in the way of putting the client's interests first.

Contractors (disbursements)

Solicitors are under a duty to honour their commitments to those instructed to assist or provide services in litigation. The solicitors' firm will usually be personally liable for third parties' fees unless there is a clear agreement with the client to the contrary. Not infrequently firms delay in paying experts and agents for no good reason other than that it helps their cashflow. Occasionally experts even have to sue for their fees. This behaviour hardly enhances the reputation of the profession.

The Court

The solicitor's duty to the court is covered below.

Publicity and advertising

The professional issues in relation to publicity and advertising are too wide to be discussed in detail in this chapter. The regulations restricting solicitors' advertising have been gradually relaxed in recent years. Increasing competition, especially in the field of personal injury work from claims organisations, has prompted much more high profile advertising by solicitors, including on television.

While there is not infrequently public criticism of 'ambulance-chasing' styles of advertisements by solicitors' firms, few complaints to the Law Society in this area have been upheld, because of the difficulties in establishing a consensus view as to what amounts to an advertisement in bad taste.

The following is a brief reminder of some of the issues in the Publicity Code which are relevant to litigation:

- individual clients must not be identified without their consent;
- there should be no 'cold-calling' either by telephone or in person, except in respect of current or former clients;
- comparisons should not be made with other solicitors' charges or quality of service;
- 'success' rates should not be quoted.

Introductions and referrals

Again only a brief reminder is appropriate in this chapter. The Law Society is, in any event, revising the Introduction and Referral Code. Currently the following are prohibited:

(a) paying any reward, e.g. by commission, to those introducing work;

(b) entering into arrangements with non-solicitors who solicit or receive contingency fees (Rule 9). The arrangements between some claims organisations and solicitors' firms in this area have been investigated by the Law Society but none have been found expressly to breach the Rule.

ADVOCACY AND CONDUCT

Solicitor advocates

The basic duty of the advocate to be independent and represent the client remains unchanged.

Solicitors need to be aware of:

- the Bar Council's Code of Conduct;
- the role of solicitors at court when 'supporting' the advocate;
- the evolving roles of solicitor and advocate;
- the new challenges posed for solicitors by easier access to higher rights of audience;
- that advocates are no longer 'immune from suit' for actions in court.

Solicitors and barristers are edging towards a level playing field. The Access to Justice Act 1999 effectively gives both parts of the profession rights to conduct litigation and appear in court. More solicitors (quite rightly in my view) are turning their hands to advocacy, for case management conferences, short hearings and fast track trials, and some are deciding to acquire higher rights of audience.

The 'balance of power' between solicitor and advocate in litigation is changing significantly. Increasingly specialist litigation solicitors are very much in charge of a case throughout, bringing in the advocate for specific tasks, except in the more complex cases where teamwork from the outset is essential. The CPR encourages this by requiring the litigator in control of the case to attend case management conferences etc.

Attending upon counsel

However, at the same time and for proportionality reasons, in fast track cases a solicitor cannot recover more than £200 for attending the trial if an advocate has been instructed, and frequently the court takes the view that there is no need to have two lawyers in court. The Law Society has changed the Code of Conduct to omit the professional obligation 'to attend upon counsel' (para. 20.04).

Yet this can conflict with the solicitor's duty to their client because:

(a) a nervous or first time litigant will often want or even need the solicitor there – going to court is a stressful experience;

(b) settlement may be discussed while waiting at court;

(c) an advocate briefed late on in the case is not well equipped to deal with the summary assessment of costs alone;

(d) if the case is lost, permission to appeal might best be sought on the spot.

Solicitors need to decide on an individual case basis whether it will be more cost effective overall and better for client care to attend trial.

In-house advocates

Some firms employ barristers or solicitors with higher rights of audience in-house so they can provide a one-stop shop service for clients. But clients must not be required automatically to use the firm's in-house advocates. It is important to give clients a real choice based on the client's, not the firm's, best interests, and on costs considerations.

No immunity from suit

Advocates no longer are 'immune from suit': it was no surprise that the House of Lords, in *Arthur JS Hall & Co.* v. *Simons* ([2000] 3 All ER 673, HL), ended advocates' immunity for decisions and actions in court, particularly in the light of the impending implementation of the Human Rights Act 1998. This should not have an impact on the duties of the advocate, but if it leads to a more measured approach to arguing hopeless points or even cases, that will be very much in tune with the CPR.

Recent case law

There has been some relevant post-CPR case law. In *Copeland* v. *Smith* (*The Times*, 20 October 1999) it was decided that advocates are responsible for advising the judge on the law, especially recent case law. (Practitioners might be forgiven for thinking it was the JSB's or the Court Service's job to keep judges up to date!) In *Memory Corp. plc* v. *Sidhu* (*The Times*, 15 February 2000), the Court of Appeal muddied these particular waters by suggesting the extent of the advocate's duty depended on 'all the circumstances' and proportionality.

THE CIVIL PROCEDURE RULES, ETHICS AND CLIENT CARE

The overriding objective, CPR Part 1

When cases do go to court, the overriding objective of the new rules, which the court must seek to effect at all times, is to enable the court to deal with cases justly. Rule 1.1(2) states that dealing with a case justly includes:

- ensuring that parties are on an equal footing;
- dealing with the case in ways which are proportionate ;
- allotting to a case an appropriate share of the court's resources, while taking into account the need to allot resources to other cases.

The parties are required to help the court to further the overriding objective (Rule 1.3). The court must further the overriding objective by actively managing cases (Rule 1.4). This may include encouraging the parties to use an ADR procedure, fixing timetables and giving directions to ensure the case proceeds quickly and effectively.

Dealing with a case in ways which are proportionate is very important. Legal representatives are expected to consider carefully, with their clients, their whole approach to a case, particularly the amount of work that might be required to progress the case and take it to trial, if necessary, and the costs which might be incurred both by their own client and by any other parties as a consequence of that work. The courts have the power to ask the parties to tell the court and other parties the amount of costs which have been incurred to date and which are likely to be incurred in the future on specific steps or stages. Orders and directions will reflect the court's view of what is proportionate. Solicitors have to explain this new power carefully to clients as it could have a significant impact on how they view their case and how they instruct the solicitor to conduct it, and on their expectations.

The courts are particularly concerned to 'level the playing field' where one party has significantly more resources than the other and is willing or can afford to spend time and costs on a case out of proportion to what is in issue or to what the other party can afford. This particular change in culture has conduct implications. There have been a few reported cases on this particular rule, some with perhaps surprising results. In *Maltez* v. *Lewis* (*The Times*, 4 May 1999) a litigant in person's challenge to the other party's right to have a QC failed (not a very Woolf-like decision?), but in *R* v. *Bow County Court, ex parte Pelling* ([1999] 1 WLR 1807) the Court of Appeal said LIPs would usually be allowed to have a *McKenzie* friend at trial.

Although the solicitor's duty remains to do what is best for the client the courts are much less willing than before to allow every arguable point, technical or otherwise, to be pursued regardless of cost and court time. No surprise, then, in *Grobbelaar* v. *Sun Newspapers Ltd* (*The Times*, 12 August 1999) it was held that the courts have the power to exclude evidence, although the implementation of the Human Rights Act 1998 may have a bearing on any excess zeal shown by a case managing judge in this respect.

The duty to help the court

Solicitors are officers of the court and as such have a clear duty to the court as well as to their client. This duty includes not misleading the court (the Access to Justice Act 1999, s.42 tries to go further and impose on employed lawyers that their first duty, when acting as an advocate, is to the court and that this overrides any other obligations, including contractual ones to the employer).

With regard to 'parties helping the court' look at *Adoko* v. *Jemal* (*The Times*, 8 July 1999): it is not proportionate for three Court of Appeal judges to spend time sorting out papers in a muddle for an appeal hearing.

Other conduct implications of the enhanced duty of solicitors to help the court include:

(a) not unduly delaying proceedings, particularly on tactical grounds – a not infrequent ploy in the past, particularly when acting for a defendant, in the hope that the claimant would run out of money or patience or both;

(b) not using procedural tricks or making unnecessary applications deliberately to cause problems for the other party; the Rules and Practice Directions, especially CPR Part 18, make it clear that applications should be used sparingly. In *Burt* v. *Montague Wells* (unreported, 10

183

July 2000 CA) the pragmatic message was to reply to requests which might have gone a bit too far if this caused minimal detriment: to over argue might incur costs penalties. Also the costs of such applications are now summarily assessed and often payable forthwith!;

(c) not carrying out more work than is 'proportionate' or justified. The costs of this are not recoverable at best even if the case is 'won' and at worst both parties' costs occasioned by the unnecessary work may have to be paid.

Conduct implications of the requirement to respect the court's limited resources might include:

(a) ensuring the solicitor with conduct of the action attends at all key court hearings and with the client when issues such as settlement will be discussed: see *Baron* v. *Lovell* (*The Times*, 14 September 1999, CA) when the absence of the fee earner merited judicial criticism;

(b) not applying for late adjournments of hearings especially trials: see *Matthews* v. *Tarmac Bricks and Tiles Ltd* ([1999] CPLR 463, CA) when failure to explain the non-availability of an expert for a planned trial date led to that being fixed in any event.

The court's powers re conduct

The court also has wide powers to take into account the conduct of legal representatives both pre-action and during proceedings (CPR Rule 44.3(5)). This includes:

- whether it is reasonable for a party to raise, pursue, or contest a particular issue;
- the manner in which the party dealt with the case or issue;
- whether a claimant exaggerated the claim.

CPR Rule 44.5 provides that the court, when deciding costs, must have regard to conduct including before as well as during proceedings and to efforts made to resolve the disputes.

The courts are expressly empowered to apply sanctions much more readily than they have done in the past for failure to comply with timetables and orders. The principle is that the party in default has to apply for relief, and that extensions to timetables are only to be permitted where these will not affect important milestones, especially the trial date. Evidence served late may not always be relied upon and there is greater use of costs penalties, including payment of costs 'on the spot', and wasted costs orders. Striking out all or part of a statement of case will continue, but on notice. The practitioners' 'nightmare' of RSC Order 17 Rule 11 should not be repeated.

Assessment 18 months after implementation showed that the courts seemed to be using the 'carrot' rather than the 'stick' approach – 'in the interests of justice' (or with half an eye to the Human Rights Act 1998?):

(a) first time orders did not usually include default penalties, except when a party had already breached court rules and/or had a flimsy case;

(b) the Court of Appeal was not upholding strike out or debarring orders when the fault had been minimal or very technical and/or had caused little prejudice to the other party;

(c) instead, costs penalties were the preferred remedy: summary assessment of costs at the end of short hearings, and orders for prompt payment, were proving to be very effective in controlling unecessary or frivolous applications;

(d) however, judicial case management provided more opportunities for the courts to strike out or summarily dispose of weak cases, and these were being taken;

(e) practitioners also came in for strong judicial criticism if they did not attend case management conferences personally or ensure whoever did so was fully briefed.

Looking at the case law, the following are the main trends:

(1) The courts will not usually strike out statements of cases or prevent reliance on evidence for minor infringements of rules or orders: see *Mealey Horgan plc* v. *Horgan* (*The Times*, 6 July 1999, re witness statements served slightly late); *Reed* v. *Swanlux Cleaning Services Ltd* (unreported, 7 June 1999) and *Biguzzi* v. *Rank Leisure plc* [1999] 1 WLR 1926 which decided that costs penalties are preferable to a strike out for late service of documents.

(2) Also the court will not embark on a mini trial to establish whether a cause of action is made out on a strike out application: see *Morris* v. *Bank of America National Trust* (*The Times*, 25 January 2000), and proportionality and prejudice are relevant issues, especially when the defendant has a substantial counterclaim: see *Tekna Design Ltd* v. *Davenport Properties Ltd* ([2000] CP Rep 63, CA). But a wholesale disregard of the CPR will justify a strike out: see *UCB Corporate Services Ltd* v. *Halifax Ltd* (*The Times*, 23 December 1999).

(3) First instance case management decisions will nearly always be supported on appeal. In *Sony Music Entertainment Inc* v. *Prestige Records Ltd* (*The Times*, 2 March 2000) a challenge to a Master's costs order on grounds of over-aggressive behaviour pre-action by the successful party failed.

(4) Disproportionate applications for minor breaches of orders or too close to trial will be dismissed with costs: see *Adams Phones Ltd* v.

Goldschmidt (*The Times*, 18 August 1999) re a 'trivial' breach of a seize and search order, and *SBJ Stephenson Ltd* v. *Mandy* (*The Times*, 21 July 1999) which held that an interlocutory injunction two weeks before trial was pointless.

(5) Acting unreasonably in contesting issues unjustifiably right up to trial is 'conduct' punishable in costs: see *Riley* v. *Shell (UK)* (The Lawyer, 10 April 2000) when Shell's last minute admission that they did occupy the jetty where the claimant had the accident meant they were deprived of their costs even though they 'won' on liability.

(6) In a similar vein, attempts to strike out cases started in the wrong court or using the wrong procedure will fail – the court's task is to transfer/or manage the case to enable it to continue: see *Cala Homes (South) Ltd* v. *Chichester District Council* (*The Times*, 15 October 1999); *Keene* v. *Martin* (*The Times*, 11 November 1999) and *Re Dicksmith (manufacturing) Ltd (in liquidation)* (*The Times*, 7 July 1999).

Looking more specifically at costs issues

(7) *Piglowska* v. *Piglowski* (*The Times*, 25 June 1999, HL) may be a family law case but it provides useful guidance across the board on proportionality: here the costs in an ancillary relief case wiped out the matrimonial assets.

(8) Conduct is very relevant in assessing costs: see *Mars UK Ltd* v. *Teknowledge Ltd (No 2)* (*The Times*, 8 July 1999) in which Jacob J held it was unreasonable to run up unforeseeably large bills without warning the other side. Look also at *Liverpool City Council* v. *Chavasse* ([1999] CPLR 802, Ch D) when Neuberger J particularly criticised 'head in the sand' conduct pre-action and badly prepared bundles (ever a judicial obsession!) as very relevant to conduct in relation to the costs of a successful party.

(9) Some good news – wasted costs are not automatic when a hopeless claim is dismissed: see *Jones* v. *Chief Constable of Bedfordshire* (unreported, 30 July 1999) and disputes on points of principle mean a summary assessment is not appropriate: see *R* v. *Cardiff City Council, ex parte Brown* (unreported, 11 June 1999).

Pre-action protocols

This subject is covered in more detail in Chapter 9 below.

During his inquiry, Lord Woolf became convinced that pre-action protocols were needed for particularly adversarial areas of litigation, to encourage a climate of openness, a 'cards on the table' approach, and early settlement without resort to proceedings.

The Protocols were first published by the Lord Chancellor's Department in July 1998. In a foreword the Lord Chancellor identified three main underpinning objectives:

- to encourage openness in communicating perceived problems and in the investigation of adverse outcomes;
- to promote timeliness in the investigation and management of potential disputes;
- to sponsor awareness of the options open to those involved in a dispute.

The Protocols are now annexed to the CPR with their own Practice Direction. Many more protocols for other types of litigation are in progress and are likely to be adopted in the next few years.

In all cases, whether or not there is an adopted protocol the courts expect:

(a) parties through their legal representatives to have exchanged information pre-proceedings (the 'cards on the table' approach);
(b) claimants to provide to defendants detailed letters of claim;
(c) defendants to reply also in detail and to be clear as to whether they are admitting or denying liability with reasons;
(d) parties to discuss sharing experts;
(e) parties holding discussions with a view to settlement.

The courts attach considerable importance to compliance with the Protocols and have powers when making case management and costs orders:

- to penalise a party for issuing proceedings prematurely;
- to penalise a party for inappropriate pre-action conduct generally;
- and particularly to penalise a party for not complying with the spirit of the Protocol.

Few cases have been reported on the Protocols. It seems that the Personal Injury and Clinical Negligence Protocols are working well.

Little use seems to be being made of the court's new powers on pre-action disclosure. But the court will order pre-action disclosure 'to aid fair disposal and save costs': see *Burrells Wharf Freeholds Ltd* v. *Galliard Homes Ltd* ([1999] 2 EGLR 81, QBD).

In *Macdonald* v. *Thorn plc* (*The Times*, 15 October 1999) the defendant's failure to reply to a letter before action was held to be insufficient on its own as a 'knock out blow' to refuse to set aside judgment in default of a defence – perhaps a surprising approach.

But the basic message from the pre-CPR cases must hold good: be prepared to put all cards on the table early and to negotiate. See *Butcher* v. *Wolfe* (30

October 1998, CA). when the court penalised a claimant for refusing to settle pre-action and then accepting the same offer during the proceedings.

The decision to sue/defend and statements of case

There is an expectation in the CPR that starting/ defending proceedings is such a key step that parties and their solicitors must stocktake and not drift into litigation. Clients often pressurise solicitors to issue proceedings in an attempt to frighten or put pressure on an opponent. This may now be viewed as unreasonable conduct.

Statements of case replace pleadings: these should summarise facts, allegations, law and evidence, and state the required remedy in plain English. Defences must answer all allegations with reasons. Bare denials will be struck out.

Statements of truth

Statements of case and witness statements must all contain a *statement of truth* of their contents.

If there is no statement of truth attached to a statement of case the court has the power to strike it out and if there is no statement attached to a witness statement or expert report, the court may order that it shall not be received in evidence. Proceedings for contempt may be brought against a party for giving a false statement of truth with dishonest intent.

Statements of truth on statements of case may be signed by the client (or insurer) or by the legal representative. Generally (although the solicitor is testifying to the truth of what the *client* and not what the solicitor believes) it is preferable for the client to sign. On occasions it may be actually inappropriate for the solicitor to sign: see *The Guide to the Professional Conduct of Solicitors 1999*, Principle 21.21, Note 4. Solicitors cannot cross-examine their own clients on the accuracy of every detail of their case. This would lead to serious conflicts of interest and make it impossible to represent the client.

It is vital, however, that solicitors ensure the client fully understands the importance of the statement of truth and the implications of signing it. The client must sign the completed document – no obtaining signatures on blank claim forms!

If the solicitor is to sign on the client's behalf, the client's authority to do so must be obtained. This means the client must see and approve the document. Solicitors should be very wary of signing for clients who through inefficiency, lack of time or a cavalier attitude have not done their homework on their own case.

Witness statements, CPR Part 32

This is an area which has not seemed to be causing problems, probably because the CPR do not change very much from the old rules.

But the Court of Appeal has stressed that solicitors should not use statements from witnesses of fact to put forward legal arguments outside the witnesses' experience: see *Alex Lawrie Factors Ltd* v. *Morgan* (*The Times*, 18 September 1999), and solicitors must not massage witness statements.

Offering payment to witnesses of fact, other than expenses in connection with providing a statement, or to attend court, is not ethical. Witnesses should not be pressurised or coached (see the *Guide*, Principle 21.10–12).

There is 'no property' in a witness: this means, in theory, that witnesses can, quite properly, be approached by either or both parties, and that one party can call another party's witness to give oral evidence, when the first party chooses not to call a witness, whose statement has been disclosed.

Disclosure of documents, CPR Part 31

This is discussed more fully in Chapter 12 below.

Under the CPR, disclosure (discovery) of documents is more limited and more controlled. The court may even decide to dispense with disclosure in some cases. The 'standard' requirement is to disclose only those documents which support either parties' case or are adverse to it.

It will be rare for additional disclosure to be allowed in the fast track. The parties and the judge decide on further specific disclosure in the multi-track, with reasonableness and proportionality being the governing factors.

Parties are required to serve a disclosure statement which explains their search for documents.

The new test for standard disclosure seems likely to lead to satellite litigation as it will not always be apparent early in an action which documents support or are adverse to each side's case, and what amounts to a reasonable search for them.

The new disclosure rules are designed to prevent cases being delayed and costs being increased by disclosure of irrelevant or unnecessary documents.

In spite of the limited nature of the standard test of disclosure, solicitors are under a duty not to mislead the court (see the *Guide*, Principle 21.01). The duty of search, and the need to include a disclosure statement and signed certificate in the list of documents, will need to be explained to clients carefully, as these are duties of the parties, not just of the legal representatives

The demise of the *Peruvian Guano* relevance test has not as yet caused any obvious problems. This could be because solicitors have not really changed their habits; this may not matter in the majority of cases with a small number of documents, but could lead to adverse costs orders where excessive disclosure has not benefited the other party. It may just be too early for case law giving guidance on reasonable searches and the meaning of the standard test.

But a solicitor applying for an 'unless' order on a failure to disclose must be sure it is very specific or it will be set aside: see *Morgans* v. *Needham* (*The Times*, 5 November 1999).

If a solicitor mistakenly discloses privileged documents, the opponent should still hand them back, as under the pre-CPR law: see *Breeze* v. *John Stacey & Sons Ltd* (*The Times*, 8 July 1999).

If applying for third party disclosure take a look at *Anselm* v. *Anselm* (unreported, 29 June 1999, Ch D) where Neuberger J said the balancing act is different than when dealing with applications between parties (or prospective ones). The order will usually have a narrower ambit and the rights of the third party, such as privacy, may need to be better protected.

The particular conduct/ethical risks for solicitors in failing to handle the new disclosure regime may well include:

(a) leaving decisions on searching for standard disclosure documents too much to the client;

(b) the corporate client may delegate inappropriately and/or take decisions not to search when they know documents exist;

(c) disclosing the existence of documents on a list without viewing them relying on unreasonable to search/disproportionality/irrelevant /privilege grounds and then being ordered by the court to disclose;

(d) clients trying to persuade solicitors to support non-disclosure of adverse documents;

(e) deliberately or carelessly 'snowing under' the other party with excessive documents.

These dangers are best protected against by clear letters of advice from the outset, meticulous attendance notes, and retention of files of documents reviewed but not disclosed with the reasons why and on whose instructions.

Expert evidence, CPR Part 35

This is covered in more detail in Chapter 8 below.

The courts are seeking to economise on expert evidence. It is the general duty of the court and the parties to restrict expert evidence to that which is reasonably required to resolve the proceedings.

On the fast track, expert evidence is normally only allowed from one or two disciplines, and oral evidence given only in exceptional circumstances and with permission. On both tracks parties are encouraged to share expert evidence, particularly in lower value claims, and for the purposes of quantification.

The court also has the power to appoint single experts. Lord Woolf was strongly in support of a court appointed expert system but he and the Rule Committee were persuaded that this would be difficult to graft onto an adversarial system. Parties may already have their own experts by the time the court gives directions, or will appoint their own 'behind the scenes' to advise on the single expert's evidence.

Instructions to experts who are preparing reports for the court may have to be disclosed to try to avoid overt 'steering' of experts' opinions, and experts are required to accept that their overriding duty is to the court and not the party who instructed them.

What are the ethical/conduct issues for solicitors to bear in mind on expert evidence?

(1) The expert's duty is to the court, certainly from the time when the court allows reliance on that expert and possibly from when he is first instructed.

(2) An expert can be instructed early to 'advise' and 'stay behind the scenes', but the costs are unlikely to be recovered, and if the expert is later retained to give evidence in the litigation the early instructions may become disclosable.

(3) Known 'partisan' experts should be avoided.

(4) Experts must never be asked to work on a contingency basis as this would compromise their independence.

(5) The court wants experts to cover the spectrum of opinion in reports and the strengths and weaknesses of a case; once a named expert has been agreed by the court it will be very difficult not to disclose the report even if the solicitor or the client is not happy with it.

(6) Never ask an expert to change the opinions in his/her reports; changes to correct facts etc. are permissible.

(7) Do not ask an expert to write 'side letters'; an expert's report must reflect the whole of his/her opinion.

(8) Remember that experts can apply to the court for directions themselves.

(9) Keep single experts particularly at arm's length – private instructions to them are not permissible.

(10) Do not send experts privileged material; if they refer to it in the report privilege is waived.

(11) Beware of asking too many oppressive questions of experts about their reports which go beyond clarification.

(12) Do not attempt to over-control an experts' discussion, particularly by instructing an expert not to agree, or requiring a sight of the experts' agreed note before it is signed/disclosed to the other party.

Questions and expert meetings are sometimes being used to bully the other side: one expert on a fast track case received 50 intricate questions, and experts have expressed concerns about being dispatched to meetings with an opposing expert who has years of courtroom experience with, at best, a woolly agenda and no solicitor at the end of a phone to assist with problems. The Draft Code of Guidance on Expert Evidence and the Clinical Dispute Forum guidelines on experts' meetings need to be adopted quickly to fill this vacuum.

Unusually a pre-April 1999 case is still essential reading. In *Vernon* v. *Bosley (No. 2)* ([1997] 1 All ER 614), the same psychiatrists were retained as experts in related personal injury and family cases for the same client. In reports prepared only a few months apart for the two actions, the experts appeared to argue very different cases regarding the client's psychiatric condition: in the personal injury case he was still suffering significantly from post-traumatic stress, in the case concerning residence and care of his children he had made a surprising recovery. Thorpe J criticised both the solicitors and the experts.

While the Court of Appeal generally has struggled hard to find cases under the Civil Procedure Rules from which 'to fly the Woolf flag' the expert ' industry', sadly, has provided some easy targets. The main emerging issues from the case law on the ethical and conduct issues of expert evidence seem to be:

(1) *Stevens* v. *Gullis* (*The Times*, 6 October 1999, CA) made an example of an old style inefficient expert whose uncooperative behaviour not only resulted in his report being 'debarred' but in 'his side' losing the case. The lesson here for solicitors is to find the right expert!

(2) *Rollinson* v. *Kimberley Clark Ltd* (*The Times*, 22 June 1999, CA), *Matthews* v. *Tarmac Bricks and Tiles Ltd* ([1999] CPLR 463, CA) and *Baron* v. *Lovell* (*The Times*, 14 September 1999, CA) emphasise to solicitors and experts that in general, late expert reports are a 'no go' area and that adjourning trials for experts' convenience is a thing of the past. Sadly, the Court of Appeal's comment in *Matthews* on medico-legal experts 'having to fit their commitments to court time-tables' did not suggest any real understanding of the current pressures on NHS consultants. Also in *Jenkins* v. *Grocott and Hoyle* ([2000] *Gazette*, 2 February) late expert evidence was admitted because on the facts it was not prejudicial to the claimant.

(3) *Thermos Ltd* v. *Aladdin Sales and Marketing Ltd* (*Independent*, 13

December 1999) was a warning about when experts may not be reasonably required, here in a patents design case. And in *Thomas Coker* v. *Barkland* (LTL, 6 December 1999, CA) when an engineering expert was not needed in a personal injury case, the claimant could not recover the costs even when he won.

(4) In *Field* v. *Leeds City Council* ([1999] CPLR 833) Lord Woolf emphasised that a single joint expert would be a better option in a local authority housing disrepair case, rather than the local authority proposing an in-house surveyor as their expert. But he did not rule out the latter option, provided that the particular expert could demonstrate an understanding of the expert's independent role. It is difficult, in our view, to square this with the universal ban on experts working on contingency arrangements when an in-house expert would be well aware that their job could be on the line if their report favoured the other side.

(5) However in *S (a minor)* v. *Birmingham Health Authority* (*The Times*, 23 November 1999) it was decided, on appeal, that restricting expert evidence to a single joint expert too early in a clinical negligence case could be unjust.

Offers to settle, CPR Part 36

This is covered in more detail in Chapter 9 below.

Either party can now make an offer to settle at any time, including pre-action. A defendant needs to reinforce any pre-action offer by a payment into court once proceedings are issued; the costs consequences of payments in remain as pre-CPR. If a claimant makes an offer which the defendant does not accept, and which is equalled or beaten at trial, the court can award the claimant interest at up to 10 per cent above base rate, and indemnity costs plus additional interest.

Ethical and conduct issues for solicitors on offers to settle include:

(a) it is the client's agenda that matters when settling a case, not the solicitor's;

(b) it is vital to explain offers and the costs consequences to a client and to take their informed instructions before settling;

(c) a solicitor must never be tempted to suggest settlement to a client just because he/she is acting on a CFA and wishes to get out of the case fast or can see advantages in fees to the firm;

(d) there are risks if the claim is exaggerated to influence the track allocation or to put pressure on the other party – even if a party 'wins' they may not receive all their costs.

Again, the anecdotal evidence is that CPR Part 36 is working well. Claimants in particular are making early offers which defendants are accepting.

Claimants will be pleased that on a claimant's offer the starting point is an award of 10 per cent above base rate on the entire judgment, and the court will then look at whether this creates an injustice: see *Little* v. *George Little Sebire & Co* (*The Times*, 17 November 1999). But *Burgess* v. *British Steel* (*The Times*, 29 February 2000) should serve as a reminder that payments into court should still be taken very seriously. Here, non-acceptance on the ground that the claimant wanted to clear his name on an allegation of malingering did not protect the claimant in costs when a payment in was not beaten at trial.

In *Ford* v. *GKR Construction* (*The Times*, 4 November 1999, CA) the Court of Appeal made it clear that evidence relevant to an offer/payment in had to be served with the offer if the costs protection under the rules is to bite. Here, the fact that the defendant only obtained video evidence during an adjournment of the trial had to be taken into account when assessing the costs order when the claimant failed to beat a payment into court.

In *Commsupport Ltd* v. *St Giles Hotel Ltd* (unreported, 23 July 1999), the defendant was awarded costs on an indemnity basis when costs in the case were greatly increased due to the claimant grossly exaggerating the claim.

Stays for settlement

As referred to earlier, the courts have a new power to stay the timetable while parties try to settle, through traditional bilateral negotiation or mediation. It is too soon to know how this may impact on most litigation. The slow take-up of the ADR pilot schemes suggests that solicitors are being cautious about this unfamiliar dispute resolution technique. Enthusiasm for mediation amongst the judges, who may want cases to settle in order to reduce their workloads, and ADR providers, who see a commercial opportunity, may not find favour with some solicitors who, in the main, remain sceptical that ADR can add value to traditional negotiations.

Negotiations

The less adversarial approach demanded by the CPR requires:

- demonstrating a willingness to negotiate;
- a more cooperative style in negotiation than in the past with the aim of:
  - maintaining cordial relations;
  - looking for the common ground;

194

- making reasonable concessions and offers;
- establishing an atmosphere of trust;
- finding options for mutual gain;
- avoiding brinkmanship and ambush.

Specific consideration is required of the need for a stay and the advantages of ADR: see CPR Rule 26.4.

CONCLUSIONS: WHAT THE CIVIL JUSTICE REFORMS MIGHT MEAN FOR SOLICITORS

The development of litigation as a separate discipline and major source of fees in many solicitors' firms in the last 20 to 30 years has been based on a culture of knowledge and application of specialist 'black letter law', skilful application of procedural tactics to achieve 'a win' and the solicitor's monopoly on the conduct of litigation. But this has caused costs and delay to increase.

The Woolf reforms should encourage a more client-centred approach, particularly in areas of litigation where compensation is not the only remedy on the client agenda. Solicitors who embrace the reforms seek to put their clients' needs and wishes first: setting objectives with the client at the first meeting, deciding on the remedy the client is really seeking, evaluating the options including using the complaints system or ADR, and setting a timescale and a budget.

More sophisticated approaches to analysing and managing complex litigation are developing. These will become more essential if in future most litigation is conducted on a conditional fee basis, or to meet the requirements of demanding funders. Techniques such as case theories and case analysis, and project management, should transform litigators from 'losers or cruisers' to 'dynamos' (S. Mayson, *Making Sense of Law Firms* (Blackstone Press, 1977)). Pro-active litigators will aim to be ahead of the procedural judge and the other party by the time of the first case management conference.

Increasingly, solicitors might provide more of a one-stop shop service: tight timetables and costs controls will make it more difficult to justify the involvement of both a solicitor and counsel, except in more complex litigation, and here they will need to work as an efficient team. It is likely that specialised solicitors will increasingly draft their own statements of case, rely less on counsel for advice on evidence, and will develop advocacy skills, not just for court hearings, but also for negotiations and mediations.

Solicitors' firms are already introducing quality controls to meet the requirements for franchises and contracts with the Legal Aid Board, and for the costs and efficiency controls of insurers. To be able to achieve tighter court time-tables and costs controls, the caseloads of fee earners may have to reduce. Solicitors' firms will also need to develop more sophisticated delegation, super-vision and teamwork systems. Diary planning and case management skills are already becoming commonplace: the use of case management IT packages will assist in the future.

Ethics and conduct must not be forgotten – they must be rediscovered. Case-loads will have to be reviewed and systems put in place to provide back-up for those on holidays or overworked.

Clients will also need to be carefully advised and/or educated. This will mean:

- more detailed retainer letters; and
- explanations of the new philosophy.

How to avoid negligence claims

- Know your client – understand their objectives and manage their expectations.
- Check for and avoid conflicts of interest with your client from the outset.
- Advise clients carefully on funding options and keep an eye on changes in their financial position.
- Follow and believe in good client care practices.
- Identify and flag up in more than one system key dates (and a date two weeks ahead?) – limitation periods, dates for service of the claim, and all important CPR milestones for serving questionnaires and evidence and keep them under careful review.
- Find out about the other party and their solicitors – check on solvency/insurance and again check for conflicts, including whenever a new party is added.
- Adopt a cooperative approach to disputes in the firm, and a settlement culture, treating opponents and others with courtesy, making and responding to offers (with the client's full instructions), and using ADR when appropriate.

As stated in the *Gazette* in May 1999: 'solicitors who cannot comply with the spirit and detail of the Woolf new code of conduct can expect a bumpy ride' – and perhaps more negligence claims?

PART II
Litigation as a project

CHAPTER 6

Project management of a litigation case

Tim Aspinall

WHY WE NEED TO KNOW ABOUT PROJECT MANAGEMENT

A litigation case is like any other project, whether that is a major civil engineering project or a social event like a wedding. Like any other project, it needs to be properly planned and executed so that it is kept under control and finishes on time and on budget to an agreed outcome. That is what project management is all about.

Think of cases that you may have done or been involved in over the years which have gone wrong. Fee earners often refer to these as their nightmare cases, the ones that they leave in a filing cabinet for days or weeks on end. Fee earners find

199

it hard to take cases like this out of the filing cabinet because they are out of control. They might be out of control because the fees are significantly more than anticipated; or because the case has gone down a blind alley and is taking far longer than anticipated; or because the client's expectations of what is going to happen are very different to what, in reality, is likely to happen. Indeed, there are lots of reasons why the case might be out of control. The reasons, however, usually centre on cost, time and outcome. From the client's point of view these are the critical issues in every case and as every managing partner or other complaints handling partner knows, these are the issues clients complain about more than any other.

In fact, although every client potentially wants a unique solution to every problem, all clients want one thing and that is certainty: certainty about what is going to happen, when it is going to happen and how much it is going to cost. These were (amongst others) the problems identified in Lord Woolf's *Access to Justice* Report, in particular the fact that:

- cases under the system have taken too long to be completed;
- the cost of cases was not always proportionate to the amount in dispute;
- solicitors have, before the Woolf Reforms, been unable to change their approach.

Lord Woolf's solution to the problems was to create new rules and in particular to give the responsibility for case management to judges. Of course judges cannot manage cases without the cooperation of the parties and the solicitors. Consequently, the Civil Procedure Rules provided penalties for parties and solicitors who failed to change their approach to litigation.

In practice, therefore, although the judges have responsibility for case management, in the sense that they will make and enforce the timetable, the real responsibility for progressing the case in a proper manner from the beginning to the end will remain with the fee earner; and fee earners who fail to progress their cases and manage them are likely to face financial penalties (costs that they will have to pay) or ultimately claims (from clients whose cases have been struck out or lost because of the fee earner's default).

How can litigators best cope with the new situation they find themselves in? How can they ensure they comply with pre-action protocols, the fast track timetable and multi-track directions? How can they comply within the new financial constraints that are imposed by the CPR or by judges in case management conferences? How can they prevent disputes arising with their own client about whose responsibility it is that a costs order has been made (payable within 14 days) for failing to comply with a direction or losing an interlocutory application?

I believe litigators have to learn skills that help them to progress their cases more effectively, that recognise a litigation case is like any other project that has to be achieved on time, on budget and to an agreed outcome. That is what this part of the book is about: using project management skills to stay in control of our litigation cases; to help us comply with the new rules and the new culture in the post-Woolf period; and to help us to manage our clients' expectations better so that they have far greater certainty about what is going to happen, when it is going to happen and how much it is going to cost.

Project planning should also reduce the risks a solicitors' firm faces when taking on any new client or a new case, particularly in a 'no win no fee' situation.

THE IMPORTANCE OF PROJECT PLANNING IN FAST TRACK AND MULTI-TRACK CASES

Project planning should enable lawyers to manage their caseload effectively in fast track and multi-track cases by helping with the following:

(1) Complying with pre-action protocols by ensuring that the appropriate work is done before issuing proceedings, or, in the case of defendants, by ensuring that appropriate investigations are carried out immediately the letter of claim is received so that an answer can be supplied within three months.

(2) Complying with the fixed timetable in a fast track action: once proceedings are issued in a fast track action the case moves quickly to a conclusion with little opportunity for either side to obtain extensions of time to comply with the CPR. There is no natural break in a case now once proceedings are issued. Project planning will set out all the steps that have to be taken before and after the issue of proceedings. The plan will make sure that the relevant fee earner has the time available to complete the tasks required and that the client is available and aware of what he or she has to do.

(3) Producing a timetable for the conduct of a multi-track action at case conferences: those fee earners who attend case conferences with clearly mapped out timetables are more likely to persuade the court that their analysis of the time and resources required for the project are the right ones. Moreover as the court considers limiting the amount of fees that can be recovered by the successful party, the fees outlined in the project plan become a very important tool. Furthermore, more and more costs decisions are likely to be made by summary assessment with reference to estimates given at the allocation stage or in case management conferences. A failure to invest the appropriate time in

preparing a project plan will almost certainly result in financial loss being suffered.

OVERVIEW

Because every litigation case is no more and no less than any other project it can be managed using project management techniques.

Every litigation case begins with a problem and a client. Our starting point is to find out more about them both. This involves gathering data. Once we have done this we need to evaluate the data and create a project plan. The plan should include a defined project goal, a review of the resources needed to achieve the goal, a budget, an agreed course of action and a review mechanism.

After preparing the plan we need to implement it. This means putting the plan into effect and, just as importantly, monitoring progress against the plan. Of course, things do not always go according to plan, as most litigators know to their cost! Implementation will often, therefore, include a rewrite (sometimes many rewrites) of the project plan to take into account new issues and facts that are discovered. We may need new goals, different resources, a more expensive budget and a different timetable. There is, therefore, a constant refining and adjusting process during the life of the project.

Finally, there is closure of the project. Closure should be easy if we have a well-defined goal because we will know when we have arrived at it. Closure also gives us the opportunity to look back at what has happened, evaluate our own performance and learn from the experience. Ideally, it should also give us the opportunity to sell more work to a delighted client who has seen the project delivered on time, on budget and to the agreed outcome.

BEGINNING: THE CLIENT AND THE PROBLEM

As we have seen the project always begins with a client who has a problem and we need to find out more about both. This involves listening to what the client has to say and obtaining information about the problem itself and about the client's needs and priorities. This sounds easy but isn't.

The biggest obstacle to getting it right is time; the one thing that all fee earners are short of. Take this as a typical example of a meeting with a new client. We arrange to see Mrs Smithers, for that is what we shall call this typical client, in our offices at 10 a.m. At 9.55 a.m. we are told she has arrived. Unfortunately, though, we have been working for the last 45 minutes on another matter that we have been meaning to look at for the last week. Inevitably, it is taking a lot longer than we thought. We really need to finish reading a particular document or the whole morning's work will be lost. We decide therefore to carry on reading as it will only take another 15 minutes and as soon as we have finished we will go and see Mrs Smithers. At 10.05 a.m. we have almost finished the document and the telephone rings. It is another solicitor we have been trying to speak to for three days about settling yet another matter. We really must take the call and then we will go and see Mrs Smithers (we will finish reading the other document later). At 10.20 a.m. we put the telephone down. We have not settled that case and we have not finished the document we started reading at the start of the day. We decide that we have kept Mrs Smithers waiting as long as we dare and we will have to go and see her now. We remember that we made some notes when we spoke to her on the telephone but we can't find them and our secretary is on the phone so we set off for the interview room with a fresh pad of paper and the harassed look of the average litigator.

After saying hello to Mrs Smithers we get straight down to it, as we haven't that much time for pleasantries as our next meeting is at 11 a.m. and we have to drive there! After obtaining some basic details about Mrs Smithers we start to find out more about the problem. Like a lot of clients, though, Mrs Smithers is not particularly focused on the really important facts that we need to know and the interview begins to wander as she tells us how she feels about the whole thing. We get as much detail as we can, draw the meeting to a close and hand the client our card. We say we will be back in touch soon. Rushing back upstairs we put Mrs Smithers' papers to one side and dash off to our next meeting.

I am sure this is not typical of all meetings with new clients, but it is a rare litigator indeed who can say they have never experienced this sort of situation and who always has the right amount of time available at the right time to handle every case. In my experience almost every litigator is under pressure, often crisis managing, and there often just isn't enough time in the day to do everything. Why is this the case? One of the basic problems is that litigators are, on the whole, unable to control the flow of work into their firms (or the speed at which cases settle). Consequently there is a temptation to take on every case that comes through the door because a litigator can never be sure where or when the next job is coming from. I often wonder if there is a fear that all litigators secretly share, namely that all their cases will settle next week/month/year leaving them nothing to do and unable to meet their targets. Perhaps this is unfair but, whatever the reasons, it seems that litigators often have too many cases to handle properly at any one time – and there are inherent dangers in this approach.

Let us look at some of the consequences of the meeting with Mrs Smithers.

Our relationship with her

We are unlikely to have created the best impression. We all know when we are talking to somebody who is harassed and busy and does not appear particularly prepared for the meeting or focused on the subject matter. Think of some conferences that you may have had with counsel or experts when it looked as though counsel or the expert had picked up his instructions and looked at them for the first time as the conference started. We feel slighted by this sort of behaviour (although we may not say anything) and it is likely to result in us not using that counsel or expert again once the case has finished.

If we behave like this to our clients they are likely to have the same sorts of feelings towards us. As we are all ambassadors for our firms that means that Mrs Smithers has a poor impression of the whole firm. Although she may stay with us for this particular matter she is less likely to refer her friends or business colleagues to us and she may not use us again for any other services.

Our understanding of her priorities

We may not have a clear understanding of Mrs Smithers' attitude to the problem. If, of course, we are dealing with a client that we know, whether it is a commercial client or a private client, we should already have a clear understanding of how they approach particular problems and what their priorities are. Every new client, however, has a different need and a different expectation. For some clients, possibly Mrs Smithers, speed is more important than anything else is. This should have an impact on the recommendation we make as to the way in which the case should be run. For other clients speed may be less important and Mrs Smithers may, for example, be willing to spend significantly more time and money on detailed preparation in order to explore every possible angle.

Our knowledge of the case

We may not have obtained important information about the case. There is a temptation when we are in a rush to make assumptions and cut corners. If we miss an important piece of information at the beginning of the case then that is likely to have a serious impact on the decisions that we subsequently make about how the case should proceed. In the most extreme cases it can lead to complaints by the client and even negligence claims.

Furthermore, by allowing insufficient time after the meeting to open the file we are likely to forget some of the detail of the conversation that we have had (not all of which will have been written down or written down legibly in the rush to conclude the interview). Later, when we come back to it and try and evaluate the data and decide what to do next we will almost certainly have to contact the client again. It always looks inefficient asking for more information two or three days after the meeting and if we try and obtain it by writing to our client it is a slow and cumbersome process (compared with the original face to face meeting, or even a telephone conversation).

Financial consequences

The less efficient we are in obtaining information the less profitable we are going to be. Our client may object to paying for our inefficient use of time (and our apparent lack of interest will make this more likely). If we are hoping to recover fees from our opponent they are more likely to object for similar reasons and if the costs are disproportionate to the amount in dispute they are likely to be disallowed. Furthermore, in 'no win no fee' cases there will be serious financial consequences if we have to pull out of a case at a later stage because insufficient information was obtained at the outset.

Benefits of spending time with Mrs Smithers

There are significant benefits, therefore, in making sufficient time for that early meeting with Mrs Smithers. We are likely to:

- have a better relationship with her from the beginning;
- find out more about her approach to the problem;
- discover all the information relevant to the problem; and
- be paid for the time we spend with her at this important meeting.

HOW LONG SHOULD WE SPEND WITH THE CLIENT?

The amount of time that we will need to spend with the client will depend on the nature of the problem and its complexity. Our aim, however, by the end of the meeting, or if it is a more complex problem, at the end of several meetings, should be to have sufficient information to be able to evaluate the problem with the client's needs in mind and plan a way forward. That will involve:

(a) agreeing an achievable and realistic objective with our client;

(b) identifying the resources that will be needed to achieve that objective (in particular the legal team and the time that legal team will need);

(c) assessing the financial cost of achieving the goal and preparing a budget in a form that is acceptable to the client; and

(d) setting out a plan of action with, preferably, a timetable identifying how long each task will take, when it will be completed by and which member of the legal team will be responsible for completing it.

HOW DO WE MAKE SUFFICIENT TIME AVAILABLE?

Work smarter not harder

The simple answer is of course to work smarter, not harder. Have you noticed how when you become busier and busier and the work piles up your time recording actually goes down? Why does this happen? I suspect it is because when we become very busy, in fact overloaded with work, we are constantly having to pick files up and put them down to sort out immediate and urgent problems. We are in fact crisis managing our caseload. Because one crisis is occurring after another with the phone ringing incessantly, constant meetings with clients and court appointments, we just do not have the time to complete our time records. As we all know, if we do not complete our time records as the day, or days, unfold, we are rarely able to remember exactly what we did and when we did it at the end of the day or the end of the week. Time is, therefore, lost. Furthermore, when we crisis manage, we are constantly looking for files as we have to react to a new crisis. The file could be in one of several places and time is wasted finding it and often disrupts other people, such as support staff who might be working on it. All this wasted time is not recorded. Ironically, therefore, the busier litigators become, the less time they record and the less money they recover at the end of the case. Poor time recording also means valuable management information is lost. We need that information if we want to know the profit or loss made on any case. In the future, if fixed fees are introduced in the fast track, this information will be essential.

The prerequisite of successful project management, therefore, is to have a balanced workload that allows us the time to start cases off properly (and of course manage them to a successful conclusion). This is not necessarily an easy thing to achieve. Most of us know intuitively, however, when we are too busy because we inevitably find ourselves in the position that I have described. If that situation starts to happen to us we should stop taking on new cases. Alternatively we should recruit new people who can do those cases for us.

Saying 'no' to new cases

I am sure that all our firms are committed to client care and a quality service. The real test of this commitment, though, is being able to say no to new work when we know that we do not have enough time to take on another case. This is hard to do and frequently the commitment to service quality will be abandoned in favour of another case in the hope that our litigators will be able to juggle their caseload and manage.

Stop juggling

More experienced and successful litigators learn how to deal with the pressure of too many cases by juggling. Great juggling feats are recounted in the pub on a Friday night about how many balls (cases) or flaming torches (cases in crisis) have been kept in the air that week. This has become a status symbol and a measure of success in itself – the litigator as 'Master of the Universe'.

The new Civil Procedure Rules, however, will simply not give litigators the opportunity to juggle caseloads around. In particular, slowing some cases down and speeding others up, to accommodate the lack of available time, will be very difficult because of the new imperative actually to comply with the court timetable! We have, therefore, to be prepared to say no to some cases and clients in the future.

BENEFITS OF SAYING 'NO'

There are many benefits in doing this. Not only are litigators going to have more chance of complying with the CPR there is also, as we have seen, the likelihood of establishing a better client relationship and making more efficient use of the time available to gather relevant information.

There is another huge benefit if we pick and choose the cases we want to take rather than accepting everything that comes our way. By being selective we can pick those clients and those cases which are likely to deliver the greatest profit for our firm. We can also, by being selective, reduce the risk to our firm in relation to 'no win no fee' cases and problem clients.

Many litigators I have spoken to who are overloaded with work say they spend a disproportionate amount of time working on the wrong cases. By this they mean cases where the client (or funding third party) is unwilling or unable to pay for all the work that is being done but where the client is very demanding and is always on the telephone or in the office. Very often these clients are unlikely to provide repeat work in the future.

This leaves the litigators with less time to deal with those cases where clients want more time spent on their cases and are willing to pay for the work that could be done. Very often these clients would be willing to refer more people to the firm. But they do not because the impression they have is that the litigator is too busy. They assume the litigator does not have the time or the desire for more work and they are probably worried that referring another client with a new case will mean that there is even less time for their matter to be dealt with.

HOW DO WE MONITOR THE CASELOAD MORE EFFECTIVELY?

Knowing intuitively that we are too busy is perhaps the least satisfactory way of monitoring our workload and capacity. This is because we are likely to have a problem by the time we realise we are too busy. Although we can stop taking new work we may already be in difficulty in complying with court timetables and suddenly find ourselves facing cost penalties, complaints and even claims as deadlines are missed.

CALCULATING THE OPTIMUM WORKLOAD

Ideally, therefore, we need a more scientific way of monitoring our caseloads and in particular identifying what the optimum caseload is for ourselves and for other litigators in our firms. Modern practice management systems provide us with the tools that we need to achieve this.

These systems enable firms to create templates and work flow charts for particular types of action. For those who have, or acquire, such systems it is possible to work out how long it should take to complete certain types of case. In fact it is possible to work out how long it should take to complete each part of such cases. This is a particularly suitable methodology for more straightforward cases that are sometimes described as commodity cases. These are the sort of cases that will be in the fast track and which make up the vast majority of cases by number in most firms.

Fast track cases

The number of hours to complete such a fast track case will depend on many factors including the type of case, the seniority and experience of the person doing it and the approach the firm has to the conduct of such an action.

Let us take a particular kind of fast track case, say an undefended personal injury action where the injury is straightforward and the special damages limited, and see what the optimum caseload should be. Using our workflow analysis and data from similar cases we have closed over the last 12 months we may conclude that this case should be dealt with by a legal executive. Let us say it should typically take the legal executive 11 hours to complete. We will also need to know over what period of time the case will be finished. Let us say that the average time for completing the matter from the date we are instructed to the date the matter is billed and closed, is 12 months. Finally, let us assume that the legal executive who will do these cases is expected to record 1,100 chargeable hours per annum. Using this information we can build up the optimum case-load for the legal executive doing this sort of work.

The calculation is this:

- number of chargeable hours available in the year divided by the number of hours that should be worked on each case per year equals the optimum caseload.

In this particular example this means:

- 1,100 (chargeable hours per year)/11 (number of hours that should be worked on each case per year) = 100 (optimum caseload).

If we gave the legal executive 100 brand new clients on 1 January each with a case that fits the profile (undefended personal injury actions with straight-forward injuries and simple special damages) then we know that all the cases should be completed by 31 December. The legal executive would have spent 11 hours on each of the 100 files during the course of the year, achieving the chargeable hours goal of 1,100 hours. This is, therefore, the optimum caseload for this particular paralegal.

Of course there will always be some variation from the optimum caseload as life is never quite as simple as statistics suggest. Nevertheless, using these tools it is much more likely that fee earners will have balanced caseloads and be able to recognise when they are reaching capacity before the crisis is on them and it is too late to do anything about it.

WHAT HAPPENS IF THE OPTIMUM CASELOAD IS EXCEEDED?

Using the same example we can see what might happen if the legal executive were given 200 cases on 1 January.

The legal executive could spend 11 hours on each case, as the workflow model requires for best practice. As there are 200 cases, though, it will take 2,200 hours to complete the caseload. As the legal executive is only likely to work 1,100 chargeable hours a year this means that the cases will not, on average, finish for about two years. (It is possible that the legal executive will work more than 1,100 chargeable hours in the year to cope with the pressure, and this would reduce the total time for completing the whole caseload to less than two years. However, working unacceptably long hours is ultimately likely to lead to stress, dissatisfaction, a loss of morale and, finally, resignation; it can also lead to claims against the firm.)

Completing cases over a longer period

Completing cases in two years instead of one is likely to have all sorts of implications for the firm and the client:

(1) If these cases are being dealt with on a conditional or contingent fee basis (as most personal injury actions for claimants will be) then the firm will have to fund those cases for twice as long as necessary. This would have significant cash flow consequences.

(2) Clients may well be disappointed that their case has taken two years to finish particularly if competitor firms are marketing the fact that they can complete simple personal injury actions within one year. This will lead to fewer referrals.

(3) Finally, and perhaps most importantly, these sorts of cases would have to be dealt with in accordance with the pre-action protocol and the fast track rules. It is unlikely that a fee earner who had such a large caseload could comply with the requirements of the protocol and the fast track. This will lead to cost penalties and, possibly, negligence claims if cases are struck out or lost through inadequate preparation at trial.

Cutting corners to achieve deadlines

An alternative approach, therefore, is for the legal executive to cut corners when dealing with the cases (to comply with the pre-action protocol and fast track time limits). This might result in, say, five and a half hours being spent on each of the 200 cases instead of the 11 hours that best practice requires in the workflow analysis.

This would in fact result in the caseload being completed within 1,100 chargeable hours (5.5 hours × 200 cases = 1,100 total hours). That means each case would be finished within one year as, on the face of it, best practice expects. There are, however, serious consequences that are likely to arise in this situation:

(1) The chances of a mistake being made, if each case has been done in half the time it should be, increases dramatically. Personal injury work is high risk in the sense that a significant number of claims arise from it. It is likely, therefore, that mistakes would be made and claims arise that would reduce or wipe out the profit the litigator was expected to make for their caseload.

210

(2) The chances of the client being unhappy are greatly increased, as it is unlikely that the litigator will have spent sufficient time managing the client's expectations and finding out about their needs. This could lead to complaints and damage to the firm's reputation. The firm's reputation is probably its biggest single asset so damaging it causes huge harm to its long term financial position.

(3) The litigator may be placed in a difficult professional position. An offer to settle by the opponent may be unattractive but tempting for the litigator to accept in order to finish the case off.

(4) Due to insufficient preparation and action by the litigator the case may be lost. In a 'no win no fee' case this would have serious financial consequences for the firm.

(5) There is a significant financial consequence if these matters are being charged by the hour. The average bill for each of these 200 files will be half (probably less than half as the legal executive will be so busy that he or she will not record all the time) the size of the bills rendered by the person with the optimum caseload.

BUILDING TEAMS TO COPE WITH EXCESS CASELOADS

It would certainly make a lot more sense if a firm were opening 200 files of this kind to take on a second legal executive to work with the first. If the work were actually being done by a senior fee earner, as is often the case in smaller firms, this would have the double advantage of creating a more leveraged team to do the work. In turn this would allow the more senior person time to develop a more demanding and better paid caseload. Larger teams also allow work to be moved around if one fee earner becomes overloaded, although this can often be a sensitive issue for clients. Introducing the whole team to each client at the start of the case (not necessarily personally but by identifying all the team members in the letter of engagement in a positive and reassuring way) can help.

OPTIMISING COMPLEX CASELOADS

The more complex the work that a fee earner handles the more difficult it is to calculate the optimum number of cases for that person. Nevertheless modern case management systems do allow time data to be gathered for different categories of case and it should be possible to build up averages regarding complex work types if there is sufficient work in each work type area. Fee earners who deal with more complex cases inevitably say that their work is too complicated to be analysed and put into work flow modules with time goals. The facts

211

suggest that more and more work is routine and less and less cutting edge. As such, more and more of it is capable of being deconstructed into work flow patterns (although there will always remain cutting edge work that really is 'one off' as it is so new and/or unusual). The Woolf Reforms also demonstrate a commitment on the part of the rule-makers to simplify procedure and do away with many of the 'tactical' areas of litigation in favour of more routine and less complex approaches.

Inevitably, with more complicated types of work the averages that we uncover will, almost certainly, be less straightforward than for simple cases. Our analysis may well need to break cases down into sub-types and/or into more stages. For example, we may see that for every 10 trade mark infringement cases we open a certain percentage will settle without a fight following a letter before action, another percentage will fight to an interlocutory injunction hearing and then settle, and a further percentage will fight to trial. We should be able to construct work flow patterns for these cases and their different outcomes and calculate how many hours each of those cases/stages will take and over what period.

Let us take some very hypothetical figures to demonstrate the principle. I have ignored team members who would work on the cases and focused on the fee earners who would have day to day conduct of these cases and be responsible for completing many of the tasks in the work flow analysis. Let us say that of every 10 cases being handled by this fee earner:

- *Simple cases*: five cases settle with a letter before action and each take 18 hours of the fee earner's time over three months (30 hours per month; 360 per year);

- *Medium cases*: four cases settle after an interlocutory hearing and each take 60 hours of the fee earner's time over six months (40 hours per month; 480 hours per year);

- *Complex cases*: one case goes to speedy trial and takes 360 hours of the fee earner's time over 12 months (30 hours per month; 360 hours per year).

In the first quarter the fee earner will be committed for 100 hours if the work is spread evenly (or 1,200 hours per annum). In the second quarter, at least five new simple cases or three medium cases will have to be opened to maintain this rate. In the third quarter, four medium cases will have to be opened as well as five simple cases and so on. It is the balance of the different levels of cases that needs to be maintained each month to ensure that the fee earner can cope within the time available. A fluctuation in that balance will have a dramatic effect on the ability of the fee earner to do the work in the time available. The workload would have to be regularly reviewed to ensure that this did not happen or the same sort of problems we saw in the simple personal injury case study will occur.

For more complex work like this, though, a more detailed analysis of how the time is spent during the duration of each case would be desirable. This would help ensure an optimum caseload for the fee earner, not just for the current month, but projected forward for the coming months based on what is likely to happen to each case in the caseload. Moreover, in complex cases a number of fee earners will work on the action and we need to know the time commitment of each fee earner and whether that time is going to be available when it is needed. So exactly how do we prepare the project plan?

CREATING THE PROJECT PLAN

The basis of every project plan

Having balanced our caseload we should know whether we have the time to take on a new client's case. We should, therefore, be able to spend the appropriate amount of time with our new client creating the right impression, finding out more about that client's needs and finding out about that client's problem. Having done this we need to produce a project plan that will enable us to take the case forward.

The project plan will be different in every case. There are, however, some common headings that every plan should include:

(1) Objective: every plan needs a goal. This is a simple statement of what we are hoping to achieve as a result of implementing the plan. The goal should be SMART: i.e. a Specific, Measurable, Attainable and Realistic Target.

(2) Resources: to achieve the goal we need resources. In litigation cases the resources will, generally, be people – fee earners, experts. But they need to be people with the time available at the appropriate moment.

(3) Budget: once we know what resources (people) are needed we should be able to calculate their cost for the time required, look at any other expenses that might be incurred and create a budget for achieving the goal.

(4) Case plans: what are the tasks we need to complete in order to achieve the goal and when and in what order should we undertake each task?

(5) Review mechanism: the project plan needs to be reviewed regularly to monitor performance against what is expected to happen and to amend the project plan accordingly.

The process of creating the project plan is a dynamic one and each of the headings interact with the others. For example, the cost of using counsel will depend on the time that we need counsel for and that will depend on the tasks that counsel will need to complete. The resource issues, budget issues and task lists will, therefore, be inextricably linked together. The process of planning is, in fact, an iterative one, constantly considering and refining the issues until the plan comes together as a whole.

Let us look at the planning process in relation to a simple personal injury action and then a more complex intellectual property action to see how the process works in practice.

THE PROJECT PLAN

Consider the following case study.

Case study 1: the simple personal injury action

We have been consulted by Mr Jonas. He tells us he was involved in a road traffic accident three months ago. He was driving his car. He was stationary at some (red) traffic lights when another vehicle hit him from behind. The driver of the other car admitted he was not paying attention. Mr Jonas took the names of two witnesses who saw what happened. He had some damage to his car which has been repaired for £300 (within his excess). He obtained three quotes from different garages and used the cheapest.

Since the accident Mr Jonas, who says he has previously enjoyed good health, has been to see his GP several times. She has told him he has a mild whiplash and should recover fully in another three months. He is already feeling much better and took no time off work.

Mr Jonas tells us that the other driver's insurer is Sensible Insurer Plc who we have dealt with many times before and who we know are reasonable and businesslike. We agree to act for Mr Jonas under a conditional fee agreement with an uplift of 10 per cent. We know a private GP who we can instruct to prepare a medical report and who will not charge us until the case is settled.

The objective

The temptation for many personal injury litigators in a case like this is to say that they will recover the maximum amount of compensation as quickly as possible with the least cost to the client. (I have experimented by asking litigators this question at various conferences around the country and invariably they give this sort of answer.)

214

There are lots of reasons why litigators want to set objectives in these very general terms:

(1) In part it is because of the way litigators are trained. They are trained in the law. Litigators are not trained to be project managers nor to agree SMART objectives with their clients.

(2) Litigators are, understandably because of the rising numbers of complaints and claims, often defensive about volunteering too much information. There is a general fear that it may be used against them later on.

(3) Litigators are, as we have seen, busy people who often do not have the time to think about what a realistic goal might be or work out when the case is going to settle and how much it will cost. Even if they could it is often more convenient to keep options open so that the caseload can be juggled as new cases come in.

SMART objective

What might a SMART objective be in this case? We have a great deal of information and assuming we are experienced in this type of case we should be able to agree a goal like this:

- obtain compensation from Sensible Insurer Plc of between £1,500 and £1,800 (inclusive of the car repair cost); achieve this within 12 months of the initial meeting without issuing court proceedings; cost to Mr Jonas should be nothing as we expect to recover our fees, including the premium and success fee, from Sensible (assumptions: the medical report confirms what the GP has said; Sensible accept Mr Jonas' account of what happened and no argument about repair costs).

Advantages of the SMART objective

(1) A SMART objective is likely to give the client a great deal of certainty. All clients want certainty about what is going to happen, when it is going to happen and how much it is going to cost. A SMART objective gives that certainty. It also sets out the assumptions behind the objective so that the client will not be taken by surprise if the objectives have to change because new information comes to light.

(2) A SMART objective gives us and the client something to aim for. Each of us knows when we have achieved our goal. There is no temptation, therefore, on either side to prolong the case to try and do that little bit better with the opponent. As soon as we have achieved the goal either

215

through negotiations, a settlement offer or a trial, the matter can be quickly disposed of. This is particularly important in the post-Woolf world as the amount of costs that can be recovered have to be proportionate. Very often the act of squeezing that little extra out of the opponent is disproportionate to the benefit it achieves. A SMART objective therefore should help our client bring the case to a sensible and early conclusion and mean that the fees are more likely to be proportionate to the amount in dispute (and therefore more likely to be paid by the opponent). In turn this is more likely to mean the best net position for our clients.

(3) A SMART objective helps us to place pressure on our opponent to settle at an earlier stage as we know what we want from the litigation. This makes it easier to put forward a CPR Part 36 offer sooner rather than later, or accept such an offer if it is within the range of our SMART objective.

(4) Of course, in a complex action it would be unrealistic to try and agree a SMART objective that sets out the final outcome in the action before all the facts are known. In a complex action, therefore, the SMART objective will be amended and developed as the case proceeds from stage to stage until a final goal can be identified.

The resources

A simple whiplash case would probably need a paralegal (preferably with access to a case management system) who had, say, 11 hours available during the course of the next 12 months to dedicate to the job. We would need to check, therefore, that we had a paralegal with that time available. As we have already seen earlier we should be able to assess this quickly by looking at our paralegal's caseload: if the optimum number of live cases is 100 then if the paralegal has less than this they should have the time. We will also need a more senior lawyer to supervise the work of the paralegal at the moments of highest risk to make sure that a mistake is not made. There should only be a few such moments in a simple whiplash case and we may only need an appropriately experienced solicitor who had one hour available during the course of 12 months. Ideally, the paralegal we have selected would always be supervised by the same solicitor. That solicitor's caseload should be balanced so that he or she always has the time available to supervise the paralegal's 100 cases. (If the solicitor was expected to do 1,000 chargeable hours a year then he or she should be able to supervise 10 paralegals each doing 100 cases (1 hour per case each year × 1,000 cases).) In addition, we will need a doctor. I know that some personal injury practitioners always prefer to use an orthopaedic surgeon whilst others are happy with specialist GPs who have experience in preparing medico-legal reports. Given the need to do reports quickly (for cashflow reasons and because they are likely to fall within the fast track) whichever sort of doctor we prefer we need to be confident they can prepare a report within, say, four weeks of being instructed. It is unlikely that we would need counsel for this particular type of case.

In summary, therefore, the resources are:

- one paralegal with 11 hours of time available in the next 12 months;
- one supervising solicitor with one hour of time available during the next 12 months; and
- one GP able to return the report within four weeks of being instructed.

Budget

The budget is quite easy to plan once we have identified the resource implications and the time required by the fee earners. In our personal injury action the budget is represented by the cost of the paralegal for 11 hours, the supervising solicitor for one hour and the cost of employing the doctor. As this action will be done on a conditional fee basis all monies will be payable at the end. The GP should be asked to defer payment to the end of the action as well. That will only leave the after the event insurance fee to pay. The total cost of the case (on the assumption that the recoverable hourly rate is, say, a blended rate of £120 with a 10 per cent success fee) will be £1,440 plus 10 per cent plus VAT plus the doctor's fee of, say, £200 and the insurance premium of, say, £100. This gives a total budget of £2,161.20.

The case plan

The case plan should set out the various tasks which have to be performed in order to achieve the goal, who they are going to be performed by, how long they will take and, ideally, what each task will cost. We do not want to go into so much detail that the plan becomes confusing. Equally we do not want to give too little detail so that it does not really help us progress the matter quickly from beginning to end.

There are different ways of setting out the case plan. It could be in tabular form or it could be a series of headings. In either event it should set out what is going to happen, who is going to do it, when it is going to happen, how long it is going to take and how much it should cost. Here is one example of how it could be done. In a simple whiplash case, we can see that it takes the case to a conclusion based on certain assumptions. If things develop differently during the implementation phase the plan would need to be revised to take account of the new information.

Table 6.1 The personal injury case plan

Date of action	Task	Person responsible	Estimated time to complete	Estimated costs
1 December	See client and obtain instructions	paralegal	1 hour	£120
2 December	Open file Draft letter of engagement to client including SMART objectives Draft letter to other driver Draft letter to other insurer seeking permission to use GP of our choice Draft letter to own insurer	paralegal	2 hours	£240
3 December	Approve letter of engagement and objectives and choice of doctor All letters sent out	solicitor	30 minutes	£60
23 January	Write to GP as no objection from other insurer	paralegal	30 minutes	£60
30 January	Hear from other insurer saying await detailed letter from us Short letter to client	paralegal	30 minutes	£60
28 February	Receive and read report from doctor Send to client for comments and approval Confirm no specials	paralegal	1 hour	£120
14 March	Draft detailed letter of claim to other side with CPR Part 36 offer of settlement	paralegal	1 hour	£120
15 March	Supervising solicitor approves draft letter and actions proposed and sends to client for approval subject to any comments on medical report	solicitor	15 minutes	£30
16 April	Client approves medical report and draft letters Send letter of claim to other side setting out full circumstances of accident, medical report and CPR Part 36 offer to settle	paralegal	30 minutes	£60
16 June	Write to other side reminding them they have a further four weeks to respond under the terms of the protocol Write to client with copy letter	paralegal	30 minutes	£60

Table 6.1 (*Continued*)

Date of action	Task	Person responsible	Estimated time to complete	Estimated costs
6 July	Letter from other side admitting responsibility and making counterproposal Ring insurer and get them to increase offer	paralegal	2 hours	£240
7 July	Supervising solicitor to approve recommendation to client to accept offer	solicitor	15 minutes	£30
8 July	Ring client and recommend acceptance and obtain client approval	paralegal	30 minutes	£60
10 July	Write to other side confirming acceptance and sending schedule of costs	paralegal	30 minutes	£60
10 August	Receive cheque from other side paying compensation and costs	paralegal	30 minutes	£60
31 August	Report to client, sending compensation and copy bills showing whole amount paid by insurer and advising terms on which file will be closed and papers held	paralegal	30 minutes	£60
TOTAL TIME		paralegal solicitor	11 hours 1 hour	£1,420

This is a reasonably detailed case plan setting out each task that has to be completed. It has the added benefit of being a detailed work flow guide for the paralegal and could be used as a template in a computerised case management system to prompt the paralegal to carry out certain tasks and to seek guidance and approval from the supervising solicitors. These systems prompt the solicitor if tasks have not been carried out by the paralegal within the time required in the case plan or if supervision is not sought. This helps manage the risk associated with doing the work at a lower level.

It is self-evident that the case plan sets out the time it will take to complete the case, who will be involved and how much the case will cost. The objective, the resource implications and the budget cannot therefore be completed without the case plan having been drafted. Nor can the case be allocated to the relevant fee earner until a check has been made on the size of that fee earner's caseload and current time commitments compared with what this case will require. The planning process, therefore, is an iterative and interdependent process.

The planning process also enables us to produce more sophisticated optimisation of workload calculations as we identify specialist sub-types. For example we may find that a case against Not Quite as Sensible Insurers Plc will take on average two more hours of the paralegal's time as the negotiating process is slower and this insurer needs to be reminded to respond more often. A paralegal dealing with Not Quite as Sensible will, therefore, be able to handle fewer cases than the paralegal dealing with Sensible Insurer Plc.

Of course the particular case plan outlined above may not be appropriate for the way that you or your firm work. The figures I have used are indicative only (and easy to use arithmetically). The time it should take a paralegal may be more or less than the 11 hours in any example. A good way of starting the process in a firm is to look back at the last 50 simple personal injury cases completed and see how long each of them took on average. Once this has been done you should have a basic model for a case plan which can then be improved. Alternatively, rôle plays can be organised with the fee earners who do this work to build up a model of best practice (and/or re-engineered practice).

THE CASE PLAN

Now consider this alternative case study.

Case study 2: intellectual property infringement action

We act on behalf of a company (Funchair Ltd) that manufactures a chair that can be placed on any of its sides and still be functional. It has a distinctive design and is marketed under the brand name 'Funchair'. The mark has not been registered. Another company (Phunnyseat Ltd) has come into the market with a similar, but not identical design of chair, sold under the brand name 'Phunnyseat', which has some similarities but may not, on the face of it, cause an association to be made by a customer with our client's product. Our client is very concerned about the competitor's product as it is being sold for 25 per cent of the price of their own and huge interest has been generated amongst buyers for shops that stock these sorts of 'gadget' products. At least two buyers have said they were confused and thought that the competitor product was manufactured by our client company.

Objectives

In a complex case like this it would be foolish to say, categorically, at a first meeting whether or not our client was likely to be successful in obtaining an injunction restraining the competitor from selling their product and using their version of the brand name. For example, there may be complex arguments regarding the ownership of any design right. The design may be one that is commonplace. Their brand name may not be sufficiently similar to ours to cause confusion or association in the minds of customers. There is a temptation, therefore, to say nothing or to say it is impossible to give any advice at all. This is quite a turn off for clients. What we really need to do is break the case down into different stages and agree an objective with the client for first stage and make sure that it fits the SMART criteria.

SMART objective

A SMART objective in this situation, therefore, may finish up looking like this:

- we will carry out an investigation to determine whether or not Funchair Ltd can show they own design rights in the chair, whether or not there are other similar articles in the marketplace that might give rise to a commonplace defence and whether or not customers in the marketplace associate the competitor's product and brand name with ours; we will prepare a report within four weeks answering these questions and setting out what Funchair can do to protect their position against Phunnyseat Ltd for a cost of £5,000–£6,000.

This SMART objective gives our client a great deal of certainty about what is going to happen, when it is going to happen and how much it will cost. Once the report is available and the objective has been achieved then a new objective can be set for the next stage of the project. What that objective will be will depend on the answers to the questions we have set in the original SMART objective. The new SMART objective might, for example, be that we will obtain undertakings from the competitor within four weeks, or apply for an injunction that the competitor shall not infringe our client's design right. Alternatively it may be that our client will decide to leave the competitor alone as the case is not strong enough. Instead the client may wish to focus on improving its internal procedures to ensure that a design right audit trail is maintained with the development of every new product and trade marks are registered to protect them in the future.

Resources

The resource implications in the IP action are significant. In order to carry out the investigation several solicitors might be needed, supervised by a partner. Key individuals at Funchair Ltd will need to be available and we will need to speak to several customers to see if they have been or are likely to become confused between the competitor product and our client's product.

This is a case where counsel is likely to be needed if a settlement cannot be reached with the opponent quickly, so we would need to find out whether a barrister of the right call and the right experience would be available once the data had been gathered and assimilated. This would be a much more intensive project than the personal injury one and more solicitor/paralegal time would need to be available during the initial four week period than during the whole of the personal injury case! If the solicitors and the partner who deals with IP disputes in our firm did not have the right amount of time available within the four week period then they should not take on the project (as a failure to seek an interlocutory injunction within six weeks of discerning the infringement will almost certainly result in the loss of the right).

Budget

Our IP case is likely to have a large budget for the first four-week period. The budget will depend on the time required to carry out the tasks in the project plan. If there is a financial limit set by the client then we may need to moderate our plan to meet our client's financial expectations (or work for a lower margin to try and win the next stage of the case). We would want to agree a payment schedule with our client, ideally I suspect, obtaining a decent amount of money in advance of the work commencing, particularly if this were a new client who we had not worked with before.

The project plan

In our IP case we could produce the plan in the same way as with the personal injury action, in a table. Alternatively we could produce it in more of a report form, which is probably easier in a more complicated case where there is more discretion available for the solicitor/partner in relation to the performance of each task:

Box 6.1 The intellectual property case plan

Obtaining preliminary data

Meeting with client to obtain preliminary information regarding the problem to identify, broadly speaking, what the issues are.
(Day 1)

Partner time: 2 hours @ £200 an hour = £400

Design right investigation

John Smith, solicitor, to interview the third party designer of the chair and obtain all necessary documentary evidence to show when and how the design was created and who owns any design rights by reference to contractual and other supporting documentation. John Smith will also need to interview head of research and development who commissioned the design for further information regarding the circumstances of its commission and to obtain any other relevant documents.

John Smith will explore in the interviews the 'commonplace' defence.
(Days 2–7)

Total time for travelling, interviews, considering documentation and writing up results: 6 hours @ £150 an hour = £900

Investigation of other issues

Freda Jones, solicitor, to interview head of production and head of marketing at Funchair Ltd to consider similarity of other products in the marketplace, our client's reputation and to obtain appropriate documentary evidence including brochures of competitor products.
(Days 2–7)

Total time to conduct interviews, obtain documents and examples and write up results: 6 hours @ £150 an hour = £900

Confusion amongst buyers

Sarah Brown, Legal Executive, to interview the two 'confused' buyers and a sample of other customers provided by head of marketing.
(Days 2–7)

Total time for interviews including travelling and writing up results and having them approved by witnesses: 5 hours @ £100 per hour = £500

Preparation of report

Assimilating all the information obtained by Freda Jones, John Smith and Sarah Brown and writing draft report to answer the questions set out in the objective.
(Days 8–10)

Total partner time: 5 hours @ £200 an hour = £1,000

Follow up work

Obtaining additional information and clarification of facts as required from witnesses interviewed.
(Days 10–11)

Solicitor time: 2 hours at £150 per hour = £300
Legal executive time: 1 hour at £100 per hour = £100

Finalising report and meeting with client

Finalise report with all new information.
(Days 12–13)

Meeting with the managing director of Funchair Ltd to discuss report and agree a way forward.
(Day 15)

Provision for contingency events (unless counsel's opinion needed in which case dates will be put back one week, see below).
Total partner time: 5 hours @ £200 an hour = £1,000

Paralegal

Assimilating documents, providing bundles and copies for clients.
(Days 12–13)

Total time: 4 hours @ £50 per hour = £200

Opinion from counsel

If counsel's opinion is required before the report can be finalised then instructions will need to be sent to counsel and the opinion obtained prior to the report being prepared by the partners. Partner to draft the Instructions and paralegals to prepare necessary documentation.
Total partner time will increase by 2 hours @ £200 = £400
Paralegals' time will increase by 1 hour @ £50 = £50

Can we use a template for a more complex case plan?

In a complex action like this it is less likely that a case plan could be pulled up from the computer that would fit these particular facts. Nevertheless, in any design right case the same sorts of issues are likely to arise and so we could produce a skeleton template which we can build on when we open a new file. This would make project planning in a more complex case easier and the template could be linked to precedent letters and documents and contain notes setting out the experience of others in the firm who have done similar cases. This is when project planning begins to link up with knowledge management. It is, however, true to say that the more complex the case, the more experience the partner brings to the project and the less routine the action becomes. Because of this, premium rates can be charged by the fee earners for this highly complex work.

IMPLEMENTATION

We have spent a lot of time looking at the beginning of an action. The reason for this is simple. *Projects fail because of a lack of proper planning and preparation.* Let us return to the nightmare cases that you may have come across as a litigator. Those cases were nightmares because they were out of control. Very often in cases which are out of control the client's expectation of what is going to happen is very different to the solicitor's expectation. This is when 'a perception gap' arises and the bigger the gap, the greater the cause for concern and the greater likelihood of a complaint and a claim.

Proper preparation and planning at the beginning of the action means these sorts of problems are much less likely to arise once we begin work. Let us consider this in a non-legal context. If we were going to build a house we would not expect to have a short meeting with the builder and for him to start work straightaway. We would expect there to be a great deal of preparation of the issues so that all the problems that might be associated with the project could be thought of. We would expect a thorough survey of the site to see if there were any problems with it such as a propensity to flooding, or contaminated land. We would then expect detailed plans of the building to be prepared so we could see what it will look like and what features it would have. It is likely that we would want to change the design and the layout of the original drafts. We might also amend the design to reflect what we could afford. Only when we were happy with the design and the costs would we want to proceed. At that stage we would sign a formal agreement setting out what was going to be built, by reference to the plans and detailed schedules of works, when it was going to be built by (with penalties for late completion) and how much it was going to cost. The construction of the house could well take less time than the preparation work, as all the problems that might be encountered in the building phase will have been anticipated and resolved. Of course there will be some minor problems but we would review these with the builder and resolve them with any appropriate amendments to the plans. Compare the preparation, planning and organisation of this building project with what often happens in a litigation case.

By planning effectively and properly, the implementation and execution stage of our litigation should go comparatively smoothly. Let us look again at our case studies.

Personal injury case study

It is hard to see what can go significantly wrong with this particular action. We have obtained all the relevant data at the beginning of the case and we know, from our previous experience, how this case is likely to develop. We have obtained our client's agreement to the objectives and to the plan and to the cost. We have allowed reasonable times in the plan for people to respond to letters. So it is highly likely that once we begin work the action will proceed much as expected.

Nevertheless the key to successful implementation is to monitor what actually happens against what should happen according to the plan on a regular basis. If we look at our original plan there is in fact no review process. When should that review process take place? A review could take place every time a task is completed to see whether or not it was on time and on budget. Alternatively, or additionally, a review could take place every 28 days to see what was happening. The review could be carried out by the paralegal responsible for addressing the case or by the partner who is supervising it. It is probably as well for both people to be involved in reviews at different times.

If, during the review, it becomes clear that matters are not proceeding as quickly as expected and dates have to be put back, then this needs to be communicated to the client immediately with a clear explanation and with a new timetable so that everybody knows what the new plan is. Of course if this happens several times without any good explanation being offered, it is likely that the client will become dissatisfied and so it would be prudent to keep a careful note as the project progresses of why dates have had to be rescheduled.

A review might draw attention to a new piece of information that requires us to re-evaluate the objective associated with the project. In our personal injury case, for example, a report from a doctor which says that the client will not recover for three years would have a profound effect on the objectives, the resources, the budget and the plan itself. Equally a letter from our reasonable insurer denying liability on the grounds that their insured has a completely different version of events which is supported by an independent witness, would also cause our case to be thrown into some confusion. This sort of information is so significant that a meeting with the client is obviously called for and will result in a completely new project plan being produced or, possibly, the case being abandoned altogether. The client will, however, be part of this process of re-evaluation and should have little cause for complaint or concern because the original objectives were based on certain assumptions which were spelt out in the original project plan and which have now been challenged.

The intellectual property case

The reviews that would be carried out during the initial four weeks that the project plan comprises would probably be of a very different kind to the personal injury action. It is unlikely that these reviews will involve the managing director of the client company (until the report has been completed). In this sense the case plan has taken us up to the review point with the client. Nevertheless there may be reviews that take place within the internal project team. For example John Smith, Freda Jones and Sarah Brown will probably need to keep each other informed of exactly what information they are obtaining as they are interviewing witnesses and obtaining documents. This is because information or documentation obtained by one of them may well help the others in their tasks. The partner may also want to keep in touch with all of them on a daily basis. Review meetings could be scheduled, therefore, for 6 p.m. every evening when the internal project team could come together for 15 minutes or so just to touch base and to exchange any relevant or important information or highlight any significant documents that the others might wish to read.

Indeed, on a large-scale piece of litigation, the project plan must include regular and frequent communication between all project team members so that the team is working together in a coordinated and businesslike way. Where third parties, such as experts or counsel or investigators, are used they should be invited to attend regular review meetings as well as they are part of the project team.

In the intellectual property case it is unlikely that things will go wrong during the investigative stage but it is possible that information will be obtained that is unhelpful to the client's position. Nevertheless it is far better that this information is obtained in this structured way at the beginning of the action and reviewed in the report that is prepared by the partner prior to any further work and cost being incurred. Further, the original SMART objective warned the client that the report would only produce recommendations for the fee. So whilst the client may be disappointed with a recommendation that no further action should be taken, the client should be satisfied that the project has been completed, on time, on budget and to the agreed outcome.

CLOSURE

Closure should be easy if there has been effective project planning, effective implementation and review of the plan and client involvement in the process. Our objective should always be SMART. As a SMART objective is one that is realistic and achievable our client's expectations should be realised. Of course, certain clients are gamblers and insist on objectives which are inherently riskier and which may not, therefore, be obtained. In such a case we should have factored that into the objective and made it clear that there is a real risk that the goal may not be achieved. In those circumstances, even the best managed project may well not deliver the preferred outcome but the blow should be softened if the client's expectations have been moderated by a carefully worded objective.

Closure in most cases, however, is relatively straightforward. Because the objective is SMART, we know when we have achieved it. That is the time to conclude the action and declare a win. Winning will be different in each circumstance but as long as it falls within the parameters agreed with the client and set out in the project plan objectives then it is a clear win for you and your client.

The danger in all projects is that as the time for closure approaches, the client wants to do a bit better because things appear to be going well. The solicitor, anxious to please the client, agrees to carry on. So even though the objective has been attained the case has still not been finished. The difficulty that arises here is, when do we now finish? In a case with a comparatively small amount of money at stake, will the cost of trying to squeeze that little bit extra out of the opponents make the total costs disproportionate to the amount in dispute and, therefore, irrecoverable from the opponent (if the opponent has to pay) or from your own client (if he or she has to pay)?

Moreover, when acting on a conditional fee it seems to me to be extremely dangerous to allow the case to continue once the agreed objective has been obtained, because if a new objective is set that is less realistic and attainable (or even worse, no new objective is set) it is possible that the conditions in the conditional fee agreement will never be attained and you will never be paid.

If you do decide to carry on with the case at the client's request to try and obtain a better deal than that which was previously in the agreed objectives then do make sure that new objectives and a new project plan are completed so that there is certainty as to what is going to happen next, when it is going to happen and what the outcome should be.

SUMMARY

It is not enough just to be a good technical lawyer. To succeed in the modern world of civil litigation we also need to be good project managers (and have good interpersonal skills to communicate effectively with our clients).

We have looked at a whole range of issues in this chapter. Some firms may have begun to implement changes along the lines suggested already; others may be further behind. Whichever position you are in do remember that implementing change of this kind requires determination and persistence. There are no instant solutions and even if you understand what needs to be done, it will be necessary to persuade others in the team as well. Furthermore, as with all change it requires an investment of time to make things happen. Given that we are all too busy anyway this extra time can be hard to find. My recommendations would be:

(1) Do not be too ambitious too quickly. Implement change one step at a time and do not try to do everything at once. Short term goals not only make the process of change seem more manageable but also provide immediate benefits. This can be very motivating to a team and help them invest their time in the next stages of change.

(2) Win over the team so that they 'buy into' what you are trying to achieve. Discuss things with them, involve them in decisions and make them feel part of the solution. This includes support staff as well as fee earners.

(3) Do not be disheartened by failure. To succeed we also have to be prepared to fail because when we implement new ideas some will not work first time around. Accept this from the start.

(4) Measure progress in implementing changes. It is easy to forget where you started from and this can lead to those involved becoming disillusioned with the pace of change. Be sure to keep a record of what has been achieved and publish this.

(5) Be brave. Saying no to new work is difficult to do. So is recruiting more staff to optimise caseloads. So is reducing your own caseload.

(6) Be confident about the value of proper planning and preparation and others (including clients) will learn to value it as well.

Above all, welcome change. Without new challenges our work can become mundane and we can become stale.

229

I am sure that all those who see the benefits of project management will find the time and be determined to make the necessary changes to working practices. I am also sure that these changes will bring success and deliver better results, on time and on budget to happier clients.

CHAPTER 7

Costs and financing

David Marshall and Sarah Ahmed

Introduction: greater opportunities, greater risk
Different funding options
Advising about the different funding options
Maximising recovery from the losing party
Conclusion

INTRODUCTION: GREATER OPPORTUNITIES, GREATER RISK

Traditional funding

Dispute resolution is a complex business. Despite the long overdue simplification of both litigation procedure and the language of the law, it usually requires the application of professional judgement and the exercise of risk and project management skills. Such skills have a price and, traditionally, litigation has been costed on a time and expenses basis.

The price combined with the indemnity principle have been obstacles impeding access to justice. The indemnity principle has inhibited solicitors from taking on a case for free or at discounted rates in the hope of recovering their full fees from the other side if successful.

The new legal landscape

The new Civil Procedure Rules (CPR):

The CPR seek to lower the price of litigation and give more certainty about cost levels. In response to the burgeoning level of complaints about solicitors' cost estimates in litigation the CPR impose on solicitors much stricter duties to advise clients and the court about costs. This, combined with fixed trial fees in fast track cases, the concept of proportionality and summary assessments, potentially restricts solicitors' ability to recover costs which actually reflect the amount of time spent. An extension of fixed costs to all stages of fast track litigation is awaited.

The CPR's 'carrot and stick' approach to the resolution of disputes to secure early settlements also seeks to minimise legal costs. Parties are encouraged to put their cards on the table before issue of legal proceedings through pre-action protocols and to consider the use of ADR. The court is also empowered to stay proceedings for ADR. There are adverse cost consequences for not exploring early settlement through negotiation, ADR and ultimately, a CPR Part 36 offer to settle.

The Access to Justice Act 1999 (AJA):

The AJA builds on the Courts and Legal Services Act 1990 which introduced the concept of (legal) conditional fee agreements ('CFAs'). The AJA explicitly acknowledges the different variants of CFAs (see below) and provides for the successful party to recover success fees (and any related after the event insurance premium subject to assessment). The application of the indemnity principle has been modified accordingly as has Solicitors' Practice Rule 8 which allows fee arrangements which are permitted by statute or common law.

The stakeholder society is a key feature of New Labour policy and its impact in a legal context is reflected in the encouragement, through the AJA, of risk-sharing funding options as between solicitor and client. Indeed, the withdrawal of legal aid for many types of litigation and its replacement with CFAs means that solicitors (and insurers) are now stakeholders in the litigation process.

Faced with these changes, it is perhaps natural for solicitors to concentrate upon the real or imagined risks arising out of the use of these various funding options. This is of course important and we deal with the risks (and there are many) fully below. However, this new world is also a world of opportunities. Many of the artificial rules governing the way in which solicitors can charge their clients and recover costs from the losing side in cases they win have been abolished or severely curtailed.

The combination of CFAs and after the event insurance may well open up the courts to a new breed of litigant from 'middle England' whom many commentators consider to have been previously dispossessed from the legal process (the famous 'MINELAs, those of 'middle income not eligible for legal aid'). Therefore, although solicitors are required to take on new degrees of risk there are also business opportunities for expansion. It is essential that solicitors understand the basis on which legal services can be paid for in this new world.

Navigating the new legal landscape

Solicitors need to know:

- what the different funding options are;
- how to choose the best option for any particular case; and
- how to maximise recovery of those costs from the losing party.

Because insurance underpins many of the new funding arrangements, solicitors need to understand the underlying insurance law.

Choosing the best option now needs to take into account not just the client's risk, but also that of the solicitor and the insurer. As stakeholders in the litigation process through CFAs, solicitors need to develop the skills to manage their own financial risk and balance it with the needs of individual clients and the demands of the market generally.

The purpose of this chapter is to:

- outline the different funding options now available to clients;
- examine the risks attached to the various funding options; and
- summarise the rules for recovery of costs from the client and the other side.

Explaining each of the funding options could itself occupy a whole book. This chapter aims to give an outline description of the options, together with pointers about their respective pros and cons.

DIFFERENT FUNDING OPTIONS

Introduction

A plethora of different payment options are now available for solicitors to offer to their clients. Some of these are traditional, such as the hourly rate plus disbursements (in effect, a 'time and materials' basis). Some are a legitimisation of widespread previous unlawful practices, such as CFAs replacing the 'speccing' of cases. Some are entirely new, such as some of the insurance products discussed below.

The various payment options dealt with in this chapter are as follows:

- full hourly rates plus expenses;
- fixed/capped fees;

- contingency fees;
- legal expenses insurance (LEI) (before the event);
- legal expenses insurance (AEI) (after the event);
- CFAs with success fee ('no win no legal fee');
- CFAs ('no win lower legal fee' or 'no win fixed legal fee');
- CFAs without any success fee (i.e. payment at normal rate);
- legal aid.

The options

Full hourly rates plus expenses (the privately paying client)

Traditionally, the privately paying client has paid for work as it is done. The solicitor agrees to take on the case for the client and will deliver bills for the work done on the basis of an hourly rate for the solicitor's fees and by passing on to the client out-of-pocket expenses at cost. Even this method of payment has not been unaffected by recent changes to the legal landscape.

First, for reasons both of enforceability against the client and recovery of costs by the client from the opponent, it has become increasingly important for the terms of the private retainer to be written down expressly and clearly. It may seem obvious common sense that a solicitor should ensure that his agreement with the client is in writing and clearly expressed. However, until recent years many cases were dealt with on the basis that the solicitor would do the work and afterwards (or on an interim basis) render a bill. The solicitor would expect the client to pay without question, and/or would anticipate recovering the costs or a proportion of them from the other side if and when the case was won. Doing so, without agreeing with the client in advance the basis of the charges, was of course unacceptable and poor practice.

The profession has got its act together with increasing detailed guidance in respect of costs information to be given to clients. This has now been further expanded and codified in the new Solicitors Cost and Information Code 1999 (see below).

Much of the litigation which was previously funded by privately paying clients paying whilst the work is being done will continue to be dealt with on the basis of hourly rates plus expenses. A change permeating this marketplace is a move towards using an hourly rate which is inclusive of any 'mark-up'. Traditionally, solicitors have presented their charging structures to clients on the basis of 'expense' and 'mark-up'. This was on the basis of a standard mark-up on expense of 50 per cent (but with a higher mark-up in the case of more complex cases). This reflected the old method of recovery of costs 'between the parties' whereby a full bill for detailed assessment would include the expense rate (the 'A' rate) and the mark-up for care and conduct (the 'B' rate). The standard 50 per cent mark-up reflected the assumed mix of a solicitor's costs reflecting one-third salary, one-third other expenses and one-third profit.

In the modern world, a variable element for care and conduct as between solicitor and client (to be determined at the end of the case) is subject to criticism (and possible striking out as an unfair contract term: see the Unfair Contract Terms Act 1977 and the Unfair Terms in Consumer Contracts Regulations 1994, SI 1994/3159). It is impossible for the client to know at the outset the rate for the work that the solicitor is doing if the retainer letter is expressed in this fashion. If, however, the mark-up is fixed (whether at 50 per cent or otherwise), what is the point of splitting the rate rather than calculating the total rate inclusive of mark-up?

It has become more common for most solicitors to express their agreement with the client in the retainer letter on the basis of an hourly rate inclusive of mark-up for care and conduct. This practice is now preferred by the new costs and information code. It has also been recognised by the courts in respect of assessment of costs 'between the parties'. Bills under the CPR are expected to include a single rate for each grade of fee-earner rather than an 'A' (expense) rate and a 'B' (care and conduct) rate as previously used. It is submitted that in a short period of time the old 'A' and 'B' rates and all the descriptions of 'care and conduct' will be a thing of the past.

Thus it is essential that solicitors consider at the outset what is the right rate for that job. This rate must include any additional element of mark-up for care and conduct that the solicitor would have been seeking to charge under the old regime. It follows that a solicitor's charges for routine litigation may, for example, be £150 per hour plus VAT and expenses, reflecting an old 'A' rate of £100 per hour and a 'B' rate for care and conduct of 50 per cent. If the case will require exceptional speed or is of exceptional complexity, then this rate might be increased by the solicitor to, say, £200 per hour, reflecting an old 'A' rate of £100 per hour with a 100 per cent mark-up for care and conduct for an exceptional case. If 'A' and 'B' rates disappear, it is essential that the initial hourly charge-out rate does reflect the complexity of the case. As a matter of good practice this has to be clear and agreed up-front with the client.

There are many pitfalls with regard to the delivery of bills under the old regime which continue into the new regime. Some of these are dealt with below. However, details such as whether the bill is an interim or final bill, whether it has been signed by a partner in the firm and so on still apply and must be considered carefully whenever bills are delivered and whenever the retainer letters are drafted. (See *The Guide to the Professional Conduct of Solicitors 1999*, published by the Law Society.)

Fixed/capped fees

The agreement of fixed fees (perhaps for each stage of the case) entitles a solicitor to charge a set amount for work done, irrespective of how much time has been spent on the matter. Capped fees preclude the solicitor from charging fees in excess of the cap. Fees within the cap will be charged by reference to hourly rates.

Proper, detailed analysis of a bulk of cases of a similar sort might provide the basis for the solicitor accurately to fix or cap fees which more or less reflect time spent and normal hourly rates. However, there is scope for fixed fees in particular either to be unfair to the client or unfair to the solicitor.

Solicitors, like any other trade or profession facing a project of uncertain size, length and complexity, have always been wary of agreeing fixed or capped fees with their clients. These have become commonplace in simple non-contentious transactions such as residential conveyancing. However in litigation, resistance to fixed fees has continued. There are two reasons for this. One is practical and the other is obscurely technical.

The practical reason is that litigation is inherently uncertain and a promise to take a case for a fixed fee can carry dangers for the solicitor. There has been a great deal of public pressure (from public bodies such as the Legal Aid Board and the Government) for fixed fees. Indeed, Lord Woolf in his Interim and Final Reports, *Access to Justice*, has stressed the need for the costs of litigation to be more certain, which in his view requires fixing fees to proportionate levels. However, there has been little progress in actually assessing how fixed fees should be determined.

The Lord Chancellor did commission research and then issue a consultation paper, *Fixed Costs in the Fast Track*, dealing with proposals for fixed fees for a solicitor's preparation work in the fast track. This was deferred until after the fast track procedures had been up and running and could be evaluated, partly because of the difficulty in assessing what the fixed fee should be. However, in a further consultation paper, *Controlling Costs*, the Lord Chancellor's Department has indicated that it will be revisiting these issues.

It is important to remember that fixed fees are easier to implement and to police for 'between the parties' costs and for costs paid by a public body such as the Legal Aid Board (from 1 April 2000, the Legal Services Commission). Most public proposals for fixed fees relate to this. The solicitor must retain the right as a matter of contract in a free market to agree whatever rate he chooses with his client. The fact that clients may decide to negotiate a fixed solicitor and client fee based on any fixed 'between the parties' fee does not derogate from this point of principle. Many commentators and legislators seem, however, to have misunderstood this distinction.

The second reason why solicitors have been reluctant in litigation matters to agree fixed fees with their clients is the obscure technical point of the 'indemnity principle' (dealt with more fully below). Up to now, a solicitor has not been able to recover from the other side more than he has agreed with his client that he should be paid for the work. If, therefore, the solicitor had agreed a fixed fee with his client, he would not be able to recover a full hourly rate from the other side. It is, however, now likely that the indemnity principle itself will be abolished (see the Government's conclusions following consultation on *Collective Conditional Fee Agreements* (September 2000)).

Until it is abolished, solicitors will remain reluctant to agree with their clients to charge a fixed amount if this will mean that they cannot seek to recover the full time expended from the losing party in the litigation. However, as will be seen below, it is possible to combine private fee paying agreements, discounted rates or fixed fees with a CFA. This will have the effect of allowing a solicitor to agree with a client a fixed fee in the case of a loss, but a full hourly rate if the case succeeds.

Contingency fees

English law has long frowned on 'contingency fees' for litigation work. A contingency fee is *any* payment that is contingent upon the result. This definition therefore embraces:

- percentage cuts of the damages won (American-style);
- uplifts on normal costs if the case is won;
- normal costs only if the case is won; and
- lower costs only if the case is lost.

Solicitors' Practice Rule 18(2) defines a contingency fee as meaning 'any sum (whether fixed or calculated either as a percentage of the proceeds or otherwise howsoever) payable only in the event of success in the prosecution of any action, suit or other contentious proceeding'.

It has been argued that contingency fees are not prohibited for work done before court proceedings are commenced, as they do not relate to 'the prosecution of any action, suit or other contentious proceeding'. However, the AJA has also widened the statutory definition of 'proceedings' to catch pre-proceedings work.

CFAs are a statutory exception to the prohibition on contingency fees to litigation. CFAs must comply strictly with the statutory requirements otherwise the agreement with the client will be an unlawful contingency fee agreement.

It had been thought that the common law had also developed to enable fees to be charged contingent upon the result, but without allowing any 'success fee' (see *Thai Trading Co.* v. *Taylor* [1998] QB 781). However, the Court of Appeal in *Awwad v. Geraghty & Co.* ([2000] 1 All ER 608) has overturned this and ruled that contingency fees in litigation remain unlawful save as sanctioned by statute. Although this area of law is subject to possible further twists and turns, it is submitted that the only safe mechanism for both pre-proceedings and post-proceedings litigation is now a lawful CFA complying with the requirements of the Courts and Legal Services Act 1990 and the AJA.

LEI (pre-purchased)

All solicitors must check with their client whether they have pre-purchased (or 'before the event') LEI. Many clients do not know that they have purchased this cover as it may be an 'add-on' to household insurance or motor insurance policies.

Such policies usually operate by way of indemnity whereby the solicitor acts on a normal hourly fee paying basis for his client, but that client is indemnified by the legal expenses insurer. However, because the legal expenses insurer is paying the bills, there is a third party in the solicitor/client relationship. Indeed, that third party often seeks to influence that relationship even to the extent of suggesting or directing the client to its own panel of solicitors. This can be a tricky relationship to manage and some of the risks are set out below.

However, a growth in the market of pre-purchased LEI should be a business opportunity for solicitors' firms as these policies are an alternative avenue to access to justice, particularly for middle income clients. These people may have been effectively excluded from the justice system. It remains to be seen whether the before the event pre-purchased LEI market takes off so that most of the population is covered by such a policy, as the authors believe to be the case in other European jurisdictions such as Germany. Alternatively, it may be that the introduction of conditional fees will operate to restrict the growth of this market. Only time will tell.

LEI (after the event)

Strictly speaking, after the event insurance is not usually a method of paying for legal services. Most after the event insurance policies are purchased in combination with a client paying privately on an hourly rate basis or in conjunction with a CFA. In other words, the after the event insurance policy simply covers the client's liability to pay the other side's costs if the case is lost. Some of these policies do cover the client's own disbursements and occasionally counsel's fees.

A hybrid form of agreement is that such as is provided by 'LawAssist' from Greystoke. This covers the client's own solicitor's costs and disbursements as well as the other side's costs and disbursements, subject to the overall level of indemnity. Under this agreement, the client pays a more substantial premium, but does not have to pay a success fee if the case is successful as the solicitor is acting on a normal hourly basis underwritten by the policy.

Some new products seek to roll up the premium as an insured disbursement so that that too is only paid out at the end of the case when the case is won.

Many of these products are new and all have their own strengths and weaknesses. Some will be appropriate for some clients, but not for others. Some of the risks are set out below. However, once again it should be stressed that solicitors must also view these as opportunities. The variety of products that are available may increase the number of clients in a position to litigate to enforce their rights or to defend themselves in civil proceedings. Provided the solicitor is aware of the multitude of products he will be well placed to take advantage of this. The new world carries risks and is subject to change, but this should not be allowed to paralyse action.

The AJA has provided that in principle these AEI premiums should be recovered as costs from an unsuccessful opponent. It is likely to be difficult for the court to assess whether the premium is reasonable and it is likely that there will have to be a series of cases of court decisions to establish the principles. One issue is that there is no real consumer market to set premiums if premiums are recoverable and payable by the other side. This is particularly so if the payment of the premium to the insurer is deferred to the end of the case and is itself insured so is not paid at all if the case is lost. The premium may also consist of numerous elements, not all of which are likely to be recoverable. For example, marketing costs, commissions and other insurance may all be rolled up in one sum and bear little relationship to the sum actually to be paid to underwriters for providing cover. The Costs Practice Direction (to CPR Parts 43–48, PD 11.10) does, however, give some guidance for policies covering both sides' costs – the premium should be compared with the sum of a success fee and AEI premium for opponent's costs only in a comparable case.[11]

CFAs ('No win, no legal fee')

The Courts and Legal Services Act 1990 s.58 was not brought into force until 1995 (see the Conditional Fee Agreements Regulations 1995, SI 1995/1675). Until then, it was unlawful for a solicitor to agree to act in litigation for a client on the basis that the solicitor would only be paid on condition that the case was won. Indeed, 'maintenance' of actions and 'champerty' have been criminal offences. Although the crime was abolished in the 1960s, any such agreement remained unenforceable at law.

The principle also applied to charging a higher fee if the case was won than if it was lost. In *Aratra Potato Co. Ltd* v. *Taylor Joynson Garrett* ([1995] 4 All ER 695), a law firm was unable to recover the balance of its fees from the client on the basis that they had entered into an unlawful contingency agreement.

From 1995, solicitors were for the first time in litigation cases allowed to agree not to charge their clients unless certain specified conditions were met. However, the maximum increase on solicitors' normal solicitor and client costs ('the success fee') was limited to 100 per cent (in other words, the solicitor could charge up to double his costs) and CFAs were limited to personal injury proceedings. The scope of CFAs was in 1998 extended to all civil litigation under the Conditional Fee Agreements Order 1998, SI 1998/1860, although they remained unlawful for matrimonial and criminal proceedings.

The principle behind the introduction of success fees in CFAs was that solicitors should be allowed to charge extra fees in cases they won:

(a) to compensate for the risk that they would get paid nothing if the case was lost ('the risk element'); and

(b) as a subsidy to cover the loss of cashflow from being unable to deliver interim bills on account of costs (and/or disbursements) during the lifetime of the case ('the subsidy element').

However, the legislation does not anywhere set out these principles clearly. Some in the profession have viewed the risks as being such as to justify an across the board charge of a 100 per cent uplift on their usual costs even though personal injury cases have historically been very likely to succeed. However, the Law Society's model agreement for conditional fees (which according to Stella Yarrow (*The Price of Success* (Policy Studies Institute, 1999)) has been almost universally adopted by solicitors) states that the success fee reflects the risk that the solicitor is running that fees will not be earned if the case does not succeed and the absence of payments on account.

The legislation does not limit the amount of the success fee by reference to the amount of damages (a 'cap'). A client could win the case but recover nothing because all of the winnings might be taken to pay the success fee. The client might even face a bill for any excess. To mitigate these problems, the Law Society proposed a voluntary cap on the success fee of 25 per cent of the damages.

Between 1995 and 1 April 2000, the profession has almost universally adopted the 25 per cent cap so that the success fee charged to the client did not exceed 25 per cent of the damages won (see Stella Yarrow, *The Price of Success*). This would in most personal injury cases mitigate the effect of charging the maximum success fee in simple cases. It is, however, submitted that charging the maximum success fee of 100 per cent in all cases would lead to a likely reduction on a solicitor and client assessment and possible investigation by the Office for Supervision of Solicitors (OSS) for over-charging. If a case is 90 per cent likely to win, but the success fee is 100 per cent, we cannot see how that could be justified, even with the *ex post facto* reduction by the operation of the 25 per cent cap on damages.

There has been no case of a client taking a solicitor to a detailed assessment of the success fee of which we are aware. However, this may to some extent reflect the difficulties that clients have in understanding how CFAs work and in particular the interrelationship between the success fee percentage and the 25 per cent cap on damages.

The AJA has provided that, subject to rules of court, success fees (and indeed any premiums for after the event insurance – see below) should be paid by the loser in the litigation along with other legal costs (Courts and Legal Services Act 1990 s.58A (6) and (7), as amended by AJA s.27 (1)). Before the implementation of the AJA, the Courts and Legal Services Act 1990 made it clear that the loser paid only normal 'between the parties' costs and any success fee came out of the winning client's damages. After implementation of the AJA, the client should be in a position to retain most of the damages and have both costs and success fees paid by the losing party. The losing party is likely to have a keener interest in a detailed assessment and reduction of unreasonable success fees, particularly as most will be repeat litigation players such as insurance companies.

The new Conditional Fee Agreements Regulations 2000, SI 2000/692, governing this distinguish between the risk element and the subsidy element, which together comprise the success fee. They must be separately identified in the conditional fee agreement. Only the risk element can be recovered from the opponent. Further, in effect, the solicitor is barred by the 2000 Regulations from charging the client any part of the risk element which is not recovered from the other side, unless the court gives its permission to do so. However, the subsidy element of the success fee is not to be paid by the opponent and can only be charged to the client after the case is won. Calculation of the subsidy element of the success fee can be problematic. There is, of course, no obligation on the solicitor to charge anything for the subsidy element and time will tell as to whether market forces will allow it to be applied routinely.

The principle of 'proportionality' does not apply to the detailed assessment of success fees 'between the parties' (see Practice Direction to CPR Parts 43–48, PD11.9). The court will, however, consider the availability of other funding arrangements (e.g. pre-purchased LEI (see Practice Direction to CPR Parts 43–48, PD11.8)) to the client (as, if used, these would not have given rise to any 'additional liability' on the losing party to pay the success fee).

After 1 April 2000, the Law Society model agreement no longer includes the cap on the success fee to 25 per cent of the damages. The point of the cap was to protect an excessive amount of the client's damages from being eaten up by the success fee. The recoverability of the risk element of the success fee from the opponent means that danger is unlikely to occur so the need for a cap is obviated.

At the time of writing, all CFAs have to be conducted on an individual case-by-case basis with a separate CFA which complies with the AJA and subordinate legislation for each case. However, regulations to permit 'collective conditional fee agreements' ('CCFAs') will be brought in. These will allow a single master agreement (e.g. between a trade union and its solicitors) to be signed with the specific details for individual cases (e.g. the success fee) to be scheduled. This will simplify procedure and may be of benefit to insurers and commercial clients as well as trade unions and their members.

CFA ('No win, lower legal fee or no win, fixed legal fee')

CFAs are traditionally known as 'no win, no fee' or 'no win, no legal fee' agreements. In the personal injury field this has been on the basis that clients cannot or will not pay any money to their solicitor unless the case is won, damages have been recovered and a costs order obtained against the (insured) losing party.

However, neither the Courts and Legal Services Act 1990 nor the AJA make it a requirement that if the case is lost the solicitor charges nothing. The wording in the legislation relates to payment in 'specified circumstances' rather than 'success' as such. It is the Law Society's model agreement for personal injury cases which has provided that if the case is lost the client pays nothing and if the case is won the client pays the full rate, with or without a success fee on top.

However, these arrangements may not be appropriate for clients or for solicitors in all types of proceedings. In particular, it would seem that commercial clients and their solicitors may be attracted by agreements providing for:

(a) a lower fee (or fixed fees) if the case is lost;
(b) full rates (which should largely be recoverable from the other side) and a success fee if the case is won.

The solicitor is running less of a risk than a solicitor who takes cases on a 'no win, no legal fee' basis as he knows that he will be paid something whatever the result of the case. There will also be some cashflow assistance to the solicitor as interim bills can be delivered (even though at a reduced rate). It may well be that these arrangements are used to cover the costs of dealing with the work as some sort of 'insurance policy' for the solicitor's firm against a total loss in difficult and complex cases.

However, it cannot be reasonable to charge the same level of success fee in a 'no win, lower fee' arrangement as the risk that the solicitor is running is lower than in a 'no win, no legal fee' arrangement. The amount that the solicitor is actually receiving in fees whatever the result must be taken into account when calculating the level of uplift the lawyer seeks to obtain if the case is successful.

'No win, fixed legal fee' might be particularly attractive to clients who need to budget for the cost of the litigation precisely. The solicitor might be reluctant to take on the case on a pure fixed fee basis (because such fees might well be lower than the time that is actually spent would justify and which would otherwise be recoverable from the other side at the end of the case). However, until it is abolished, care must be taken not to otherwise offend the indemnity principle especially where the bill is looked at on an item by item basis on detailed assessment (see *General of Berne Insurance Co. Ltd* v. *Jardine Reinsurance Management Ltd* [1998] 1 WLR 1231).

It is of course important fully and clearly to explain these arrangements to the client. It may well be a much more suitable arrangement for sophisticated commercial clients than for individual clients unless great care is taken to explain the potential costs liability to the client in advance.

CFAs (without success fees)

This form of CFA provides that the solicitor's fee is contingent on the result in that the solicitor will charge nothing (or possibly a lower fee, see above) if the case is lost, but their normal fee (with no uplift or success fee) if the case is won.

This arrangement (known in the profession as 'speccing') was unlawful, but not uncommon, before the decision in *Thai Trading Co.* v. *Taylor* ([1998 QB 781). In that case, Mr Taylor, a solicitor, acted for his wife in a dispute arising out of the purchase of some furniture. When Mrs Taylor brought proceedings against the company, unsurprisingly Mr Taylor acted without any written retainer from his wife. It was accepted that this work was done on the basis that if the case had been lost, Mr Taylor would not have sought a fee from his wife. However, he wished to circumvent the operation of the indemnity principle so that on winning the case he was entitled to recover his normal costs. The Court of Appeal in *Thai Trading* held that public policy had moved on and that this was now a lawful arrangement.

One of the attractions of a so-called '*Thai Trading* agreement' has been their simplicity. There was no requirement at common law that these needed to be in writing, although if they were not in writing the terms of the retainer may be unclear. However, the Government took the opportunity of regulating this whole area of law in the AJA (see the Courts and Legal Services Act 1990 s.58 (2)(a), (3), as amended by AJA s.27 (1)). This means that any such agreement now has to be in writing and is known as a CFA, albeit one without a success fee. The AJA also provides that regulations may be made to set out matters that must be included in any such agreement or discussed with the client beforehand.

The Court of Appeal in *Awwad* v. *Geraghty & Co*. ([2000] 1 All ER 608, CA) provided a further twist. In this case Geraghty & Co. agreed in 1993 to conduct libel proceedings for Mr Awwad on the basis of 'normal' fees if he won and lower fees if he lost. He lost. Geraghty & Co. sought to recover their fees at the lower rate. They lost. This was because they had entered into an unlawful contingency fee agreement. This was obviously correct for a 1993 agreement, but the Court of Appeal went further by saying that the Court of Appeal in *Thai Trading* had been wrong, public policy and the common law had not moved on and, save as provided by Parliament, contingency fees for litigation remain unlawful. All such agreements should now only be conducted by solicitors under a CFA which fully complies with the statutory requirements.

It may well be asked why any solicitor would choose to enter into such an agreement rather than a CFA with a success fee. However, in certain areas of litigation it may well be that as a matter of market forces the client is not prepared to pay a success fee and, for whatever reason, does not believe that the solicitor will necessarily be able to recover this. Otherwise, the likelihood of recovering success fees under CFAs as costs from the losing party does seem to mean that there would usually be very little purpose in entering into a *Thai Trading* agreement now that the AJA has been implemented.

Legal aid

For all its faults, the legal aid scheme has over recent years provided a long-stop protection for those of limited financial means to enable them to defend or exercise their rights through the civil courts. Legal aid was a demand-led scheme enabling any client who was financially eligible and who had a meritorious case to retain a solicitor in private practice. There were very few exceptions (for example, libel proceedings). The availability of legal aid was however viewed to some extent as a passport to the courts for the poor, but excluding the bulk of 'middle England'.

In the AJA, the new Labour Government implemented fundamental changes to the legal aid scheme. The very words 'legal aid' disappear from the lexicon, together with 'green form' and 'ABWOR'. Not every solicitor will be able to obtain publicly funded legal representation or legal support for his client. This will be limited to franchised firms and, in due course, firms with a contract to provide legal aid in certain specified areas of law. The budget will now be capped and civil legal aid will have to compete with criminal legal aid for a share of the funds. The Government say that they will be using the new contracted and capped budget to re-focus legal aid spent on priority areas of work.

Many of the criticisms of the changes have concentrated upon the removal of legal aid from certain traditional areas of work. In particular, no legal aid is to be made available for most personal injury cases. As 80,000 or so certificates each year were issued in personal injury cases before the implementation of the new legal aid regime, this is a fundamental change. The Government's view is that most personal injury cases that are currently brought under legal aid can be brought by way of CFAs. The AJA provisions enabling success fees to be recoverable mean that this should not be at the expense of the client, but at the expense of the losing party.

The Government says that in a world where the public is not prepared to spend additional taxpayers' money on legal services, it is essential to get best use for the money out of such publicly funded services as can be provided. If such services can be provided by the private sector (by way of CFAs) it is the New Labour philosophy that they should be provided by the private sector, leaving the public sector to deal with matters where such options do not exist. In other words, the Government's promise is that by removing legal aid from personal injury cases there will be more opportunity to focus the budget on priority areas such as those dealing with social exclusion.

The proof of the pudding will be in the eating. The savings that the Government will make from removing most personal injury cases from legal aid will be minimal in relation to the total budget (perhaps £35 million out of £1.6 billion on the Legal Aid Board's own figures in *Testing the Code*). The conditional fees and after the event insurance market is immature and may not be able to cope with the new volume of work. However, whatever solicitors may think of the changes (whether as the Government would say from self-interested motives or because they fear that their clients will no longer be able to get access to justice), they have to live in the real world.

Some form of publicly funded legal services will remain. Some solicitors will be able to provide services to their clients and be paid by way of legal aid even after 1 April 2000, the date of implementation of the AJA provisions.

So far as civil litigation is concerned, the only substantial area of work to remain within the scope of legal aid will be housing and administrative law cases. As has been noted, most personal injury cases will be removed. Also, cases arising out of the conduct of the business are excluded. Clinical negligence cases remain within the scope of legal aid, at least for the time being.

The new Funding Code sets out strict criteria for the grant of legal aid and all practitioners must be conversant with its principal provisions. In particular, strict calculations of cost/benefit ratios are applied. The world of legal aid has changed, but there are still opportunities for solicitors to provide services to the poor and socially excluded in the Government's priority areas. However, solicitors will need to live by the new Funding Code. They will need to be franchised and in contracts with the Legal Services Commission. They will need to apply the strict criteria for funding. They will need to concentrate upon priority areas.

The reward is still likely to be payment at a less than commercial rate by the Legal Services Commission for cases where the client effectively pays for the services out of damages by way of the statutory charge or where the Commission itself pays the solicitor. However, if 'between the parties' costs orders were to be obtained solicitors will continue to be able to claim full normal costs from the losing party. In this case, the work is a little like a CFA on a 'no win, lower legal fee' basis. However, payments on account of costs and disbursements are a great benefit, particularly in a world where much other litigation may be on a deferred payment basis under CFAs.

ADVISING ABOUT THE DIFFERENT FUNDING OPTIONS

Introduction

Solicitors' Practice Rule 15 and the Solicitors' Costs Information and Client Care Code 1999 ('the Code') contain detailed provisions about client care in the context of costs advice.

The consequences of non-compliance are a finding of inadequate professional services under the Solicitors Act 1974 s.37A in respect of which the OSS may disallow all or part of a solicitor's costs and award compensation to the client of up to £5,000.

Getting started

The first point solicitors must appreciate is the duty to advise clients about the range of funding options which may apply to their case and when any costs are to be met.

This duty is a requirement of para. 4 of the Code which deals with the client's ability to pay. It specifically refers to considering the applicability of legal aid (including advice and assistance), LEI (pre-purchased or after the event) and employer/trade union schemes.

Breach of the Code exposes solicitors to disciplinary action and, if there is loss, to a negligence claim. Negligence may occur, for example, if a solicitor neglects to check with the client if they have LEI. Many clients do not realise that they have LEI as an 'add on' to household, car or credit card insurance and, if the solicitor does not remind them of this possibility and the client pays privately, they will suffer loss. If the client enters into a conditional fee agreement then the success fee and any after the event insurance premium may not be recoverable from the opponent unless there are very good reasons for not using the pre-purchased LEI.

Solicitors' Practice Rule 1 stipulates that a solicitor must not do anything which compromises or impairs his ability to act in the best interests of the client. The new funding options raise issues about what this means in the context of after the event insurance, specifically, does this require the solicitor to find the best insurance policy for the client and what does 'best' mean?

It is doubtful that the rule imposes a positive duty to get the best deal for the client having surveyed the market for the best insurance premium. However, if a solicitor is recommending a particular policy, any relationship and incentive must be disclosed. The Association of British Insurers Code of Practice provides that a policy should only be recommended if the solicitor is satisfied that the policy is suitable for the needs and resources of the client. It would also seem sensible for the solicitor to inform the client about what steps s/he has undertaken to survey the market and invite the client to do their own investigations.

Confirming the basis of charging

Once the appropriate funding option has been selected, the solicitor should confirm the basis of charging in writing as soon as possible (see para. 3(c) of the Code). A CFA must meet the strict requirements of the AJA.

Under para. 4(e) of the Code, solicitors must make it clear if any estimate, quotation or other indication of costs is not intended to be fixed.

Under para. 4(f), solicitors must explain how the firm's fees are calculated. If the basis of charging is hourly rates this must be made clear and the client must be told if rates may increase. Paragraph 3(b) states that the information must be given clearly and at a level which is appropriate for the particular client.

Advance costs information

Solicitors Practice Rule 15 requires solicitors to give information about costs at the outset of instructions and the specific information requirements are set out in the Code. Paragraph 3(a) of the Code provides that costs information must not be inaccurate or misleading.

In summary, the Code requires solicitors to give *'the best information possible'* about the overall costs, including a breakdown between fees, VAT and disbursements. This includes:

(a) agreeing a fixed or capped fee, or explaining the time likely to be spent and giving a realistic estimate or forecast within a range of costs if hourly rates apply. If this is not practicable, solicitors must explain why and give the best possible information about the next stage of the matter;

(b) advising clients about when payments, either to them or third parties, (e.g. experts or counsel) are likely to be needed; and

(c) advising whether the likely outcome of the case will justify the risk and about any exposure to adverse costs' orders.

Additional information requirements are specified depending on whether the client is legally aided or paying privately and these are covered below as points to consider for these funding options.

Paragraphs 2(d) and (e) of the Code make it clear that the costs information requirements have equal application to legal aid, CFA and contingency fee agreements. Paragraph 2(b) of the Code recognises that it may be inappropriate to give the full information required by the Code in certain circumstances, e.g. for existing clients, or where it is insensitive or impracticable.

Keeping the client informed

Paragraph 6 of the Code requires solicitors to update clients about costs at regular intervals of at least every six months.

Solicitors should inform clients of any circumstances affecting the amount of costs, the degree of risk or cost-benefit to the client of pursuing the case. Clients should be informed as soon as possible if an estimate or upper limit may or will be exceeded. This requires solicitors to have costs tracking systems in place.

Reviewing the basis of charging

There is only one constant in life – change. Solicitors should always keep the basis upon which they are charging under review. Paragraph 6 of the Code specifically requires solicitors to consider eligibility for legal aid if they become aware of a material change in the client's means.

A review may be agreed at the outset of the case, for example, a client may pay privately for initial investigative work to enable the solicitor to assess the chances of success and quantum, following which the solicitor may agree to act under a CFA. It may also be in a client's interests to swap to a CFA where the case is legally aided but the client is required to make a significant contribution.

If the basis of charging changes, the solicitor must take equal care to document the new basis in order to comply with Practice Rule 15.

Points to consider with different funding options

In this section, we raise practical issues which require to be considered by both solicitor and client when choosing a funding option. We do not pretend that the issues raised are comprehensive, but they should form a useful checklist of points to consider.

Client paying privately

This section covers privately paying clients (i.e. where LEI does not apply) paying hourly rates plus expenses and fixed/capped fees.

As mentioned above, using hourly rates as the basis for charging is the traditional means of funding cases, both privately and under legal aid. In both spheres it has recently been challenged resulting in the introduction of alternative funding methods. Solicitors would do well to bear in mind that clients can vote with their feet and hourly rates may no longer be feasible for certain areas of work. If hourly rates are acceptable to clients, this may only be on the basis of bulk discount rates being agreed.

Clients paying privately may also require solicitors to agree fixed or capped rates for the litigation as a whole, stages of the litigation or even for all work done over a year through an annual retainer. Such arrangements require deft risk assessment skills of solicitors and considerable expertise estimating costs.

Points to consider include the following.

The requirements of the Code: specific requirements for privately paying clients focus on explaining to clients their primary liability for their own legal fees and exposure to adverse costs orders. Readers are referred to para. 5(b) of the Code. In particular solicitors should ensure clients understand that, even if they win, their opponent may be unable to pay their costs.

The client's credit-worthiness: can or will the client actually pay? In contentious matters solicitors can and, it is recommended, should ask for money on account of costs, both at the outset and throughout the different stages of the case. It will limit exposure to bad debts and guard against the situation where a deadline is imminent but no funds are in place.

If solicitors are willing to give clients credit, it is recommended that this is only after credit checks have been undertaken unless the firm is willing to take the risk for commercial reasons. It is not untypical in a family context to secure fees against the matrimonial home and, in common with other businesses, there is no reason why solicitors should not request charges or guarantees from third parties.

However, care should be taken where security is given over shared assets, such as a matrimonial home, that the co-owner receives independent advice before entering into the security or charge. Otherwise, as illustrated by *Barclays Bank Plc* v. *O'Brien* ([1994] 1 AC 180) the security may not be enforceable against the co-owner. Guarantees must be in writing to be enforceable.

Interim bills: few solicitors can afford to wait until the outcome of a case to be paid and firms' cashflow will come under increased pressure as they take on a mixed portfolio of traditionally funded cases and CFAs. Interim bills should be rendered at regular intervals.

Interim bills also benefit the client by keeping them informed of costs and assisting them to budget for litigation. The Code (see above) provides that solicitors should keep clients informed of costs by rendering interim bills at agreed intervals.

Solicitors need to be careful to distinguish between interim bills on account and interim statute bills and it is recommended that they confirm the position in writing in the letter of retainer. Interim bills on account have the advantage of flexibility since they do not represent final quantification for the relevant period (subject to the principles set out in the *General of Berne Insurance Co.* case, see below). Statute bills are a final costing for the period in question and the solicitor cannot reassess such bills to reflect a successful outcome.

The disadvantage of interim bills on account is that solicitors cannot sue on such bills; equally clients cannot apply to have such bills assessed.

Challenging hourly rates: a solicitor cannot assume that the client's agreement of hourly rates enables them to charge for whatever time they have spent; see above regarding the Code and the comments below about the court rules governing recoverability of costs.

If solicitors seek to bill sums which vary substantially from any estimates, including revised estimates, then there must be a risk that such sums will be disallowed by the OSS as misleading or inaccurate in breach of para. 3(a) of the Code. A substantial variance may also be indicative of negligence or overcharging.

Sophisticated clients paying hourly rates may well require integrated networks allowing them to have access to solicitors' costs information so that they can keep track of costs and assess the value of work done. They may also employ costs draftsmen to review bills.

Fixed/capped fees and risk assessment: a capped fee has no risk for the client, but significant risk for the solicitor if they underestimate the amount of time/cost. For fixed fees, the risk is shared, the solicitor may either under or overestimate the cost.

Solicitors need to consider carefully the variables in each case to determine if fixed or capped fees are suitable, for example the nature of the case, the character of the client, the identity of the opponent and the court. If an annual retainer is to be agreed then it is recommended that solicitors both research the client's business sector and carry out due diligence on the client's own business. For example, it would be helpful to know about the number of claims brought or threatened by and against the client in the last few years and contracting/employment procedures as appropriate.

It is particularly important, therefore, that solicitors produce case management plans and case budgets to plot the broad strategy of the case and its cost at the outset. As to cost, if fixed/capped fee agreements are to succeed, solicitors will need to capture and analyse costs data so that they can accurately estimate costs for different types of litigation. This is likely to require use of sophisticated, computerised costs tracking systems. As with any statistical exercise, accuracy will depend upon firms being able to produce estimates from a large pool of data.

Whilst you cannot legislate for the actions of the court or the other side, you can for your client by attaching conditions or caveats to the agreement. However, depending on how extensive these are, your client may rightly say that, in reality, there is no fixed fee and this could be unattractive if the aim is to attract clients.

Fixed/capped fees and managing clients' expectations: it is recommended that solicitors warn clients of any adverse consequences of fixing or capping fees, for example, if this will translate into lower (but adequate) standards of service delivery or have consequences for the staffing of the case.

Contingency fees

Prohibitions: Solicitors' Practice Rule 8 prohibits contingency fees where a solicitor is *'retained or employed to prosecute or defend any action, suit or other contentious proceeding'* save where permitted by common law or under statute.

Solicitors should ensure that contingency agreements are lawful or they risk forfeiting payment altogether and disciplinary action. The definition of contingency fees in Solicitors' Practice Rule 18(2) focuses on fees payable only in the event of success. It is not limited to agreements where solicitors take a cut of the damages. However, CFAs are permitted by statute under the Courts and Legal Services Act 1990 and AJA, subject to meeting those Acts' provisions (and dealt with in more detail below).

As a matter of construction, it had been widely considered that contingency fees were lawful where no court proceedings were on foot in relation to pre-action advice and in respect of employment cases in the Industrial Tribunal (because such matters do not constitute an 'action, suit or other contentious proceeding'). However, the position is not entirely clear.

At common law the *Geraghty* case (see above) suggests that solicitors who wish to offer clients any fee arrangement pursuant to which either all or some part of their fees will depend upon a successful outcome must utilise a CFA which complies with the Courts and Legal Services Act 1990 and/or the AJA. Further, the AJA itself defines 'proceedings' as 'any sort of proceedings for resolving disputes (and not just proceedings in a court), whether commenced or contemplated' (s.58A (4)).

In conclusion, the sanction of statute is the only guarantee of enforceability of any contingency fee agreement since neither freedom of contract nor the principles of fair conduct (see *Panchaud Frères SA* v. *Etablissements General Grain Co.* [1970] 1 Lloyd's Rep 53) will override illegality or public policy arguments which make contingency agreements champertous (see below under CFAs generally).

Risk assessment: contingency fees are only payable in the event of success. They typically represent a fixed sum or percentage of the proceeds. Accordingly, in addition to assessing carefully the merits of the case, solicitors should carefully assess whether such fixed sum or percentage of proceeds is likely adequately to remunerate them for work done (see below in relation to CFAs generally).

Legal expenses insurance ('LEI')

Many of the key points to consider about LEI arise from the fact that LEI policies are:

(a) contracts as between the insurer and the insured client (there is no contractual relationship between the solicitor and the insurer), the terms of which require to be considered in detail like any other contract upon which a client is relying;

(b) insurance contracts which are subject to the principles of insurance law and require an understanding of, for example, the concepts of utmost good faith and subrogation; and

(c) contracts of indemnity: the insurer's obligation is to make good the insured's loss (i.e. legal expenses), for which the insured has primary liability.

However, it is important to remember that there are many different insurance products available and each policy should be considered individually. The pointers below apply to both before the event and after the event LEI unless expressly stated otherwise.

Points to consider include the following.

Panel solicitor restrictions: solicitors should check whether they can act under the policy or panel solicitors must be instructed.

The most established AEI schemes, such as 'Accident Line Protect', relate to personal injury cases carried out under CFAs and require panel membership. Panel firms are vetted for quality standards and membership is reviewed having regard to members' administration of the scheme, the number of claims undertaken, their cost and the solicitors' claims/loss record.

Outside such schemes, the Insurance Companies (Legal Expenses Insurance) Regulations 1990, SI 1990/1159, provide that the insured has freedom to choose their lawyer 'to defend, represent or serve the interests of the insured in any enquiry or proceedings' whenever recourse is had to LEI with certain exceptions (reg. 7).

The Guide to the Professional Conduct of Solicitors 1999, published by the Law Society, interprets this as giving freedom of choice once proceedings are imminent or on foot or there is a conflict of interest between the insurer and the insured. However, the insurance ombudsman has indicated that he would expect a restriction of choice of solicitor to be made clear to the client on inception of the policy. In practice, the insurer rarely does this.

The risk of losing a case to a panel member suggests it is commercial sense for solicitors to obtain panel memberships if possible.

The initial basis of charging: LEI cover is rarely retrospective and written confirmation of cover is required before cover is granted. This usually requires the solicitor to certify reasonable prospects of success.

However some AEI schemes extend cover automatically to panel firms and premiums are fixed. In return, panel firms are required to take out cover for all CFA cases, irrespective of the merits of the case. The Association of British Insurers Code of Practice provides that a policy should only be recommended if the solicitor is satisfied that the policy is suitable for the needs and resources of the client. This potentially raises an ethical issue because, in a very strong case, a solicitor may have otherwise advised the client against paying for AEI. That said, there is no such thing as a cast iron case. If a solicitor is recommending a particular policy, any relationship and incentive must be disclosed. As long as solicitors are open about any 'ties' or constraints imposed by schemes which they have chosen or developed, this should overcome any ethical problems.

Newer AEI schemes which extend beyond the safety of PI tend to review cases individually (i.e. there is no automatic acceptance). Premiums will be set according to the insurer's perception of the merits. Solicitors will be required to submit application forms, perhaps with a fee setting out details about the case and their view of the merits.

Where claims require solicitors to report on the merits, solicitors need to consider and agree with the client the initial basis of charging for advising on the scope of the policy, the investigatory work in connection with the claim itself and the report to the insurers.

Primary liability of the client: solicitors should make it clear to the client that they are primarily liable for their fees even if they have LEI unless there is a CFA in place which provides for the solicitor's fees to be paid only on a win.

This is because technically, LEI is a contract of indemnity. In addition the insurer may object to paying some part of the solicitor's fees on the basis that the client has been unreasonable or any cap has been exceeded. Alternatively, it may transpire that the insurer is entitled to avoid the policy.

Validity of the policy and risk of avoidance: for before the event insurance solicitors should check the proposal and renewal notices to ensure that there has been no failure to disclose which will entitle the insurer to avoid the policy.

Ensure the client understands the duty of utmost good faith and the importance of full disclosure of material facts, otherwise cover will be avoided. It is irrelevant whether non-disclosure arises from indifference or a mistake.

It is equally irrelevant that the reason for non-disclosure is the client's failure to understand that a fact was material. This imposes an obligation on solicitors to ensure that clients appreciate what facts are material to any particular legal action.

Solicitors must themselves, as the client's agent, disclose those material facts which are in their knowledge.

Guidance as to what is material is given in the Marine Insurance Act 1906 s.18 (2), which provides that every circumstance is material which would influence the judgement of a prudent insurer in fixing the premium or determining whether he will take the risk.

It is a breach of the duty of utmost good faith if the insured seeks to benefit from the policy by wilful misconduct such as acting in such a way as to invite the peril insured against into being.

Scope of cover: solicitors should check the scope of cover, for example, is the event covered, is there a cost/benefit analysis restriction, are there any cost limitations, is an excess payable?

The solicitor should advise the client and the insurer if any financial limits compromise his/her ability to achieve a successful outcome.

Exclusion clauses in insurance contracts are specifically excluded from the application of the Unfair Contract Terms Act 1977. However, for consumer clients, the Insurance Ombudsman has stated that he will apply the spirit if not the letter of that Act (*Annual Report for the Insurance Ombudsman 1990*) and the Unfair Terms in Consumer Contracts Regulations 1994, SI 1994/3159 do apply.

Continuing requirements under the policy: solicitors should check the policy for reporting requirements about, for example, costs and the prospects of success. In *DAS Legal Expenses Insurance Co. Ltd* v. *Hughes Hooker & Co.* (1994, unreported) a legal expenses insurer successfully sued a firm of solicitors for misrepresentation. The solicitors had obtained, but not disclosed, an unfavourable counsel's opinion.

Solicitors should also check for warranties about future conduct, for example, to the effect that information is *and will remain accurate.* Ensure that the client understands that the duty of utmost good faith is continuing. Breach of a warranty will entitle the insurer to avoid the policy and repudiate liability from the date of breach.

Mitigating loss: as a contract of indemnity, the insured must mitigate their loss: they cannot use a sledgehammer to crack a nut and expect the insurer to pick up the cost. Solicitors should ensure that the client understands that they cannot adopt a blank chequebook approach and should seek to settle the case as appropriate – the policy does not guarantee a day in court.

If a solicitor considers the client is being unreasonable, the prudent course is to seek the insurers' views and warn the client that they may themselves have to pay for any step which is unreasonable.

Not doing so runs the risk of an application under the Solicitors Act 1974 s.71 (1) which enables a third party, such as an insurer who is liable to pay a bill, to apply for an assessment. Michael Feldman also submits (in *Legal Expenses Insurance* (CLT Professional Publishing, 1998)) that the wording of the Supreme Court Act 1981 s.51 is probably sufficiently wide to allow the insurer to seek to obtain wasted costs orders against a solicitor acting for the insured.

Recovery of costs from the insurer: generally, solicitors dealing with insurers who cover solicitor-own-client costs will find them tough on rates and bills alike: they often employ costs draftsmen and frequently require solicitors to have their costs assessed.

Policies typically expressly provide that costs and disbursements should be reasonably and properly incurred. The case should be pitched at a fee earner of the right level of experience and expertise.

If solicitors wish to render interim bills, it is sensible to say so at the outset, although some insurers only provide for payment at the end of the case or after specified periods.

Cover for adverse costs orders: generally, insurers do not cover exposure to the other side's legal costs save for under AEI policies. Solicitors should check the terms of the cover and, if it does not extend to adverse costs orders, they should ensure that the client understands this (although they are primarily liable in any event).

However, even if the insurance policy does not provide for cover of the other side's costs, the insurer will be exposed to third party costs orders if they exert a substantial degree of influence or control over the conduct of proceedings. In *TGA Chapman Ltd* v. *Christopher* ([1998] 1 WLR 12, CA) the insurer was effectively conducting the matter, putting forward various defences which failed. The court exercised its power to award third party costs under the Supreme Court Act 1981 s.51 (1).

For AEI policies which are aimed at covering adverse cost orders, solicitors should carefully review any qualifications attached to such cover and advise clients accordingly. It is not uncommon for policies *not* to pay out in the event of the client being 'successful', however it is not inconceivable for a client to be 'successful' and yet exposed to an adverse costs order. For example, a client may lose a claim but successfully defeat a counterclaim; the CPR suggest that the courts are more likely to carve up liability for costs for example, to penalise a claimant who has pursued multiple causes of action or heads of loss, some of which are unsuccessful.

Confidentiality and conflicts of interest: it is important that the solicitor remains clear in their own mind who the client is – it is not the insurer. This can give rise to conflicts of interest because the solicitor has a duty to keep clients' affairs confidential but the insured has obligations of disclosure to the insurer.

Therefore a solicitor must obtain consent from the insured before allowing the insurer to inspect the file and the client should be reminded of their duties to the insurer when consent is sought.

If a solicitor becomes aware of a fraud by the client on the insurer or a material non-disclosure there is no duty to warn the insurer (and this would probably be in breach of duty to client). However, principle 17 of *The Guide to the Professional Conduct of Solicitors 1999* provides that solicitors must not act towards anyone in a way which is fraudulent or deceitful or otherwise contrary to their position as solicitors. Nor must they use their position to take unfair advantage for themselves or others. It imposes a duty to stop acting and terminate the retainer.

In such circumstances, it may be best to advise the client to take independent advice from another solicitor about whether or not there has been non-disclosure.

Panel referrals: panel solicitors may accept referrals from legal expenses insurers provided they comply with the provisions of the Solicitors' Introduction and Referral Code 1990 (para. 6.03). The referred client must be treated as any other private client.

Solicitors cannot enter into an agreement which insists that a particular solicitor must act: the client is entitled to instruct the solicitor of their choice (see above). It is a breach of the Code for solicitors to reward introducers by the payment of commission or otherwise. This is, however, at the time of writing under review by the Law Society and is likely to be modified or abolished.

Selecting AEI cover: it has already been noted that solicitors should be careful about assuming duties to advise clients about which policy to select and qualify any recommendation as appropriate.

However it makes sense to check out the proposed insurer since the AEI market is relatively untried and tested outside the established personal injury schemes. What is the insurer's reputation: are they good claims handlers in terms of efficiency and fairness, in particular, what is the quality of their claims assessors and how accessible are they? Care should also be taken as to the flexibility of the policy in terms of amount of cover and increasing cover. A negligence claim may arise if a client becomes embroiled in litigation on the incorrect understanding that LEI will meet all their costs if they have to discontinue or settle on poor terms.

Considerations for solicitors themselves include the policy wording: is it in plain English or will you have to spend time explaining it to clients with associated hidden costs? Does the insurer have explicit success rates expectations and what are the consequences of not meeting these? Do they plan to be in the market long-term (particularly important if the insurer requires the solicitor to give them all their business).

Do you think that the amount of the premium is reasonable in relation to the risk and is it an amount which is likely to be recoverable from the opponent if the case is won?

Conditional Fee Agreements ('CFAs')

CFAs are an innovative form of funding litigation or arbitration (see *Bevan Ashford* v. *Geoff Yeandle* [1998] 3 WLR 172). On the face of it, CFAs have enormous appeal for clients. However, whether or not to offer CFAs to clients raises complex issues about both the merits of the case and a firm's ability to bear the cost of the litigation for the duration of the case and, in the worst case scenario, at the end of the day.

From clients' perspective, when CFAs were first introduced, a CFA may not have been the best way forward because they could afford to fund the case without conceding a success fee, especially where the case had high chances of success. Another disadvantage of CFAs when they were initially introduced was that the damages might be swallowed up by the success fee. These disadvantages have been removed by s.27(1) of the AJA for CFAs entered into after 1 April 2000, which provide that the losing party can be required to pay the risk element of the success fee. (Under the transitional arrangements, this must be 'the first' CFA in the case, so it is not possible to replace an existing CFA and expect to recover the success fee.) However, the matter is ultimately in the court's discretion and subject to assessment.

In certain, complex cases, it may not be in a client's best interests to have a CFA because the solicitor cannot realistically be expected to carry the costs of the case and it would compromise the client's chances of success for the solicitor to run the case on such basis as they can afford to run it. However, the different variants of CFAs mentioned above should not be forgotten: CFAs do not necessarily require a 'no win, no legal fee' arrangement. This section raises points related to all three types of CFA mentioned above.

From the solicitor's perspective, s/he would be well advised to consult detailed works on the subject (e.g. O'Mahoney, Ellson, Marshall and Bennett, *Conditional Fees: Law and Practice* (Sweet & Maxwell, 2000); Kerry Underwood, *No Win, No Fee, No Worries* (Central Law Training)). If it is intended to do any volume of CFA work, solicitors should carry out in-depth business planning and consult with their bank manager before dipping their toe into the water. This is because solicitors offering CFAs are themselves taking a gamble on the outcome of the litigation, the amount of any damages recovered and the enforceability of any judgment.

Points to consider when assessing risk issues for solicitors include those listed below. For the purposes of this chapter, it is worth emphasising that the body of experience of CFAs to date is based upon personal injury litigation, the success of which tends to revolve around factual evidence of a single event and which is relatively low risk. Solicitors should not base their perception of how successful CFAs are on personal injury data alone.

Client commitment and good faith: where a client's personal exposure is limited, they may be prepared to take greater risks than if they were paying their own legal fees and perhaps have less commitment to the litigation. In short, they have 'nothing to lose'. It is important that solicitors seek to address the risk of untruthful or unreasonable conduct by the client through:

(a) careful risk analysis: what evidence can the client produce to back up what they say?

(b) explicit discussion and agreement of the client's role: it must be explained to the client what is expected from them in terms of instructions and speed of response given the stricter regime of the CPR;

(c) escape clauses in the CFA: it is important to legislate in advance for termination of the CFA if, for example, the client has not given instructions or is tardy giving instructions, or if there has been material non-disclosure or deceit.

The Law Society model provides for clients to pay 'basic costs', i.e. at the solicitor's usual rate with no success fee uplift in the event of inadequate, improper, unreasonable or misleading instructions, failure to pay disbursements (if relevant) or lack of cooperation.

The form of CFA: the agreement must comply with the conditions set out in the Courts and Legal Services Act 1990 s.58 as amended by s.27 of the AJA otherwise it will be unenforceable as champertous and/or contrary to public policy.

Whilst maintenance and champerty are no longer punishable by imprisonment, fee agreements which amount to maintenance or are champertous are unenforceable as contrary to public policy and the solicitor will not be able to recover any fees at all. Therefore, whilst the new developments encourage creativity, there are still pitfalls for the unwary.

In particular it is important not to confuse American style contingency agreements (see above) with CFAs, as a claims assessor handling personal injury claims found to its cost in 1999. Following allegations of champerty, the DTI presented a winding up petition which stated that the 'business consists of generating profits out of the proceeds of its clients' claims, and accordingly is contrary to public policy and the rule against champerty'.

Solicitors should also bear in mind that, since CFAs are a contract, the Unfair Contract Terms Act 1977 and the Unfair Terms in Consumer Contracts Regulations 1994, SI 1994/3159 apply and affect enforceability of unfair or unclear terms.

For the above reasons, whilst precedents make bad masters, they are good slaves and solicitors should make full use of the Law Society model agreement and any other such model precedents which emerge to avoid falling foul of the laws of champerty and maintenance and consumer legislation. Care must also be taken explaining how CFAs work and, in particular the success fee and payments in respect of insurance and disbursements. It is recommended that solicitors remind clients at key points in the case that the success fee will be taken out of damages if (and to the extent to which) it cannot be passed on to the other side.

Defining 'success': the definition of success will determine whether or not a solicitor is paid. It is therefore extremely important that it is carefully defined in the CFA to take account of counterclaims and the likelihood that either through offers to settle, negotiation or ADR, 90 per cent of cases typically end in compromise, with each party making concessions. Solicitors should also take care not to focus narrowly on legal redress in their definition of success: settlement through negotiation or ADR may lead to different forms of redress.

A compromise may well affect the client's perception of success, although arguably the fact that they are prepared to settle suggests that they have secured some measure of success. Nonetheless, to avoid conflict solicitors should be clear with clients about what constitutes success and identify this in the CFA. This should assist generally to manage the client's expectations from the outset.

A side benefit is that there will be an explicit discussion about what the client regards as a successful outcome which can inform a settlement strategy.

The take on decision: a solicitor's decision to take on a case under a CFA is an investment decision with implications for the firm's cashflow and financial well-being. Under the Law Society model form CFA, the solicitor cannot pull out of a case because it is getting risky, but can lawfully pull out if it is no longer likely to succeed at all.

Given the consequences of the take on decision, it is recommended that solicitors establish a written policy for taking on CFAs with set criteria. The policy document should be agreed by the partners and aim to maintain the firm's exposure at an acceptable level.

The policy document should be supported by formal risk assessment case analyses to be completed by all fee earners for each CFA case which requires a methodical analysis of the case's strengths and weaknesses. Analyses with checklists and guidelines as to what type of and how much information is required can greatly assist better decision-making and avoid time-wasting

It is recommended that no CFA case should be taken on without the approval of an objective fee earner ('the CFA Manager'), probably a partner and, in particularly complex, time and cost intensive cases, a panel of CFA managers.

Whilst no-one can avoid a 'bolt out of the blue' which destroys a case, those firms who have 'been there before' and invested in building up a body of specialist knowledge might be expected to achieve the highest success rates.

Assessment of the success fee: the court can be required to assess the success fee and accordingly it is important for solicitors to be able to demonstrate how they assessed the risk, and therefore the success fee of individual cases. Solicitors should create pro forma risk assessment documents for completion by fee earners at the take on stage so a contemporaneous record is available.

Cover for adverse costs orders: CFAs do not cover the client against exposure to the other side's legal costs. Solicitors should ensure that clients understand this exposure and in most, if not all cases, the client should be advised to take out after the event insurance cover to protect their position (see above for pointers about LEI cover). The Conditional Fee Agreements Regulations 2000, SI 2000/692 impose a duty on solicitors in conditional fee cases (but not, bizarrely, those utilising insurance policies paying both sides' costs) to inform the client of the availability of AEI and of the suitability of any policy recommended.

As between solicitors and third parties a CFA is still arguably champertous maintenance; case law suggests that what makes it acceptable is the fact that the maintainer pays the costs of the other side if the litigation fails. (See *Orme* v. *Associated Newspapers*, *The Times*, 4 February 1981; *Singh* v. *Observer Ltd* [1989] 2 All ER 751; *Mainwaring* v. *Coltech Investments*, *The Times*, 19 February 1991; *McFarlane* v *EE Caledonia* (No. 2), *The Times*, 8 December 1994.) This suggests that it is in the solicitors' interests to ensure that insurance cover is available to cover against an adverse costs order. That said, in *Hodgson* v. *Imperial Tobacco Ltd* [1998] 2 All ER 673, the court indicated it would be slow to make costs orders against solicitors in such cases. The decision reviews the three circumstances in which solicitors can be personally liable for costs: pursuant to a wasted costs order under the Supreme Court Act 1981 s.51(6), under the court's inherent jurisdiction to make a costs order against a solicitor, or pursuant to its general jurisdiction as to costs under the Supreme Court Act 1981 s.51(1), (3) (but only if the solicitor is acting over and above their capacity as a legal representative in the proceedings).

Important considerations for solicitors undertaking volume CFA work are the insurer's terms and their claims record with the insurer. Whilst schemes such as Abbey Legal Protection (ALP)'s established 'National Accident Line Protect' scheme can offer very competitive premiums (although they have nearly doubled since October 1999 as a result of a greater number of claims), such schemes may tie the firm to the insurer. ALP object to any form of intermediate funding, therefore it is not possible to enter into non-contentious businesses agreements for cases expected to settle without issue of proceedings.

Such schemes often require panel membership with members being required to demonstrate quality standards and expertise in the relevant area of law. Nonetheless, firms may be and have been suspended or expelled from such schemes for losing too many cases. An alternative is to self-insure, building up a war chest individually or in association with other firms to meet adverse costs awards and charging clients 'premiums' or a higher success fee to cover it. This might be done in combination with external AEI to avoid getting a bad claims record with the insurer. Self-insurance places even greater risk on solicitors and accordingly, their risk assessment skills.

A new development in the CFA insurance market is 'only if you win' insurance such as Royal & Sun Alliance's 'Pursuit'. It offers protection against adverse costs orders and covers clients' own fees and disbursements but the client is required to pay no premium unless they win.

When acting for a client whose opponent may have a CFA, you must advise your client that any costs award against them may include payment of the success fee and the winning party's insurance premium in addition to their normal costs. There is a safeguard in that the success fee and insurance premium can be challenged in the courts.

Recoverability of costs and the success fee: as the solicitor falls to be paid costs by the loser it is incumbent on solicitors to investigate the financial standing of the other party. Again, the body of experience of CFAs is in the personal injury field where the majority of defendants can look to their insurer's deep pocket.

In order to protect solicitors' reputation and in the public interest, the Law Society model CFA previously recommended capping the success fee at 25 per cent (for the success fee element only of legal costs, exclusive of VAT). The cap was not mandatory and has now been removed from the model agreement. As success fees are now to be largely recoverable from the opponent the rationale behind the cap (protecting the client's damages) has disappeared.

Monitoring the case: the prospects of success in a case can nosedive dramatically as some new piece of evidence comes to light. Concern about 'new facts' being known to the client before the take on decision could be a basis for termination. An offer to settle or simply to mediate may also require a difficult judgement call to decide if the case should be settled.

Having regard to the serious consequences for a firm of losing a CFA case it is important that firms create a formal framework to enable CFA cases to be regularly reviewed to maintain objectivity. Reviews should take place in times of difficulty as well as regularly through periodic reports to the CFA manager.

Termination: if termination is because of non-disclosure or deceit this places the solicitor in a difficult position since there will be issues of proof, interpretation, etc. If the solicitor withdraws, the client has to pay the basic costs under the Law Society model CFA. If they cannot pay, it may be better to continue or press for a settlement or discontinuance.

In terms of client care, pulling out because the solicitor perceives there to be no hope of success will require the solicitor to be frank with the client about their assessment to maintain their confidence. If clients' expectations have not been well managed, the solicitor can expect to spend non-chargeable time dealing with complaints.

Cashflow: this is potentially the biggest headache for solicitors' firms. In a 'no win, no legal fee' case there will be no payment whatsoever until after the conclusion of the case (and any enforcement proceedings). If the case is lost there will be no payment at all. Moreover, solicitors may have to bear the disbursements which a client cannot afford to pay, although this is a factor which can be reflected in an increased success fee.

Some insurers cover the client's disbursements under the scheme, although there may be exceptions. For example, many policies do not cover counsel's fees. This means that either a CFA should be negotiated with counsel with the success fee carved up between solicitor and counsel, or the client or solicitor must pay counsel's fees.

Whilst counsel can work under a CFA, it is illegal for experts to do so. It will be important for solicitors to maximise cashflow in relation to disbursements by negotiating CFAs with counsel and deferred payments and free screening with experts. Another means of minimising disbursements will be to exploit the single expert rules under the CPR (where this is not disadvantageous to the client). Some insurance schemes offer to insure and/or fund disbursements by way of a loan at commercial rates. Solicitors will have to keep a weather-eye to the economy and the cost of borrowing.

The upshot is that solicitors' fee income will be more volatile because it will be impossible to predict success and whether or not the swings and roundabouts principle will work: i.e. the success fee will cancel out the loss of unsuccessful cases. Solicitors will need to monitor their overall exposure carefully with systems in place which give a 'helicopter vision' of the number of CFA cases taken on, won and lost, the number of hours for which payment is contingent on success, the amount of disbursements being funded and the recoverability of fees, including the success fee element from cases which have been won. Thus, limiting the number of high risk CFA cases and also the total exposure to CFAs the firm is willing to bear, will help firms spread the risk of a CFA portfolio.

Inevitably CFA cases will be lost and it is important that there is a firm-wide understanding that success fees are supposed to compensate solicitors for such cases; they are the fighting fund for other CFAs and not bonus income for partners to draw.

Advertising and CFAs: solicitors' firms have been criticised by the Advertising Standards Authority for advertising 'no win, no fee' funding arrangements since this does not alert readers to the fee for insurance cover and other disbursements which they may have to pay.

Law Society guidance before the introduction of CFAs had indicated that the phrase was well understood by clients and permissible. However research by Stella Yarrow and Pamela Abrams, *Nothing to Lose? Clients' Experiences of Using Conditional Fees* (University of Westminster, 2000) since the introduction of CFAs has indicated that there is widespread discontent amongst clients about its use.

The Advertising Standards Authority have recommended that if a client is required to make any payment whatsoever, this should be mentioned in the advertisement. This recommendation should be followed.

Unbundling

Unbundling effectively involves the solicitor acting as a 'sub-contractor' to whom specific tasks are outsourced by the client. Chapter 5 above deals with the different forms which unbundling can take.

It is assumed that, if clients are willing to deal with solicitors at all, the reason for unbundling a case is because none of the aforementioned options are available or affordable. Typically, the client pays the solicitor at hourly rates or a fixed or capped fee for different aspects of their advice. Points to consider on these types of fee arrangement in general are set out above. The key points to consider specific to unbundling are as follows:

The take on decision: it is not difficult to imagine unbundling where you are dealing with an in-house lawyer or client of similar sophistication. However, solicitors should not assume that clients understand the litigation process or the substantive law in issue. It is this understanding which should inform the client's decision as to who will be responsible for what and as to whether unbundling is a realistic option.

Unless the solicitor is willing to invest non-chargeable time or the client is willing to pay for general advice at the outset, the take on decision will require skilful, rapid screening.

Since unbundling will involve a more interdependent style of working, solicitors will need to form a view on whether or not they feel they can work with the client as part of a team.

Giving the client an overview: it is recommended that clients are given information generally outlining the litigation process including cost rules and the key legal points to be proved: e.g. for a breach of contract, the existence of a contract, breach of contract and damage. Such information could be provided through an Internet service for a nominal fixed charge.

At the outset of instructions and throughout a case, clients should be advised about the importance of court deadlines and limitation periods, both in connection with work for which they are responsible and work for which the solicitor is responsible.

Without transparency of the different stages of litigation and an understanding of the breakdown of tasks for each stage and the legal principles, solicitors risk at best, mismanagement of clients' expectations and, at worst, a case being struck out because matters have been left to the client with which they cannot deal.

The case of *Stephens* v. *Gullis* (*The Times*, 6 October 1999) illustrates the dangers. The claimant instructed an expert themselves with minimal input from their solicitors and, in consequence, the report was served late and did not consider the evidence or address the relevant issues. The court debarred the claimant from calling the expert at trial.

General advice contained in letters, standard information packs or on the Internet should be stated to be of general application and clients invited to consult the solicitor for advice (for which the solicitor may charge at their discretion) on their specific case.

The division of responsibilities: as in any project involving different players, it is extremely important that it is agreed who will be responsible for leading a project and what role each player is to have; otherwise there is a danger of tasks falling between two stools.

Having discussed the division of responsibilities with the client, the agreed roles should be confirmed in writing by the solicitor so it is clear what service(s) they are and are not supplying under an unbundling arrangement and what the client is to do.

Instructing counsel: clients should be aware that, should they wish to use counsel, counsel must be instructed through a solicitor.

Recoverability of costs: whilst a solicitor is not on the record, the client is a 'litigant in person' and solicitors should ensure that clients understand the rules which apply to and restrict recovery of costs by litigants in person.

CPR Rule 48.6 provides that costs (but not disbursements) allowed to a litigant in person must not exceed two-thirds of the amount which would have been recoverable if they had been represented by a lawyer. The amount allowed to a litigant in person will reflect any financial loss or, if this cannot be proved, an amount for time reasonably spent doing the work at the rate specified in the costs practice direction (as at 1 November 1999, £9.25 per hour).

Under CPR Rule 48.6, the client can also recover 'payments reasonably made by him for legal services relating to the conduct of the proceedings' and also for expert assistance in connection with assessment of costs. This suggests that solicitors need not be on the record if the client is to recover legal costs. The *New Law Journal*, 1 July 1994, at p. 890 reported a case where a client recovered costs in excess of £59,000 for obtaining legal assistance from solicitors who were not on the record.

Solicitors should impress upon clients acting in person the importance of keeping records to evidence financial loss, including payments made to solicitors.

Going on the record: a solicitor's authority and duty to the client and the court continues as long as they are on the court record. Care should be taken in deciding whether or not to go on the record and also to follow the proper procedures for coming off the record as necessary. Otherwise there is a risk that the solicitor or client will not have the right to be heard at hearings and/or documents may be misdirected albeit correctly served.

Legal aid

A part of the Government's reasoning behind controlling the legal aid budget and regulating its relationship with solicitors (its suppliers) through contracts is to gain further controls on cost. The Government, through its agent, the Legal Services Commission (formerly the Legal Aid Board) will be able to use its position as a bulk purchaser of legal services to control price.

It is quite possible that once the current set of changes have been effected, the next set of changes will be to introduce competitive tendering for blocks of work based on price subject to certain quality safeguards. It is, therefore, not a certain environment for solicitors, nor is it likely to be a well paid one.

Points to consider include the following.

Administering legal aid: the requirements for franchising and its associated quality assurance system may involve expensive irrecoverable costs for solicitors, not to mention the time involved setting up the system in the first place. For example, the new contract documentation requires solicitors to maintain records for average costs per case.

However in today's competitive market, the existence of quality systems is likely to be key to survival in any event.

Performance assessment: the Commission is likely to be increasingly interested in outcome measurements and performance against prediction. This is already intimated as the case for clinical negligence cases.

The Commission is now able to assess the performance of individual solicitors in terms of prediction and outcome by reason of the new legal aid numbers incorporating the solicitor's roll number. Records of costs per case are likely to be used to determine whether or not firms should remain on their approved panel of legal aid suppliers. Solicitors can expect to lose their franchise or have it suspended if their performance is deemed inadequate.

Prescribed rates: prescribed rates already exist for certain areas of work. However, it is also likely that the Commission will move closer towards payment of benchmark costs per case rather than paying costs on a case by case basis. Records of costs per case are likely to be used to set benchmark cost figures for different categories of case.

Costs limitations: the old rarely enforced 'cost conditions' under legal aid cases have now been replaced by strictly enforced 'limitations'. These limitations set out specifically the maximum that can be claimed from the Legal Services Commission in costs (meaning profit costs, counsel's fees and disbursements) from specific dates. Computerised time recording and warning systems are now essential.

Specialist panels: some areas of work under legal aid will be increasingly restricted to specialists. For example, clinical negligence work is now restricted to firms who have members of either the Law Society's Medical Negligence Panel or the AVMA Referral Panel. It is recommended that firms of solicitors focus on franchise areas accordingly.

Client benefits: until the implementation of the AJA provisions allowing recoverability of success fees and insurance premiums, there was seldom any doubt that a client would be better off under legal aid than under a CFA. This is no longer obviously the case, because the client's damages can be effectively ring-fenced and possible liability for the other side's costs can be insured. In areas where legal aid remains, the solicitor must carefully consider with the client the pros and cons of all of the funding options.

As for firms who have the requisite specialist expertise, the obvious danger is that individual solicitors who carry the qualifications may be increasingly mobile and able to command huge salaries. The partners who have invested considerable time and resources in systems may not personally be the holders of the relevant qualifications and may see no return on their investment if the relevant staff walk out.

MAXIMISING RECOVERY FROM THE LOSING PARTY

The indemnity principle

Whatever arrangements may have been made for the client to pay his solicitor, the client and the solicitor have the same interest in maximising the amount of those costs which can be recovered from a losing opponent.

The starting point for ensuring that costs are recovered is the 'indemnity principle'. Expressed long ago by the House of Lords in *Gundry* v. *Sainsbury* ([1910] 1 KB 645), this costs principle provides that a successful party cannot recover from the loser more than he has agreed to pay his own solicitor.

The advent of CFAs might seem to obviate the need for such a principle. As the client will not be paying the solicitor anything unless the case is won (triggering an obligation on the defendant to pay costs) it might be argued that the client has very little interest in the headline hourly rate set out in the CFA. The CFA does not, however, breach the indemnity principle because the client's liability to pay the costs on a solicitor and client basis is created if the case is won.

Indeed, many solicitors would like to simplify the explanation of costs with their clients. They would like to be able to say that under a 'no win, no legal fee' CFA the client has no liability to pay any costs if the case is lost (because it is a 'no win, no legal fee' agreement). They would also like to be able to say that the client would also have no liability to pay any excess costs if the case is won. In other words, many solicitors would like to agree in advance with a client not to charge any excess solicitor and client costs over and above the costs recoverable from the other side. There is nothing to stop a solicitor agreeing to waive any excess solicitor and client costs after the event (indeed, this is commonly done in personal injury cases). If, however, such an agreement were made beforehand, then under the indemnity principle, the solicitor who has won the case would not be able to recover any costs at all from the losing party. This is because there would be no liability on the client for the loser to indemnify by paying the costs.

However, the indemnity principle has been revived by recent court decisions. First, in *Bailey* v. *IBC Vehicles Ltd* ([1998] 3 All ER 570) the question of a trade union's retainer with its solicitors was examined. Following that decision the chief taxing master issued Supreme Court Taxing Office Practice Direction 2/1998. This made it clear that the indemnity principle was alive and well. It required solicitors to summarise the terms of their retainer in the bill (or an annexure to the bill) and to certify that there had been no breach of the indemnity principle. Furthermore, in *General of Berne Insurance Co. Ltd* v. *Jardine Reinsurance Management Ltd* ([1998] 2 All ER 301) it was held that not only did the indemnity principle apply to the total amount of costs billed to the client and sought to be recovered from the other side, but also to each individual item of work. In other words, if interim bills are delivered expressly for certain portions of the work then no more than that sum can be recovered from the other side for that work. This is so even if the totality of the bills to the client exceed the totality of the costs sought from the other side.

It is submitted that in the light of the payment options discussed in this chapter the indemnity principle is becoming increasingly artificial and redundant. Indeed, there has been mounting pressure on the Lord Chancellor's Department to modify or abolish it. The Lord Chancellor's Department has just, at the time of writing, indicated that it should be abolished. It is to be hoped that the indemnity principle will soon either be abolished or will be sufficiently modified to at least enable solicitors to agree in advance to waive any element of additional solicitor and client costs. This will simplify the procedure for explaining costs (irrecoverable) procedures to the client at the outset of the case.

The Civil Procedure Rules

The overriding objective (Rule 1.1)

Although the CPR contain a number of rules specifically dealing with recovery of costs which are dealt with below, the importance with which the cost of the litigation is viewed is emphasised by this being expressly dealt with in Part 1 of the CPR which sets out the overriding objective.

CPR Rule 1.1 sets out the overriding objective which is to enable the court 'to deal with cases justly'. Dealing with a case justly expressly includes for the first time 'saving expense' (Rule 1.1(2)(b)), and most importantly:

> dealing with the case in ways which are proportionate:
> (i)   to the amount of money involved;
> (ii) to the importance of the case;
> (iii) to the complexity of the issues;
> (iv) to the financial position of each party.

The Rule also implicitly accepts that the resources that are likely to be available to the court service are limited and that each case will have allotted to it only 'an appropriate share of the court's resources, while taking into account the need to allot resources to other cases'.

The overriding objective therefore requires that the costs of proceedings form a fundamental part of the decision-making process of the court and the parties in connection with the conduct of the dispute. This is new and follows from the fundamental re-think by Lord Woolf in his Interim and Final Reports on *Access to Justice*. He identified the evils of the then current court system as being cost, complexity and delay. In the old world, the Rolls-Royce system used for litigation may have been designed for those most complex and valuable of cases, but could be used (even if completely inappropriate) for small low value cases. There were some crude measures to prevent this such as the small claims limit and county court scale costs. However, in the old world the idea was that the solicitor did the work that the solicitor considered necessary to bring the case to trial or settlement. The solicitor would then, broadly speaking, recover the cost of the work done, unless the court, after the event, considered the work to be unreasonable in nature or amount.

The new rules are designed to move the world of litigation closer to a world of binding estimates, fixed costs and benchmark costs. Some, probably including Lord Woolf, would have wished to go further. However, the CPR is a compromise in that it moves in that direction but retains many of the features of the previous system at least on an interim basis. However, the guiding spirit behind the rule changes should not escape any litigation solicitor who wishes to recover costs both now and in the future.

Scope of the Costs Rules (CPR Part 43)

This Part schedules the new costs forms introduced by the CPR. These new forms, including a new model form of bill, are a major change to the previous costs procedure. In many respects they are a great improvement. In particular, the new form N252 (Notice of Commencement of Assessment of Bill of Costs) sensibly sets out the full total costs claimed in the bill for use both by the paying party and the client of the receiving party.

The new form of bill is in some ways clearer than the old form which was rather archaic. However, there has been confusion as to whether it is mandatory or advisory and this confusion has spread to different practices being adopted in different courts. For cases where all the work was done before 26 April 1999 it can be more sensible to prepare a bill in the old form provided that the local court will accept this. For mixed cases it is probably more sensible to use or adapt the new model form of bill.

It seems that although the rules do allow for the production of bills on disk and seem to imply that bills, objections and responses to objections and the final assessed bill could be dealt with electronically, this has not happened to any great extent so far. Although the technology is in theory here, so many different systems are in use that it is quite hard to merge the various forms. However, no doubt as technology advances and comes into more widespread use and there are more common protocols for file merger this will simplify the process considerably.

The opportunity has also been taken to simplify and improve the various legal aid forms and costs certificates, which is welcomed.

General rules about costs (CPR Part 44)

This Part of the CPR sets out the way in which the court would go about assessing costs. Although many of the rules and the terminology have a basis in the old regime, there have been important changes both of terminology and principle. The court retains an overriding discretion as to 'whether costs are payable by one party to another; the amount of those costs; and when they are to be paid' (CPR Rule 44.3(1)(c)).

The so-called 'English rule' that the 'loser pays' is retained (CPR Rule 44.3(2)(a)), but 'the court may make a different order' (CPR Rule 44.3(2)(b)). The court must have regard to all circumstances including the conduct of the parties, whether a party has succeeded on part of the case even if not wholly successful and to any payment into court or offer to settle (whether or not under CPR Part 36) (CPR Rule 44.3(4)). Expressly requiring the court to take account of the conduct of parties is a change in emphasis and is expanded upon in CPR Rule 44.3(5). This refers to conduct pre-proceedings (such as whether a protocol was followed) as well as after proceedings. It also says that the court must take into account whether it was reasonable to raise, pursue or contest allegations or issues and the manner in which the party pursued or defended the case or allegation or issue.

It therefore follows that simply winning a case does not mean that the court will order the loser to pay all the costs. How this will all work in practice is difficult to say. These are early days.

The case of *Mars UK Ltd* v. *Teknowledge Ltd* ([2000] ECDR 99) is a very important decision by Jacobs J. This was a substantial claim for infringement of copyright and breach of confidence. The claimant succeeded in a primary claim for infringement of copyright, but failed in the claim for breach of confidence. The claimant's costs of the action were reported to be £550,000. An interim order was sought by the claimant on account of the costs payable. The judge concluded that taking into account the pre-action conduct of the claimant and the way in which the claim had been pursued, the claimant should not be able to recover more than £120,000 on a detailed assessment and ordered an interim payment of only £80,000 by the defendant.

In particular, the pre-action conduct criticised included an over-aggressive and over-long letter of claim setting an unreasonable deadline for response. The claimant also ignored the defendant's suggestion of 'without prejudice' negotiations before issue. The judge also considered that although the breach of confidence claim had been arguable, it had not been necessary and the claimant had lost on this issue.

The judge was also concerned about how high the costs had been and that this was not reasonably foreseeable by the defendant. It is certainly advisable that if an expensive step is about to be undertaken by any party to litigation (or proposed litigation) full details of those steps, why they are necessary and their likely extent should be made clear to the other party in advance. If that is done there is a much better chance of recovering most or all of those costs.

Solicitors should now be very wary of implying to their clients that if the case is won the costs will be recovered. Whilst this was the case before the introduction of the CPR in many forms of litigation (and in particular in personal injury cases for claimants) it is far from certain that this will be the case in the new world of the CPR. It is a little ironic that one of Lord Woolf's principles was that costs should be more 'certain'. Before the introduction of the CPR, solicitors could be quite certain that all or virtually all of the costs would be recovered if the case was won and could tell their clients so (and if the indemnity principle had been modified or abolished could have been absolutely certain of this). Since the CPR, no solicitor could make such a claim to the client who therefore does not know how much the costs they will actually have to bear (as opposed to the total costs of the case) will be.

Basis of assessment

The basis of assessment will be on the standard basis or the indemnity basis as previously. The indemnity basis broadly reflects the old definition. The standard basis, however, adds an additional test that the court will 'only allow costs which are proportionate to the matters in issue' (CPR Rule 44.4(2)(a)). Proportionality is again another fundamental principle of Lord Woolf's recommendations for the civil justice system. Proportionality, as we have seen, is first mentioned in Part 1 of the CPR as part of the overriding objective. CPR Rule 44.4(2)(a) gives concrete expression to this. The Practice Direction to this Rule, however, expressly states (at para. 3):

> The relationship between the total of the costs incurred and the financial value of the claim may not be reliable guides. A fixed percentage cannot be applied in all cases to the value of the claim in order to ascertain whether or not the costs are proportionate. In any proceedings there will be costs which will inevitably be incurred and which are necessary for the successful conduct of the case. Solicitors are not required to conduct litigation at rates which are uneconomic. Thus in a modest claim the proportion of costs is likely to be higher than in a large claim, and may even equal or possibly exceed the amount in dispute. Where a trial takes place, the time taken by the court in dealing with a particular issue may not be an accurate guide to the amount of time properly spent by the legal or other representatives in preparation for the trial of that issue.

This Practice Direction is a welcome guidance to the profession as to how proportionality is to be viewed. There were suggestions in Lord Woolf's reports that fixed percentages might be applied to determine whether or not the cost expended on a case is proportionate to the amounts involved and the value to the client. The Practice Direction makes it clear that this is not so, at least not 'in all cases'. Until costs decisions have been appealed and there is authoritative guidance about how the courts are to interpret the principle of proportionality, exactly what it means, however, will remain unclear.

Many costs judges seem to be taking the view that they know a case is disproportionate when they see it, but find it impossible to describe. It is appreciated this is not particularly helpful guidance to those working within the civil justice system! The best that can be said in the absence of any firm guidance in the rules or any authoritative court decision is that Lord Woolf's initial views seem to have been that 25 per cent of the value of the claim is proportionate as a rough rule of thumb. The consultation issued by the Lord Chancellor's Department, *Fixed Costs in the Fast Track*, suggested a figure of 50 per cent of the claim.

It does seem very unlikely that many cases will succeed in obtaining recoverable costs exceeding the value of the claim. Special reasons that might allow this are those cases, which involve matters other than money (for example, injunctions) or cases where the matters of principle are exceptionally important to the individuals (perhaps, for example, professional negligence cases).

Summary assessments

Another principle of the new costs rules is that as much of the costs should be assessed on a 'summary' basis during the course of the case as possible leaving any detailed assessment to sweep up any extra costs at the end. This is a change in emphasis whereby under the old rules almost all costs were determined at the end of the case rather than whilst it was going along. Summary assessment of interlocutory costs was introduced prior to the CPR and is supposed now to be the general rule for interlocutory hearings (which last less than one day) and fast track trials. The Practice Direction to CPR Part 44 sets out the procedure.

If costs are to be costs in the case then the general rule is that no summary assessment of costs will be made (Practice Direction 44, para. 4.4(3)). This presumably also applies to orders of 'claimant's costs in case' and 'defendant's costs in case'. Costs cannot be summarily assessed if the receiving party is a child or a patient (unless the solicitor has waived the right to further costs) (Practice Direction 44, para. 4.9(3)).The court cannot make a summary assessment of costs if the receiving party is in receipt of legal aid (Practice Direction 44, para. 4.9(1)).

However, if the paying party is a child or patient the court may make a summary assessment (Practice Direction 44, para. 4.9(4)). If the paying party is in receipt of legal aid the court may make a summary assessment (Practice Direction 44, para. 4.9(2)). But this is not an order that the paying party has to actually pay the costs as summarily assessed as this is still dealt with under the

Legal Aid Act 1988 s.17 (whereby liability actually to pay costs awarded against a legally aided party is normally postponed). The Practice Direction does not expressly deal with the question of what happens if the paying party has signed a CFA. Guidance was given by the Vice Chancellor before the introduction of the CPR. This indicated that provided notice was given to the receiving party and to the court of the existence of the CFA, liability to pay any sums summarily assessed would be postponed (similar to awards against legally aided parties). It appears that many courts are continuing this procedure, but the position remains unclear.

Experience to date of summary assessment has been mixed. There have been anecdotal reports of difficulties and somewhat arbitrary assessments. Some anecdotal reports suggest that costs being allowed on interlocutory applications are too high. Other anecdotal reports suggest that there has been arbitrary cutting of costs claimed by judges. Some judges have no previous experience whatsoever in assessing costs. This has been less of a problem in the county court where district judges have traditionally filled both the functions of procedural judges and costs judges. It is anticipated that guidance as to benchmark costs for interlocutory applications is to be published by the senior costs judge. Whilst not mandatory, this will be a welcome guidance both to the profession and to the judiciary. Similarly, the guideline rates that have been published are not mandatory even though they have apparently been treated as mandatory by some district judges on assessment. The position remains very unclear.

Solicitors need to take care in ensuring that where a summary assessment of costs is a possibility they do provide the required statement of costs within the required timescale. Otherwise the court is likely to award that no sums be paid and the solicitor will not then be able to claim subsequently on a detailed assessment for the work done for that hearing.

Similarly, at the end of fast track trials the intention is that the costs of the case will be summarily assessed. It is essential that either counsel is fully briefed as to the costs or that the solicitor's representative is able to make representations to the court as to the level of costs to be awarded. In difficult cases it is likely that a submission that costs be referred for detailed assessment may meet with success if the judge is unused to assessing costs and there is a limited time after the end of the trial. However, as time goes on it is likely that more and more fast track cases will be summarily assessed at the end of a trial, at least until the introduction of fixed costs which is still on the agenda.

Fixed Costs (CPR Part 45)

This part of the costs rules broadly replicates the old rules for fixed costs in the case of early judgments (summary judgment, judgment in default, etc.).

Fast track trial costs (CPR Part 46)

The actual cost of the trial itself on the fast track will no longer be subject to detailed or summary assessment. Instead, fixed costs under CPR Part 46 will apply. This awards a variable amount of costs to the advocate depending on the 'value of the claim'. If the claimant wins the case this means the total amount of the judgment excluding interest and costs and any reduction for contributory fault. If the costs are to be awarded to the defendant, the value of the claim is the amount specified in the claim form (excluding interest and costs); or if none was specified, then the maximum amount the claimant reasonably expected to recover according to the statement of value in the claim form (Practice Direction 44, para. 4.9(2)).

Solicitors need to decide whether they propose to undertake the advocacy and fast track trials or to brief counsel. If counsel is to be briefed the solicitor should seek where possible to limit the liability of the client to pay no more by way of brief fee than the amount recoverable as fixed costs on the other side.

It is also possible that no costs will be paid for any attendance on counsel at a trial. There is an allowance for payment of an additional £250 in respect of fees for sitting behind counsel. This is not, however, automatically awarded. Solicitors need to discuss with individual Chambers the requirement for counsel to be clerked at fast track trials.

Detailed assessment (CPR Part 47)

Part 47 of the CPR sets out the procedure for detailed assessment (previously 'taxation') of costs. There have largely been many sensible improvements on the previous costs procedures. There has also been a welcome simplification of terminology.

The intention of the rules is that disputes about the costs that are to be paid in respect of proceedings are resolved quickly and if they cannot be resolved between the parties that the role of the court is limited to resolving those real issues of dispute. There are also provisions for interim payments which are designed to prevent paying parties objecting to bills simply for the purpose of delaying payment.

Solicitors should ensure that they are fully familiar with the procedures set out in CPR Part 47. In particular, as soon as a detailed bill has been drawn and notice of commencement of detailed assessment proceedings has been served on the paying party, close watch should be made to ensure compliance by the paying party in respect of the timetable set out. If objections are not lodged within the relevant time period, application can be made for a default certificate. Even if the paying party sets the certificate aside it is very likely that they will be ordered to pay a proportion of the costs immediately.

If objections are received within time, the solicitor for the receiving party should check whether a request and/or an application can be made for an interim certificate to cover the amount of the costs which are not disputed by the paying party.

A welcome change to the rules is the provision that costs draftsman's fees should be paid by the paying party in addition to the solicitor's costs and expenses set out in the bill. The costs draftsman should, however, be charged out on the same basis as a fee earner. Therefore the number of hours spent on the rate claimed should be set out in the bill. The fee should not be expressed as a percentage of the costs as drawn in the bill even if that is the way in which the costs draftsman as the solicitor's agent or sub-contractor is charging the solicitor for the work.

It is not entirely clear from the rules and Practice Direction, but probably the detailed assessment hearing itself is a hearing to which the rules with regard to summary assessment of costs applies. Presumably therefore both parties should serve and lodge a statement of costs in the same way as set out above for summary assessment at interlocutory hearings.

Appeal procedures have been substantially revised and thankfully the 'review' step of applying to the same costs judge who made the original decision has been removed from the sequence.

Special costs cases (CPR Part 48)

Part 48 of the CPR sets out various miscellaneous costs provisions which have been brought forward from the old rules, but which do not fit into the other sections on costs. In particular, they deal with rules relating to non-parties, pursuant to a contract, trustees, patients and children.

The second section of Part 48 deals with costs relating to solicitors and other legal representatives. In particular Rule 48.7 deals with wasted costs and Rule 48.8 sets out the procedure for detailed assessment of solicitor and client costs. Rule 48.9 provides for the detailed assessment of success fees by clients under CFAs. It is expected that similar provisions will be introduced to deal with 'between the parties' detailed assessments.

Part 36 offers (CPR Part 36)

Although CPR Part 36 is dealt with elsewhere, an offer or payment made under Part 36 has important costs consequences and so is dealt with briefly here. So far as defendants to money claims are concerned, CPR Part 36 broadly replicates the procedures of the old 'payment into court'. The court will order the claimant to pay costs incurred by the defendant after the latest date on which the payment or offer could have been accepted without permission unless the court considers this unjust. It follows that the claimant will also not be able to recover his costs over that period from the defendant.

The big change is extending the provisions of CPR Part 36 to claimants. The costs consequences for defendants where a claimant does better than proposed in a Part 36 offer are set out in CPR Rule 36.21. Unless the court thinks it unjust, it will:

(a) order interest on the damages awarded to the claimant at a rate not exceeding 10 per cent above base;

(b) will cost the claimant on the indemnity basis;

(c) award the claimant interest on those costs at a rate not exceeding 10 per cent above base.

The interest provisions (on both damages and costs) run only from the last date on which the defendant could have accepted the Part 36 offer. It therefore follows that the earlier that an appropriate Part 36 offer can be made, the better the prospects that the claimant can obtain the benefit of these costs provisions.

However, the other important point is that the costs payable by the defendant after the last date on which the Part 36 offer could have been accepted will be on the indemnity basis. As has been seen, the indemnity basis does not bring into play the concept of 'proportionality', whereas the standard basis does. This could be an important safeguard to the client to ensure that the client maximises recovery of the costs expended on the litigation from the other side if the case is won. Solicitors must therefore be alert to making Part 36 offers at appropriate levels, revising them when appropriate and doing so at the earliest possible stage.

Conclusions

In maximising recovery of costs for the client the following points should be noted:

(1) The solicitor should ensure that there is a clear and enforceable retainer with the client. Whilst the indemnity principle exists in any shape or form, there is a danger that the solicitor will not be able to recover any costs if the retainer is not clear, in writing and enforceable. The danger of an unenforceable retainer is perhaps magnified by the increased and complex payment options that are now available.

(2) Nothing in the CPR (save for the introduction of fixed costs) reduces the need for a solicitor to maintain clear, accurate and detailed file

notes recording the work undertaken on the case (see *Brush* v. *Bower Cotton & Bower* [1993] 4 All ER 741).

(3) It is essential that full computerised records of time being spent are also maintained. A solicitor needs to know quickly and accurately how much time has been spent on a file. It is very difficult to have the file costed by a costs draftsman for the purposes of summary assessment of costs. This is because of the time that would be needed and the likelihood that the file would have to be removed from the solicitor at the time when the solicitor most needs it (i.e. immediately before a hearing).

(4) Solicitors must get used to preparing estimates for their clients and for the courts. Solicitors must also analyse the costs benefit ratios so as to ensure that if the client succeeds in the case the costs that have been incurred are likely to be held by the court to have been proportionate to the issues. No client will thank a solicitor for a bill which exceeds the damages obtained because the costs recovered were reduced on the grounds of proportionality. It is also quite likely that a solicitor would find it difficult to enforce payment of the bill against the client in those circumstances.

(5) Defendants should make even more use of CPR Part 36 payments than previously. They are a very effective costs weapon against claimants. Claimant's solicitors must make use of Part 36 offers at a realistic level as early as can reasonably be done.

(6) Solicitors must be preparing for the future. The current state of costs rules is not complete. Fixed costs for the fast track remain on the horizon as do benchmark costs for multi-track cases. Solicitors should be using their computerised records to maintain a database of costs so that they can measure whether fixed costs when they are brought in will properly reward the solicitor for the work expended and if not how procedures can be changed to ensure that profitability is maintained.

CONCLUSION

The plethora of funding options means that, in order to discharge their duty to act in clients' best interests, solicitors must know what the different options are and which option best suits the client and their case. Where a solicitor is a stakeholder in the litigation, the funding option must also meet the firm's own risk management criteria.

Risk assessment skills should always have been an important part of the litigation lawyer's skill set and the survival instinct should ensure that these skills become particularly well-honed. This will require solicitors to adopt the type of project management tools and quality standards systems mentioned in this chapter and other chapters in the book. Firms must carefully consider their investments in training, IT and supervision accordingly.

The risks of conducting litigation under a CFA and the investment of time, money and energy required to manage those risks may be off-putting. However, solicitors must balance these risks against the risk of losing clients to competitors who are prepared to be more creative and risk-taking in their approach to funding litigation.

CHAPTER 8

The external team

Simon Parrington, Neil Hext, Roger Clements and Anthony Cherry

---

C. EXPERTS

A. INSTRUCTING COUNSEL

The legal team should aim to promote a complete legal service to its clients whether private, corporate or institutional. Part A of this chapter deals with the selection and briefing of counsel in general terms.

'HORSES FOR COURSES': CHOOSING COUNSEL

Counsel may be instructed by a solicitor at any stage in litigation and in some instances it may be appropriate to instruct counsel prior to the commencement of litigation. He or she may be instructed to advise on the merits before issue and then to draft statements of case (pleadings) after commencement, attend on applications, advise on evidence pre-trial and ultimately attend court.

While some firms are increasing the number of their solicitor advocates, it is still usual to brief counsel to appear at longer trials. The solicitor who deals with a varied caseload is sometimes considered to be the general practitioner of the legal profession with counsel being akin to the consultant. Barristers in general are more experienced than solicitors in court procedure, and the handling and presenting of evidence in court. But this is changing, especially as more solicitors specialise in particular areas of litigation and develop drafting, project management and advocacy skills through interim hearings, case management conferences and, for some, fast track trials.

The relationship between counsel and solicitor is an important one and one which may be developed over a number of years. The process begins on first instruction. The solicitor is the professional client of the barrister. The solicitor is always responsible for providing counsel with proper instructions and for negotiating and paying the barrister's fee.

Unless the client has a pre-arranged agreement with a particular set of chambers, the solicitor with conduct of a case should choose which barrister to instruct on any particular matter. London or provincial counsel may be chosen but, in each instance, the instructing solicitor must ascertain for himself which barrister is suitable for each individual matter.

The solicitor must assess whether his chosen counsel has sufficient knowledge of the particular aspects of law involved in the case and whether the value and importance of the case warrant instructing counsel of many years call. However, a complex or high profile case or a case proceeding in a specialist court may benefit from the instruction of a high profile counsel.

There are no set guidelines for choosing one barrister as opposed to another although the following may be considered:

(a) counsel must be able to work with his instructing solicitor and the client as part of a team;

(b) counsel should not only have an in-depth knowledge of the law but also be able to take a commercial and sensible approach to litigation;

(c) counsel should be skilled in the drafting of statements of case (pleadings) and presentation of the case efficiently and effectively.

Leading counsel may be used in a wide variety of difficult litigation whether in high court, county court, tribunals or elsewhere. Criteria to be considered include:

- the complexity of the case;
- the value of the case;
- the importance of the case to the client;
- the potential for publicity;

- the budget for legal fees;
- that the use of leading counsel may dispense with the need for a junior;
- the added value which the instruction of leading counsel may give.

INSTRUCTING COUNSEL IN CIVIL LITIGATION

The small claims court (see also Chapter 10)

Counsel's role is likely to be limited in small claims to the hearing. This is because of the limited costs available and the informality of the hearings. The court has a very wide discretion as to how such hearings should be conducted. Costs are limited by CPR Rule 27.14 to fixed costs, expenses, loss of earnings, to a limited extent experts' fees and increasingly, legal costs occasioned by 'unreasonable conduct'.

Usually small claims will be conducted either by litigants in person or by solicitors or their representatives. However, the small claims court is a place at which junior counsel in pupillage or in the first years of call may be briefed for a small fee.

Fast track (see also Chapter 11)

Cases in the fast track tend to be less complex than multi-track cases but more complex than small claims. They can involve difficult issues and technical areas of law so counsel is more likely to be briefed in such cases.

Counsel may also settle a statement of case or defence and in certain cases may be asked to advise. If briefed at trial then fixed costs for the advocacy will apply even if the trial takes more than one day.

Multi-track (see also Chapter 13)

Such cases as proceed in the multi-track are by virtue of value alone likely to be more complex. Counsel may be engaged on a more pro-active basis than on either the fast track or the small claims track. In larger and more complex claims counsel should settle the statement of case (and defence) together with schedules and other 'pleadings'. When a case is allocated to the multi-track, the court may fix a case management conference for which it may be appropriate for counsel to be briefed. If not and there is a pre-trial review (PTR) then if there is a prospect of settlement counsel should certainly be briefed at that stage.

TEAMWORK

The importance of competent case management (as encouraged by the CPR) is critical in large scale and high value litigation. One of the most under-valued aspects of this is the early involvement of specialist senior counsel. It is for the solicitor to appoint the team. He should carefully select senior and junior counsel as well as experts as early as possible in the litigation or even before proceedings have begun. The client should be included as part of the team and should understand his role as well as the role of each other member of the team.

GIVING INSTRUCTIONS AND WORKING WITH COUNSEL

In cases of complexity, it is possible that leading counsel may wish to retain a set of papers throughout the currency of the claim which can be updated and revised as the litigation progresses. Detailed instructions should be given ensuring that counsel is supplied with all relevant documents, statements and pleadings.

Be sure to instruct or brief counsel in good time so as to give him or her the opportunity to prepare the case properly. Poor instruction dispatched late can reflect on the outcome of a case.

To achieve identification of all key issues, leading counsel may be instructed to work with junior counsel in connection with the settling of statements of case. This will ensure that only the facts material to the case are pleaded and that all relevant facts and issues are identified at the outset.

Disclosure in this type of claim is likely to be extensive and vitally important – early contact with counsel might assist but be aware of overuse of counsel, the costs of which will not be recoverable.

Early identification of appropriate witnesses is important. Whilst the solicitor will gather documentary and witness evidence and, with the witness, will draft the statement, selection of witnesses whose evidence is to be adduced should be considered by counsel in more complex cases.

Despite the emphasis of the CPR upon restricting use of experts, large scale and/or valuable litigation will require the involvement of specialist experts (see Part C below). Early involvement of leading counsel will enable him or her to have an input on issues such as specialist expertise, relevance of experience, the quality of an expert as a witness and ability in drafting reports.

Counsel may have a role to play in advising on settlements. Timely and tactical use of CPR Part 36 offers to settle can be vital to the outcome of a case and to costs recovery (see Chapter 15). 'Court door' deals done by counsel in the court corridor should be a thing of the past.

Counsel should be instructed to provide a final opinion in good time prior to trial so as to allow time for counsel's advice to be acted upon. Detailed instructions prior to trial should assist or facilitate early and comprehensive drafting of a skeleton argument. A conference with counsel may prove of assistance.

STATEMENTS OF CASE (PLEADINGS)

Although pleadings as such no longer exist under the CPR, the expression is still used to describe the particulars of claim, statement of case, defence, counter-claim and reply, CPR Part 20 proceedings and replies to requests for further information.

Because the rules impose time constraints upon the parties, counsel might be instructed to settle the statement of case or other pleadings and, if so, as soon as possible. The CPR provides for each party to certify the truth of the statement of case. Therefore it will be necessary for counsel to be provided with specific instructions in order that he or she might plead the case accurately. Solicitors should check all statements of case very carefully to ensure accuracy and compliance with the CPR – there are still too many 'pleadings' taken straight from precedent books which do not set out the facts or respond fully to allegations made by the other party. A party cannot be expected to sign the certificate of truth if the statement of case does not accurately reflect the true facts.

PREPARING FOR TRIAL WITH COUNSEL

Preparation

The brief should be delivered as soon as is reasonably practicable: counsel must be given a proper opportunity to master the issue in the case. However, because of the need to keep an eye on proportionality in costs, it is also important not to brief counsel too soon. If there is a prospect of settlement prior to trial then you should be prepared to negotiate (with the client's approval) prior to preparing the brief to counsel.

In complex cases involving expert evidence or numerous witnesses, it may be necessary to hold a pre-trial conference with the expert witnesses present. Where appropriate, counsel ought to be given the opportunity to meet the experts in advance of the trial in order that he or she might review not only their evidence but also the way in which the expert will present at trial. A great deal of time and money can be saved by holding a pre-trial conference.

The skeleton argument

The skeleton argument is an abbreviated note of the argument to be used by counsel at trial. Use of skeleton arguments has developed through the Chancery and Admiralty courts and is now more often used in mainstream litigation. The skeleton argument should identify the issues in the case, the facts which are relied upon, relevant points of law and it should cite authorities where appropriate. The court will be assisted if the summary includes a chronology of events – in complex cases such a chronology will be a necessity.

Although the skeleton argument is only a summary of the relevant points to be considered by the court, it will save the court time and will assist the judge during the hearing of the case and when considering his judgment. The skeleton argument will provide a framework for the hearing itself and enable counsel to restrict the amount of time to be spent on submissions.

A case summary will frequently be the subject of a direction by the procedural judge. Usually the court will require the claimant's solicitor to file a case summary (of not more than 500 words) before the trial. This may be prepared by solicitor or counsel.

ADVOCACY

Barristers and solicitors all have rights to appear in any court in the land subject only to qualification.

Advocacy is a skill which for some is a natural talent but for most has to be learned and practised. Save in a few cases, trial advocacy used to be the preserve of the Bar. That is no longer so. Solicitors regularly appear in the county court before a circuit judge and a good many are the equal of many barristers as advocates. That said, the profession still looks to the Bar for the bulk of its trial advocacy.

Use of advocacy skills is called for in two main areas of work in the county courts and high courts:

- pre-trial applications and hearings;
- trials.

PRE-TRIAL HEARINGS

The vast majority of what used to be called interlocutory hearings are dealt with by solicitors, legal executives and outdoor clerks. They are heard before district judges and masters. However, introduction of the CPR has reduced the need for interim hearings because the directions orders on allocation to track and the case management conferences provide a framework for the progress of each case.

Of course there will still be mortgage re-possession summonses, bankruptcy proceedings etc. to be heard. However, the really important pre-trial hearings are the case management conferences and pre-trial reviews.

Whether or not you employ counsel will depend upon whether you feel confident enough to deal with the matter yourself and the size and complexity of the case. Remember that the court will require the person dealing with the case to attend or, if not, someone with a thorough working knowledge of the file including the costs position. Preparation is the most important part of these cases:

- prepare;
- know the file and the issues in the case;
- know the witnesses and their availability for trial;
- know the experts and their availability;
- know the costs incurred to date and the estimates of future costs and whether these are proportionate;
- consider the consequences of failure.

Attending court is really the easy part!

If you brief counsel then do so in good time and give proper instructions. Counsel is only as good as the instructions given. If the application is complex or the case management conference is large and difficult then, in addition, you should be prepared to discuss the case with counsel before the day of the hearing to ensure that counsel has a proper understanding of the case and to give counsel an opportunity to discuss the case with you. Ensure that, if an order with time limits is to be made, counsel is told how long is needed for compliance; counsel should not be permitted to submit to or agree a direction that provides, say, for medical reports to be exchanged before the date upon which examination by the expert is due to take place or to agree a trial date on a day when a lay witness is not available. Failure to give counsel the information that the court is likely to require will leave you with only yourself to blame, and the client to answer to, if the order or directions are not what you wanted.

TRIAL

The main factors to be considered are:

- cost;
- skill;
- necessity.

Small claims

Often it is cheaper to brief junior counsel than for a solicitor to attend at a small claims hearing. The small claims court provides a good training ground for young advocates to practise their skills. A fee should be agreed with counsel's clerk in advance of the hearing in every case and, if appropriate, collected in advance from the client. Once a fee has been agreed for attending a small claims hearing then that fee should be paid to counsel without delay after the hearing. Counsel should be given instructions in good time, making sure he or she has all the papers that will be before the court, particularly if counsel is to attend court without an instructing solicitor.

Fast track

It is with one day fast track trials that the Bar is likely to see most competition from solicitors. Having run a straightforward case to trial there is no real reason why the solicitor should not handle the advocacy. The approach is different in fast track cases, as there is much less time for submissions. Being on top of the facts, evidence and issues in dispute is the key. Costs allowed as advocacy fees are fixed by scale to a maximum of £750 (as at March 2001). Assessment of costs will usually take place summarily at the end of the case. You must always remember to prepare, file and serve the statement of costs.

It should be a reasonably straightforward exercise to brief counsel for a fast track trial, but it is important to make sure that counsel has all the facts before him or her, particularly if he or she is to be accompanied by a junior fee earner or to appear without an instructing solicitor. If counsel is required to deal with the summary costs assessment at the end of the case then he or she must have detailed instructions in that regard both as to the client's and the opponent's claims for costs.

Multi-track

In most multi-track cases, advocacy at trial will be conducted by counsel. Costs will be subject to a detailed assessment and therefore will be much less restricted than in the fast track.

ATTENDING AT TRIAL

It is often desirable for the solicitor who has the conduct of the file or at least one who has a strong working knowledge of it, to attend the final hearing with counsel. In addition to being able to deal with queries raised by counsel before, during and after the hearing, the solicitor's representative will look after the party his firm is representing and also be in the best position to take down a detailed note of all the evidence and the judgment. The solicitor's note of the judgment may be the only accurate note of the judgment available in the event that an appeal is lodged.

The requirement of the CPR for summary assessment of costs in fast track trials reinforces the importance of solicitors' attendance. Traditionally the issue of costs remains within the expertise and knowledge of the solicitor rather than counsel who may have received little or no training in the assessment of costs. It may be appropriate for the solicitors to take over the conduct of the case from counsel at the conclusion of the trial if the judge orders a summary assessment. It is unlikely that counsel will be familiar with issues such as charging rates, time spent or proportionality unless he or she is given specific instructions.

It must be remembered that CPR Rule 46.3(2) provides for a fee (currently) of only £250 in fast track trials for attendance by instructing solicitor and that it will be for the judge to exercise his discretion to allow such a fee should he consider that it was appropriate for the solicitor's representative to attend.

CONCLUSION

In summary:

    (a) consider whether it is really necessary to instruct or brief counsel;

    (b) bear proportionality in mind when instructing counsel;

    (c) choose counsel who you consider to be best suited to the case and the client;

(d) teamwork is the key, particularly in complex cases; without proper instructions, evidence and documents, counsel cannot present the client's case in the best light;

(e) prepare the case properly before instructing or briefing counsel: take proper instructions from the client, proof witnesses effectively, gather expert evidence with care and quantify the claim realistically.

B. COUNSEL'S ROLE: THE BARRISTER'S PERSPECTIVE

Part B of this chapter deals with instructing counsel from the barrister's point of view.

IS THERE STILL A PLACE FOR COUNSEL?

The role of the barrister in the context of the legal profession as a whole has never been more under scrutiny than it is today. With the gradual expansion of solicitors' rights of audience and the increasingly competitive environment that all lawyers now find themselves in, there are those who question the very existence and viability of this 'half' of the legal community.

However, before one can answer the question 'Is there a need for the Bar at all?', one must first ask, 'what do barristers do?' Broadly speaking, counsel's main function is that of an advocate. This is a skill that evolves in an individual primarily through practice. Few advocates would say that they honed their skills in, say, cross-examination in the classroom and it is trite that someone who performs in court every day will tend to be a more competent advocate than someone whose experience is sporadic.

It follows from this that whether or not the professions merge, those who hold themselves out as advocates will probably need to work on a referral basis. The lawyer who takes on the role of an advocate only in his or her own cases will not build up the experience necessary to become competent.

Thus the real debate is not about whether the client needs two lawyers or just one: rather, it is about whether these services can be better provided from within a fused profession or whether there is still room for an independent Bar.

Here a number of factors come into play. First, cost: there can be little doubt that at the junior end, the Bar offers a service which is cheaper on an hour for hour comparison than a solicitor of equivalent experience can ever hope to offer. The reason for this is that currently the Bar does not have the overheads of a typical firm of solicitors. They employ few staff and do not need extensive premises. As one moves up the profession the disparity reduces, but arguably, except for the few 'stars' of the Bar, when one compares like with like, counsel is probably less costly.

Secondly, the existence of a competitive Bar means that the lay client has more choice. He or she is not tied in to the advocates who are employed by the firm of solicitors he or she instructs. This can be a great advantage where the case involves a specialised area of law. A smaller firm of solicitors, even if it has a specialist advocate, is unlikely to have the capacity to cater for the full range of types of case which might walk through the door. It is a feature of the Bar that it is becoming increasingly specialised. Apart from a very few at the top of the profession, who are frequently instructed more for their intellectual abilities or showmanship than their pre-existing knowledge, the barrister as 'jack of all trades' is a dying breed. Many Chambers, recognising that specialism is potentially their only lifeline, are now developing discrete practice groups whose members profess specialist knowledge of particular areas.

On the other side of the coin, the great advantages that solicitors have is primary contact with the client and control of the day to day work on the case. It is a selling point to be able to present the client with a seamless package. During the interlocutory stages, this freedom of access is probably more efficient. For the barrister to deal with a particular question the client must first ask it of the solicitor who then passes it up the chain.

The new forms of funding that are being introduced create practical difficulties for the barrister. Solicitors are much better placed than barristers to meet the challenges of 'no win no fee'. In addition there is the element of trust. The client may well feel happier with an advocate who is with the firm they have come to trust than with an outsider whose reputation is unknown to them. There are also practical benefits to the client in that it reduces the scope for the lawyers to be able to sidestep responsibility by blaming each other.

Finally, the changes in the environment in which barristers work mean that there is a discernible upward pressure upon their fees. Barristers' Chambers are behaving more and more like commercial concerns. They now spend large sums on marketing (which continues to shock the more traditional elements of the Bar). Information technology and the need for more support staff mean that overheads are on the rise. As a result, counsel's ability to undercut solicitors may not survive into the long term.

Currently, experience suggests that the reform of rights of audience has not had the impact that was feared by the Bar (and hoped for by its supporters). It is still relatively unusual to be opposed by a solicitor advocate. This applies as much to fast track trials as it does to bigger cases. The low levels of recoverable fees fixed by the CPR mean that only the simplest cases requiring the least preparation are a realistic target for most firms.

High Street firms of solicitors, who are required by their clients to provide a service over a huge range of areas of law, still rely very heavily upon counsel, not only for advocacy but for advice as well. Many of these firms would find it hard to operate without. Few can have their sights on the work currently done by the Bar. The biggest challenge to the Bar therefore is the current trend towards larger and larger firms of solicitors. Because of the nature of the job and the fact that it is essentially a referral service, it is only the bigger firms that can seriously hope to be able to provide their clients with specialist advocates in-house. Even if that trend continues, it is likely that the Bar will survive, although perhaps in a smaller form. For larger, more complex cases, it is unlikely that any but the very biggest firms will be able to offer their clients advocates who are as specialist and experienced as those that currently exist at the Bar.

SILKS AND JUNIORS

It usually takes between 15 and 20 years for a barrister to take silk. It is not an automatic promotion and there are many advocates who, despite their seniority, for one reason or another have not taken silk (indeed some choose not to apply because of the inevitable change it would mean in the volume and type of work that they would receive). At the moment silks make up about 10 per cent of the profession. The award is designed to be a recognition of distinction in advocacy and the selection process places heavy weight on consultation with the judiciary and other senior members of the legal profession. That selection process is not without its critics. However, there is no doubt that broadly speaking the QC system enables some sort of judgement to be made about the experience and quality of the advocates concerned. In addition, perhaps not uncontroversially, there is the further, somewhat nebulous benefit that a silk can bring authority to a case that can be particularly useful in the higher courts.

All of these virtues are, as one would expect, reflected in the fees that silks generally charge. It goes without saying that they tend to be instructed in more complex cases and those of particularly high value.

In the past, if one instructed a silk one would almost always instruct a junior as well. That is something that is changing and silks are often more than happy to appear alone without a junior. However, the complexity of the case, whether it is because of the legal issues or the sheer weight of evidence involved, can mean that the case is unmanageable by one person on his own and a junior, sometimes a team of juniors, is required.

The role of the junior is to deal with 'pleadings', attend interim hearings, consider statements and provide tactical guidance. This is an area where the Bar is particularly vulnerable. There is no obvious need for the junior to be a barrister and solicitors, particularly the large commercial firms, are starting to supply the service in-house. From the point of view of the client there is something to be said for having a junior who has had experience as an advocate in his own right. There is nothing like having to defend one's pleading before the trial judge to give one a keen sense of what is necessary to plead and what can be left out. But for the sets of Chambers who dominate in this area – who find it hard to find 'small work' for their very junior members – that sort of experience towards the bottom of the board may well be no greater than that of their instructing solicitors.

THE CAB RANK RULE

As long as he is available to do so, it is part of counsel's professional duty to accept any instructions in relation to work that he holds himself out as competent to carry out. However, this is now subject to an important exception. Counsel is not obliged to take instructions where his remuneration is to be by way of a conditional fee. In some areas of work, e.g. claimant's personal injury, conditional fees have become widely accepted by the Bar. But the decision as to whether or not to take a case on conditional fee lies with the barrister concerned and it is something that must be negotiated at the outset.

TEAMWORK: COUNSEL'S VIEW

In the context of a profession which is guilty at times of prima donna behaviour, and sometimes sheer arrogance, teamwork is not something that automatically springs to mind! Yet frequently solicitors and the counsel they instruct regard themselves as being part of a team based upon professional relationships that have built up over many years. The level of interaction between the solicitor and counsel will depend upon the type of case, its size and complexity. However, counsel can be a useful resource to consult on all aspects of the litigation as it develops, from the initial drafting of statements of case, through disclosure, witness statements, expert evidence, tactics, procedure and settlements. Often it is unnecessary to prepare formal instructions. Many barristers are more willing than their clients realise to give informal advice on the telephone. Chambers may also be able to provide extra pairs of hands from the junior end to help out with the legwork on bigger cases.

Of course it would be misleading to suggest that the whole Bar is as responsive as this. Some barristers simply are not good team players. Some of these will be worth instructing for other reasons. However, it is important to remember that the Bar is like any other market: if you do not get the service you require, you can always go elsewhere.

GIVING INSTRUCTIONS: COUNSEL'S VIEW

Instructions to counsel are prepared in a wide range of styles, from a minimalist 'the facts of this case will be apparent from the papers herewith', to a lengthy treatise on the history of the case and the development of relevant areas of the law. From counsel's point of view, the most important thing to include is what he is being instructed to do. That may simply be asking him to draft a defence or represent a party at trial. In the context of an advice, it may be the question he is being asked to answer. Sometimes the instructions need contain no more than this. However, there are usually a number of other things that should be included. They are as follows:

(a) a list of the enclosures with a meaningful description of the contents of each;

(b) a very brief outline of what has happened, perhaps with a summary of the main issues that are in dispute;

(c) the date and venue of the court appearance, or the date by which the work needs to be produced;

(d) who to contact (with a telephone number) if any queries arise.

For 'pleadings', counsel will usually need to see detailed instructions from the lay client, either in the form of an attendance note or a witness statement and possibly from a liability expert. This is particularly important now that statements of case have to be verified by a statement of truth. In the case of a defence, it is very helpful if the defendant himself has been asked to comment upon the allegations in the particulars of claim, one by one. In the case of instructions to advise, if the solicitor has his own views on the issues he should state them.

It is worth asking counsel to telephone upon receipt of papers. It gives both solicitor and counsel an opportunity to discuss the issues and counsel may well be able to give a preliminary view which can be passed on to the client. More importantly, it provides an opportunity to agree time limits for the work. This can be one of the biggest sources of aggravation between solicitors and counsel. If there is no clear deadline for when the work needs to be produced, counsel will prioritise it at the bottom of the pile and it will be done later rather than sooner. Where there is urgency, it is important to make counsel aware of this and get him to commit to producing the work by a certain date. Sometimes counsel will simply be unable to produce the work in that timescale in which case it is better to know that on day one than on the day that the work is due. Equally, in fairness to counsel, one should not insist on unreasonably tight timescales where there is no urgency for the work that would merit it. Finally, a telephone call can avert disaster by revealing that counsel is on holiday, off sick or that the papers have not arrived.

Before leaving the question of instructions, what should you do if you are not happy with the service that counsel has provided? Of course there are formal steps that can be taken where it is suspected that substantial mistakes have been made which have caused real loss. However, in situations which fall short of this, the solicitor should not hesitate to contact counsel and make the concerns known. Too often, little or no feedback is given because the solicitor does not want to offend. But the solicitor and the lay client are entitled to a proper service and the matter should not be allowed to rest when a telephone call might provide a solution to the problem.

STATEMENTS OF CASE (PLEADINGS): COUNSEL'S VIEW

Lord Woolf's intention (see *Access to Justice*, Final Report, p. 5) was to simplify the pleading process and do away with tactical allegations designed cynically to obscure the issues rather than clarify them. However, in two respects the CPR have made pleadings, now statements of case, more significant.

First, a defendant who wishes to deny an allegation must give his reason for doing so (CPR Rule 16.5(2)). This represents a cultural shift for the defendant. It means that he has to have everything in order virtually as soon as the claimant starts the proceedings so that he can plead the allegations upon which he will rely at trial in detail. It is essential that investigation takes place during the pre-action phase. If for any reason that has not happened, advantage should be taken of the provisions in the CPR to extend time. The High Court procedure of putting in an acknowledgement of service has been applied across the board to all cases, allowing the defendant up to four weeks to file a defence (CPR Rule 15.4). The parties can agree between themselves an extension of time for a further 28 days (CPR Rule 15.5) but further time must be obtained by a court order. In cases where, perhaps for limitation reasons, the claimant has issued without proper notice to the defendant, he should be prepared to consent to an extension of time. An unreasonable refusal could result in an order for costs against him (CPR Rule 44.3(5)).

Secondly, the client has to sign a statement of truth verifying the contents of the statement of case. In theory this means that the lay client can no longer say in the witness box that he had never seen the particulars of claim before and that the misrepresentations contained within it are nothing to do with him.

One would have thought that these two aspects of the CPR would actually mean that more attention was paid to the pleading process leading to increased use of counsel. In fact anecdotally there appears to have been a decline in instructions in this respect, particularly defences.

This may be a pity because drafting is a technical skill. Bad 'pleadings' can lead to disproportionate expenditure during the course of the case, not to mention heartache for the client at trial when the possibility that his case might not be determined on its proper basis becomes a real one. It is therefore something that it is important to get right. Obviously in low value cases, particularly fast track cases, where the issues are not difficult, the statements of case can be prepared simply by adapting a standard form which complies with the CPR. However, in more complex cases (and this does not necessarily mean higher value ones) individual attention is required and it is important that the drafting is carried out by someone competent to do it.

ADVICE FROM COUNSEL

The current trend seems to be that solicitors are becoming more discerning about spending money on getting advice from counsel. This may be an application of the principle of proportionality under the new regime. Apart from the question of hourly rate, there is often no reason why it should be any easier for counsel to research a tricky legal point than his solicitor. Indeed, once one adds in the cost of preparing instructions it may well be cheaper for the solicitor to come to a view on his own. Certainly in non-publicly funded fast track cases it has become the norm to get to trial without counsel ever being asked to advise, whether on liability, quantum or evidence.

Nevertheless, with bigger cases there are large numbers of solicitors who still choose to use counsel, particularly where the case is factually or legally complex. Counsel can offer the benefit of specialist experience in a particular field. Advice can be either in writing or orally in conference. The advantage of the latter is that questions can be addressed as they arise. The advantage of the former is that it can be cheaper, once one takes account of all of the costs associated with attending a conference. Of course it is possible (but more expensive) to combine the two.

PREPARING FOR TRIAL: COUNSEL'S VIEW

Collection and analysis of evidence is a central part of the role of the litigation solicitor and frequently this can and is done without any input from counsel. It is becoming less and less easy to justify obtaining a general advice on evidence, which is likely to tell the solicitor no more than he knows already.

However, there are three ways in which counsel can become involved. First, particularly in larger cases, he may be asked to comment upon witness statements or expert reports. There is a distinction between finalising a witness statement and taking a statement from a witness. Although the old rules preventing a barrister from interviewing a witness have been relaxed, it is still regarded as inappropriate for trial counsel to take or draft a witness statement himself, rather than advise on it on the basis of information provided to him (see the Bar Council's guidance on 'Preparing Witness Statements for use in Civil Proceedings'). The CPR states that, where practicable, a statement must be in the witness's own words (Practice Direction to CPR Part 32, para. 18.1). But the witness's 'own words' are sometimes not very coherent and the statement does not always cover all the aspects that it should in order to prove the case. It is legitimate for counsel to suggest changes to statements, pose questions for the witness or for the expert and ask for the substance of the statement to be rearranged.

The second way in which counsel can become involved in the collection of evidence is giving advice on a specific point, for example whether expert evidence is necessary on a particular issue. This is the kind of advice which can often be dealt with over the telephone.

Finally, there is the pre-trial conference. This may not always be necessary – smaller or more straightforward cases will not require it – but if it is, it usually takes place a few weeks prior to the trial and is an opportunity to identify any gaps in the evidence and any further investigations that need to be carried out.

PRE-TRIAL HEARINGS: COUNSEL'S VIEW

At the interim level, arguably the Woolf reforms reduce the scope for instructing counsel. At a multi-track case management conference the legal representative of each party must be familiar with the case and have sufficient authority to deal with issues that are likely to arise (CPR Rule 29.3). The person most qualified for that position is likely to be the solicitor who has conduct of the case. Except where the issues are particularly complex (which is perhaps the type of case where counsel might already have been involved), there is generally no reason why the solicitor should not be in a position to deal with any of the matters that can arise at the case management conference.

However, there may be some cost advantages in instructing counsel. Particularly where the court is not local, a junior barrister will generally be cheaper to instruct than a fee earner charging on an hourly rate and is likely to be more effective than an agent. For this reason, in practice counsel is still frequently asked to attend case management conferences. Proper briefing means that the instructions must contain the full history of the case including all of the orders that have been made, all of the correspondence and all the evidence collected. Counsel will also need to know as much about the tactical position as possible. Are there any more experts who are to be instructed? Is the appointment of a joint expert appropriate? What about a split trial? He or she must also be fully briefed about the costs and provided with costs schedules and an explanation of the assumptions behind them.

Whether or not to instruct counsel on other applications will depend upon their complexity. Some applications will be as important to the client as the trial itself, and occasionally as involved, e.g. summary judgment applications, applications to strike out and applications for security for costs. The flexibility of the new approach under the CPR means that case management questions can arise at the hearing of any application. Frequently, after the hearing of an application the court will take the opportunity to consider the management of the case. Thus if counsel is to be instructed, it will be important for him to be in a position to deal with these matters.

TRIAL: COUNSEL'S VIEW

Having booked counsel to appear, the first step is preparation and delivery of the brief. This can be a bone of contention between solicitor and counsel. On the one hand, the solicitor does not want to brief too early because if the case settles the client will still have to pay counsel's fee. On the other hand, the barrister does not want to be in the position where he is struggling to get to grips with a difficult case the night before the trial. This system of payment on the brief is a controversial one. There are those who say that it should be scrapped and that counsel should be paid on an hourly rate, perhaps with a booking fee. From the client's point of view, however, it is obviously a huge advantage not to become bound to pay anything until it is fairly clear that the trial is going to go ahead. Moreover, the system creates a cut-off point at which costs will escalate which can provide the necessary pressure for parties to settle.

An associated problem that arises is that the barrister who has been booked to appear is no longer available when the brief is delivered, sometimes because he has simply been double-booked. There is no doubt that this phenomenon is one of the Bar's least attractive features. It is to some extent a by-product of the briefing system itself: where counsel is not guaranteed payment until the brief is delivered, it is inevitably a temptation to hedge the position by accepting a booking on another matter.

For practical purposes, in the absence of systemic change in the way that barristers are paid, there are things that can be done to alleviate the problems. It is possible to negotiate in advance that there will be a reduction in the brief fee if the case does settle, thus allowing the brief to be delivered in good time.

Clearly, the nature of counsel's job means that returning briefs is unavoidable, for instance where another trial runs over. However, double-booking is recognised by the Bar itself as being bad business practice. Practice Management Standards issued by the Bar Council provide that a solicitor should be notified promptly if there is a conflict in the diary. By adopting such a transparent approach potential problems can be avoided, perhaps by agreeing that an appropriate alternative will shadow the commitment in case the first choice does not become free. From the solicitor's point of view it is a good idea to obtain an express representation from Chambers that counsel is not booked for something else. If all else fails and Chambers continues to provide an inadequate service in this respect, the only answer is to vote with one's feet.

ATTENDING AT TRIAL: COUNSEL'S VIEW

At the trial itself, at least in multi-track cases, both counsel and solicitor usually attend. This apparent duplication of resources is not wholly without justification. Problems do arise at trial, e.g. with witnesses and documents, which the solicitor is the appropriate person to deal with. In addition, the solicitor is the one who has the most detailed knowledge of the way in which the case has proceeded, which can be essential when it comes to the question of costs.

On the fast track, the CPR envisage that a solicitor will not normally attend as well as the advocate. The court has the power to award a further (currently) £250 in respect of a legal representative's attendance at trial but must be convinced that his attendance was necessary (CPR Rule 46.3(2)). This raises a potential problem in that on the fast track, a summary assessment of the costs is supposed to take place at the end of the trial. Realistically, it is often difficult for counsel to make effective submissions on costs; first because he is not traditionally familiar with the intricacies of detailed assessment; secondly, because he has not had detailed conduct of the case and so will usually know no more than that which is contained in the costs schedule, which is by no means a detailed description of the work that has been done.

The first of these problems could be overcome by appropriate education; there is at the very least a need for a practical guide to the 'nuts and bolts' of assessment, going beyond the CPR rules and dealing with questions like what rates are district judges awarding in any given area, etc. The second problem is more fundamental and is in fact no more than a reflection of what was intended by the summary assessment system. By its very nature summary assessment is a process to be approached in a broad brush manner. The judge is supposed to take a overall view of the time spent on the file and determine the costs accordingly. An element of rough justice is inherent in such a system. Experience shows that by far the biggest influence upon the level of costs awarded on a summary assessment is the amount of costs claimed by the other side in their schedule.

CONCLUSION

In the modern litigation world there is no doubt that there is a need for the specialist advocate. The real question is whether there is room for the independent Bar or whether the role will be absorbed within the solicitor's branch of the profession. Certainly that has not yet happened and an equilibrium exists in which the position of the Bar is not threatened by the traditional High Street or provincial solicitor. However, that equilibrium will be upset if the current trend towards larger and larger firms of solicitors continues and develops.

C. EXPERTS

INTRODUCTION

In his report, *Access to Justice*, Lord Woolf considered experts to be one of the principal causes of expense and delay in the civil justice system. Part 35 of the Civil Procedure Rules addresses many of these concerns and encourages a climate of openness and cooperation between the parties. Two principal themes can be seen as dominating CPR Part 35:

- the overriding duty of the expert to the court;
- the proportionality of cost to the value of the claim (in conformity with the overriding objective in CPR Part 1).

The changes taking place as a result are:

- fewer experts;
- less money for experts;
- less time for experts to respond;
- less oral evidence.

In general, the CPR:

- favours single experts;
- requires objective unbiased reports;
- requires a standard format for expert reports;

300

- provides for written questions to experts;
- encourages expert discussions;
- gives the expert the right to ask the court for directions.

It should be borne in mind, however, that guidance in the case law (e.g. *National Justice Compania Naviera SA* v. *Prudential Assurance Co. Ltd, (The Ikarian Reefer)* [1995] 1 Lloyd's Rep 455, CA) as to how experts should be used and should conduct themselves remains good law.

IS AN EXPERT REQUIRED?

Under the new regime of the CPR, greater attention must be given to the initial question whether an expert in a particular discipline is required at all, or whether more cost-effective solutions might be found. While it is certainly hard to imagine valuing a construction claim without a quantity surveyor, or the prognosis for a broken leg without an orthopaedic surgeon, perhaps, e.g., the 'Situations Vacant' column of the local newspaper might give sufficient help on a small loss of earnings claim.

This may, however, be a difficult decision for the claimant's solicitors. If it is decided not to have an expert in a particular field, then it may be impossible to prove the claimant's case, or the case may be pleaded the wrong way. However, if the solicitors retain an expert whom the court does not subsequently permit, they will usually be unable to recover the cost from the defendant.

If there is a significant chance that the court may consider expert evidence in the particular field entirely unnecessary, the best course is to nominate an expert and give the defendant an early opportunity to challenge the need for such expert evidence. Although the procedural judge may still subsequently disallow the expert, he is less likely to do so if the defendant has acquiesced in obtaining evidence in that field.

WHO IS AN EXPERT?

CPR Rule 35.2 defines an expert, for the purposes of the CPR, as one who has been instructed to give or prepare evidence for the purpose of court proceedings; but experts are instructed by litigators or their clients for many other purposes than to give or prepare evidence for the purpose or court proceedings. The new Code of Guidance for Experts (last published draft appeared in *Clinical Risk*, vol. 5 no. 5 pp. 168–72) distinguishes between the activities of an expert as *adviser* and as *an expert witness*. In the past experts have found difficulty in distinguishing and separating these roles; CPR Part 35 is helpful in creating a practical distinction. Experts who give or prepare evidence for the purpose of court proceedings have a duty (CPR Rule 35.3) to the court which overrides any obligation to the person from whom they have received instructions or by whom they are paid. But that duty arises only when the expert is instructed to prepare a report, which might be used before a court. Until such time, the expert has an obligation to the party as *adviser*.

But the difficulties do not end there. The two roles cannot be separated in time for the expert continues to have a role as adviser throughout the course of litigation, not excluding court proceedings. In written and in oral evidence to the court the expert's duty to the court is clear but during conference with counsel experts also have a duty in the preparation of the case. In the event of an oral hearing the expert will often be required to advise counsel in the cross-examination of experts called by the opposing party, thus continuing the role of adviser.

There is tension between the roles; experts as well as lawyers often have difficulty in understanding their proper limits.

THE DUTIES OF THE EXPERT

The expert's duties are set out clearly in CPR Part 35. Not only does the expert (CPR Rule 35.3) have an overriding duty to the court but also the content and form of the expert's written evidence (CPR Rule 35.10) is clearly prescribed. The Practice Direction to CPR Part 35 adds further detail. In providing written evidence to the court experts are required to declare that they understand their duty to the court and have complied with that duty (CPR Rule 35.10(2)). The form of that declaration must be for the individual expert but one such model, closely modelled on *Access to Justice*, III, 13.35 is illustrated in Box 8.1. However, experts also have duties to the parties who instruct and pay them and these duties, in the form recommended by the Expert Witnesses Institute, are set out in Box 8.2.

Box 8.1 The expert's declaration

The Expert's Declaration

1. I understand that my overriding duty is to the court, both in preparing reports and in giving oral evidence.
2. I have set out in my report what I understand from those instructing me to be the questions in respect of which my opinion as an expert are required.
3. I have done my best, in preparing this report, to be accurate and complete. I have mentioned all matters which I regard as relevant to the opinions I have expressed. All of the matters on which I have expressed an opinion lie within my field of expertise.
4. I have drawn to the attention of the court all matters, of which I am aware, which might adversely affect my opinion.
5. Wherever I have no personal knowledge, I have indicated the source of factual information.
6. I have not included anything in this report which has been suggested to me by anyone, including the lawyers instructing me, without forming my own independent view of the matter.
7. Where, in my view, there is a range of reasonable opinion, I have indicated the extent of that range in the report.
8. At the time of signing the report I consider it to be complete and accurate. I will notify those instructing me if, for any reason, I subsequently consider that the report requires any correction or qualification.
9. I understand that this report will be the evidence that I will give under oath, subject to any correction or qualification I may make before swearing to its veracity.
10. I have attached to this report a summary of my instructions.

I believe that the facts I have stated in this report are true and that the opinions I have expressed are correct.

303

Box 8.2 The expert's duties to the parties

EXPERT WITNESS INSTITUTE

Fundamental Principles

1. A Member will only accept instructions in matters where he/she has the knowledge, experience, academic qualifications, professional training and resources appropriate for the assignment.
2. A Member will maintain client confidentiality except where there is a legal or overriding professional duty to disclose.
3. When providing evidence, whether written or oral, the primary duty of a Member is to the court.
4. A Member will not accept instruction in any matter where there is an actual or potential conflict of interest. If there is any such conflict of interest a Member must inform the instructing solicitor and will only act if the lay client agrees in writing.

Ethical Standards

5. A Member will comply with the code of professional behaviour/ethics of any body of which he/she is a member.
6. A Member belonging to a professional body will observe any professional declaration relating to experts issued by that body. In the absence of the foregoing, careful consideration must be given to the observance of the Institute's Expert's Declaration and to its inclusion with any reports.

The Expert/Client Relationship

7. A Member will only accept an instruction that is clear, precise and unambiguous. Orally accepted instructions should be confirmed in writing by the expert.
8. A timetable must be agreed and where this cannot be met, notice of the delay must be communicated at the earliest opportunity to the relevant parties.
9. Where a Member requires specialist assistance with any part of the assignment, prior agreement must be obtained from those issuing instructions and the name of the specialist (or organisation) to be engaged together with details of relevant experience and qualifications must be provided.
10. Where a practice has been instructed, the names of the expert(s) to be assigned and details of their experience and qualifications must be provided on request.

11. A Member will not enter into an arrangement to receive a contingency or conditional fee in respect of any proceedings.

Liability

12. A Member is required to maintain appropriate professional indemnity cover in respect of the full liability of the expert service itself.

Passing Off

13. A Member must not use any title or letters to which he/she is not entitled by means of qualification and/or experience or in any sense misrepresent him or herself.

CHOOSING AN EXPERT

Some professional bodies maintain lists of qualified and appropriately trained members who are prepared to give expert evidence. The quality of these lists is variable. Whilst in some professions the accrediting and training professional body had a direct interest in the preparation of members to give expert evidence, most do not. Most professional bodies are concerned only with their members' ability to function within their profession and know little of their skills as an expert witness. Certainly in medicine, most of the Royal Colleges provide information which amounts to little more than a list of volunteers.

There are few published lists to which the solicitor, seeking an expert, can turn with any confidence. The requirements for entry into such lists are in any event somewhat modest. They can seldom match the expert to the case. The Academy of Experts ('the Academy') and the Expert Witness Institute ('the Institute') can supply lists of members but again are ill equipped to match experts to cases. Specialist firms and support organisations such as Action for the Victims of Medical Accidents (AVMA) keep lists of tried and tested experts but such information is usually jealously guarded and not for publication! Published case reports can be helpful in identifying an expert who has previously given evidence in a satisfactory manner and can also prove a helpful hazard warning when occasionally a judge finds the performance of the expert inadequate or inappropriate. News, in this respect, seems to travel rather slowly and it is a constant source of wonderment that experts who have been severely castigated by courts still find employment from solicitors who remain ignorant of (an often widely published) adverse judgment.

Liability experts in professional negligence actions require special care. In issues relating to breach of duty it is essential that the expert was in practice at the time of the alleged negligence and is familiar with the type of practice to which the case relates. Experts who are retired from practice quickly become out of date and cannot be relied upon to know the 'state of the art' at the time in question. Experts called to assist the court in relation to causation, on the other hand, do not need to take account of the 'state of the art' at the time of the incident but must assist the court with the latest and best available knowledge.

TRAINING AND ACCREDITATION OF EXPERTS

Experts, ignorant of the law within which they operate, can be a menace to the courts for they waste time, addressing the wrong questions and applying the wrong standards. There is no longer any excuse for this, as there is ample training available for those who wish to avail themselves of it. Three bodies exist for the support of experts: the Academy, the Institute and the Society of Expert Witnesses ('the Society'). All of these bodies run conferences and both the Academy and the Institute run training courses, which in the case of the Institute includes a course in basic law for experts. Membership requires only modest evidence of expert experience, usually in the form of references from solicitors. The Institute has a category of membership (provisional) specifically for those seeking to learn how to become effective experts. In providing such education the Institute was responding to the challenge laid down by Lord Woolf in *Access to Justice* (III, 13.54):

> I certainly support the provision of training for experts, both through attendance at courses and through the dissemination of published material . . . Professional people who take on responsibilities as expert witnesses need a basic understanding of the legal system and their role within it. They also need to be able to present their evidence effectively, both in written reports and orally under cross-examination. Training in presentational skills, however, should never lose sight of the fundamental point that the expert's duty is to assist the court. Otherwise it is not in the interest of justice because it may result in the truth being concealed.

What is required is that the expert should be educated, not just trained. The qualities required of an expert are:

- relevance;
- professional status/accreditation;
- forensic training/skill;
- reputation;
- track record.

If there is to be training should there also be accreditation? For those who instruct experts a system of accreditation is attractive but in practice a credible and effective system of accreditation is difficult, if not impossible to achieve. However, accreditation does occur, it is already here; the problem is how to make it better. Accreditation exists in the form of lists, some of them formal and published, some of them informal, but the requirements for entry to any of the published lists are pathetically modest. Once on the list it is difficult at present to see how the expert could be removed, because there is no monitoring or feedback which would lead to the expert's name being removed from any of the formal published lists. To be effective, accreditation would have to be run by a neutral body such as the Academy or the Institute and would require a rigorous standard of admission; that is difficult enough but any system of monitoring and continuous reassessment would prove extremely expensive.

In any event no system of training and accreditation should seek to be exclusive. There are those who make their living, or a substantial part of it, by giving evidence to the courts. It is entirely reasonable that they should be trained, their training properly validated and that they should be accredited. But what of the occasional expert? What of the scientist whose expertise is so rarefied that he is called upon only once or twice in a lifetime to give evidence? It would be unreasonable to expect him or her to jump through the same training or accreditation hoops.

Nevertheless, accreditation in a different form is on the horizon. Because of concern about the standards of scientific evidence in the criminal courts, reflected in the *Report on Forensic Science* by the House of Lords Select Committee on Science and Technology published in 1993, a new body has been created with Home Office funding and approval and with the support of the Royal Society of Chemistry. The Council for the Registration of Forensic Practitioners has started work assessing and ultimately accrediting practitioners in the criminal courts to give scientific evidence. The Council's main task will be to register forensic practitioners, to publish the register and to maintain quality standards. But the ambition of the Council is much broader than the criminal courts. The definition of forensic practitioners is 'persons who practice the application of science to produce evidence in the courts of law and other legal processes'. For this purpose science is defined as 'a craft, trade or occupation requiring a trained skill'. Thus the Council's ambit is broad and will eventually encompass experts of all kinds in all courts. Initially, emphasis will be on forensic scientists in the criminal courts. Six working parties have been set up to deal with:

- court competence;
- discipline competence;
- fingerprint experts;

- document examiners;
- blood and body fluids;
- discipline.

EXPERTS PRE-ACTION

Many organisations are able to call upon in-house experts for preliminary advice when litigation is threatened. Increasingly, parties with no funding or only limited public funding require screening reports from experts to determine whether a conditional fee arrangement is worthwhile, to advise legal expenses insurers or to satisfy the Legal Services Commission that further funding should be extended. For a modest fee the instructing party requires a simple overview based on perhaps one or two hours of work and a limited number of papers to be examined. In the medical negligence field AVMA recently published guidelines for the assistance of experts and those instructing them in the preparation of such screening reports (see Box 8.3).

Also the pre-action protocols for personal injury and clinical negligence claims (see Chapter 9) require the parties to cooperate on expert evidence.

Box 8.3 AVMA guidelines for medical experts

AVMA Guidelines for Medical Experts in Preparing Screening Reports in Clinical Negligence Cases

Screening Reports may be required in the following circumstances:
 To apply for Community Legal Service funding;
 To provide initial report to a privately funded client;
 To advise a conditional fee insurer;
 To advise a legal expenses insurer;
 To satisfy the Legal Services Commission on a subsidiary issue of negligence or causation where funding has been granted to obtain an expert's preliminary opinion, e.g. reporting on histopathology slides, x-rays/scans.

The remit of the Screening Report is to highlight/narrow down the medical issues and summarise the strengths and weaknesses of a potential case.

The solicitor must contact the expert prior to instruction to ask as to the availability of the expert and should agree, with the expert, when instructions are to be sent.

The report is to be prepared within the time agreed with the solicitor which in most cases would be within 4 weeks of receipt of instructions.

The expert should have the benefit of the client's statement, a detailed chronology (prepared by the solicitor/in house para-medical) and paginated core medical notes. These core medical documents should be no more than 20 pages.

The expert should have the option of being able to contact the solicitor for further information.

The Screening Report should not be regarded as disclosable. It should be headed 'Screening Report – Disclosable only to the client and his/her legal advisors'.

The Screening Report is to include points/issues that require investigation and therefore the benefit of a full report. It should comment on areas of possible negligence and the important issues on causation.

The expert should indicate whether or not his/her speciality is appropriate and whether or not a further expert is required.

The expert should indicate, at the end of the report, his/her details of availability to be able to discuss the contents of the report with the solicitor on the telephone.

The fee for the Screening Report is to be £250 to include a review of the chronology and paginated core medical notes and a telephone discussion with the solicitor on receipt of the report. This further clarification should be limited to the evidence supplied with the initial instructions unless an additional fee is agreed.

INSTRUCTION

The Code of Guidance enjoins the expert not to accept instructions unless clear. The instructing solicitor must state clearly whether the expert is required to give advice or to prepare evidence for the purpose of court proceedings, in which case he will need to be told in which track and in which court the action is likely to be heard.

The information required by the expert on first instruction includes:

- the identity of the parties;
- the nature and extent of expertise called for;
- the purpose of requesting the advice or report;

- fast track or multi-track;
- the court;
- the timescale;
- the fees: when they are to be paid and by whom.

PRIVILEGE

Since the introduction of the CPR there has been considerable confusion, doubt and concern about how much of what an expert says or writes must be disclosed to the other side, apart from the formal report to the court. CPR Part 35 is not clear in this regard. Adrian Whitfield QC has helpfully reviewed the subject (in *The Status of the Expert in Giving Advice in Preparing a Report for the Court* (2001) *Clinical Risk* vol. 7 no. 2, pp. 60–2) and advises that:

(a) pre-litigation reports by an expert need not be disclosed (see *Waugh v. British Railways Board* [1980] AC 521);

(b) post-litigation advice by an expert, unless it indicates a departure from the view expressed in the report, is advice to the client and need not be disclosed;

(c) instructions to experts remain privileged save only for the circumstances outlined in CPR Rule 35.10.

CPR Rule 35.10(3) requires the expert to 'state the substance of all material instructions, whether written or oral, on the basis of which the report was written'. The difficulty for the expert is the next paragraph (Rule 35.10(4)):

The instructions referred to in paragraph (3) shall not be privileged against disclosure but the court will not, in relation to those instructions:

(a) order disclosure of any specific document; or

(b) permit any questioning in court, other than by the party who instructed the expert,

unless it is satisfied that there are reasonable grounds to consider the statement of instructions given under paragraph (3) to be inaccurate or incomplete.

As far as I am aware this provision has not been tested in a report and experts remain confused about just how much detail of their instructions the court expects to be included in this statement.

Where the expert, having written a report or having given evidence in court, changes his view, that change of view must be communicated to the court at the earliest opportunity.

THE SINGLE JOINT EXPERT (SJE)

CPR Rule 35.8 provides for parties to agree or the court to appoint a single expert to advise the court. In practice, this may remain a contentious issue for solicitors and their clients: while most practitioners can probably relate quite easily to the idea of a single joint expert (SJE) on quantum, the question of a SJE on liability is more difficult, as an opinion one way or the other may go to the heart of the case. The CPR makes no distinction between the two, although the developing case law provides some guidance. See especially *S (a minor)* v. *Birmingham Health Authority* (*The Times*, 23 November 1999, CA) in which the Court of Appeal made it clear that SJEs are not usually appropriate on liability in complex professional negligence cases and *Daniels* v. *Walker* ([2000] 1 WLR 1382, CA) in which the Court of Appeal said that second experts might be allowed, and the costs recovered, if a quantum SJE's report could be shown to be wrong.

SJEs must take care that their conduct is determined by the principles of fairness and transparency. Instructions must begin in writing and it is essential the SJE receives written instructions from *both* sides. It is not enough for one side to issue instructions and to inform the expert that they are jointly instructed. The expert requires, at the very least, a written acquiescence by the other party. Ideally the expert should be appointed by a joint letter of instruction. If that is not possible then separate letters of instruction must be exchanged so that each side knows what the other side's instructions are. It follows therefore that the expert cannot accept instructions by telephone for they cannot effectively be shared. Every communication from the expert to one party must be copied to the other parties.

The Code of Guidance suggests that if an expert is required to attend a conference with counsel, the solicitor(s) for the other parties should be invited to attend that part of the conference which the SJE attends.

CPR Rule 35.8(5) provides that unless the court otherwise directs the instructing parties are jointly and severally liable for the payment of the expert's fees and expenses. The prudent SJE discovers, in advance, exactly what arrangements are to be made for the payment of his fees so that he knows to which party he may look in the event of difficulty.

FEES

The court (CPR Rule 35.1) has the responsibility to restrict expert evidence to that which is 'reasonably required to resolve the proceedings'. The court's power to restrict expert evidence is dealt with in Rule 35.4 and in particular:

'The court may limit the amount of the expert's fees and expenses that the party who wishes to rely on the expert may recover from any other party'.

Before undertaking instructions the expert should agree with those instructing him how and when he is to be paid. In publicly funded cases, expert fees can be paid as disbursements under contracts or certificates and payment on account is available for all certificated work. Prior authority from the Legal Services Commission guarantees payment. In the last resort the contract between the expert and the solicitor governs the payment of fees and the expert must establish at the outset whether he is agreeable to any delay in payment of his fees or the interference with that contract by a third party such as the Legal Services Commission, the client or the costs judge.

THE REPORT

The Code of Guidance for Experts makes a clear distinction between *advice* and *report.* In many cases the distinction will be irrelevant for only one 'report' will be written. Thus in a straightforward personal injury case the medical expert will usually write only one report which will serve both as advice and evidence to the court.

However, in professional negligence litigation the liability expert, whether instructed by the claimant or the defendant, will usually have a somewhat 'one-eyed' view when first asked to advise. The first document prepared for the instructing solicitor/client will be an initial advice to enable the lawyers to determine the merits of the case and to draft the letter of claim or statement of case. Only after the exchange of lay witness evidence will the expert have a complete view of the case and be able to construct a report, for the purpose of court proceedings. It is this final report which must be accompanied by all the trappings set out in CPR Part 35.

For the purpose of court proceedings, an expert report must:

- be addressed to the court;
- give details of the expert's qualifications;
- give details of any literature or other material which the expert has relied upon in making the report;
- state who carried out any test or experiment;
- state whether or not the test or experiment has been carried out under the experts' supervision;
- give the qualifications of the person who carried out such test;

- where there is a range of opinion, summarise the range of opinion and give reasons for his own opinion;
- contain a summary of the conclusions reached;
- contain a statement that the expert understands his duty to the court and has complied with that duty;
- set out the substance of all material instructions;
- be verified by a statement of truth;
- comply with the requirements of the Code of Guidance for Experts.

The precise wording of the statement of truth is set out in the Practice Direction to CPR Part 35: 'I believe that the facts I have stated in this report are true and that the opinions I have expressed are correct'.

SHADOW EXPERT

Where the court directs or the parties agree on a single joint expert there is nothing to prevent each of the parties appointing their own expert, so as to challenge, if necessary, the single expert's view. Similarly, there is nothing to prevent any party engaging an expert solely as an adviser, that expert being exempt from the requirements of CPR Part 35 under whose influence he will never fall – nothing, that is, except that the costs of such an expert will not be recoverable. Recovery of costs is only possible when the calling of expert evidence is sanctioned by the courts. This effectively creates inequality, since only a party with unlimited resources (usually the defendant) can afford the luxury of the unrecoverable cost.

QUESTIONS TO THE EXPERT

CPR Rule 35.6 allows a party to put written questions to an expert of another party about the report but the questions may be put only once and must be within 28 days of service of the expert's report. They 'must be for the purpose only of clarification of the report'. There is no time limit set for the answers to the report. In cases on the fast track, this may be the only effective way of challenging the report of the opposing expert who will not usually be called to give oral evidence.

THE EXPERT ON THE FAST TRACK

The fast track is reserved for cases worth not more than £15,000 and in which the trial is likely to last for no longer than five hours. Expert evidence will not necessarily be permitted. When it is, there will be an expectation that the evidence will be given by a single expert, jointly instructed by the parties. An expert on the fast track, whether singly or jointly instructed, will have limited time in which to respond since the standard period between the giving of directions and the trial would be no more than 30 weeks. The principle of proportionality will determine that the costs recoverable for expert evidence on the fast track will be modest. The standard directions on the fast track will determine the timetable for questions to experts and the answers to them. Oral evidence will not normally be called in the fast track unless the court specially directs it. In such circumstances the evidence in chief will normally be contained in the report and the time for cross-examination strictly limited.

In short, the expert in the fast track will encounter:

- the expectation of single joint experts;
- a strict timetable;
- capped fees;
- usually no oral evidence.

EXPERTS' DISCUSSIONS

Part 35 of the CPR (Rule 35.12) allows for discussions between experts of opposing parties, to identify the issues in the proceedings and where possible to reach an agreement on an issue. There is some anxiety on the part of solicitors that experts' discussions may effectively settle cases in a manner which the solicitors cannot control. In this context, it is important to bear in mind CPR Rule 35.12(5), which takes account of these anxieties: 'Where experts reach agreement on an issue during their discussions, the agreement should not bind the parties unless the parties expressly agree to be bound by the agreement'.

The agenda is key to the success of any discussion. The agenda provides the opportunity for solicitors (and through them the parties) to control the content of the meeting. In those cases in which resolution will be dependent upon expert evidence, a meeting should be held as early as possible, so as to save costs. Many cases which at present proceed towards trial could be resolved earlier if experts were encouraged to meet with an appropriate agenda. There must, however, be some understanding on each side of the opposing experts' views, in order for the agenda to be set. Provided that the experts have all the relevant documents and have formulated their opinion on them, many cases would benefit from an early expert discussion.

There is a distinct advantage in a face-to-face discussion. Video links and telephone conferences are a poor second best and in practice do not resolve issues with the same facility. Nevertheless the rules refer to 'discussions' rather than to meetings and in the interests of saving costs and time, there will be occasions on which experts cannot reasonably be expected to be in the same room. In such circumstances discussions by telephone or video link are permissible but are only likely to be successful if strict guidelines are observed. Such guidelines have been suggested for the conduct of such meetings in the context of clinical disputes ('Guidelines on Experts' Discussions in the Context of Clinical Disputes', (2000) *Clinical Risk* vol. 6 no. 4 pp. 149–52).

The purposes of an experts' discussion is to identify:

- the extent of the agreement between the experts;
- points of disagreement and the reasons for disagreement;
- action which may be taken to resolve the outstanding points of disagreement;
- any issues not raised in the agenda and the extent to which those issues can be agreed.

Without a properly constructed agenda, discussions are unlikely to be fruitful and the parties, their solicitors and experts should cooperate to produce a concise agenda, which should:

- be prepared by the claimants' solicitors with the experts' assistance;
- be supplemented by the defendant's solicitors;
- be mutually agreed;
- contain clearly stated closed questions applying the correct legal test.

Before the discussion, the expert should be provided with appropriate documents. If the proceedings have not been issued there should at least be an agreed chronology together with witness statements and such expert opinion as had been exchanged. If proceedings have been issued, the statement of case, the claimant's chronology, the defendants' comments on the chronology, the witness statements and the expert's reports (as exchanged) should be provided.

At the close of the discussion it is essential that points of agreement, disagreement and further action should be captured and acknowledged. In a face-to-face meeting this can usually be achieved by signatures on a document based closely on the agenda. Where experts are separated and discussions occur by telephone or video link, it is essential that each expert writes and signs a document, at the end of the discussion, which can be exchanged immediately.

There is considerable controversy as to whether solicitors should be present. In most cases it will probably not be necessary or appropriate for any one other than experts to be present for the discussion. However, during the public consultation on the Guidelines for Experts' Discussions in the Context of Clinical Disputes a powerful case was made, in the specific context of medical negligence, for the solicitors to be present at the discussion at least in those cases where the issues to be discussed were complex, if only so that the solicitors (who would play no part in the meeting) could understand the reasons for the conclusions drawn and be able to account for the final document to their clients. Unless solicitors do understand the reasons for the experts' conclusions they are unlikely to be able to compromise the case or to establish such agreement between the parties that the time at trial can be significantly curtailed.

The expert's duty is to the court and no expert should accept instructions not to agree any item on the agenda.

THE EXPERT'S RIGHT TO ASK QUESTIONS OF THE COURT

CPR Rule 35.14 gives the expert the right to file a written question for directions to the court, without giving notice to any party. This may be particularly helpful in circumstances in which the expert believes that there is a conflict between his instructions, his professional responsibilities and his duty to the court.

THE WITNESS SUMMONS

The subject of witness summonses tends to be rather inflammatory. Most experts resent the service of a witness summons unless specially requested. Occasionally it may be helpful to an expert in escaping from his employer but it does not generally assist the expert in managing his timetable and attending to his duties.

With procedural judges now increasingly unwilling to consider expert availability when setting down cases for trial, double and treble bookings of experts is a frequent event. Since most cases set down for trial settle beforehand, this does not usually present any insuperable difficulty in attending court. It does, however, cause considerable anxiety to solicitors who are aware that their expert is also booked to appear in another court in another part of the country. The issue by all parties of witness summonses to the expert does nothing to

316

resolve the difficulty. By mutual agreement and cooperation between professionals it is usually possible to overcome conflicting commitments without the unnecessary costs and aggravation generated by witness summonses.

Courts are increasingly intolerant of experts who, having committed themselves to give evidence are unavailable for trial. Lord Woolf, giving judgment in the Court of Appeal in *Matthews* v. *Tarmac Bricks and Tiles Ltd* ((2000) 54 BMLR 139) said:

> I hope that the message will be understood by both the medical profession and the legal profession, that it is essential that if parties want cases to be fixed for hearing in accordance with the dates which meet their convenience, those dates should be fixed as early as possible. The parties cannot always expect the courts to meet their convenience. If they hold themselves out as practising in the medico-legal field doctors must be prepared to arrange their affairs to meet the commitments of the courts where this is practical. If there is no agreement as to the dates which are acceptable to the court, the lawyers for the parties must be in a position to give the reasons why certain dates are not convenient to doctors.

PART III
New procedures

CHAPTER 9

Early settlement and the protocols

Nigel Tomkins

INTRODUCTION

This chapter will consider how the new Civil Procedure Rules have changed the way we deal with civil litigation from the outset. It will look at pre-issue conduct and the pre-proceedings protocols, including the background to the changes, the development and aims of the pre-proceedings protocols and how to manage expert evidence and to involve the client, both lay and institutional. The chapter will also consider other changes impacting on pre-issue conduct, including alternative dispute resolution (ADR), pre-action offers to settle, judicial control and pre-action disclosure. The chapter ends by considering whether the changes are working, and with a look towards the future.

PRE-ISSUE CONDUCT AND PRE-ACTION PROTOCOLS

The background to the changes

The road to change can be traced back for many years. There were many previous attempts to sort out the civil justice system and none of them did more than succeed in part and tinker rather than transform. Lord Woolf was well aware of this when he began his review. He did not mean to waste years of effort and get nowhere. He knew that a revolution was needed to force a change in the thought process of most lawyers. What was needed was not just another set of rule changes but a complete change in culture.

His statement quoted in *The Times* on 23 June 1994 that: 'It is only those with the deepest pockets who can risk going to law', was an early signal of the fact that such a change in our legal culture was likely to be on its way sooner rather than later. The expense was clearly a barrier to ordinary people having access to the judicial system. By June 1995 when the *Access to Justice* Interim Report to the Lord Chancellor on the civil justice system in England and Wales was published, there could no longer be any doubt at all. Change was coming and Lord Woolf was to ensure that it was coming in a big way.

Included in its most significant findings was the view that the main procedural tools for conducting litigation efficiently under the old rules had been subverted from their proper and intended purpose. The old rules simply did not work. It questioned whether this was through incompetence or deliberate acts. It was clear that the suspicion was that it was deliberate, and I do not have a moment's doubt that often the suspicion was well founded.

Pleadings frequently said as little as possible in an effort to keep all options open. Witness statements, an earlier innovation aimed at a 'cards on the table' approach had rapidly begun to follow the same route, with 'the draftsman's skill often used to obscure the original words of the witness'. The conclusion was that this led to a fundamental deficiency, the failure to establish the issues in the case at a reasonably early stage, and many other problems resulted from this, including additional expense.

Lord Woolf had no doubt that the expense of litigation was one of the most fundamental problems confronting the civil justice system. He quoted Sir Thomas Bingham, then the Master of the Rolls, who described it as 'a cancer eating at the heart of the administration of justice'. He saw the combined problems of cost fuelled by the excessively combative environment in which so much litigation was conducted. This in turn led to the settlement of cases almost routinely not happening until a very late stage in any proceedings.

Statistics were used which showed that in the High Court in 1993, of those cases set down, the vast majority settled with or without an order of the court.

Only 13 per cent were determined after trial and 9 per cent settled during the course of the trial or at the doors of the court. In the county court a much higher proportion, 57 per cent, were determined after trial. Twelve per cent settled during the course of the trial and 17 per cent settled but the parties attended court for approval. The evidence was damning. Clearly something had to be done.

During the inquiry there was unprecedented consultation with all those involved in the civil justice system. Judges, practitioners and consumers worked together to hammer out new ways of tackling problems and contributed to the creation of an entirely new framework for civil justice, designed to fit simultaneously with a new culture. This all came together in *Access to Justice*, the Final Report, published in July 1996.

In it, Lord Woolf set out his blueprint for the future conduct and resolution of civil disputes in England and Wales. He set out his vision of a new landscape with features, the first and most important of which was that litigation was in future to be avoided wherever possible. This was the basis of his change of culture. Be open with each other. Settle your disputes. Keep them out of court.

People would be encouraged to start court proceedings to resolve disputes only as a last resort, and only after using other more appropriate means when these are available. Alternative dispute resolution (ADR) was flagged up as a new option to be encouraged. We were promised legal aid funding would be available for pre-litigation resolution and ADR. Even now, although we know that legal aid funding is never likely to happen, the encouragement to settle and not to litigate remains at the core of the reforms.

Perhaps most important was to be the introduction of pre-action protocols backed by additional powers for the court in relation to pre-litigation disclosure. The aim of this new pre-action process was to enable the parties to obtain information much earlier and to promote early settlement. Lord Woolf promised that before commencing litigation, both parties would be able to make offers to settle the whole or part of a dispute, supported by a special regime as to costs and higher rates of interest if not accepted.

Everything was to be aimed at avoiding litigation and where it could not be avoided making it less adversarial and ensuring cooperation between the parties. This has happened and there is now an expectation of openness and cooperation between parties from the outset, supported by pre-litigation protocols. The courts are able to show their disapproval of a lack of cooperation prior to litigation through the new rules and Practice Directions.

A claim should now set out the facts alleged by the claimant, the remedy the claimant seeks, the grounds on which the remedy is sought and any relevant points of law. The response should set out the defendant's detailed answer to the claim and make clear the real issues between the parties. The fact that both 'statements of case' have to include statements of truth has helped focus the minds of the parties.

In chapter 10 of the Final Report Lord Woolf set out his proposals for the development of pre-action protocols. The intention was to build on and increase the benefits of early but well-informed settlements that genuinely satisfy both parties to a dispute. The purposes of protocols was said to be to focus the attention of litigants on the desirability of resolving disputes without litigation and to enable them to obtain the information they reasonably needed in order to enter into an appropriate settlement. Failing that, if a pre-action settlement was not achievable, their aim was to lay the ground for expeditious conduct of proceedings.

The development of pre-action protocols

The pre-action Personal Injury Protocol came directly out of the civil justice review process. The pre-action protocols working party included people who had usually been directly opposed to each other in disputes. They very often had little good to say about each other. They certainly did not start out trusting each other. Trust grew and the 'culture' changed. By a step-by-step process of negotiation a protocol was worked out and agreed by all parties. The dictionary definition of negotiation is 'to discuss with the goal of finding terms of agreement'. To some this will give a false impression. Unfortunately too many people interpret negotiation as being the skill of persuading other people to accept their point of view. If it is said of a man or woman that he or she is a good negotiator it usually means that they gets the best of the deal. Frequently when a deal is struck to the advantage of one party and the detriment of the other, seeds of disagreement and retaliation are sown, which can have unforeseen future results. Members of the working party did not seek to do that. All were aware of the risk and worked very hard to avoid it.

The aims of pre-action protocols

The aims of the pre-action protocols fit exactly with the new culture:

- more pre-action contact between the parties;
- better and earlier exchange of information;
- better pre-action investigation by both sides;
- to put the parties in the position where they may be able to settle cases fairly and early without resort to litigation;
- to enable proceedings to run both to the court timetable and efficiently, if settlement is not achieved and litigation does become necessary.

THE CLINICAL NEGLIGENCE PROTOCOL

Two protocols were introduced with the new Civil Procedure Rules, one for clinical negligence cases and the other for personal injury claims. The Clinical Negligence Protocol was prepared by a working party of the Clinical Disputes Forum. The Clinical Disputes Forum is a multi-disciplinary body which was formed in 1997, as a result of Lord Woolf's *Access to Justice* inquiry. One of the aims of the Forum was to find less adversarial and more cost-effective ways of resolving disputes about healthcare and medical treatment. It had the support of the Lord Chancellor's Department, the Department of Health, the NHS Executive, the Law Society, the Legal Aid Board and many other key organisations.

The number of complaints and claims against hospitals, GPs, dentists and private healthcare providers was growing as patients became more prepared to question the treatment they are given, to seek explanations of what happened, and to seek appropriate redress. The group felt that it was clearly in the interests of patients, healthcare professionals and providers that patients' concerns, complaints and claims arising from their treatment are resolved as quickly, efficiently and professionally as possible. There was a climate of mistrust and lack of openness on both sides. They concluded that the mistrust had to be removed, and a more cooperative culture developed. The protocol highlighted that the courts increasingly expect parties to try to settle their differences by agreement before issuing proceedings. It reminded parties that most disputes are resolved by discussion and negotiation, emphasising that carefully planned face-to-face meetings may be particularly helpful in exploring or narrowing the issues in dispute and, if the timing is right, in helping to settle the whole matter. The steps of this Protocol were kept deliberately simple. An illustration of the likely sequence of events in a number of healthcare situations is shown at Annex A of the Protocol and is reproduced in Figure 9.1.

Patient (P)   Healthcare provider (HCP)

INITIAL STAGES

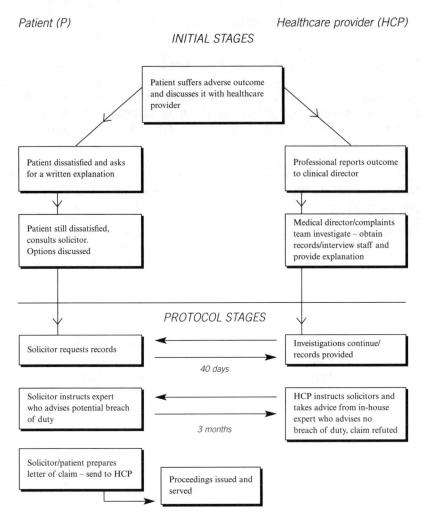

Figure 9.1 Sequence of events under the Clinical Negligence Protocol

THE PERSONAL INJURY PROTOCOL

The Personal Injury Protocol is intended to apply to all claims with a personal injury element and not just to the personal injury element of the claims. It excludes occupational disease cases as they are to have their own protocol. The Protocol is principally designed for claims with a personal injury element of less than £15,000 which are likely to be allocated to the fast track. This figure was introduced on the basis that admissions of liability where cases had a value up to £15,000 would be maintained. In *Hackman* v. *Hounslow LBC* (unreported, 1 December 1999), *Gale* v. *Superdrug Stores Plc* ([1996] 1 WLR 1089) was held not to have survived the introduction of the CPR as their purpose was to make litigation more certain. CPR Rule 14.1(5) gives the court power to allow a party to withdraw an admission, the burden resting upon the party applying. Reference was made to the Personal Injury Protocol because it indicates that admissions are expected to hold good and this seems to have influenced the decision.

The main elements are:

(1) Letter of claim: this should contain a clear summary of facts, an indication of the nature of injuries and of any financial loss suffered. The letter should provide sufficient information to enable investigation to be carried out. The defendant or their insurers should reply within 21 days of the posting of the letter. It is suggested that the letter should contain sufficient information to enable the defendant's insurer to assess the risk.

(2) Investigation period: the insurer has three months, additional to the 21 days acknowledgement period, to investigate and respond, indicating whether liability is accepted or denied, before the claimant issues proceedings subject only to any limitation problems.

(3) No admission of liability: the response must be full and explain the reasons for the denial or allegations of contributory negligence. In *Northfield* v. *DSM (Southern) Ltd* (unreported, 12 May 2000) Fuller J in the Basingstoke County Court considered 'unreasonable conduct' to include a defendant's failure to state its case on liability before issue. This was a small claim. Under CPR Rule 27.14(2) the court may not order a party to pay a sum to another party in respect of that other party's costs except in very limited circumstances. That includes under CPR Rule 27.14(2)(d) a power to order 'such further costs as the court may assess by the summary procedure and order to be paid by a party who has behaved unreasonably'. The defendant argued that they had made a commercial decision to settle after issue of proceedings. The judge held that that was not acting reasonably. The defendant's failure to state its case on liability before issue amounted to unreasonable conduct for the purposes of the CPR.

(4) Documents: where the defendant denies liability he should enclose with the letter of reply any documents material to the issues and that are likely to have to be disclosed in the course of any litigation whether they have been listed by the claimant or not. The Personal Injury Protocol contains non-exhaustive lists of documents for disclosure.

(5) Contributory negligence: if there is an allegation of contributory negligence on the part of the claimant the defendant's insurer should disclose any documents relevant to that aspect as well.

(6) Special damages: details should be sent as soon as practical, together with a schedule of special damages.

(7) Experts: there is a system for selecting and instructing experts in the Protocol and it should always be followed. It is much misunderstood; details are set out below.

(8) Non-compliance: the aim is that a party should not benefit by their failure to comply with the Protocol. The court should take whatever steps are needed to ensure this does not happen and that the parties are in effect put into the position they would have been in if there had been compliance. Sanctions should be proportionate and simply designed to redress any unfair advantage that may have been gained.

(9) Before proceedings are issued, a pre-issue stocktake should be carried out (see below) and parties should always consider making a CPR Part 36 offer to settle (see further below).

How to manage expert evidence under the Personal Injury Protocol

The parties should try to use a mutually acceptable expert on any issue where an expert is needed. With non-medical experts, such as an expert on a liability issue, either party may begin the process. However, with medical evidence the claimant should always take the initiative. A claimant has to prove the nature and extent of the injury and, if proceedings are to be issued, the medical evidence must be attached to the statement of case. It is not appropriate in most cases to seek to instruct a doctor before dealing with liability – that ignores proportionality. Where there proves to be no liability, in most cases, neither side will need to see medical evidence at all. If the insurer seeks to take the initiative they should be reminded that liability is the first matter to be dealt with. It would not be unreasonable for the claimant to refuse a request from them to proceed with the instruction of a doctor until liability has been dealt with.

At a time of his choice the claimant should provide the insurers with a list of the names of doctors to whom he/she is considering sending instructions. This may be in the claim letter, should the claimant wish to deal with it then, or at any other point in the process. The choice lies with the claimant. It is his choice but if he proceeds too soon he may have to accept the cost of the medical report as a lost disbursement. Usually instruction will follow the response from the insurer on liability.

The insurers have 14 days (35 days if the nomination is in the letter of claim) to object to any expert suggested before they are instructed. A positive objection is needed. To say that one doctor is agreed or to express a preference is not raising an objection to others. The claimant is still free to instruct any expert nominated. There is deliberately no provision for joint instructions in the

Protocol as that would mean the waiving of privilege by the claimant. The defendant has no input at all at the instructions stage.

A report need only be disclosed if relied upon. If the report is relied upon and disclosed each party can seek answers from the expert on aspects of the report relevant to the issues. Questions and answers are sent via the claimant's solicitors. There is no provision for questions to be sent directly to the doctor by the defendant, nor is there any provision for answers to be sent directly to the defendant by the doctor. The questions should be sent to the claimant. The claimant should send a full copy of the letter asking questions to the doctor and a full copy of the reply to the defendant.

If the Protocol is followed by the claimant when obtaining a medical report, the insurer or defendant cannot instruct their own doctor without either the claimant's agreement or the permission of the court.

OTHER PRE-ACTION PROTOCOLS

The Personal Injury Protocol produced by the working party was an excellent example of the new culture Lord Woolf wanted to achieve. Many have found this hard to accept and there has been some criticism of the Protocol, suggesting that it provides too much dispensation to one side or the other depending on which side it is viewed from. More often than not the loudest complaints have come from those solicitors who usually act for defendants claiming that it unfairly favours the claimant. Those who criticise have not yet grasped the need to change their outlook and accept that the culture they lived under for so long is obsolete. Other protocols are now following the example set by the Personal Injury Protocol. Two came into force on 2 October 2000: the Pre-action Protocol for Construction and Engineering Disputes and the Pre-action Protocol for Defamation.

Pre-action Protocol for Construction and Engineering disputes

The Construction and Engineering Protocol applies to all construction and engineering disputes (including professional negligence claims against architects, engineers and quantity surveyors). A claimant is not required to comply before commencing proceedings for the enforcement of the decision of an adjudicator to whom a dispute has been referred under s.108 of the Housing Grants, Construction and Regeneration Act 1996. He is not required to comply if his claim includes a claim for interim injunctive relief, or if he intends to seek summary judgment pursuant to Part 24 of the CPR. Nor does he have to comply if the claim relates to the same, or substantially the same, issues as have been the subject of recent adjudication under the 1996 Act, or some other formal alternative dispute resolution procedure.

The aims mirror the earlier protocols. Prior to commencing proceedings, the claimant or his solicitor must send to each proposed defendant a copy of a detailed letter of claim which must contain the following information:

    (a) the claimant's full name and address;

    (b) the full name and address of each proposed defendant;

    (c) a clear summary of the facts on which each claim is based;

    (d) the basis on which each claim is made, identifying the principal contractual terms and statutory provisions relied on;

    (e) the nature of the relief claimed: if damages are claimed, a breakdown showing how the damages have been quantified; if a sum is claimed pursuant to a contract, how it has been calculated; if an extension of time is claimed, the period claimed;

    (f) where a claim has been made previously and rejected by a defendant, and the claimant is able to identify the reason(s) for such rejection, the claimant's grounds of belief as to why the claim was wrongly rejected;

    (g) the names of any experts already instructed by the claimant on whose evidence he intends to rely, identifying the issues to which that evidence will be directed.

Within 14 calendar days of receipt of the letter of claim, the defendant should acknowledge its receipt in writing and may give the name and address of his insurer if he has one. If there is no acknowledgement by or on behalf of the defendant within 14 days, the claimant is entitled to commence proceedings without further compliance with the Protocol.

Should the defendant intend to object to all or some part of the claim, on the basis that the court lacks jurisdiction, or that the claim should be referred to arbitration, or that they are the wrong defendant, then they must raise this within 28 days of receipt of the claim letter. The letter of objection needs to specify the parts of the claim to which the objection relates, setting out the grounds relied on, and, where appropriate, identifying the correct defendant if known. However any failure to take such objection will not prejudice the defendant's rights to do so in any subsequent proceedings, but the court may take such failure into account when considering the question of costs. When notice of objection is given, the defendant is not required to send a letter of response dealing with the claim or those parts of it to which the objection relates.

Within 28 days from the date of receipt of the letter of claim, the defendant must send a letter of response to the claimant containing the following information:

(a) the facts set out in the letter of claim which are agreed or not agreed, and if not agreed, the basis of the disagreement;

(b) which claims are accepted and which are rejected, and if rejected, the basis of the rejection;

(c) if a claim is accepted in whole or in part, whether the damages, sums or extensions of time claimed are accepted or rejected, and if rejected, the basis of the rejection;

(d) if contributory negligence is alleged against the claimant, a summary of the facts relied on;

(e) whether the defendant intends to make a counterclaim, and if so, giving the information which is required to be given in a letter of claim;

(f) the names of any experts already instructed on whose evidence it is intended to rely, identifying the issues to which that evidence will be directed.

The parties may agree to extend the 28 day period up to a maximum of four months. If a response is not received by the claimant within that period he is entitled to commence proceedings without further compliance with the Protocol. If a counterclaim is made the claimant must provide a response within the equivalent period allowed to the defendant to respond to the letter of claim.

An innovation of the Construction and Engineering Protocol is the requirement for the parties to have a meeting. As soon as possible after receipt by the claimant of the defendant's letter of response, or receipt by the defendant of the claimant's letter of response to the counterclaim, the parties should normally meet. The aim of the meeting is for the parties to agree what are the main issues and to identify the root cause of disagreement in respect of each issue. This is a means to effect a pre-issue stocktake. Issue by issue or on the dispute as a whole, the parties should consider whether some form of alternative dispute resolution procedure would be more suitable than litigation, and if so, endeavour to agree which form to adopt. If the parties are unable to agree on a means of resolving the dispute other than by litigation they should try to agree whether, if there is any area where expert evidence is likely to be required, a joint expert may be appointed and if possible who that should be. They should also try to agree the extent of disclosure of documents with a view to saving costs; and the conduct of the litigation with the aim of minimising cost and delay.

If there is a pre-action meeting the parties may disclose to the court the fact that the meeting took place, when and who attended and what agreements were concluded between the parties. If the meeting did not take place a party may tell the court why not; who refused to attend, and the grounds for their refusal. Other than that, everything said at a pre-action meeting must be treated as 'without prejudice'.

Clearly, if by complying with the Protocol a claimant's claim might become time-barred then the claimant must commence proceedings without complying with the Protocol. However in those circumstances, a claimant must apply to the court on notice for directions on the timetable and form of procedure to be adopted, at the same time as he requests the court to issue proceedings. The court will consider whether to order a stay of the whole or part of the proceedings pending compliance with the Protocol.

Pre-action Protocol for Defamation

The Pre-action Protocol for Defamation is intended to encourage exchange of information between parties at an early stage and to provide a clear framework within which parties to a claim in defamation, acting in good faith, can explore the early and appropriate resolution of that claim. There are important features distinguishing defamation claims from other areas of civil litigation, and these must be borne in mind when both applying, and reviewing the application of, the protocol. In particular, time is always 'of the essence' in defamation claims; the limitation period is (uniquely) only one year, and almost invariably, a claimant will be seeking an immediate correction and/or apology as part of the process of restoring his/her reputation.

The claimant should notify the defendant of his/her claim in writing at the earliest reasonable opportunity. The letter of claim should include sufficient details to identify the publication or broadcast which contained the words complained of and, if known, the date of publication; where possible, a copy or transcript of the words complained of should be enclosed. If it is claimed that there are factual inaccuracies or unsupportable comment within the words complained of the claimant should give a sufficient explanation to enable the defendant to appreciate why the words are inaccurate or unsupportable. The nature of the remedies sought by the claimant should also be identified. If necessary, the letter of claim should also include any facts or matters which make the claimant identifiable from the words complained of and details of any special facts relevant to the interpretation of the words and/or any particular damage caused by the words. Ideally the claimant should identify the meaning he or she attributes to the words.

The defendant should provide a full response as soon as it is reasonably possible to do so. If they believe that they will be unable to respond within 14 days (or any shorter time specified in the letter of claim), then they should specify the date by which they intend to respond. The response should say whether or to what extent the claimant's claim is accepted, whether more information is required or whether it is rejected. If the claim is accepted in whole or in part, the defendant should indicate which remedies it is willing to offer. If more information is required, then the defendant should specify precisely what information is needed to enable the claim to be dealt with and why.

If the claim is rejected, then the defendant should explain the reasons why it is rejected, including a sufficient indication of any facts on which the defendant is likely to rely in support of any substantive defence. The defendant's response should include the meaning they attribute to the words complained of.

The need for the parties to act reasonably to keep costs proportionate to the nature and gravity of the case and the stage the complaint has reached is made clear in the protocol. So too is the fact that the parties will be expected by the court to provide evidence that alternative means of resolving their dispute were considered and some suggested forms of ADR (see below) are listed.

INVOLVING THE CLIENT, BOTH LAY AND INSTITUTIONAL

Acting for a claimant in a claim running under a pre-action protocol requires more involvement between lawyer and client. Better investigation and clarification of evidence is needed than in the past before a letter of claim can be sent. Solicitors need to keep in touch with the client, both to keep them up to date and to ensure a speedy response can be sent dealing with any developments. Claimants have obligations under protocols not just defendants and the claimant needs to understand this.

Defendants need to have systems in place to deal with protocol claims. There are a series of things that institutional defendants can do to protect their position:

(1) Any letter of claim received should be passed immediately to the insurer, or if the company is self insured, to the in-house claims department. This is essential so that they can issue the initial response letter to the claimant or solicitors on the company's behalf.

(2) The company should be reminded that if a deadline is missed, the claimant may commence legal proceedings and build up legal costs without sanction.

(3) The company should provide those dealing with the claim on its behalf with full information as soon as possible. All protocols have tight timetables from the date of acknowledgement of the letter of claim in which to reach a decision on liability and notify the claimant.

(4) As time is of the essence, the company needs to ensure that its nominated personnel are conversant with the requirements of any relevant protocol and that systems and procedures are in place to obtain and provide the required documentation within the prescribed timescales.

(5) A senior officer within the organisation should be appointed to act as a focal point for communications and have responsibility for the collection and collation of information and for verification of the accuracy and truth of documentation in case it needs to be lodged with a court.

(6) The comany should be reminded that speed of response will have a major impact on its ability to defend claims effectively. Failure to do so could result in its position being prejudiced or in an increase in costs or other penalties being imposed by the court.

(7) It is important to stress that protocols may show up failures in unexpected ways. For example, the Personal Injury Protocol may impact on health and safety. The onus on an employer to produce safety documents before court action starts needs to be addressed. If the expected documents are missing then that is likely to have an adverse effect for the employer in terms of the outcome of the claim. The lack of documents may be taken to show their failure to comply with relevant health and safety law.

OTHER CHANGES IMPACTING ON PRE-ISSUE CONDUCT

Protocols are only part of the changes. A settlement culture means there must be negotiation. The first rule for successful negotiation is not to attribute your own motives to other people. Sometimes we have such a high regard for our own opinions and motives that we assume that any other intelligent person must think the same way. This is quite simply wrong. People who think like that need to ponder on their approach or they will find that they are constantly having a very hard time in the world of the new settlement culture.

ALTERNATIVE DISPUTE RESOLUTION (ADR)

Alternative dispute resolution (ADR) was proposed by Lord Woolf as another key element in the plans for change. ADR is a name used to cover various means of settling disputes outside the courtroom. In the USA over recent years, a number of states have experimented with ADR programmes as court time delays together with the rising cost of litigation continued to plague their system. Some states have voluntary ADR systems, others mandatory.

In our system mediation is the usual form of ADR. It can in fact be almost any sophisticated form of organised and facilitated negotiation. It is regularly used in disputes relating to banking or financial services, insurance, construction, probate, computer law, contracts, professional negligence, and many other commercial disputes. So far it is less common in clinical negligence and personal injury cases. Mediation is normally private. Those who use it believe it to be cost effective and fast. A mediation meeting can sometimes be set up in a matter of days. It can be used simply to reduce litigation costs but it can have other benefits such as to avoid unwanted publicity and obtain an early settlement. It has had a great deal of use in disputes between parties with an ongoing relationship. There, a court battle of the old fashioned type might have left both sides feeling that the relationship was terminally damaged. ADR should, at least in theory, avoid this.

When is ADR appropriate?

ADR even without legal aid funding is still firmly on the agenda. This was shown in the case of *Dyson* v. *Leeds City Council* ([2000] CP Rep 42, CA), where the Court of Appeal (Lord Woolf MR, Ward LJ, Laws LJ) ordered a retrial. The trial judge preferred the evidence of one expert witness to another but gave no reasons. Damages had been substantially agreed and it seemed to the court that the case was pre-eminently of the category of cases in which the ADR process should be adopted. The defendant was reminded of the court's power to take a strong view about rejection of the court's suggestion of ADR by implementing an order for costs on an indemnity basis or possibly awarding a higher rate of interest to be paid on any damages recoverable. They may have ordered a retrial but clearly they did not want one to take place, they wanted the parties to settle.

ADR is not going to be suitable in all cases and the early fear that it would be forced on reluctant parties seems to have receded. In *Federal Bank of the Middle East Ltd* v. *Hadkinson (Stay of Action)* (FC3 1999/7317 A2, Ch D), Arden J considered whether ADR was appropriate to resolve a number of outstanding issues in a case following judgment.

This was an action concerning complex business agreements and monetary claims. In proceedings after judgment the defendant sought a stay of proceedings pursuant to CPR Rule 26.4 for an initial period of one month in order for the parties to engage in mediation under an accredited mediator. The defendant submitted that the overriding objective encouraged resolution of proceedings by ADR and that this was a case where, the issues having been somewhat defined by the preceding judgment, ADR was appropriate.

The claimant, however, submitted that ADR was inappropriate at that time, given the nature of the allegations and the degree of confidence between the parties. Arden J felt the claimant was right and this was not an appropriate case for ADR at that time. There was considerable mistrust between the parties. He pointed out that mediation had to involve the free flow of information between the parties. There was in this case a state of uncertainty over the issues, which would be the subject of any mediation, so that it was most unlikely that ADR would have been successful. ADR was not ordered.

ADR and other forms of negotiation

With ADR and any other form of negotiation there must always be some element of willingness on the part of those involved to trust each other. There also has to be a significant degree of certainty on the issues in the dispute before they can be tackled.

Negotiation is a process civilised people use to reach agreement. The goal of negotiation is not to win or defeat your counterpart, it is to succeed in reaching that agreement. The mechanism of true negotiation is collaboration, the work of a partnership rather than a means for setting out different entrenched positions. The most common mistake people make in negotiation is to treat it as warfare. Most of the negotiating we do in life is with the same people over and over again. They may be colleagues, spouses, family, friends, partners, as well as opponents in our cases. We need to try to consider each negotiation as an episode in an ongoing relationship. If we can do that our behaviour will be much more appropriate and we will do a vastly better job for our clients.

In the distant past, when two parties (with deep pockets) had a disagreement they would hire knights to act as mercenaries and 'wage war' to determine who was right. Later lawyers became the replacement for 'knights' and for many centuries we have been 'waging law' to resolve our civil disputes. The new culture proposed by Lord Woolf means that negotiation is the preferred means. In essence we should use negotiation to 'wage peace' and try to avoid 'waging law' if possible. This is just as big a change for some people to take on board as using law rather than single combat must have been in ancient times.

PRE-ACTION OFFERS TO SETTLE

The Pre-Action Protocol for Personal Injury Cases was amended on 3 July 2000. One change is that, following an admission, pre-issue disclosure of the medical evidence has now been added as a requirement in para. 3.21:

> Where the defendant admits liability in whole or in part, before proceedings are issued, any medical report obtained by agreement under this protocol should be disclosed to the other party. The claimant should delay issuing proceedings for 21 days from disclosure of the report, to enable the parties to consider whether the claim is capable of settlement. The Civil Procedure Rules Part 36 permit claimants and defendants to make offers to settle pre-proceedings. Parties

should always consider before issuing if it is appropriate to make a Part 36 offer. If such an offer is made, the party making the offer must always supply sufficient evidence and/or information to enable the offer to be properly considered.

The encouragement to try to settle, and in particular the section on CPR Part 36 offers, is good practice whatever type of civil litigation is involved. Part 36 offers get results and cases settle. Pre-action offers are covered by the rules in CPR Part 36. The motive is the same as for *Calderbank* offers, namely that a party should not reject reasonable offers of settlement. Part 36 enables the court to impose sanctions in terms of interest and costs in those circumstances where a Part 36 offer has been made, within the requirements of the rules, but not accepted.

The rules cover offers made before the start of proceedings ('pre-action offers') as well as after issue, offers made by claimants as well as by defendants and offers in respect of non-money claims as well as money claims. If the defendant's pre-action offer includes an offer to pay money and the claimant rejects it and sues, the defendant cannot claim the benefits of CPR Part 36 unless the sum offered, or more, is paid into court within 14 days of issue in accordance with CPR Rules 36.3 and 36.10(3).

If a claimant makes a pre-action offer within CPR Part 36 and the defendant rejects it but is ultimately held liable for more, or the judgment is more advantageous to the claimant than the proposals contained in a claimant's Part 36 offer, costs consequences are laid down by CPR Rule 36.21. One consequence is that the court may order higher interest on the whole or part of any sum awarded: CPR Rule 36.21(2). Another is that the court may award the claimant costs on the indemnity basis from the latest date upon which the defendant could have accepted the offer, plus interest at a high rate: CPR Rule 36.21(3).

A CPR Part 36 offer is treated as 'without prejudice except as to costs' and should not be disclosed to the court until questions of liability and, where appropriate, quantum have been determined or the Part 36 offer or payment has been accepted: CPR Rule 36.19. It is not appropriate to include a Part 36 offer by the claimant in any document the claimant may need to put in evidence. It should not therefore be included in a letter before action although it may be sent at the same time.

On the other hand it may be that a defendant makes a pre-action offer later backed by a Part 36 payment and the claimant decides not to accept. Where at trial the claimant fails to match the payment or fails to achieve in substance what was offered the court will order the claimant to pay any costs after the time for acceptance of the offer or payment unless it considers it unjust to do so: CPR Rule 36.20(2).

An offer to settle may be made in any form and upon any terms a party may choose. The court retains its discretion in relation to costs where there has been an offer to settle. However, to protect a party in relation to costs, the form and content of an offer (including the period for which it is to remain open) are regulated by the rules. If an offer is mixed (both an offer to pay a sum of money and the giving of some other form of relief) to provide effective protection to the offeror the money offered must be paid into court if it is not accepted pre-issue.

THE PRICE OF FAILURE TO CHANGE

The world has moved on very quickly. The Court of Appeal did not even wait for the new rules to be published before it showed what it expected in this brave new world and furthermore that they meant the Civil Justice Review proposals to be taken seriously and would see that they were. In their judgment in *Butcher* v. *Wolfe* (*The Times*, 9 November 1998) the court sent out a strong message.

The defendants in the case were the plaintiff's brothers, all three holding farm-land in Hampshire as beneficial tenants in common in equal shares. Following disagreement on the dissolution value of tenancies, the plaintiff sought an order for sale of the land and the winding up of the family partnership. She also wanted vacant possession as opposed to the tenanted basis of valuation, which added as much as 40 per cent to the estimated value of the property. When she settled the proceedings it was more or less on the basis which her brothers had offered before proceedings had started. The court pointed out that if she had accepted before issue the legal costs of the proceedings would not have been incurred. The court held that the plaintiff should have to pay the costs of the action. Litigation was not a last resort, indeed it was not even necessary and the plaintiff paid the price.

Unfortunately there has been great and understandable fear that unless those involved in the legal system act within the spirit of the reforms, the changes may create even more conflict than had existed previously. Pre-action protocols have, for example, been a major worry to both sides. Ensuring that full information is provided by all parties at an early stage is clearly now required. It must be a step forward provided there is goodwill on both sides. If Richard Nixon with all of his paranoia could reach the point where he could say 'an adversary is not necessarily an enemy' it must be within the capacity of members of the legal profession to reach the same conclusion.

JUDICIAL CONTROL

By tradition the conduct of civil litigation in England and Wales, as in other common law jurisdictions, is adversarial. That remains the case. What has changed is that the main responsibility for the initiation and conduct of cases, both before and after the commencement of proceedings, no longer rests with the parties. The role of the judge is not just to adjudicate on issues selected by the parties when they choose to present them to the court. There is now judicial control to stop the adversarial process and culture from degenerating into a battlefield, as frequently happened in the past. Previously, questions of expense, delay, compromise and fairness seemingly had only low priority. The consequence was that expense was often excessive, disproportionate and unpredictable; and delay was frequently totally unreasonable and unjustifiable.

An early example of the judiciary grasping the mood of change, following implementation of the new rules, came from a report in the *APIL Newsletter* (August 1999). It reported how Buckley J, sitting in the Queen's Bench Division on 21 May 1999, had applied costs sanctions because of the conduct of a party following settlement by consent order in an asbestos-related disease claim. Exposure to asbestos dust had led to the development of terminal and untreatable mesothelioma. The allegation was that exposure only happened during what the victim saw as continuous employment from 1962 to 1990. That was not in fact the case.

Several changes had occurred in the corporate legal personality of the employers, meaning that it was in the end necessary to sue three defendants. The third defendant was a FTSE 100 listed company with insurance. The second defendants were without any assets, but they were a wholly owned subsidiary of a functioning company with assets more than sufficient to satisfy any judgment. The holding company happily intimated an intention to satisfy any award that was made against the second defendants.

There were also arguments in the case between the first and second defendants about how to apportion liability between themselves. These were made especially keen since one of the insurers was in receivership. To make things worse Lloyd's Underwriters disputed the existence of cover for another element of the exposure period.

Eventually the defendants agreed terms between themselves and liability was conceded on behalf of all defendants on the third working day before trial. The defendants, however, could not reach any agreement on damages. The dispute between the defendants became so bad that no offers were made to settle the case, and there was no money in court.

The third defendants and their solicitors and insurers intimated a willingness on a compromise basis to accept a settlement offered on behalf of the claimant.

The second defendants refused to agree those terms. Eventually, on the third day of trial, the case was settled at the figure proposed by the claimant with costs on standard basis. The litigation was funded under a conditional fee agreement with a success fee. Buckley J held that the conduct that caused the loss of the second and third days was improper or unreasonable within the meaning of Rule 44.14 of the CPR. He ordered the second defendants to pay the claimant's costs of the second and third days on an indemnity basis, including indemnifying the claimant in respect of the success fee for which he was liable in respect of those days. The party who delayed the settlement paid the price.

Judicial pressure and control is being used day after day to enforce the message that we have a new culture aimed at early settlement and that all must aim to achieve it. Failure to do so can be a painful and expensive exercise. The decision of the Court of Appeal sitting in Cardiff on 22 October 1999 in *Ford* v. *GKR Construction* (*The Times*, 4 November 1999) illustrates this extremely well. This was an action for damages for personal injury sustained by the claimant in a road traffic accident. Liability was admitted. The hearing to assess damages began on 17 September 1998 and continued on 18 September, when the case was adjourned. At this point the defendants decided, for the first time, that they would employ an enquiry agent to follow the claimant for a time and video her, and the recordings were of assistance to the defendants' case. The video evidence was disclosed to the claimant's solicitors on 26 October and the claimant wanted to settle at this stage but the defendants refused.

The video evidence was admitted and when the trial resumed the claimant returned to the witness box where she was cross-examined about the results of the surveillance. In his judgment, Gaskell J referred to the impact of this evidence saying:

> I find that some of her [the claimant] evidence is unreliable if taken to reflect the totality of her state. Her evidence concentrates on the worst times. It is not balanced by what she was able to achieve when she was better. What she says about her limitations accurately reflect what she can and cannot do when she is in the depths of her despair, but that is not the situation all the time, and the video evidence does disclose an ability to manage to a significantly greater extent than she was prepared to admit.

The video had produced the desired effect. Damages were assessed and judgment was entered for the claimant for £89,323 including interest. Well in advance of the trial on 16 April 1998, the defendants had paid into court a total of £95,000. Under the old rules all post-payment in costs would have been paid by the claimant. Under the new rules she might well have expected even worse. However, perhaps at first sight surprisingly, the judge ordered that the defendants were to pay the claimant's costs of the entire action. Significantly, the judge made this express finding: 'I do not think that the plaintiff was deliberately lying'. Without that the outcome might well have been very different. The defendants appealed and the Court of Appeal upheld the decision. The judges made clear their reasons and they were linked directly to the new settlement culture.

Judge LJ said:

> Civil litigation is now developing into a system designed to enable the parties involved to know where they stand in reality at the earliest possible stage, and at the lowest practicable cost, so that they make may make informed decisions about their prospects and the sensible conduct of their cases. Among other factors the judge exercising his discretion about costs should consider is whether one side or the other has, or has not, conducted litigation with those principles in mind.

He was backed up totally by Lord Woolf who said in his own judgment:

> I would like to stress the importance of the comments made by Lord Justice Judge as to the need when conducting litigation to make prompt disclosure of all relevant matters . . . The principle to which Lord Justice Judge referred as to the parties conducting their litigation making full and proper disclosure is even more important now that the CPR have come into force. Under the CPR it is possible for the parties to make offers to settle before litigation commences. As to the disclosure required in relation to that procedure, protocols in specific areas of litigation make express provision. Even where there is no express provision contained in a relevant protocol which applies to the particular litigation, the approach reflected in the protocols should be adopted by parties generally in the conduct of their litigation. If the process of making Part 36 offers before the commencement of litigation is to work in the way which the CPR intends, the parties must be provided with the information which they require in order to assess whether to make an offer or whether to accept that offer.
>
> Where offers are not accepted, the CPR make provision as to what are to be the cost consequences (CPR 36.20 and 36.21). Both those rules deal with the usual consequences of not accepting an offer which, when judged in the light of the litigation, should have been accepted. I also draw attention to the fact that the rules refer to the power of the court to make other orders and make it clear that the normal consequence does not apply when it is unjust that it should do so.
>
> If a party has not enabled another party to properly assess whether or not to make an offer, or whether or not to accept an offer which is made, because of non-disclosure to the other party of material matters, or if a party comes to a decision which is different from that which would have been reached if there had been proper disclosure, that is a material matter for a court to take into account in considering what orders it should make.
>
> This is of particular significance so far as defendants are concerned because of

the power of the court to order additional interest in situations where an offer by a claimant is not accepted by a defendant. We have to move away from the situation where litigation is conducted in a manner which means that another party cannot take those precautions to protect his or her position which the rules intend them to have.

The message could not be clearer: change your ways or you will pay the price. This case sent alarm bells ringing throughout the profession.

PRE-ACTION DISCLOSURE

The quest for openness is further reflected in the simplification and extension of the court's powers to order pre-action disclosure as had been promised. In *Burrells Wharf Freeholds Ltd* v. *Galliard Homes Ltd* in the Technology and Construction Court on 1 July 1999, Dyson J removed any doubt about the validity of the new rules having made pre-action disclosure possible in cases other than personal injury. He concluded that the Lord Chancellor was entitled to invoke the powers in s.4 of the Civil Procedure Act 1997 for the purpose of amending the Supreme Court Act 1981 and bringing CPR Rule 31.16 into effect.

The judge also confirmed that pre-action disclosure would be ordered where the criteria in CPR Rule 31.16(3) were satisfied and in unusual cases.

In the case of *Wilma Elsie Hatcher* v. *Plymouth Hospitals NHS Trust* in the Plymouth County Court on 27 July 1999, Tromans J showed that he fully understood the new culture. He ordered that comments and statements prepared by clinicians to meet a lay complaint were not prepared in anticipation of legal proceedings and were not protected by legal professional privilege. They were properly disclosable before a claim under CPR Rule 31.16(3)(d). The claimant's medical records had already been disclosed before the application was made but the defendant refused to disclose the complaints file. The claimant believed that the complaints file contained the statements of the two clinicians present during the operation, as well as other potentially relevant papers. The defendant argued that disclosure was inappropriate and, as a preliminary point, that the documents in the complaints file were covered by legal professional privilege, but lost. The documents had to be disclosed before issue of proceedings.

THE NEED FOR OPENNESS

By pure coincidence on the same day, 27 July 1999, in *Baron* v. *Lovell*, the Court of Appeal sent out the same message as Tromans J on the need for openness. The claimant saw defendant's medical report long after directions for service had expired, for the first time on the day of a hearing before a trial on quantum, when a CPR Part 36 offer was made. The judge decided that the defendant could not call the expert, trial to be in August on claimant's expert's evidence only.

The Court of Appeal held that the judge had exercised his case management powers under the CPR correctly in accordance with the overriding objective contained in CPR Part 1. It was not in the spirit of the CPR for a report to be disclosed on the day that an offer under CPR Part 36 was made. The CPR would not be effective if the previous practices were allowed to continue.

This again shows how keen the courts are to ensure an open approach. It is far more important than any 'interests of justice' argument, which would almost certainly have succeeded under the old rules, with costs being the means of dealing with the position. Under the old rules the powers of the courts had fallen behind the more sophisticated and aggressive tactics of some litigators. The orders for costs made were an ineffective sanction applied after the damage was done. The delay in being able to obtain effective intervention by the court both encouraged rule-breaking and discouraged the party who would be prejudiced from applying for preventive measures.

Contrast that with the Court of Appeal decision in *Long* v. *Tolchard & Sons Ltd* (*The Times*, 5 January 2000). The case arose out of a back injury allegedly sustained by Mr Long in August 1983 in the course of his employment by the defendant as a brewery drayman. The writ was not issued until February 1990, Long contending that he had only been in a position to consider a claim after consulting an orthopaedic registrar in March 1987. At a hearing in December 1993 issues of limitation and liability were determined in favour of the claimant, with McIntosh J accepting the claimant's contentions in relation to s.11 of the Limitation Act 1980. The judge also indicated that he would also have found in his favour under s.33 of the Act had he needed to do so.

The trial of the issue of quantum was eventually heard in July 1998 before a different judge, Grigg J. The claimant adduced the evidence of a chiropractor to show that his back problem had continued from 1983 until he was dismissed from the defendant's employment in February 1988. The chiropractor produced notes where he had recorded that Long told him in July 1985 that he had suffered his back injury at work in 1983. It also came out that Long had complained of back problems in 1979 and 1980 whilst he was in the Army. Even so, Long was awarded damages of £10,000. He then appealed on quantum. The defendant cross-appealed out of time against the earlier judgment on limitation and liability.

The Court of Appeal held that the new evidence clearly established that the claimant had the knowledge necessary to start his proceedings in July 1985. This meant that his action was statute-barred when it was issued unless the provisions of s.11 of the 1980 Act could be disapplied under s.33. The earlier exercise of the judge's discretion counted for little as it was based on a false picture. The primary limitation period would only be disapplied where it was equitable to do so. Here, although the claimant had a strong case on liability, it was only one circumstance, albeit an important one, which the court had to consider. They took into account the extensive periods of delay on the part of the claimant and, most importantly, his failure to disclose relevant documents and to give a true and accurate account of his condition. Claimants, just like defendants, must disclose all relevant details if they want the courts to have any sympathy for them. He lost the appeal.

IS CHANGE WORKING?

I spent over 30 years in practice, often treating litigation like a war game. The rules were largely ignored in terms of compliance but they were never ignored when they could be used as a tactical weapon in the battle. All was fair in 'law' and war and this was war. Little thought was ever given to the final outcome of the case if there was an opportunity of finding a procedural argument to have on the smallest of points. I have changed along with many others. The new settlement culture is much better for our clients. The evidence available shows that to a large extent it is working. There has been a significant reduction in the number of new sets of proceedings issued. Cases are settling earlier and therefore they are costing much less overall when both costs and damages are taken into account. Parties want their dispute resolved quickly.

In personal injury cases, where we have had a protocol from the outset, insurers seem happy to pay reasonable compensation to settle cases early, particularly the smaller ones that make up the vast majority of claims. The new system with the new culture provides them with a far better opportunity to do this than they have ever had before. The less they need to place themselves in the hands of their solicitors, the better they like it. If there are losers then those who are being hardest hit are the defendants' lawyers and there are clear signs that the changes are biting in many firms.

Protocols do seem to work. If not, the court should put matters right. Speedy timetables and court control should stop opponents from going back to the old ways.

PRE-ISSUE STOCKTAKE

The new culture is all about settling cases that should be settled at the earliest possible time and for the minimum legal cost. Sometimes that will not happen and litigation will still be needed. Always carry out a pre-issue stocktake of the case. This checklist may be helpful:

- review the prospects of success;
- does the defendant have the ability to pay?
- check the costs incurred to date;
- prepare future costs estimates;
- narrow the issues as far as possible;
- plan a timetable for the case;
- check for compliance with any protocol or general protocol 'spirit';
- have your witnesses been interviewed?
- have you assembled documents for disclosure?
- have you sorted out any experts?
- is the evidence all ready?
- which track will you be in?
- what directions will you need?
- have you tried to settle?
- have you made a CPR Part 36 offer?
- is a stay post-issue worthwhile?
- might ADR resolve the dispute?
- have you made an offer to settle?
- have you reviewed any offer to settle received?

THE FUTURE

Further pre-action protocols to cover other types of litigation such as commercial work are likely to follow those already in place. The basic approach can and should be adopted in all cases pre-litigation. The general protocol 'spirit' can and should be fitted to almost any dispute. The parties involved normally want a speedy resolution, not a long drawn out and expensive process. Pre-action protocols or protocol behaviour bring this about in many disputes.

Most of us are familiar with Charles Dickens' novel *Bleak House*, set against the background of an apparently perpetual court case. Who would have wanted

345

to be a party in *Jarndyce* v. *Jarndyce* where the best anyone could say year after year was 'I expect a judgment shortly'.

Many parties to real litigation felt just as frustrated by the legal system before the reforms. Cases seemed to drag on for an eternity. The old culture was centered on the lawyers and worked to their benefit first. That was completely wrong and those of us who believed in it were wrong. The new culture puts the parties and their needs first, with the legal profession where they should be, in a supporting role.

Many practitioners, both sides, claimant and defendant alike have found it hard to change. A tourist in New York stopped a passer-by and asked, 'How do I get to Carnegie Hall?' The response was 'practice, practice, practice'. That has to be the message for us too. Learn to love the new settlement culture. Keep trying until you succeed. There is no alternative to it. The judges are already seeing to that, whether we like it or not.

CHAPTER 10

Small claims

Suzanne Burn

INTRODUCTION

Most solicitors regard small claims as outside the realm of legal work: they are trained to think that lawyers are not needed to help consumers with disputes over faulty washing machines and, even if they are, the work is not cost effective.

But the litigants who use the small claims court like it because of the informality and 'no costs' rule. Also the increased jurisdiction of up to £5,000, implemented in the civil justice reforms in April 1999, the changing methods of funding civil claims and the increased demands from more knowledgeable clients for specific help only when they need it, create the climate for a new role for lawyers in smaller claims.

£5,000 is a considerable sum of money for most individuals and small businesses. When the amount at stake is towards the upper end of the new small claims limit it will be economically viable for a client to seek legal advice, and possibly, representation: some individuals will be prepared to pay modest legal fees to pursue or defend a good case even when the costs recoverable from the losing party are fixed and very limited. Moreover, many commercial clients will want and pay for help in setting up systems for routine small claims work, especially debt recovery and straightforward insurance claims. If solicitors do not do this work then others, including debt collectors, claims assessors and the growing breed of 'lay' advisers and *McKenzie* friends will do so (see *R* v. *Bow County Court, ex parte Pelling* [1999] 1 WLR 1807, CA).

As two leading district judge commentators have said: 'Solicitors should not brush aside Part 27 of the Civil Procedure Rules as being of no importance or interest or applicability to them' (Holloway J); 'Practitioners will be wrong to think they will never touch a small claim. Increasingly it will be expected that legal advice will be sought by litigants before small claims are issued. I do not consider that £5,000 is small change by any means. Neither will most of the public' (Michael Walker J).

This chapter is an attempt to whet solicitors' appetites for small claims work. It does not provide a full commentary on the new rules or a detailed 'how to' guide to following the procedures. These exist elsewhere. The growing importance of small claims in the civil justice system is explained; the 1990s research, which largely prompted the increased limit, is considered briefly; the main changes in the CPR are discussed; funding and costs are considered; an 'unbundled' approach to small claims work is suggested; problems in enforcing small claims are referred to briefly, and, finally, some practical pointers to solicitors' potential new role are suggested.

BACKGROUND TO THE SMALL CLAIMS COURT

The county courts were created in the 1840s to provide a local, cheap and simple system for the recovery of small debts which it was too expensive to pursue in the Queen's Bench Division – the jurisdiction was then £20!

By the early 1970s, the county courts' jurisdiction had expanded so much that it was felt necessary to create a separate system for small claims. Informal 'arbitration' was introduced for claims up to £100. The financial limit was raised gradually over the years to £1,000 in the early 1990s.

However, the access to justice debate of the 1980s and 1990s highlighted the problem of costs as an obstacle to bringing a claim in the higher courts. Successive governments also realised the potential for reducing public expenditure on legal aid by increasing the small claims limit: legal aid was only rarely made available for small claims.

Accordingly, immediately after Lord Woolf suggested in his Interim Report (*Access to Justice*, 1995), that the (then) £1,000 limit might be reviewed (subject to the safeguard of providing better advisory services in the courts, which were not implemented) the Lord Chancellor announced a significant increase to £3,000, relying upon the 'popularity' of the 'no frills', low cost procedure.

This was brought into effect in January 1996. The only concessions made to the extensive criticisms raised by parts of the legal, voluntary sector and consumer communities was to keep the limit at £1,000 for personal injury claims and to introduce some very limited recoverable legal costs in cases involving applications for specific performance or injunctions.

Certainly by volume of cases disposed of in the county courts, small claims have fast outstripped open court trials, as Table 10.1 shows.

Table 10.1 County court proceedings disposed of by open court trial and by arbitration

	By open court trial	By arbitration	Total	% by arbitration
1990	22,000	52,000	74,000	70
1991	26,000	62,000	88,000	70
1992	27,000	80,000	107,000	75
1993	25,000	106,000	131,000	81
1994	24,000	88,000	112,000	78
1995	24,000	88,000	112,000	78
1996	20,000	94,000	114,000	83
1997	15,000	97,000	112,000	87
1998	14,000	99,000	113,000	88
1999	13,000	88,000	101,000	87

Source: Judicial Statistics: LCD annual

In the 1980s and 1990s rates of litigation dropped steadily in all courts but the exception was small claims. This trend has continued after the implementation of the CPR: new proceedings in the Royal Courts of Justice fell by 70 per cent, and in the county courts by 20 per cent but the numbers of small claims are holding steady.

THE 'SUCCESS' OF THE SMALL CLAIMS COURT

The last 10 to 20 years has seen a major, largely 'unplanned', growth in the numbers of litigants acting in person (LIPs) in all our courts, probably for a number of different reasons:

(a) there are no bars on individuals acting in person in any proceedings, as there are in other jurisdictions;

(b) a dwindling percentage of the population is eligible for Legal Services Commission legal help or representation;

349

(c) many middle income citizens do not have access to any third party funding but cannot afford legal fees and 'resort to going it alone';

(d) with increasing education more citizens have the confidence to act for themselves;

(e) some litigants manage to pursue or defend actions with advice and/or assistance from the voluntary sector, including the 'duty desks' which operate in many county courts, or from specific services or publications aimed at LIPs, e.g. the training courses now offered in Bristol by the National Council for Access to Law;

(f) there is a growing number who positively choose to act for themselves; some have had unfortunate experiences with courts and lawyers, others develop a taste for litigation and may pursue several actions.

The popularity of the small claims court is one, significant, manifestation of this trend.

Detailed studies of small claims were conducted in the 1990s by the National Audit Office (*Handling Small Claims in the County Court* (NAO, 1996)) and, for the Lord Chancellor's Department by Professor Baldwin. Baldwin's first study (*Small Claims in the County Courts in England and Wales* (Clarendon Press, 1997)), carried out when the financial limit was £1,000, involved an examination of 1,800 files, observation of more than 100 hearings and interviews with 33 district judges and 260 litigants. The second (*Monitoring the Rise in the Small Claims Limit* (LCD, 1997)), was a specific study to compare the experiences of litigants in the small claims courts and open court hearings, in cases with a value of £1,000 to £3,000: this involved interviews with 160 litigants.

The key findings from these studies were the following.

(1) The main users of the small claims court are small businesses, professionals and middle class individuals pursuing or defending cases concerning consumer goods and services, debt, contract and non-personal injury road traffic claims.

(2) Very few cases reach the small claims court which involve social welfare issues, including housing.

(3) The majority of litigants taking cases in the small claims court do not seek legal advice nor are represented by lawyers at the hearing: many of these do not feel at a disadvantage, express satisfaction with the quality of the service provided by the court, and would choose to represent themselves again.

These studies and the statistics suggested to the Government that the small claims procedures were a great success and led to the further proposal in 1997 that the limit could 'safely' be raised again to £5,000 and that this would enhance access to justice.

However, there are a number of important contra-indications in the research which successive governments have chosen to overlook.

(1) Both the NAO and Baldwin's first study showed that parties who were represented by lawyers had a higher success rate than those who were unrepresented. The NAO recommended further specific research on this but it was not undertaken.

(2) Rates of legal representation in small claims hearings rose with the increasing financial limits. In Baldwin's first study, in 18 per cent of the cases at least one party was represented, but in the second study 50 per cent were represented, especially in the larger value claims. Claimants were more likely to be represented than defendants, especially insured claimants in road traffic accident cases. So much for Baldwin's comment that with the rising small claims limit, the county courts could soon become a lawyer free zone!

(3) The numbers of litigants seeking legal advice also increased: only 25 per cent did so in the NAO study, but 40 per cent did so in Baldwin's first study, and 50 per cent two years later.

(4) Informal procedures are problematic for more complex higher value cases. Baldwin found that many litigants adopted a casual approach to completing claims forms, and that the court leaflets and other information provided by the court staff were insufficient help. He concluded that it was asking too much of the judges to sort out legal difficulties at hearings, when there were points of law which the parties had not understood in advance.

(5) The out of court settlement rate for small claims was much lower than in other litigation, because it is solicitors who negotiate. In Baldwin's second study, almost none of the small claims settled before trial but 25 per cent of the 'open court' control did so. He found that some LIPs thought that initiating contact with the other side would be regarded by the court as improper.

Baldwin concluded in his first study:

> The expansion [of the small claims limit] has enhanced access to justice for a limited segment of the population. The genuinely poor make few appearances at small claims hearings and when they do it is typically as defendants to a landlord or money lender . . . If litigants are to perform adequately in the small claims arena then they require some familiarity with the rules of the game in advance of the hearing. What this means in practice is that litigants must receive advice

351

beforehand about the validity of a claim (or defence) if the principle of lay people presenting their own cases is to work . . . In the writer's view there comes a point where serious injustice might result from expecting lay litigants in person to go it alone.

SMALL CLAIMS AND THE CIVIL PROCEDURE RULES

What has not been changed

The small claims track is now a separate regime designed to meet CPR Part 1, the overriding objective, i.e. that the court should seek to deal with cases in ways which save expense and are proportionate to the amount of money involved.

It should not be viewed in isolation – all the basic principles in CPR Parts 1, 3 and 26 apply, although, based on the previous County Court Order 17, Part 27 of the CPR is a considerable improvement both in content and drafting style, largely thanks to the Association of District Judges who carried out much of the reshaping work.

The basic framework of the small claims system has not been changed by the CPR:

(a) the aim is still to decide most small claims quickly at only one hearing;

(b) the hearing will remain informal with the district judge having wide powers to adopt any method or approach which is appropriate, as long as it is fair; there is no need to take evidence on oath and the judge may limit cross examination (CRP Rule 27.8);

(c) many of the rules of evidence designed for larger and sometimes more complex cases are disapplied: interim remedies (Part 25); disclosure (Part 31); expert evidence (Part 35), and offers to settle (Part 36);

(d) generally only very limited costs are recoverable (fixed costs attributable to issuing proceedings and allocation to track; witness travel expenses and loss of earnings up to £50 a day; expert fees to a maximum of £200 and legal fees of up to £260 when an injunction is sought: CPR Rule 27.14(2)–(3) and Practice Direction to Part 27 para. 7.3);

(e) district judges still have to apply the law!

As Professor Baldwin very graphically described small claims hearings:

> no place for standing on ceremony, for airs and graces or pomposity . . . hearings characterised by good humour and robust common sense, seasoned with large doses of legal and judicial pragmatism.

What has been changed by the CPR

Although the basic framework remains, the changes introduced by the CPR *are* significant, particularly as they should encourage solicitors to reappraise their role in small claims.

The main changes are as follows:

(1) The small claims track is the 'normal' track for claims with a value of up to £5,000, previously £3,000, except for personal injury and housing disrepair when it is £1,000 (CPR Rule 26.6). Larger claims can only be allocated to the track with the consent of all parties.

(2) It is a track, not a separate court, and the inappropriate description 'arbitration' has been dropped, although sadly not the equally inappropriate 'small'. The LCD apparently gave up on trying to find a new label. My suggestion of the People's Court did not find favour as being too American!

(3) There is no longer any automatic reference into the track. The court has to take a case management decision to allocate a case to the small claims track based on the parties' statements of case and information on the allocation questionnaire, and the claimant has to pay the allocation fee (CPR Rule 26.5) (although this requirement was dropped from 2 May 2000 for claims under £1,000, following serious criticism by the Civil Justice Council).

(4) Automatic transfer to the defendant's home court has been restricted: it applies only when the claim is for a 'specified amount' and the defendant is an individual (CPR Rule 26.2).

(5) The court has the jurisdiction to order any remedy, including injunction and specific performance, thus confirming the Court of Appeal decision in *Afzal* v. *Ford Motor Co. Ltd* [1994] 4 All 720, CA (CPR Rule 26.3).

(6) The district judge has a clear power to strike out hopeless claims or defences, confirming the unofficial practice adopted in some of the more enlightened courts for some time pre-CPR (CPR Rule 27.6).

(7) Summary judgment is available for the first time in small claims for either claimant or defendant, with the test being 'no reasonable prospect of success', the *Saudi Eagle* (*Alpine Bulk Transport Co. Inc.* v. *Saudi Eagle Shipping Co. Inc.* [1986] Lloyd's Rep 221) test (CPR Part 24).

(8) Preliminary hearings are intended to be unusual: there is more use of detailed paper directions. New standard form templates are available for contract, road traffic accident, building, landlord and tenant, holiday, wedding and neighbour cases (see the Practice Direction to CPR Part 27).

(9) The court can dispense altogether with a hearing, with the parties' consent, e.g. where the case could be decided on the documents, or it would be disproportionately expensive for a party to attend (CPR Rule 27.10).

(10) Hearings, in common with the other tracks, are 'in public' unless the district judge orders otherwise (CPR Rule 39.2) (which might be where publicity could cause damage to confidential matters), although they are usually still in the judge's room (CPR Rule 26.10).

(11) Parties will not be penalised for not attending the hearing on distance/proportionality grounds provided the court is told seven days in advance (CPR Rule 27.9).

(12) Companies may be represented as of right at the hearing by a company official (see the Practice Direction to Part 27, para. 3(4)).

(13) The judge has to give reasons for the decision, albeit briefly (not an extended essay), and the decision is tape-recorded (see the Practice Direction to Part 27, section 5).

(14) Costs, if any, should be assessed by the summary assessment procedure at the end of the hearing. Small claims track costs only apply from allocation (CPR Rule 44.9), any costs order made before allocation is not affected by later allocation (CPR Rule 44.1), and in higher value claims allocated to the small claims track by consent, fast track costs will apply from that date. This will also be the position if a claim is transferred up to the fast track, from the time of transfer (CPR Rules 27.14, 27.15 and 44.9).

(15) Slightly enhanced rights of appeal were implemented in April 1999 (CPR Rule 27.12) but on limited grounds and within 14 days. The circuit judge could decide an appeal without a hearing, to weed out hopeless cases quickly. But following consultation, the Lord Chancellor decided that Part 52 (in force from 2 May 2000) should also apply to small claims from October 2000 (except where appeals were filed before that date). CPR Rules 27.12–13 were revoked and the Practice

Direction to Part 27 was amended. The current regime for appeals in small claims is:

(a) permission to appeal is now required from the first instance judge or the appeal court;

(b) appeals will lie to the next level of judge, usually the circuit judge;

(c) when permission is given there has to be a hearing, usually to dispose of the case, not to send it back to a district judge for a rehearing;

(d) appeals are reviews, not rehearings, so there is very limited scope to adduce new evidence;

(e) appeals will be allowed when the decision of the lower court was:

    (i) wrong;

    (ii) unjust because of a serious procedural or other irregularity;

(f) second appeals will only be allowed exceptionally.

THE POTENTIAL PROBLEM AREAS IN THE CPR

These are probably fewer in number than in other parts of the CPR but are nonetheless significant.

Do the pre-action protocols apply?

The following are some points to consider.

(1) The Protocols and Practice Direction do not cover this (I have to admit the protocol working parties, which I coordinated, simply did not consider this when drafting the Protocols).

(2) The Protocols are not aimed at and could cause problems for litigants in person.

(3) Not many personal injury, and very few clinical negligence or defamation claims, will be within the small claims track band.

(4) Proportionality strongly suggests that a letter of claim with short time to respond and a willingness to try to settle pre-action should be sufficient (see the Protocols Practice Direction). The courts, in my view, should not expect extensive pre-action collaboration on documents and experts in a small claim.

(5) Sanctions for failing to comply with a Protocol will be difficult to apply when only limited costs are recoverable, unless conduct is very unreasonable.

The track definitions, particularly for personal injury and housing disrepair, are problematic and which may lead to satellite litigation (CPR Rule 26.6(1)).

Personal injury

It is the pain and suffering element alone which needs to be greater than £1,000 and the total damages greater than £5,000 for the fast track to be the normal track. This at least clarifies the very ambiguous position in the pre-1999 CPR but lay litigants will not be able, without help, to value separately the different heads of claim on the claim form. It may be very difficult, therefore, for the court to assess the likely general damages at allocation stage based on the limited information provided. It could also encourage some claimants to 'exaggerate' the pain and suffering element of the claim to try to escape into the fast track and attract recoverable costs.

It would have been simpler to exclude all personal injury claims from small claims except by consent, as proposed by APIL and the Law Society.

Housing disrepair

Despite many attempts at the drafting, and after several rounds of consultation, including with the Law Society and the Housing Law Practitioners' Association, the track definition test is a complex one, which could be difficult to operate in practice:

(a) to be allocated to the fast track *both* the costs of the repairs *and* the value of any claim for damages have to be greater than £1,000 separately, which is effectively a £2,000 limit for any claim involving both elements;

(b) if there is no repair claim, perhaps because the repairs have already been carried out, then any claim with a value of less than £5,000 will be allocated to the small claims track, even though proving causation between disrepair and damage, and estimating compensation, invariably needs skilled advice, including from an expert.

It seems that the Rule Committee and LCD compromised the clear political intention to treat housing claims in a similar way to personal injury by accepting the arguments of the social landlords and the DETR that housing repair budgets were being unfairly eroded by successful legal claims.

Allocation to track

Why should a claimant with a case which is definitely in the small claims track by value have to be put to the trouble of completing the long complex allocation questionnaire and, if the value of the claim is over £1,000, pay the allocation fee, only to have their choice of track confirmed, especially when the issue and allocation fees combined could be disproportionate to the value of the claim? This is hardly consistent with the proportionality principle in the overriding objective.

Also, many lay litigants need legal help to complete the form if useful information is to be provided to the court.

The real reason for requiring the allocation fee to be paid is to enable the Court Service to balance its books, as the costs of running the service now have to be covered entirely from court fees. (Most other jurisdictions have decided that the civil courts are a public service, which should, in the public interest, be financed at least in part from general taxation.) The increase in the small claims limit means fewer cases on the other tracks. These will not usually 'pay their way' as the defended cases which run through or close to trial, in particular, take up considerably more Court Service resources, especially judicial ones, than most small claims (despite paying some additional court fees for applications and at listing stage). The alternative, of raising court fees for fast and multi-track claims, was presumably rejected because those fees could then be so high they would act as a deterrent to access to the courts in some cases. With falling caseloads in the more senior courts, the Court Service and Government are faced with a serious quandary; put up fees again and continue the vicious spiral or return to subsiding the courts as a public service.

However, it is certainly not wise for a claimant to inflate the value of the claim to encourage allocation to the fast track, because when this becomes apparent the claimant might lose entitlement to fast track costs. Aware defendants will provide the court with their own estimate on the value of a claim when filing the defence or allocation questionnaire to secure a tactical advantage.

Stays for settlement

Will courts make use of the power in CPR Rule 26.4 to stay small claims for settlement, including by ADR? Again there is anecdotal, but not reported, evidence of very small claims being referred out to mediation by the judges on the grounds that they should not be using court resources! But is this fair, especially if a fee for mediation has to be paid?

Transfer to the defendant's home court

While the new rules are preferable to the old for claimants in particular, any automatic transfer may causes problems, especially where a party subsequently applies for a re-transfer, as the courts not infrequently lose files when they are being 'shuttlecocked' around.

In addition, the new rules on automatic transfer only apply to claims for a 'specified amount'. This is not necessarily the same as an unliquidated claim. A claimant in a personal injury or holiday claim might choose to limit their 'specified amount' to secure an allocation to the small claims track, only then to find the case has been transferred to a court some distance away for the defendant's benefit. A better solution might have been only to consider transfer at allocation stage.

Default judgment

The new rules should enable claimants in a damages action to apply for default judgment for a specified amount within the small claims track and avoid the old style 'interlocutory judgment' with damages to be assessed which could attract a costs order. Defendants, of course, might be caught out by this.

Summary judgment

Undoubtedly the introduction of summary judgment in small claims is to be welcomed, enabling weak claims and defences to be terminated early in cases which the court has not felt able to strike out on the basis of the statement of case alone.

But the fact that this is now an available option prior to allocation may lead to problems, especially where a litigant in person is required to pay the costs of the other party's successful early application for summary judgment, without having been aware that such costs would be recoverable. This needs to be given greater prominence in the claim form and response packs and in the small claims leaflets.

Offers to settle

It may have seemed logical to exclude CPR Part 36 from general application to the small claims track, but incentives to settlement are even more necessary in low value claims for proportionality reasons, particularly as litigants in person are inexperienced in, and less often use, negotiation. A limited recoverable costs regime for small claims might have been the answer, but there is the possibility of applying for costs on the 'unreasonable conduct' basis.

Listings and time estimates

In theory these could cause difficulties too; it would not be in keeping with 'allocating an appropriate share of the court's resources' (CPR Rule 1.1(2)(e)) if small claims hearings were listed further ahead than 30 weeks from allocation, or for more than one day (the fast track guidelines). However, the political pressure was on to be seen to make the fast track work well with an intention to reserve resources for fast track trials if courts were under pressure. In practice, the falling workloads in the courts has meant only limited slippage in setting hearing dates for small claims.

Hearings

There is some confusion in the CPR and Practice Directions about who can represent a litigant at a small claims hearing. Clearly:

- litigants can represent themselves;
- company employees can represent their employer; and
- a solicitor, barrister, or fellow of the Institute of Legal Executives can represent a client, even when the client is not in court.

However, the Lay Representatives (Rights of Audience) Order 1999, SI 1999/ 1225, states that a lay representative is not permitted when the client is not present at the hearing. Also the Practice Direction to CPR Part 27 implies that 'unqualified' trainees, legal executives and paralegals are to be regarded as 'lay representatives'. This could mean they are not able to appear unless the client is present or the court gives express permission. This may be because small claims hearings are now 'in public'. Judges have a discretion to say no to lay representatives including *McKenzie* friends. But in *R* v. *Bow County Court, ex parte Pelling* [1999] 1 WLR 1807, the Court of Appeal suggested that *McKenzie* friends should usually be permitted at hearings.

Restricting representation to qualified lawyers is hardly consistent with the overriding objective to 'save expense' or with Article 6(1) of the European Convention on Human Rights (ECHR). It will often only be cost effective for solicitors' firms to provide a small claims service if the work, including representation at hearings, is carried out by junior staff, under supervision as necessary. One possibility might be for firms to seek 'blanket approval' from their local court for junior staff to appear rather than to seek individual approval on a case by case basis.

Costs

It is very arguable whether the 'no recoverable costs' rule remains fair to small claims litigants who need legal advice on the merits of their case and/or help to prepare documents or representation, especially in the larger or more complex claims, if these are not allocated to the fast track on application. It could be argued that the rule offends the compensatory tort principle and Article 6 of the ECHR. From a more practical standpoint it also discourages settlement and can encourage a determined opponent to delay, prevaricate, unreasonably deny liability, and simply be intransigent, to wear down the other party.

The position on recovering costs is unclear in a number of respects because the CPR are silent about the following:

(1) What happens when liability of a claim within the scope of the small claims track is not disputed by the defendant, and is settled pre-issue or before allocation to track, except as to costs? The costs are now at the discretion of the court. There were a number of cases decided on this issue under the old rules, but in different ways. As the costs regime of the small claims track only applies once a case is allocated to track, the starting point perhaps should be the value of the claim provided it has not been exaggerated. The Costs Rules and Practice Direction preserve the right for a party to issue solely to resolve costs (Costs Practice Direction) and in July 2000 a new Rule was added, CPR Rule 44.12A, to implement a specific procedure to resolve disputed costs starting with a CPR Part 8 claim.

(2) What is the situation when a defendant admits/agrees to pay part of a sum claimed pre-allocation so that the amount 'remaining in dispute' is within the scope of the small claims track? The result should be as above (see Rule 44.11(1) and the Costs Practice Direction, para. C5), but this is an area which seems likely to lead to satellite litigation if it is used by defendants tactically to try to avoid having to pay costs.

(3) What happens when the claim is on behalf of a child or 'patient' where the court still has to approve any settlement? Costs might be recoverable in this type of case, but what if the defendant is an individual rather than an insurer who, again, did not anticipate having to pay costs?

The main exception to the 'no costs' rule in small claims is where a party has been guilty of 'unreasonable conduct' (CPR Rule 27.14(2)(d)). This preserves the pre-CPR rule. There were very few reported decisions on this issue, even after the increase in the small claims financial jurisdiction in 1997. The likelihood that more parties will seek legal advice or be represented following the further substantial increase in the jurisdiction in April 1999 suggests that possible arguments to advance with regard to unreasonable conduct might be:

(a) issuing/pursuing a hopeless case/defence specifically to embarrass/ inconvenience the other party;

(b) issuing prematurely without any attempt to negotiate or discuss settlement;

(c) refusing or failing to provide essential information/evidence pre- or post-issue, especially if this is in breach of a court order or might assist settlement;

(d) deliberate or unreasonable delay or lack of cooperation, e.g. paying in full just before the hearing, seeking a very late adjournment of the hearing or failing to attend without giving notice and then trying to set the judgment aside.

Where costs may be recoverable on this ground, should the party seeking their costs serve a costs schedule for summary assessment before the hearing? How will LIPs know that they should do this? How will the court decide the amount of costs? There are no guidelines in the CPR or Practice Directions. I suggest the court should apply fast track principles/proportionality and that the indemnity principle will also apply, when both parties have legal representatives (so that costs recoverable from the paying party should not exceed the amount the receiving party would pay his own solicitor).

A steady trickle of cases reported in *Current Law* from late 1999 onwards suggests that unreasonable conduct costs awards are becoming more common.

Appeals

While including small claims in the ambit of Part 52 of the CPR is generally to be welcomed, there is as yet no guidance from case law on what might amount to a 'serious procedural or other irregularity'. It seems highly likely the courts will interpret this new rule restrictively on proportionality grounds, and to avoid highly speculative small claims appeals taking up an 'inappropriate amount' of court time.

Procedural arguments alone seem destined to fail: the applicant would need to show that, e.g. determinative evidence had been unreasonably excluded by the judge, or that he had refused to allow a party to cross-examine on very weak evidence, or that the decision had been based on matters on which evidence had not been offered.

The CPR have not changed the small claims regime significantly in the short term, but the increased financial limits bring into the track more complex claims some of which are more seriously contested. This means more litigants seeking legal advice and/or representation, and probably longer and more traditionally adversarial hearings, more (successful?) claims for costs on 'conduct' grounds and more appeals. Will the next move be to introduce a 'fast track 2' with a limited scale of recoverable costs and a 'super small claims court or track' from which lawyers are banned or strongly discouraged? History has a habit of repeating itself!

FUNDING SMALL CLAIMS

Insurance

Solicitors must, in any value of claim, on taking instructions, check first whether the client has access to any means of third party funding, particularly insurance – in small claims, typically for road traffic accident property damage claims. 'Before the event' legal expenses insurance is increasingly available as a cheap add-on to domestic motor and holiday insurance policies, or through trade union membership, or more recently to small businesses.

Many liability and legal expense insurers offer telephone helplines which may be sufficient for the client's needs. There may be financial limits on the legal expense cover (typically £5,000, £10,000 or £25,000 which may include the other party's costs if the case is lost and these costs are recoverable) or restrictions on the choice of solicitor (most insurers restrict initial pre-action work at least, to those on their panel, who provide a (sometimes limited) service for an 'economical' retainer).

With the cutbacks in state funding of civil claims, legal expenses insurance (LEI) is likely to an expanding market. In Germany for instance, where state-funded legal aid is very limited, a high percentage of the population has legal expenses insurance. There are also fixed recoverable costs in most courts and a much higher rate of litigation than here.

LEI could offer many citizens and small businesses improved 'access to justice' in the small claims track in future.

Legal help, help at court and representation (legal aid)

State funding for help at court or representation through the Legal Services Commission will only very rarely be available for small claims track cases in future; the Access to Justice Act 1999 Funding Code states that 'an application will be refused if the case has been or is likely to be allocated to the small claims track'.

Housing cases are the exception; they will be considered for funding where the damages are over £1,000.

However, firms with a civil franchise/contract will be able to provide 'legal help', i.e. advice initially limited to two hours' work 'where there is sufficient benefit to the client, having regard to the circumstances of the matter, including the personal circumstance of the client, to justify work, or further work being carried out'. These are even harsher tests than under the previous funding regime, where legal aid for representation in proceedings was usually refused under the unreasonableness test, would only be granted where there were exceptional circumstances justifying the use of a solicitor, and where such representation would produce tangible benefit to the client. The issue of cost benefit had to be considered very carefully, but occasionally legal aid could be obtained for a small claim.

The *Legal Aid Handbook* also stated that legal aid would not usually be granted to assist a client in putting the case for the claim to be taken out of small claims. The Funding Code is not so specific but it seems very unlikely funding will be available in the new stricter regime.

As there is no longer any automatic reference into small claims, solicitors should press the LSC, in cases when the appropriate track is not obvious or is in dispute, to at least provide funding to cover work until the allocation to track stage, and/or to cover any summary judgment application, because a costs liability may be incurred before allocation which could cause severe hardship to someone on a low income.

In my view, some claims towards the upper limit of the small claims track band *ought to* qualify for funding for legal representation throughout the proceedings on cost/benefit grounds, particularly if the prospects of success are good, the matter in issue is of importance to the client, or he/she will have particular difficulty in pursuing or defending the claim, or needs help with a particular step, especially at court (and Professor Baldwin's research showed that represented parties did do better at small claims hearings).

Conditional fees

In theory there is no difference between a small claim and a fast or multi-track case with regard to conditional fee funding. In July 1998 conditional fee agreements became lawful in all money claims (see the Conditional Fee Agreements Order 1998, SI 1998/1860) and in July 2000 success fees and insurance premiums became recoverable from the losing party (Civil Procedure (Amendment No. 3) Rules 2000, SI 2000/1317). However, in practice, even on a £5,000 claim, charging a success fee will not be very attractive (to lawyer or client) unless the basic charge (to which the success fee is added), is kept very low. Also it is not clear whether the courts would order recovery of a success fee and insurance premium as part of an 'unreasonable conduct' costs order in a small claim.

But keeping within the Law Society's recommended voluntary cap on the success fee (of 25 per cent of the damages) should not be an additional handicap, as few clients with a small claim will be willing to lose perhaps one-third or even one-half of their money in costs.

Private funding

In most small claims, in any event, it will be uneconomic for the client, and disproportionate, for solicitors' firms to charge for work on an open-ended hourly rate basis, because the client will want certainty on their likely financial outlay before deciding whether the claim is worth pursuing. Fixed, or at least capped, fees will be a much more attractive proposition because the client will at least know the maximum downside if they lose the case.

The issue for the solicitors' firm is whether fixed fees in small claims can be made to pay. For claims up to £2,000 to £3,000, fees of more than 10 per cent of the value of the claim are unlikely to appeal to clients on proportionality or cost benefit grounds: but this may only buy a very few hours' work, even at trainee or junior fee earner rates. For claims of £4,000 to £5,000 in value, fees of up to 20 per cent of the value of the claim may be worthwhile, especially in strong cases for commercial clients, provided court fees do not rise any more.

However, business and commercial clients, including insurers, are willing to block purchase services for volume small claims work, e.g. road traffic accident vehicle damage claims, debt recovery, or even defendant holiday claims, provided a streamlined cost effective system is set up, using junior staff in the solicitors' office, and junior barristers for the advocacy at hearings in distant courts.

The other attraction for the firm could be offering greater responsibility and job satisfaction for the junior staff, provided the client is made fully aware of the type and level of service they are buying and the local court will allow non-solicitors to conduct the advocacy at the hearing.

Firms also need to know their bottom line: at what level of funding, in comparison with hours worked, will a small claim be profitable? Some firms will be prepared to break even, or lose money, on small claims because of their commitment to the local community and/or disadvantaged clients, or because the work is a 'loss leader' for an important commercial client.

UNBUNDLING

Another approach to providing a cost effective service is to 'unbundle' the work between the solicitor and the client.

Most solicitors' firms offer, and clients expect, a traditional 'full service' package, especially in litigation, which is usually regarded by lawyers as too technical and complex for clients to understand. Typically the client 'retains' the solicitor, who, often unilaterally, decides the scope of the service, runs the case, does all the work, and bills the client, usually on an open-ended hourly basis.

However, there are other approaches. In the USA a limited service approach, known as 'unbundling' is rapidly gaining popularity. The term was coined by Forrest 'Woody' Mosten, who has been running a successful family law practice in Los Angeles in this way for some years. A possible definition of unbundling is: 'providing legal help to those of moderate means by sharing the work between the lawyer and the client, i.e. by dividing up the tasks in the legal bundle'.

Unbundling can take a number of different forms:

(a) providing advice to a client willing and able to conduct their own case: through an initial consultation for a flat fee, or from time to time during the case as determined by the client and his/her needs and means;

(b) agreeing to share the specific tasks required in a case between the lawyer and the client, with the lawyer usually remaining 'in charge' and conducting any litigation.

The reaction of lawyers, clients, and judges in the USA to unbundling is very positive because of the potential for increasing access to justice. The benefits for the clients are obvious: they pay only for what they need, they retain ownership of their problem and its resolution, and may develop a better understanding of the legal system. But there are potentially equal benefits to the lawyers in gaining new clients or new areas of work (or at least not losing work), and in acquiring new skills. Also if lawyers become less paternalistic and remote, respect for the profession might even improve!

It would be wrong to pretend that there are no problems with the unbundled approach, particularly in the post-Woolf world of tightly timetabled litigation:

(a) skilful screening is required as only some clients will be able to work in partnership in this way;

(b) the division of tasks needs careful planning and recording in writing – important work must not slip down the middle or be expensively duplicated;

(c) financial arrangements must be crystal clear;

(d) either the lawyer or the client must be and stay on the court record to avoid muddle for the other party and the court.

However, so far, clients who agree to work in this way with their solicitor appear to be happier, pay their bills on time, complain and sue less often. The professional indemnity insurers are also being supportive of the approach.

Many solicitors in this jurisdiction probably adopt the unbundled approach without attaching the label. The advice sector and solicitors' firms who specialise in welfare and community law frequently offer no or low cost surgeries and help with small claims or tribunal hearings. At the other end of the spectrum many businesses and insurers conduct the pre-action stages of claims themselves, only bringing in lawyers for specific tasks when proceedings are issued.

An unbundled approach to a small claim might include:

(a) providing pre-prepared information/DIY packs for a nominal charge to clients or to referrals from advice sector agencies (although experience suggests these may be of limited value without some face to face contact);

(b) giving advice on the merits, law and procedure on a one-off interview basis at a firm or advice agency surgery for no or a very limited fee;

(c) drafting letters of claim or response, completing claim forms/defences and/or allocation questionnaires;

(d) advising on the value of the claim, including locating and instructing an expert where necessary;

(e) checking documents including witness statements and statements of losses and costs;

(f) providing a letter, note, skeleton argument or schedule of expenses or costs for the hearing;

(g) providing advocacy at the hearing.

In the light of Professor Baldwin's research the most useful of these are probably advice at the outset, help with assembling the evidence and drawing up a note for the hearing. District judges do not welcome over-adversarial or long-winded advocacy and cross-examination at small claims hearings, but on the other hand they can find it difficult to reach reasoned and fair decisions when no, limited or confused evidence is presented, especially if this is not available in advance of the hearing.

Prompted by the results of Professor Baldwin's research, the LCD even suggested, in a consultation paper on small claims in 1998, that lawyers might be banned entirely from small claims hearings. The threat was not carried through, possibly because the *quid pro quo* would have been allowing larger claims only to be conducted by a lawyer (as is the case in many other jurisdictions).

CHECKING THE CREDIT-WORTHINESS OF THE OPPONENT AND ENFORCING THE JUDGMENT

The majority of litigants assume that a judgment will automatically be enforced by the court. It is a considerable disappointment for many litigants, and a source of disillusionment with the court system, that obtaining a judgment may only be the start of the process for recovery of the money.

The National Audit Office study on small claims and the Home Affairs Select Committee were very critical of the rates of enforcement of judgments generally and especially of small claims judgments. A major LCD initiative on reviewing enforcement is in progress, which is looking at earlier judicial involvement in the process, including means enquiries during or at the end of liability hearings, more court-led and streamlined integrated enforcement procedures and improved collection machinery, but changes are not likely to be implemented soon.

In the meantime, the role of the solicitor, particularly in a potential small claim, is clearly to help the client check the credit-worthiness of the opponent, by searching the Register of County Court Judgments and advising on carrying out local inquiries. Advice and trading standards agencies will often have local knowledge of bad payers if the solicitors' firm does not.

For commercial clients pursuing debts against individuals or small businesses, the issue may be differentiating between 'can't pays' and 'won't pays' but there is at present no means of establishing a debtor's means with the assistance of the court until after judgment has been obtained.

THE SOLICITOR'S ROLE IN SMALL CLAIMS

As District Judge Frenkel has said:

> the guidance clients want [in small claims] is the same as solicitors provide for family and friends. They want a list of crucial points, a reminder of what is relevant, a warning about common traps and perhaps a piece of standard text. The advice will be business like and jargon free and given for a fixed fee. First time litigants may want to be represented, even if they carry out the preparation work themselves. Professional litigants . . . may want a litigation support system. They require a set of standard forms, an intelligent litigation checklist and access to specialist advice if they hit a problem beyond their experience. If this desert island advice falls short of the traditional service usually considered necessary to protect their client's interest, it is an infinite improvement on having no access to legal advice whatsoever.

The following is a checklist for a solicitors' firm considering taking on small claims work:

- Have a clear policy on taking on small claims work, who can take the decision to accept instructions and on who does the work.
- Let the local advice agencies know the firm offers a service for small claims and for which types of case.
- Set up a simple fixed fee or discounted charging structure. This could be task-based, e.g. advice on merits/law = £100, drafting letters or particulars of claim = £50, but with a cap on total fees as a percentage of the value of the claim.
- Consider providing regular free or low cost initial advice surgeries and/ or facilities for clients to look up information themselves in a library or online.
- Prepare a small claims variation of the firm's client care letter which covers the funding arrangements and the level of fee earner who will do the work.
- Make available some basic information packs for different types of case covering the essentials of the rules and procedures (this could include a set of the Court Service small claims leaflets, checklists of steps and standard letters). If there is a demand for a particular type of small claim in the locality the packs could also include notes on the relevant law.

- Ensure junior staff who run the cases are well supervised and the local courts have no objection to them representing clients at hearings in the absence of the client.
- Negotiate arrangements with barristers' chambers and any organisations willing to provide a representation service for a low, fixed or even no fee.
- Offer a (free) debriefing service for clients and the junior staff who run the cases.
- Keep a database of small claims decisions, especially in the local court, as so few are reported.

The following is a checklist for a solicitor helping a client with a small claim:

- advice on the law, prospects of success and the likely value of the case;
- agreeing the funding arrangement and the scope of the firm's work;
- advice to the client on how to check whether the defendant is worth suing;
- advice on alternative ways of resolving the dispute;
- drafting a letter of claim or reply;
- advice on, or help with, negotiations and attempts to settle;
- helping the client to assemble documents, including photos;
- helping the client locate and interview witnesses;
- advice on obtaining an expert's report, preferably in conjunction with the other party;
- explaining the court procedures and providing copies of leaflets, forms and standard directions;
- help with completing the claim form, defence and/or allocation questionnaire and/or in making any specific applications, e.g. for striking out the other side's case, summary judgment, allocation to a higher track or for specific non-standard directions;
- advice/help in complying with directions;
- preparation for the hearing:
  - assembling the 'bundle' of evidence
  - compiling a schedule of losses, expenses and costs including where appropriate for unreasonable conduct;
  - writing a note to the judge on the law (with any authorities attached);

- writing a list of the key points: the court could be invited to treat this as a substitute for an appearance if it is uneconomic for the client or the solicitor to attend.

- Coaching the client for the hearing or arranging or undertaking the representation but in a low key unadversarial manner, taking the cue as to approach from the district judge. District Judge Richard Holloway has said: 'Probably the most effective practitioner who frequently came to small claims hearings in front of me was a very clever solicitor . . . who seldom cross examined at all. He would, in a few sentences, plus some references to statute or legal authority, sink his opponent's case . . . He was a "one point advocate". He defeated one HP company so often they began instructing him themselves. And it was all done without any ritualistic advocacy at all'.

- Advising on and helping with any appeal and/or enforcement.

CONCLUSIONS

The small claims track is here to stay. The informal, low cost, low risk, relatively speedy approach suits many litigants. Moreover, the Government's agenda is only to provide very limited legal help to those who cannot pursue small claims on their own, through the Community Legal Service by legal help (advice) only in selected franchised, contracted, committed and low price solicitors' firms. In addition, the civil justice reforms emphasise that litigation, even a small claim, should be viewed 'as a last resort' and the courts are increasingly encouraging those with disputes to settle them by non-litigious means such as mediation.

The numbers of litigants acting in person has grown significantly in recent years and the courts, especially the district judges in the small claims track, are trying hard to meet their needs and dispense justice by edging the adversarial process towards the inquisitorial. This could easily spread to the fast track, particularly if very restricted fixed costs are introduced.

The challenge for solicitors' firms is whether and how to retain a role in this market, either for economic 'survival' reasons, or because of commitment to a particular client base, especially the local community. The limited service approach, fixed fees for hiring junior staff, or unbundling are probably the only ways forward, with some scope for conditional fee arrangements at the upper end of the track band. But abandoning small claims work will certainly not enhance solicitors' reputations and should not be the option of choice for community-based firms, not least because they could in due course also lose some of the fast track work.

If solicitors' firms cannot offer a cost effective value-added service in small claims, can they do so in mainstream litigation in an era when legal information is increasingly available, virtually free, on the Internet and when accountants, loss adjusters and claims assessors are more than ready to pick up the work which the legal profession cannot handle?

CHAPTER 11

Surviving the fast track

Jane Ching[1]

INTRODUCTION

As it is the author's view that in order to survive the fast track, as much work as possible should be carried out as early as possible, this chapter starts with

[1] I am indebted to my colleague Jenny Chapman for her invaluable comments on an early draft of this chapter together with her important insights into the practicalities of the fast track insofar as they affect personal injury practitioners. I am also grateful to the Professional Ethics Division of the Law Society for kindly confirming the current status of Principle 20.04.

the trial before then examining in detail the tactical approach which will enable the practitioner to reach the trial as efficiently as possible. The procedure is taken in stages, each of which begins with a checklist of matters to be considered at each stage so that the practitioner can make the best possible use of the time available.

SOME TERMINOLOGY

(1) *Fast track time*: the period of the case between allocation and trial during which the case is subject to the fast track directions which will be difficult to dislodge, certainly as far as the trial date and the listing questionnaire are concerned (CPR Rule 28.4); see *Taylor* v. *Graham* ([2001] CP Rep 11, CA).

(2) *Pre-allocation time*: the period of the case between issue and allocation where time limits for statements of case and allocation questionnaire are crucial but are subject to some flexibility (such as extension of time for defence by 28 days);

(3) *Premium time*: the period before issue when, subject to the limitation period and the practical advantages of issuing early, there are almost no restrictions on time. Indeed, as appears from Table 11.2 below, in a Personal Injury Protocol case, this period could easily last six months or more.

Table 11.1 Generic timetable

Stage	Date by which activity complete	Activities
Initial client interview	Week 0 (January)	Obtain initial information, evaluate alternatives to litigation, decide how to fund the case, decide on the legal issues at stake, and consider initial fact investigation.
Fact investigation	Week 13 (early April)	Produce first estimate of costs, draft case summary and timetable. Make contact with opponent by letter of claim and begin to establish matters in issue in the case leading to a first draft of particulars of claim/defence. Consider early Part 36 offer. Attempt to carry out disclosure by consent. Comply with pre-action protocol. (Approved protocols exist for personal injury, clinical

373

Table 11.1 (*Continued*)

Stage	Date by which activity complete	Activities
		negligence, defamation, and construction and engineering disputes. Others in the course of development include those for professional negligence and debt collection. Protocols may be used on an individual firm or ad hoc basis: see, e.g. Eversheds commercial pre-action protocol in [2000] *Solicitors' Journal*, 15 September, 826). Proof witnesses and consider (and discuss with opponent) appropriate use of expert witnesses. Sound out possible experts for availability and instruct them if there is a pre-action protocol.
Issue of claim form with particulars of claim, filing of defence	Week 14 (mid-April)	Reconsider matters in issue. Consider making/renewing Part 36 offer on issue. Consider applying for summary disposal. Define parameters of search for disclosure exercise. Adjust interim case summary.
Receipt and return of allocation questionnaire	Week 18 (mid-May)	Liase with opponent and agree parameters of dispute, suitable directions, particuarly proposals about expert witnesses. File first costs estimate with allocation questionnaire. On receipt of directions, instruct expert and notify witnesses of fact and advocate of likely date of trial.
ALLOCATION (it is assumed that the court is able to process allocation questionnaires within days)		
Disclosure	Week 22 (mid-June)	Many documents should have been disclosed pre-action or been attached to statements of case. On receipt of documents, revise draft witness statements, refine case summary and re-evaluate whether documents need to be sent to expert.
Witness statements	Week 28 (end July)	Narrow issues further by consent, notices to admit. On receipt, evaluate whether expert needs to see statements, refine case summary.

Stage	Date by which activity complete	Activities
Experts reports	Week 32 (end August)	Consider asking for comments on opponent's report/questions to expert. Refine case summary. Consider meeting of experts. Update costs estimate. Reconsider Part 36 position.
Receipt and return of listing questionnaire	Week 40 (end October)	Plan and agree timetable for trial with opponent. Liaise with advocate. File second costs estimate with listing questionnaire. Finalise case summary.
Trial	Week 44+ (end November+)	Bundles, witness summonses. Prepare costs estimate for summary assessment of costs at end of trial.

GENERAL PRINCIPLES OF SURVIVAL

The key to survival in the fast track will be whether you are in control of your case and the procedure or whether they are in control of you. Maintaining control requires a shift of emphasis from pre-1999 practice: an assumption that the bulk of the work is done pre-action or very early in the life of the proceedings rather than by gradually focusing on the narrow issues of the case in the hiatus just before discovery (now 'disclosure').

Given the dictates of the overriding objective (particularly CPR Rules 1.3, 1.4(2)(a)) we may find or already have found that the only sensible way to survive is to engage in the kind of cooperative behaviour that historically broke out in the period shortly before trial, by necessity, much earlier in the action than we (or our colleagues then in practice) did before 1999. It is in everyone's interests to get as much done as possible in the premium and pre-allocation time. There are less active periods within the fast track time that can be exploited but not many of them: once the directions begin, for our own safety and that of our clients, we have to work on the assumption that there are very few places to hide.

It should not be thought that engaging in cooperation is weak or against the client's interests. It is possible to be assertive without being aggressive, proactive without being weak. Early cooperation may indeed lead to achieving the client's goals whilst avoiding the time, stress and expense of taking the case towards trial. What the new régime does mean, if it is implemented by individual courts and judges as Lord Woolf intended, is that there is no scope for taking your eye off the ball.

In this chapter we will see a way of developing a simple template for the management of a fast track case which can then be adapted for individual cases or multiplied to take in caseloads consisting of numerous similar cases.

This template is based on a conservative estimate of the time to trial using the 'typical timetable' set out in the Practice Direction to CPR Part 28, para. 3.12 (assuming, for example, that no acknowledgement of service will be filed). On the basis that it is easier to expand the working period than to contract it, this template could be regarded as representing the tightest timetable to which the parties might have to work. It is provided as an example of a possible plan for surviving the fast track in a generic case. In Personal Injury Protocol cases a different (and quite possibly longer) pre-action period is demanded by the Protocol: this is set out in Table 11.2.

It is assumed in the table that the claimant's case takes four weeks to investigate fully but that afterwards the Protocol time limits are complied with. Time periods are extended if the accident is outside England and Wales or if the defendant is out of the jurisdiction.

Table 11.2 The pre-action stage in a Personal Injury Protocol case

Stage	Date by which activity complete	Activities
Initial client interview	Week 0 (January)	Obtain initial information, evaluate alternatives to litigation, decide how to fund the case, decide on the legal issues at stake, and consider initial fact investigation.
Fact investigation	Week 4 (February)	Produce first estimate of costs, draft case summary and timetable. Obtain initial information, evaluate alternatives to litigation, decide how to fund the case, decide on the legal issues at stake, and consider initial fact investigation. Consider early Part 36 offer. Proof witnesses and consider proposed expert witness(es). Sound out possible experts for availability.
Letter of claim	Week 5 (early February)	Send letter of claim with appropriate documents, pre-action Part 36 offer (possibly) and proposals about experts. The latter could be sent separately – perhaps once the response to the letter of claim had been received but to gain the maximum time to instruct experts it should be sent as early as possible.

Table 11.2 (*Continued*)

Stage	Date by which activity complete	Activities
Defendant's initial interview and beginning of fact investigation	Week 5 (early February)	Will cover very similar issues to the claimant, including the pre-action Part 36 offer.
Defendant's acknowledgement of letter of claim	Week 8 (March)	Defendant has 21 days to acknowledge receipt of the letter of claim.
Defendant's response to proposals about experts	Week 10 (mid March)	Defendant has 14 days to respond to proposals about experts but 35 days to respond if the claimant's proposals about experts were in the letter of claim (para 3.16). After that stage the expert(s) can be instructed. It is assumed that the expert takes three months to complete the report. If the expert is jointly instructed, however, s/he may not be able to complete the report until the defendant's response to the letter of claim is available. Even in separate expert cases it may be wise not to finalise the report until the defendant's response is available.
Defendant's considered response with disclosure documents	Week 20 (June)	Defendant has three months from the acknowledgement to respond in detail.
Claimant obtains expert's report	Week 22 (June)	This should be disclosed to the defendant to establish whether the claim can be settled.
Defendant responds to expert's report	Week 25 (July)	Claimant should not issue proceedings until the defendant has had three weeks to consider expert's report.
Claimant may now issue if dispute unresolved.	Week 26 (mid July)	Consider making/renewing Part 36 offer on issue.

DOCUMENTS

Repeated references are made in this chapter to three documents which the author considers will assist in managing the fast track case. It is suggested that drafts of these documents are produced as early as possible and then continually refined at each stage of the proceedings.

A draft case summary

A case summary not exceeding 250 words may well be required in the trial bundle (see Practice Direction to CPR Part 25, Appendix). Its format can be modelled on that required in multi-track cases (see Practice Direction to Part 28, para. 5.7), and include:

- a chronology;
- the issues agreed/in dispute;
- the evidence needed to decide the issues in dispute.

If work is commenced on this from the outset it will provide a focus for a number of activities:

- analysing the legal and factual components of the case, so that the statement of case can be drafted;
- identifying the areas on which to focus fact investigation;
- identifying areas which can be admitted/not proceeded with;
- narrowing the issues which have to be resolved at trial so that they fit comfortably into a single day's trial.

There seems no reason in the light of CPR Rules 1.3 and 1.4(2)(a) not to have this document in a format which can travel between and be agreed between the parties (as well as shown to the court if and where necessary).

A costs schedule

If at the outset you can produce a reasoned estimate of costs this of course assists in complying with the professional obligations to ensure that the client is appraised of the likely cost of the case. If it is corrected and updated regularly, then you will also be better able to:

- assist the court with its general obligations under CPR Rules 1.1(2)(b) and (c);
- persuade the court that any individual step proposed is consistent with CPR Rule 1.4(2)(h);
- easily comply with obligations to file costs schedules on allocation and on listing;

- deal with summary assessment of costs for interim applications;
- deal with summary assessment of costs at trial (especially since the costs of the trial themselves are fixed under CPR Part 46).

A case management timetable

At both allocation and at listing the parties are invited to submit proposed directions. At any hearing you should be prepared to deal with directions (Practice Direction to CPR Part 28, para. 2.5). A focus both for achieving this and for maintaining control of the management of the case is a timetable of some kind. Whatever format it has, it should be easily alterable (as, e.g. the court may not approve the agreed directions). A simple timetable which can be kept on the front of the file will assist in:

(a) keeping your client properly advised about the likely length of the litigation;

(b) providing an easy indication of the stage the case has reached accessible to you and colleagues;

(c) providing an easy way of keeping client, expert, counsel etc. advised of the key dates and the stage the case has reached;

(d) planning the directions you wish to seek and showing the court (and opponent) that the proposed timetable is proportionate;

(e) recording unmissable dates, especially where judgment or strike out is the potential penalty (i.e. filing of statements of case, including a defence to counterclaim (contrary to the previous CCR position, see CPR Rule 12.3(2)(b)), return of allocation and listing questionnaries).

Of course only a minimum of cases reach trial, especially in the light of CPR Rule 1.4(2)(e) and (f). But at what stage can those that will proceed to trial be isolated from those that will not? Even those that reach trial will do so in a more truncated format than in the past. We start with that truncated trial in order to put the remainder of the fast track procedure into context.

TRIAL: WEEK 44 ONWARDS

This is a day's trial (five hours) (Practice Direction to CPR Part 26, para. 9.1(3)(a)). However, the need for a longer trial, at least if the reason is not a counterclaim or other CPR Part 20 claim, does not necessarily justify taking the case out of the fast track (para. 9.1(3)(c) and (e)). Split trials are available in the fast track (paras 9.1(3)(d), 12).

However, in order to fit the trial in an ordinary case into a day, oral opening speeches, oral examination in chief and oral evidence of experts will probably have been discarded (Practice Direction to CPR Part 28, paras 8.2, 8.4(2), 7.2(4)). Cross-examination may be limited in time or limited to particular issues (para. 8.4(1)). It will be important to have identified as early as possible those issues which *only* the trial can resolve (and within those the issues which can *only* be dealt with by oral examination in chief, or by oral cross-examination). Time spent on the peripheral issues is time wasted: the key is to think in terms of minima, identifying the 'triable issues' not in the old sense of RSC Order 14 but in the sense of those issues which can *only* be resolved at trial.

In terms of the trial day itself, effective use of the written forms of advocacy – skeletons, witness statements, case summaries, clear and comprehensible expert's reports, intelligent questions to the expert(s) – will be imperative. Much of the advocacy therefore devolves on the solicitor with conduct of the file rather than on the advocate conducting the trial (and perhaps increasingly the solicitor with conduct of the file and the advocate for the one day trial will be the same person). Be aware of and prepare for the summary assessment of costs at the end of the trial (Practice Direction to CPR Part 28, para. 8.5) (see *Stevens* v. *Watts*, unreported, 22 June 2000, where the Birmingham County Court declined to give general principles for the summary assessment of costs after fast track trials but nevertheless sanctioned fast track trial costs of £4,500). If you keep a running schedule of costs from day one it should not be too difficult to update it for trial and to explain any differences between it and the estimate filed on allocation. The costs of the trial are fixed by CPR Part 46, which provides a further impetus if one were needed to deal with the trial day in as streamlined a way as possible. Note the letter from the Vice Chancellor published in [1999] *Gazette*, 3 June to the effect that until the solicitors' conduct rules are amended, it will continue to be 'necessary' for the purposes of recovery of the costs of a solicitor attending on counsel under CPR Part 46 for counsel to be attended.

The parties can of course have an effect on the running of the trial day by agreeing sensible and proportionate directions, filed with the listing questionnaires. If these are sensibly thought out and demonstrably proportionate to the case and the remaining issues to be resolved at trial, they will no doubt be attractive to the court. Liaison in producing these is encouraged (Practice Direction to CPR Part 28, para. 6.1(4)).

Knowing what we are working towards, we move on to consider how to use the time available to reach the trial (or to avoid trial altogether).

INITIAL CLIENT INTERVIEW: WEEK 0

The following is a suggested checklist for the initial client interview:

- take client's proof;
- establish means of funding (written agreement if you wish to recover from client more than is recovered from opponent) (CPR Rule 48.8(1A);
- collect documents brought in by client and identify further documents client must locate;
- ask client to identify where all documents of possible relevance are stored;
- identify witnesses to be interviewed;
- discuss ADR and parameters of settlement, including CPR Part 36;
- identify reporting and billing structure (by costs schedule, timetable and case summary). Deal with other client care and Practice Rule 15 issues;
- advise on;
  - demands of overriding objective;
  - likely timescale to trial;
  - disclosure obligations: set up mechanism with client to find, collate and evaluate disclosure documents when preparing list;
  - obligations/court's powers relating to experts;
  - court's power to require clients to attend any hearing;
  - court's case management powers;
  - penalties for failure to comply with protocol/protocol-like behaviour;
  - penalties for failure to accept a claimant's Part 36 offer;
  - statement of truth and its consequences;
- identify suitable person to sign statements of truth and disclosure statement;
- other general advice on issues involved in case, strength of case, availability of welfare benefits etc.

It is a fact of life that defendant solicitors are likely to be brought into the process later than claimant solicitors and that they will have to make more efficient use of the time available against the pressure of the threat of the claimant losing patience and simply issuing proceedings. It is to be hoped that the facts that:

(a) failure to comply with a pre-action protocol can be penalised against both parties and

(b) that in any event pre-action behaviour can be taken into account on costs (CPR Rule 44.3(5)(a) and Protocols Practice Direction, paras 2 and 4)

will educate both solicitors and clients to make sensible use of the pre-action period. In theory, the parties have unlimited time to work out what the case is about and to define the issues that need to be developed through to trial. In practice the demands of the limitation period and of the cashflow of clients who need to recover damages or at least an interim payment will put some sort of limit on this period: but would a voluntary interim payment cause the claimant to hold off issue and give the defendant more time to investigate?

How should the parties behave in non-protocol cases? Ideally, as closely to the model of the available protocol(s) as possible (Protocols Practice Direction, para. 4). The court can hardly criticise behaviour which is virtually identical to the sanctioned protocol behaviour. Where the parties need to depart from the protocol model because of the demands of the case it would be as well to have the reasons for doing so in writing and agreed as far as possible. An agreed protocol for an individual case is not impossible.

Put at its simplest, it would be as well for the standard debt collection letter before action to give more detail than was commonly the case in the recent past, to have attached copies of relevant contract and invoices and, consistently with the Personal Injury Protocol, to allow the defendant at least 21 days to respond (although it should be noted that the draft Debt Collection Protocol only requires 14 days' notice). That, if nothing else, marks the radical shift in behaviour demanded by the CPR.

FACT INVESTIGATION: WEEKS 0 TO 14

The important actions to take in this stage are:

- identify cause(s) of action/lines of defence (including contributory negligence/failure to mitigate);
- identify issues of law;
- estimate quantum;
- for each element of duty, breach, causation and loss, identify;
  - probative documents: arrange with client to locate these now;
  - witnesses;
  - experts;
  - points of law;
  - real evidence;

- identify documents to attach to letter of claim/response to letter of claim;
- plan letter of claim/response to letter of claim;
- produce first draft case summary;
- report to client.

Much can be done in this premium period in the following areas:

Proving the case

The important issues are as follows:

(a) Defining the legal issues involved in the case (if not admitted); drafting an outline statement of case;

(b) identifying the evidence which will be required to prove each legal issue (if not admitted);

(c) inviting the opponent to identify matters in dispute (in Personal Injury Protocol cases this is provided for within the Protocol);

(d) taking initial proofs of evidence;

(e) sounding out experts. Although the Personal Injury Protocol allows the parties to negotiate about the instruction of experts, in any other case the position is vague. In a multi-track case, the Practice Direction to CPR Part 29, para 5.5(2) provides that 'a party who obtains expert evidence before obtaining a direction about it does so at his own risk as to costs, except where he obtained the evidence in compliance with a pre action protocol'. The fact that similar wording does not appear in the fast track Practice Direction is perhaps related to the early assumption that fixed pre-trial costs would imminently be imposed in fast track cases in any event. It would seem prudent, however, in the interim to warn the client that early instruction of experts might lead to irrecoverable costs.

(f) carrying out exchange of probative documents by consent;

(g) drafting an interim case summary that can be adapted as the case progresses but which will provide a simple aide memoire for reference throughout.

Fact investigation

There are a number of methods of fact investigation to which you may have been introduced in training. Put at its simplest any claim for damages (for the claimant) can be broken down into the following:

- a duty (a duty of care, a contractual duty based on specific express or implied terms);
- breach of that duty (by some sort of failure on the part of the defendant which can be identified);
- causing loss (the causal link can be established as can the extent of the loss).

On the face of it, evidence will be needed to support each of these. Any defence (other than contributory negligence) is normally an attack on one of more of these issues.

However, it is in the interests of both parties in a fast track case to narrow the issues as far and as quickly as possible, ideally during the premium time. Duty can often be admitted in contractual and road traffic cases. If the claimant can set out the extent of the loss carefully and conclusively (and as soon as the claimant can do that the claimant can clearly make a persuasive CPR Part 36 offer) then the extent of the loss (if not its causation) should be susceptible of agreement. However, beware a change of mind afterwards (see the Personal Injury Protocol, paras 2.9, 3.9) as at the very least the court will be invited to take a dim view in exercise of its case management powers. Individual particulars of loss can perhaps be disposed of: if there are 14 particulars of loss in a case where the claimant need only substantiate one to succeed the claimant should perhaps think seriously about agreeing not to proceed on some of the more peripheral particulars (the court will be interested in trying to strike out or simply not proceed on such issues in any event).

Those who generally act for defendants will need especially to take a grip on the procedure early on: in the absence of any limitation problem, the claimant has the leisure of as much time as it takes to organise, assimilate facts and documents, interview witnesses and so on before contacting the defendant or engaging the pre-action protocol behaviour. Consider inviting the client to refer cases to you as soon as any dispute arises which they might need to defend so that you gain as much time as possible.

Perhaps the most significant incentive to take a firm grip of the definition and management of the case from an early stage is provided by the courts and their uncompromising attitude towards failure to comply with the fast track timetable. So, for example, in *Taylor* v. *Graham* ([2001] CP Rep 11) the Court of Appeal unequivocally reminded practitioners that allocation to the fast track meant that compliance with the timetable was of even greater importance than in other cases.

Managing the case

The most important issues are:

- plan and make proposals to the opponent for:
  - points that can be admitted/not proceeded with/disposed of by a consensual CPR Part 24 application;
  - experts;
  - parameters of search for CPR Rule 31.6(b) documents: be able to set search in motion quickly;
  - ADR;
  - directions and timescale if proceedings are issued (including contents of allocation questionnaire);
- identify with the client a signatory for statements of truth and disclosure statements;
- consider:
  - contentious CPR Part 24 applications;
  - making an early (pre-action?) offer under CPR Part 36;
  - starting the running costs schedule;
  - who will carry out advocacy at the trial.

In protocol cases, however, the early management and fact investigation is prescribed and given a structure by the protocol. As suggested earlier, in other cases the protocol(s) should be regarded as a guide to good practice.

However, in the premium time you can make plans which include:

(a) planning an appropriate timetable for the case within the fast track parameters which can be put to the opponent for discussion and agreement and subsequently to the court as agreed directions;

(b) producing a similar plan of the costs of the case;

(c) setting up reporting systems with the client including identifying within a corporate client the appropriate person to sign statements of truth and disclosure statements;

(d) once sufficient information is available both about the likely quantum of the case and the likely degree to which it will be defended, proposals for negotiation, ADR, early CPR Part 36 offers.

Systems in the office

Survival systems that you will need to survive the fast track include:

- an efficient diary system with all the fast track dates marked in it;
- a mechanism for creating schedules of costs to date and projected costs for the future easily and quickly;
- a system for delegation of work;
- good relations with experts and counsel;
- a system to obtain instructions and signatures from the client within short timescales;
- a timetable for the case available to client, counsel, expert, client and matter partner.

It is entirely possible that the whole dispute can be resolved during the premium time. Even if this is not the case, the 'triable' issues should be identified as far as possible and the probative documents placed in the common domain. At least where there is no limitation problem, the issue of proceedings should be the last resort.

ISSUE OF CLAIM FORM WITH PARTICULARS OF CLAIM, FILING OF DEFENCE: WEEK 14

The following checklist lists the essential points:

- Claimant files with court (a response pack and notes for the defendant must be included on service).
  - Legal Services Commission funding certificate (if any);
  - copy(ies) notice of funding;
  - fee;
  - claim form (×3 depending on number of defendants and to ensure a sealed copy for oneself);
  - particulars of claim (×3 as above) if serving at the same time;
  - statement of special damages (referred to by Practice Direction to CPR 16, para. 4.2 as a 'schedule of details of any past and future expenses and losses' which may be wider than the strict definition of 'special damages') (×3 as above);
  - medical report(s) (×3 as above);

- copies of any documents, lists of names of witnesses, points of law attached to particulars;
- consider arrangements for service – court will normally carry this out;
- consider making/renewing a Part 36 offer on issue;
- consider early applications e.g. under Part 24.

- Defendant considers:
  - filing acknowledgement of service;
  - contents of defence, and whether to attach documents, names of witnesses, points of law;
  - issuing counterclaim/other Part 20 claim;
  - filing defence;
  - early applications, e.g. under Part 24, CPR Rule 3.4;
  - making Part 36 payment.

- If there is a counterclaim, claimant must remember to file defence (CPR Rule 12.3(2)(b), abolishing the previous CCR rule);

- Once all statements of case served:
  - review and adjust draft case summary, timetable, proposed parameters for search, draft costs schedule;
- Identify areas still in dispute, then:
  - consider requests for further information under Part 18;
  - consider narrowing issues: CPR Rule 3.4, Part 24, notice to admit;
  - review plans for and agree parameters of search for CPR Rule 31.6(b) documents;
  - produce first draft of allocation questionnaire and discuss with opponent (to the extent that this did not take place pre-issue);
  - consider any other applications, interim payments etc.;
  - report to client.

If sufficient activity has taken place during the premium pre-action time then the issue and statement of case stage should be able to proceed simply and without a great deal of surprise. A reasoned claimant's CPR Part 36 offer will frequently accompany the proceedings. The contents of the particulars of claim and defence should not hold surprises. There is of course the option to extend time by filing of an acknowledgement of service (CPR Rules 10.3 and 15.4). (The acknowledgement (except in the Commercial Court) falls in a different place to the old High Court acknowledgement: after the particulars of claim if served separately, rather than before them). Time may also be extended by consent for up to 28 days (CPR Rule 15.5) and it is likely that defendants caught out by the issue of proceedings will attempt to use these mechanisms to catch up. The court may well, however, be critical of attempts to slow the procedure down simply to compensate for inefficiency. It is for this reason amongst others that it is suggested that defendant solicitors would be well advised to educate their clients to pass on matters to their solicitors (or at least warn their solicitors of disputes) as soon as litigation is in prospect rather than waiting for a letter of claim.

Once statements of case have been filed, the areas of dispute will have crystallised, ideally entirely consistently with the indications about the claim and defence given in the pre-issue period. Optimum use of the premium time means in theory that no further narrowing of issues need take place as the parties have defined them in their entirety before trial. In practice, in any case with a degree of complexity further narrowing will take place. However, the running case summary can be refined again at this stage and the parameters of the disclosure exercise finalised. In parallel with the statements of case stage both parties should be considering appropriate interim applications.

INTERIM APPLICATIONS

Actions to take at this stage are:

- evaluate risks of winning/losing application;
- prepare summary assessment costs schedule;
- consider suitable advocate;
- prepare evidence so that it can be filed with application;
- make application;
- review opponent's evidence;
- consider whether a separate bundle/skeleton argument necessary;
- be prepared to deal with other case management issues (see Practice Direction to CPR Part 28, para. 2.5);
- report to client on result (specifically if there is a contrary costs order (CPR Rule 44.2));
- evaluate whether result has any impact on case summary, timetable and/or costs schedules.

Much of the above also applies to the respondent to an application.

It is to be hoped that the Court Service use its best endeavours to list such applications so that they do not prejudice the timetable to trial, especially where the application itself, if successful, will dispose of the case entirely or at least significantly narrow the issues for trial (Practice Direction to CPR Part 28, para. 2.9). (If the application is due to a delay by one or other party, this will not normally be allowed to prejudice the trial date: Practice Direction to CPR Part 28, para. 5.4.)

The CPR indicate that all applications should be made as soon as possible and that in particular applications for summary disposal should be made before allocation or on return of the allocation questionnaire (Practice Directions to Part 23, para. 2.7, Part 26, para. 5.3). Until resolved the application will normally delay allocation (Practice Direction to Part 26, para. 5.3(2)) although costs orders made prior to allocation cannot be affected by subsequent allocation (CPR Rule 44.11(1)). The effect of CPR Rule 44.9 is negligible in relation to costs pre or post-allocation since the 'special rules' in this context apply only to the trial and not to the interim stages.

Where a trial date or window has been fixed it is important to realise that a pending application will not normally be allowed to prejudice the trial date (CPR Rule 28.4), thus increasing the amount of work that has to be done on the case concurrently with the progress of the remainder of the directions towards trial. (See also *A.C. Electrical Wholesale plc* v. *IGW Services Ltd* (unreported, 10 October 2000, CA).)

Applications for summary disposal need not be highly contentious. A possible use of CPR Part 24 includes the previous RSC Order 14A procedure for early disposal of issues of law and construction extended to circumstances where the application will not dispose of the entirety of the case but only of part of it or of a subsidiary issue.

Note however that even if the parties decide *not* to bring an application, the court is entitled to convene a hearing of an application of its own motion (especially summary disposal under CPR Part 24 (CPR Rule 24.5(3)) or strike out under CPR Rule 3.4) (CPR Rule 3.3 and Practice Direction to Part 3, para. 4.1).

Nevertheless, unless the court makes separate provision for or dispenses with allocation (often at an earlier interim hearing), the filing of a defence triggers the issue of an allocation questionnaire to which the parties have 14 days to respond (CPR Rule 26.3) (although the court has power to dispense with this stage and might exercise it, for example, if all relevant issues are dealt with at an earlier hearing).

RECEIPT AND RETURN OF ALLOCATION QUESTIONNAIRE: WEEK 18

Use this stage as a general review of the case so far:

- update costs schedules and project to trial;
- review timetable to trial: are there any stages that can be dispensed with allowing the trial to be brought forward (disclosure, experts etc.)? (Practice Direction to Part 28, para. 3.13);
- review position on ADR/settlement/Part 36;
- review proposals for disclosure, including parameters of search;
- review plans for witnesses of fact;
- review proposals for experts;
- review position on suitable advocate for trial;
- agree directions as far as possible with opponent (also agree and submit case summary?);
- file allocation questionnaire together with any agreed documents;
- report to client.

The 14 day period for the return of the questionnaire is simply not long enough to work out what the case is about and how to manage it, especially when this case is only one of a substantial caseload. In order to avoid significant difficulties at this stage it is essential that prior planning and liaison has taken place. (The penalties for failure to deal with the allocation questionnaire on time culminate in striking out: Practice Direction to CPR Part 26, paras 6.6, 2.5(1).) The allocation questionnaire should be a focus for recording decisions that have already provisionally been made rather than a spur to make those decisions in the first place.

It is suggested that the allocation process should be regarded as one of cooperation and transparency (see Practice Direction to CPR Part 26, para. 2.3) and that discussion between the parties about the decisions to be recorded on the questionnaire are an integral part of the process from first instruction. Agreement of a timetable for trial in collaboration with the opponent but within the parameters of the usual fast track directions will provide a simple focus on which to establish such cooperation. Agreed documents filed with the questionnaire will be considered by the court if they cover the issues set out in the fast track practice direction: Practice Direction to CPR Part 28, para. 3.5. The Appendix to the Practice Direction setting out standard fast track directions can be usefully used as a template. Although it is not required until trial, the production of an agreed case summary even at this stage can assist in concentrating the minds of the parties on defining those issues which need to go to trial.

It is not insignificant that there is a substantial fee payable by the claimant (currently £80) for filing of the allocation questionnaire. If nothing else it will concentrate the minds of the parties. In terms of the overriding objective it can be thought of as a failure on the part of the parties if they have got this far without either resolving the case entirely or at least resolving a substantial number of the issues in the case.

This is also a stage to revisit the prospects of settlement. Even if there is no prospect of resolving the entire dispute, consider whether negotiation or mediation can assist in narrowing the issues which need to proceed to trial.

DIRECTIONS

If there is a directions hearing be prepared to demonstrate your proposed timetable very clearly to the court, possibly by chart or calendar. Otherwise on receipt of directions:

- review and adjust;
  - case summary;
  - timetable in accordance with directions given;
  - costs schedule if it was prepared on assumptions (such as use of separate experts) which are no longer correct;
- instruct expert(s) – if joint liaise with opponent: include clear instructions and timetable of crucial dates, meeting, final report etc.;
- notify client, expert, advocate, witnesses of expected date/window for trial;
- review draft witness statements and fact investigation generally;
- review position on CPR Part 24 and Part 36.

It goes without saying that if directions are requested which will cause the trial to be anything further than 30 weeks away, you will have difficulty justifying these to the court. The result may simply be to take the case out of the fast track. Certainly if limitations on costs were ever to be imposed on the fast track one might expect the court, if it took the case out of the fast track at all, to do so on condition that the fast track costs limitations continued to apply to it unless there was good reason not to do so.

So, to take a common situation in personal injury cases where quantum cannot be finalised until the medical condition has stabilised after a considerable period, the options (short of delaying issue of proceedings until the condition had stabilised which might itself cause limitation problems) would appear to be:

(a) to keep the case in the fast track with a split trial, the trial of quantum taking place once the medical condition has stabilised;

(b) to keep the case in the fast track without a split trial but with a trial once the medical condition has stabilised; if the proposed trial date is likely to be further away than the 'typical' 30 weeks from allocation, this option is unlikely to be attractive to the court (see Practice Direction to CPR Part 28, para. 3.6(2));

(c) to ask for the case to be taken out of the fast track and to set a trial date once the medical condition has stabilised.

Arising from this is the need to be able to demonstrate to the court when a trial of quantum can sensibly take place. Medical experts should therefore be asked to predict in the initial report when they consider the medical condition is likely to stabilise.

Once notice of allocation has been received with directions, the timetable for the case can be adjusted and any outstanding matters of fact investigation followed up. Assuming that the court has allowed expert evidence, the expert can be instructed with impunity (but bearing in mind that his or her instructions will no longer be privileged: CPR Rule 35.10(4)). It is suggested that even in a non-protocol case the model letter of instruction contained in the personal injury pre-action protocol might be used as a template for the letter of instruction.

DISCLOSURE: WEEK 22

The following are the essential issues:

- is disclosure of any documents not previously disclosed necessary?
- check client was advised early on of disclosure obligations;
- review documents provided by client;
- review documents attached to statement of case, provided under pre-action protocol or protocol-like behaviour, provided in support of a Part 36 offer;
- review issues in dispute: go back to fact investigation and identify the documentary evidence necessary to prove each element still in dispute, these will be the documents on which you rely;
- have you agreed parameters of search with your opponent, or at least set out in early correspondence what categories of document you consider to be relevant and proportionate?
- review client's instructions on location and nature of documents not relied on;

- carry out search for negatively probative documents (bring into operation agreed mechanism to do this, own resources and those of client);
- evaluate which of documents retrieved in search fall within CPR Rule 31.6(b);
- evaluate for privilege and for disproportionate inspection under CPR Rule 31.3(2);
- draft list;
- arrange for disclosure statement to be signed by person identified as suitable to do so within client's organisation (allow time to carry this out);
- evaluate opponent's list (including whether search is in accordance with agreed parameters);
- inspect;
- consider whether any applications for specific disclosure etc. necessary;
- review witness statements in light of documents received;
- send appropriate documents to expert;
- review case summary in light of documents received;
- ensure a system in place to identify and deal with disclosure of any documents which come to light after exchange of lists.

For further discussion of disclosure in the fast track context, see Chapter 12 'Disclosure'.

WITNESS STATEMENTS FOR TRIAL: WEEK 28

Actions to be taken at this stage are:

- review case summary, especially consider any issues that are not proceeding to trial by consent, or by order under CPR Part 24, Rule 3.4 or otherwise;
- review disclosure documents;
- review any witness statements/lists of witnesses attached to statements of case;
- review details of witnesses given in your own and in opponent's allocation questionnaires;
- review initial proofs;
  - do you still have evidence to cover all the matters in issue?
  - are there any witnesses who you no longer require?
  - is there any further information now required from witnesses?

- finalise witness statements;
- identify hearsay;
- invite advocate to consider drafts;
- exchange;
- after exchange;
  - review opponent's statements;
  - respond to evidence adduced as hearsay;
  - consider notices to admit;
  - adjust case summary;
  - send statements to expert witness where necessary;
  - review Part 36 position and position on ADR/negotiation;
- report to client.

It is foreign to the nature of most solicitors to give away evidence early but if there is a witness statement whose content will not be affected by subsequent developments in the case why not attach it to the statement of case and have done with it? (Practice Direction to CPR Part 16, para. 14.3 refers to the attaching of names of witnesses and/or attaching of documents, which could include witness statements.) It is impossible to avoid having a witness statement of the client, because although you could rely on the statement of case signed by the client as evidence at an interim hearing (CPR Rule 32.6(2)(a)), the statement of case will not do for trial. However, in circumstances where it is known that there is a clear dispute (for example as to the words said on a particular occasion) it will continue to be necessary to have the statements of the opposing witnesses prepared in isolation in order to obtain their untainted testimony.

A number of comments about witness statements, which appear in Lord Woolf's Report, are not carried through explicitly into the rules. For example: 'On the fast track the witness statements should be no more than a succinct summary of the evidence which the witness can give' (Interim Report, *Access to Justice* (1995) ch. 22). 'If the courts are flexible about allowing a reasonable degree of amplification of witness statements at trial, then they can expect the lawyers to be less concerned to draft absolutely comprehensive statements. This is not to be taken as encouragement deliberately to omit relevant material, but simply to rein back the excessive effort now devoted to gilding the lily. In the interim report, I recommended that courts should disallow costs where they thought the drafting of witness statements had been disproportionate. Trial judges, and to some extent procedural judges, will need to make a real effort, especially in the early phase of the new system, to scrutinise witness statements rigorously. This is the only way in which they will be able to pinpoint repetitious or inappropriate material, such as purported legal argument or analysis of documents. This is a fault which must in the main be attributed to the legal profession and not to its clients; wasted costs orders may therefore be appropriate in some instances of grossly overdone drafting. Only if the legal profession is convinced by demonstration that it has an active judicial critic over its shoulder will it be persuaded to change its drafting habits' (Final Report, *Access to Justice* (1998), ch. 9). That said, if witness statements are built up from an initial analysis of the issues in dispute in the case, dealing with principally those issues which only that witness can deal with and only then with issues of corroboration, Lord Woolf's complaints can be forestalled.

Since it will no longer be normal for separate hearsay notices to be sent (CPR Rule 33.2(1)) it becomes more important than ever to be able to identify and deal with hearsay evidence.

EXPERT WITNESSES: WEEK 32

The following checklist deals for completeness with the position of experts throughout the proceedings. A detailed consideration of the role of experts is outside the scope of this chapter and is dealt with comprehensively in Chapter 8 above. What follows are some issues which can be regarded as specific to the fast track. Bear in mind that the emphasis is on a single jointly appointed expert as far as possible: see the Practice Direction to CPR Part 28, para. 3.9(4).

Pre issue/initial interview with client:
Advise client on:

- need for expert at all;
- obligations and role of the expert (including the fact that expert's duty is to the court);
- likely costs of expert, risk of irrecoverability;
- court's powers relating to experts, including unlikelihood of expert giving oral evidence at trial;
- need to provide information to the expert (and under CPR Rule 35.9).

Fact investigation:

- identify areas where expert evidence needed and whether oral evidence will be necessary;
- sound out proposed expert(s) for availability;
- comply with protocol (if any);

- discuss arrangements for expert evidence with opponent;
- include time for working with expert(s) in draft timetable;
- consider whether pre-action order for preservation/inspection necessary.

Issue to allocation:

- attach copy report to particulars of claim/defence where required/ desirable.

On filing allocation questionnaire:

- review arrangements for expert(s) with opponent, including need to inspect, meetings of experts etc.;
- review whether oral evidence at trial will be necessary;
- list names and/or specialities of proposed expert(s) in allocation questionnaire;
- agree directions (including direction for questions to the joint/ opponent's expert) and timetable for expert evidence and attach to questionnaire.

On allocation:

- consider carefully the issues on which expert should report and the documents he/she should see;
- book expert(s);
- instruct expert, including guidelines on content and format of report (see Practice Direction to CPR Part 35), duties and obligations, copy of timetable etc.;
- consider whether a meeting of experts is advisable.

Towards exchange/service of report(s):

- consider whether expert needs to see further disclosure documents/ witness statements;
- consider likelihood of questions to the joint/opponent's expert.

After exchange/service:

- review opponent's report (if any);
- finalise questions to joint/opponent's expert;

- consider whether further assistance from expert needed (such as sitting in on the trial, even though this is unlikely to be recoverable).

There is a conflict between the desire to book an expert as early as possible and not to instruct an expert prior to the directions stage, thereby running the risk of irrecoverability of that expert's fees. The demands of the Personal Injury Protocol requiring at least an attempt to agree on the identity of an expert have an effect on the timing of the premium pre-action time.

There will be those cases where a report of some kind has had to be obtained without any reference to the proposed defendant simply to establish whether or not there is a case and to identify the appropriate defendant. This distinction between 'advice' and 'report' experts is acknowledged in the Code of Guidance for Experts. It is to be hoped that courts accept that there are cases in which pre-empting the directions or even the pre-action protocol is entirely reasonable and that the costs of obtaining such a report will frequently be recoverable. The costs of obtaining such a report may in other cases have to be written off (as was of course always the case under the old procedure, although the risk of an interventionist court refusing to allow an expert was perhaps less). The client must, of course, be advised of this risk.

MANAGING EXPERTS IN THE FAST TRACK

One answer to the preceding question is to develop a relationship with experts (perhaps on a local law society basis with a locally agreed panel of experts) for a provisional booking to be confirmed after instructions have been given, knowing that a percentage of instructions will be confirmed. Consider also the prospect of multi-tasking experts: in *Townshend* v. *Superdrive Motoring Services Limited* (unreported, 4 February 1999) an order that a care consultant could deal with employment issues (rather than calling a separate employment consultant) and that an othopædic surgeon could also deal with maxillo-facial issues was upheld by the Court of Appeal (see also Practice Direction to CPR Part 35, para. 5).

You will also need to build the time requirements of the expert into the timetable for the case, giving the expert a clear indication of the time constraints to which he/she must work.

PRE-ACTION PROTOCOLS

Where an expert is instructed under a pre-action protocol, the costs should, it is suggested, be regarded as prima facie recoverable (even where the expert is not subsequently allowed). The parties should hardly be penalised, except where it is immediately apparent that the use of experts is superfluous, for complying with a protocol. The effect on the premium time of use of an expert in personal injury cases is demonstrated above in Table 11.2. It is also worth noting that dependent on the defendant's response, the Personal Injury Protocol can result in an unusual use of a single expert: where the claimant calls an expert and the defendant calls no expert evidence. This is fundamentally different in principle (although perhaps ultimately not in practice) to the use of a jointly instructed expert (see *Carlson* v. *Townsend* [2001] EWCA Civ 511, CA).

QUESTIONS TO EXPERTS UNDER CPR RULE 35.6

The standard fast track directions allow for a timetable to be given for questions to experts at the stage of giving directions (Practice Direction to CPR Part 28, Appendix). Where there are separate experts you will need to consider retaining your expert to review the opponent's report and to assist in formulating questions to the other expert.

TRIAL

Experts will not give oral evidence at trial except in exceptional cases (CPR Rule 35.5(2) and Practice Direction to CPR Part 28). Therefore you might consider, when instructing an expert, to ask him or her to make it easy to present the expert evidence to the court by using diagrams, photographs and models as well as making the report itself straightforward to understand, as the expert will not be able to expand on it or clarify in the witness box. Acceptance of a norm that experts will not give oral evidence also may mean that priorities in choice of expert change: you will need experts who can guarantee to provide a report within a very limited timescale but much less concern need be given to their performance in the witness box or limited availability for trial. We can assume that if there are separate experts and you wish to instruct yours to sit in on the trial to assist the advocate, that the costs of doing so will normally be irrecoverable.

LISTING QUESTIONNAIRE: WEEK 40

Use this opportunity to review the case generally:

- review steps taken towards ADR/settlement;
- review expert(s) reports: are there issues on which oral evidence would be of assistance?
- review witness statements: are there statements that can go in by consent? Are there issues on which oral evidence in chief would be of assistance?
- review documents: can you agree bundles?
- are there any further directions required: could they be agreed with opponent?
- can a trial timetable be agreed in outline with opponent for proposing to the court?
- propose to opponent exchange of draft listing questionnaires (see Practice Direction to CPR Part 28, para. 6.1(4))?
- finalise case summary: is there anything else that can be admitted?
- produce final costs schedule (compare with schedule filed on allocation and be prepared to explain any differences);
- what notice of trial will you need?
- who is the advocate? What preparatory assistance will he/she need?
- file listing questionnaire in time (three days late and it will be vulnerable to being struck out);
- review Part 36 position: should your offer be improved?
- report to client.

The fee for filing a listing questionnaire is very substantial (currently £200), but with the sweetener that it is refundable if the action is settled before the trial date is fixed or at least seven days before trial. (See also CPR Rule 44.10 on the extent to which the costs of preparation for a fast track trial may be recoverable if the case settles close to trial.) Remember that if the questionnaire is three days late, it risks being struck out (Practice Direction to CPR Part 28, para. 6.5). Completion of the listing questionnaire should, like the allocation questionnaire, be the culmination of a process rather than a last minute attempt to cram everything into the one-day trial. It does no harm to look at both the listing questionnaire and allocation questionnaire early on, to estimate how far in the future you are likely to be required to complete them (entering these dates on the running timetable) and to use them actively as a guide to the questions that you should be easily in a position to answer by that stage.

CONCLUSION

Managing the case efficiently towards trial involves as a first step organising yourself, your office and your caseload. More difficult is organising third parties: clients, counsel and especially busy expert witnesses. Clear early definition of the issues in the case followed by the creation of an appropriate timetable will demonstrate firm expectations of the client and the external team from the outset. If you are organised enough to manage your own team effectively, you cannot help but impress the court with your approach.

CHAPTER 12

Disclosure

James Burnett-Hitchcock

INTRODUCTION

Of the three evils of civil litigation identified by Lord Woolf in the research which led up to publication of *Access to Justice* (delay, complexity and expense) two, he considered, were routinely displayed to excess in what was then called discovery of documents. He concluded that he had to produce a system which would put an end to such excesses: in effect, an end to the way in which litigants and their lawyers exploited the opportunities afforded by the decision in *Compagnie Financière du Pacifique* v. *Peruvian Guano Co.* (1882) 11 QBD 55.

The question was, how? If we were to retain any form of discovery of documents in litigation, it would have to be strictly controlled, and yet still ensure, so far as reasonably practicable, that the documents which could really influence the outcome of the dispute were produced early, cheaply, and with minimal chance of procrastination or obfuscation.

The new rules (substantially embodied in CPR Part 31) go a long way towards achieving this. But, in introducing fresh criteria for 'disclosure' (as it is now called), they inevitably raise fresh problems. ('Discovery' used to mean what 'disclosure' means today: Defoe, *Robinson Crusoe* (1719) 'discovering himself to the savages'; but today that meaning is routinely conveyed by 'show' or 'disclose', so Lord Woolf was merely opting for modern usage.) This step in the conduct of a lawsuit is therefore likely to remain a battleground for litigators – and the sting is in the tail. Contrary to popular belief, *Peruvian Guano* is not dead, or, if it is, then only in the sense that the Transylvanian Count is 'dead'. The concept survives into the third century (nineteenth, twentieth and now twenty-first) courtesy of the Commercial Court (see below).

But arguably the most important change is that disclosure, as well as being greatly restricted, will, thanks to a number of innovations, now commence at a much earlier stage in the proceedings: indeed, significant disclosure will occur before proceedings start.

SOURCES

The sources for a consideration of the new rules on disclosure are as follows:

- CPR Parts 1, 3, 16, 24 and Practice Direction to Part 16;
- CPR Part 31 and Practice Direction to Part 31;
- CPR Part 23 and Practice Direction to Part 23;
- *Commercial Court Guide 1999*, Section E and Appendix 9;
- law of privilege, generally;
- Practice Form N265;
- specialist rules/Practice Directions and pre-action protocols/Protocols Practice Direction.

Part 31 contains the basis rules (and as always the Practice Direction to that Part is just as important as, and should be read together with, the rules themselves).

Part 23 and its Practice Direction govern applications, and are therefore relevant when seeking to obtain further disclosure or, for example, to challenge some aspect of an opponent's disclosure.

The *Commercial Court Guide 1999*, Section F and Appendix 9 represent, one might say, the coffin in which, Dracula-like, the decision in *Peruvian Guano* is preserved.

The law of privilege is thought by most commentators to remain unaffected by CPR Part 31, since it is a matter of substantive law and cannot be altered except by primary legislation. (The flanking attack on legal professional privilege mounted in CPR Rule 48.7(3) (wasted costs orders), which provides that: '(3) For the purposes of this rule, the court may direct that privileged documents are to be disclosed to the court and, if the court so directs, to the other party to the application for an order' was defeated in a first instance judgment in July 1999, on the basis that the removal of privilege by the creation of new rules by the Rules Committee was ultra vires the latter; primary legislation would be required.) Bear in mind, however, the continuing distinction between disclosure and inspection: save in exceptional circumstances, a privileged document must still be disclosed: it is inspection which may, in certain circumstances, be legitimately withheld.

As to specialist rules and Practice Directions, there are as yet only a couple which are directly relevant; and pre-action protocols are dealt with later.

Disclosure must be made in Form N265, the layout of which contains few surprises, the main one being the need for a disclosure statement.

BASIC PRINCIPLES

The thinking behind *Access to Justice* and, in turn the new Civil Procedure Rules, was that, if the enormous majority of lawsuits which settle before trial (but often only at the door of the court) could somehow be made to settle earlier – and, ideally, without the need for proceedings – then:

(a) dispute resolution would be faster and cheaper;

(b) the overall service to clients would be enhanced;

(c) the courts would be relieved of much unwanted business, and could concentrate on those cases which genuinely required judicial intervention or trial;

(d) delay in getting to trial would be much reduced (because the queues would be shorter).

But, self-evidently, in order to be able to advise on the merits of the case generally, and on a suitable level for settlement in particular, a solicitor needs to know:

- how his opponent puts his case;
- what the evidence is;
- what help, if any, the documents can give – to either side.

Thus, early settlement, if it is to be achieved, must involve an element of early disclosure, including pre-action disclosure; and the steps by which disclosure of documents should be undertaken should start well before the issue of a claim form. The following is a chronological checklist showing the steps in the disclosure process:

Before proceedings start:

(1) Explain nature and extent of disclosure obligation to client including:
   (a) reasonable search;
   (b) standard disclosure criteria;
   (c) disclosure statement.

(2) Identify 'appropriate person' to make disclosure statement.

(3) Consider the extent of 'reasonable search':
   (a) will this differ from the extent of the documents you could/should read to advise on merits?
   (b) if Yes: explain possible risks of reading/not reading the larger category, and agree approach;
   (c) if No: no problem (be grateful!)

(4) Select documents to accompany letter before action or response, pursuant to common sense, pre-action protocol or Practice Direction.

(5) Consider making request for voluntary pre-action disclosure by any potential party to proceedings: if so decided, make written request, followed, if necessary, by application for order.

After proceedings start:

(6) Consider making request for voluntary disclosure by non-party; if so decided, make written request, followed, if necessary, by application for order.

(7) Select documents for service with statement of case/bespeak copies of documents mentioned in opponent's statement of case.

(8) Consider use of IT for disclosure and discuss with client and opponent.

(9) Agree (if possible) with opponent issues on which disclosure to be given.

(10) Prepare own list of documents in Form N265, with disclosure statement signed by 'appropriate person', and serve.

(11) Consider opponent's list of documents, and possible request/application for specific disclosure and/or special disclosure (Commercial Court) based on:

(a) challenge to claim to be entitled to withhold inspection (usually because of privilege or proportionality); or

(b) challenge to alleged reasonableness of search; or

(c) compelling extraneous reason for believing disclosure incomplete, backed by evidence.

(12) Review own and opponent's witness statements and experts' reports and consider giving/requesting disclosure of any document mentioned.

(13) Consider making disclosure of 'late arrivals' (i.e. documents received/discovered since initial disclosure) on an ongoing basis.

When preparing for trial:

(14) Agree selection of documents for bundle with opponent.

(15) Consider and discuss with opponent and then also with judge at pre-trial review use of IT to manage documents at trial.

Note that 'disclosure order' appears well down the list: disclosure proper is *not* automatic either, it will only occur pursuant to an order of the court.

Finally, remember that the amount of disclosure that will be ordered depends upon a combination of the track to which the case is allocated (or likely to be allocated), the issues involved (litigation under the CPR being essentially issue-driven) and the overriding principle of proportionality found in CPR Part 1.

As to the tracks:

(a) on the small claims track, CPR Part 31 does not apply, so, in practice, there will be little or no disclosure;

(b) on the fast track there will be standard disclosure only, save in exceptional circumstances;

(c) on the multi-track standard, plus 'specific' or (in the Commercial Court) 'special' disclosure may be ordered, depending on the circumstances.

However, because of the extent of the disclosure which will routinely occur 'up front' there will be many cases in which, by the time statements of case and witness statements have also been served, there will be few documents remaining to be disclosed. Do not ever consider advising a client to 'run the case up to discovery, and then take stock'; those days are over.

Thus, whereas in the past 'discovery' was largely viewed as a single event occurring at a comparatively late stage in proceedings, today it should start *before* proceedings commence, and progress through a number of stages culminating in the delivery by each party of a list of documents in Form N265. Accordingly, in addressing the disclosure process as a whole, it makes sense to adopt a chronological approach.

PRE-ACTION PROTOCOLS

Pre-action protocols are a guide to best practice in the exchange of information and documents between the parties to a dispute, before litigation is commenced. They are not Rules or Practice Directions; but (see below) failure to comply with them will generate much the same consequences as non-observances of a Rule or Practice Direction.

Their introduction was considered necessary to remedy the bad habits which litigants and their solicitors have slipped into over the years. Amongst other things:

- claimants provide too little information before suing;
- defendants investigate too late to avoid being sued;
- core issues are, in consequence, not identified before proceedings commence;
- settlement is achieved at the door of the court.

The objectives of pre-action protocols are set out in the Protocols Practice Direction:

> 1.4 The objectives of pre-action protocols are:
> - to encourage the exchange of early and full information about the prospective legal claim;
> - to enable parties to avoid litigation by agreeing a settlement of the claim before the commencement of proceedings;
> - to support the efficient management of proceedings where litigation cannot be avoided.

Four pre-action protocols have so far been approved by the Vice-Chancellor, namely those relating to:

- personal injury claims;
- the resolution of clinical disputes;

- defamation;
- construction and engineering.

However, further protocols are being planned and others have already been drafted, including protocols on:

- professional indemnity claims;
- holiday claims;
- housing disrepair;
- debt collection;
- commercial disputes.

The prospect of uncontrolled proliferation of pre-action protocols is uninviting. Consideration might usefully be given to (a) restraining the number of 'stand-alone' protocols and (b) for the rest, establishing a 'core' or 'general' protocol, with specialist appendices tailored to the needs of the many different categories of proceedings routinely encountered in practice.

The importance of the protocol to the disclosure process is apparent from the Personal Injury Protocol, which requires:

(a) claimant to send letter of claim, in recommended format, to proposed defendant when sufficient details are available to substantiate claim;
(b) defendant to reply within 21 days;
(c) defendant (or insurers) to state whether liability is denied, within three months;
(d) if liability is denied, defendant to enclose with his reply: 'documents in his possession which are material to the issues between the parties, and which would be likely to be ordered to be disclosed by the court either on an application for pre-action disclosure or on disclosure during proceedings'.

The Protocol also contains succinct standard disclosure lists for use:

- in road traffic accident cases;
- in highway tripping claims;
- in workplace claims;
- where specific regulations apply.

There are many reasons why you should comply with a protocol, for instance:

(a) CPR Rules 3.1(4) and (5) and 3.9(1)(e) enable the court to take non-compliance into account when giving directions for case management;

(b) CPR Rules 44.3 and 44.4 enable the court to take non-compliance into account when considering whether and if so what order to make on costs;

(c) the Protocols Practice Direction empowers the court, in cases where non-compliance has led to the unnecessary institution of proceedings or the unnecessary incurring of costs;

    (i) to award costs against the defaulting party;

    (ii) on an indemnity basis;

    (iii) to deprive an otherwise successful claimant who has defaulted of part or all of his interest claim;

    (iv) to award penalty interest against a defaulting defendant, in respect of sums found due to the claimant ('penalty' meaning Base Rate plus up to 10 per cent).

Where the cause of action is not covered by an existing protocol, pre-action behaviour should nevertheless conform with the spirit of the protocols as required by the Protocols Practice Direction:

4. In cases not covered by any approved protocol, the court will expect the parties, in accordance with the overriding objective and the matters referred to in CPR 1.1(2)(a), (b) and (c), to act reasonably in exchanging information.

PRE-ACTION DISCLOSURE ORDERS

A further key innovation under Lord Woolf's reforms is to remove the former restriction whereby pre-action disclosure orders could only be made in relation to personal injury and death claims. The criteria are now to be found in CPR Rule 31.6(3)(a) to (d):

(3) The court may make an order under this rule only where:

    (a) the respondent is likely to be a party to subsequent proceedings;

    (b) the applicant is also likely to be a party to subsequent proceedings;

    (c) if proceedings had started, the respondent's duty by way of standard disclosure, set out in rule 31.6, would extend to the documents or classes of documents of which the applicant seeks disclosure; and

    (d) disclosure before proceedings have started is desirable in order to:

- dispose fairly of the anticipated proceedings;
- assist the dispute to be resolved without proceedings; or
- save costs.

The rules are not unfamiliar, but three points should be particularly noted.

Rule 31.16(3) refers to 'applicant' and 'respondent', there is no mention of 'claimant' or 'defendant'. It follows that there is no reason why pre-action disclosure should not be sought by or from a third party (strictly, a 'Part 20 person').

The rule which (since at least the Administration of Justice Act 1970) has permitted orders for pre-action discovery in personal injury cases of *categories* of document has survived the removal of the personal injury/death restriction. To obtain the order you do not now have to be able to identify each document individually: identifying a category suffices, it appears.

The key word in CPR Rule 31.16(3)(d) is *'desirable'* – a modest threshold, it is submitted, consistent with the view that pre-action disclosure should help avoid litigation, and therefore be freely available. Surprisingly little use appears to be made of this useful weapon, to date. Why not include in the letter of claim a paragraph requesting prompt disclosure of documents perhaps by reference to a schedule, backed with the threat of an application for an order? After all, the criteria are not, it seems, very demanding.

DISCLOSURE ORDERS AGAINST A NON-PARTY

Once again, this is an old rule expanded by Lord Woolf: hitherto, it was only available in personal injury and death claims. In removing the restriction, a powerful new tool to help gather evidence has been created. Previously, if you wanted to obtain documents from an uncooperative witness or potential witness, all you could do was issue a subpoena duces tecum. It was not possible obtain a discovery order in advance of trial against a 'a mere witness'. But the subpoena duces tecum had serious defects. Thus, in theory, it would only produce documents on the day of the trial, far too late to be able to put them to best use (even the device of the 'early trial date' still delayed production too long). Moreover, it was necessary to specify precisely each document which the witness was required to bring with him, and that was often impossible (accurate description of documents you have never seen can be tricky!): it was, however, not good enough merely to request *categories*.

Under the new rules, both problems are gone: a disclosure order can be sought against a non-party at any time after proceedings have commenced, and you can call for categories of document, not just separately-identified documents.

However, two points should be noted:

(a) the standard of proof, in this case, is rather higher: the applicant must show that disclosure is *necessary* (to dispose of the claim fairly or to save costs); the mere witness is not to be easy game, after all;

(b) the costs of a non-party disclosure order will almost always be awarded (at least initially) against the successful applicant.

The relevant provision is CPR Rule 31.17(3):

(3) The court may make an order under this rule only where the documents of which disclosure is sought are likely to support the case of the applicant or adversely affect the case of one of the other parties to the proceedings; and disclosure is necessary in order to dispose fairly of the claim or to save costs.

SERVICE OF DOCUMENTS WITH STATEMENT OF CASE

Assuming that:

(a) a fully-particularised 'letter before action' was sent on behalf of the claimant, seeking damages for, say, breach of contract;

(b) the spirit of the pre-action protocols was fully complied with by the protagonists, in exchanging information;

(c) a pre-action disclosure order was made and complied with by a potential second defendant;

(d) proceedings could not be avoided,

the next step in the disclosure chain will be the service of documents with statements of case. Two important paragraphs of the Practice Direction to CPR Part 16 on statements of case must be considered, namely paras 10.3(1), (2) and 11.3(2), (3):

10.3 Where a claim is based upon a written agreement:
(1) a copy of the contract or documents constituting the agreement should be attached to or served with the particulars of claim and the original(s) should be available at the hearing, and

(2) any general conditions of sale incorporated in the contract should also be attached (but where the contract is or the documents constituting the agreement are bulky this practice direction is complied with by attaching or serving only the relevant parts of the contract or documents).

11.3 A claimant may:

(1) refer in his particulars of claim to any point of law on which his claim is based;

(2) give in his particulars of claim the name of any witness whom he proposes to call, and

(3) attach to or serve with the particulars of claim a copy of any document which he considers is necessary to his claim (including any expert's report to be filed in accordance with Part 35).

Paragraph 10.3 requires no comment, but para. 11.3 is one of the best examples of the Woolf Practice Direction being in some respects more important than the CPR Part to which it relates – for the latitude permitted the pleader by para. 11.3 of the Practice Direction is a revolutionary addition to, not explanation of, the rules contained in Part 16 itself.

The question then arises 'why should any sane litigator want to refer to a point of law/give the name of an intended witness/attach a document necessary to his claim, in/to his particulars of claim?'

The answer, it is suggested, lies in CPR Parts 1, 3 and 24, dealing with the overriding objective, the court's case management powers, and with summary judgment respectively.

CPR Part 1 imposes on the court the duty to further the overriding objective by actively managing cases; and 'actively managing cases' is defined as including, amongst other things, 'deciding promptly which issues need full investigation and trial and, accordingly, *disposing summarily of the others*' (emphasis added).

CPR Part 24 revolutionises summary judgment introducing new, readily achievable criteria for summary judgment and rethinking the procedure so that either claimant or defendant may apply, on much the same footing. CPR Rule 24.2 provides:

24.2 The court may give summary judgment against a claimant or defendant on the whole of a claim or on a particular issue if –

(a) it considers that –

(i) that claimant has no real prospect of succeeding on the claim or issue; or

      (ii) that defendant has no real prospect of successfully defending the claim or issue; and

    (b) there is no other reason why the case or issue should be disposed of at a trial.

CPR Part 3 expressly provides that the court may make of its own motion any order which it would have power to make upon the application of any of the parties: a rule-maker's hint (that judges should play a proactive role in the new case-management regime) which judges have so far not been slow to take.

So, if, either as claimant or defendant, you consider that you have an unanswerable case, either in part or in whole, take full advantage of the above rules and:

    (a) plead your case fully;

    (b) attach any key documents not so far disclosed (do *not* wait for disclosure of documents as such);

    (c) include points of law relied upon (with copy decisions attached, where appropriate);

    (d) include names of witnesses (with copy witness statements, where appropriate).

Let it be known that you intend to apply for summary judgment at an early stage, if indeed you do not receive a call from the court to say that the judge is himself considering summary judgment of his own motion.

The message is simple: the new rules positively invite the litigant to make it easy for the court to see it his way – only a fool would decline the invitation (and try to keep his cards up his sleeve).

THE NEW DISCLOSURE CRITERIA

So far, we have been concerned with situations in which disclosure and inspection are, in effect, simultaneous, because copy documents have been produced at the outset.

But the two are quite separate concepts. Thus 'a party discloses a document by *stating that the document exists or has existed*' (CPR Rule 31.2) – no more: no less.

What, then, under the new rules is a party obliged to disclose? The answer is that, on the fast track, he will routinely have to give standard disclosure, and that will almost always be that: see CPR Rule 31.6:

31.6 Standard disclosure requires a party to disclose only –

  (a) the documents on which he relies; and

  (b) the documents which –

    (i)   adversely affect his own case;

    (ii) adversely affect another party's case; or support another party's case; and

  (c) the documents which he is required to disclose by a relevant practice direction.

On the multi-track, he may have to produce additional documents.

But, whilst the new criteria appear simple, they beg the question 'how can I establish what disclosable documents I have without reviewing the whole lot?' Under the old, objective rules, the answer was 'you cannot': you had to read all the documents which you could find, and consider whether they 'related to the matters in issue'. That, of course, was the problem: it could often mean wading through boxes – even warehouses full – of old files, and then disgorging them on your opponent. This could be horrendously expensive; and the process was notoriously open to abuse, for 'strategic' purposes.

Under the new rules, the answer to the question is 'by making a reasonable search'.

THE REASONABLE SEARCH, AND THE DISCLOSURE STATEMENT

CPR Rule 31.7(1) provides that, when giving standard disclosure, a party is required to 'make a reasonable search for' documents falling within Rule 31.6(b) or (c); and the factors to be taken into account in deciding what is reasonable include:

- the number of documents involved;
- the nature and complexity of the proceedings;
- the ease and expense of retrieval of any particular documents; and
- the significance of any document which is likely to be located during the search.

In other words, 'proportionality' will be a significant factor.

But if the 'reasonable search' is to perform a pivotal function in disclosure, who is to judge what is reasonable – and how? More importantly, how can you be sure that your opponent has made a reasonable search, and, if you are not, compel him to do more? A further innovation, therefore, is the disclosure statement, the form of which appears in the Appendix to the Practice Direction to Part 31: see Box 12.1

Box 12.1 The disclosure statement

> ## Disclosure statement
>
> I, the above named claimant [or defendant] [if party making disclosure is a company, firm or other organisation identify here who the person making the disclosure statement is and why he is the appropriate person to make it] state that I have carried out a reasonable and proportionate search to locate all the documents which I am required to disclose under the order made by the court on . . . day of . . . I did not search:
>
> (1) for documents predating ....
> (2) for documents located elsewhere than ....
> (3) for documents in categories other than..
>
> I certify that I understand the duty of disclosure and to the best of my knowledge I have carried out that duty. I certify that the list above is a complete list of all documents which are or have been in my control and which I am obliged under the said order to disclose.

The disclosure statement *must* be included in the list of documents. It puts the court, and of course the opposing party, in a position to consider whether they accept that the search was indeed reasonable. It is also, in appropriate cases, the means of signalling to an opponent and the court that there may be other disclosable documents available, but that the disclosing party does not consider that it would be reasonable to search for them having regard to the requirement of proportionality in litigation set out in CPR Part 1 (the overriding objective).

THE APPROPRIATE PERSON

Curiously, while CPR Part 31 stipulates the factors to be considered in determining what would be a 'reasonable search', and the Practice Direction to that Part adds that they should be considered subject to the overriding principle of proportionality, no guidance is given on how to identify the 'appropriate person' to sign the disclosure statement. It is submitted that the guidance on 'who may sign the statement of truth' which appears at para. 3 of the Practice Direction to Part 22 may safely be relied upon.

Thus, in the case of a corporation, a statement of truth (and, it is suggested, by analogy, a disclosure statement) must be signed by 'a person holding a senior position'; and para. 3.5 goes on to define 'senior position':

3.5 Each of the following persons is a person holding a senior position:

(1) in respect of a registered company or corporation, a director, the treasurer, secretary, chief executive, manager or other officer of the company or corporation, and

(2) in respect of a corporation which is not a registered company, in addition to those persons set out in (1), the mayor, chairman, president or town clerk or other similar officer of the corporation.

DISCLOSURE ON THE FAST TRACK

In view of the amount of documents which will have been disclosed in the course of the steps already described, disclosure on the fast track, in its historical sense, is in many cases redundant: the documents on which the parties rely should already be in the common domain, attached to statements of case or disclosed pursuant to the relevant protocol or the Protocols Practice Direction. Note in passing that the only kinds of document which at present fall within CPR Rule 31.6(c) (documents required to be disclosed by a Practice Direction) are:

(a) those listed in the Personal Injury Protocol as there is a Practice Direction requiring compliance with the protocol; the documents listed in the Personal Injury Protocol therefore fall into standard disclosure under CPR Rule 31.6(c) irrespective of their probative value in any given case;

(b) those required to be attached to statements of case (although this is not explicitly described as disclosure).

Dealing with disclosure in the new regime demands proportionality: recognition that the fast track involves rationed justice. It bears much the same relationship to the desires of the client in an individual case as the intestacy rules to the desires of an individual testator. The cases in which a document that entirely disposes of the opposition's case is found lurking amongst that party's disclosure documents are rare outside fiction. On the fast track it is worth bearing this in mind.

The 'reasonable search' may have to be carried out in a number of stages. Common sense dictates that as much use as possible be made of the premium time before issue. You will always search for the documents on which you rely and for the documents which your opponent is required to disclose as part of the relevant protocol. It is the documents which adversely affect your case or support another party's case to which the parameters of the search become particularly relevant. Can you agree with your opponent in advance that a particular degree of search will be proportionate to the case? Rather than relying on your opponent's view as to the reasonable parameters of search why not set out in correspondence in advance what you consider those parameters to be (and seek your opponent's agreement to them) – this may avoid subsequent applications for specific disclosure in the precious fast track time, which (see Chapter 11 'Surviving the Fast Track') is strictly limited.

Once disclosure is prima facie complete, you will of course decide whether or not to apply to court to enforce the obligation if you consider it has not been complied with by your opponent. There is nothing in the rules stating explicitly that the court has no *jurisdiction* in a fast track case ever to order disclosure which is wider than standard disclosure, at least on a specific disclosure application. However, we can expect the court to be very reluctant to order any wider disclosure of documents which are necessarily of only speculative relevance. The approach of the court is best deduced from CPR Rule 28.3(2) and the Practice Direction to CPR Part 28, para 3.6(4), both of which refer to disclosure less than standard disclosure, but not to disclosure greater than standard disclosure. Further information is probably better dealt with by CPR Part 18.

In the interests of saving costs and making best use of time, it is suggested that applications for specific disclosure should be avoided in the fast track as far as possible. In terms of the scope of disclosure, the principal disputes will be about failures to comply with standard disclosure (disputes about relevance or about privilege) or about the scope of the search. Try to pre-empt such disputes by agreeing with your opponent the appropriate parameters of disclosure, and then put those proposals to the court with the completed allocation questionnaire.

WHICH DOCUMENTS? PROBLEM AREAS

The 'reasonable search', once decided upon, determines the extent of the efforts to be made in trying to find documents which respond to the standard disclosure criteria. But problems can still arise. The new rules substantially (but not exactly) follow the old.

'Document' means anything in which information of any description is recorded, which would include, for example, a CD, cassette, floppy disk, or video (CPR Rule 31.4). The importance of this point cannot be overemphasised. In today's commercial dispute, the material preserved in a client's computer will often be of far greater significance than the contents of the conventional correspondence file.

'Copy', in relation to a document, means anything onto which information recorded in the document has been copied, by whatever means, and whether directly or indirectly (CPR Rule 31.4).

Only one copy of a document need be disclosed *but* by CPR Rule 31.9(1), (2), a copy containing a modification, obliteration or other marking or feature and on which you intend to rely or which adversely affects your own case or prejudices or supports another party's case counts as a *separate document*, and must therefore be separately disclosed.

A party need only disclose documents which are or have been *in his control*, meaning in his physical possession, or of which he has or had a right to possession, or which he has or had a right to inspect or copy (CPR Rule 31.8(1), (2).

The duty of disclosure continues until the proceedings are concluded, which means, in practice, that you will have to serve supplemental lists to cover documents of which you become aware after carrying out the main disclosure, at any time up to the giving of judgment (or, indeed, decision on appeal, if there is one) (CPR Rule 31.11(1), (2)).

INSPECTION: WITHHOLDING INSPECTION AND WITHHOLDING DISCLOSURE

The combination of the new disclosure criteria and the principle of proportionality laid down in CPR Part 1 (and expressly referred to in the Practice Direction to Part 31) results in something of a 'Catch-22' situation over withholding of inspection. But, using a little common sense, it is not hard to see what is intended.

The basic propositions are as follows:

(a) 'disclosure' means stating that a document exists or has existed (CPR Rule 31.2);

(b) a party to whom a document has been disclosed has a right to inspect it (CPR Rule 31.3 (1));

(c) *disclosure* may be withheld (i.e. the party does not have to divulge the existence of the document or documents in question) *only* after a successful application to the court for permission to withhold disclosure 'on the ground that disclosure would damage the public interest'; such an order would, for obvious reasons, not normally be served upon, or be open to inspection by, any third party (CPR Rule 31.19(1), (2);

(d) *inspection*, by contrast, may be declined/withheld if:

(i) the document is no longer in the discloser's control; or

417

(ii) the discloser has a right or duty to withhold inspection; or

(iii) the discloser 'considers that it would be disproportionate to the issues in the case to permit inspection of documents within a category or class of document disclosed under rule 31.6(b)', (the standard disclosure criteria) (CPR Rule 31.3(2)).

The second exception would of course cover legal professional privilege.

As one would expect, the party from whom inspection has been withheld can apply to the court to challenge his opponent's claim to be entitled to withhold inspection (see below).

But a potential danger has been created by the introduction of the right to withhold inspection in reliance upon the concept of proportionality.

A party who has, for example, huge quantities of old files which might contain disclosable documents may, on grounds of proportionality, decide to refuse inspection: the refusal will be in relation to the inspection of documents which, but for the proportionality factor, would have been made available to his opponent. The objective (cutting down the scale of disclosure, to save time and money) is laudable; but it will only be fully achieved if the discloser can himself *safely* avoid reading through all the documents himself. But can he?

If the discloser claims to withhold inspection on grounds of proportionality having not read the documents himself, his opponent challenges the claim, and the challenge succeeds, the discloser will be forced to permit inspection by his opponent of documents which he has not even read himself. The risks inherent are very obvious. If, in order to avoid such risks, the discloser decides to read all the old files first, he will have to disclose any truly 'disclosable' documents which he comes across in the course of the process – for better or for worse – and he will quite possibly have to lose any chance of saving time and expense (such as the new rules were intended to provide).

It follows that the precise extent of the 'reasonable search' and of the review of old documents to be undertaken by solicitors under the new rules ought to be discussed carefully with clients, as also the problems mentioned above, before the investigation of the case, let alone the disclosure process, is embarked upon.

THE PROCEDURE FOR DISCLOSURE AND INSPECTION

The procedure for standard disclosure is set out in detail in the CPR. The key points to note on disclosure (from CPR Rule 31.10) are:

(a) a list must be served by each party on every other party in Form N265;

(b) it must indicate which disclosed document(s):

    (i) are no longer in the discloser's control (and what has happened to them);

    (ii) he claims a right or duty to withhold from inspection;

(c) the list must contain a disclosure statement:

    (i) setting out the extent of the search for documents;

    (ii) certifying that the person making the statement understands his duty to disclose, and has discharged it;

    (iii) explaining why (in the case of a corporate party) the individual concerned is the 'appropriate person' to make the statement.

The key points on inspection and copying (from CPR rule 31.15) are

(a) inspection must be permitted within seven days of notice served by a party entitled to inspect;

(b) copies must be provided within seven days of a request supported by an undertaking to pay copying charges;

(c) a party may also inspect a document 'mentioned in' a statement of case, witness statement, or summary, affidavit or expert's report (CPR Rule 31.14).

In relation to both disclosure and inspection, CPR Rule 31.13 permits the parties to agree or the court to order that either (or both) shall be undertaken in stages. This provision is frequently applied; and, in preparing the case management plan (see Chapter 13 'The Multi-track'), the practitioner should always consider whether phased disclosure would be appropriate.

SPECIFIC DISCLOSURE OR INSPECTION

Because of the change in the criteria for disclosure, applications for 'further specific discovery' (as they used to be) will not in future be made. Instead of asserting (usually by way of affidavit) that the opponent has not made full discovery of 'relevant' documents, the practitioner will, in essence:

(a) either challenge the assertion contained in his disclosure statement, that he has carried out a 'reasonable search' or

(b) challenge his claim to be entitled to refuse inspection of disclosed documents on grounds of, for example, privilege (as before) or – the new factor – proportionality.

Consequently, an order for specific disclosure or inspection will be in a new restricted form under CPR Rule 31.12:

> 31.12(1) The court may make an order for specific disclosure or specific inspection
>
> (2) An order for specific disclosure is an order that a party must do one or more of the following things:
>
> (a) disclose documents or classes of documents specified in the order;
>
> (b) carry out a search to the extent stated in the order;
>
> (c) disclose any documents located as a result of that search.
>
> (3) An order for specific inspection is an order that a party permit inspection of a document referred to in rule 31.3(2).

An application for such an order must comply with CPR Part 23 and its Practice Direction. Accordingly:

(a) it is initiated by issuing an application notice, which must specify the order sought, the reasons for seeking it, and whether a hearing is required;

(b) the application notice may itself contain/be relied upon as evidence in support, and should therefore be endorsed with a statement of truth;

(c) do not swear an affidavit: you are unlikely to recover the cost from your opponent, other than in special circumstances;

(d) do prepare the costs assessment schedule and attempt to agree it with the opponent, not less than 24 hours before the hearing, and remember to supply the court with a draft order.

The net effect of CPR Part 23 is to render applications simpler and cheaper. Any additional evidence (i.e. over and above that already contained in statements of case and witness statements) can be included in the application notice itself (see above).

SPECIAL DISCLOSURE

In addition to specific disclosure (described above), it should be noted that a 'special disclosure order' is available in the Commercial Court, in appropriate cases, and where this can be shown to be 'necessary'.

In such cases, the court may be prepared to order that:

> each party shall carry out a thorough search for all documents relevant to the issues ... including ... all documents which may *lead to a train of enquiry* enabling a party to advance his own case or damage that of his opponent (emphasis added) (*Commercial Court Guide 1999*, Appendix 9).

The order is likely to be made in a limited range of cases only, typically cases which involve allegations of fraud, dishonesty or misappropriation, or cases in which knowledge (or lack of knowledge) or, for example, non-disclosure of information (e.g. in relation to an insurance dispute) is in issue.

Thus did the judges of the Commercial Court save *Peruvian Guano* discovery from final extinction, despite Lord Woolf's best efforts.

THE USE OF TECHNOLOGY BEFORE AND DURING TRIAL

First, some reminders. Disclosure of documents under the CPR should commence before proceedings, will probably progress with the service of statements of case, will be issue-driven, and may well, in a substantial case, be undertaken in stages (usually based on discrete issues).

Consideration must be given, at the allocation questionnaire stage (and thereafter in case management conferences) to the nature and extent of the disclosure that is *necessary*: the court will not allow more.

The parties are expected to cooperate with one another: 'gamesmanship' and abuse of the disclosure process for tactical purposes are *out*.

Lord Woolf's Report *Access to Justice*, recommended more extensive use of litigation support technology to assist document management, but this idea has yet to be fully developed in the Rules and Practice Directions.

Litigation support systems are, broadly, of three types, namely:

- basic indexing;
- full text retrieval;
- document imaging.

The creation of a basic index involves the loading of objective details (carefully determined at the start) of all relevant documents (i.e. not usually confined to 'disclosable' documents) into a database, so that searches may be conducted, for example:

- by date;
- by author;
- by addressee;
- by subject matter.

Full text retrieval enables users to search the full text for key words or phrases, much in the way, for example, that a Lexis search is conducted (save that it will be carried out on your own database, and not online). To enable this to happen, it is necessary first to load all the documents in question onto the system. It may be possible simply to scan them, but, whatever method it adopted, it will not be a cheap exercise. Once accomplished, however, this task will enable patterns to be readily identified, and documents to be swiftly collated (to name but two uses). Full text retrieval is a powerful case analysis tool.

Document imaging is, in effect, taking photographs of individual documents and holding them on a computer, for ready access and display. However, whilst document imaging enables a number of individuals (for example, judge, counsel, solicitors and witnesses) all to look at the same document on their screens (without having to rummage through lever-arch files, etc.) it will not, of itself, enable you to:

(a) pull together documents whose 'vital statistics' have been loaded on to an index in accordance with pre-determined categorisations (as basic indexing will); or

(b) 'search', using computerised software, the document database, for example, for documents containing a single word, phrase or expression (as full text retrieval will).

It is obvious that the cost of such systems can be considerable, and that they must be used carefully.

It is suggested that, in the context of disclosure, IT should be employed on the following basis.

Do not treat IT as a substitute for reading the documents: it is no such thing. Consider whether and if so at which stage conduct of the particular case will be best assisted by an indexing, retrieval or imaging system. You may, for example, want to use a basic indexing system early on to help collate documents which have features in common: you may want to improve on that index later, when the issues are narrowed. You may want to reserve imaging for documents which together comprise the court bundle, with an eye to efficient display at trial.

Estimate the cost of using whatever system you opt for, in particular:

(a) will your opponent agree to share the cost of your chosen system or combination? (ask the opponent);

(b) if not, will the court order him to do so if you succeed in the action? (consider asking the procedural judge);

(c) will your client agree to the use of any such system with or without the possibility of recovering (part or the whole of) the cost, if successful?

If, but only if (even under the new disclosure criteria), it is clear that substantial numbers of documents will have to be reviewed by your opponent or the court, document imaging, at the appropriate moment, will probably save time and money. But, particularly given the new emphasis on the use of ADR, it makes sense to defer the imaging exercise until either disclosure and inspection of substantial numbers of documents is inevitable, or you are preparing for trial and, in either case, your opponent and/or the court has approved a cost-sharing regime.

CHAPTER 13

The multi-track

James Burnett-Hitchcock

INTRODUCTION

The foundation-stones for the proposals contained in Lord Woolf's Report *Access to Justice* (which led directly to the creation of the new Civil Procedure Rules) were:

(a) that in future every attempt should be made to resolve disputes *without* the need for litigation or, worse still, trial;

(b) that if litigation could not be avoided, then the 'overriding objective' (set out in CPR Part 1) must to be to deal with cases 'justly'.

CPR Part 1 goes on to explain what 'dealing with cases justly' means, and then adds a third new stipulation, namely:

(c) that the court must further the overriding objective by actively managing cases; and the meaning of 'active case management' is then in turn spelled out.

On the fast track, there is little room for 'active case management': the amount in issue is limited to £15,000 (currently): standard directions are the order of the day: time from allocation to trial is set at about 30 weeks: trial is limited to one day, with costs assessed at the end of that day.

On the multi-track, the opposite is true. Its hallmarks are:

(a) the ability to handle cases of widely differing values and complexity;

(b) the flexibility given to the court to manage a case in a way appropriate to its particular needs.

The multi-track is rather like a giant 'Lego set', a box full of tools and procedures from which the judge and the solicitors can take out what they need, to build a vehicle to carry the case efficiently from allocation (the first case management task to be performed by the court) to trial, taking advantage, along the way, of any opportunity to settle the dispute by some other means.

So the *level* of case management is very variable. Much will depend on the complexity of the issues, and identifying the issues early on is a priority task.

This chapter will consider the nature and parameters of case management by the court on the multi-track, and its effect on the solicitors' role and their relationship with the court, and will then examine the procedural framework of multi-track litigation, detailing the contributions which the solicitors should make at each stage – and how the court will impose its own decisions if they fail to do so – to ensure compliance with a pre-set timetable and budget.

CASE MANAGEMENT: THE JUDGE'S APPROACH

The meaning of active case management (by the court) is detailed as summarised below in CPR Rule 1.4:

- encouraging cooperation between parties;
- early identification of issues;
- considering whether ADR is appropriate and if so encouraging its use;
- deciding in which order different issues should be determined, to shorten the case;
- fixing timetables;
- having regard to the value of case, means of parties and complexity of issues, to ensure a level playing field and proportionality;
- dealing with as many aspects of the case on the same occasion as possible;
- dealing with a case without the parties attending;

425

- using IT where practicable;
- dealing with cases quickly and fairly.

It is a pretty full list; but note in particular the following items, which hold the key to the judge's approach:

(a) *early identification of issues:* from the issues will flow decisions on what evidence is needed, factual or expert, and, generally, the degree of court intervention which might be required;

(b) *deciding which issues can be dealt with summarily*: the judge will, from the outset, seek to limit the scope of the dispute, consistent with ensuring that it absorbs no more of the court's resources than it should;

(c) *considering whether ADR is appropriate*: the chances of resolving the dispute outside the court system will be reviewed regularly throughout the case (see further below);

(d) *fixing timetables*: above all, the judge's task is to set the timetable for the case, in consultation with the solicitors, and then keep them up to the mark;

(e) *considering cost-benefit issues*: a new and crucial element of dealing with cases justly is the concept of 'proportionality', not defined, but clearly intended to be of universal application (and possibly of particular application in relation to costs).

So the procedural judge's task is to ensure prompt analysis of the case, knock out minor issues (or, indeed, the whole case) early on if possible, consider what evidence and procedural programme is required, fix a timetable, and ensure that the parties stick to it. (The procedural judge under the CPR will normally be the same person as the one who performed the role under the old rules: a High Court Master, district judge or (increasingly) a deputy district judge. Occasionally, where a complex case (such as a multi-party action) or a specialist jurisdiction is involved, a High Court or circuit judge will be involved from the outset.) He will also ensure that the parties actively consider settlement, by ADR or otherwise, and do not litigate for the sake of it. Note also one further element of CPR Rule 1.4:

(f) Dealing with as many aspects of the case as [the court] can on the same occasion.

This is the key: in future, litigation is no longer to be conducted salami-style – taken one step at a time, and in your own good time, without an eye to the future. We now have issue-based litigation: define the issues, and design the procedure to resolve them, from start to finish. It is a good idea to treat Rule 1.4 as a checklist, to be reviewed before every trip to court. Have you taken every aspect of the case as far as you can at this stage, or are there any little jobs outstanding (which an astute judge might delve into)?

Is it, then, all to be strict obedience to rules, and much cracking of whips? Certainly not. The new rules give encouragement to the solicitors to plan the case, and secure the court's approval to the plan. However:

- if the solicitors will not produce a proper plan, the court will impose one;
- the plan must cover the ground right up to trial, with a timetable, and will contain 'milestone dates'.

Conclusion: a new approach by the profession to the planning and running of a case is essential, in order both to comply with and to succeed under the new CPR, and nowhere more so than on the multi-track.

The point was emphasised by the Senior Queen's Bench Master, in his paper 'The CPR and the proactive judge':

> Civil litigation needs to be trimmed of its unessential features in order to concentrate on the true issues. It is to this end that the courts wish to see the parties being more open from the start, with clear protocols before the litigation commences, with statements of case (especially defences) which do not try to fudge the nature of the case, and with clients properly advised as to the advantages of settling their differences by alternative means, if they can.
>
> At an early stage, a target date for the trial must be set, and all directions tailored to achieving it. The Procedural Judge's task is to determine all issues that can be determined summarily, and indeed to devise a rolling agenda for resolving issues: so often, two or three issues, if determined early on, can cause the parties to settle the whole dispute, and thus avoid an expensive trial.
>
> If, however, there has to be a trial, then the aim must be to restrict the amount of oral evidence, disclosure of documents, and reliance on experts, to the right amount to ensure a fair and just trial.
>
> None of this can be achieved unless the courts and the judges realise that it is a partnership: the role played by the profession – meaning the manner in which they co-operate and work with the courts – will be vital.

THE PROCEDURAL FRAMEWORK

The procedural framework looks like this.

The allocation questionnaire having been filed, the procedural judge allocates to the multi-track, and may do any or all of the following:

(a) issue written directions (which he probably will do, in a straight-forward case);

(b) set a timetable, fixing, as appropriate:

    (i)   a case management conference (CMC);

    (ii) a pre-trial review (PTR);

    (iii) a date for the filing of a completed listing questionnaire;

(c) set a trial date, or 'window' for trial, as soon as possible.

At this stage, the court's first concern will be to ensure that the issues are identified and the necessary evidence is prepared and disclosed. The first decision is to choose between giving immediate directions, and fixing an early CMC. A number of matters will be considered, including

(a) whether the answers to the allocation questionnaire contain sufficient information generally to enable the court to give proper directions *without* a CMC;

(b) the extent to which any relevant pre-action protocol has been complied with;

(c) whether the parties wish *or* the court considers it appropriate that the proceedings be stayed under CPR Rule 26.4 for ADR to be tried;

(d) whether any party proposes to seek summary judgment.

If the court decides to give directions on its own initiative (i.e. without a CMC) and is not aware of any steps taken by the parties other than exchanging statements of case, its general approach will be to give 'standard directions' under the Practice Direction to CPR Part 29, para. 4.10:

- filing and service of further information;
- standard disclosure;
- simultaneous exchange of witness statements;
- single joint expert unelss good reason not to do so;
- simultaneous exchange of experts' reports *unless*:
  - single joint expert or
  - evidence on liability and amount;

428

- (if experts' reports not agreed) discussion between experts and report on outcome;
- CMC listed, after date for compliance with directions;
- trial period specified.

A party can apply to vary such directions *but* under CPR Rule 29.5: 'Any date set by the court or the rules for doing any act may not be varied by the parties if the variation would make it necessary to vary any of':

- a CMC;
- a PTR;
- the return of a listing questionnaire;
- the trial, or trial period.

These, then, are the 'milestone dates': far easier to influence them in advance by filing a case management plan, than to have them altered after the event.

If, by failing to comply with a pre-action protocol or (worse still) to file an allocation questionnaire, you necessitate an allocation hearing, expect:

- to be ordered to pay the costs;
- on an indemnity basis;
- forthwith (meaning, within 14 days);
- (quite possibly) out of your own pocket.

The court may order *further* directions hearings whenever appropriate: likewise, a party may apply to vary directions. This is dealt with later in the chapter. But if you apply for directions on a matter which could/should have been dealt with at a previous hearing, you must expect to pay for the privilege of so doing.

Clearly the regime is designed to encourage practitioners to put forward their own case management plan, for the approval of the court.

HELPING THE JUDGE: THE CASE MANAGEMENT PLAN

Consider the following:

(1) CPR Rule 29.4 provides that if the parties *agree* proposals for the management of the proceedings (usually known as a case management plan or CMP) and the court considers it suitable, the court may

approve the CMP without a hearing and may 'give directions in the terms proposed'.

(2) The Practice Direction to CPR Part 29 encourages litigants to take advantage of this rule and provides (at para. 4.4): 'the court may have regard to any document filed by a party with his allocation questionnaire containing further information, provided that the document states either that its content has been agreed with every other party or that it has been served on every other party, and when it was served'.

Putting these two propositions together, the practitioner's best course becomes obvious, namely:

- to draft a case management plan and send it to the other parties;
- to try to agree it with them, and then file it *with the completed allocation questionnaire*;
- failing agreement, to send the draft to the court anyway, with a copy of the letter under cover of which it was sent to the other parties, explaining the thinking behind it/arguments in favour of it, as appropriate.

There are two points to watch.

(1) Do not delay returning the completed allocation questionnaire to the court while you seek agreement to the CMP from the other parties: *always* comply with the court's deadline for the return of the allocation questionnaire.

(2) Ensure that the CMP complies with the requirements of the Practice Direction to CPR Part 29, para. 4.7: directions which *must* be included, and para. 4.8: directions which *should* be included where appropriate, as set out below.

4.7 (1) To obtain the court's approval the agreed directions must:
  (a) set out a timetable by reference to calendar dates for the taking of steps for the preparation of the case;
  (b) include a date or a period (the trial period) when it is proposed that the trial will take place;
  (c) include provision about disclosure of documents, and
  (d) include provision about both factual and expert evidence.

4.8 Directions agreed between the parties should also where appropriate contain provisions about:
  (1) the filing of any reply or amended statement of case that may be required;

    (2)   dates for the service of requests for further information under the Practice Direction supplementing Part 18 and of questions to experts under rule 35.6 and by when they are to be dealt with;

    (3)   the disclosure of evidence;

    (4)   the use of a single joint expert, or, in cases where it is not agreed, the exchange of expert evidence (including whether exchange is to be simultaneous or sequential) and without prejudice discussions between experts.

If the court does not approve the parties' own agreed directions, it will either take them into account in deciding what other directions to give, or call for an early CMC.

PROJECT MANAGEMENT

The CMP (whether devised and agreed by the parties and then approved by the court, or handed down by the court without a hearing, and subsequently amended on an application by one or more of the parties) will specify:

(a) *all* the tasks which each party must perform to bring the case to trial;

(b) the timetable according to which they must be performed;

(c) milestone dates at which (quite apart from other interim hearings, such as ad hoc applications or additional CMCs set up by the court) progress is to be reviewed.

The idea of establishing *all* the tasks needed to get to trial some 14 days or so after the defence is served may be novel to some; but a glance at the allocation questionnaire confirms the position – it is very comprehensive. Apart from tracking information, it calls for information on interim applications, settlement/ ADR prospects, pre-action protocols, witnesses, experts' evidence, and representation at, location, and estimated duration of trial. It also contains one dramatic innovation:

> **Costs:** (only relates to costs incurred by legal representatives)
> What is your estimate of costs incurred to date, excluding disbursements, VAT and court fees? £ . . .
> What do you estimate the overall costs are likely to be, excluding disbursements, VAT and court fees £ . . .

These two questions should transform both the way in which major cases are conducted (i.e. the running of multi-track actions) *and* the relationship with the client in such cases. The reasons are simple:

(a) the court requires disclosure of both costs to date *and* a projection to the end of trial, in a document to be completed shortly after service of the defence, namely, the allocation questionnaire;

(b) when it is returned to the court, it will be usual to annex a CMP (see above);

(c) the costs information given in the replies to the above two questions is likely to be reviewed at (and should therefore be updated in preparation for) any subsequent CMC, application, listing hearing or PTR, at any or all of which the client may attend.

Conclusion: both best practice and common sense dictate that the costs information you give the court (like the other information demanded by the allocation questionnaire) should be discussed with the client before return of the allocation questionnaire *at the very latest.* Failure to do so will render subsequent embarrassment (or worse) inevitable. But if you must provide such information to a client anyway, is it wise to defer doing so until, in practical terms, the rules compel you? There is a better way.

The new ethos established by Lord Woolf (treat the court as a last resort: if you must litigate, ensure that the case is dealt with *justly*) obliges solicitors and their clients to carry out a thorough assessment of a case at the outset. Only then can sensible decisions be taken about whether, and if so at what level and how, to attempt settlement, or whether to litigate. Either way, significant amounts of information are likely to be exchanged with opponents before proceedings commence, in compliance with a specific pre-action protocol or the Protocols Practice Direction (see Chapter 12 'Disclosure').

If the resulting strategy includes litigation, costs will have to be discussed with the client, and an estimate prepared. This is the start of the process. At the latest, by the time the defence is served and an analysis of the issues can be carried out, you should devise a comprehensive plan for the conduct of the case, making provision for:

(a) the steps which must be taken to get the case to trial, divided into manageable sections;

(b) the timing of each step;

(c) the resources needed to complete those steps (partners, assistants, legal executives and trainees);

(d) the number of hours work you foresee for each individual in relation to each task (usually on a 'high/low' basis).

Items (a) and (b) can be conveniently set out on a spreadsheet: 'tasks' listed on the vertical matrix, 'timing' (in weeks or months) on the horizontal matrix. A second spreadsheet should carry items (c) and (d), and two further cost columns should then be added to it along the bottom: 'budget' and 'actual' respectively.

This will then produce a simple case management plan and a case management budget, which can be used to project manage the litigation.

The plan and the budget will help you:

- to estimate future costs for client and CMC purposes;
- to allocate personnel (between the instant case, and others);
- to anticipate (internal) manpower problems which may arise in complying with the court's, or an opponent's suggested timetable, and to provide accordingly;
- to report progress to your client (comparing 'actual' with 'budget' figures at each stage);
- to ensure compliance with the court's timetable (and, crucially, the milestone dates);
- to remain competitive in an ever more competitive profession.

But how do you provide accurate budgets in complex cases, if you have never done it before? True, case budgeting is not an accurate science; but that is not the point. If case budgets are regularly prepared, and in a consistent fashion, they will provide a huge improvement on the traditional 'impossible to forecast, but we will bill you monthly!' approach. Within most firms of solicitors which conduct litigation as a regular part of their business, there will reside hundreds, probably thousands of years (combined) experience of litigation costing and budgeting, but it has seldom been put to any formal use.

That experience, properly harnessed in the preparation of a case management plan and a case budget, will greatly enhance the service to clients, as well assisting compliance with the CPR.

KEEPING SETTLEMENT IN MIND: ADR CHECKPOINTS

The fact that a dispute could not be settled without the institution of proceedings does not mean that those involved should 'rush to trial'. The Woolf ethos is 'Treat the court as a last resort': there will invariably be opportunities to reconsider the prospect of settlement along the way, and practitioners should be on the look-out for them at all times.

Encouraging the use of ADR is one of the *duties* imposed on the court by CPR Rule 1.4: it is no accident that the first question on the allocation questionnaire is:

A. Do you wish there to be a one-month stay to attempt to settle the case?

The same question, in essence, will be raised at a number of stages on the path to trial. 'ADR checkpoints' are found in:

- the allocation questionnaire (CPR Rule 26.3);
- the case management conference (CPR Rule 29.3(1));
- the listing questionnaire (CPR Rule 29.6(1));
- the pre-trial review (CPR Rule 29.3(1));
- the listing hearing (CPR Rule 29.6(3)).

An order may be made to stay the proceedings while the parties try to settle the case by ADR or by other means *at any other time* under CPR Rule 26.4, which provides that:

(2) where:
    (a) all parties request a stay under paragraph (1), or
    (b) the court of its own initiative, considers that such a stay would be appropriate,
the court will direct that the proceedings be stayed for one month.

It goes without saying that a sound knowledge of ADR procedures – how to select the right form of ADR, and then prepare and present your case – is essential to the modern litigator, whose first task, when such an order is made, may well be to explain ADR to his client, who knows nothing whatever about it. For some, a steep learning curve will be involved.

THE CASE MANAGEMENT CONFERENCE

The key to making *any* case management conference effective is thorough preparation – it is not an occasion at which to request extra time for doing a whole row of tasks which you should already have completed, it is a *conference* at which, allotted tasks having already been performed, decisions can be made about the next steps in the action (Senior Master Turner, 'The judge in the chair', April 1999).

Thus the Senior Queen's Bench Master, and who better to learn from? The point, of course, is that if a conference is to be effective:

(a) the right people must attend;

(b) they must have done their homework;

(c) they must decide what their objectives are *in advance*, and not just work them out as the conference proceeds.

Who, then, are the 'right people'?

The Senior Master sees nothing wrong with a five-handed conference, to include:

- the (procedural) judge;
- both parties;
- both parties' legal representatives.

The legal representatives must

(a) be fully familiar with the case;

(b) have sufficient authority and information to deal with 'any matter which may reasonably be expected to be dealt with (including fixing a timetable, identification of issues, and matters of evidence)'.

Note that the penalty for sending an unbriefed, last-minute substitute who knows little or nothing of the case will be a wasted costs order.

What homework?

The legal representatives should:

(a) bring all the documents which the court is likely to want to see (including witness statements and experts' reports);

(b) consider whether the parties should attend (and, if so, ensure that they are aware of the latest position in the proceedings, or prepare to be seriously embarrassed);

(c) consider whether a case summary would be useful;

(d) consider what orders each wishes to be made, and give notice to the opposing solicitors accordingly;

(e) (if appropriate) prepare and serve a costs summary in approved form.

Under the Practice Direction to Part 29, para. 5.7:

> 5.7(1) A case summary:
>
> (a) should be designed to assist the court to understand and deal with the questions before it;
>
> (b) should set out a brief chronology of the claim, the issues of fact which are agreed or in dispute and the evidence needed to decide them;
>
> (c) should not normally exceed five hundred words in length, and
>
> (d) should be prepared by the claimant and agreed with the other parties if possible.

What are the objectives?

The court is likely to consider the following:

- is the substance of the claim clear and understandable?
- are amendments required to a statement of case or other document?
- what disclosure is needed?
- what expert evidence is needed: how should it be obtained and disclosed?
- how should it be clarified?
- what factual evidence is needed?
- should a split trial/trial of a preliminary issue be allowed?

The court will always set a timetable for compliance with its directions.

The directions given may include the holding of a further CMC or PTR, and the court 'will be alert to perform its duty to fix a trial date or period as soon as it can' (Practice Direction to CPR Part 29, para. 5.4).

If a party wishes to obtain an order not routinely made at a CMC and believes it will be opposed, he should:

(a) issue and serve the application in good time for hearing at the CMC;

(b) (if he seeks a costs order) prepare and serve a costs summary (and, of course, try to agree costs figures with the opposing party in relation to that application) not less than 24 hours before the hearing.

Remember that, consistent with the duty to deal with as many matters as possible on the same occasion, you may wish to make applications at a CMC and, at the last minute, may discover that your opponent will not agree the order(s) which you seek. Even though it is a CMC, you must still warn the court, check that there is enough time to deal with the contested items, and serve a schedule of costs relating to the application(s).

The above regime applies to *all* CMCs; but, plainly, the nature of the first CMC will depend largely upon whether any or any extensive directions were given at the allocation stage. If they were, the court's concern will be to ascertain whether the parties have complied with them, and, if not, why not.

In a substantial or complex case, a number of CMCs may be held. The parties must always:

(a) consider in advance of a hearing what orders they may wish to seek;

(b) be ready to update the court on costs incurred to date and their projections of costs up to the conclusion of the case.

NB: Always remember proportionality, the spectre at every CMC feast.

VARYING THE DIRECTIONS

Flexibility is one of the hallmarks of case management on the multi-track; but, conversely, *fixing timetables and controlling the progress of the case* is one of the (case management) duties imposed on the court by CPR Rule 1.4. In considering the extent to which the parties may be permitted to vary the court's directions without referring back to the court for approval, it is plain that a balance must be struck between these two potentially conflicting approaches. Turning to the mechanics of variation, in what circumstances is it desirable that the court should be permitted to *vary* its orders, as opposed to requiring the dissatisfied party to appeal?

The answers, for present purposes, are to be found in a combination of:

(a) CPR Rule 2.11;

(b) CPR Rule 29.5;

(c) CPR Rules 31.5, 31.10(8) and 31.3;

(d) Practice Direction to CPR Part 29, para. 6;

(e) these rules cover the procedure to be adopted:

   (i) where a party is *dissatisfied* with a direction given by the court;

   (ii) where the parties have *agreed* a variation they would like made, or

   (iii) where a party wishes to apply to vary a direction.

(f) The Practice Direction to CPR Part 29 states that it is 'essential' that any party wishing to have directions varied take the appropriate steps as soon as possible: the court will assume that a party who fails to appeal or to apply within 14 days of service of the order in question 'was content that the directions were correct in the circumstances then arising'.

437

As to 'the appropriate steps' see synopsis in Box 13.1.

Box 13.1 Procedure for variation of directions

(A) If the variation has been agreed between the parties:

Question (1) Is it an agreement to:

- vary the time specified by a rule or by the court to do any act (under CPR Rule 2.11)?
- dispense with or limit standard disclosure (under CPR Rule 31.5)?
- dispense with a list of documents or a disclosure statement (under CPR Rule 31.10(8)?
- carry out disclosure or inspection in stages (under CPR Rule 31.13)?

If Yes: Parties must record agreement in writing but need not file at court unless any of the following apply:

- Rule 3.8 (sanctions have effect unless defaulting party obtains relief);
- Rule 28.4 (variation of case management timetable, fast track);
- CPR Schedule 1: RSC Order 59 Rule 2c (appeals to the Court of Appeal);

All of which provide time limits that *cannot* be varied by agreement between the parties.

Note in particular: CPR Rule 29.5 provides that parties *must* apply to the court to vary:

- a 'milestone date' on the multi-track;
- any other date the variation of which would make it necessary to vary a milestone date.

If No: Parties *must* apply for consent order, by filing draft of order sought, with agreed statement of reasons. The court may:

- make the order, in the agreed or other terms, or
- direct that a hearing be listed.

(B) If the variation has *not* been agreed between the parties

Question (2) Was the dissatisfied party present at or did he have due notice of the hearing at which the order/direction was made/given?

If No: The dissatisfied party should apply to the court to reconsider its decision.

If Yes: Then:

438

Question (3) Has there been a change in the circumstances since the order was made?

If Yes: Dissatisfied party should apply to court to reconsider, as above.

If No: The dissatisfied party should appeal the order.

Note: An application to the court to reconsider its decision:
- will usually be heard by the same judge (or another of the same level);
- will be the subject of at least three days' notice from the court to all parties;
- may result in confirmation or variation of the original directions.

THE LISTING QUESTIONNAIRE

Assuming that:

- summary judgment was not granted;
- there is now no prospect of settlement by way of ADR;
- the trial date or period is now some three months off,

it is time for the court to check up on progress made in getting ready for trial.

For this purpose, the court will send to the parties, no less than eight weeks before trial, a listing questionnaire in Form N170, for completion and return within (usually) 14 days. Its purpose is:

(a) to check that the timetable/directions have been complied with, and, if not, to find out why;

(b) to fix a firm date for trial;

(c) it will also enable the court to decide whether a PTR is needed, or whether a PTR already fixed is still required or can be dispensed with;

(d) the parties *must* reply;

(e) if no party replies, the court will normally make an order that if no listing questionnaire is filed by any party within three days from service, the claim and any counter claim will be struck out;

(f) if only one party files a listing questionnaire, the court will normally fix a listing hearing, and may require the party in default to pay the costs on an indemnity basis.

In addition to asking whether previous directions have been complied with (and, if not, why not) and whether further directions are needed, the listing questionnaire enquires as to:

(g) experts: has permission for expert evidence been given, which experts from what fields will be called, who are they, is expert oral evidence to be given, etc.?

(h) other witnesses: how many, who, their availability, are their statements agreed, will they need special facilities (e.g. an interpreter)?

(i) representation: will counsel/solicitors or the parties appear, and when are they not available?

(j) the trial: how long will it take, how many pages will there be in the bundle?

The parties are not required by the rules to exchange copies of their completed listing questionnaires, but the Practice Direction encourages them to do so ' to avoid the court being given conflicting or incomplete information', and in order to file an agreed order for directions, if possible.

The court may include in its order any directions agreed by the parties, if considered appropriate. In order to be considered 'appropriate' the agreed directions must cover the matters prescribed by the rules. See Practice Direction to CPR Part 29, para. 9.2:

(2) Agreed directions should include provision about:
(a) evidence, especially expert evidence;
(b) a trial timetable and time estimate;
(c) the preparation of a trial bundle, and
(d) any other matter needed to prepare the case for trial.

(3) The court will include such of these provisions as are appropriate in any order that it may make, whether or not the parties have filed agreed directions.

The court must fix the trial date or week, give a time estimate, and fix the place of trial.

THE PRE-TRIAL REVIEW (PTR)

In some cases, the information in the parties' completed listing questionnaires will indicate that a PTR should be ordered under CPR Rule 29.7, if indeed one has not previously been ordered.

The purpose of the PTR is:

(a) to afford a final opportunity to explore settlement before the costs of preparing for trial, and the trial itself are incurred;

(b) (where settlement is plainly impossible) to prepare an agenda for trial.

Accordingly, the PTR should wherever practicable be conducted by the trial judge, and be attended by:

- the intended trial advocates;
- the solicitors;
- the parties (specifically, a representative with authority to settle the action).

The judge will wish, again, to check that all previous directions have been complied with, and will then wish to review a wide range of aspects of the case with a view to the production of an effective trial timetable. Now more than ever, preparation for trial is an activity which, to a large extent, should be undertaken jointly. Starting with the issues, the judge will be seeking to promote agreement on as many items as possible. The following is a suggested PTR agenda:

- Issues: is there an agreed list?
- Documents: which documents *must* be before the court?
- Witnesses: how many, who, on what issues, and have they special needs?
- Experts: how many, who, in what fields, has permission been given, have they met/agreed anything, and are they to give written or oral evidence?
- Skeleton arguments and when they will be available.
- Background reading plan/materials and when they will be available.
- Chronology and/or case summary: is it available/agreed?
- IT: should it be used for:
  - adducing evidence?
  - managing and displaying documents?
  - providing real-time transcription?

- cross-examination of overseas witnesses?
- other purposes?
- Timing: how long will be needed for each stage?
- How much in total will the court allow?

But the court will not necessarily order what the parties agree to. Always remember:

(a) that the court has power to control evidence under CPR Rule 32: in practice, this may mean declining to admit (otherwise admissible) evidence from a second or third witness, or putting a strict time limit on cross-examination;

(b) that the principle of *proportionality* (to the amount involved, the importance of the case, the complexity of the issues and the financial position of each party) is to be observed at all stages;

(c) that in addition to applying proportionality 'dealing with a case justly' includes 'allotting to it an appropriate share of the court's resources, while taking into account the need to allot resources to other cases' (CPR Rule 1.1(2)(e)).

It follows that in drafting a trial plan or timetable for discussion at a PTR, practitioners would do well to consider in advance which parts of the case (or their evidence) they would prefer to sacrifice or economise on, should the judge not agree to either the level of costs or the amount of time or evidence proposed by them. He is entitled under the new rules to say 'you may want four days, but I am only going to give you three'. *That* is case management by the court.

The touchstone for preparing the draft trial timetable should be 'no more than is necessary': do not try to introduce all the evidence you can, rather, confine yourself to *what you need as a safe minimum, to succeed on each issue.*

THE NEW INTERLOCUTORIES

CPR Rule 3.1(2) provides that the court may: '(d) hold a hearing and receive evidence by telephone or by using any other method of direct oral communication'.

CPR Part 32 provides: '32.3 The court may allow a witness to give evidence through a video link, or by other means'.

The Practice Direction to CPR Part 23 (applications) provides that the court will only order that an application be dealt with by a telephone hearing if:

- all parties have consented;
- no party is acting in person,

and it contains detailed directions on the conduct of a telephone hearing:

(1) Applicant's lawyer is responsible for making all conference call arrangements with BT 'Call me' (or a similar system, providing names and numbers for all participants, to telephone company).

(2) BT calls lawyers, counsel and judges at exact time stipulated by court.

(3) Conference call is recorded by BT/tape sent to court.

(4) Costs of call are treated as part of costs of application.

CPR Part 1 stipulates that the overriding objective of the Rules is 'to deal with cases justly' (CPR Rule 1.1(1)) and goes on to say that that 'includes, so far as is practicable . . . (b) saving expense'. CPR Rule 1.4(1) provides that the court must further the overriding objective by 'actively managing cases' and goes on to say that that '(2) . . . includes . . . (K) Making use of technology'.

CONCLUSIONS

(1): short applications, even where contested, should be dealt with by telephone, particularly where any significant travelling is required by counsel or solicitors. It remains to be seen whether a party's withholding of his consent (one of the two prerequisites to the making of the necessary order) without giving, or perhaps having, any substantive reason, will be regarded as lack of cooperation, or breach of the requirements of CPR Rule 1.3 ('to help the court to further the overriding objective') of sufficient turpitude to merit a costs sanction. In principle, there seems no reason why not.

(2): in planning a trial, consideration should be given to avoiding the need for witnesses to travel long distances (e.g. from abroad) to attend court, unless there is reason to think that they could not be effectively cross-examined by video link. Recent decisions suggest that counsel's *preference* for having the witness before him in the flesh (rather than on a video-link screen) is not by itself enough.

CHAPTER 14

Alternative dispute resolution

Susan Barty

INTRODUCTION

Recent years have seen departments within a number of different law firms dealing with contentious matters changing their names away from 'Litigation Department' to 'Dispute Resolution Department'. This change of name, cynically viewed by some, reflects a real change of emphasis in the type of contentious work carried on by solicitors. The costs of litigation have escalated during the last decade and the court procedures, as identified by Lord Woolf in his review of the civil justice system in England and Wales, had become complex, rule-orientated and slow. Although it has been widely acknowledged that some 80 to 90 per cent of cases will settle, this has tended to be at a relatively late stage of the proceedings, often at the court door. Arbitration has become tainted with the same problems of cost and delay as litigation and has become regarded by many as a form of privatised litigation, as bad or worse than the court process. In both his interim and final reports Lord Woolf advocated the use of alternative dispute resolution (ADR) for resolving disputes. This emphasis is now reflected in the Civil Procedure Rules.

There have been increasing moves over the last five to ten years in England and Wales to introduce ADR procedures in order to resolve disputes. This growth follows that which first took place in the USA and other common law jurisdictions, such as Canada, Australia, New Zealand and Hong Kong. Although in the international business arena companies and their lawyers have been using negotiation, conciliation and mediation for decades to settle their disputes, what is new is the increased formalisation of this process and how ADR has, in the last decade, become an integral part of the dispute resolution process in England and Wales, with increasing influence from the court in directing parties towards the use of ADR procedures. As confirmed by recent reports, the changes brought about with the Civil Procedure Rules can only result in increased use of ADR.

This chapter looks at what is meant by ADR, in particular under the CPR, its advantages and disadvantages, and when a case is suitable for ADR. The different routes to ADR are then addressed, with an explanation as to the likely process actually involved in a mediation and what should be included in any settlement agreement at the end of a mediation.

WHAT DO WE MEAN WHEN WE TALK ABOUT ADR?

The meaning of the term alternative dispute resolution has not been settled. The term is sometimes taken to mean 'alternative to litigation' and therefore including arbitration. However arbitration, like litigation, is a fact-finding and adjudicative process which remains more akin to litigation. Increasingly, therefore, the term 'alternative dispute resolution' is taken to mean 'alternative to the adjudicative or imposed decision processes of litigation and arbitration'.

The main methods of alternative dispute resolution currently used in England and Wales, are as follows:

(1) Early neutral evaluation/judicial appraisal: without prejudice non-binding case appraisal by a judge or some other appropriate individual to help to narrow and define the issues and thereby to assist the parties in arriving at a settlement.

(2) Expert appraisal/adjudication: an expert or other adjudicator is appointed by the parties, whose decision may be binding or non-binding as agreed between the parties.

(3) Mediation: a neutral third party participates in a structured negotiation and assists the parties in reaching a binding settlement, whilst not seeking to offer an opinion or decision on any issue.

(4) Conciliation: used increasingly to describe those circumstances where a more active role is played by the third party conciliator in informing the parties of his or her opinion on the issues.

(5) Internet schemes: in the modern e-commerce and Internet era, it is not surprising that Internet mediation schemes have been set up, although there is very little documented evidence of use of these systems: at their most simple, they will require the parties to identify their scope for settlement by placing 'bids', before narrowing these down to try and reach a settlement.

(6) Ombudsmen: used in relation to complaints from individuals in both the public and private sectors and used increasingly following the rash of privatisations in the 1980s and 1990s, for example in the banking, insurance and pensions industries, the ombudsmen have wide powers of investigation and will not necessarily confine their recommendations to what is strictly permitted as a matter of law.

(7) Adjudication: which has become common in construction disputes.

Of the above, mediation seems to have acquired a prominence in England and Wales. There has been some encouragement also to use early neutral evaluation, although this still seems to remain a little-used process, perhaps being regarded by many with some suspicion, no doubt in part borne out of unfamiliarity.

Of course, in essence, the number of possible alternative methods of resolving disputes will be almost limitless. A number of different alternative forms of dispute resolution (usually from the USA) have been identified by numerous different commentators.

ADR UNDER THE CIVIL PROCEDURE RULES

Although mention of alternative dispute resolution in the new Civil Procedure Rules is not frequent, the spirit of ADR pervades the rules. Most particularly it features in CPR Part 1, the all-important overriding objective, to which practitioners regularly need to refer during the conduct of any litigation.

The overriding objective is dealt with in detail elsewhere in this book, but in its basic terms it is the objective of enabling the court to deal with cases justly. The court's duty to manage cases is an important part of the overriding objective and active case management expressly includes 'encouraging the parties to use an alternative dispute resolution procedure if the court considers that appropriate and facilitating the use of such procedure' (CPR Rule 1.4(2)(e)).

In an ideal world this would pave the way for a new era of solicitor-to-solicitor cooperation. However, whilst genuine cooperation between the lawyers of litigants may still be a rare event, what does appear to be happening is a real increase in the number of references to ADR.

By contrast with the position under the old court rules, where any court encouragement to use ADR generally came rather late in the day, the issue now arises more frequently, and at a much earlier stage.

Under the Pre-action Protocols, parties are encouraged to resolve disputes without recourse to litigation. After proceedings have commenced, when the parties are filling in the allocation questionnaire, they are given the option of making a written request that the proceedings be stayed while the parties try to settle the case by alternative dispute resolution or by other means. Even if the parties do not request a stay, the court under CPR Rule 26.4(2) may, of its own initiative, order a stay. In either case the court will direct a stay of one month, although this period may be extended by the court, and the parties are under a duty to keep the court informed of their progress.

Notwithstanding that there is no express reference to ADR, or the option of requesting a stay in proceedings, in relation to later stages of litigation, in practice the parties can expect the court to ask at each key procedural stage whether ADR has been considered. This is perhaps unlikely in fast track cases after the case has been allocated and is on its fast track to trial. However, in multi-track cases, the issue is likely to be raised, apart from at the track allocation stage, at the very least at the case management conference and at the pre-trial review, and may be raised at any other hearing before the court. Although it may depend on the approach of different judges/masters, if ADR is not considered or attempted, the parties are likely to be asked to justify the reason for this.

The provisions in CPR Part 44 relating to costs are dealt with in more detail in Chapter 7 above, but the conduct of the parties, before and during the proceedings, will be scrutinised by the court and is a key issue in deciding what order should be made as to costs. Accordingly there will be costs sanctions for any conduct considered to be unreasonable.

There has been some debate amongst the judiciary about the merit of imposing costs sanctions for a failure to approach ADR in good faith. However, there does not appear to be wide support for specific costs sanctions and certainly costs sanctions do not appear to have been significantly applied or, in any event, publicised. This is likely to be because of the difficulty of subjective evaluation in determining how a failure to participate in good faith can be judged and by whom. As soon as some qualitative assessment is required, the question as to what precisely amounts to a lack of good faith will be difficult to determine.

However, the judges clearly intend to exercise their discretion under CPR Part 44 in relation to costs and in relation to the conduct of the parties. The manner in which they have conducted the action and the parties' approach to ADR may well be one issue taken into account.

ADVANTAGES OF ADR

There is very little in the way of detailed research which has been carried out as to the success rate of ADR in England and Wales, particularly by comparison with the USA. Professor Hazel Genn's report on the Central London County Court Pilot Mediation Scheme (Lord Chancellor's Department Research Series 5/98) was the first substantive survey into mediation in this country. However, the Pilot Mediation Scheme on which Professor Genn was reporting had a take up rate of only about 5 per cent and accordingly there is a limit as to the extent to which anyone can form a view of the likely success of the process from the study. The Centre for Dispute Resolution (CEDR) and other ADR agencies often refer to the very high success rate of their processes. Figures in the region of 80 or 90 per cent are often quoted (although, with the great increase in the number of cases being referred to mediation, this 'success' rate looks like being reduced). Clearly what cannot be determined is the number of cases which settle through that procedure, but which would otherwise not have settled or, alternatively, the percentage which settle at a significantly earlier stage than would otherwise have been the case. There are, however, clearly a number of advantages of ADR. The chief advantages of mediation are identified in the Commercial Court Practice Statement (Waller J) issued on 7 June 1996, which listed the following.

Costs savings

Clearly, if a dispute is settled as a result of ADR, the parties will save the costs which would otherwise have been incurred in the following stages of the litigation up to and including the trial. By bringing forward in time the resolution of the dispute, there will also be savings for the client in terms of their own time in dealing with the dispute. ADR should, however, not be considered simply as a cheap means of resolving disputes. The costs (including in emotional terms) of preparing for and attending at the ADR should not be underestimated by the parties.

Avoidance of delay

This advantage is likely to become even more significant with the emphasis on ADR at an earlier stage under the CPR. Mediations, in particular, can be arranged as quickly as the parties want and as early as the parties want in any dispute, even before the commencement of any proceedings.

Preservation of existing relationships and reputation

One of the key advantages to resolving a dispute by the use of ADR techniques is that such a resolution tends to assist in preserving relationships between the parties, particularly in commercial disputes. A hard fought trial is clearly not conducive to maintaining good relationships. Mediation, in particular, tends to focus on the potential benefits to both parties of some form of continuing relationship and the mediator will want to help the parties to focus on the future, on life after the dispute has been resolved. Reputation can also be preserved as a result of the confidentiality of the ADR process. However, the mediation process is often a long and tough process, which may well leave the parties feeling somewhat bruised and battered.

A wider range of settlement options

ADR provides great flexibility in terms of settlement options, which options are simply unavailable from any adjudicative process. For example, where a party considers that they have a 60 per cent chance of succeeding at trial, a mediation can reflect this percentage likelihood in the final agreed settlement. Moreover, the parties can take into account other potential benefits, apart from the simple payment of damages, for example the provision of services free of charge. In this way the parties retain control over the process and the eventual outcome and are not reliant on what some may consider to be the idiosyncrasies of the court resolution process.

More efficient use of judicial resources

This is clearly an influential factor so far as the courts are concerned. The aim is very much to eliminate the delay in the resolution of disputes and proper use of ADR techniques will in principle allow the courts to focus on those disputes which require some form of court adjudication.

Other advantages

The advantages set out above address those identified in the Commercial Court Practice Statement, but will not only apply to commercial cases. However, in non-commercial cases, there seems to have been a greater reluctance to embrace ADR, maybe more as a result of inexperience. Nevertheless, it can bring great advantages in all types of cases. The opportunity to attend a mediation gives the advantage of controlled, without prejudice, negotiation, whilst also allowing for a sense of having had the equivalent of a day in court, and an opportunity to vent feelings before an independent third party. It also allows for the alleged wrong doer to make an apology (often much sought after, yet sparingly given in court proceedings) direct to the wronged party, in a controlled environment. In a mediation, there is scope for the parties to explain, outside the usual legal and procedural constraints, what happened and how the dispute arose. One other great advantage of ADR is its confidentiality. This should assist in the relative free flow of information, without the risk of the issues disclosed being referred to later.

DISADVANTAGES OF ADR

There are relatively few disadvantages to attempting an alternative dispute resolution process. The disadvantages will only apply if the process is unsuccessful and, to a certain extent, therefore mirror the advantages identified by the Commercial Court.

Cost

ADR is not simply a low cost dispute resolution option. Parties often underestimate the cost incurred in preparing for any ADR process, both in terms of legal costs and client time. Clearly, if the process fails, these costs will usually have been incurred at least to some degree, in addition to the other costs of the litigation process. Indeed, it was a common view expressed by those participating in the Central London County Court Pilot Scheme that a failure to settle at the mediation led to increased costs. These costs are also generally irrecoverable, since the standard practice is for each party to bear its own costs of the mediation. It would be unusual for the successful party at trial to receive its costs of the process. The costs will include the cost of the third party neutral's fees, as well as the basic cost of the mediation (cost of the venue and other general expenses), which are usually borne by the parties in equal shares.

Delay

The process of setting up a mediation can be time-consuming and, if the process is unsuccessful, this will be wasted time. However the detailed preparation involved for any ADR process is likely to be of value to the parties in the future conduct of the litigation.

Effect on existing relationships

An ADR process does not always result in a 'win:win' solution for both parties, although this is clearly the ideal outcome. In certain situations there may be a 'lose:lose' result, and this clearly will not improve relations between the parties. In certain circumstances, the ADR process can even worsen relations between the parties and, particularly if the process is unsuccessful, it can push the parties further apart.

Release of information

As part of any ADR process the parties are encouraged to release information. This is particularly true of mediation, where a mediator will seek to extract as much information as possible from the parties. In doing so, the parties may end up revealing information to the other side. Although the process is confidential between the parties (indeed, the mediator will not release information to the other side unless authorised to do so), and notwithstanding that the process is conducted without prejudice, once information has been released to the other side it is clearly impossible to withdraw it. Linked to this is the risk of one party seeking to abuse the process and to take advantage of it in terms of seeking further information about the other side's case or simply to gain more time. Nevertheless, it is not unusual for a party to enter into a mediation seeking to obtain some advantage and then to get carried away by the process. Indeed, a good mediator should be able to avoid one party seeking to abuse the process.

SUITABILITY OF CASES FOR ADR

When should ADR not be attempted?

ADR can, in theory, be used for any dispute and at any stage of the dispute. There are, however, certain situations where it will be inappropriate to attempt ADR.

Need for injunction or other court assistance

If there is some need for an order of the court either to restrain someone from doing something, or to require a party to take a particular action (for example, pursuant to a freezing injunction or search order), then ADR will clearly not be appropriate. Nevertheless, in any of these disputes, it is possible that ADR will be appropriate at a later stage in the proceedings.

Precedents or test cases

There may be a number of cases or potential cases which all hinge on a particular point, for example there may be a dispute involving the wording of a particular insurance policy. There may also be a matter of great public interest or principle which requires a definitive judgment. In any of these cases, ADR will not be appropriate.

Summary judgments

One party may consider it has a very good prospect of obtaining summary judgment. If this is so, this may be a reason for that party to choose the litigation route. Litigation may therefore be considered more appropriate for straightforward debt recovery actions, where one party considers the other party's position to be intrinsically extremely weak. However, ADR, particularly early neutral evaluation, but also mediation, should not be ruled out in this type of situation. It is not unusual for what is considered to be a very strong case to fail at court.

Limitation periods

If one party finds itself up against the imminent expiry of a limitation period, then that party will not be able to delay the commencement of proceedings. However, in particular under the provisions of the CPR, and in the current favourable climate for ADR, it will be possible to ask the court for a stay in the proceedings while the parties seek to settle the case by ADR.

Publicity

Generally, parties favour the confidentiality of the mediation process. In some situations, however, a party may desire the publicity gained from proceedings. In these circumstances the privacy and confidentiality of ADR will generally not allow publicity.

Economic power

One party which has much greater commercial strength may prefer to pursue the litigation route in order to use its economic power over the weaker party, which may find it difficult to fund lengthy litigation. Most practitioners will recognise this as a tactic which often worked very well under the old Rules of the Supreme Court. However, under the CPR, with the applicability of costs sanctions and the express objective of ensuring that the parties are on an equal footing, this may mean that this tactic proves to be somewhat less effective in the future.

Effective existing negotiations

Clearly if there are effective existing negotiations going on between the parties, there is no need to seek the assistance of a third party neutral in resolving the dispute. However, there is a need to distinguish between the belief that effective negotiations will be possible between the parties and the actual existence of effective negotiations. The Central London County Court Pilot Scheme demonstrated that a number of solicitors who were offered mediation as part of that Scheme considered mediation to be unnecessary, because they considered themselves capable of negotiating without the assistance of a third party. In fact, it often proves to be the case that establishing effective negotiations is not that simple and the assistance of a third party may make all the difference.

Lack of genuine interest in settlement

Clearly if one party lacks a genuine interest in settlement, then there will be little point in seeking any form of alternative dispute resolution. However, it can be difficult to judge this issue, in particular since there is (still) a tendency for litigators to posture in the course of legal proceedings. Accordingly, there is a need to distinguish this from a lack of genuine interest in settlement. It may be that, in this situation, some encouragement from the court to attempt ADR will be particularly advantageous. Moreover, in mediation, an effective mediator can also often convince an otherwise reluctant party of the merits of finding an alternative means of resolving the dispute.

Complex or substantial cases

It has been said that ADR is not suitable for multi-party disputes, disputes involving complex legal issues or multi-million pound disputes. In fact, there is no intrinsic reason why disputes of this nature should not be subjected to an

ADR process. There may be issues in any of these proceedings where some form of early neutral evaluation would be of assistance.

Where a dispute involves complex legal issues, even if the entire dispute cannot be subjected to the ADR process, it may be that there are individual issues where an early neutral evaluation would assist. Disputes involving complex legal issues can also be mediated effectively although, on the whole, mediation will not involve a careful review of all the legal issues. Instead, a more 'broad brush' approach is generally taken.

Multi-party disputes can be, and have been, effectively mediated. There may be a need for bigger and more rooms for the process and the process may take longer, but there are a considerable number of examples now of multi-party disputes which have been successfully mediated.

Similarly, for multi-million pound disputes, there is no reason why they should not be mediated. The only issue may be that the cost savings may be proportionately less important, but the costs savings may nevertheless be considerable. Ultimately the question will be one for the client to judge the costs savings against the risk.

ROUTES TO ADR

Contract

The parties may have an existing contract between them which requires them to attempt some form of alternative dispute resolution. Increasingly in commercial agreements, parties will include a multi-layered dispute resolution clause, requiring the parties to negotiate, often with an escalation up to senior or chief executive level. The clause may also require the parties to attempt some form of alternative dispute resolution before commencing proceedings.

There is much debate as to the merit of such clauses and their enforceability. As to the merit of such clauses, there are those who advocate binding ADR clauses and those who advocate non-binding clauses. There are clearly advantages and disadvantages to both approaches. A non-binding clause may provide sufficient encouragement to the parties to attempt such processes, whilst not restricting the parties in the event that some form of swift action is required to be taken. However, some may consider there to be little point in having a clause which is not binding. Ultimately, it will be for each party to consider the relevant options during the course of the negotiations leading up to the entering into any agreement.

Although there is little in the way of case law in this jurisdiction as to the enforceability of ADR clauses, there is authority in both the USA and

Australia. In England and Wales, the case of *Channel Tunnel Group Ltd* v. *Balfour Beatty Construction Ltd* ([1993] AC 334) is of relevance. In this case, a contractual clause provided for the initial reference of disputes or differences to a panel of experts and provided for final settlement by arbitration in Brussels. The enforceability of the clause was considered by the House of Lords, which concluded that it was legitimate to use the discretionary general powers of the court to enforce a dispute resolution agreement which was 'nearly an immediately effective agreement to arbitrate, albeit not quite'. The House of Lords considered that the parties in this case were experienced large commercial enterprises which had negotiated and drafted a dispute resolution clause, and that those who make agreements for the resolution of disputes must show good reasons for departing from them. It was also considered in the interests of the orderly regulation of international commerce that, having promised to take complaints, in this case, to experts and, if necessary, to arbitrators, then this was where the parties should go. That one party now found this method too slow to suit their purposes was irrelevant.

In the case of *Halifax Financial Services Ltd* v. *Intuitive Systems Ltd* ([1999] 1 All ER (Comm) 303), the judge had to consider a dispute resolution clause which obliged the parties to submit any dispute to meetings between the parties' senior representatives and then 'structured negotiations . . . with the assistance of a neutral adviser or mediator'. There were provisions for the appointment of the neutral adviser, but no further detailed terms as to the process to be adopted. The parties had entered into direct negotiations but had not attempted mediation. On the particular wording of this clause, the court considered that the clause was not effective and that it did no more than to make provision for the parties to negotiate hopefully towards an agreement. The judge took the view that forced negotiations between the parties would be futile at that particular time.

Accordingly, each dispute resolution clause will have to be construed on the basis of its own specific terms. However, provided there is sufficient detail in an agreement as to the ADR procedure decided upon, it is likely that the courts will seek to give the clause effect. Although the specific clauses have not been tested in the courts, there may be some advantage to adopting a clause put forward by one of the established ADR organisations, since these clauses may provide a shorthand method of identifying a detailed mediation procedure. However, this will have the potential disadvantage of tying the parties to a particular organisation for pursuing the relevant alternative means of resolving the dispute.

Court intervention

The intervention of the court in encouraging the use of ADR or, in certain circumstances, directing the use of ADR in appropriate cases, has been a

455

relatively new development. The Commercial Court was probably the first to become very pro-active in this respect and, under the CPR, there is likely to be continued and even increased encouragement by the court.

The intervention of the court can be extremely useful where both parties are concerned that suggesting ADR may be taken as a sign of weakness or if one party demonstrates a reluctance to follow this route.

In addition to the likely increase in the number of court orders directing a stay of proceedings to give the parties an opportunity to attempt ADR, there are a number of specific court schemes which are designed to encourage the use of ADR.

(1) Central London County Court Scheme: the Central London County Court has extended its pilot mediation scheme, which was launched in May 1996. This scheme is now permanent and is used for cases where the sum in dispute is over £3,000.

(2) Commercial Court Scheme: the Commercial Court regularly makes ADR orders in its standard form, requiring the parties to exchange lists of individuals who are available to conduct ADR procedures and requiring the parties to take 'such serious steps as they may be advised to resolve their disputes by ADR procedures before the neutral individual or panel'. The Commercial Court also makes its own judges available to carry out early neutral evaluation where this is chosen by the parties.

(3) Court of Appeal Mediation Scheme: parties in the Court of Appeal hearing lists will receive an invitation to take up the facility of using a Court of Appeal panel mediator, at present at no cost. This still appears to be under-used as a process.

(4) District registries and regional courts: Bristol Law Society launched a pilot out-of-court mediation scheme for civil disputes in June 1994 and a scheme has been begun in Leeds. It seems likely that this practice will develop in other regional courts.

Subsequent agreement

Probably most commonly, the parties may reach agreement after a dispute has arisen to refer the matter to ADR. However, parties are sometimes reluctant to address the issue, for fear of this being taken as a sign of weakness. However, under the CPR, and as ADR becomes increasingly part of the dispute resolution process, it is less likely that this will be an issue to the same extent.

The issue can be raised either directly between solicitors representing the parties, the parties themselves, or through a third party. On occasions one party may choose to ask one of the established ADR organisations to raise the issue with the other side. In this way, the ADR organisations can offer independent advice to an otherwise suspicious party. The whole process can be set up quickly, but may take longer where there is a need to persuade the other side. It is necessary to take care with the terms of the agreement. The various established ADR organisations have standard ADR agreements. There is generally a single mediation agreement between the parties and the third party neutral. The agreement will usually be signed at the start of the mediation. The mediation agreement can be as detailed as the parties prefer, but should, at the minimum, include the following:

(a) the type of ADR process;

(b) the basic agreement to refer the matter to mediation, using wording such as 'the parties will endeavour to resolve the dispute by mediation';

(c) the appointment of the mediator;

(d) identify the representatives (if any) for the parties;

(e) address the question of authority to settle the dispute;

(f) provisions as to the confidentiality and without prejudice nature of the process;

(g) provisions as to the costs of the proceedings, generally that these will be borne by the parties in equal shares;

(h) provisions as to the conclusion of the mediation: the parties should also consider whether they would wish the mediator to provide a non-binding opinion on the merits, in the event of no settlement being agreed; most parties prefer not to seek this option, because it is likely to impact on the mediator's independence and neutrality;

(i) provision as to settlement and requirement for any settlement to be reduced to writing and signed by the parties at the successful conclusion of the mediation.

The parties may wish for more detailed provisions as to the procedure to be adopted. It may, for example, be sensible to provide that there should be a stay of the proceedings while the mediation is being conducted. For international disputes, there may be a need to provide for governing law and jurisdiction provisions. The mediator may also require further provisions, for example some exclusion of liability and provision to ensure that the mediator cannot be called upon as a witness in any subsequent proceedings between the parties.

CHOOSING THE THIRD PARTY NEUTRAL

The choice of the third party neutral is probably the most important decision of all. There are a number of well established ADR bodies which will put forward names of individuals who are properly trained in mediation, who will sit as early neutral evaluators or, indeed, who will act as the third party neutral in any form of ADR. The Commercial Court has a number of judges who will sit as early neutral evaluators.

However, there has been some concern expressed as to the relative lack of good and experienced mediators and the need to ensure quality to maintain confidence in the process.

Parties will need to consider the type of mediator. For certain disputes the parties will want a legally qualified mediator: this may be a solicitor, barrister or a judge or retired judge. Clearly much will depend upon the individual's own approach to the ADR process. Some individuals will be more likely to provide an evaluative, rather than a facilitative approach, and will tend to comment upon the relative strengths and weaknesses of the party's case. Careful consideration will have to be given as to the best approach for the dispute in question. Alternatively, the parties may seek some specialist in the field in relation to which the dispute has arisen. For medical negligence actions, someone with a degree of knowledge or experience in this field is likely to be useful. Where a mediator has relevant specialist knowledge, this may help in building up the necessary trust between the mediator and the parties. In certain instances it may be appropriate to consider appointing co-mediators with differing strengths or experience. ADR organisations may provide a pupil to work with the mediator and may provide specialist expertise in this way. Consideration may also be given as to the nationality of the mediator. For an international dispute it may be appropriate to consider appointing a mediator from another jurisdiction, provided that individual has the appropriate expertise and training.

MEDIATION

Preliminary practical issues

Consideration should be given as to the *appropriate location* for the mediation. There are no hard and fast rules as to the appropriate location. There may be a reluctance to go somewhere which is not considered independent, for example the offices of the parties or their solicitors, although this may prove to be a good practical option. In particular, this can assist in reducing the costs of the mediation. Alternatively, for example if a barrister has been selected as a mediator, the barrister's chambers may provide the facilities. There will be numerous other neutral venues available, including arbitration rooms. The parties may prefer to go to a hotel. Although there are examples quoted of a relatively inhospitable venue resulting in a swift settlement, generally it will be important to find a relatively comfortable venue for the mediation, since mediations can, and often do, last for a considerable length of time.

The main requirement, at its most simple, is that there should be a sufficient number of rooms to allow for one large room for all the parties for any joint sessions, together with individual rooms for each party. It is most helpful to have ready refreshments available and appropriate business facilities for the parties (easy access to fax, photocopying etc.).

Attendance

It is vital for the client to attend the mediation, and that the person attending has authority to settle the dispute. If the person attending does not have authority to settle, this will risk jeopardising the whole process. However, if those attending only have limited authority to settle, for example only up to a particular sum, this should not necessarily jeopardise the process. In general terms, a limitation on the ability to settle will not be particularly different from a self-imposed minimum or maximum on the settlement figure, which the parties may prefer not to divulge. Nevertheless, the mediator may seek to ascertain at the outset if there is any limitation on the authority to settle. The parties should make their own decision as to whether or not this information should be released to the mediator and, if so, at what stage.

Legal advisers will also often attend a mediation. It is generally considered easier for the mediator where legal representatives are involved, at least at the outset, although towards the end of the process the mediator may prefer to exclude the legal representatives from the settlement negotiations. The legal adviser should, however, be experienced (or at the very least, trained) in mediation and should generally take care not to adopt an adversarial or positional stance, which may not be conducive to settlement. Where a party attends without legal representation, the mediator's task is more time-consuming and the mediator will need to take additional care not to be seen to be favouring one side over the other.

There may also be a need for anyone with relevant technical knowledge to attend. This may be an expert witness or a technical representative from the client.

If the claim is one covered by insurance, it may be appropriate for the insurers also to attend the mediation.

In general terms, the parties will often want to match the representation of the other. It is therefore important to ascertain at the outset who will be appearing on behalf of each party. Care should, however, be taken not to have too many people attending the mediation for each side. Where there are larger numbers, the process can become more cumbersome.

Documentation

The parties should decide together what the mediator should see. The mediator is likely to assist in directing what documentation there should be. It is generally helpful if an agreed statement of facts can be prepared between the parties and then each party should submit written submissions, with a summary of the dispute from their point of view. In terms of supplementary documentation, this should be kept to the minimum. Careful thought should be given as to precisely what the mediator needs to see. It may also be helpful for the mediator to have a confidential briefing paper, if there are any specific issues which it is thought should be brought to the attention of the mediator in advance of the mediation, but which it is not desired to disclose to the other side.

Duration

The mediation may take any number of days. However, for most disputes, a mediation should be capable of being completed within one day, starting at, say, 9 a.m. or 9.30 a.m. and going on, often until late in the evening. For particularly complex disputes (for example those involving a number of different parties) a second or third day may be required.

Parties should, however, be aware that the mediation discussions tend to fill the time available and therefore additional time should not be allowed unless considered absolutely necessary. The system is sufficiently flexible that, if the parties reach the end of the first day without having negotiated a settlement, but consider that a limited amount of additional time is needed in order to reach a settlement, then a second day can be agreed at that stage. It may even be worth setting a time by which the mediation should finish, for example 7 p.m., so that all parties know, and can work towards, a deadline. This deadline can always be extended if it seems the parties are close to a resolution.

For certain disputes, a cooling-off period can be helpful to allow parties to reflect upon the issues raised during the mediation, although this may backfire and leave parties more entrenched. Often, where a dispute is not settled at the mediation, it will do so at a later stage, relatively soon after the mediation. The mediator will often assist in reaching a settlement, even after the formal mediation has finished.

STRUCTURE OF THE MEDIATION

Introduction

In considering the structure of the mediation, it is important to remember that the whole process is without prejudice. Nothing that either party says during the course of the mediation can later be referred to by the other party during the legal proceedings, should the mediation not be successful. However, it is important to remember that once a concession or an admission has been made during the course of a mediation then, should the mediation not be successful, it will be open to the other party to seek to take advantage of this during the continuation of the proceedings, whilst not referring directly to the concession or admission. For example, some requests for further information may be made on the basis of the concession or admission and the party which made the concession or admission may find cross-examination at trial directed accordingly.

Although the structure of the mediation is very much up to each individual mediator, essentially the mediation is likely to fall into four main stages. This is very much based on the CEDR model, but this is a model which has been adopted more widely. First, there will be opening statements by the mediator and the parties. This will be followed by an exploration stage where the mediator will assist the parties in exchanging information, fact-finding exercises and in exploring the issues. This is probably the key stage in the mediation. It is extremely important and often underrated. The negotiation stage will follow, but this will come relatively late in the day, once the issues have been fully explored. Hopefully a settlement will be agreed by the parties at the end of the process. This may be achieved earlier on, but the realities are such that this tends to happen much later on, when the parties are becoming tired and wanting to bring an end to the process.

Mediator's opening

The mediator's opening is part of the vital process of building up the necessary trust and confidence between the mediator and the respective parties. This will be particularly important for a client who has had no, or little, previous experience of the mediation process (or even the litigation process). The mediator may well have spent some time prior to the commencement of the mediation in discussions with the parties or their representatives.

In the opening, the mediator will explain his or her role to the parties and the likely conduct of the mediation. He will emphasise his neutrality and will encourage the parties to look for opportunities to resolve their disputes in a way which does not depend wholly upon legal merits and remedies. He will tell the parties that they should look for an outcome which will enable them both to win, or at least to find a resolution that they can both live with. This needs to be considered in the light of the risk of the uncertainty of litigation, which is likely to be of concern to both parties.

Opening statements by the parties

The opening statements by the parties can be extremely important. This is each party's opportunity to speak to the other side and the opportunity should not be wasted. It is important to seek to cause the other side to question their own case. It is likely to be the first time the client, or the main representative, on the other side has had an opportunity to hear the opponent's case, without the 'spin' which will have been put on it by the legal representatives.

It is important that the parties, in making their opening statements, take account of the fact that mediation is not the same as adversarial litigation. Accordingly, opening statements should be succinct, concentrating on key issues between the parties, which may not be the legal issues. Opening statements should not be inflammatory, but they may be a good opportunity for each side to make clear the strong feelings which may exist. The opening statements should be valuable in identifying to the mediator and to the parties what are the real issues.

It is generally regarded as most helpful if the parties themselves make the opening statements, although many clients may be nervous and/or reluctant to do so. All mediations are likely to be highly charged and emotional, particularly cases involving individuals. This can make it difficult for the party to feel sufficiently at ease to make the opening statement. However, opening statements by the legal representatives tend to be more adversarial and add little to the written submissions.

Opening statements should make clear the desire to settle and should mention any settlement proposals which have been made to date. If the opening statements are too inflammatory, the mediator may break the parties apart or even delay the second opening statement.

Questions and discussion

After the opening statements, there will generally follow an opportunity for parties to raise any questions and discuss with each other their respective positions. There will, however, be ample opportunity for discussion during the rest of the day and, at this stage, the opportunity is best used for clarification. Some mediators may seek to encourage the parties to deal with the issues face to face, rather than immediately breaking up into private meetings. This will very much depend on the style of the mediator, the dispute and the parties.

Meetings in caucus

Having heard the opening statements, the mediator will commence the process of exploration of the possibilities for resolution, usually speaking to each party in private. Through this process, he will expect to encourage the parties to develop a basis from which they can negotiate, with a view to achieving an acceptable settlement for both parties. The private meetings are possibly the most valuable aspect of the mediation. The mediator will meet with each of the parties separately, usually starting with the claimant, with a view to achieving a better understanding of their respective positions and concerns.

There will generally be a series of meetings during which the mediator explores the issues and uses the opportunity to find out information from both parties. The mediator will also use this opportunity to test both parties and their respective cases. Although mediators are generally reluctant to express any opinion on the merits, they can be expected to test the expectations of the parties and to ensure that they are realistic both in terms of what can be achieved through the mediation process, and also what might be achieved by continuing the litigation process through to trial.

Any information released to the mediator during the private sessions will be kept confidential, in the absence of any agreement to release the information to the other side. However, appraised of the respective parties' concerns and fears, the mediator may be able to facilitate proposals which serve to reduce the differences between the parties. This constitutes the main body of the mediation.

Where a caucus session lasts for a long time, there is the risk of an air of boredom developing for the other party or parties. The parties may also seek to draw conclusions from the fact that the mediator appears to be spending longer with one party than another. This can be dangerous and the mediator therefore will often ask the party with whom he is not meeting to undertake some particular task, for example calculating figures or considering particular issues.

Meeting between the parties

Towards the end of the process, or even earlier depending upon the mediator, the parties may be brought together to discuss particular issues, or to negotiate terms as a whole. Some mediators will use meetings between the parties quite substantially during a mediation, but it is a process which needs to be handled carefully if the mediator is to keep the trust of the parties.

The mediator may even put the parties together without legal representatives and maybe even without the mediator. It is often considered that lawyers get in the way at the final stages of the negotiations and it is very easy for the whole process to fall apart at a late stage.

It is important for the parties to appreciate that there is no element of coercion in the mediation process and that neither party can be required or forced to agree. However, parties often find that, having invested a great deal of time and energy into the mediation process, there is a real incentive to settle the dispute, rather than waste the opportunity which has been provided by the mediation process.

The role of the mediator

The mediator is not there to achieve a just and fair result, simply to bring about a settlement between the parties. The mediator is not there to form his own view on the appropriate settlement, but to broker a deal between the parties.

The neutrality of the mediator is a fundamental requirement to the process. It is important that the mediator retains, and is seen to maintain, his neutrality and that he is not persuaded to take sides or to appear to favour the position of one of the parties against the other. It is this neutrality which provides him with credibility in the process. It is important for the mediator to be trusted and respected by the parties.

The mediator must do what he can to get the parties for themselves to explore avenues for the resolution of their disputes which are imaginative, lateral, while addressing the real causes of the dispute. There has been much debate as to whether a mediator should be more facilitative (in gently encouraging the parties towards settlement) or more evaluative (testing the parties more on their respective cases). Most mediators, however, can and do move from one approach to the other depending on each case and depending on each stage of each mediation. It is possible for a mediator to test a party's case without expressing a personal opinion and whilst maintaining his or her neutrality.

The parties may ask the mediator to give an opinion on various matters in relation to the dispute between them, even where they have chosen not to. They should also consider whether or not to ask the mediator to give them a non-binding opinion as to the merits, in the event of no settlement being achieved.

The role of the parties

It is important to appreciate that the role of the advocate in a mediation is different from the role of a party in litigation. Accordingly, having made their opening statements, the parties should not regard themselves as advocates for their cause. Having established their respective opening positions, negotiations between the parties should be both rational and principled and both parties should be looking for opportunities for mutual gain.

Legal representatives attending at a mediation should support their client and advise where appropriate. This extends to full and proper preparation for the mediation. It is extremely important that the legal representative should have had proper training before representing a client in a mediation. The skills needed in playing an effective role in a mediation are different from those required at court or in day-to-day dealings with the other side. There is a need also to make sure the client has a clear idea of what can be achieved through mediation and what they should expect, both in legal and in emotional terms.

Generally it is considered helpful to have a more client-led mediation than a mediation led by the legal representatives, even though they can play an important part. However, this will depend on the client, the case and the issues involved. Nevertheless, the mediation will tend to focus less on the precise legal issues and more on the basic commercial aspects of the case.

In advance of the mediation it is important to consider what roles those attending the mediation should play and who should be chiefly involved in the negotiations.

Strategy and planning

It is extremely important for the parties to prepare carefully for any mediation and to consider not only their own case, but also the interests and position of the other side. There is a real need to make sure, in advance of the mediation, that the client focuses on its own case in a realistic way, and that the focus is on the strengths and weaknesses of both parties, including as to what might be achieved in court and as to where any compromise might be made. The parties should consider what their best alternative to a negotiated settlement agreement (the much referred to 'BATNA') would be, as well as the position in the event of losing comprehensively at trial. The parties should consider the amount of irrecoverable legal costs likely to be incurred, together with the limitations on the client's time to devote to lengthy court proceedings.

Parties should approach the mediation much as they would any principled negotiation. The mediation process is intended to bring about circumstances where the parties are able to open up negotiations where the opportunity to negotiate may otherwise have disappeared. Accordingly, they should decide upon an appropriate opening position, and whether and at what stage to make any concessions. Throughout the process it will be important to build credibility with the other side, not only with the opening statements, but also during the course of the mediation. The parties should also plan and control the flow of information. If there is a key legal issue needed to convince the other side, then this should be addressed at an early stage in the mediation.

The parties should seek the opportunity to gather information and ask questions. Where information is to be offered, the parties should consider whether it should only be offered in exchange for information received from the other side. The parties are likely to be focused on their 'bottom line' (i.e. for the claimant, the figure below which it will not go or, for the defendant, the figure it will not go above) which should have been thought through fully in advance. This is important, otherwise the parties may find themselves being pushed into a settlement, when it is late and when they are tired, which they will regret later. The mediator may seek to ascertain the 'bottom line', although many are trained not to do so; the practice may therefore vary amongst different mediators.

It can also be helpful to begin to draft a settlement agreement at a relatively early stage of the mediation, for example if the parties are agreed on a number of other issues, but the basic figure remains in dispute. This can encourage parties to focus on the settlement and life after the mediation, but can also identify issues for further clarification while the process is still continuing.

The conclusion of the process

Evidence suggests that agreement is reached in over 70 per cent of cases. Where no settlement has been achieved, what has been said during the course of the mediation cannot be used against the relevant party in court, although the parties may have gained information, helpful or otherwise, about the other party's position. What has been learnt may even assist in bringing about circumstances for a negotiated settlement at some stage in the future. At the very least, the parties should have a far better understanding of the real underlying issues in the dispute between them. Of course, if no agreement has been reached, all the inherent risks of going to trial still remain. The parties may therefore try mediation again at some later stage, or the mediator may keep a dialogue going between the parties.

Settlement agreement

Assuming resolution is achieved as a result of the process, the terms of the agreement, precisely recording the position of the parties, should be reduced to writing at the earliest opportunity. This task should be undertaken with the assistance of the mediator, who will be careful to ensure that the settlement agreement truly reflects the agreement of the parties. It is particularly important to do so before the mediation concludes, since committing the terms to writing will be done at a time when the parties have built up a degree of trust between themselves and the mediator, which might be irretrievably damaged in the event of any disputes as to the wording of any settlement agreement. The mediator may therefore retain an interest in the conclusion of the settlement following the mediation itself.

The parties will have to decide whether the agreement should be intended to be legally binding or non-binding. A non-binding agreement will be rare. If the agreement is non-binding, the parties will be recording their agreement and intent, but not in a form or manner which could be referred to a court for enforcement should either of the parties fail to comply with its terms. If a non-binding agreement is reached, the parties will need to consider in what circumstances the agreement will become binding.

The agreement should record, as near as possible, the full details of what the parties have agreed. There may, however, be circumstances where further documentation or further agreements are needed to effect the settlement. There may, for example, be some requirement for agreements as to maintenance, transfer of property or services, in circumstances where it is not feasible for all this to be agreed at the end of the mediation. Consideration should also be given as to whether court documents will be required to bring an end to any court proceedings or to issues within those proceedings.

The point of achieving a binding agreement is that such an agreement should be a contract which is legally enforceable, so that each party can have the comfort that the other is committed to the performance of the agreement and, ultimately, should it become necessary, that they will be able to secure assistance from the court.

Disputes often arise as to terms of settlement at the very end of the process or during discussions to finalise detailed terms. The mediator may retain a useful involvement to resolve any such subsidiary disputes.

Detailed settlement terms

The precise terms of any settlement agreement will depend upon the facts of the dispute. This is an important stage, where the legal representatives will have a more significant role, both in considering appropriate provisions and in explaining them, and the need for them, to the client. This will clearly be of particular importance where the client is less sophisticated and less familiar with the litigation process.

There are certain general considerations which should be addressed when preparing any settlement agreement:

(1) Warranty of authority: both parties should be required to warrant in the settlement that their representatives taking part in the mediation and executing the agreement were properly authorised to do so.

467

(2) Contractual formalities: care should be taken to ensure that contractual formalities have been properly complied with by both parties to ensure that any binding agreement will be properly enforceable by each against the other. Particular care may be required in this regard if the parties come from different jurisdictions and different systems of law. Formalities also as to transfer of property or additional agreements should be considered.

(3) Breach of agreement: consideration should also be given as to what is the intended effect of any breach. Will a breach terminate the agreement or simply render the party in breach liable in damages? There may be different consequences for the breach of different aspects of the agreement. Consideration should be given as to how any disputes arising out of the agreement should be dealt with and whether, for example, they should be referred to mediation with the same mediator.

(4) Existing proceedings: consideration should be given as to the impact of the settlement on existing proceedings and as to formalities which need to be undertaken to bring any existing proceedings to an end. Again, the mediator may retain a role here.

(5) Enforcement: consideration should be given as to whether the agreement needs to, and can, be enforced in other jurisdictions.

(6) Interests of other parties to the mediation: the parties should ensure that the respective interests of all parties to the mediation are covered, and as to all and any disputes between other parties.

(7) Unresolved issues: there may be certain issues left unresolved by the mediation. If so, the agreement should address what steps are to be taken by the parties in relation to those issues. The parties should consider whether it is intended that they should continue to be litigated, or whether they are to be referred once more to some form of alternative dispute resolution.

(8) Termination of the mediation agreement: the parties should consider whether finalising the settlement agreement serves to terminate and bring an end to the mediation process or whether the mediation remains alive pending the resolution of any unresolved issues.

(9) Any conflicting agreement: where there exists an ongoing business relationship between the parties, great care must be taken to ensure that the terms of any settlement agreement do not conflict with any continuing arrangement regulating the parties' business together.

(10) Costs: the position as to costs is generally that each party will bear its own costs, both of the litigation and of the mediation process. It is, of course, likely that consideration of the costs of the litigation have been taken into account in the settlement agreed. The parties may

seek to have some other agreement as to costs. However, to seek to have some acknowledged winner or loser in this way is not very consistent with the idea behind mediation.

(11) Confidentiality: an express term to confirm the extent of confidentiality should be considered.

ISSUES FOR THE FUTURE

Conditional fees and mediation

One issue which will be significant for the future as we see more use of mediation, is with the interrelationship with conditional fees. These are dealt with in Chapter 7 above but, in drafting any conditional fee agreement, careful consideration will have to be given as to precisely what will constitute a success so as to justify recovery of costs. The issue here will not be very different from the general position on settlement of cases where there is a conditional fee agreement, but is an important issue to bear in mind.

Training

Training and continuing professional development is of ever-increasing importance to solicitors and training in mediation is no exception. Solicitors are used to a far more adversarial approach and need to be trained in mediation skills. It is for each solicitor to consider how best to achieve the necessary degree of training and how to do so cost-effectively. There are different courses available through the recognised ADR bodies, through the Law Society or through the usual training organisations, which cover the mediator's role and also the role of the legal representative in mediation. Both aspects can provide an invaluable insight into the process before gaining actual practical experience.

CONCLUSION

ADR and, in particular, mediation has already become an integral part of the dispute resolution process in this jurisdiction. With time, proper training and a great deal of effort from all those involved in the actual process, it can achieve an effective and valuable result, and a worthwhile alternative to court proceedings. It will not be successful in all cases, but every practitioner will need to consider ADR for every dispute being handled. Clients will increasingly expect their solicitors to be able to advise them as to the pros and cons of ADR for their particular case and to represent them at the mediation itself. The court will also expect the legal representatives to have addressed this in their advice to their clients.

CHECKLIST: GETTING TO MEDIATION

- **Is it right for your case?**
  - Do you need a judgment from the court?
  - Can you negotiate without assistance?

- **What is the right stage?**
  - Can the dispute be resolved early?
  - Do you need disclosure? witness statements? expert evidence?

- **How do you get there?**
  - Is there a special court scheme in place?
  - Is there a Protocol in force
  - Have the parties agreed a month's stay in the allocation questionnaire?
  - Can an ADR organisation assist?
  - Will the court make an order at the case management conference?

- **Choose your mediator**
  - Is there need for specialist knowledge?
  - Lawyer or non-lawyer?
  - Do they have experience?
  - Do they have the right personal attributes?
  - ADR organisation recommended?
  - Local intelligence?

- **Preparation**
  - Facts
  - Law
  - Expectations

- **Who should attend?**
  - Authority to settle
  - Numbers attending
  - Specialist knowledge
  - Other influential parties, e.g. spouse
  - Anyone likely to prove obstructive to a settlement

CHAPTER 15

Other major changes

Caroline Harmer

A. OFFERS TO SETTLE

INTRODUCTION

This part of the chapter will consider how the Civil Procedure Rules Part 36 will affect litigation practice. It will look at the major changes:

- procedure for claimant's offer to settle;
- defendant's pre-action offer to settle;
- problems of mixed money and non-money claims;
- penalties for failing to beat an offer to settle or payment in.

This part will also look at practical considerations:

- how early to make offers to settle;
- getting the procedure right;
- notice of payment-in in personal injury cases;
- non-money claims;
- calculating the enhanced interest.

CPR Part 36 was clearly a difficult rule to draft. It is not an easy Part to get to grips with. It has already been amended and will no doubt be subject to further revision at some time in the future. It seems to contradict itself from time to time and there is a confusion of terms. While the rules on payments into court by defendants in money claims are very much the same as before, there are some other significant changes and additions to this area of procedure and practice.

CLAIMANT'S OFFER TO SETTLE

When?

A claimant's offer to settle may be made before proceedings commence (known as an offer to settle); after commencement of proceedings (known as a Part 36 offer); and may be made even less than 21 days before trial (see CPR Rule 36.5(7)).

How?

An offer to settle must:

- state that it is a CPR Part 36 offer;
- be in writing;
- state whether it relates to the whole or part of the claim;
- state whether it takes into account any counterclaim;
- make clear the position regarding interest (see CPR Rule 36.5).

It must be signed by the offeror or his or her legal representative.

Time limits

If the offer is made not less than 21 days before the start of the trial it must be expressed to remain open for acceptance for 21 days from the date it is made, and provide that after 21 days the offeree may only accept if the parties agree costs or the court gives permission (CPR Rule 36.5(6)). 'Made' means when received by the offeree (or his or her legal representative where there is one).

An offer may be withdrawn at any time (see *Scammell* v. *Dicker*, *The Times*, 14 February 2001, CA) and will not then have the consequences set out in CPR Part 36. It may be improved, and this will be effective when details are received by offeree (CPR Rule 38.8). Permission of the court is not needed before withdrawing an offer (see *Pitchmastic plc* v. *Birse Construction Ltd*, *The Times*, 21 June 2000).

Acceptance

This takes place when notice of acceptance is received by the offeror (for the contents of the notice see Practice Direction to CPR Part 36, para. 7.7). The defendant will need leave of the court if he wishes to accept a Part 36 offer later than 21 days after the offer was made (CPR Rule 36.12) unless liability for costs is agreed. An offer to settle made before proceedings are begun which is accepted after they have been begun appears to need the court's permission (see CPR Rule 36.10). This contradicts CPR Rule 35.6 which provides that acceptance does not need permission of the court if costs are agreed.

Costs consequences of acceptance of Part 36 offer

If acceptance does not need permission of the court, the claimant is entitled to his costs of the proceedings up to the date of acceptance (CPR Rule 36.14).

Failure to accept

In the case of an offer before proceedings, as long as it is expressed to be open for at least 21 days, the court will take the offer 'into account' when making any order as to costs. The sanctions of indemnity costs and additional interest are expressed to apply to a claimant's 'Part 36 offer' and therefore may not apply to these offers.

In the case of a Part 36 offer, if the defendant is held liable for more than the offer, or the judgment is more advantageous to the claimant than the proposals in the offer then, unless the court considers them unjust, the consequences may be:

(a) additional interest on the whole or part of the sum for some or all of the period from the date on which the defendant could have accepted the offer without needing the permission of the court; the rate of interest is a rate not exceeding 10 per cent above base rate;

(b) indemnity costs from the same date;

(c) interest on those costs at up to 10 per cent above base rate.

CPR Rule 36.21(6) was introduced on 2 October 2000 to make clear that where the court awards interest under this Rule and also awards interest on the same sum and for the same period under any other power, the total rate of interest may not exceed 10 per cent above base rate.

It had been thought that the full additional rate of interest was to be awarded over and above other interest awarded in the normal way. However, the amended Rule shows otherwise. So if the court orders interest at 8 per cent on the full award of damages, for example, the maximum rate of additional or 'penalty' interest will be, at the time of writing, 7.25 per cent: i.e. base rate (5.25%) + 10% = 15.25 less 8% already awarded = 7.25%.

In the author's view the position is less clear where a different percentage or no interest is awarded on the various heads of damage. In a personal injury case the interest on general damages is 2 per cent making the additional or penalty interest 13.25 per cent; the interest on general damages is half the special account rate of 7 per cent, i.e. 3.5 per cent making the additional or penalty interest 12.75 per cent; however, there is no interest on damages for future loss and therefore, it would seem, there will be no additional or penalty interest awarded. This seems to impose a very mild sanction in cases where there is a significant element of future loss. Alternatively the court could average out the interest it awards to a percentage of the total damages, and then apply the additional interest to the whole of the award. The difficulty is that the way in which the Rule is drafted is very unclear and seems not to have taken the personal injury case into account.

Where the claimant beats their own offer and is awarded additional interest there is no guidance in the Rules or the Practice Direction as to the approach the court should take, e.g. whether it should be awarded on all the damages. It has been held that one approach is to calculate it from the earliest date when it can be awarded and then evaluate whether that would cause an injustice (*Little* v. *George Little Sebire & Co*, *The Times*, 17 November 1999). This seems to be the approach being adopted by many courts at present.

Claimant's failure to beat own offer

Practice Direction to CPR Part 44, para. 2.4 provides that failure by a claimant to beat his or her own offer will not in itself lead to a reduction in costs.

DEFENDANT'S PRE-ACTION OFFER TO SETTLE AND PART 36 PAYMENT

When?

To settle a money claim a defendant may either:

- make a pre-action offer; or
- make a payment into court once proceedings have begun.

How?

An offer must:

(a) state it is a Part 36 offer;
(b) be in writing;
(c) state whether it relates to the whole or part of the claim;

(d) state whether it takes into account any counterclaim;

(e) make clear the position regarding interest (see CPR Rule 36.5);

(f) include an offer to pay the costs of the offeree up to 21 days after the date it was made;

(g) be signed by the appropriate person if the offeror is a company or corporation (Practice Direction to CPR Part 36, paras 5.5 and 5.6).

It may:

- be limited to accepting liability up to a specified proportion (CPR Rule 36.5);
- be made by reference to an interim payment.

A payment in must be by notice filed at court stating the amount and containing (*mutatis mutandis*) the same information as for an offer. Service is by the court or the offeror. The latter must file a certificate of service. The money must be paid into court (for the procedure see Practice Direction to CPR Part 36, para. 4).

Time limits?

The time limits are as for claimant's offers except that time starts to run in relation to a payment when the notice of payment, or of any increase in the payment, is served on the offeree.

However, it is important to note that if a defendant makes a pre-action offer which is not accepted, then this must be followed by a payment of not less than the sum offered within 14 days of service of the claim form. Clarification of a defendant's offer or payment may be requested within seven days.

Withdrawal or reduction of payment in

A payment in may not be withdrawn without the permission of the court although it may be increased at any time. CPR Rule 36.6(5) was amended on 2 October 2000 to confirm that a payment into court may only be *reduced* with permission of the court.

Acceptance

Acceptance of a payment in must be in writing to the defendant within 21 days of the offer or payment being made, and does not require the court's permission. The acceptance must be received by the offeror within the time limit. If made less than 21 days before trial then the court's permission is needed unless liability for costs is agreed. Whether liability for costs means the amount of costs is not clear.

Costs consequences of acceptance

In the case of acceptance of a pre-action offer, the defendant will pay the costs as offered.

In the case of acceptance of a payment in, the claimant is entitled to the costs of the proceedings on a standard basis up to the date of serving the notice of acceptance unless permission of the court is required. If the payment in relates to part of the claim only and on acceptance the claimant abandons the rest of the claim, he is entitled to the costs of the proceedings.

If the notice of payment in takes into account any counterclaim, the costs include those attributable to the counterclaim. There are special rules relating to acceptance where the offer or payment is made by one or more, but not all, defendants (CPR Rule 36.17). Payment out of court should be requested as set out in Practice Direction to CPR Part 36, para. 8.1.

Failure to accept

If the claimant fails to better a Part 36 payment, the court will, unless it considers it unjust to do so, order the claimant to pay the defendant's costs from the last date for acceptance without leave of the court.

GENERAL PRACTICAL POINTS

Offers

If the defendant makes an offer rather than a payment into court after proceedings have been commenced, or if the claimant makes an offer which does not comply with CPR Part 36, is the offer effective in relation to costs and possibly interest?

In *Petrotrade Inc* v. *Texaco Ltd* (*The Times*, 14 June 2000, CA) the Court of Appeal considered this in relation to summary judgment and a Part 36 offer by the claimant. They asked does there have to be a trial? The answer was probably yes for CPR Part 36 to apply. However, the Court of Appeal went on to hold that:

Where an offer is made by a claimant, that offer is not accepted and the claimant recovers more as a result of summary judgment, it is possible for the court, exercising its general jurisdiction, to award a higher rate of interest than the standard rate. Courts should bear this in mind, otherwise claimants might not wish to apply for summary judgment because they could achieve higher rates by going to trial.

The status of offers which do not fall within CPR Part 36 was further considered in *Amber* v. *Stacey* ([2001] 1 WLR 1225, CA) where it was held that a written offer is not to be treated as a precise equivalent of a payment in when the court is considering costs.

Fast track cases

These will be particularly difficult as the amounts being argued over are relatively low. Further in certain types of litigation it is very difficult to predict the amount the judge may award, e.g. general damages in personal injury cases.

How will the court view parties who have gone to trial over, say, £500? The defendant may have made a pre-action offer of £5,000 and then paid this into court and the claimant may have made an offer to settle of £5,500. Is it in accordance with the overriding objective and proportionate to use up the court's time fighting over such a small amount? Might clever wording of letters lead to this being argued on costs at the end of a fast track trial (assuming the judge is prepared to hear anything but the sketchiest arguments on costs on the summary assessment)? The fact that 10 per cent of the costs is at stake is not so strong an argument when that amounts to £500 rather than the £50,000 that might be being argued over in a multi-track case.

Clarification

The offeree who wishes to seek clarification of a Part 36 offer or payment has seven days from receipt to do so (CPR Rule 36.9). If none is forthcoming, the offeree may apply for an order. Case law is inconsistent on the meaning of clarification.

Timetable

A close eye should be kept on the timetable. It is important to accept within 21 days if possible, as accepting late could have adverse costs consequences, i.e. additional costs to be agreed with offeror, or costs imposed by the court if permission is needed.

Improving the offer or payment

Consideration should be given to the need to improve the offer or payment. In some cases, the longer it takes to settle the action, the more the damages increase. In other cases, changes in circumstances may mean that the damages decrease, so that it might be desirable to revise the offer.

Are the rules on additional interest enforceable?

Certain commentators have suggested that the rules on additional interest are unenforceable because they are ultra vires. This argument is discussed by Stephen Stewart QC in [1993] *Journal of Personal Injury Litigation* 145. Until this is clarified by amendment to primary legislation or in case law, a real problem exists.

There has been one case that has considered this question (*All-In-One Design and Build Ltd* v. *Motcomb Estates Ltd*, *The Times*, 4 April 2000) which held that the rules are not ultra vires.

Counterclaims

In cases where there is a counterclaim, the offer or notice of payment must be carefully drafted to make it clear whether the counterclaim is taken into account.

Interest

The general rule is that any offer or payment will be treated as inclusive of interest until the last date on which it could be accepted without requiring the permission of the court (CPR Rule 36.22). If the offer or notice of payment is expressed not to be inclusive of interest, it is important to remember that it must also state whether any interest is offered and if so the amount, the rate or rates offered and the period for which it is offered.

Clearly the most straightforward approach is to make an offer or payment which includes interest.

PRACTICAL POINTS FOR CLAIMANTS

Level of offer

It is important not to make either too high an offer or too low; the first is dangerous on costs, the second will lead to an under-settlement. This approach goes against all that one is taught in relation to negotiating techniques where the advice is to aim high.

Assessing quantum early

Claimants will need to pay special attention to quantum perhaps earlier than in the past, so that they can take advantage of the offer to settle procedure.

Early offers

The higher interest and indemnity costs are not available to a claimant who beats the defendant's offer or payment, therefore a claimant ought to be aiming to put in an offer to settle *before* the defendant comes in with a pre-action offer or payment into court. It is unclear what will happen if the claimant beats the payment in and their own offer.

Procedural questions

A claimant should consider whether to withdraw the offer to settle made before proceedings are begun and turn it into a Part 36 offer on commencement of proceedings. This ensures that the claimant is eligible for indemnity costs and additional interest and enables updating of the offer. The pre-trial period will be 'taken into account on costs'.

It is important not to make an offer too early. The court may not allow additional interest or indemnity costs when the offer is beaten because the information available to the offeree at the time the offer was made was not sufficient to enable a decision on acceptance to be made (see CPR Rule 36.22). Even worse, if the party has not been open and prompt about information, the result might be a wasted costs order. This is illustrated and emphasised by para. 3.21 of the Personal Injury Protocol, which now concludes with the following:

> Parties should always consider before issuing if it is appropriate to make a Part 36 offer. If such an offer is made, the party making the offer must always supply sufficient evidence and/or information to enable the offer to be properly considered.

It is also vitally important to get the procedure right, as if not, the costs and other consequences set out in the Rule do not apply and the party will have to rely entirely on the discretion of the court.

Failure to beat the defendant's offer or payment

Under the old rules the costs sanction, although discretionary, was almost invariably applied to the maximum whatever the circumstances and whether the payment in was not beaten by £1 or £1,000. The CPR place emphasis on applying costs sanctions unless it is unjust to do so. If the claimant fails to beat the payment in by £1, he or she should be ready to argue that it would be unjust to apply the full costs sanction and make the claimant pay all the defendant's costs from payment in. The court may feel, however, that continuing to fight on after what was clearly a very accurate payment in does not accord with the overriding objective of seeking to avoid litigation.

There have been some decided cases on this issue. In *Ford* v. *GKR Construction* (*The Times*, 4 November 1999, CA), the claimant failed to beat the defendant's payment into court. Nevertheless the Court of Appeal upheld a costs order in the claimant's favour. The defendant had left it until after an adjournment of the trial to produce video evidence of the claimant which led to the lower award of damages. Comments were made by the Court of Appeal about the importance of the offeree being in possession of all relevant information before an offer is effective.

In *Jones (Marilyn)* v. *Jones (Margaret)* (*The Times*, 11 November 1999, CA), the claimant failed to beat the payment in and argued that she should have her costs up to a date some four months later than the payment in which was when the defendants disclosed a further medical report. The Court of Appeal disagreed.

In *Burton* v. *Cannon* ([2000] LTL, 4 May 2000), the claimant was awarded £2,000. She alleged she had had to leave the police force because of her injuries. Video evidence showed otherwise. There had been an offer of £10,000 three days before trial. The claimant had to pay the costs of the three day trial (around £15,000) but was awarded the majority of her pre-trial costs.

PERSONAL INJURY CASES

Road traffic accidents

Practice Direction to CPR Part 36, para. 11.2, reminds defendants in road traffic accident cases that if they pay damages for hospital expenses directly to the hospital, then notice of that payment must be given to the court and all other parties.

Deduction of benefits

The compensation recovery system creates difficulties where payments are concerned. The new rules have tried to make the position clearer than it was before. CPR Rule 36.23 provides that a notice of payment must state:

- the gross compensation;
- the name and amount of any benefit deducted;
- that the sum paid in is the net amount after deduction of benefits.

Before this Rule came into effect it was not clear that the payment notice had to contain all this information. Many notices were unclear and there was particular difficulty in discovering exactly which benefits had actually been deducted. There had also been debate about whether it was necessary to beat the net or the gross payment in, in order to avoid the adverse costs consequences. It is now clear from the Rule that the claimant must beat the gross sum.

A payment in may be made some time before there is an application to take the money out of court. Where this is the case, the court may reduce the amount to be paid out to take account of any further benefits to be deducted and pay out accordingly, i.e. reduce the amount to paid to the claimant and pay out the balance to the defendant for reimbursement of DHSS.

Defendants may wish to make an offer or payment to try to settle the case and otherwise protect themselves on costs but may not yet have the necessary certificate of recoverable benefits. If proceedings have commenced, the defendant may, instead of paying into court, make an offer provided that at the time he does so he has applied for the certificate and provided that he makes a payment not more that seven days after he receives the certificate.

B. STATEMENTS OF CASE

INTRODUCTION (A)

This part of the chapter will look at the new rules on drafting statements of case (formerly pleadings), amendments to statements of case, and requests for further information. It will consider the major changes:

- the rules on particulars of claim are now inclusionary rather than exclusionary;
- defences are required to be more detailed;
- further and better particulars and interrogatories have been replaced by requests for further information.

This part will also look at practical considerations:

- how much to include in the particulars of claim;
- ensuring that defences are not defective;
- using statements of case to achieve other objectives.

PARTICULARS OF CLAIM: IN GENERAL

The rules on particulars of claim are to be found in CPR Part 16 and the accompanying Practice Direction.

Contents

Particulars of claim must include:

- a concise statement of facts;
- a claim for interest (if being sought) and details of that claim;
- a claim for aggravated, exemplary or provisional damages and the grounds for claiming them (if relevant);
- if relying on a conviction, details of that conviction (Practice Direction to CPR Part 16, para. 10.1);
- particulars of any devolution issues raised (Practice Direction on Devolution, para. 16.2).

This part of the CPR (Rule 16.4) and the Practice Direction are the same as the previous rules.

Statement of truth

Particulars of claim must be verified by a statement of truth (see CPR Part 22 and the Practice Direction to that Part as to who may sign the statement of truth). If the particulars of claim are being filed and served with the claim form, then it seems that the signature on the claim form will suffice, but if the particulars are filed and served separately then the statement of truth will be required. To make or cause to be made a false statement without honest belief in its truth, is a contempt of court (CPR Rule 32.14). However, proceedings for contempt may not always result as the court can use other sanctions (see *Blue Triangle Cars Ltd* v. *Phillips* (unreported, 3 Feb 2000): statement of truth obviously incorrect, held to be abuse of process).

Serving the particulars of claim

If practicable the particulars should be filed and served with the claim form but if not within 14 days of service of the claim form (see Practice Direction to CPR Part 16, para. 3). In the latter case the claim form must state that particulars of claim will follow. In the Commercial Court particulars are served after the service of the acknowledgment of service (see *Commercial Court Guide*).

Particular types of claim

Paragraph 4 of the Practice Direction to CPR Part 16 sets out specific matters which must be included in certain types of claim. It covers:

- personal injury claims;
- fatal accident claims;
- recovery of land;
- hire purchase claims;
- defamation claims.

Nothing in para. 4 should come as a surprise as it largely replicates what was in the old rules on pleadings.

Other matters to be included

It is here (para. 9) that we find the major changes. In particular:

(a) where a claim is based on a written contract, a copy of the contract or documents constituting the agreement and any general conditions of sale which are part of the contract should be attached (unless it is bulky in which case it is enough to serve part of the documentation);

(b) where a claim is based on an oral contract, the contractual words used and details of who made them to whom and when and where they were spoken should be set out;

    (c) where a claim is based on an agreement by conduct, details must be set out.

Further, in para. 10.2 we see that the claimant must specifically set out the following if they are being relied on:

- fraud, illegality, misrepresentation;
- breaches of trust;
- notice or knowledge of a fact;
- unsoundness of mind, undue influence, wilful default;
- any facts relating to mitigation of damage.

Under the old rules these matters were required to be set out in a defence but there was no particular requirement for them to be included in the particulars of claim except as far as was necessary under the general rules of pleading.

While it may be sensible to require details of most of the allegations in the above list, it seems strange to require the claimant to plead positively to mitigation. In the past, if the defendant wished to argue failure to mitigate he did so in the defence, it was not for the claimant to plead a positive case on mitigation.

PRACTICAL MATTERS

Details of contracts

Important questions are how far will it be necessary to include this information? Will particulars be struck out, or will the court refuse to issue proceedings if details of contracts are not included? There appears to be no consistent approach at present.

For example, if a solicitor is running a debt collection service for a business client who takes most of the orders over the telephone, how much information should be in the particulars of claim? In the past, the solicitor may have started (or the computerised debt recovery case management system might have provided) particulars of claim as follows:

> The plaintiff's claim is for £500 being the price of law books sold and delivered by the plaintiff to the defendant on 1st April 1999 and for interest thereon under section 69 of the County Courts Act 1984.

Now it may be necessary to draft that paragraph as follows:

1. On 1st April 1999 Lovely Law Books agreed to sell and deliver legal text-books to Caroline Harmer.
2. The price of the legal textbooks was £500.
3. The agreement to sell legal textbooks was made over the telephone between Tracy for Lovely Law Books and Samantha for Caroline Harmer.
4. The legal textbooks were delivered to Caroline Harmer on 26th April 1999.

Mitigation

Will it now be necessary for the claimant to include a paragraph in every particulars of claim to the following effect?

The claimant has made every effort to mitigate his losses including in particular the following:

a. he has attended 25 job interviews without success;
b. he has borrowed a neighbour's car while his was off the road awaiting repair;
c. he has undergone private physiotherapy treatment;
d. he has attended all medical consultations required of him and completed all recommended treatment.

The author's view is that this was included in the requirements for particulars of claim by an oversight. There is no mention of it in the requirements for the defence. Perhaps, however, a paragraph such as the above would be useful in order to discover what the defendants are arguing on mitigation. How will they respond?

> The defendants neither admit not deny paragraph X as they have no knowledge of the facts stated therein. However, the defendants deny that he has fully miti-gated his loss as he has not returned to work when the medical evidence of Dr Bones clearly states that he is fit to do so.

A recent case (*Cooper* v. *P & O Stena Line Ltd* [1999] 1 Lloyd's Rep 734) has said that where the defendant alleges malingering then, because it is effectively an allegation of fraud, it must be pleaded specifically. This case was decided under the old rules but, in the author's view, is even more relevant under the new rules.

PERSONAL INJURY CASES

Contents of particulars of claim

Under the Practice Direction to CPR Part 16, para. 4.1, the particulars must contain the claimant's date of birth and brief details of the claimant's injuries. This was required under the old rules. It seems that recent practice is to include more detail of the injuries than before.

Fatal accident cases

In fatal accident cases (see Practice Direction to CPR Part 16, para. 5.1) further details are required namely:

(a) that it is a Fatal Accidents Act 1976 claim;

(b) the name and date of birth of the dependants on whose behalf the claim is brought, and

(c) details of the dependency claim.

The particulars of claim should also include details of any claim for bereavement damages where relevant.

The Fatal Accident Act 1976 claim may be combined with a claim under the Law Reform (Miscellaneous) Provisions Act 1934 on behalf of the estate. If this is the case, then care must be taken to make this clear. It is suggested that the particulars should be clearly set out in two different sections with the relevant Act being stated in each section.

Provisional damages

If provisional damages are being claimed then further details need to be included as was also the case under the old rules. The chance of a serious deterioration or disease developing must be set out and the disease or deterioration specified.

Accompanying documents

Any personal injury claim form must generally be accompanied by, or if not followed by, the particulars of claim together with a report from a medical practitioner, where the claimant is relying on the evidence of such a person, and a schedule of details of any past and future expenses and losses which he or she claims. The medical report should be 'about the personal injuries which he alleges in his claim'.

There may be some debate about whether claiming for such heads of damage as loss of congenial employment or loss of earning capacity needs to be specified in the schedule or whether they follow naturally from the facts of the case. In the author's view, a claimant should, as a matter of good practice, set out all the heads of damage claimed. Further, they may wish to use the Scott Schedule approach to heads of claim, particularly as this will lead to greater clarity in any defences that comply with the CPR.

OTHER PARTICULAR TYPES OF CLAIM

Recovery of land

The particulars of claim must contain those matters set out in the Practice Direction to CPR Part 16, para. 6. These largely replicate what was in the previous rules.

Hire purchase claims

Paragraph 7 of the Practice Direction to CPR Part 16 sets out the many details required to be provided in the particulars of claim. These are the same as under the old rules; however, the language is clearer and plainer than before.

FURTHER SIGNIFICANT MATTERS TO NOTE

Human rights

The Practice Direction to CPR Part 16, para. 16 provides that any party who seeks to rely on any provision of, or right arising under the Human Rights Act 1998, or seeks a remedy available under that Act, must state that fact in his statement of case and provide the details required by the Practice Direction.

Declaration or injunction

If a claim is made for a declaration or injunction relating to land then the claim must state whether or not it is in respect of residential premises and identify the land by reference to a plan where necessary.

Consumer credit

A useful reminder is that where a claim is brought in the High Court relating to a consumer credit agreement, the particulars of claim must state that it is not one which must be brought in the county court (see Practice Direction to CPR Part 16, para. 9.6). If a case is started in the wrong court, then it may be struck out or transferred down with possible costs consequences.

Foreign currency

If the claim is for a sum of money expressed in foreign currency then the details in Practice Direction to CPR Part 16, para. 11.1 must be set out.

Points of law

Paragraph 16.3 at the very end of the Practice Direction to CPR Part 16 sets out a few lines which could lead to the biggest change of all in how cases are stated, if both practitioners and judges embrace its objectives.

It provides that a party may refer to any point of law on which his claim or his defence is based. Points of law were not generally to be pleaded under the old rules although they sometimes were. Legal argument can therefore be set out and in a straightforward case this might be very useful as the statement of case could effectively be the skeleton argument for the fast track trial.

Evidence

Paragraph 16.3 also provides that a party may name any witness he or she proposes to call. This may give added weight to an allegation or point raised in a defence.

Documents

Paragraph 16.3 further provides that a party may attach to or serve with the statement of case a copy of any document which is necessary for the claim or defence, and this includes an expert's report. In fast track cases, the statement of case could therefore be compendious and could, in effect, be the trial bundle. This has the advantages, first, that the other side can see the strength of the serving party's case thereby, it is to be hoped, promoting settlement, especially if the statement of case is backed by an updated offer to settle or payment in; secondly, it may remove the need to make disclosure, which is something to be avoided in fast track cases particularly when trying to make costs proportionate;

thirdly, the compendious statement of case becomes in effect a trial bundle with the result that very little further paperwork needs to be prepared for the bundle; and lastly, the district judge or Master when considering the papers at the allocation stage may be so impressed by the strength of the case, that he or she decides of their own volition to arrange a summary judgment hearing (see below).

THE DEFENCE

It is here that real changes have been made. Although many defences, particularly in commercial cases, were pleaded in a detailed way by specifically answering allegations made in the statement or particulars of claim, others, particularly in personal injury and other negligence cases, were no more than bare denials.

Even before the Civil Procedure Rules were implemented some district judges had started to strike out bare denials of their own motion, but the practice was not widespread.

The rule of implied admissions in the High Court meant that defences in High Court proceedings needed to be more carefully drafted than in the county court where no such rule existed.

The main changes are:

- all defences must be specifically pleaded;
- bare denials are no longer acceptable;
- the rule of implied admissions applies to all courts.

CPR Rule 16.5 provides that a defendant in his defence must state:

(a) which of the allegations he denies, the reasons for so doing and if he intends to put forward a different version of events, his own version;

(b) which allegation he is unable to admit or deny and therefore requires the claimant to prove;

(c) which allegations he admits.

The Rule further provides that if the defendant fails to deal with an allegation, he shall be taken to admit it unless on considering the defence it is clear that he has 'set out . . . the nature of his case in relation to the issue to which that allegation is relevant'.

Rule 16.6 allows a defendant who claims he is entitled to money from the claimant and is relying on this as a complete or partial defence, to include this in the defence without having to bring a separate CPR Part 20 claim. As the note to this rule in the Green Book explains 'The law relating to set off is complex and often depends on the nature of the relevant transaction'. Explanation is given of some of the main principles concerning set off and the distinction between a set off alone and one by way of counterclaim is outlined. It is recommended that practitioners should make certain that the rules and case law on this topic are understood before deciding which course of action to adopt.

Paragraphs 11 to 14 of the Practice Direction to CPR Part 16 set out further requirements for the drafting of defences.

Personal injury cases

In addition to dealing properly with every allegation in the particulars of claim, the Practice Direction to CPR Part 16 provides that the defendant should in relation to a medical report served with the particulars of claim, state whether he agrees, disputes (and if so why) or neither agrees nor disputes but has no knowledge of the matters in the report. If the defendant has obtained his own medical report then this must be attached to the defence.

Further where the claimant has complied with the CPR and filed and served a schedule of past and future expenses and losses, the defendant should attach a counter schedule stating which items he agrees, which he disputes (and if so supply alternative figures 'where appropriate') and which he has no knowledge of.

All cases

As with particulars of claim, the defence may include any point of law on which the defence is based, the name of any witnesses to be called, and there may be attached any documents which are considered necessary to the defence including any expert's report.

Additional requirements

If the defendant wishes to dispute the claimant's statement of value in the claim form, he must state this in the defence and say why and if possible give his statement of value. If defending in a representative capacity, this must stated and explained. If no acknowledgement of service has been filed, an address for service must be given in the defence. Details must be given of the expiry of any limitation period if that is being relied on. The defence of tender has to be set out as required in CPR Rule 37.2.

Statement of truth

Defendants must ensure that defences contain a statement of truth. If there is no such statement, the claimant might apply to strike out the defence or wait until trial and deal with the matter at that stage. It is important to make certain that the right person signs the statement of truth.

FAILURE TO COMPLY WITH THE CPR

If statements of case are not properly drafted there are a variety of possible sanctions.

(1) Rule 3.4 and the Practice Direction to CPR Part 3 make it clear that the court has the power to strike out statements of case which do not comply with the rules either on application by a party or on its own initiative.

(2) Badly drafted statements of case which need amendment may lead to adverse costs orders, summarily assessed and payable within 14 days.

(3) Summary judgment may be granted, e.g. where the defendant has failed properly to respond to an allegation in the particulars of claim.

(4) Early and sequential exchange of witness statements may be ordered against a party whose statement of case is defective, rather than an order that amendments be made.

Parties should be advised against taking too many detailed points on statements of case. In *McPhilemy* v. *Times Newspapers Ltd* [1999] 3 All ER 775, CA, a libel action, Lord Woolf remarked that contests over the terms of pleadings were to be discouraged.

Defence to counterclaim

Failure to file a defence to a counterclaim entitles the party making the counterclaim (CPR Part 20 claimant) to judgment in default (CPR Rule 12.3(2)). This will not surprise those used to dealing with High Court litigation under the old rules, but it may well catch out those who were county court litigators because under the old rules failure to file a defence to counterclaim in the county court did not entitle the defendant to judgment.

Reply to defence

There is no requirement that one be filed (see CPR Rule 16.7). If one is filed but it fails to deal with a matter raised in the defence this is not fatal to the claimant's case for the Rule provides that in this case the claimant shall be taken to require the matter to be proved.

It is important to remember that a statement of truth will be required as before.

Amendments

Paragraph 11.2 of the Practice Direction to CPR Part 16 reminds us that a later statement of case must not contradict or be inconsistent with an earlier one. If that were the case, any resulting delay or confusion could easily rebound on the party in default through costs orders.

The Practice Direction advises that if new matters have come to light the appropriate course 'may be' to seek leave to amend. If a party wishes to alter the factual basis of a claim or defence, his credibility is suspect because he will already have signed the statement of truth as to the facts initially included in his statement of case. Where new facts have come to light since the signing of the statement of truth, an amendment will not have this consequence.

Requests for further information

The old rules on interrogatories and further and better particulars have gone (and we may say good riddance to them). In their place, CPR Part 18 provides that each party may apply for an order that the other party clarify any matter in dispute or give additional information whether or not the matter is contained or referred to in a statement of case. This will be subject always to keeping an eye on the overriding objective and proportionality. The old tactic of using further and better particulars to create delay should be less easy to indulge in under the new rules. Applying for further information is not subject to any other limitations. The application is made under CPR Part 23 following a written request for further information. The request for information and the answer must be set out in the same way as the old request and reply to further and better particulars. Answers must be verified by a statement of truth.

Before applying for further information, alternatives should be considered. It may be better, e.g. to seek early exchange of witness statements possibly on a sequential basis. This reduces the number of stages to go through and incurs less costs.

C. SUMMARY DISPOSAL

This part of the chapter looks at what used to be called Order 14 proceedings, namely applying for summary judgment. In the past the application was reasonably straightforward but success was more difficult, particularly outside the Royal Courts of Justice where the district judges were always said to adopt a more lenient approach than the Masters.

We will consider the following major changes:

- defendants may apply for summary judgment;
- the test to be applied has changed;
- the procedure is different.

We will also look at practical considerations:

- when to apply;
- use by defendants;
- when not to apply;
- streamlining the procedure.

WHO MAY APPLY FOR SUMMARY JUDGMENT?

Both the defendant and the claimant may now apply for summary judgment. The application may relate to the whole of the claim, or any issue in the claim. Previously the defendant was unable to apply but if the plaintiff applied could, in certain circumstances under RSC Order 14A, walk away from the application with judgment in his or her favour. However, the court could only give judgment for the defendant where the application fell within Order 14A which was concerned with points of law or interpretation of contract.

Another change concerns small claims. Under the previous rules it was not possible to apply for summary judgment if the claim was a small claim. This no longer applies. (See CPR Rule 24.3 which lists the proceedings where summary judgment is unavailable, namely certain possession proceedings in relation to residential premises; admiralty claims *in rem*; contentious probate.)

Under CPR Part 3 the court has power to dispose of the claim, or part of it, of its own motion in furtherance of the overriding objective. Thus, in theory at least, the court may grant summary judgment without any party making an application. Time will tell how far courts will be prepared to do this. Anecdotal

495

evidence in the time since implementation of the new rules suggests that this power is being used, albeit infrequently.

THE TEST TO BE APPLIED

CPR Rule 24.2 sets out the test to be applied. It is that the claimant has no real prospect of succeeding on the claim or issue; or the defendant has no real prospect of successfully defending the claim or issue; and there is no other reason why the case or issue should be disposed of at trial.

Under the previous rules the ground for applying for summary judgment was that 'the defendant has no defence to the claim or to a particular part of the claim' (county court). The previous High Court rules meant that the plaintiff had to prove that there was no defence and deal with any grounds for defence raised by the defendant.

The Practice Direction to CPR Part 24 originally contained a paragraph which when read together with the Rule appeared to contradict the Rule and suggest that the test was, in fact, the same as under the old rules. This anomaly was removed by the amendments to the Practice Direction which came into effect in September 1999.

Now there is no difference between the tests in either court although exactly where the burden of proof lies, i.e. whether it is more akin to the old High Court rather than the old county court approach, is hard to determine from the rules. Following the amendment to CPR Rule 24, the test is now the same as that which is applied to an application to set aside judgment: the *Saudi Eagle* test ([1986] 2 Lloyd's Rep 221, CA). See also *S* v. *Gloucestershire County Council* [2000] 3 All ER 346, CA.

The judge must not conduct a mini-trial of the issues which would be better investigated at trial and thus should not summarily dispose of issues which require this approach (*Swain* v. *Hillman* (*The Times*, 4 November 1999, CA)).

PROCEDURE

An application may be made once the defendant has filed an acknowledgment of service or a defence unless the court gives permission or a Practice Direction provides otherwise (CPR Rule 24.4(1)). If the claimant applies after the acknowledgment of service, the defendant is not required to file a defence before the hearing.

At least 14 days notice of the hearing must be given as must notice of the issues to be decided at that hearing unless, of course, the court decides to grant summary judgment of its own motion, in which case CPR Rule 3.3 applies.

The application will be made according to the general requirements of CPR Part 23. It should be noted, however, that the time limits in CPR Part 23 are overridden by those in CPR Part 24.

Part 24 provides that written evidence does not have to be filed or served if this has already been done. Indeed, it seems that it is not mandatory to file and serve written evidence at all.

It also provides that if the applicant wishes to rely on written evidence then this must be filed and served at least three days before the hearing. If the respondent wishes to rely on written evidence, then the time limit is at least seven days before the hearing.

If the court fixes the hearing of its own initiative, then any party who wishes to rely on written evidence must file and serve it within seven days of the hearing and must file and serve any evidence in reply within three days of the hearing.

The court's powers are: to give judgment on the claim or any issue in it; striking out or dismissal of the claim; dismissal of the application; a conditional order which is one which requires a party to pay a sum of money into court and gives directions as to the filing and service of a defence and provides strike out as a sanction for non-compliance. If a conditional order is made the court may make any further case management directions it wishes. The footnote to para. 5 of the Practice Direction to CPR Part 24 emphasises that the court will not follow its former practice of granting unconditional or conditional leave to defend.

The Practice Direction also makes specific reference to claims where an account or inquiry is sought (para. 6) or where specific performance is sought (para. 7).

Costs will be either fixed costs or interim costs which may be summarily assessed if the hearing lasts a day or less.

PRACTICAL CONSIDERATIONS

When to apply

In accordance with the overriding objective it would seem right to apply as soon as possible. For the claimant this is likely to be after the acknowledgment of service in a very clear cut case, or in a less clear cut case possibly waiting until a defence has been put in and then making the application at the same time as returning the allocation questionnaire. If the application is made when returning the allocation questionnaire, many courts do not require the completion of the rest of the questionnaire until the application for summary judgment has failed.

For the defendant it would seem right to apply after returning the acknowledgment of service if the argument is that the claim discloses no cause of action. If the argument is that the defendant has a complete defence to the claim, then this should wait until the defence is filed and served, giving the claimants the opportunity to discontinue and thereby controlling the costs.

Defendants making use of CPR Part 24

There appears to be nothing in the rules which stops a defendant applying for summary judgment against him or herself. This might seem a very unusual application. However, in a case where liability is in dispute the application might be a clearer way of disposing of quantum arguments than a payment into court which involves parting with money and risking acceptance by the claimant in a case where the defendant believes he or she has a strong defence.

Defendants may wish to apply for summary judgment in relation to some of the issues where the claimant has listed several heads of claim in their particulars of claim. Although parties may be penalised in costs at the end of the case for pursuing unnecessary issues, their opponents might also be criticised for not seeking to dispose of these issues at an earlier stage.

D. WITNESS STATEMENTS AND EVIDENCE

EVIDENCE: CPR PART 32

CPR Part 32 gives wide powers to the court to control evidence. CPR Rule 32.1 provides that through directions the court may decide which issues it wishes to hear evidence on, what type of evidence that may be (witnesses, statements etc.) and the way in which evidence is to be put before the court, e.g. by video link (see CPR Rule 32.3).

CPR Rule 32.2 gives the court power to exclude otherwise admissible evidence. This may work in favour of a party, e.g. where the court excludes evidence which is more prejudicial than probative (see *Grobbelaar* v. *Sun Newspapers Ltd* (*The Times*, 12 August 1999, CA).

CPR Rule 32.1(3) allows the court to limit cross-examination. This may be done by laying down a trial timetable in advance which sets out the time allowed for cross-examination, or it may be done at the trial itself by the judge trying to control the time the trial is taking.

Practical points

In seeking to comply with the overriding objective the court may, in its attempt to narrow the issues and cut costs and delay, take control of how a case is to be prepared or presented. Imagine a situation where the statement of case reveals a number of issues on which the solicitor knows he or she has evidence in the form of witnesses or documents. At the directions stage, the court decides that the case is to go forward on some of the issues only and that the number of witnesses is to be limited to two on each side. Disclosure is to be limited to those issues alone. The solicitor has three witnesses, all of whom are essential to presenting the factual story to the court: what is to be done? First, the solicitor should make certain that the allocation questionnaire is completed carefully. To take a simple example: if there are three witnesses to a road traffic accident or an accident at work where the value of the case is clearly within fast track limits, it should be anticipated that some district judges will limit the number of witnesses that may be called on the grounds of proportionality. If all three are to say the same thing, there may be some merit in the district judge's approach. However, if each of the three tells a part of the story – before the accident, the accident itself and after the accident – and all of these facts are necessary, then the solicitor will need to call all three. This should be made clear in the allocation questionnaire. If this is not done, then it may become necessary to appeal the directions, which may not be successful and which could rebound in costs whether successful or not.

If a party is denied the evidence of a witness who it thinks is essential to its case, or if perhaps a case is lost because such evidence has been denied, consideration might be given to a challenge under the Human Rights Act 1998, as Article 6 of the European Convention on Human Rights enshrines the right to a fair trial at a public hearing. Similarly, if the court has limited the right to cross-examine, a Human Rights Act challenge should be considered. Bear in mind always that Lord Woolf in *Daniels* v. *Walker* ([2000] 1 WLR 1382) commented that it was essential that counsel, and those who instructed counsel, took a responsible attitude as to when it was right to raise arguments based on the Human Rights Act 1998 and judges should be robust in resisting inappropriate attempts to introduce such arguments.

CPR Rule 32.2 suggests that witnesses will give oral evidence at trial but paper evidence otherwise. A solicitor may choose to present witness evidence at trial by witness statement alone subject to notice (see below). This of course will save costs. If a witness or party is desired to give oral evidence at any other hearing, then an order of the court must be sought and justified on costs grounds.

The ability to give evidence by video link may be useful, for example where witnesses live in another country and the cost of getting them to the court is disproportionate, or where they refuse to come to this country to give evidence. Video link evidence of lay or expert witnesses may also be useful in seeking to fix an earlier trial date than would be possible were the witness to have to attend court for the trial. However, in these circumstances consideration should also be given to the use of witness statements or the use of depositions (see below).

WITNESS STATEMENTS AND AFFIDAVITS

The CPR have not made major changes to this area, but the following are significant:

- witness statements are preferred to affidavits;
- there is power to order filing of witness statements;
- power to direct the order of exchange;
- power to refuse to allow a witness (see above);
- once served any party may put the witness statement in as evidence;
- evidence at hearings rather than trials may be in any written form;
- use of witness summaries;
- the rules on hearsay notices have been amended;
- there are amended rules on admissibility of plans, photographs etc.

Form of witness statement

The Practice Direction to CPR Part 32 sets out how a witness statement should be headed, what format it should be in and how the body of the witness statement should be drafted. Many of these points were previously in specialised Practice Directions, e.g. *Guide to Commercial Court Practice*, but not in the general rules. The important points to note are that the statement should set out:

(a) name, place of residence or business address, name of employer and position he holds;

(b) occupation or if none description;

(c) that he is a party to the proceedings or the employee of the party;

(d) which, if any, statements are matters of information and belief and if so the source of the matters;

(e) verification and identification of any exhibits (which should remain separate from the statement);

(f) a statement of truth as follows: 'I believe that the facts stated in this witness statement are true' unless the witness is unable to read or sign the statement when it must contain a certificate made by an authorised person (see para. 21). Any alterations must be intialled (para. 22).

Most importantly, the witness statement should be in the witness's own words and should be in the first person.

If the statement or affidavit is not in the correct form then the court may refuse to admit it as evidence and may refuse to allow the costs of its preparation.

The above apply to affidavits as they do to witness statements.

Witness summaries

If it is not possible to obtain a witness statement where ordered to do so, then an application may be made without notice for permission to serve a witness summary instead. A witness summary is one which contains a summary of the evidence the witness will give (if known) or the matters on which the witness will be questioned (if the evidence is not known). The name and address of the witness must be included unless the court orders otherwise.

Use of witness statements in court

There is a stronger presumption that witness statements will stand as evidence-in-chief (CPR Rule 32.5(2)).

It is made clearer than under the old rules, that a witness may amplify his witness statement, and as before give evidence on any new matters that have arisen since exchange (CPR Rule 32.5(3)).

In the past a witness statement, once exchanged, could not be used by the other side if the witness was not called to give evidence and/or the witness statement was not relied on by the serving party. Now it is clear that where a witness statement has been served and the serving party then decides not to call that witness, the other party may make use of it in evidence (see CPR Rule 32.5(5)). The court has no power to order the serving party to call the witness: *Society of Lloyd's* v. *Jaffray* [2000] 2 All ER (Comm) 181.

However, where the purpose of putting in the other side's witness statement (which substantially conflicted with the case being put forward) was to discredit that evidence, it might not be used: *McPhilemy* v. *Times Newspapers Ltd* ([1999] 3 All ER 775, CA).

Under the old rules most applications had to be supported by affidavit. Now it is much easier. Applications must be supported by evidence but the choice as to how this evidence is to be presented is largely that of the applicant. The only proviso is that it must generally be written and in a very few cases must be by affidavit (e.g for freezing orders (once *Mareva* injunctions) or search and seize orders (once *Anton Piller* orders). The other side has the right to apply to the court for permission to cross-examine the person giving the evidence (see CPR Rule 32.7).

A witness may be cross-examined on his witness statement whether or not it was referred to in examination in chief (CPR Rule 32.11). However, the general rule is that the statement may not be used for any other purpose other than the proceedings in which it is served unless the witness consents, the court gives permission or the statement has been put in evidence at a hearing held in public. If it has been put in evidence in chief then it is in any event open for inspection unless the court otherwise directs during the course of the trial.

Filing and serving of witness statements

CPR Rule 32.4(3) provides that the court may give directions as to the order in which witness statements are to be served and whether or not the witness statement is to be filed (see also para. 23 of the Practice Direction to CPR Part 32).

The general approach of the court in fast track cases will be to order simultaneous exchange (see Practice Direction to CPR Part 28, para. 3.9 and Appendix) within 10 weeks from the notice of allocation. The practice at present is to order exchange by a particular date. In multi-track cases the general approach is the same (see Practice Direction to CPR Part 29, para. 4.10). However, para. 4.2 points out that the court will seek to tailor its directions to the needs of the case.

Sequential exchange might be ordered, for example, where a statement of case was defective and where its defects could most easily be remedied by the early exchange of witness statements by that party.

Hearsay evidence

It is made clear that if the hearsay evidence is to be given orally or is contained in a witness statement of a person not being called, notice under Civil Evidence Act 1995 s.2 is given by serving the witness statement and informing the other party that the maker of the statement is not being called and why (see CPR Rule 33.2).

In other cases a notice must be served in accordance with CPR Rule 33.2(3), (4). This would apply to hearsay contained in documents, for example.

As under the old rules, there is provision for the court to order a witness to attend for cross-examination (CPR Rule 33.4) and for the other party to challenge the credibility of the maker of the hearsay statement (CPR Rule 33.5).

Plans, photographs and models etc.

Under the old rules the automatic directions provided for much of this hearsay evidence to be admitted. Now CPR Rule 33.6 provides that as a general rule, a party may only use this evidence if notice has been given to the other side. Notice has to be given where the plan etc. is not contained in a witness statement, or is to be produced by a witness orally at trial or is to be produced in conjunction with a hearsay statement where notice has to be given. Evidence under this rule could include tape recordings and video recordings. The other party must be given an opportunity to inspect it and to agree its admission without further proof.

PRACTICAL MATTERS

Preparation of witness statements and affidavits

The Practice Direction to CPR Part 32 should be followed. The Practice Direction provides in para. 25 that if it is not and the statement or affidavit is not in the correct form, then the court may refuse to admit it as evidence and may refuse to allow the costs of its preparation. It is open to the party who has prepared a defective statement to seek permission to file or use it but as this may not be forthcoming it is obviously better to follow the Practice Direction in the first place.

Judges had been dissatisfied with the way in which witness statements were being prepared for some time (see comments in *ZYX Music GmbH* v. *King* [1995] 3 All ER 1). Not only must they contain the truth and the whole truth but they must not have been edited or improved upon in any way. Solicitors and counsel should resist the temptation to smarten them up – to moderate the language or improve the grammar. A witness statement which on paper reveals a very different character, e.g. in style or manner, to the one appearing in the witness box can only serve to cast doubt on the evidence-in-chief. Witnesses are unlikely to be able to comment on how the law applies to them. Including a comment on the law in a witness statement is not appropriate even though it might be thought useful to have an argument on the law included in the statement for the judge to read. The proper place for legal comment is elsewhere. In the case of *Alex Lawrie Factors Ltd* v. *Morgan* (*The Times*, 18 September 1999, CA), one witness statement contained a comment that the witness had read *Barclays Bank* v. *O'Brien* and indicated how it applied to the case. This was criticised. Witness statements were not the place for lawyers to put forward complex legal argument on which the witness would not be able to speak if cross-examined.

Preparation of witness summaries

There may be occasions where it is not possible to complete a witness statement and where a witness summary will be all that is possible or all that is cost effective. For example, the witness may be unavailable at the time it is necessary to sign and serve the statement; the witness may be in another country where there are difficulties and expense in preparing the statement; the witness may have the right to refuse to give a statement; the witness may not be prepared to sign a statement. Of course, if a party does not know what the witness will say and merely knows the questions that will be put to the witness, that party is indulging a high risk strategy by seeking to rely on that witness.

Any party may make use of witness statement

As any party may make use of a witness statement in evidence, it is clear that statements must be prepared with the issues in mind and not as some kind of 'catch-all' of any of the facts that the witness can remember that may or may not have a bearing on the ultimate issues. It is also clear that witness statements are not exchanged just because they are there: they need proper analysis to see whether they support a party's own case (in which case serve them), they are neutral (in which case do not list the witness on the allocation questionnaire), or even worse they contain evidence which even if it does not actively support the other side casts some doubt on the party's evidence. For example, putting in a witness statement of an eye-witness who does not actually support the party's version of the facts even though it equally does not support the other side, could be dangerous bearing in mind the burden and standard of proof.

Inspection of witness statements

If the witness statement has been put in evidence-in-chief then any person may apply to inspect it; this could include members of the press, or a business rival of the party concerned. Just because it has not been read out in court does not mean that the contents may not be revealed. In fact it is essential to a system of open justice, that evidence given in court is available for scrutiny. With this in mind, however, consideration should be given as a matter of course and particularly in any high profile cases, to seeking a direction that inspection is not to be allowed. The rule gives two obvious examples of when inspection might not be allowed: the nature of any expert medical evidence in the statement, and the nature of any confidential information, e.g. personal financial matters, as well as more general exceptions, e.g. the public interest, and interest of children or patients. This exclusion from inspection may relate to the whole or part of the statement.

Amplifying witness statement

Long witness statements in fast track cases may not be appropriate. If the issues are relatively straightforward and the value of the claim is low, it may be better to keep costs proportionate by providing a witness statement that deals with all the issues but does not include absolutely every single fact. If the case settles no more is needed; if the case goes to trial then the witness may amplify their statement. Costs will have been saved. However, none of the evidence given in amplification should come as a surprise! The CPR Part 32 provides that permission will only be given for amplification or new evidence if there is good reason not to confine the evidence to that in the original statement.

Experience suggests, however, that many judges are reluctant to allow any examination-in-chief, whatever the rules may say.

Hearings

Evidence at an interim application hearing is to be given by witness statement and not affidavit unless the CPR, a Practice Direction or some statutory provision requires an affidavit (CPR Rule 32.6). It may not even be necessary for a separate witness statement to be drafted as the statement of case (signed with the statement of truth) or even the application notice (also signed) may either together or alone provide all the evidence needed. If it is not to be in the form of an affidavit, then the evidence should be in whatever form is most easy to assemble. Much of it may already have been prepared, e.g. statement of case, witness statements. Re-drafting it all for the purpose of an application may not be cost effective. If the litigation plan envisaged applying for summary judgment then this can be anticipated by the way in which the statement of case is put together, e.g. with references to documents and copies attached, with references to witnesses' names. The application notice itself will not need to refer to any other evidence save that the defendant has put in a defence and what the claimant thinks of it! If the statement of case is being used as evidence in support of an interim application, it seems it must again be verified by a statement of truth (see Practice Direction to CPR Part 32, para. 26).

The hearsay rules provide that the other side may apply to cross-examine any witness whose witness statement rather than oral evidence is being relied on and importantly, the failure of that witness to attend if ordered to do so will mean that his evidence may not be used unless the court gives permission. It will therefore be sensible to make certain that witnesses are available on the day fixed for the hearing in the probably unlikely eventuality of needing to attend for cross-examination.

Filing and serving witness statements

In the fast track, consideration should be given as to whether it is necessary to serve witness statements at all or in relation to every witness. If the party's statement of case properly signed with the statement of truth contains all the factual evidence, a witness statement may be unnecessary. If police report statements are sufficient, exchange of witness statements may be avoided. It will, of course, depend on the circumstances of the case. To keep costs proportionate, it is one of the options to take into account when planning the case.

Sequential exchange of witness statements may be appropriate in certain cases, e.g. this may be ordered to fill in missing details in a statement of case rather than ordering more costly amendment. Filing of witness statements might be asked for where an opponent has not been complying with the timetable laid down by the court. The court should then be able to check whether the order has been complied with and apply any sanction laid down in that order for non-compliance.

If statements are not served within the time laid down by the court, then the CPR provide that the parties may agree to a different timetable for exchange provided first that the date for the listing questionnaire and the date for trial are not compromised, and secondly that the timetable did not build in sanctions for late exchange. If a party has served statements late without agreement of the other side or the court, then the trial judge has the discretion to allow or refuse to allow the evidence to be put forward. Buckley J held in *Mealey Horgan plc* v. *Horgan* (*The Times*, 6 July 1999), that a court would use its power to exclude evidence of a party which had failed to serve witness statements only in exceptional cases.

The attitude of the courts to delay seems to have moderated since the introduction of the CPR. In *Cank* v. *Broadyard Associates Ltd* ([2001] CP Rep 47, CA) the Court of Appeal reinstated a defence and counterclaim which had been struck out for failure to file and serve witness statements in time. *Biguzzi* was followed as was *Bansal* v. *Cheema* (unreported, 2 March 2000). In the latter case the judge had failed to apply the factors in CPR Rule 3.9(1) systematically; the judge in *Cann* had failed to consider the checklist of factors; in both cases the judge had erred in imposing a sanction.

In *Kotia* v. *Dewhirst* (unreported, 6 October 1999) the claimant exchanged witness statements late; the claim was allowed to continue but there were costs penalties. The court also made the point that time orders should specify a specific date and time for compliance and the old custom of 'within x days' should be dispensed with.

E. THE TRIAL

The main changes in this area are:

- that fast track trials will last no longer than a day;
- that fast track trial costs are fixed;
- that there will generally be summary assessment of fast track costs at the end of the trial;
- that a trial timetable will be laid down either before the trial or even on the day of the trial itself.

FAST TRACK TRIALS

To last no longer than a day

Fast track trials will be held within 30 weeks of the case being allocated to the fast track. They will last for no more than a day. If for some reason the trial does go into a second day, the costs available to the winning party will still be limited to the fixed costs for a one day trial.

In preparing for a fast track trial, thought should be given to the number of witnesses that are needed and whether or not expert evidence is required at all, is to be given in the form of a report only or is to be given orally. If the number of witnesses or the need for oral expert evidence is such that the trial is likely to last longer than a day, then the district judge will either allocate the case to the multi-track or make directions that limit the number of witnesses of fact and the way in which expert evidence is to be put before the court.

Fixed trial costs

The maximum costs for a fast track trial are limited to £750 where the value of the claim is more than £10,000; £500 where the value is between £3,000 and £10,000 and £350 where the value is below £3,000. Solicitors who attend the trial to sit behind counsel will not be able to claim any costs for so doing unless it is necessary for them to be there in which case the maximum that may be claimed by the winning party is £250. In planning a fast track trial, therefore, the choice of advocate will need careful thought. Will it be possible to instruct counsel within the fast track costs limit or will there be a shortfall in costs paid by the losing party? If the latter is the case, then the winning party will have to pay the difference. If the case is complex, necessitating more senior counsel, then the case could be taken out of the fast track and into the multi-track if the court will allow this to be done.

Summary assessment of costs

At the end of a fast track trial, the general rule is that the costs of the whole of the case will be summarily assessed. A possible, even probable, scenario is as follows: costs will be decided by a judge who has little experience of assessing costs after listening to argument on costs by the advocates on each side who have little experience of dealing with solicitors' costs. If this is the likely scenario, then it is the solicitors' job to ensure that the communication gap is bridged. It will be sensible, in addition to preparing the required schedule of costs, to prepare a short brief to counsel about how the costs were incurred and e.g. why they may seem out of the ordinary in places. Documents may need to be attached, such as letters passing between the parties, which explain how costs of this level came to be incurred.

In the time since the introduction of the Civil Procedure Rules, there has still been no consistency about the judges' approach to summary assessment of costs. Some deal with the matter in a very few minutes, others take considerably longer; some hardly bother to inquire into the costs at all, merely deducting a percentage from the receiving party's bill or, less frequently, allowing it in full; others adjourn the matter for detailed assessment at a later date.

THE TRIAL TIMETABLE

Rather than let a trial take its course with the risk that it may significantly overrun its time estimate, the CPR now provide that a timetable may be laid down for the trial. In both the fast track and the multi-track, as soon as practicable after the date specified for filing a completed listing questionnaire, the court will not only fix the date for trial but give directions for trial including a trial timetable (see CPR Rule 28.6 and Practice Direction to CPR Part 28, para. 8; CPR Rule 29.8 and Practice Direction to CPR Part 29, para. 9). The judge will 'generally have read the papers in the trial bundle and may dispense with an opening address'. He or she may confirm or vary any timetable previously given, or if none set his or her own. In order to ensure that the timetable is as far as possible appropriate to the case, parties should make sure that they comply with the Rule and Practice Direction by giving accurate time estimates, that they know which issues are important and need time given to them, that they agree a timetable before returning the listing questionnaire and therefore seek an agreed direction as to the timetable, and that at the trial itself the time limits are kept to.

F. THE DIFFICULT OPPONENT

The new rules provide many more opportunities than before to try to control the difficult opponent. A good case analysis, clear grasp of the issues, a structured case plan and thorough understanding of the CPR will arm a party's legal adviser with all he or she needs to drive forward the litigation.

Even the difficult client may be brought to a realisation of what is at stake through use of the CPR.

The one real difficulty that has not been addressed by the changes, however, is the service provided by the courts: long hearing dates; trials aborted at the last minute through failure to find a judge; being moved half way round the country for trial; insistence on case management conferences attended by the lawyers from miles away which take 10 minutes and merely confirm what the parties had agreed; allocation questionnaires taking time to be sent out and no timetable imposed upon the court for allocating cases – are all problems encountered daily by practitioners.

The following are suggestions where use of the CPR may help to control the difficult opponent.

MAKING USE OF PROTOCOLS

There are four official Protocols which relate to personal injury claims, to clinical disputes, to construction and engineering disputes and to defamation. Protocols give guidance as to pre-action practice. Failure to comply with a Protocol may lead to orders for indemnity costs against those failing to comply and additional interest or a reduction in interest being awarded against the defaulting party.

The Personal Injury Protocol is particularly relevant to simple fast track claims. More complex claims and larger value claims are not suitable for all the detail of the Protocol but it may be adapted for use in these cases. Industrial disease claims will be the subject of a separate protocol in the near future.

Where there is no official protocol that applies, the Protocols Practice Direction provides that parties act reasonably in exchanging information and documents relevant to the claim and generally to try to avoid the necessity of issuing proceedings. There are many draft protocols in existence but these have not yet been adopted as official protocols. They may nevertheless provide good guidance.

A difficult opponent should be invited to comply with an existing Protocol, or if one is not relevant, with the spirit of protocols. They should be reminded of para. 4 of the Protocols Practice Direction.

A claimant should emphasise in their full letter of claim that they are writing a letter in accordance with a Protocol, or protocol-type behaviour, and should offer the other side an amount of time to respond fully to the letter of claim. If this offer is not taken up by the recalcitrant defendant, then there seems no reason why, if proceedings have to be issued, that this same defendant should be given any extra time for drafting a defence or otherwise preparing to defend the case.

MAKING USE OF CPR PART 36

Pressure may be put on an opponent by the use of CPR Part 36 offers or payments into court. A claimant or defendant may put additional pressure on their opponent by making an offer of settlement before proceedings are commenced. The threat of indemnity costs and penalty interest may be enough to bring a difficult defendant to heel.

MEDIATION

CPR Rule 1.4 provides that the court must further the overriding objective by actively managing cases, which includes 'encouraging the parties to use alternative dispute resolution procedures and helping the parties to settle the whole or part of the case.' Clearly the court cannot suggest mediation until proceedings have been started. Once they have, however, there are various occasions in the CPR which give power to the court to stay for settlement and for mediation. Some courts have a history of encouraging mediation, e.g. the mediation project in the central London County Court and the Practice Directions which encouraged mediation in the Commercial Court.

If the other side is refusing to communicate at all, then it is unlikely that mediation will be of any use whatsoever. However, if one of the problems being faced by the solicitor for other side is an unrealistic expectation by the party concerned, it may be that the other party's solicitors would be happy to suggest mediation.

PUSHING AHEAD WITH LITIGATION

If all attempts at reasonable pre-action behaviour have failed, then the CPR provide a way of dealing with the difficult opponent. Having made certain that every opportunity has been given to the other side to respond and lay their cards on the table, proceedings should be issued. A careful case plan should be drawn up with an expected timetable for the litigation. The plan should include shortening the time limits and the steps necessary for litigation as much as possible.

The issues upon which the case is to be fought should be drawn as narrowly as possible. The statement of case should be drafted within the confines of these issues in a way which leaves the other side very little room to manoeuvre. Bearing in mind how defences now have to be drafted, a defendant can be put on the spot by particularised drafting of statements of claim.

Defendants faced with unnecessary litigation or difficult opponents should make certain that they comply with any pre-action procedures so that when and if litigation starts they are in a position to respond, to make payments in, and to ensure that the claimant does not use time as a weapon to try and force a settlement in a case where there is a good defence.

Using summary judgment

Both sides should consider whether they will be able to use summary judgment in order to attempt to dispose of the litigation as quickly as possible. If it is not possible to dispose of the litigation entirely through the summary judgment procedure, then consideration should be given to narrowing the issues between the parties by disposing of some of them in this way.

Completion of allocation questionnaire

A party completing an allocation questionnaire should do so as fully as possible. This has the advantage of showing that they understand the case and are progressing it sensibly. It also has the added advantage of indicating to the district judge that they have done all that they should have done. If the other side has been obstructive by refusing to comply with the Protocols, refusing to discuss settlement etc., then reference can be made to this in the allocation questionnaire.

Case management conferences

Case management conferences are essential for more complex claims but may not necessarily be useful for more straightforward claims. However, where a difficult opponent is concerned, the case management conference will concentrate the parties' minds. Attendance at the case management conference not only by the parties' lawyers but by the parties themselves may be a very useful way of ensuring that they face the realities of the situation.

Laying down detailed timetables with sanctions

If litigation has commenced and the difficulty being faced is delay, then asking the court to lay down a detailed timetable for the litigation, possibly with sanctions built in such as strike out, may be the way to control the delay. Although such a timetable with sanctions built in is most likely to be imposed at the second attempt to give directions, it might be possible to persuade the district judge or Master to lay down such a timetable from the outset if you can show a history of delay.

Notice to admit facts or documents

Another way to put pressure on a dificult opponent and also to narrow the issues is to make use of the rules which provide for notices to be served to admit facts or to admit documents (see CPR Rules 32.18 and 32.19).

COSTS

Costs estimates

At various stages in the litigation, estimates of costs will have to be given, e.g. with the allocation questionnaire and with the listing questionnaire. No doubt the district judge or Master will also want to hear an update on cost estimates at any case management conference. This may be the first time that the party has really faced up to the cost of litigation. It will also enable the court to attempt to control the costs. If the costs are in danger of becoming disproportionate due to the behaviour of the other side, then it is sensible to be prepared to explain to the court the reason for the excessive costs, namely the difficult behaviour of the opponent.

Summary assessment of costs

If it is necessary for a party to make an interim application to control the other side's behaviour in the litigation, then the party will generally be entitled to an order for costs, assuming it is successful in the application, which are to be summarily assessed and payable within 14 days. As Lord Woolf said in *Biguzzi v. Rank Leisure* (*The Times*, 5 October 1999), 'The ability of the court to make indemnity costs orders and to order that they be paid forthwith was a valuable sanction. For a solicitor to have to justify to his client why he had to be put in funds to meet such an order was particularly valuable for bringing home to the solicitor and the party the consequences of default; particularly if costs were assessed summmarily'.

Costs orders

Finally, if the difficult opponent has led to additional and unnecessary work in the case, an unnecessarily long trial for example, then the court can be invited to make cost orders which reflect its view of the opponent's behaviour. This may include indemnity costs or indeed costs orders against the legal advisors of the opponent (see e.g. *Mars UK Ltd* v. *Teknowledge Ltd (No 2)* (*The Times*, 8 July 1999); *Baron* v. *Lovell* (*The Times*, 14 September 1999, CA). In *Liverpool City Council* v. *Rosemary Chavasse Ltd* ([1999] CPLR 802, Ch D), the claimant was awarded half its costs rather than the three-quarters which it would have received had it behaved reasonably before the issue of proceedings. As the trial bundle contained a great many unnecessary documents, it was awarded only five-eighths of the costs of preparing it.

Practice Rule 13
(supervision and management of a practice)

In this rule, words in italics are defined in the notes.

(1) The *principals* in a practice must ensure that their practice is supervised and managed so as to provide for:

    (a) compliance with principal solicitors' duties at law and in conduct to exercise proper *supervision* over their admitted and unadmitted staff;

    (b) adequate *supervision* and direction of clients' matters;

    (c) compliance with the requirements of sections 22(2A) and 23(3) of the Solicitors Act 1974 as to the direction and *supervision* of unqualified persons;

    (d) effective *management* of the practice generally.

(2) Every practice must have at least one *principal* who is a solicitor *qualified to supervise.*

    (3) (a) Except as provided in (b) below, every office of the practice must have at least one solicitor *qualified to supervise*, for whom that office is his or her normal place of work.

        (b) Without prejudice to the requirements of paragraph (1) of this rule, an office which undertakes only property selling and ancillary mortgage related services as defined in rule 6 of these rules, survey and valuation services, must be managed and supervised to the following minimum standards:

        (i) the day-to-day control and administration must be undertaken by a suitably qualified and experienced office manager who is a fit and proper person to undertake such work; and for whom that office is his or her normal place of work; and

        (ii) the office must be supervised and managed by a solicitor *qualified to supervise*, who must visit the office with sufficient frequency and spend sufficient time there to allow for adequate control of and consultation with staff, and if necessary consultation with clients.

(4) This rule is to be interpreted in the light of the notes, and is subject to the transitional provisions set out in note (k).

    (5) (a) This rule applies to private practice, and to solicitors employed by a law centre.

        (b) The rule also applies to other employed solicitors, but only:

        (i) if they advise or act for members of the public under the legal aid scheme; or

(ii) if, in acting for members of the public, they exercise any *right of audience* or *right to conduct litigation,* or supervise anyone exercising those rights.

Notes

(a) Principals' responsibility for the practice

Principals are responsible at law and in conduct for their practices, and compliance with the rule does not derogate from this responsibility. Under rule 6 of these rules, property selling or mortgage related services to one party to a conveyance, and conveyancing services for the other party, may not be supervised by the same solicitor.

(b) 'Supervision' and 'management'

(i) *'Supervision' refers to the professional overseeing of staff and the professional overseeing of clients' matters.*

(ii) *'Management' is a wider concept, which encompasses the overall direction and development of the practice and its day-to-day control and administration. Management functions include business efficiency as well as professional competence.*

(iii) *Operationally, supervision and management may be delegated within an established framework for reporting and accountability. However, the responsibility under paragraph (1)(a) of the rule, and the responsibility referred to in note (a) above, remain with the principals.*

(iv) *'With sufficient frequency' in paragraph (3)(b)(ii) would normally mean daily; but if the office is open at weekends it may be possible to defer consultations with clients until a weekday and be available only at need to staff.*

(c) Evidence of effective supervision and management

Where a question arises as to compliance with paragraph (1) of the rule, principals will be expected to be able to produce evidence of a systematic and effective approach to the supervision and management of the practice. Such evidence may include the implementation by the practice of one or more of the following:

(i) *guidance on the supervision and execution of particular types of work issued from time to time by the Law Society including:*

(A) *guidance on solicitors' responsibilities for the supervision of clerks exercising rights of audience under section 27(2)(e) of the Courts and Legal Services Act 1990; and*

(B) *good practice guidelines on the recruitment and supervision of employees undertaking investment business;*

(ii) *the practice's own properly documented management standards and procedures;*

(iii) *practice management standards promoted from time to time by the Law Society;*

(iv) *accounting standards and procedures promoted from time to time by the Law Society;*

(v) *external quality standards such as BS EN ISO 9000 or Investors in People; and*

(vi) in the case of solicitors employed by a law centre, any management standards or procedures laid down by its management committee.

(d) 'Qualified to supervise'

A solicitor is qualified to supervise if he or she:

(i) has held practising certificates for at least 36 months within the last ten years; and

(ii) has completed the training specified from time to time by the Law Society for the purpose of the rule.

(e) 'Normal place of work'

(i) A solicitor's 'normal place of work' is the office from which he or she normally works, even though the day-to-day demands of practice may often take the solicitor out of the office.

(ii) If a solicitor normally works from a particular office for a part of the working week, that office is his or her 'normal place of work' for that part of the week. The solicitor may have a different 'normal place of work' for another part of the week.

(iii) A solicitor who has a different 'normal place of work' for different parts of the week could be the sole solicitor qualified to supervise at different offices at different times in the week. However, no solicitor can be the sole solicitor qualified to supervise at two different offices for the same part of the week.

(iv) For compliance with paragraph (3) of the rule, an office must, for every part of the working week, have a solicitor qualified to supervise for whom that office is his or her 'normal place of work' for that part of the week. This could be a different solicitor for different parts of the week.

(v) The working week of an office includes early mornings, late evenings and weekends if work is carried on, and if so the office must have a solicitor qualified to supervise for those times. However, it is not required that the solicitor qualified to supervise normally works at those times, provided that he or she:

(A) is available for emergency consultation; and

(B) pays occasional visits to the office during such times.

(f) Working away from the office

It is particularly important that systems of supervision and management encompass the work of:

(i) those persons from time to time working away from the office – e.g. at home, visiting clients, at court, at a police station, at a consulting room open only for a few hours per week, or staffing a stand at an exhibition;

(ii) any person who normally works away from the office, such as a teleworker or homeworker.

(g) Absence of solicitor qualified to supervise, or office manager

(i) When the solicitor qualified to supervise at an office is away on holiday, on sick leave, etc., suitable arrangements must be in place to ensure that any *duties to clients and others are fully met. A similar standard applies to the absence of an office manager with responsibility for the day-to-day control and administration of a property selling office.*

(ii) If the solicitor qualified to supervise will be away for a month or more, the arrangements will normally need to include the provision of another solicitor qualified to supervise at that office. A similar standard applies to the absence of an office manager with responsibility for the day-to-day control and administration of a property selling office.

(h) 'Right of audience' and 'right to conduct litigation'
'Right of audience' and 'right to conduct litigation' are to be interpreted in accordance with Part II and section 119 of the Courts and Legal Services Act 1990.

(i) Recognised bodies
'Principal', in relation to a recognised body, means a director of that body.

(j) Registered foreign lawyers
(i) A registered foreign lawyer who is a principal in the practice may fulfil the role of a 'solicitor qualified to supervise' for the purpose of paragraph (2) of the rule, provided that:

(A) the practice has at least one principal who is a solicitor; and

(B) the practice does not exercise or assume responsibility for any right of audience or any right to conduct litigation; and

(C) the registered foreign lawyer has practised as a lawyer for at least 36 months within the last ten years; and

(D) he or she has completed the training specified under note (d)(ii) above.

(ii) A registered foreign lawyer who is a principal in the practice may fulfil the role of a 'solicitor qualified to supervise' for the purpose of paragraph (3) of the rule or note (k)(ii)(C) below, provided that:

(A) no right of audience or right to conduct litigation is exercised or supervised from that office; and

(B) the registered foreign lawyer has practised as a lawyer for at least 36 months within the last ten years; and

(C) he or she has completed the training specified under note (d)(ii) above.

(k) Transitional provisions
For a period of 10 years from 23rd December 1999:

(i) a solicitor or registered foreign lawyer who would not satisfy the requirements for a solicitor qualified to supervise can nevertheless fulfil that role for the purpose of paragraph (2) of the rule or note (k)(ii)(C) below, provided that:

(A) immediately before 12th December 1996 he or she was qualified to supervise an office under practice rule 13(1)(a) as it then stood, or any waiver of that rule; and

(B) any requirements of that rule or of any waiver continue to be met;

(ii) *a person who would not satisfy the requirements for a solicitor qualified to supervise can nevertheless fulfil that role for the purpose of paragraph (3) of the rule, provided that:*

> *(A)* *immediately before 12th December 1996 he or she was managing or employed to manage an office in compliance with practice rule 13(1)(b) as it then stood, or any waiver of that rule; and*
> *(B)* *any requirements of that rule or of any waiver continue to be met; and*
> *(C)* *the office is attended on a daily basis by a solicitor qualified to supervise.*

Practice Rule 15
(costs information and client care)

Solicitors shall:

(a) give information about costs and other matters, and

(b) operate a complaints handling procedure,

in accordance with a Solicitors' Costs Information and Client Care Code made from time to time by the Council of the Law Society with the concurrence of the Master of the Rolls, but subject to the notes.

Notes

(i) A serious breach of the code, or persistent breaches of a material nature, will be a breach of the rule, and may also be evidence of inadequate professional services under section 37A of the Solicitors Act 1974.

(ii) Material breaches of the code which are not serious or persistent will not be a breach of the rule, but may be evidence of inadequate professional services under section 37A.

(iii) The powers of the Office for the Supervision of Solicitors on a finding of inadequate professional services include:

(a) disallowing all or part of the solicitor's costs; and

(b) directing the solicitor to pay compensation to the client up to a limit of £1,000.

(iv) Non-material breaches of the code will not be a breach of the rule, and will not be evidence of inadequate professional services under section 37A.

(v) Registered foreign lawyers, although subject to Rule 15 as a matter of professional conduct, are not subject to section 37A. However, solicitor partners in a multi-national partnership are subject to section 37A for professional services provided by the firm.

APPENDIX 3

Solicitors' Costs Information and Client Care Code

1. Introduction

(a) This code replaces the written professional standards on costs information for clients (see paragraphs 3–6) and the detail previously contained in Practice Rule 15 (client care) (see paragraph 7).

(b) The main object of the code is to make sure that clients are given the information they need to understand what is happening generally and in particular on:

    (i)   the cost of legal services both at the outset and as a matter progresses; and

    (ii) responsibility for clients' matters.

(c) The code also requires firms to operate a complaints handling procedure.

(d) It is good practice to record in writing:

    (i)   all information required to be given by the code including all decisions relating to costs and the arrangements for updating costs information; and

    (ii) the reasons why the information required by the code has not been given in a particular case.

(e) References to costs, where appropriate, include fees, VAT and disbursements.

2. Application

(a) The code is of general application, and it applies to registered foreign lawyers as well as to solicitors. However, as set out in paragraph 2(b), parts of the code may not be appropriate in every case, and solicitors should consider the interests of each client in deciding which parts not to apply in the particular circumstances.

(b) The full information required by the code may be inappropriate, for example:

    (i)   in every case, for a regular client for whom repetitive work is done, where the client has already been provided with the relevant information, although such a client should be informed of changes; and

    (ii) if compliance with the code may at the time be insensitive or impractical. In such a case relevant information should be given as soon as reasonably practicable.

(c) Employed solicitors should have regard to paragraphs 3–6 of the code where appropriate, e.g. when acting for clients other than their employer. Paragraph 7 does not apply to employed solicitors.

(d) Solicitors should comply with paragraphs 3–6 of the code even where a client is legally aided if the client may have a financial interest in the costs because contributions are payable or the statutory charge may apply or they may become liable for the costs of another party.

(e) The code also applies to contingency fee and conditional fee arrangements and to arrangements with a client for the solicitor to retain commissions received from third parties.

3. Informing the client about costs

(a) Costs information must not be inaccurate or misleading.

(b) Any costs information required to be given by the code must be given clearly, in a way and at a level which is appropriate to the particular client. Any terms with which the client may be unfamiliar, for example 'disbursement', should be explained.

(c) The information required by paragraphs 4 and 5 of the code should be given to a client at the outset of, and at appropriate stages throughout, the matter. All information given orally should be confirmed in writing to the client as soon as possible.

4. Advance costs information – general

The overall costs

(a) The solicitor should give the client the best information possible about the likely overall costs, including a breakdown between fees, VAT and disbursements.

(b) The solicitor should explain clearly to the client the time likely to be spent in dealing with a matter, if time spent is a factor in the calculation of the fees.

(c) Giving 'the best information possible' includes:

    (i)   agreeing a fixed fee; or

    (ii) giving a realistic estimate; or

    (iii) giving a forecast within a possible range of costs; or

    (iv) explaining to the client the reasons why it is not possible to fix, or give a realistic estimate or forecast of, the overall costs, and giving instead the best information possible about the cost of the next stage of the matter.

(d) The solicitor should, in an appropriate case, explain to a privately paying client that the client may set an upper limit on the firm's costs for which the client may be liable without further authority. Solicitors should not exceed an agreed limit without first obtaining the client's consent.

(e) The solicitor should make it clear at the outset if an estimate, quotation or other indication of cost is not intended to be fixed.

Basis of firm's charges

(f) The solicitor should also explain to the client how the firm's fees are calculated except where the overall costs are fixed or clear. If the basis of charging is an hourly charging rate, that must be made clear.

(g) The client should be told if charging rates may be increased.

Further information

(h) The solicitor should explain what reasonably foreseeable payments a client may have to make either to the solicitor or to a third party and when those payments are likely to be needed.

(i) The solicitor should explain to the client the arrangements for updating the costs information as set out in paragraph 6.

Client's ability to pay

(j) The solicitor should discuss with the client how and when any costs are to be met, and consider:

    (i) whether the client may be eligible and should apply for legal aid (including advice and assistance);

    (ii) whether the client's liability for their own costs may be covered by insurance;

    (iii) whether the client's liability for another party's costs may be covered by pre-purchased insurance and, if not, whether it would be advisable for the client's liability for another party's costs to be covered by after the event insurance (including in every case where a conditional fee or contingency fee arrangement is proposed); and

    (iv) whether the client's liability for costs (including the costs of another party) may be paid by another person e.g. an employer or trade union.

Cost-benefit and risk

(k) The solicitor should discuss with the client whether the likely outcome in a matter will justify the expense or risk involved including, if relevant, the risk of having to bear an opponent's costs.

5. Additional information for particular clients

Legally aided clients

(a) The solicitor should explain to a legally aided client the client's potential liability for the client's own costs and those of any other party, including:

    (i)   the effect of the statutory charge and its likely amount;

    (ii) the client's obligation to pay any contribution assessed and the consequences of failing to do so;

    (iii) the fact that the client may still be ordered by the court to contribute to the opponent's costs if the case is lost even though the client's own costs are covered by legal aid; and

    (iv) the fact that even if the client wins, the opponent may not be ordered to pay or be capable of paying the full amount of the client's costs.

Privately paying clients in contentious matters (and potentially contentious matters)

(b) The solicitor should explain to the client the client's potential liability for the client's own costs and for those of any other party, including:

    (i)   the fact that the client will be responsible for paying the firm's bill in full regardless of any order for costs made against an opponent;

    (ii) the probability that the client will have to pay the opponent's costs as well as the client's own costs if the case is lost;

    (iii) the fact that even if the client wins, the opponent may not be ordered to pay or be capable of paying the full amount of the client's costs; and

    (iv) the fact that if the opponent is legally aided the client may not recover costs, even if successful.

Liability for third party costs in non-contentious matters

(c) The solicitor should explain to the client any liability the client may have for the payment of the costs of a third party. When appropriate, solicitors are advised to obtain a firm figure for or agree a cap to a third party's costs.

6. Updating costs information

The solicitor should keep the client properly informed about costs as a matter progresses. In particular, the solicitor should:

(a) tell the client, unless otherwise agreed, how much the costs are at regular intervals (at least every six months) and in appropriate cases deliver interim bills at agreed intervals;

(b) explain to the client (and confirm in writing) any changed circumstances which will, or which are likely to, affect the amount of costs, the degree of risk involved, or the cost-benefit to the client of continuing with the matter;

(c) inform the client in writing as soon as it appears that a costs estimate or agreed upper limit may or will be exceeded; and

(d) consider the client's eligibility for legal aid if a material change in the client's means comes to the solicitor's attention.

7. Client care and complaints handling

Information for clients

(a) Every solicitor in private practice must ensure that the client:

(i) is given a clear explanation of the issues raised in a matter and is kept properly informed about its progress (including the likely timescale);

(ii) is given the name and status of the person dealing with the matter and the name of the principal responsible for its overall supervision;

(iii) is told whom to contact about any problem with the service provided; and

(iv) is given details of any changes in the information required to be given by this paragraph.

Complaints handling

(b) Every principal in private practice must:

(i) ensure the client is told the name of the person in the firm to contact about any problem with the service provided;

(ii) have a written complaints procedure and ensure that complaints are handled in accordance with it; and

(iii) ensure that the client is given a copy of the complaints procedure on request.

Pre-Action Protocol for Personal Injury Claims

December 1998

1 Introduction

1.1 Lord Woolf in his final Access to Justice Report of July 1996 recommended the development of pre-action protocols: 'To build on and increase the benefits of early but well informed settlement which genuinely satisfy both parties to dispute.'

1.2 The aims of pre-action protocols are:

- more pre-action contact between the parties
- better and earlier exchange of information
- better pre-action investigation by both sides
- to put the parties in a position where they may be able to settle cases fairly and early without litigation
- to enable proceedings to run to the court's timetable and efficiently, if litigation does become necessary.

1.3 The concept of protocols is relevant to a range of initiatives for good litigation and pre-litigation practice, especially:

- predictability in the time needed for steps pre-proceedings
- standardisation of relevant information, including documents to be disclosed.

1.4 The Courts will be able to treat the standards set in protocols as the normal reasonable approach to pre-action conduct. If proceedings are issued, it will be for the court to decide whether non-compliance with a protocol should merit adverse consequences. Guidance on the court's likely approach will be given from time to time in practice directions.

1.5 If the court has to consider the question of compliance after proceedings have begun, it will not be concerned with minor infringements, e.g. failure by a short period to provide relevant information. One minor breach will not exempt the 'innocent' party from following the protocol. The court will look at the effect of non-compliance on the other party when deciding whether to impose sanctions.

2 Notes of guidance

2.1 The protocol has been kept deliberately simple to promote ease of use and general acceptability. The notes of guidance which follow relate particularly to issues which arose during the piloting of the protocol.

Scope of the protocol

2.2 This protocol is intended to apply to all claims which include a claim for personal injury (except industrial disease claims) and to the entirety of those claims: not only to the personal injury element of a claim which also includes, for instance, property damage.

2.3 This protocol is primarily designed for those road traffic, tripping and slipping and accident at work cases which include an element of personal injury with a value of less than £15,000 which are likely to be allocated to the fast track. This is because time will be of the essence, after proceedings are issued, especially for the defendant, if a case is to be ready for trial within 30 weeks of allocation. Also, proportionality of work and costs to the value of what is in dispute is particularly important in lower value claims. For some claims within the value 'scope' of the fast track some flexibility in the timescale of the protocol may be necessary, see also paragraph 3.8.

2.4 However, the 'cards on the table' approach advocated by the protocol is equally appropriate to some higher value claims. The spirit, if not the letter of the protocol, should still be followed for multi-track type claims. In accordance with the sense of the civil justice reforms, the court will expect to see the spirit of reasonable pre-action behaviour applied in all cases, regardless of the existence of a specific protocol. In particular with regard to personal injury cases worth more than £15,000, with a view to avoiding the necessity of proceedings parties are expected to comply with the protocol as far as possible e.g. in respect of letters before action, exchanging information and documents and agreeing experts.

2.5 The timetable and the arrangements for disclosing documents and obtaining expert evidence may need to be varied to suit the circumstances of the case. Where one or both parties consider the detail of the protocol is not appropriate to the case, and proceedings are subsequently issued, the court will expect an explanation as to why the protocol has not been followed, or has been varied.

Early notification

2.6 The claimant's legal representative may wish to notify the defendant and/or his insurer as soon as they know a claim is likely to be made, but before they are able to send a detailed letter of claim, particularly for instance, when the defendant has no or limited knowledge of the incident giving rise to the claim or where the claimant is incurring significant expenditure as a result of the accident which he hopes the defendant might pay for, in whole or in part. If the claimant's representative chooses to do this, it will not start the timetable for responding.

The letter of claim

2.7 The specimen letter of claim at Annex A will usually be sent to the individual defendant. In practice, he/she may have no personal financial interest in the financial outcome of the claim/dispute because he/she is insured. Court imposed sanctions for non-compliance with the protocol may be ineffective against an insured. This is why the protocol emphasises the importance of passing the letter of claim to the insurer and the possibility that the insurance cover might be affected. If an insurer receives the letter of claim only after some delay by the insured, it would not be unreasonable for the insurer to ask the claimant for additional time to respond.

Reasons for early issue

2.8 The protocol recommends that a defendant be given three months to investigate and respond to a claim before proceedings are issued. This may not always be possible, particularly where a claimant only consults a solicitor close to the end of any relevant limitation period. In these circumstances, the claimant's solicitor should give as much notice of the intention to issue proceedings as is practicable and the parties should consider whether the court might be invited to extend time for service of the claimant's supporting documents and for service of any defence, or alternatively, to stay the proceedings while the recommended steps in the protocol are followed.

Status of letters of claim and response

2.9 Letters of claim and response are not intended to have the same status as a statement of case in proceedings. Matters may come to light as a result of investigation after the letter of claim has been sent, or after the defendant has responded, particularly if disclosure of documents takes place outside the recommended three-month period. These circumstances could mean that the 'pleaded' case of one or both parties is presented slightly differently than in the letter of claim and response. It would not be consistent with the spirit of the protocol for a party to 'take a point' on this in the proceedings, provided that there was no obvious intention by the party who changed their position to mislead the other party.

Disclosure of documents

2.10 The aim of the early disclosure of documents by the defendant is not to encourage 'fishing expeditions' by the claimant, but to promote an early exchange of relevant information to help in clarifying or resolving issues in dispute. The claimant's solicitor can assist by identifying in the letter of claim or in a subsequent letter the particular categories of documents which they consider are relevant.

Experts

2.11 The protocol encourages joint selection of, and access to, experts. Most frequently this will apply to the medical expert, but on occasions also to liability experts, e.g. engineers. The protocol promotes the practice of the claimant obtaining a medical report, disclosing it to the defendant who then asks questions and/or agrees it and does not obtain his own report. The protocol provides for nomination of the expert by the claimant in personal injury claims because of the early stage of the proceedings and the particular nature of such claims. If proceedings have to be issued, a medical report must be attached to these proceedings. However, if necessary after proceedings have commenced and with the permission of the court, the parties may obtain further expert reports. It would be for the court to decide whether the costs of more than one expert's report should be recoverable.

2.12 Some solicitors choose to obtain medical reports through medical agencies, rather than directly from a specific doctor or hospital. The defendant's prior consent to the action should be sought and, if the defendant so requests, the agency should be asked to provide in advance the names of the doctor(s) whom they are considering instructing.

Negotiations/settlement

2.13 Parties and their legal representatives are encouraged to enter into discussions and/or negotiations prior to starting proceedings. The protocol does not specify when or how this might be done but parties should bear in mind that the courts increasingly take the view that litigation should be a last resort, and that claims should not be issued prematurely when a settlement is in reasonable prospect.

Stocktake

2.14 Where a claim is not resolved when the protocol has been followed, the parties might wish to carry out a 'stocktake' of the issues in dispute, and the evidence that the court is likely to need to decide those issues, before proceedings are started. Where the defendant is insured and the pre-action steps have been conducted by the insurer, the insurer would normally be expected to nominate solicitors to act in the proceedings and the claimant's solicitor is recommended to invite the insurer to nominate solicitors to act in the proceedings and do so 7–14 days before the intended issue date.

3 The protocol letter of claim

3.1 The claimant shall send to the proposed defendant two copies of a letter of claim, immediately sufficient information is available to substantiate a realistic claim and before issues of quantum are addressed in detail. One copy of the letter is for the defendants, the second for passing on to his insurers.

3.2 The letter shall contain **a clear summary of the facts** on which the claim is based together with an indication of the **nature of any injuries** suffered and of **any financial loss incurred**. In cases of road traffic accidents, the letter should provide the name and address of the hospital where treatment has been obtained and the claimant's hospital reference number.

3.3 Solicitors are recommended to use a **standard format** for such a letter – an example is at Annex A: this can be amended to suit the particular case.

3.4 The letter should ask for **details of the insurer** and that a copy should be sent by the proposed defendant to the insurer where appropriate. If the insurer is known, a copy shall be sent directly to the insurer. Details of the claimant's National Insurance number and date of birth should be supplied to the defendant's insurer once the Defendant has responded to the letter of claim and confirmed the identity of the insurer. This information should not be supplied in the letter of claim.

3.5 **Sufficient information** should be given in order to enable the defendant's insurer/solicitor to commence investigations and at least put a broad valuation on the 'risk'.

3.6 The **defendant should reply within 21 calendar days** of the date of posting of the letter identifying the insurer (if any). If there has been no reply by the defendant or insurer within 21 days, the claimant will be entitled to issue proceedings.

3.7 The **defendant**('s insurers) will have a **maximum of three months** from the date of acknowledgment of the claim **to investigate.** No later than the end of that period the defendant (insurer) shall reply, stating whether liability is denied and, if so, giving reasons for their denial of liability.

3.8 Where the accident occurred outside England and Wales and/or where the defendant is outside the jurisdiction, the time periods of 21 days and three months should normally be extended up to 42 days and six months.

3.9 Where **liability is admitted,** the presumption is that the defendant will be bound by this admission for all claims with a total value of up to £15,000.

Documents

3.10 If the **defendant denies liability**, he should enclose with the letter of reply, **documents** in his possession which are **material to the issues** between the parties, and which would be likely to be ordered to be disclosed by the court, either on an application for pre-action disclosure, or on disclosure during proceedings.

3.11 Attached at Annex B are **specimen**, but non-exhaustive, **lists** of documents likely to be material in different types of claim. Where the claimant's investigation of the case is well advanced, the letter of claim could indicate which classes of documents are considered relevant for early disclosure. Alternatively these could be identified at a later stage.

3.12 Where the defendant admits primary liability, but alleges contributory negligence by the claimant, the defendant should give reasons supporting those allegations and disclose those documents from Annex B which are relevant to the issues in dispute. The claimant should respond to the allegations of contributory negligence before proceedings are issued.

Special damages

3.13 The claimant will send to the defendant as soon as practicable a Schedule of Special Damages with supporting documents, particularly where the defendant has admitted liability.

Experts

3.14 Before any party instructs an expert he should give the other party a list of the **name**(s) of **one or more experts** in the relevant speciality whom he considers are suitable to instruct.

3.15 Where a medical expert is to be instructed the claimant's solicitor will organise access to relevant medical records – see specimen letter of instruction at Annex C.

3.16 **Within 14 days** the other party may indicate **an objection** to one or more of the named experts. The first party should then instruct a mutually acceptable expert. It must be emphasised that if the Claimant nominates an expert in the original letter of claim, the Defendant has 14 days to object to one or more of the named experts after expiration of the period of 21 days within which he has to reply to the letter of claim, as set out in paragraph 3.6.

3.17 If the second party objects to all the listed experts, the parties may then instruct **experts of their own choice**. It would be for the court to decide subsequently, if proceedings are issued, whether either party had acted unreasonably.

3.18 If the **second party does not object to an expert nominated**, he shall not be entitled to rely on his own expert evidence within that particular speciality unless:

(a) the first party agrees,

(b) the court so directs, or

(c) the first party's expert report has been amended and the first party is not prepared to disclose the original report.

3.19 **Either party may send to an agreed expert written questions** on the report, relevant to the issues, via the first party's solicitors. The expert should send answers to the questions separately and directly to each party.

3.20 The cost of a report from an agreed expert will usually be paid by the instructing first party: the costs of the expert replying to questions will usually be borne by the party which asks the questions.

3.21 Where the defendant admits liability in whole or in part, before proceedings are issued, any medical report obtained by agreement under this protocol should be disclosed to the other party. The claimant should delay issuing proceedings for 21 days from disclosure of the report, to enable the parties to consider whether the claim is capable of settlement. The Civil Procedure Rules Part 36 permit claimants and defendants to make offers to settle pre-proceedings. Parties should always consider before issuing if it is appropriate to make Part 36 Offer. If such an offer is made, the party making the offer must always supply sufficient evidence and/or information to enable the offer to be properly considered.

ANNEX A. LETTER OF CLAIM

To Defendant

Dear Sirs

Re: **Claimant's full name**
     Claimant's full address
     Claimant's Clock or Works Number
     Claimant's Employer (name and address)

We are instructed by the above named to claim damages in connection with an *accident at work / road traffic accident / tripping accident* on   day of *(year)* at *(place of accident which must be sufficiently detailed to establish location)*

Please confirm the identity of your insurers. Please note that the insurers will need to see this letter as soon as possible and it may affect your insurance cover and/or the conduct of any subsequent legal proceedings if you do not send this letter to them.

The circumstances of the accident are:
(brief outline)

The reason why we are alleging fault is:
(simple explanation e.g. defective machine, broken ground)

A description of our clients' injuries is as follows:
(brief outline)

(In cases of road traffic accidents)
Our client *(state hospital reference number)* received treatment for the injuries at *(name and address of hospital)*.

He is employed as *(occupation)* and has had the following time off work *(dates of absence)*. His approximate weekly income is *(insert if known)*.

If you are our client's employers, please provide us with the usual earnings details which will enable us to calculate his financial loss.

We are obtaining a police report and will let you have a copy of the same upon your undertaking to meet half the fee.

We have also sent a letter of claim to (***name and address***) and a copy of that letter is attached. We understand their insurers are (***name, address and claims number if known***).

At this stage of our enquiries we would expect the documents contained in parts (***insert appropriate parts of standard disclosure list***) to be relevant to this action.

A copy of this letter is attached for you to send to your insurers. Finally we expect an acknowledgment of this letter within 21 days by yourselves or your insurers.

Yours faithfully

ANNEX B. PRE-ACTION PERSONAL INJURY PROTOCOL: STANDARD DIS-CLOSURE LISTS, FAST TRACK DISCLOSURE

RTA cases

Section A

In all cases where liability is at issue –

(i)   Documents identifying nature, extent and location of damage to defendant's vehicle where there is any dispute about point of impact.

(ii)   MOT certificate where relevant.

(iii)   Maintenance records where vehicle defect is alleged or it is alleged by defendant that there was an unforeseen defect which caused or contributed to the accident.

Section B

Accident involving commercial vehicle as potential defendant –

(i)   Tachograph charts or entry from individual control book.

(ii)   Maintenance and repair records required for operators' licence where vehicle defect is alleged or it is alleged by defendants that there was an unforeseen defect which caused or contributed to the accident.

Section C

Cases against local authorities where highway design defect is alleged.

(i)   Documents produced to comply with Section 39 of the Road Traffic Act 1988 in respect of the duty designed to promote road safety to include studies into road accidents in the relevant area and documents relating to measures recommended to prevent accidents in the relevant area.

Highway tripping claims

Documents from Highway Authority for a period of 12 months prior to the accident –

(i)   Records of inspection for the relevant stretch of highway.

(ii)   Maintenance records including records of independent contractors working in relevant area.

(iii)   Records of the minutes of Highway Authority meetings where maintenance or repair policy has been discussed or decided.

(iv)   Records of complaints about the state of highways.

(v)   Records of other accidents which have occurred on the relevant stretch of highway.

Workplace claims

(i)   Accident book entry.

(ii)   First aider report.

(iii)   Surgery record.

(iv)   Foreman/supervisor accident report.

(v)   Safety representative's accident report.

(vi)   RIDDOR report to HSE.

(vii)   Other communications between defendants and HSE.

(viii) Minutes of Health and Safety Committee meeting(s) where accident/matter considered.

(ix)   Report to DSS.

(x)   Documents listed above relative to any previous accident/matter identified by the claimant and relied upon as proof of negligence.

(xi)   Earnings information where defendant is employer.

Documents produced to comply with requirements of the Management of Health and Safety at Work Regulations 1992 –

(i)   Pre-accident Risk Assessment required by Regulation 3.

(ii)   Post-accident Re-Assessment required by Regulation 3.

(iii)   Accident Investigation Report prepared in implementing the requirements of Regulations 4, 6 and 9.

(iv)   Health Surveillance Records in appropriate cases required by Regulation 5.

(v)   Information provided to employees under Regulation 8.

(vi)   Documents relating to the employees' health and safety training required by Regulation 11.

Workplace claims – disclosure where specific regulations apply

Section A – Workplace (Health Safety and Welfare) Regulations 1992

(i)   Repair and maintenance records required by Regulation 5.

(ii)   Housekeeping records to comply with the requirements of Regulation 9.

(iii)   Hazard warning signs or notices to comply with Regulation 17 (Traffic Routes).

Section B – Provision and Use of Work Equipment Regulations 1992

(i)   Manufacturers' specifications and instructions in respect of relevant work equipment establishing its suitability to comply with Regulation 5.

(ii)   Maintenance log/maintenance records required to comply with Regulation 6.

(iii)   Documents providing information and instructions to employees to comply with Regulation 8.

(iv)   Documents provided to the employee in respect of training for use to comply with Regulation 9.

(v)   Any notice, sign or document relied upon as a defence to alleged breaches of Regulations 14 to 18 dealing with controls and control systems.

(vi)   Instruction/training documents issued to comply with the requirements of Regulation 22 insofar as it deals with maintenance operations where the machinery is not shut down.

(vii)   Copies of markings required to comply with Regulation 23.

(viii) Copies of warnings required to comply with Regulation 24.

Section C – Personal Protective Equipment at Work Regulations 1992

(i)   Documents relating to the assessment of the Personal Protective Equipment to comply with Regulation 6.

(ii)   Documents relating to the maintenance and replacement of Personal Protective Equipment to comply with Regulation 7.

(iii)   Record of maintenance procedures for Personal Protective Equipment to comply with Regulation 7.

(iv)   Records of tests and examinations of Personal Protective Equipment to comply with Regulation 7.

(v)   Documents providing information, instruction and training in relation to the Personal Protective Equipment to comply with Regulation 9.

(vi)   Instructions for use of Personal Protective Equipment to include the manufacturers' instructions to comply with Regulation 10.

Section D – Manual Handling Operations Regulations 1992

(i)   Manual Handling Risk Assessment carried out to comply with the requirements of Regulation 4(1)(b)(i).

(ii)   Re-assessment carried out post-accident to comply with requirements of Regulation 4(1)(b)(i).

(iii)   Documents showing the information provided to the employee to give general indications related to the load and precise indications on the weight of the load and the heaviest side of the load if the centre of gravity was not positioned centrally to comply with Regulation 4(1)(b)(iii).

(iv)   Documents relating to training in respect of manual handling operations and training records.

Section E – Health and Safety (Display Screen Equipment) Regulations 1992

(i)   Analysis of work stations to assess and reduce risks carried out to comply with the requirements of Regulation 2.

(ii)   Re-assessment of analysis of work stations to assess and reduce risks following development of symptoms by the claimant.

(iii)   Documents detailing the provision of training including training records to comply with the requirements of Regulation 6.

(iv)   Documents providing information to employees to comply with the requirements of Regulation 7.

Section F – Control of Substances Hazardous to Health Regulations 1988

(i) Risk assessment carried out to comply with the requirements of Regulation 6.

(ii) Reviewed risk assessment carried out to comply with the requirements of Regulation 6.

(iii) Copy labels from containers used for storage handling and disposal of carcinogenics to comply with the requirements of Regulation 7(2A)(h).

(iv) Warning signs identifying designation of areas and installations which may be contaminated by carcinogenics to comply with the requirements of Regulation 7(2A)(h).

(v) Documents relating to the assessment of the Personal Protective Equipment to comply with Regulation 7(3A).

(vi) Documents relating to the maintenance and replacement of Personal Protective Equipment to comply with Regulation 7(3A).

(vii) Record of maintenance procedures for Personal Protective Equipment to comply with Regulation 7(3A).

(viii) Records of tests and examinations of Personal Protective Equipment to comply with Regulation 7(3A).

(ix) Documents providing information, instruction and training in relation to the Personal Protective Equipment to comply with Regulation 7(3A).

(x) Instructions for use of Personal Protective Equipment to include the manufacturers' instructions to comply with Regulation 7(3A).

(xi) Air monitoring records for substances assigned a maximum exposure limit or occupational exposure standard to comply with the requirements of Regulation 7.

(xii) Maintenance examination and test of control measures records to comply with Regulation 9.

(xiii) Monitoring records to comply with the requirements of Regulation 10.

(xiv) Health surveillance records to comply with the requirements of Regulation 11.

(xv) Documents detailing information, instruction and training including training records for employees to comply with the requirements of Regulation 12.

(xvi) Labels and Health and Safety data sheets supplied to the employers to comply with the CHIP Regulations.

Section G – Construction (Design and Management) Regulations 1994

(i) Notification of a project form (HSE F10) to comply with the requirements of Regulation 7.

(ii) Health and Safety Plan to comply with requirements of Regulation 15.

(iii) Health and Safety file to comply with the requirements of Regulations 12 and 14.

(iv)   Information and training records provided to comply with the requirements of Regulation 17.

(v)   Records of advice from and views of persons at work to comply with the requirements of Regulation 18.

Section H – Pressure Systems and Transportable Gas Containers Regulations 1989

(i)   Information and specimen markings provided to comply with the requirements of Regulation 5.

(ii)   Written statements specifying the safe operating limits of a system to comply with the requirements of Regulation 7.

(iii)   Copy of the written scheme of examination required to comply with the requirements of Regulation 8.

(iv)   Examination records required to comply with the requirements of Regulation 9.

(v)   Instructions provided for the use of operator to comply with Regulation 11.

(vi)   Records kept to comply with the requirements of Regulation 13.

(vii)   Records kept to comply with the requirements of Regulation 22.

Section I – Lifting Plant and Equipment (Records of Test and Examination etc.) Regulations 1992

(i)   Record kept to comply with the requirements of Regulation 6.

Section J – Noise at Work Regulations 1989

(i)   Any risk assessment records required to comply with the requirements of Regulations 4 and 5.

(ii)   Manufacturers' literature in respect of all ear protection made available to claimant to comply with the requirements of Regulation 8.

(iii)   All documents provided to the employee for the provision of information to comply with Regulation 11.

Section K – Construction (Head Protection) Regulations 1989

(i)   Pre-accident assessment of head protection required to comply with Regulation 3(4).

(ii)   Post-accident re-assessment required to comply with Regulation 3(5).

Section L – Construction (General Provisions) Regulations 1961

(i)   Report prepared following inspections and examinations of excavations etc. to comply with the requirements of Regulation 9.

(ii)   Report prepared following inspections and examinations of work in cofferdams and caissons to comply with the requirements of Regulations 17 and 18.

N.B. Further Standard Discovery lists will be required prior to full implementation.

ANNEX C. LETTER OF INSTRUCTION TO MEDICAL EXPERT

Dear Sir,

Re: (*Name and Address*)
D.O.B. –
Telephone No. –
Date of Accident –

We are acting for the above named in connection with injuries received in an accident which occurred on the above date. The main injuries appear to have been (**main injuries**).

We should be obliged if you would examine our Client and let us have a full and detailed report dealing with any relevant pre-accident medical history, the injuries sustained, treatment received and present condition, dealing in particular with the capacity for work and giving a prognosis.

It is central to our assessment of the extent of our Client's injuries to establish the extent and duration of any continuing disability. Accordingly, in the prognosis section we would ask you to specifically comment on any areas of continuing complaint or disability or impact on daily living. If there is such continuing disability you should comment upon the level of suffering or inconvenience caused and, if you are able, give your view as to when or if the complaint or disability is likely to resolve.

Please send our Client an appointment direct for this purpose. Should you be able to offer a cancellation appointment please contact our Client direct. We confirm we will be responsible for your reasonable fees.

We are obtaining the notes and records from our Client's GP and Hospitals attended and will forward them to you when they are to hand/or please request the GP and Hospital records direct and advise that any invoice for the provision of these records should be forwarded to us.

In order to comply with Court Rules we would be grateful if you would insert above your signature a statement that the contents are true to the best of your knowledge and belief.

In order to avoid further correspondence we can confirm that on the evidence we have there is no reason to suspect we may be pursuing a claim against the hospital or its staff.

We look forward to receiving your report within _____ weeks. If you will not be able to prepare your report within this period please telephone us upon receipt of these instructions.

When acknowledging these instructions it would assist if you could give an estimate as to the likely time scale for the provision of your report and also an indication as to your fee.

Yours faithfully

APPENDIX 5

Practice Direction: Protocols

General

1.1 This Practice Direction applies to the pre-action protocols which have been approved by the Head of Civil Justice.

1.2 The pre-action protocols which have been approved are specified in the Schedule to this Practice Direction. Other pre-action protocols may subsequently be added.

1.3 Pre-action protocols outline the steps parties should take to seek information from and to provide information to each other about a prospective legal claim.

1.4 The objectives of pre-action protocols are:

(1) to encourage the exchange of early and full information about the prospective legal claim,

(2) to enable parties to avoid litigation by agreeing a settlement of the claim before the commencement of proceedings,

(3) to support the efficient management of proceedings where litigation cannot be avoided.

Compliance with protocols

2.1 The Civil Procedure Rules enable the court to take into account compliance or non-compliance with an applicable protocol when giving directions for the management of proceedings (see CPR Rules 3.1(4) and (5) and 3.9(1)(e)) and when making orders for costs (see CPR Rule 44.3(5)(a)).

2.2 The court will expect all parties to have complied in substance with the terms of an approved protocol.

2.3 If, in the opinion of the court, non-compliance has led to the commencement of proceedings which might otherwise not have needed to be commenced, or has led to costs being incurred in the proceedings that might otherwise not have been incurred, the orders the court may make include:

(1) an order that the party at fault pay the costs of the proceedings, or part of those costs, of the other party or parties;

(2) an order that the party at fault pay those costs on an indemnity basis;

(3) if the party at fault is a claimant in whose favour an order for the payment of damages or some specified sum is subsequently made, an order depriving that party of interest on such sum and in respect of such period as may be specified, and/or awarding interest at a lower rate than that at which interest would otherwise have been awarded;

(4) if the party at fault is a defendant and an order for the payment of damages or some specified sum is subsequently made in favour of the claimant, an order awarding interest on such sum and in respect of such period as may be specified at a higher rate, not exceeding 10% above base rate (cf. CPR Rule 36.21(2)), than the rate at which interest would otherwise have been awarded.

2.4 The court will exercise its powers under paragraphs 2.1 and 2.3 with the object of placing the innocent party in no worse a position than he would have been in if the protocol had been complied with.

3.1 A claimant may be found to have failed to comply with a protocol by, for example:

(a) not having provided sufficient information to the defendant, or

(b) not having followed the procedure required by the protocol to be followed (e.g. not having followed the medical expert instruction procedure set out in the Personal Injury Protocol).

3.2 A defendant may be found to have failed to comply with a protocol by, for example:

(a) not making a preliminary response to the letter of claim within the time fixed for that purpose by the relevant protocol (21 days under the Personal Injury Protocol, 14 days under the Clinical Negligence Protocol),

(b) not making a full response within the time fixed for that purpose by the relevant protocol (3 months of the letter of claim under the Clinical Negligence Protocol, 3 months from the date of acknowledgement of the letter of claim under the Personal Injury Protocol),

(c) not disclosing documents required to be disclosed by the relevant protocol.

Pre-action behaviour in other cases

4 In cases not covered by any approved protocol, the court will expect the parties, in accordance with the overriding objective and the matters referred to in CPR 1.1(2)(a), (b) and (c), to act reasonably in exchanging information and documents relevant to the claim and generally in trying to avoid the necessity for the start of proceedings.

Information about funding arrangements

4A.1 Where a person enters into a funding arrangement within the meaning of rule 43.2(1)(k) he should inform other potential parties to the claim that he has done so.

4A.2 Paragraph 4A.1 applies to all proceedings whether proceedings to which a pre-action protocol applies or otherwise.

(Rule 44.3B(1)(c) provides that a party may not recover any additional liability for any period in the proceedings during which he failed to provide information about a funding arrangement in accordance with a rule, practice direction or court order).

Commencement

5.1 The following table sets out the protocols currently in force, the date they came into force and their date of publication:

Protocol	Coming into	Publication force
Personal Injury	26 April 1999	January 1999
Clinical Negligence	26 April 1999	January 1999
Construction and Engineering Disputes	2 October 2000	September 2000
Defamation	2 October 2000	September 2000

5.2 The court will take compliance or non-compliance with a relevant protocol into account where the claim was started after the coming into force of that protocol but will not do so where the claim was started before that date.

5.3 Parties in a claim started after a relevant protocol came into force, who have, by work done before that date, achieved the objectives sought to be achieved by certain requirements of that protocol, need not take any further steps to comply with those requirements. They will not be considered to have not complied with the protocol for the purposes of paragraphs 2 and 3.

5.4 Parties in a claim started after a relevant protocol came into force, who have not been able to comply with any particular requirements of that protocol because the period of time between the publication date and the date of coming into force was too short, will not be considered to have not complied with the protocol for the purposes of paragraphs 2 and 3.

Schedule

1. Personal Injury Protocol.

2. Clinical Negligence Protocol.

APPENDIX 6

Useful addresses

Academy of Experts
2 South Square
Grays Inn
London
WC1R 5HP
website: www.academy-experts.org

Association of Personal Injury Lawyers
11 Castle Quay
Castle Boulevard
Nottingham
NG7 1FW
tel: 0115 958 0585
website: www.apil.com

Action for the Victims of Medical Accidents
44 High Street
Croydon
Surrey
CR0 1YB
tel: 020 8688 9555
website: www.avma.org.uk

British Standards Institution
389 Chiswick High Road
London
W4 4AL
tel: 020 8996 9001
website: www.bsi-gobal.com

Capsoft UK Ltd
24 Palmerston Place
Edinburgh
EH12 5AL
tel: 0131 226 3999
website: www.capsoft.co.uk

Centre for Dispute Resolution (CEDR)
Princes House
95 Gresham Street
London
EC2V 7NA
tel: 020 7600 0500
website: www.cedr.co.uk

Child Poverty Action Group
94 White Lion Street
London
N1 9PF
tel: 020 7837 7979
website: www.cpag.org.uk

Commerce and Industry Group
The Law Society's Hall
113 Chancery Lane
London
WC2A 1PL
tel: 020 7320 5801
website: www.commerceandindustry.org.uk

Expert Witness Institute
Africa House
64–78 Kingsway
London
WC2B 6BD
tel: 020 7405 5854
website: www.ewi.org.uk

Forum of Insurance Lawyers
The Law Society's Hall
113 Chancery Lane
London
WC2A 1PL
tel: 020 7323 4632

Freelance Solicitors Group
5 The Link
West Acton
London
W3 0JW
tel: 020 8992 3885
http://members.ad.com/pjmiller00/freelance.html

Investors in People UK
4th floor
7–10 Chandos Street
London
W1M 9DE
tel: 020 7467 1900
website: www.iipuk.co.uk

LSLA London Solicitors Litigation Association
(no one address)
website: www.londonsla.f9.co.uk

Legal Aid Practitioners Group
The Law Society's Hall
113 Chancery Lane
London
WC2A 1PL
tel: 020 7336 8565

Management Charter Initiative
Russell Square House
10–12 Russell Square
London
WC1B 5BZ
tel: 020 782 9000
website: www.bbi.co.uk.mci

The Law Society
113 Chancery Lane
London
WC2A 1PL
tel: 020 7242 1222
website: www.lawsociety.org.uk

Laserform International Ltd
LFM House
231 Higher Lane
Lymm
Cheshire
WA13 0RZ
tel: 01925 750 000
website: www.laserform.co.uk

Legal Services Commission
85 Gray's Inn Road
London
WC1X 8AA
tel: 020 7759 0000
website: www.legalservices.gov.uk

Local Government Group
The Law Society
113 Chancery Lane
London
WC2A 1PL
tel: 020 7320 5801
website: www.localgov.com

Pan-European Organisation of Personal Injury Lawyers (PEOPIL)
130 Loyd Road
Northampton
NN1 5JA
tel: 01604 628 213
website: www.peopil.com

Society of Expert Witnesses
PO Box 345
Newmarket
Suffolk
CB8 7TU
tel: 0845 702 3014
website: www.sew.org.uk

Trainee Solicitors Group
The Law Society's Hall
113 Chancery Lane
London
WC2A 1PL
tel: 020 7320 5794
website: www.tsg.org

Young Solicitors Group
The Law Society's Hall
113 Chancery Lane
London
WC2A 1PL
tel: 020 7320 5793

Index

IT (*cont*)
supervision 80–1
CD-Roms 86–8
databases 86
debt collection systems 67
diary 73–4
disclosure of documents, and 421–3
e-mail 74–5
pitfalls 75–7
EgamiLegal 89
electronic court room 88–90
electronic interface with court offices 90
electronic transcripts 88–9
forms software 72–3
generally 30–1, 65–71, 111–12
hardware 70
Internet *see* **Internet**
intranets 86
know-how and knowledge management 85–6
legal research and sources 86–8
litigation support software 89–90
LiveNote 89
local area network (LAN) 69–70, 87
marketing, and 135–6
networking, and 146
operating system software 70–1
project management software 83–5
R/KYV 89
skills 90–1
software 70
spreadsheet software 72
time recording 77
unbundling, and 111–12
word processing 71–2, 86

Jones, Peter 11
Judicial control 339–42

Know-how and knowledge management 85–6

Land, recovery of
statement of case 489
Law schools 11
LawAssist 239
Legal aid
administering 266
client benefits 267
costs limitations 267
generally 244–6, 266
growth in litigation, and 2
new Funding Code 245–6
performance assessment 266
personal injury cases 245
prescribed rates 266–7
small claims 363–4
specialist panels 267
Legal Aid Board

Community Legal Service Quality Mark at Specialist Help Level 52–4
Franchise Quality Assurance Standard 45
franchising model 23–4
Legal Aid Franchise Quality Assurance Standard (LAFQAS) 52–4, 77, 80
Legal expenses insurance
Accident Line Protect 117, 167, 253, 261
advising client as to 247, 253, 257
after the event (AEI) 238–9, 247, 253, 254, 256, 261
selecting 257
confidentiality 256–7
conflicts of interest 256
continuing requirements under policy 255
cover for adverse costs orders 256
exclusion clauses 255
fraud by client 256
freedom to choose lawyer 253
generally 28, 252–3
initial basis of charging 253–4
mitigating loss 255
nature of policies 252
panel referrals 257
panel solicitor restrictions 253
pre-purchased 238, 246–7
primary liability of client 254
recovery of costs from insurer 255–6
risk of avoidance 254
scope of cover 254–5
small claims 362
validity of policy 254
warranties about future conduct 255
Legal profession
unification of 29–30
Legal professional privilege 175–6
Legal research and sources 86–8
Legal Services' Commission Scheme 47
Lexcel 40, 48–52, 62
Litigants in person 38, 178, 183, 349–50
see also **Small claims; Unbundling**
Litigation
growth in 1–2
last resort, as 154–5
support software 89–90
LiveNote 89
Local area network (LAN) 69–70, 87

Management
rise of 10
Management Charter Initiative 61
Marketing
aims of 129–30
brochures 139
client relationship ladder 132–3
developing relationships 143–4
firm's overall strategy, and 130–1
generally 128–9